# NO
# ROOM
## IN THE
# INN

## Reading
## The Bible
## Today

TOM HIGGINS

Published by:    Tom Higgins,
                 Currach, Castlebar,
                 Co. Mayo, Ireland.

Unless otherwise stated, Scriptures selections are from the Good News Bible (GNB), Bible Societies/Collins. There are some selections from other Bibles, as follows: The Jerusalem Bible (JB), "The New Jerusalem Bible" (NJB) and the "New Revised Standard Version Catholic" (NRSVC). The Catechism of the Catholic Church is referenced as CCC.

**ISBN: 978-1-5272-8639-9**

Design and layout:    Sinéad Mallee, Graphic Designer, Knock, Co. Mayo.
Printed by:           IngramSpark.com

# Acknowledgements

There are a number of people to whom I owe my gratitude for reading my manuscript. Each of them brought his or her own particular perspective to bear on the text, whether as helpful comment, suggestions, or calling for further clarification in parts therein. Their names are as follows: Sean Nestor, Anne Higgins-Petz, Kenneth Lyons, Bernard Gallagher, Tony Burke, Ann Jordan and Kieran Higgins.

Last, but not least are the many contemporary Biblical scholars whose writings helped me in my effort to make this the kind of book I wanted to be. I acknowledge my gratitude to them in the many footnote references throughout the book.

I want to thank my wife, Mary, sons Kieran and Brendan, daughter Ann, daughter in-law Rebecca and late daughter in-law Iana, all of whom supported me throughout my years of research and writing.

## Dedication

*For my grandchildren:*
*Conor, Cormac, Iman, Neel, Maeve and Senan.*

# CONTENTS

## CHAPTER 3
## Abraham, Isaac and Jacob

## CHAPTER 4
## Exodus and Deuteronomy

## CHAPTER 7
### The Prophet Jeremiah

## CHAPTER 8
### Ezekiel and Second Isaiah

## CHAPTER 12
### The Later Galilean Ministry (3:7-6:6a)

## CHAPTER 13
### Jesus Shares and Extends his Ministry (6:7-8:21)

## CHAPTER 14
### The "Way" to Jerusalem (8:27-10:52)

# Introduction

## Two Testaments

The English word "bible" comes from the Greek words *ta biblia*, which means "the books." The Bible is not a single book, rather a collection of books written over a period from about 800 BC to 90 AD.

The Christian Bible is divided into two parts – the Old Testament and the New Testament. There are forty-six books in the Old Testament and twenty-seven in the New Testament. The Old Testament begins with the account of the creation of the world and continues with the story of God's dealings with humanity down to the time of Jesus. The New Testament is an account of Jesus and his immediate followers.

The New Testament begins with the four gospels, which are four separate accounts of the life and teachings of Jesus and his redemptive work on behalf of humanity. The gospels are followed by The Acts of the Apostles, which is a history of the early Church. Then come the letters to the new Christian communities (mostly from the pen of St. Paul). The Bible ends with the Book of Revelation, which is a revelation of human destiny in a new creation at the end of time.

For both Jews and Christians, the Bible is the story of the Creator God and his self-communication to human beings (known as revelation), making the Bible of great importance to their lives. The ancient Hebrews (Israelites) were able to see God reflected in his creation (Psalm 29, 104, 148), in the unfolding of their history and in their daily lives. Israel learned from its history. Its history brought its people's flaws out into the open and revealed to them the consequences of their failure to trust in God and their disobedience. In reading the Bible, we ourselves can learn much from the experience of Israel. We get to know God, to experience God more deeply in our lives, as the One inviting us to participate in his ongoing work of creation.

## What Kind of Book?

In approaching any book, there are a number of questions we may ask. What sort of book is this? Is it a treatise or a work of fiction such as a novel; is it history or biography? And what authority does the author have to deal with his or her subject? In the case of a novel or drama, we might expect the author to shed some light on the human condition and inspire and enlighten the reader. Other questions might be, who wrote this book? Is the person a contemporary author or from an earlier period? A creative writer from a past age can still have something of value to say to us today, Shakespeare, for example. We often choose a book because we know that the author has an expertise, either in a particular field of study or because of his or her reputation as a creative writer. Readers will be able to determine how useful the book is to them, depending on the answers to those questions.

The same questions might be asked with reference to the Bible. I will discuss them when commenting on individual books of the Bible. For the present, it may be enough to state that, although the Bible contains seventy-three different books, it is a single story, with a beginning, middle and end. As with any story, when we begin reading the Bible, the suspense of the narrative soon urges us on, as we wonder how the author will resolve the difficulties and problems encountered by his characters, in order to bring everything to a satisfying conclusion. What we often look for in a story is a happy ending or some kind of redemption for its characters as a climax to the narrative. The ancient Hebrews thus saw history, not as an unending cycle of events, but as a story that was going somewhere. They believed and hoped that God was leading them to a glorious future.

Although the books of the Bible have different authors, writing at different times, both Jews and Christians believe, that in a certain sense, God is the author of the Bible. God is the author, in the sense that he inspired the human authors to write what he wanted them to write. Thus, inspired by the Spirit of God, the human authors freely and passionately devoted themselves to the mission of communicating the good news of God's love to his people. (Isaiah 6:8; 61:1-2; Jeremiah 20:9; Ezekiel 2:1-7). As well as being author, God is there in the biblical story as one of its characters. God is the chief protagonist of the Bible. He appears in almost every page of the book, sometimes in the background, but always directing the course of events towards his good purposes. He respects the freedom of human beings; he never compels them to act in a particular way. He leads and guides us on "the right path" and invites us to follow him. (Psalm 23:3; 25:4-5, 8-10; Isaiah 30:20-21; 58:10-11; John 16:13). We often choose to turn a deaf ear to God and refuse to be guided by him. (Isaiah 42:18-19; 48:17-18; Jeremiah 6:16-17). But he never gives up on us. (Isaiah 49:14-16). God's words and actions resonate throughout the whole Biblical narrative. His words are creative and effectual. (Genesis 1:3). His words and his "ways" are superior to human thoughts, words and actions. (Isaiah 55:8-11). His words can become metaphorically fruitful, once human beings begin to listen to him and follow in his ways.

As we read the Bible, we soon discover that the sovereignty of God is the main theme giving unity and coherence to the whole narrative. (Genesis 1:1; Isaiah 40:25-31; 45:7-9; Mark 14:36). God created the world and is, therefore, sovereign over his creation. Although created in his image, human beings are dependent on God, and are thus limited in what they can do. (Genesis 1:26). It is only the Creator of the universe who has the power to deal definitively with the disabled condition of humanity (Mark 2:1-3; 5:39-41; 16:5-6; Luke 10:33-35) and bring his characters (human beings) home to a happy ending. (Psalm 23:5-6). Thus, it is only in the denouement of the Biblical story that God's purposes become fully manifest and his sovereignty over all malign forces revealed in all its power and splendour. (Isaiah 11:6-9; Revelation 21:3-4).

## The Question of the 'Big Book'

The Bible is one of the oldest books in the world. And the reason often advanced for not reading it is that it is a big book, written a long time ago and thus not easy to understand. Perhaps, for these reasons it may scare some people away from opening its pages. Furthermore, seeing that it is such an ancient book, there is a question about its relevance in today's world. I will now try to deal with these questions.

With regard to the problem of the 'big book,' I will share with readers the approach I have adopted in my book. Opening page one of the Bible, with the intention of reading the whole book from cover to cover might be a task not likely to succeed. I have adopted a selective approach to the Bible. I have selected some books for more detailed consideration than others, e.g. Genesis, Exodus, the writings of the Prophets and the Gospel of Mark. I group a number of books together for more general treatment: Joshua, Judges, Samuel and Kings. Of the books I choose for detailed treatment, I still omit certain passages, e.g. Exodus 26-30, which include details about civil and religious laws. I also omit the Books of Leviticus and Numbers, apart from some brief reference to them, e.g. Leviticus 19:18. Much of Leviticus is dealing with regulations for religious worship in ancient Israel. These may not be of any great interest to people today. The Book of Numbers covers more or less the same events as Exodus. I devote just one chapter to the books of Joshua, Judges, Samuel and Kings, while dealing in more detail with the first three kings of Israel: Saul, David and Solomon. Of great importance are the books of the prophets. I deal briefly with Amos and Hosea, two of the twelve minor prophets. These two were the first of the prophets with books to their names. They were active in Northern Israel from about 750 to 721 BC, the date in which that kingdom fell to the Assyrian empire. I comment on the major prophets in more detail - Isaiah, Jeremiah and Ezekiel, all of whom appeared in the period of the later kings of Israel and Judah. The Book of Isaiah can be recommended for reading in its entirety – not just for its literary artistry and its great poetry, but because of its revelation of God as the Creator of the universe and saviour of humanity.

There is a group of books in the Bible known as the wisdom books. These are the Books of Job, Psalms, Proverbs, Ecclesiastes, Ecclesiasticus, the Song of Songs, and the Book of Wisdom. I have omitted these for consideration, because they are not strictly concerned with salvation history, (the history of God's relationship with humanity down the ages), which is the main theme of my book. The wisdom books have an important place in the Bible. Wisdom is God's gift to us. Wisdom guides us towards righteous living. It is a way to live our lives that does not bring us a lot of pain and regret. The Book of Job is a long and beautiful poetic account in which the principal character, Job, questions God about his innocent suffering. (See Job 7:1-11). Despite his sufferings, Job was at last able to see God as his "redeemer." (Job 19:25-27, NRSVC). The question of innocent suffering was fully answered in the life, death and resurrection of Jesus. The Book of Psalms was the hymnbook of the Jerusalem temple. For Christians, it is the prayer book of the Church. There are five different kinds of psalms: praise of God, wisdom, thanksgiving, royal psalms and psalms of lament. Down the ages and today, the psalms of lament have given suffering persons the trust that God is with them in their pain and the hope that he will listen to their cries for help. (See Psalms 80, 85, 126, 137, 42:6-11). The psalms foreshadow Jesus. In psalm 23, for example, Jesus is the shepherd who gives us all we need, leads us to meadows of green grass and restful streams, thus satisfying our hunger and thirst for meaningful life. (Psalm 23:2). He strengthens us for our journey and leads us on the right path (23:3). He accompanies us and consoles us in times of darkness. (23:4). It is Jesus who ultimately prepares a welcoming home banquet for us in God's own house. (23:5-6). I reference and quote extensively from the Psalms and from most of the other wisdom books.

Now for a brief outline of the content of the books I have selected for commentary. The Books of Genesis and Exodus (the first two books of the Bible) are important as an introduction to salvation history. The name *Genesis* means 'origin.' The book opens with the creation of the world. The main theme of Genesis is God's relationship with the whole of humanity. God is the chief protagonist of Genesis. The other principal characters in the book are Adam, Eve, Cain, Abel, Noah, the builders of Babel, Abraham, Jacob and his sons. These are archetypes of humanity. They represent ourselves in our own relationship with God – how we lose faith in him and go our own way, but then may learn to trust him and begin our journey of following him all over again. (Isaiah 49:10-11; Psalm 23:2; 77:20; Mark 10:32). God did not create human beings and then leave them to their own devices. He wants to establish a relationship with the human beings whom he created in his own image and likeness (Genesis 1:26), so that they may become more like himself. God establishes his relationship with Adam and Eve by blessing them and appointing them to a mission of caring for the earth and all of its creatures and its people (Genesis 1:28; 2:15). God thus honours and dignifies human beings through inviting them to participate in his ongoing creative work. (See Psalm 8:5-6). But they reject his offer of responsible stewardship and go into hiding from him (Genesis 3:8), choosing instead to care only for themselves. This is the first act of disobedience in the Bible. (Genesis 2:16-17; 3:6). It is to have dire consequences. (Genesis 2:7b; 3:19). The persistent refusal of this mission of caring is very much the story of the Old Testament. But the story does not end there. Only what the prophets called a remnant would remain faithful to God. (Isaiah 4:3-4). The remnant was at last reduced to one man – Jesus of Nazareth.

Abraham is a major figure in Genesis. He is the great man of faith in the Bible. In the story of Abraham, we learn that faith means trust in God, and that such trust leads to obedience, which is a decision to be led and guided by God. Abraham represents humanity as a whole. Because human beings (through Adam) have disobeyed God and refused their God-given mission of caring (Genesis 2:16-17; 3:6), God then chooses one man (Abraham), and because of this man's faithfulness and obedience, God promises to give him "as many descendants (people of faith everywhere) as there are "stars in the sky or grains of sand along the seashore." (Genesis 22:17). Because of Abraham's trust and obedience, God promises to bless (save) his descendants of all nations. (Genesis 22:18). However, after a few generations, through rivalry and enmity, Abraham's family breaks up and scatters. And as a result, its members find themselves in exile in Egypt, where they are eventually enslaved. (See Genesis 37).

The name *Exodus* means 'departure.' The Book of Exodus tells the story of God appointing Moses to a mission of rescuing the Israelites (descendants of Abraham) from slavery in Egypt. (Exodus 3:7-10). It is notable that the mission of Moses is also one of caring for God's people. Having been saved from slavery, God does not leave his people alone, wandering about the Near East. He tells them that their earthly journey has a goal and purpose, and he wants to lead them towards that goal. In order to give them hope and encouragement, he promises to bring them to the land of Canaan, later named Israel. They are told that this is a rich and fertile land, where they will live long. (Exodus 3:8; Deuteronomy 11:9). This was the land first promised by God to Abraham (Genesis 12:1b, and again to Abraham's descendants through Moses (Exodus 3:8, NJB). Ever after, it became known as the 'promised land,' which the people understood as their destiny. Exodus continues with an account of the people's journey through a semi-arid wilderness to Mount Sinai, where God reveals the Ten Commandments to them. (Exodus 20:1-17). The purpose of the Commandments is to bind the scattered Hebrew tribes together so that they might live in a right relationship with God and with one another in the promised land, where they would eventually become a nation. While commenting on Exodus, I refer briefly to the Book of Deuteronomy, which is composed in the form of a long speech delivered by Moses to the Israelites just before they entered the promised land. Moses appeals to the people never to forget the God who rescued and saved them, the one who promises to be with them always. It is to this God, and no other, that they owe their loyalty and obedience. (Deuteronomy 32:45-47). The Exodus story foreshadows Jesus' rescue of the whole of humanity from evil, and our journey through this life to our promised land destiny of eternal life with God.

The books of the Bible that deal with salvation history in the promised land (Canaan) are Joshua, Judges, Samuel and Kings. In the first part of this period (Joshua and Judges), the people try to form a loose confederation of the twelve tribes. This largely proves to be a failure. So there then arose the desire to have a king ruling them like the other nations. This is the story told in the Books of Samuel and Kings. In these books, God tries to form a relationship with one nation Israel, but with the expectation that Israel (descended from Abraham) would be the means of bringing his blessing of salvation to all nations. (Genesis 22:18). In the Bible, at this stage, salvation is understood as no more than God establishing his people in obedience to himself and giving them a rich and fertile land as their destiny.

The long period of the kings of Israel gave rise to prophecy. God called the prophets to be his spokespersons on earth. He filled them with his Spirit and appointed them to a mission (giving further meaning to the idea of mission) of speaking the truth to the Kings of Israel when they deviated from obedience to God and led their people astray. (Amos 5:10-15). The prophets warned that disobedience would have dire consequences for Israel. (Jeremiah 5:1, 5-6).

Because of its turning away from the Lord, Israel came to an end as a nation in 587 BC. Its leading people, including its last king, were then taken away to slavery in the Babylonian empire (the land of the rivers Tigris and Euphrates). The prophet Isaiah reminded the people why God allowed them to be taken into exile ("plundered and locked up in dungeons," Isaiah 42:22). Their new experience of bondage was because they would not live as God wanted them to live, or obey his teachings about creating a caring society, one in which justice and mercy would prevail (Isaiah 42:24), so that they might be the means of bringing the blessing of justice and mercy to the wider world (Isaiah 42:6-7). This was God's plan for Israel and the world ever since the time of Abraham.

The Book of Ezekiel, and Isaiah chapters 40-55 deal with the period of the Israelite exile in Babylon (587-537 BC). The exile wasn't all bad. It was God's plan to bring his people to their senses, testing them "in the fire of suffering" like silver in a burning fire. (Isaiah 48:10; see Psalm 66:10-12). They had been seduced and led away from God by the material riches of the promised land and by their own schemes for salvation: militarism, political power and the affluence that only benefited a small number of people. Far away in Babylon, they would learn that human beings cannot live on bread alone (material things), but on obedience to God's word spoken to them in their Scriptures. (Deuteronomy 8:2-3). The people had lost their way (Isaiah 53:6a) by turning God's gifts of land and nation into false gods who could never save them, thus abandoning the God who cared for them and liberated them from Egypt. But God had not abandoned or forgotten his people. (Isaiah 49:8-9; 14-15, 22). Having being sent into a metaphorical wilderness (Babylon), like their ancestors of old in Egypt, they would find God, once again, speaking to them - preparing them for their return home (Isaiah 40:1-3). Yes, God would restore them to their destiny, thus fulfilling their deepest desires for salvation (Isaiah 55:1-2) and renewing their mission to be a "light to the nations," so that, in the words of God himself, "my salvation may reach the remotest parts of the earth." (Isaiah 49:6; see 60:1-3).

So far in the Bible, we are beginning to get a picture of human limitation and failure. God does not give up on human beings. He continually responds to such failure with a renewal of his love covenant with his people. (Isaiah 50:10; Jeremiah 31:31-34; Ezekiel 11:19-20; 36:26). No matter the disobedience of Israel, God's offer of salvation still holds firm. He will continue freeing his people from the bondages which lead them away from him. (Isaiah 14:3; Galatians 5:1). His promise of a destiny (promised land) is not withheld. Jesus will interpret the ideas of liberation and destiny in a new way, thus fulfilling, in a deeper sense, the vision of the Old Testament.

## Relevance of the Bible Today

A question is often asked, 'Because the Bible is an ancient religious text, how can it make sense of life today?' The world has certainly changed since Biblical times. But deepest human needs and desires remain constant – the need for true freedom, peace, love, community, hope. The Bible has a relevance in today's world, because it raises the question about the meaning of human life.

People today say that the human race has advanced and matured over the millennia, making us wiser, more knowledgeable and more sophisticated than ever before. To be sure, great progress has been made in areas of invention and discovery, in science and technology. Such developments have brought us many benefits. Advances in modern medicine have improved human wellbeing in untold ways. Science, however, cannot explain everything about us or provide answers to our deepest needs. It is only one avenue to truth. It cannot create states of perfection in this world. No matter what the mastery of science, unaided human reason and knowledge can never conquer the suffering and evils that enslave and disable humanity (Mark 2:2-3), the greatest evil of all being death. This can only be the work of the Creator and sovereign God. (Ezekiel 37:11-12; Isaiah 26:19; John 6:40; Mark 2:10; 16:6; 1 Corinthians 15:23).

The Bible has nothing to say about science. The Bible is a great book of wisdom. While we may, indeed, have become more sophisticated and more knowledgeable today, it is a matter of debate whether humanity has progressed very much at all in its wisdom. The Bible understands wisdom as the practical knowledge - aided by the word of God - by which human beings gain true and lasting happiness. Wisdom is trusting and hoping in God as the reliable guide to human life, and not in many of the things in which we often place our faith and hope, such as the false gods of instant gratification, unlimited freedom, fame, status and possessions. These things are false gods because they cannot give us true and lasting fulfilment, although that is what they always promise. They can tie us up in bondages, often only bringing us grief. (See Mark 10:21-22, NRSVC). Placing all our hopes in what is ephemeral may be delusional. It can lead to disappointment and a loss of a sense of meaning. The Bible deals with fundamental questions about human life: what is the meaning of life, how should we live our lives in order to find peace and fulfilment, where do we come from, do we have a purpose in the world, and where are we going, i.e. do we have a destiny beyond this world? These questions are as relevant today as they were 2,500 years ago, when much of the Old Testament was finally completed. Moreover, the Bible provides the kind of answers to them that can make human life meaningful and fulfilling.

What is meant by a meaningful life? Life has meaning if there is a purpose behind it. A life lived with purpose can be a fulfilled and happy life. The human being is a searcher for meaning. So, for example, we find meaning in our work and in loving and caring for our families. But in so doing, or having done all of that, we are still left searching, these things seemingly not fully satisfying our deepest desire for happiness. Because the things of this world never fully satisfy us, we continue the search for ultimate meaning. So we ask if there are higher meanings that will more deeply satisfy us: do our lives as a whole have a meaning and purpose? There is a belief abroad today that human beings are nothing more than the material product of a blind evolution. In other words, we come into the world without any purpose. We are born, we live for a while and then we die. But other than that, we are going nowhere. This is a false, materialistic philosophy. It can lead people into depression and despair. It is false and delusional, because it leaves the deepest yearnings of the human heart unfulfilled.

If our lives as a whole are to have meaning, such meaning has to be a given. It must come from outside ourselves – from the Creator God who made us for a purpose. The message of the Bible is that God responds to our search for ultimate meaning, by giving us a meaning, which, left to ourselves, we could never discover. Living in the present moment, no matter how gratifying, is not enough. Human beings need a story that leads somewhere. This is what gives us hope – as a counteract to grief and despair. (Mark 10:22, NRSVC). Hope looks for fulfilment of our desires, but because nothing in this world can fully satisfy us, our restless hearts have a longing for a happiness that only God can give us, by sharing his eternal life with us beyond death. (*Confessions of St. Augustine*, chap.1; see Revelation 21:3-4; Psalm 63:1,3, 5, 7-8).

As we live our lives, God begins to fulfil our deepest desires by giving us a job to do. At the beginning of the Bible we find that God blesses human beings and appoints them to missions of caring for the earth and one another. (See Genesis 1:28; 2:15; Psalm 8:5-8). This gives us a reason for living (meaningful life) and sets us on a journey, leading to ultimate fulfilment. Our mission in life represents the first steps of our journey to our promised land destiny. (Hebrews 11:16; Revelation 21:3-4). Through serving and caring for the earth and our neighbour, God guides us on a path that leads to eternal life. (Mathew 25:34-35; Mark 10:21; see Psalm 23:3). God is preparing a welcoming-home banquet for us. (Psalm 23:5-6; Luke 15:22-24). This gives meaning and purpose to our lives. It inspires us with courage and hope and empowers us for our journey through the trials and tribulations of this life.

Speaking through the prophet Isaiah, God reveals that caring is equated with service. (See Isaiah 42:5-7). Like Israel of old, we are called to be God's servants. (Isaiah 43:10). Serving others is what rescues us from being overly concerned with the self. It amounts to losing our old life centred on the self. (Mark 8:34-35). Moving away from the comfort zone of the self can be difficult and painful. But God does not leave us alone when he calls us to do his creative work on earth. He is with us on our journey, to strengthen and encourage us. (Exodus 3:12a; 4:11-12; Jeremiah 1:18-19; Luke 24:49; Matthew 28:19).

God, however, has a problem with human beings. From the beginning, God wants to form a relationship with human beings, so that they might become more like himself –caring, just and merciful. (Exodus 34:6; Deuteronomy 32:4; Psalm 10:18; 11:7; 146:6-9). In imitation of him, God's people are exhorted to "learn to do right and seek justice." (Isaiah 1:17). In order to seek and establish justice, our concerns must be directed towards others. (Matthew 25:35-36). But from the beginning, humanity decides to go its own individualistic way, symbolized by the departure from Eden. (Genesis 3:8). Salvation history reveals that, although promising to be faithful to God (Exodus 24:3), human beings continually reject their call to service, in disobedience of God. (Genesis 1:28; 3:6,8; Jeremiah 38:20; Isaiah 53:6a). They want to go their own way and create their own meanings. (Isaiah 53:6a). The Old Testament has much to say about the consequences of human 'wandering' (Genesis 3:19b; 4:16), which began with the flight from the Garden of Eden. Disobedience is one of the main themes of the Books of Judges, Samuel and Kings. The kings are judged for leading their people astray and according to their loyalty to God. A turning to false gods, such as affluence, elitism and power, only leads to disaster. (1 Kings 11:3-6, 11).

The Old Testament ends with the writings of the great prophets of Israel. God revealed himself to the prophets as a God of justice and mercy. The mission of the prophets was to communicate God's justice and mercy to a spiritually blind, deaf and rebellious people. (Isaiah 42:18-20; Ezekiel 12:1-2). The people's failure to create a just and merciful society in the promised land (Israel) was a failure of obedience, a refusal of their mission of caring. It led to exile in the far country and separation from God. (Isaiah 48:18-19; Jeremiah 22:3, 5, 8-9; Ezekiel 45:9; Luke 15:13-14). The prophets finally came to the conclusion that disobedience was so all-pervasive, that nothing short of a divine intervention in the world could deal with it. The prophets then foretold that a new King in the line of King David would come. This king would know the will of God and obey it. (Isaiah 11:1-3). Thus, there arose the hope for a future Messiah (one to finally deal with evil and put everything right), who, with the Spirit of God living in him, would at last accomplish what no human being ever could, i.e. lift human beings up from their lost and wounded condition and carry them home. (Genesis 2:17b; 3:19; Luke 10:30-35; 15:4-6a, 22-24).

## Jesus: God's Servant, Messiah and Son

The New Testament is a continuation of the Old Testament Bible. Its main theme is the fulfilment of God's Old Testament promises and plans for humanity. In his disobedience in the Garden of Eden, the first human representative failed in his God-given mission of service, which was caring for the earth and one another. He then went into hiding from God. (Genesis 1:28; 2:15; 3:8). In a later phase of salvation history. God appointed Israel to be his servant, to trust in God and to see that justice was done on earth, and to open its blind eyes to its sins of disobedience, reminding Israel that he was the only God. (Isaiah 41:8-9; 42:6-7, 18-20; 43:10; 49:6). But disobedient Israel only gave lip service to God, proving to be a blind and deaf servant. (Isaiah 29:13; Amos 5:14-15, 24; Ezekiel 12:2). Israel disobeyed its God-given mission to practice justice at home, thus failing in its role of being a guiding light to the other nations.

Isaiah's servant foreshadows Jesus, who is God's perfect and obedient servant. Jesus fulfils what the prophets only saw as a dim horizon for Israel. Jesus is the servant who succeeds in his task. (Isaiah 52:13; 63:10). It is he who establishes justice among the nations. (Isaiah 42:1-4, 6-7). As the new embodiment of Israel, Jesus is the "light of the world"– so that the people of all nations might come into a union with one another in obedience to God. (John 8:12).

Jesus is also God's Messiah, the king who, at last, will put everything right and establish his reign over evil for ever. (Isaiah 9:7). At the beginning of his earthly ministry, Jesus revealed the content and aims of his mission as Messiah. In the Nazareth synagogue, he quoted the prophet Isaiah (61:1-2) in words he then applied to himself. (Luke 4:18-19, NRSVC). Jesus is the one who opens eyes (Luke 4:18c) that have been blind to their sins. It is he who sets people free from a variety of oppressions. (Luke 4:18b; Genesis 3:1a; Mark 1:32-34). The time has come for God to intervene in the world to put everything right and "save his people." (Luke 4:19).

More than Messiah, Jesus is the Son of God, meaning that he has a deep filial relationship with the Father. (Mark 1:11; 9:7). Jesus was filled with God's Spirit and named the "beloved Son" of God (Mark 1:10), confirming him in his obedience and empowering him to do what Israel of old failed to do. God appointed Israel to be his "son." (Exodus 4:22; Jeremiah 30:9c, 31:20; Hosea 11:1). But because of its disobedience of God and blindness to its sins, Israel failed to be a true son of God. It failed to care for the most vulnerable in its society. (See Hosea 11:2-4). In the Garden of Gethsemane, Jesus proved himself the be a true Son, in that he offered a perfect obedience to God his Father (Mark 14:36). Further, in offering himself as a substitute for us, he suffered the consequences of human rebellion against God, which is death, so that we (the rebellious ones) might be freed from the bondage of death and obtain eternal life as our destiny – his great act of service. (Isaiah 53:5). After God raised him up from death, he came back again to forgive all who had a hand in his death, i.e. rebellious humans (Luke 24:36, 46-47; John 20:19), thus liberating everyone from their vengeful and murderous ways. (Genesis 4:8; Mark 3:6, 12:7-8; 14:63-64). His great act of forgiveness brings the whole of humanity into his own obedience and union with God. This is the union for which Jesus prayed for his disciples shortly before his death. (John 17:20-21).

Thus, both as obedient Son and as the new human representative in the new garden (Gethsemane), Jesus restores humanity to a filial relationship and union with God, as originally in the Garden of Eden before the 'fall.' (Genesis 2:8, 15). Human beings are then empowered to resume their mission of caring.

The Christian gospel is God's word to us, offering us hope, and presenting us with a challenge. We too, are called to follow Jesus on his journey of service (Mark 1:16-17, NRSVC; John 20:21; Matthew 28:19), to stay with him and not run away into hiding (Mark 14:50), in his ongoing mission of liberating and caring (Luke 4:18-19), as our own task in life. (Matthew 25:35). Although the disciples abandoned Jesus when he was arrested by the religious authorities, he did not abandon them. In his last words on earth to them (and to us too), he told them that he would be with them "always." (Matthew 28:20; see Isaiah 41:10; 49:15-16; Deuteronomy 31:6; Romans 8:38-39). The human story is going somewhere. Being with us always implies an eternal love relationship with God, as our destiny. This is the promised land towards which we can journey in hope.

## An Approach to the New Testament

There are reasons why I could not include the whole of the New Testament for consideration in this book. Accordingly, I have chosen the Gospel of Mark for detailed commentary, while also making reference to the gospels of Matthew, Luke and John, the Acts of the Apostles and the Letters of St. Paul. Mark's gospel (meaning 'good news') was the first of the gospels to be written. It is thus the closest in time to Jesus. Although this is the shortest of the gospels, it contains the whole of the Christian message within its pages. Mark's gospel presents the life of the Christian as a journey of obedient service, of following Jesus on the road he has already gone ahead of us. The good news is that it is a road leading to resurrection, as the fulfilment of our destiny. As a work of literature, and in its unique and glorious vision of human life, Mark's gospel sets a headline for the authors of the other three gospels.

My hope for this book is that it will encourage lay people to read the Bible, while, at the same time, they should feel free to adopt a selective approach similar to what I follow here. In this introduction and throughout the book, I make innumerable references to other verses and parts of the Bible. While reading the book, I encourage readers to have a Bible close to hand, with the intention of looking up the references, as these will open up new layers of meaning and understanding.

CHAPTER 1

# THE BIBLE: A LITERARY WORK

## Inspiration

Unlike a science book or indeed any factual book or treatise, the Bible is a literary work, and as such, it is inspired. But in the case of the Bible, the inspiration comes from God, through the Holy Spirit. "No prophetic message ever came just from human will, but people were under the control of the Holy Spirit as they spoke the message that came from God." (2 Peter 1:21).

Because the Bible is the inspired word of God, it follows that its books "must be acknowledged as teaching solidly, faithfully and without error the truth which God wanted put into sacred writings for the sake of salvation."[1] (See 2 Timothy 3:16-17). Because the Bible is only concerned with religious truth, the fact that it may not always be correct in the matter of historical or scientific truth is irrelevant. "Genesis, chapter 1 (the creation story) appears not as a scientific treatise, but rather as a theological meditation on the sovereignty of God over all creation and the place of the Sabbath observance within the fabric of creation."[2]

It can be truly said of all great human creations – art, architecture, literature, music – that they are inspired by the author of all creation. But biblical inspiration is different from all other kinds of inspiration in that it arises out of the human authors' experience of God speaking to them and revealing to them what he wants to teach about human life and human destiny. In almost any passage of the Bible - whether in its formal poetry, prayers, prophecy, historical accounts, or the parables of Jesus, his sayings and miracles - the words excite wonder and awe, and we in turn, are inspired by their power to move us.

The Bible is both inspired itself, and in turn, inspires us to undertake the challenging faith journey of following the way of Jesus. The Bible can inspire us because of the beautiful language in which it is composed – the language of poetry, some of it written in formal poetry, such as the Psalms and much of the writings of the prophets. Because poetry is full of metaphor and symbol, the language of poetry can disclose

---

[1] *Dei Verbum, Dogmatic Constitution on Divine Revelation, Vatican II*

[2] Daniel J. Harrington, S.J, *How Do Catholics Read the Bible?* (Rowman and Littlefield Publishers, Inc), P. 38.

multiple meanings in biblical texts. It is understandable that God would speak to us in the most beautiful language of all, namely that of poetry. This is amply illustrated in any passage, in any story from any part of the Bible. (See 1 Kings 3:5-12; Mark 4:35-41; Matthew 14:22-32).

## Divine and Human Authorship of the Bible

Just as Jesus was fully divine and fully human, the Bible is at the same time the word of God and the words of human beings; it is both divine and human. As in the case of Jesus, it is a place where the divine and the human meet and overlap. The Second Vatican Council says that the books of the Bible were written under the inspiration of the Holy Spirit, that they have God as their author and have been handed on to the Church.[3] The same document also states that the human authors are "true authors."[4] How can this be; is there not a contradiction here? How can God work on human minds while yet leaving them free human minds? Is there something mysterious about the authorship of the Bible?

God, as Creator, is present always, in and to his human creatures and to the wider creation, sustaining them in their existence and in everything they do, whether it is authoring a book of the Bible or anything else. All creative work reveals something of its creator's mind, feelings and imagination. This means that any created work resembles its creator in some way. Similarly, the created world mirrors God. "How clearly the sky reveals God's glory." (Psalm 19:1). In a deeper sense, human beings resemble God in certain ways. "God said, 'Let us make man in our own image, in the likeness of ourselves.'" (Genesis 1:26, NJB). This means that there is a spark of the divine within each and every one of us. Thus, God works creatively in and through his image bearing human creatures, so that as co-creators with God, some of them are called to author a book of the Bible. Thus, as a creative work, the Bible could be said to be a reflection of the mind of God.

However, this sustaining presence of God, in and through human beings doesn't destroy their autonomy to act as free beings. Because freedom is an attribute of God, we resemble God also in our freedom. So, as free beings (through the God present in us), it can be said that both God and human beings are authors of the Bible. Having called us to be stewards of his creation, God always needs his human image-bearing partners in furtherance of his creative purposes, which are ongoing in the world.

In the same way God enters his creation, in and through Jesus, so that we can say that Jesus is the perfect reflection, the perfect image of God. God was not pretending to be man in Jesus; he became man. In the same way, God was not pretending to use human beings in authoring books of the Bible. In using the gifts given to them by God, and inspired by God, the authors were acting as themselves.

We may put it like this: God granted a limited autonomy to the human authors of the Bible, and inspired by him, they fulfilled their God-given task. Yes, a limited autonomy! Absolute autonomy would mean complete separation from God, a rejection of him as a partner. So perhaps we could look on the Bible as a partnership between the Creator God and his co-creators, made in his image.

---

[3] Vatican II, *Dei Verbum,* 11.

[4] Vatican II, *Dei Verbum.*

We have a spark of the divine within us. God's hand has to be at work in all creative endeavour, whether it is writing a novel, painting a picture or building a gothic cathedral. The results are not all due to human beings' own efforts, however skilled or talented they may be. We are dependent creatures. We are not totally autonomous.

Because the Bible was produced by human beings in partnership with God, it was not dictated by God in any sense. Dictation would imply coercion, imposition, prescription. God would be doing all the work; his creatures would merely be cyphers. Dictation would have made human beings the slaves of God, depriving them of the possibility of freely responding to him. God is like a loving Father, not a dictator. Love does not compel. Love is kind and merciful. Love waits for a loving response. Love creates partnership. So for example, did God *literally* dictate the Ten Commandments to Moses? Perhaps the Commandments were gradually brought to finality over a number of generations, and eventually, under the inspiration of God, edited for inclusion in the Bible, and then ascribed to Moses who prepared the Hebrew slaves for the reception of God's law after their liberation from Egypt – the story told in the Book of Exodus.

One of the central themes of the Bible is the notion of covenant – God speaking to us out of love and calling us to respond to him in a loving manner. This means that, far from dictation or coercion, God is continually inviting and empowering his human partners (created in his image), while respecting their freedom, to follow him in his ongoing creative work.

We recognise that the human authors, as human beings, were limited in many ways; they were products of a particular time and culture. They were ignorant of science, and as we will see later, sometimes ignorant of theology. In earlier times they were incapable of receiving a full idea of who God is.

## Interpreting the Bible

The human authors of the Bible didn't have to know about many things, including science and the early history of the earth. But as a literary work, there is no reading of the Bible without interpretation.

> Since God speaks in Sacred Scripture through human beings, in human fashion, the interpreter of Sacred Scripture, in order to see clearly what God wanted to communicate to us, should carefully investigate what meaning the sacred writers really intended.[5]

The contents of a science book, or indeed any factual book, can only have one meaning. On the other hand, a literary work like the Bible can have multiple meanings, and as such, it needs to be interpreted, in order to arrive at its meaning. In the opening lines of one of his greatest poems, W. B. Yeats says, 'I went into a hazel wood because a fire was in my head?'[6] We ask, 'What does Yeats mean by that?' It can have multiple meanings. The parable of the Prodigal Son (itself a poetic text), for instance, can have many layers of meaning.

[5] *Dei Verbum* 12.

[6] *The Song of Wandering Aengus.*

Thus, interpretation unlocks the key to what God is saying to us in the Bible. However, interpretive skills are not something we can take for granted. The Pontifical Biblical Commission says that an understanding of Biblical texts is only granted to the person who can see them on the basis of life experience. Divine intervention in human history comes to us through faith, which is a slow maturing process.

> As the reader matures in the life of the Spirit, there grows in him or her the capacity to understand the realities of which the Bible speaks. In exploring the meaning of Biblical texts, we must accept that they actually speak to us of the present and not just the past. Secondly, we must hold the conviction that the divine intervenes in human history.[7]

In order to interpret any part of the Bible - among other things - we must pay attention to literary forms. "For truth is set forth and expressed differently in texts that are variously historical, prophetic, poetic, or of other forms of discourse."[8]

The Bible contains practically every known literary genre, including myth, legend, parable, epic, folklore, history, story, poetry, prayers, proverbs, letters, hymns, prophecy and apocalyptic. These cannot all be interpreted in the same way. For example, a story written as an epic, cannot be interpreted in the same way as a historical account. Some parts of the Bible are meant to be interpreted literally, and others metaphorically. The Babylonians really captured Jerusalem and burnt it down in 587 BC. Jesus was put to death on a cross by Puntius Pilate, the Roman governor. On the other hand, the creation stories, the story of Adam and Eve, the Tower of Babel, the account of the Flood, the parables of Jesus and many other stories and teachings are to be understood metaphorically. When Jesus said, 'I am the vine and you are the branches,' he was speaking metaphorically. There are also parts of the Bible which are literally true, but which can also be interpreted metaphorically.

The second point about interpretation is that the Bible must be interpreted in the spirit in which it was written, and especially, in the light of the Bible as a whole. This means that serious attention must be given to the content and unity of the whole of Scripture if its meaning is to be correctly worked out. For this reason, many contemporary literary interpreters insist that isolated parts of a text are to be understood in the light of the text as a whole, that is, in the context of the large work to which the text belongs, in this case, the Bible.

This raises the question: How do we interpret the "dark" passages of the Old Testament which may cause difficulties for believers? Some parts of the Bible may be culturally conditioned, so that we would not interpret them as applicable to today's world.

> Biblical revelation is deeply rooted in history. God's plan is manifested progressively and accomplished slowly, in successive stages, and despite human resistance. God chose a people and patiently worked to educate and guide them.

---

[7] Pontifical Biblical Commission, 1993.

[8] Ibid.

Revelation is suited to the cultural and moral level of distant times and thus describes facts and customs such as cheating and trickery, and acts of violence and massacre without explicitly denouncing the immorality of such things.[9]

As the Bible evolved, so did its teachings. The earlier books of the Bible teach concepts and practices that later books modify or reject. The ancient Israelites were a primitive society. They were not always ready to receive the fullness of revelation. Only in the later stages of their evolution were they more open to the truth of what God was saying to them. Thus, the later prophets of Israel taught about the love and mercy of God for all people, and condemned every kind of injustice and violence. They were God's best teachers in preparation for the Christian gospel. And so, we should interpret difficult texts in their historical-literary context and in the light of Christ who is the fulfilment of the law and the prophets. Even Jesus' own disciples exhibited a hardness of heart to the word of God. (See Matthew 28:17; Mark 9:32). We can all be slow to grasp and receive God's true message. Jesus himself is the best interpreter of Scripture. (See Luke 24:25-27).

An example of a difficult biblical text comes from a lengthy speech attributed to Moses in the Book of Deuteronomy, in which Moses reminds the Hebrew tribes that they will have to fight the native peoples and capture their cities when they enter Canaan, the land promised to Abraham and his descendants. The Lord said, 'When you capture cities in the land that the Lord your God is giving you, kill everyone. Completely destroy all the people.' (Deuteronomy 20:16-18).

The question arises, does God's choice of Israel (divine election) entail violence and the ethnic cleansing of other peoples? Is the God of Israel an intolerant and cruel God? How could ethnic cleansing be of the will of God, who commanded "thou shall not kill?" In choosing Israel, God is revealed as loving and caring, and from the time of Abraham, the choice of Israel was so that Israel would eventually bring God's blessing of salvation to the other nations. (Genesis 22:18). In ascribing violence to God, the author of Deuteronomy, and others, may have been projecting their *own* violent tendencies on to their limited understanding of God at a particular time– an instance of bad theology. They may have seen God as morally, no better than themselves. (In international relations how often do we see violence still being adduced as the first option in order to rid the world of some evil)? With reference to the conquest of the promised land in the Book of Joshua, even if the Canaanite people are depicted as involved in all kinds of evil, even child sacrifice, this does not justify the notion of God calling for their destruction.

The biblical theologian, R. W. L. Moberly says that the command to kill other peoples in Deuteronomy was written in retrospect. It was a utopian law that was not realized within Israel's history. The Canaanites were neither exterminated nor expelled from the promised land. (See Book of Judges 1:21-23; 1 Kings 9:20-21). Modern biblical scholars hold that this law was purely theoretical and was never in effect.[10]

How are we to interpret such texts which begin with the words: "The Lord said?" We are not to imagine that God literally appears and whispers commands into the ears of

---

[9] Pope Benedict XVI, *Verbum Domini,* (Catholic Truth Society), p. 58.

[10] R. W. L. Moberly, *Old Testament Theology,* (Baker Academic, Grand Rapids, Michigan), p. 61-2, 65.

the prophets or biblical authors. What is at stake here is that leading men speak and act in accordance with what they discern as the will of God at a particular time.

By the time of the final editing of the books of Deuteronomy and Joshua in the 7th century BC, the Canaanites had been long assimilated within Israel, but may have still held onto many of their traditional religious practices.

Moses did not write the Book of Deuteronomy. Biblical scholars think that the book originated during the 7th century BC, and that it was only finally edited, with new material included, after the return of the Jews from the Babylonian captivity in 537 BC, a time when final editions of the Hebrew Scriptures were being produced and collected as a single volume.[11]

As we have already noted with reference to interpretation, in the context of the Bible as a whole, such actions in the Books of Joshua and Deuteronomy are superseded in the teaching of Jesus. In the First Letter of John, we read that "God is love." (1 John 4:8). The thrust of the Bible as a whole is to prescribe love and forgiveness of enemies and to value and cherish all human life, because God loves all people everywhere. Love is not vindictive, but seeks the good of the other. The later prophets condemned militarism and preached a God of justice and mercy, the compassionate and caring one, especially caring for the weak and vulnerable. Jesus never condemned anyone for wrong-doing. His way was forgiveness, mercy and love. He turned the other cheek to evil so as to create a new world of union and harmony. He expected the same in his followers. (See Matthew 5:38-39, 43-44).

How do we come to a resolution if there is little or no agreement about the interpretation of a particular passage of the Bible? Who finally decides the meaning of a particular text? Because the Old Testament Scriptures were accepted into the early Church, and the New Testament had its origin in the Church, it follows that "interpreting Scripture is subject finally to the judgement of the Church, which carries out the divine commission and ministry of guarding and interpreting the word of God."[12]

## How did the Bible Come to be Written?

In the case of most books of the Bible, there was a long oral history of perhaps hundreds of years; stories passed down, some written accounts, and with the addition of new insights relevant to life in later times. There were some written fragments dating possibly from about 1,000 BC – some stories of creation, stories about Abraham and accounts of the Israelites in Egypt and their rescue by Moses, as told in the Book of Exodus. When the final editing of all of this material took place, probably during the Babylonian exile (587-537 BC), both oral and written sources would have been taken into account in the compilation of the first five books of the Bible and the books of the prophets.

Biblical scholars are not in complete agreement about the timing and methods of all of this. But in all ancient cultures, the main reliance, initially at any rate, was on oral transmission. The first stories originating in all ancient cultures are myths and legends. Irish myths and legends, for example, were passed on orally down the ages before being

---

[11] Lawrence Boadt, *Reading the Old Testament*, (Paulist Press, New York), p. 75.

[12] The Pontifical Biblical Commission.

committed to writing after Christianity began to take root in Ireland in the late 5th century AD.

When the Israelites were in exile in Babylon (587-537 BC), they became familiar with a culture, in some ways, greater than their own. All of this influenced their own unique understanding and relationship with God. First of all, they learned of the Babylonian creation myths, which became the basis of their own creation story and the stories of Noah and the Flood. The prophets of the exile (Ezekiel and Second Isaiah), who wrote their own accounts, thus received new revelations of God through their experience of exile in Babylon. They discovered God, not just as the God of one nation Israel, but as the creator of the universe. This means that God would have the interests of all nations at heart. All of these revelations found their way into the shaping of the Old Testament Bible as we have it today.

## The Bible and Science

Before going on to the Genesis creation stories in the next chapter, let us deal briefly with a question that often arises today in reference to the Bible: does science disprove the Bible?

Many people today hold the view that the world and human beings can be understood and explained, simply from a scientific perspective, without reference to the Bible or the God of the Bible. The mindset that science can explain the *whole* of reality is derived from modern science, which according to some people, is supposed to be the source all our reliable knowledge, everything else being merely opinion. There is a belief today that knowledge should be reduced to facts, as if facts were the only truth. But what about wisdom, ideals, values, meaning? Science has nothing to say about these aspects of reality. Are values not also important? Facts are simply informative, while values and ideals have the power to transform our lives. It is not a question of one or the other. To say that science can explain the whole of reality is not a finding of science. It is really a faith.

The purpose of science is to provide descriptions and explanations about the physical universe through empirical and mathematical means. Science is about explanation, telling us *how* the world works and the causes of things. The Bible, on the other hand, is a literary work (stories, poetry, prayers, history). Therefore, its meaning is disclosed through interpretation. Who would say that there is no truth, nothing about values in stories, poetry and history?

The Bible is concerned with religious truth. "The purpose of Sacred Scripture, is to provide us with the truths that God wanted to reveal to us for our salvation."[13] Therefore, the seven-day creation story in Genesis is not an explanation or description of the origin of the physical universe. It has nothing to say about cause and effect. Rather it tells us that, however the world began, it did not create itself. God is ultimately responsible for all of creation. The seven-day account should be understood metaphorically and interpreted as the good news of God's love-relationship with the world and human beings.

From start to finish, the Bible is concerned with fundamental questions about the meaning and purpose of life. These questions are outside the domain and competence

---

[13] Pope Pius xii, *Divino Afflante Spiritu*, 1943.

of science. They open up a whole new world of meaning. So we ask why is there anything rather than nothing? Why is there evil in the world, and is there a solution to the problem of evil? Science asks how does the world work, while the Bible asks why do we exist at all, and what ought we do?

When science shows that the earth and life on earth evolved over hundreds of millions of years, religion accepts that as factual. Let us digress with a brief reference to what became known as the Ussher chronology! In 1650 AD the Protestant archbishop of Armagh, James Ussher, published his theory of the age of the earth. This theory was based on a literal interpretation of the Old Testament, especially the Book of Genesis. Ussher deduced that the first day of creation took place on October 23, 4004 BC! This was actually like what most people believed before the age of science. However, with the discovery of the age of the earth through geology and the study of the development of ancient life through rock fossils, modern science put paid to Ussher's calculations. Then all of a sudden in late 19th century England, the cry went up, 'Science disproves the Bible.' This resulted in a crisis of faith for many people and an emptying of churches all over England.

In point of fact, the discoveries of science had a beneficial effect on the interpretation of the Bible. It was then that Biblical scholars began to cast a critical eye on Sacred Scripture. This opened the way to the discovery of its true meaning. Slowly, the recognition dawned that the Bible is a literary work, which in many of its pages, must be interpreted metaphorically. The seven-day creation account in Genesis, for example, is pure poetry, and as such, should not be interpreted literally. Although science investigates *how* the world developed through natural causation (the theory of evolution), the Bible reveals that this came about through the creative activity of the sovereign God, and for a purpose. Thus, God is the ultimate cause of everything. The existence of laws presupposes a lawgiver. The laws of nature (e.g. gravity) are God's laws. The only thing that science can disprove is bad science.

Although, as believers, we accept the proven discoveries of science, this does not mean that we can accept every supposedly "scientific" statement made in the name of science. Statements such as "there is no reality beyond this physical world" and "there is no transcendent reality beyond this world" are philosophical, not scientific statements. Behind such thinking is the belief (yes, a belief) that religious people are living by blind faith, while non-believers in God are grounding their position on evidence and reason. To state that there is no transcendent reality and that science is the only arbiter of truth, are not findings of science. Such statements are merely beliefs. When some scientists claim that there is no spiritual dimension to reality, that there is no God, and therefore no God-given purpose to the world, these are claims which cannot be proven by science. And believers cannot agree with them. If as some scientists claim, life emerged and developed by pure chance, blind and random, the result of a purposeless natural process that did not have human beings in mind, then that particular interpretation of the theory of evolution is incompatible with both the Jewish and Christian understanding of creation, which sees the world and human life as intended by God for a purpose, revealing that human life is worthwhile and meaningful.

## God and the Idea of Purpose

Purpose is fundamental in considering the existence of God. Any system is bound by rules that govern events within the system. In reference to the system that governed the evolution of life, the rules are the laws of nature. These rules explain how the system works, but not why it came into existence, which has to do with purpose. The so-called 'blind' processes of evolution only serve to explain the *workings* of the system as discovered by science; the *purpose* of evolution is another matter entirely, and can only come from outside the system.

First of all, if we describe any system or object, solely in terms of its physical properties, we are left with an incomplete explanation or understanding of the object. For example, to describe a kettle just as a material object made of metal would not give a full understanding of the kettle. For that, we must look to its purpose, which is to boil water. Its purpose is not found within its physical properties, but is given to it by its maker, someone outside itself. Once we know its purpose, the kettle then becomes a meaningful object. So, with regard to the question, why is there a universe, we need to look at a Creator God as the One from outside the system, who gives the universe meaning and purpose. The created world couldn't have emerged, nor could it exist apart from God's purpose for it.

But hold a minute! Materialists readily agree that all human creations from a pen knife to a steam engine have purposes assigned to them by human beings as their creators, but that we ourselves come into the world without any purpose at all; we are just the chance material products of a blind evolution. In this context, let us call to mind, the post-war French existentialist philosopher, Jean-Paul Sartre. As with all materialists, Sartre's first premise is a denial of the existence of God. If there is no God, then there are no God-given purposes granted to the world or to human beings before their birth. What Sartre is saying, is that human beings have no destiny, no *ultimate* purpose, and when they die, they will merge with the dust of the earth. If we are to have an ultimate destiny, it has to be God-given. But no God, therefore no human destiny! The conclusion to be drawn from that is the one which Sartre himself accepted - that human life is absurd and meaningless. "Everything that exists is born for no purpose, continues through weakness and dies by chance."[14] The first part of that statement is merely an assertion. This rejection of God is passed off as supposedly scientific, as something empirically verified, which it is not. When scientists look into biology, they cannot see such a reality as meaning and purpose, but equally there is no evidence that such a reality does not exist.

As a materialist, Sartre would hold that the only meanings and purposes we have are ones we assign to ourselves, and according to him we have unlimited freedom to do so in any way we choose. Indeed, many of our choices are good; we can find meaning in loving relationships, in raising children, in our work, in artistic creation, in building and inventing things. Through the exercise of such choices we participate in the creative power of God, whether consciously or not. Creative pursuits satisfy our desire for fulfilment, because implicitly, they involve a search for God himself. But in themselves, do they satisfy our deepest hungering for the perfect and permanent? How could they give lasting

---

[14] Jean-Paul Sartre, from his book, *Being and Nothingness*.

satisfaction if we feel that all of them will come to nought when we die? Probably the deepest human hungering is to love and to be loved. However, even the best loving relationships end with death. But does love itself end with death? The Christian answer is no. (1 Corinthians 13:8-9).

So do our lives as a whole have an ultimate purpose? Can true meaning be found only in God, who gives us a permanent existence through a love that lasts into eternity? Implicit in all desire – even in sensual pleasure - is a longing for intimacy with God, as the only one who can fulfil our deepest desires. "As a deer longs for running streams, so longs my soul for you, my God." (Psalm 42:1). Thus, it is belief in a Creator God, who loves us into existence and fulfils our deepest longings for a permanent love and happiness, that gives ultimate meaning and purpose to our lives. Therefore, belief in God is not irrational. It makes perfect sense of human existence.

Can the existence of a Creator God be reconciled with the theory of evolution? In the evolution of the universe, God is the one *outside the system* whose purpose was that eventually a species (human beings) would evolve with a deep yearning for fullness of life, such a yearning to be fulfilled by God himself, who wants to share his love and his life with us as our fulfilment and destiny. Our destiny is life with God, and in order to help us along the road towards that goal, he creates a world through which we can journey in hope.

The above tells us much more about ourselves than what science can disclose. Science has nothing to say about the hungering of the human heart for a love that is permanent. Science can only deal with the visible aspects of reality. The hidden aspects are no less real than what can be observed by science. We arrive at the idea of God in an attempt to account for *all* aspects of reality, so we can say that God encompasses reality in its totality – the hidden no less than the visible aspects. In other words, the real is much larger than the physical, and bigger than what can be demonstrated by science.

It would seem that purpose is built into the universe. Francis Collins, the scientist who headed the human genome project - together with many other leading scientists - thinks that the universe is fine tuned for the emergence of life. There are innumerable examples of this fine tuning. To give but one such example: If the force of gravity after the big bang differed by one part in a hundred million million, from what it is, there would have been no galaxies, stars, or planets, and therefore, the emergence of life would have been impossible.

Francis Collins is a believer in God. He sees no conflict between religion and science. "The God of the Bible is also the God of the genome. He can be worshiped in the cathedral or in the laboratory. His creation is majestic, awesome, intricate, and beautiful – and it cannot be at war with itself. Only we, imperfect humans, can start such battles. And only we can end them."[15]

## The Universe: God's Work of Art

All created works reveal something of their creator. Does the created world point in some

---

[15] Francis Collins, *The Language of God, A Scientist Presents Evidence for Belief,* (Pocket Books, Simon & Schuster, UK), 2007, p. 211.

ways to a Creator God; does it reflect something of the Creator? We observe the world as awe-inspiring, wonderful, beautiful, marvellous – qualities surely reflecting the Creator God himself. It takes the poetry of the Psalms to put into words our response to the awesome wonders of the world. In a certain sense, his creation gives glory and praise to God. "The heavens declare the glory of God; the vault of heaven proclaims his handiwork." (Psalm 19:1, NJB). "For so many marvels I thank you; a wonder am I, and all your works are wonders." (Psalm 138:14, NJB). Human beings, especially, reflect something of the glory of the Creator. "You have made human beings inferior only to yourself, you have crowned them with glory and honour." (Psalm 8:5). The wonder and glory of creation both reflect, and then direct our attention, in praise and thanks to the Creator.

Most scientists agree that mutation and the development of species is never entirely blind or random. Instead of pure randomness, blind processes and chance outcomes, we can look at the world as a creation, with an intelligent God as its Creator. Law plus an element of chance are the basis of all creative work, as any artist will tell us. In the creation of the world, it is the laws of physics which are operative. There are always two elements in creativity – yes, the element of chance, but chance combined with rules and directed towards a purposeful outcome.

Many natural processes in evolution will have the appearance of chance, but that does not mean total randomness, which would only lead to chaos. It is doubtful if a work of art could ever emerge from the random flinging of paint at a canvas without giving some attention to rules and having some purpose in mind. Otherwise no coherent or meaningful whole would emerge. The creation of order out of randomness (chaos) must be the purpose of all true creative work.

A cursory glance at the evolution of the universe might see nothing but randomness and chance. On reflection, we might begin to observe a system always striving and tending towards completeness, eventually ending up with human beings as its crowning glory. In a manner utterly transcending the efforts of human artists, the Creator God, with a clear purpose in mind for his creation, and allowing for the freedom and autonomy of elements of chance, brings order out of chaos, coherence and union out of disharmony in his great creative work. (Genesis 1:1-3). Although chance happenings may be the only things we can observe in the evolution of life, hidden behind these appearances is the hand of God, guiding the whole system towards his good purposes. We can imagine a kind of unconscious purposefulness at work in the evolution of life – a system moving towards a goal without having an apprehension of what is taking place.

Through purposeful evolution, God actually made creation creative. He did not make a static universe, a mere machine, allowing no place for creative freedom. The laws of nature cannot be wholly deterministic. God did not plan every detail of evolution from the start. In a universe open to chance, there will be some unwelcome outcomes, genetic imperfections, for example. And if volcanic eruptions happen according to the laws of physics, God would never intend that people would be smothered by burning lava. Only miracles would prevent such happenings, but continuous miracles would undermine the structure of God's own law. The same is true of mutations that drive evolution – some will be harmful, as by chance. That is the necessary price of building chance or randomness into a physical system. God created the world "good," not perfect. (Genesis 1:31).

God made us creative too. Yes, through our freedom, we too have been given a degree of autonomy. But as is true of the universe, we have not yet attained the goal that God has set for us, which is one of lasting fellowship and loving communion with him. The evolutionary movement towards that goal, though frustrated by human evil, still justifies the faith that God's purpose of uniting humanity to himself will ultimately be realized.

Human beings are genetically programmed towards aggression and self-interest – traits that were naturally selected over millions of years of evolutionary competition and struggle. So, we should expect that these negative traits would be overcome only slowly. The price of an emerging universe is that co-operation and altruism will be slow in coming. But in the furtherance of his purpose, God does not leave us alone in our helplessness. He enters into a personal relationship with us, by offering us his love, a love which he wants us to share with one another. By so doing, he invites us to cooperate with him (as his creative partners) in shaping the future of the world in line with his good purposes, aiding our good intentions and seeking to block the worst effects of our evil tendencies. Thus, our relationship with God, also involves the freedom of an open system; everything is not determined solely by law. The randomness and indeterminacy in nature and in ourselves are what is required.

## Does God Intervene in His Creation at Certain Times?

Does the Bible say that God intervened in his creation to create the first human beings? (Genesis 2:7, 21-23). This would be a wrong interpretation of the creation stories in Genesis, which are not intended as factual accounts. In the biblical creation stories, God is revealing the uniqueness and dignity of the human person created in his image, one with whom he can have a relationship. As believers, we accept the findings of evolution – the gradual development of life from lower to higher more complex forms. We do not postulate the special intervention of God to create any particular species.

However, scientists still have no clue as to how the first living cell emerged from the slime of the earth. But this does not mean that we should draw on what was once known as the "God of the gaps" theory in order to account for the existence of something that science at a particular time cannot explain. The emergence and development of life at all stages is a natural process, and because God is *always* involved in his creation, working through natural causation, he does not have to intervene directly at any given time in order, so to speak, to correct a flaw in his handiwork. We should look on the natural evolution of life as God's wonderful way of creating the world. How life evolved from non-living matter to a living cell is a scientific question, for which science, one day may find an explanation.

## The Wish-Fulfilling God

Belief in God almost disappeared from human consciousness in the course of the 19th century. This may have arisen from too literal an interpretation of the creation stories in the beginning of the Book of Genesis, leading people to think that the Bible was untrue.

The German philosopher, Ludwig von Furebach (1804-1872) said that it is human beings who invent God by projecting a hungering for immortality and meaning on to an imaginary God. Thus, God is imaged as an illusion born of wishful thinking, as something people invent to comfort them in the face of life's troubles. We might describe this idea of God as the wish fulfilment God.

But this is not the God of the Bible, who is not an indulgent God at all, but rather a God who calls us away from our comfort zone to costly journeys of service to humanity, what Jesus calls carrying our cross. (Genesis 12:1-2; Exodus 3:7-9; 1 Samuel 16:11-13; Jeremiah 1:4-10; Matthew 4:18-22, 28:16-20; Acts 1:6-8). The God we encounter in the Bible is the God of covenant, a God of love to be sure, but it is tough love. Love is always costly, loving our neighbour can be difficult, loving enemies more so. Love involves obedience to God's law, and failing in that, we might face the prospect of eternal separation from God. All of this is a long way from the coddling, wish-fulfilling God of Furebach. The God in whom we believe is a God who challenges us to undertake difficult journeys of service, which involve feeding the hungry. (Matthew 25:33-34).

People do not believe in God from some emotional or comforting need, but because such belief makes perfect sense of their experience of life. Furebach was right about one thing: human longing and yearning for perfection and fulfilment. In our endless yearning, we hunger for many things: fame, status, possessions, power, but more deeply, for knowledge, truth and love; more deeply still, for a permanent happiness and existence - for a love that will never end. (See Psalm 42:2-3; 63:1). "Lord, you are great, and worthy of our praise. You stir in us the desire to praise you... For you have made us that we long for you, and our heart is restless until it rests in you." (*Confessions*, St. Augustine, Ch. 1). The Christian gospel offers us the comfort and joy of knowing that there is a God who responds to human hungering for fulfilment. (See CCC 27-30). This God loves us with an eternal love, but is also a God who calls us to responsible stewardship.

The reality is, if we have a hunger for certain things, there is always something there to satisfy it. We hunger for food, and food is there to satisfy this hunger. We hunger for material things, but these satisfy us only up to a point. Because of their ephemeral nature, material things never give us full happiness or satisfaction. Our yearning seems to be infinite, so it would seem that it is only the infinite God who can satisfy it, through a love and a happiness that is perfect and everlasting. This God is far from an illusion; it is reasonable to suppose that he exists, and that he wants to have an eternal relationship with us. It is this above all which gives human life meaning and purpose. "All religions bear witness to man's essential search for God." (CCC 2566) If this natural human hoping and yearning were to be frustrated, life would be absurd.

Love does not compel or control. We live in an unfinished world, a world open to experimentation, risk and chaos. We ourselves give full expression to our humanity when we engage in risk-taking and adventure, although not of course in a reckless manner! This is what gives rise to faith, which is always open to new possibilities. God shares his divine, creative powers with all of creation, and calls on his human creatures to be partners with him in his continual work of creation. This is but another way of saying that the world is not perfect, but for ever tending towards the fullness of perfection which is God's goal for his creation.

Thus, the existence of God is not only compatible with the theory of evolution but makes that theory much more probable. Belief in God is reasonable, and consistent with scientific knowledge.

## Translations of the Bible

Before the invention of printing in the 16th century, all copies of the Bible had to be made by hand. As this was slow and laborious work, very few copies of the Scriptures were available to believers. The first translation of the Old Testament from Hebrew into Latin was done by St. Jerome in the late fourth century AD. It was from Greek that Jerome translated the New Testament into Latin. The first major English translation was done in early 17th century England. This was known as the King James Bible. There have been a number of Catholic translations, one of the more recent being the Jerusalem Bible in 1966, and now The New Jerusalem Bible. In the Jerusalem Bible, God is referred to as Yahweh. This was the name God gave to Moses in his burning bush experience when God called him to free the Hebrew slaves from Egypt. Most other English translations of the Bible refer to God as the "Lord'"– the name for God in the translation of Hebrew to Greek of the Old Testament. Catholic editions of both the NRSV Bible and the Good News Bible are now available. The NRSV Bible follows the tradition of the King James version, while presenting the text in a style that appeals to contemporary readers.

## CHAPTER 2

# CREATION AND 'FALL'

## Introduction to the Book of Genesis

The name "genesis" means "origin" or "beginning," and comes from the title given to the book by those who translated the Hebrew Old Testament into Greek in about 100 BC. The Book of Genesis tells about the origin of the universe, of humankind, of human disobedience and of God's plan to redeem humanity from its disobedience. Throughout the first book of the Bible, the main character is God, who creates the universe, judges those who do wrong and leads and helps human beings through history. Genesis was written to record the story of a people's faith and to help them to keep that faith alive.

The purpose of the early chapters of Genesis is not to provide a factual account of the world's beginnings. According to geologists, the earth is about five billion years old, and some anthropologists think that human beings have been living on earth for about two million years. The authors of the first two chapters of Genesis did not know anything about this long history, nor were they concerned about it. Their purpose was to seek a religious meaning for the existence of the world and humankind. They wanted to teach the religious truth that both the world and human beings have their origin in the Creator God who created them in an act of love, and who wants to have a loving relationship with them.

We cannot speak of history in Israel until the exodus of Israel's ancestors from Egypt (ca. 1,250 BC), as narrated in the Book of Exodus, and written long before the creation stories in the first two chapters of Genesis. We must bear in mind that the creation stories, and what follows them in chapters 4-11 of Genesis are really the fruit of centuries of reflection, modified, and with new material added to them in their final editing. There are two creation accounts in the opening chapters of Genesis. There is a measure of agreement among scholars that the second creation account (Genesis 2:5-25) had its origin in the tenth century BC, during the kingship of David and Solomon.[16] The first creation account (Genesis 1) was composed much later, during the Babylonian exile (587-537 BC). For events leading up to the Babylonian exile, see 2 Kings, chaps. 23-25.

By the end of the Babylonian exile (537 BC), the authors of the still evolving Book

---

[16] Lawrence Boadt, Reading the Old Testament (Paulist Press), p. 78.

of Genesis wanted to show that the God who liberated his people from the slavery of Egypt had been involved in the world and in their story long before the exodus from Egypt. God's liberating action and his creation of them as a people devoted to him, were not just for Israel, but for the whole world, because – and this was the new prophetic insight – he created the universe. (See Isaiah 40:21-26). It was probably with the new revelation of God as Creator of the universe that strict monotheism (belief in the existence of one God only) began to take hold in Israel. Monotheism is implied in the creation account in Genesis 1.

The first eleven chapters of Genesis are concerned with the existence of God, the wonder of his creation, the joys of life, the human capacity for evil, and God's love and patience with human beings despite sin and human failure. While the creation accounts in Genesis 1 and 2 tell the story of God as Creator, the remaining chapters up to chapter 11 could be regarded as accounts of human beings themselves trying to replace God as Creator, but with disastrous consequences.

Then as a follow-up to the first eleven chapters of Genesis, the biblical authors wanted to record a number of traditions about their ancestors as a kind of preface to the Book of Exodus. Thus, 80 per cent of Genesis (chapters 12-50) is devoted to the founding patriarchs of Israel, Abraham, Isaac and Jacob, and Jacob's twelve sons, who were the founders of the twelve tribes of Israel. Then follows the account of the twelve tribes and their descendants in exile in Egypt, where they were eventually enslaved, setting the scene for their rescue from slavery in the Book of Exodus. In Genesis 12-50, the authors want to show that God had guided their ancestors, through his promises, up to the events of the Book of Exodus (the second book of the Bible).

The Adam and Eve account, is a story of great beginnings in paradise (God's ideal world), and then a 'fall,' which can be interpreted as a metaphor for humanity's enduring quest for absolute autonomy (self-exaltation), leading to self-ruin, and followed by exile. It was probably their reflection on their history in the promised land, leading up to the Babylonian exile in 587 BC that inspired much of the Book of Genesis. Self-exaltation, followed by humiliation, is a recurring theme in the Bible.

## Genesis 1 and the Babylonian Myths

While in exile in Babylon (587-537 BC), the Israelites became familiar with the Babylonian creation myths, and these had an influence on the creation account in Genesis 1. To the modern mind, myth is something untrue. So how are we to understand myth in the biblical sense? All ancient cultures are intrigued by beginnings – where did human beings come from, how can both natural and social order be created and maintained, and what is the meaning and purpose of human life? The human being is a searcher for meaning. Myths are a search for ultimate meaning. They are stories that represent a search for wisdom and an understanding of the world and human life. Because human beings are limited and imperfect, the belief may have arisen that the creation of order and harmony in the world cannot be the work of mere humans. It must be due to the power of a god or gods, usually the principal god of a city or region in which the story is told.

All myths, including those of Babylon, deal with creation - fights among the gods to establish order in a chaotic world, the defeat of chaos by a hero god, and the making of human beings from earthly clay. Myths are not to be interpreted literally. The truth in myth is conveyed metaphorically and symbolically. These stories are not factual. They have nothing to do with science. They are religious interpretations of human beings' struggles to find meaning, through their relationship with God or gods.

During their exile in Babylon, the Israelites became familiar with, and were influenced by the old Babylonian creation myth, the *Enuma Elish*, which originated in the late 12th century BC Mesopotamia (the land of the rivers Tigris and Euphrates).[17] The *Enuma Elish* was discovered written on clay tablets unearthed by archaeologists.

In all creation myths, the gods are seen as the powers that control the universe, and the act of creation is thought of as bringing order from disorder. The *Enuma Elish* tells about the struggle between the creator god Marduk, (the chief Babylonian god, the god of light) and the dragon Tiamat, goddess of the sea (representing the forces of chaos, see Genesis 1:2). Having slain Tiamat and thus banishing chaos, Marduk divided her body in two, and formed one half as the sky and human beings, and the earth with the other half. Thus, according to this myth, there is something sinister at the origin of the world. The myth depicts creation as a product of violence, and it sees something dragon-like and demonic in human beings. In such a view of the world, only an absolute ruler, the king of Babylon, who is the representative of Marduk, can control the demonic and bring order to the world. The *Enuma Elish* thus represented one vision of the world and of the discomfiting reality of human beings' struggle to live in harmony among themselves. To be sure, often enough the world really does look like a dragon's lair and human blood as dragon's blood. "Blood I will mass and cause bones to be. I will establish a savage. "Man" shall be his name. Verily, savage man I will create. He shall be charged with the service of the gods, that they might be at ease." (*Enuma Elish*, Ancient Near Eastern Texts, 68). In the *Enuma Elish*, human beings were thus created to do the work that the gods had previously been doing, so that the gods would have a life of ease. Human beings are thus, slaves of the gods. In the Genesis accounts, God created man as good, not a savage.

There is a close correspondence between the first creation account in Genesis 1 and the *Enuma Elish*.[18] Genesis 1:2 mentions darkness and the waters of chaos. *Enuma Elish* speaks about primeval chaos and gods warring against the god of the sea, symbol of chaos. In both accounts, there is a seven-day creation sequence, and both of them end with the creation of man on the sixth day, followed by a seventh day of rest for God or the gods. Both accounts deal with the same elements (a divine spirit or spirits as creators, the creation of the world, day and night, light and darkness, chaos and order, and they follow the same ordered sequence.

The authors of Genesis used this myth to explain the origins of the world as *they* saw it. They did not accept the theology of *Enuma Elish*. In the biblical creation account, there are no warring gods battling for power, no violence, and no demonic dragon made from the body of a god. There is but one God who exists outside and beyond his creation,

---

[17] Boadt, p. 91. *The Enuma Elish* is published in a document called *Ancient Near Eastern Texts* (ANET 60f), and is available today as a paperback book.

[18] Boadt, p. 93.

and no warring gods battling for supremacy. The Creator God speaks his word and creation springs into being. "In the beginning, God created heaven and earth. Now the earth was a formless void, there was darkness over the deep, with a divine wind sweeping over the waters. God said, 'Let there be light,' and there was light" (Genesis 1:1-4, NJB). In Genesis, "a divine wind" (God's Spirit) simply moves over the turbulent waters (primeval chaos) and brings them to order. It is the formless void alone that stands against the power of God. God then speaks his word, and the powers of darkness are banished. (See Genesis 1:1-31).

The great contribution of the Jews to humanity was monotheism, the notion of God as One, as opposed to polytheism (many gods). While polytheism symbolized competition and strife, monotheism was important, in its revelation of one unifying principle in the universe – the Creator of union, the one who can bring order out of chaos. While the Babylonians worshiped the sun and moon as gods, the Biblical authors saw God as distinct from natural forces, and creating and controlling the sun and moon. The attention of the reader is thus directed to the One who has created these marvellous lights. And the Creator God is infinitely superior to anything he has made. This creation account in Genesis 1 probably derives from the one composed by the prophet Isaiah, who lived in Babylon with the Jewish exiles. (See Isaiah 40:25-31). In his account, the prophet may have wanted to wean the exiles away from allegiance to Marduk and from polytheism in general, by expanding the idea of God as the benevolent creator of the universe, and thus superior to all national gods such as Marduk, the god of Babylon.

The Babylonian myths represent the values of empire - power, domination and subjugation, presented as a battle in which the strong overcome the weak - leading to the scattering of peoples rather than union. (See Genesis 11:8-9). Instead of reflecting such disorder into the world, the Creator God creates harmony out of disunion. The Babylonians were very uncertain about what the gods wanted and what would please them. What would please one god might anger another one. So there was a struggle to appease the gods.

God's creation is not a chance or random act. It has a purpose given to it by God who wants to provide a home for human beings (Genesis 2:15), whom he created in his image and likeness, so that they can relate to him and share in his own creative powers. (Genesis 1:26-28). In contrast to the gods of polytheism, the Creator God is personal. He has a moral character. He loves human beings, who having been created in his image (1:27), have the *capacity* to love him in return. He wants his human creatures to enjoy his creation in fellowship with himself and with one another. In contrast to what the Babylonian myth says, everything that God creates is "good." (Genesis 1:10b, 12b, 18b, 21b, 25b, 31).

When the Jewish people were in exile in Babylon, their condition was one of slavery. Inspired by their prophets, they looked forward to a liberation that only the Creator God could give them. (See Isaiah 40:9-11). This would bring order to their chaotic world in Babylon. Living with such a hope, they may have discovered God as the creator and sustainer of the world. As distinct from Marduk, this God wants to establish a loving relationship with human beings and to liberate them from slavery.

The creation narrative in Genesis 1 is thus about liberation - the liberation of the world from primordial darkness, analogous to the liberation of the Jewish people from slavery (Egyptian and Babylonian), bringing them home to the promised land and a new intimate relationship with God. This foreshadows Christ's liberation of humanity from the chaos of all enslavements, leading to the dawn of a new creation, thus further deepening our relationship with God, who makes us his children and thereby sharers in his divine life.

## Genesis 1 – What Kind of literature?

In order to interpret the seven-day creation account we must examine its literary genre. Is it science or history? Neither! It is poetry, and as poetry, it must be interpreted metaphorically. Like a poem, it is schematic. Its orderly layout reflects the order of creation itself. The account follows a formula of repetition similar to poetry: God said... 'let there be'... "and it was so; he saw that it was good... and it was evening and morning,'" The account ends (2:4) with a climax of rest on the seventh day, to be known as the Sabbath. (The Hebrew word "Sabbath" means "rest"). The meaning of Genesis 1 is thus revealed in its literary character.

This creation account reveals the transcendent aspect of God as utterly other, and distinct from his creation. It has been attributed to priests of the Jerusalem temple. Evidence for its priestly source is found in its orderly structure and its emphasis on Sabbath worship. It may have been intended for liturgical celebration in the newly-built temple after the return of the Jewish exiles from Babylon in 537 BC. It functions as a hymn of praise and thanks to God for the benevolence and goodness of his creation, and for revealing his love for human beings, through the beauty, wonder and magnificence of the world.

The phrase "in the beginning" means that creation marks the start of time and the course of history. Time and history have a beginning. They did not emerge purely by blind fate or chance; they have their origin and final goal in God, about which the Bible will tell us more, when it speaks of a new creation. (Revelation 21:1). In the light of the New Testament, we know that God created all things through his eternal word, Jesus Christ. (See John 1:1; Colossians 1:16-17).

"And God saw that it was good." (Genesis 1:10, 12, 18, 21, 25, 31, NJB). Everything God created is good. God does not create evil. The Babylonian myths saw evil coming from the gods. But evil does not come from the Creator God. As the Jewish exiles discovered under the Babylonian yoke, it is human beings who bring the chaos of evil down upon themselves – exemplified in domination, exploitation, strife, when they walk away from partnership with God.

When God said, "Let there be light" (Genesis 1:3; see Psalm 33:6-7, 9), he was liberating the world from the chaos symbolized by darkness: disorder, anarchy, strife, fear and ignorance, to name but a few. God's creative activity goes on in the world, through the work of human beings, in cooperation with God, to find the correct balance between order and chaos. A little chaos can be a good thing. We can become strong by being exposed to a little chaos, to danger and adventure–as long as they don't overwhelm us.

Light is associated with order, darkness with chaos. Light has a metaphorical meaning. In the New Testament, light is associated with Christ, the light of the world, who has shone on us, giving us the light of the knowledge and wisdom of God, liberating us from the chaotic darkness of sin. (See John 1:9, 8:12). John's Gospel says that Jesus is the source of life, and that this life has brought light to humanity. (John 2:4). It is Jesus who will liberate humanity from the darkness of death, in a new creation at the end of time. When that day comes, there will be "no need for the sun or moon, because the glory of God will shine on everyone," and Christ will be God's lamp, the people of the world walking in that light. (Revelation 21:23-24).

The creation of the seventh day (Genesis 2:1-3) is meant as a day of rest for God and his creatures, a day in which human beings should reflect on the wonders of creation and on the bountiful God who gifted all of this to them. We need 'time out' in order to contemplate the meaning of life. We did not float into existence by pure chance. We came into the world with a meaning and purpose assigned to us by a loving God who wants to have a relationship with us. We have a purpose in the mission of responsible stewardship to which God calls us. (Genesis 1:27-28).

The sabbath rest reminds us that we should not try to outdo God. If we behave as though everything depends on us, we reject God as sovereign Lord of creation, and set ourselves up in his place. (Genesis 3:6). We need to stand back and reflect on our dependency on God, because everything we have and enjoy does not depend on us. Limited as we are, we cannot do everything we want. The sabbath rest is an acknowledgement of this. Even when troubles assail us, we may begin to see them as of lesser account once we reflect on the wonder and magnificence of God's bountiful world. (See Job 38:1-14). Because of the loss of a sense of dependence on God today, the Sabbath day of rest may have lost some of the meaning it once had for everyone.

## The Creation of Man in the Image of God

God said, 'Let us make man in our own image, in the likeness of ourselves, and let them be masters of the fish of the sea, the birds of heaven, the cattle, all the wild animals and all the creatures that creep on the ground.' God created man in the image of himself, in the image of God he created him, male and female he created them. God blessed them, saying to them, 'Be fruitful, multiply, fill the earth and subdue it. Be masters of the fish of the sea, the birds of heaven and all the living creatures that move on earth.' God also said, 'Look, to you I give all the seed-bearing plants everywhere on the surface of the earth, and all the trees with seed-bearing fruit; this will be your food. And to all the wild animals, all the birds of heaven and all the living creatures that creep along the ground, I give all the foliage of the plants as their food.' And so it was. God saw all he had made, and indeed it was very good. Evening came and morning came: the sixth day. (Genesis 1:26-31, NJB).

Created "in God's image!" (1:26). As a way of making himself present to his people, the Pharaoh of Egypt placed statues, images of himself throughout his kingdom, symbolizing his authority and outreach to his subjects. Human beings are God's images placed on earth

(God's dominion), as his representatives, in order to continue his work of creation. In the Bible, God alone is King. God places his image in human beings, all of whom thus share in the sovereignty and creative power of God. As image-bearers of God (resembling him in some ways), we are called to the awesome responsibility of co-creators, in a partnership with God.

It's as if God created the world as a temple in which he placed his image: human beings made in his likeness, so that he could live for ever with them in mutual harmony. Thus, the two spheres of created order, called in Genesis, "heaven" and "earth," are not to be seen as separate or detached from one another. They are the twin halves of God's good creation, so that the God who lives in heaven, is also mysteriously present on earth through his human creatures. We live in a heaven-and-earth world, with God's image (human beings) placed within it. The sovereign God is present as caretaker in his world but calling on his image bearers to participate in his plans for the world – as good stewards of his creation. (Genesis 1:27-28).

"Created in his image" also means that God has written on our hearts the desire for him, a desire which will not be fully satisfied until we reach the fullness of union with him in the hereafter. This natural desire for God is evident in our constant yearning for perfect goodness, truth and love. Were such yearning to be frustrated, then life would be meaningless. The journey back to God begins on earth as we form unions with one another. Through such unions, we can glimpse something of the perfect love for which we continually yearn. Thus, through God's image in us, we have the *capacity* for a relationship with him, so that he is with us as companion on our earthly journey towards our destiny, when we will see him as he is. Without his image placed in us, we would not have the gift of love, and would thus lack the capacity of sharing in God's life of love as our eternal destiny.

In the foregoing passage, God reveals his purpose in creating human beings in his image. He appoints them to be "fruitful, multiply," to be "masters" of all the creatures of the earth, and to "fill the earth and subdue it." (1:27-28).[19] The phrase about subduing the earth may have been interpreted in the past as encouraging the exploitation of nature. A wrong interpretation! The God in whom we believe is a loving and caring God. So it is unthinkable that he would want his human creatures to abuse the work of his hands, or to exploit it for material gain. It is rather that God calls human beings to a mission of caring stewardship of the earth and all its creatures. It is by faithfully discharging this mission, that God forms a relationship with us. God shares his creative powers with human beings, and he expects them to use these powers responsibly. When human beings selfishly pluck the forbidden fruit of exploitation, they disobey the Creator and go their own way and away from God. The earth belongs to God. It is he who created it. As we see today, it is when human beings claim ownership of the earth, that exploitation and destruction take place. The earth and everything in it are gifted to us by God. It is to him we are accountable for the use we make of his gifts. "The world and all that is in it belongs to the Lord; the earth and all who live on it are his. He built it on the deep waters beneath the earth and laid its foundations in the ocean's depths." (Psalm 24:1-2). "Animals are God's

---

[19] The NRSV Bible uses the word "dominion" over the earth's creatures.

creatures. He surrounds them with his providential care. By their mere existence, they bless him and give him glory." (CCC 2416). The material world possesses a dignity of its own: "and God saw that it was very good." (Genesis 1:31). "By the very nature of creation, material being is endowed with its own stability, truth and excellence, its own order and laws." (CCC 339).

The way to be "fruitful" and "multiply" is to bring God's unfinished work to completion. These words represent a call to human beings to be co-creators. We are called to a mission of creating fruitfulness, not only biologically, but also by creating love, joy, peace, patience, kindness, generosity, faithfulness and gentleness. We are called to reproduce in our daily lives the fruits of God's Spirit breathed into us by the Creator. (Genesis 2:7b; See Galatians 5:22). We can be fruitful by developing the world's hidden potentials – the arts, science, technology, medicine, commerce, agriculture, social life, to name but a few.

## Creation Psalms

A number of Psalms were composed as hymns of praise to God for his creation. Psalm 8 is one of the best known of these.

> O Lord our Sovereign,
> how majestic is your name in all the earth!...
> When I look up at your heavens, the work of your fingers,
> the moon and stars that you have established;
> what are human beings that you are mindful of them,
> mortals that you care for them?
> Yet you have made them a little lower than God
> and crowned them with glory and honour.
> You have given them dominion over the work of your hands;
> you have put all things under their feet,
> sheep and oxen and all the beasts of the field,
> the birds of the air and the fish of the sea…
> O Lord, our Sovereign,
> how majestic is your name in all the earth!
> (Psalm 8, NRSVC, see also Psalms 19:29, 93, 104; 74:12-17; 104:1, 5-9; 148:3-4,
> 7-8, 11-13; Job 9:1-10 and chapters 38-41).

God's name is "majestic" above and beyond anything else on earth. God is King because he is Creator. His name tells what he does. He creates, and being "mindful" of human beings, he loves and cares for what he creates. Human beings being "crowned with glory and honour" may be another way of saying that they are created in the image of God. Giving human beings "dominion" over the work of his hands is a call to a mission of stewardship. Psalm 8 looks ahead to Jesus. In the New Testament, it is Jesus who really crowns us with glory and honour by sharing the glory of his risen life with us.

## The Second Creation Account

> Then the Lord took some soil from the ground and formed a man out of it; he breathed life-giving breath into his nostrils and the man began to live. Then God planted a garden in Eden, which is in the East, and there he put the man he had formed. He made all kinds of beautiful trees grow there and produce good fruit. In the middle of the garden stood the tree that gives life and the tree that gives knowledge of what is good and what is bad... Then the Lord placed the man in the Garden of Eden to cultivate it and guard it. He said to him, 'You may eat the fruit of any tree in the garden, except the tree that gives knowledge of what is good and what is bad. You must not eat the fruit of that tree; if you do, you will die the same day.' Then the Lord God said, 'It is not good for the man to live alone. I will make a suitable companion to help him.' God created the animals, but not one of them was a suitable companion to help the man... Then the Lord God made the man fall into a deep sleep, and while he was asleep, he took out one of the man's ribs and closed up the flesh. He formed a woman out of the rib and brought her to the man. Then the man said, 'At last, here is one of my own kind – bone taken from my bone, and flesh from my flesh.' That is why a man leaves his father and mother and is united with his wife, and they become one. The man and the woman were both naked, but they were not embarrassed. (Genesis 2:7-9, 15-18, 21-25).

The reader of Genesis will be aware of a second creation account in Genesis 2:5-24). It is thought that this creation account originated in the northern kingdom of Israel, and was composed long before the first account in Genesis 1. Israel was divided into two kingdoms after the reign of King Solomon – the northern kingdom of Israel and the southern kingdom of Judah. (See 1 Kings 12). Some northerners fled south to Judah after the fall of the northern kingdom to the Assyrian empire in 721 BC (2 Kings 17), and it is thought that they brought their own creation story with them to Jerusalem, the capital of the kingdom of Judah. That creation story was then combined with the priestly account (Genesis 1) during the following centuries in Judah.[20] The kingdom of Judah continued in existence until 587 BC, when the Babylonian empire destroyed Jerusalem and brought its people into exile in Babylon. (2 Kings 25).

Though the second creation account is different in style and content from the first, the final editors of Genesis wisely incorporated the two together. The two accounts complement one another in their theology. In the first account (Genesis 1), God is portrayed as a distant King, at whose command the whole creation comes into existence. Thus, God's magnificent creation of the world in Genesis 1 sets the stage for his intimate concern for the man and woman (humanity as a whole) in Genesis 2. God is awe-inspiring, mysterious, beyond anything that we can conceive, but is also as close to us as parents to their children - as revealed in the second creation account.

In the second creation story (Genesis 2:5-25), God is envisaged, not as a far-away

---

[20] Lawrence Boadt, *Reading the Old Testament*, p. 74-75.

king as in Genesis 1. He reigns over his creation with loving care, and in a personal way. The good God is with human beings, seeking a relationship with them, because he loves what he creates. God is intimate with the man and woman, accompanying them in the Garden of Eden – a metaphor for the world. God is metaphorically depicted as a potter who "forms" the first human person from clay. He breathes life-giving breath into the man's nostrils and the man begins to live. (2:7; see 1:27). Despite race, colour or culture, human beings are all the same, one humanity, all of us made from God's good earth. But there is something more to us than earthly dust. God breathes the breath of his own life – a share of his life - into this human being, made in his image. (2:7b). God plants a garden in Eden (2:8), fully providing for human needs. God takes a walk in this garden. (3:8). He makes clothes for Adam and Eve. The second account is less repetitious, more dramatic, and more down to earth than the first. Instead of "male and female" we have "man and wife." Instead of "create" we have the phrase "to form."

How can we make sense of these two different ways of picturing God which recur throughout the Bible? Both of these models of God are equally valid, and indeed, complementary. The seven-day creation account in Genesis 1 represents the first model. This account is structured and almost abstract. Here, God is pictured as utterly distinct from the world, and remote from human beings. This is the transcendent God in all his majesty and immensity, in total control of the world–the king ruling his creation from afar.

The other way of representing God is exemplified in the second creation account and elsewhere in Genesis (2:5–3:24; 4:1-16; 6:13-7:24; 11:1-9). These accounts are based on a completely different model. They are not to be interpreted literally. In them, God appears incarnated as a human being, as personal, possessing human emotions, communing with human beings in God's garden (this world) – God as immanent. We are so accustomed to the first model of God that the second model strikes us as strange and almost incredible. But it may be more significant and meaningful for our lives than the first model, because it pictures God, not just as a remote deity, but with us (immanent), guiding and caring for us on our earthly journey–God as a partner of humanity. In our daily lives, we can experience the caring hand of God through the help and care we receive from one another. It is only in the New Testament that the notion of God incarnated in human beings reaches its fullness of meaning in Jesus. (See Acts of the Apostles 17:28).

The "garden," symbolizing this world, contained "all kinds of beautiful trees producing good fruit." (2:9). Such gardens were common in the ancient Near East, planted, irrigated and walled-off around the palace of the king, symbolizing his bountiful outreach to his subjects. Here in Genesis, the garden symbolizes God's bounty to humankind. The trees in the garden are good for food. All creation is good. (2:9). God supplies all human needs. The garden is a home which sustains life, nourishes and protects. God renews his call to humanity to a mission of stewardship of the garden – the earth. (Genesis 2:15)

The garden is not to be interpreted literally. It is God's vision of the world. It represents the world and human life as God always wanted it to be. When we live in right relationship with God and other people, we are in peace with ourselves and the world. Yet we know that this is not how things are. This vision of heaven united to earth is only fulfilled through Jesus Christ in an end-of-time creation of the "new heaven and the new earth" when God will make his "home with human beings." (See Revelation 21:1-5). As Isaiah 51:3 and Ezekiel 36:35-36 prophesised, the bliss of Eden will reappear in the future, as the Kingdom of God fully established, into which God calls his adopted children. (See CCC 736).

"It is not good that the man should be alone." (2:18). Human beings who cut themselves off from their fellow men and women, cannot live lives of love. Therefore, God is not reflected in their lives. Love comes into the picture when the man has a partner. In their relationship, the man and woman reflect the love-life of God. Eve has the same human nature as Adam – "bone of my bone and flesh of my flesh." (2:23). They complement each other. The "not good to be alone" phrase is resolved in the union of the two. Genesis 2:24 is a reference to the institution of marriage and the human community. Human beings depend on one another, and can only flourish and be creative in a spirit of harmony and cooperation. The man and the woman are called by God to live together in loyalty and trust, in a union that mirrors the love-life of God himself. They are called to make a gift of themselves to each other, in imitation of God's bounty to them.

For a summary of the teaching of the Church on the theme of creation, see CCC 280, 282-284, 286, 289, 341, 349, 356, 397-398.

## Forbidden Fruit

> Now the serpent was more crafty than any other wild animal that the Lord God had made. He said to the woman, Did God say, 'You shall not eat from any tree in the garden?' The woman said to the serpent, 'We may eat the fruit of the trees in the garden; but God said, 'You shall not eat of the fruit of the tree that is in the middle of the garden, nor shall you touch it, or you will die.' But the serpent said to the woman, 'You will not die; for God knows that when you eat of it your eyes will be opened, and you will be like God, knowing good and evil.' So when the woman saw that the tree was good for food, and that it was a delight to the eyes, and that the tree was to be desired to make one wise, she took of its fruit and ate; and she also gave some to her husband, who was with her, and he ate. Then the eyes of both were opened, and they knew that they were naked, so they sewed fig leaves together and covered themselves. (Genesis 3:1-7, NRSVC).

There are echoes of the Babylonian *Epic of Gilgamesh* [21] in the Adam and Eve story. (Genesis 3:1-13). *The Epic of Gilgamesh* is a long poem from Mesopotamia (the land of the Tigris and Euphrates rivers). It was written on clay tablets sometime between 2,700 BC and 600 BC. It is the earliest known piece of literature in the world. In this myth, immortality and great wisdom are two qualities that distinguish heavenly beings from human beings. The hero Gilgamesh, half god and half human, goes on a quest for immortality - trying to be like the gods. (See Genesis 3:5). He fails to find immortality, but he receives a plant that will renew his youth as long as the plant lasts. Then the plant is stolen from him by a snake. The author of Genesis borrows a number of elements from

---

[21] *The Epic of Gilgamesh* is available today as a published book.

Gilgamesh: the tree, the plant (tree) of life, the snake, the search for the unattainable–the longing for unlimited wisdom, knowledge and power.

In contrast to Gilgamesh, the biblical author does not say that human beings are half God, but are created in God's image. God offered the gift of immortality to us, but in the context of working along with him as good stewards of his creation.

Venomous serpents were greatly feared in the ancient Near East, as a threat to human life. (Genesis 49:17; Exodus 4:2-3). The movements and tactics of this reptile make it a powerful symbol of shrewdness, cunning and deceit. (Genesis 3:1 Matthew 10:16; 2 Corinthians 11:3). More than anything else, the serpent is a symbol of evil in the Bible. It may symbolize the human ego, the pride which wants to gratify itself and to have things its own way, no matter what the consequences. The serpent may be symbolic of the temptations which can often arise from the evil lurking in human hearts.

The question posed in the Garden of Eden story is whether God's splendid and orderly world will collapse back into chaos, thus reversing his work of creation. The signs are not good. The serpent (literally a snake) is there, symbol of chaos. The garden is an enclosed world, full of beautiful trees and watered by some of the world's great rivers. (Genesis 2:10, 13-14). Eden is a symbol of order, while the serpent plays the role of chaos, suddenly appearing where everything is orderly and full of light. It seems that nothing, not even a world of bliss and light can be walled off from the rest of harsh reality. The serpent is really ourselves, and our proclivity for evil. If humans choose a life of autonomy, they leave themselves open to the possibility of death-dealing chaos. (Genesis 2:17; 3:19). According to Genesis, humanity has chosen the latter. (Incidentally, ancient literature seems to portray the human being as incapable of coping indefinitely with a world of bliss.) There is always the human hungering for adventure and risk. [22]

The command that God gave to Adam and Eve was not to eat from "the tree of the knowledge of good and evil." (2:17). The fruit which was forbidden to the man and woman, can have multiple meanings. It could symbolize the infinite knowledge and power of God, which human beings are utterly incapable of attaining in its fullness, although they never cease claiming such knowledge and power as their own right. Human beings are dreamers and searchers. We are never satisfied with the degree of knowledge, power and happiness we have at a given time, but are ever reaching out for more and more. Being made in the image of God, we have a divine fire within us which can propel us into arrogance, grandiosity and the misuse of freedom (forbidden fruits). We may then use power for purposes of domination, aggrandisement and exploitation. But the image of God in us can also propel us towards nobility, righteousness, mercy and compassion – life-enhancing fruits that God wants to share with us. Because our judgement can be mistaken and defective, too often, we choose what is forbidden rather than what is life-enhancing. Thus, more often than not, we desire and reach out for something harmful, but which we still perceive as "good to eat" (possess). We are like a young child who is told by a parent not to go near a fire. When the child disobeys this command, death could be the outcome.

In Genesis 3:4 the serpent distorts the truth of God's command in 2:17, and thus,

---

[22] See the Irish myth, *Oisin in Tír na nÓg*.

cunningly tries to sow doubt, confusion, dissension and conflict in the minds of the human pair. (3:12-13). The tempter accuses God of being a liar and appeals to the vanity and pride of the man and the woman. He tells them that they could become all knowing, all-powerful. The phrase "you will be like God" is almost a repetition of the phrase "created in God's image" in the first creation account, but this time, it is a temptation to self-aggrandisement and self-exaltation.

Human beings cannot be like God – all knowing and all powerful. It is wisdom to accept God as sovereign, and human beings as dependent. When human beings usurp God, they grasp the forbidden fruit of glory and sovereignty (attributes belonging to God alone) for themselves. They want to be completely autonomous, claiming unlimited power and freedom to go their own way. When human beings claim absolute autonomy, they may gain some God-like knowledge and power, but it can be knowledge without wisdom, power without responsibility and freedom without limits. Down through history, human beings have plucked the forbidden fruit of trying to organize the world without God, but they have done so by turning on their fellow humans and consigning them to death. "You must not eat the fruit of that tree; if you do you will die." (Genesis 2:17; 3:3, 3:8, 17-18). The author of Genesis is saying that this is how human beings are tempted, and this is how they behave. The eating of forbidden fruit is repeated again and again down through history. This 'eating' is freely willed, and it represents a perennial failure on the part of the human being to be what God intends him or her to be.

Succumbing to the temptation of wanting to be like God, Adam and Eve eat the forbidden fruit. Then they notice that they are "naked," while formerly they were not ashamed of their nakedness. (Genesis 3:7 in the foregoing passage). "Naked" following the 'fall' means that the man and woman are no longer drawing their strength from union with God. They want to be independent and to rely entirely on their own resources. Once they begin trying to be whatever they themselves intend (creating their own meanings), rather than what God intended them to be, they run up against the new world of their own limitations, imperfections, powerlessness and inadequacy. This frustrates them. It causes them all kinds of pain and anxiety. Thus, being 'naked' means to be vulnerable in the face of harsh reality. (See Genesis 3:17-18). God then brings them back to the harsh reality of their mortality; he reminds them that they were made from soil and will become soil again, in other words, they will die. (3:19b).

What is at issue in eating the forbidden fruit is disobedience. God appoints Adam and Eve (all of us) to a mission of caring for his good 'garden' (Genesis 2:15), which means caring for the earth, for all of its creatures and one another. This is what God wants human beings to be: carers of his good creation. But they frustrate God, reject their God-given mission of stewardship and thus disobey him. They are given a mission of service, but they choose the path of self-service and self-indulgence – in obedience to their own will. (3:6). The history of God's people Israel is a failure of obedience. Adam and Eve are archtypes, representatives, whether of groups, cultures, nations or humanity as a whole. "All subsequent sin would be disobedience of God and lack of trust in his goodness." (CCC 397). St. Paul looked on Adam's sin of disobedience as the archetypal sin that was only reversed by the obedience of Christ, the new Adam. (See Romans 5:12-14).

## Hiding from God

> That evening Adam and Eve heard the Lord walking in the garden, and they hid from him among the trees. But the Lord God called out to the man, 'Where are you?' (Genesis 3:8-9, see Luke 15:13).

Their hiding from God can be interpreted as hiding from their true selves as images of God, a denial of their true nature and the purpose for which they were created. Their hiding may represent a retreat into individualism, an evasion of responsibility, an abandonment of their God-given mission as gardeners (carers), which was what God wanted them to be. Before this, God walked with Adam and Eve in the garden. Now the primordial couple are afraid to walk with God, and they go into hiding. This is an understandable fear, because God's standards are high; his judgement is real. It may be best to try and avoid him, so run away, pretend he doesn't exist, rely on oneself.

God called out to them, 'Where are you?' (3:9). Even when we reject God's offer of stewardship and go our own way (Isaiah 53:6a), he still loves us, and when we go astray and hide from him, he wants us to come back to himself again. We are the lost coin hiding in the darkness of the house. In his plan to find us, God lights the lamp of Jesus Christ, who searches us out in all the dark corners of a room. He rejoices when he finds us. (Luke 15:8-10). Having plucked the forbidden fruit of his inheritance, the prodigal son walks away into hiding from the Father. But he soon finds that this only leaves him starving and thirsting (naked), vulnerable and lost. During all his years of hiding, the Father of the lost and starving son is on the road calling out, 'Where are you?' The father welcomes his son home with a celebratory banquet for the whole village. (Luke 15:23). The Lord says, 'Come everyone who is thirsty – here is water.' (Isaiah 55:1; see 45:22-23; 49:9-10).

## Life East of Eden

God hears out the defence of each of the actors in this story. Where formerly all was peace and harmony, now there is tension and discord - each character blaming the other for the disaster that has ensued. (Genesis 3:12f). They become aware and understand what it is like to be envious, angry and resentful. This will result in a loss of trust in one another, each one blaming the other. (3:12-13). And that in turn, will lead to enmity, strife, separation, family break-up, and lone "wandering over the earth." (Genesis 4:1-8, 15-16).

God said to the snake, 'I will put enmity between you and the woman, and between your offspring and hers. It will bruise your head and you will strike its heel.' (Genesis 3:15, NJB; see CCC 412). God promises ultimately to crush the tempter's head, to defeat the destroyer Satan, and ultimately to overcome the forces of evil that fragment and disfigure his good creation. The woman's offspring (the offspring of Eve) will bruise the serpent's head but the serpent will bite her offspring's heel. Jesus will be the woman's offspring, the one to finally defeat Satan and the tempter's weapon of death. It will be costly for Jesus, because the snake will "bite his heel." Victory over evil will eventually be brought about by God's Messiah, Jesus Christ. Because Mary (the new Eve) gave Jesus to the world, she has a role in God's victory over evil. She is the offspring of Eve.

The task of hard work allotted to Adam and Eve is not intended as a penalty.

(3:17). It may be understood as the renewal of God's call to creative and responsible stewardship of the earth. But this will be a painful mission. It will not be paradise. When we fall out of right relationship with God and one another, we no longer experience paradise. With regard to the ground being under God's curse (3:17), in the Old Testament such curses should not be interpreted as punishment, or seen as God wishing evil on something or someone. Since God created the earth, he loves all of it and wants it to flourish. "Curse" in this sense is but an expression of judgement. It's as if God is saying to the snake (3:14) and the man and woman (3:15), 'This is what you have done and these are the consequences of your behaviour. Even nature itself will suffer from your disobedience, because your labours will be fruitless,' symbolized by "weeds and thorns." God appointed human beings as stewards of the earth, to care for it and all its creatures. The outcome of this good stewardship would be fruitfulness – the flourishing of human lives and the earth.

As regards our earthly home, we see today what human greed and exploitation (forbidden fruits) are doing to the earth - violating the covenant God made with Noah. (Genesis 8:21; see Isaiah 24:4-6). Our failure to carry out our mission of caring amounts to disobedience, and its consequences are clearly evident today in the harsh reality of climate change, which may eventually lead to death. However, a time will come when God will restore the earth to his good purposes. (See Romans 8:21-23).

With their eyes now opened to the future, the man and woman (representing humanity) must plan and prepare for it. They must literally sow now so that they can enjoy the fruits of their labour in the future. (3:17b). In other words, they must sacrifice the present (defer gratification - the reverse of plucking the forbidden fruit) so as to provide for future wellbeing and security. But they will suffer frustration and disappointment, because their painful labouring will often be spiritually fruitless. (3:18).

Genesis seems to be saying that life is suffering. We should always try to eliminate pain wherever we find it, but much of the suffering in the world results from the harm we do to ourselves, to one another and to planet earth. In following base impulses, human beings succumb to selfish desires, doing what's expedient rather than acting responsibly and altruistically for the good of others and the earth itself. These are the forbidden fruits we pluck when we pursue the pleasure of the moment, rather than defer gratification for a greater future good: sow now so that we will have fruits in the future. We don't want to hear about sacrificing now for future benefit. That would be too costly. Instead of fruitfulness, the outcome is the metaphorical "weeds and thorns," leading to frustration and death. (Genesis 3:18-19).

In his encyclical about the relationships between ourselves, God and the world, Pope Francis says that these have been broken by our refusal to acknowledge our limitations and dependency as human beings, leading to our lack of caring for the image of God in one another and for the earth. As a result of that, instead of producing the good fruit of righteous living, all our efforts end up as "weeds and thorns." This uncaring mindset amounts to a rejection of God himself.

Human life is grounded on three fundamental and closely intertwined relationships: with God, with our neighbour and with the earth itself. According to the Bible, these have been broken, both outwardly and within us... in our presuming to take the place of God and refusing to acknowledge our creaturely limitations.[23]

In making clothes for Adam and Eve clothes (3:21), in a sense, God is covering up, compensating for human failure and inadequacy, with the gift of his love. He does not allow his human creatures to go naked, alone and vulnerable in the world, but wants to clothe them in his love, so that they may still reflect his image into the world by their selfless service.

> Then the Lord God sent the man out of the Garden of Eden and made him cultivate the soil from which he had been formed. (Genesis 3:23).

The expulsion of Adam and Eve from the Garden of Eden should be interpreted as God's judgement rather than punishment. What they are being expelled from is their desire to be like God. Before expulsion, they had already made their choices – to walk away from God and go into hiding. (3:9). Much of the punishment human beings endure (Genesis 3:16-19) is but the consequence of their disobedience of God.

God's people Israel saw meaning in their history. the story of their past taught them a lesson. When the story of Adam and Eve's expulsion from the Garden of Eden was being finally edited for inclusion in the new Jewish Scriptures during the Babylonian exile, the authors-editors could have been mindful of the people, who due to their disobedience, had been expelled from their Garden of Eden homeland (Israel) and carried off as slaves to Babylon, to life East of Eden. (See 2 Kings 24:18-29 - 25:1-29). They hadn't died physically, but as a community and nation, they had disintegrated, because they had walked away from the Creator God for the gods of materialism (the riches of the promised land - silver and gold). This left them naked, in a kind of death, because they had cut themselves off from the source of life, from the God who created and loved them. Cut off from God's empowerment, all their toil and labours only produced the "weeds and thorns" of exile and enslavement. (Genesis 3:18a; see John 15:5).

## A Revelation of the Human Condition

The story of the 'fall' has universal significance. The fall of Adam and Eve can be viewed not just as an original fall from grace, but as a parable of the human condition. It is not that we are born in a state of guilt over an offence that originated with our distant forbears. This story is about the concrete situation of human life, always and ever, rather than about some kind of taint or blot passed on biologically down through history. The wrongs of centuries have made the world what it is. We are born into a world that is already broken. Theologians refer to this as the mystery of iniquity.

The story of the 'fall' is a revelation of the social nature of the human person. By nature, we are social beings, not simply individuals "doing everything my way." Instead of living out our relationships in cooperation, mutual respect and interdependence, we

---

[23] Pope Francis, *Laudato Si*, 66.

violate our nature as images of God. In seeking to be competitive (as programmed by evolution), we end up in situations of exploitation, greed and self-aggrandizement, leading to enmity and strife – the fruitlessness of life East of Eden. (Genesis 4:1-8). We are born into a world damaged by egoism, exploitation, injustice, violence and war. Death as well as life is at work in us. There is a solidarity of evil that we cannot escape, symbolized in the Satan. The 'fall' is a metaphor for the fallen world today and ever. The Genesis stories are mirrors reflecting our own faces.

"The tree of the knowledge of good and evil" symbolically evokes the insurmountable limits that man, being a creature, must freely recognise and respect with trust. "Man is dependent on his Creator, and subject to the moral norms that govern the use of freedom." (CCC 396). One of the teachings of Genesis is that there are boundaries in life that we must not traverse, or we will end up in untimely death. Two such boundaries are freedom and power. Human freedom is not an absolute. Power in human hands is not an absolute. Only in God are these attributes held to be absolutes. Man's freedom is limited through his obligation and commitment to other people, to the God present in them, and to the earth itself. In the modern world, freedom is seen as a licence to do whatever the individual wants. So walking away from God and going our own individualistic way is seen as an exercise of freedom. On the contrary, we should view freedom as liberating us from our base instincts and destructive desires. True freedom takes the individual out of the self and gives one a purpose for living, by directing one's concern towards others, and thus fulfilling our God-given mission of caring. True freedom is not a license to do whatever we want, but to do what is good and right, in alinement with the will of the Creator God. In human hands, power is limited, and must be exercised responsibly and with justice for all. We are expected to enjoy the fruits of God's garden (Genesis 2:8) - God's created gifts, all our endowment in this world - but doing so by exercising responsible stewardship (Genesis 2:15), and not by succumbing to individualistic base instincts. Going beyond the boundaries of freedom and power leads to exile from God – to death, not life (Genesis 2:17).

In the modern world, our reaching out for 'God knowledge' and power have been a source of evil as well as good. The good it has brought is visible in the many benefits of technology and the discoveries of science. But in plucking the forbidden fruit of knowledge, power and unlimited freedom, human beings become aware of their capacity for evil as well as good. Our 'God knowledge' has brought creative benefits to humanity but in its misuse of science, it has also produced ever more efficient weapons for killing. Twentieth-century technological innovations in farming and transport are proving to be destructive of the earth, and are partly responsible for climate change. New products and farming practices are destroying wild life and natural habitats. All of this may ultimately pose a threat to human life itself.

However, everything is not chaos and darkness in the world. God's Spirit is quietly at work in the midst of human folly and brokenness. Despite all the chaos, the miracle is that societies in most places still function in an orderly and beneficial manner. And at last, there are some signs of international cooperation to tackle climate change. The question is, will this happen before it is too late? We must not lose hope in the future. The human being can be self-destructive and will suffer for it, but God knows how to bring good out of the evil we do. However, the journey from evil to good can be painful.

## Jesus, the New Adam

St. Paul contrasts the universality of sin and death with the universality of salvation in Christ. (Romans 5:18-19; see CCC 402). In Adam, the relationship between humanity and God was broken. The gospels present Jesus Christ as the new Adam, who clothes us with the warmth of a close relationship with God, making us sons and daughters of God. (Galatians 3:27). St. Paul instructs believers to "put on Christ." (Romans 3:14; Colossians 3:12). And this involves the transformation of our bodies. (1 Corinthians 15:53). We are called to put on the characteristics, qualities and virtues that reflect our identity as children of God. "Clothe yourselves with compassion, kindness, humility, gentleness, patience and forgiveness." (Colossians 3:5-14). Jesus came among us as God's new human representative, standing in solidarity with us. His obedience to God, even as it meant his death, undoes the disobedience of our first representative, and its consequence, namely death.

## Sacrifice in the Ancient Near East

At the dawn of history, human beings must have awakened to their limitations and mortality, and to their capacity for bringing evil and suffering down on their own heads and those of others. But in face of their vulnerability, imperfection and powerlessness, there must have been a yearning, either for a lost or future paradise, together with a recognition of the difficulty of ever getting there. People must have wondered if there was anything human beings could do in order to arrive at something better than their present condition, which clearly was not paradise. Having a sense of their dependency, vulnerability and powerlessness (the nakedness of Adam and Eve), they might have dreamed of a power in the universe greater than themselves, who might come to their aid and make everything better. What could they do to contact this power; could they form a relationship with it? What if this power was the very God from whom they had gone into hiding? In some such manner, the idea of sacrifice may have been born.

Making sacrifices to the gods was common to all ancient cultures. What is the purpose of sacrifice? In the Bible, sacrifice is one of the principal means of ratifying, renewing and repairing the relational bond between God and his people.[24] In the biblical patriarchal period (Genesis), sacrifice was a natural offering of gifts to God by ordinary people. (Genesis 4:3-4; 12:7-8; 13:18; 29:9; 26:25; 35:7). All public actions of sacrifice were performed by the head of the family. What is given up as an offering (animals, birds, a part of crops) must be part of the property of the offeror, so that it has meaning as representing oneself. Patriarchal religion was a form of natural family religion. which was distinct from the later and more formal sacrificial cult instituted by Moses, and later carried out in the Jerusalem temple. (See Leviticus 9:1-10).

Sacrifices are symbolic actions, giving outward and public expression to man's devotion to God. By means of sacrifice, man recognises his dependence on God and

---

[24] *Catholic Bible Dictionary*, p. 791.

acknowledges the authority of God over his life.

Probably at the dawn of history, human beings discovered that something better might be attained in the future by giving up (sacrificing) something of value in the present, in other words, by deferring gratification. Existence could be made bearable and meaningful through work, painful work. (Genesis 3:19). Work is delayed gratification. Finding meaning and value in work could make it sacrificial. (The realization that pleasure can be usefully forestalled dawned on humans with great difficulty. We are still struggling with the idea). The fruits of work benefit others as well as oneself. They could bring eventual and mutual rewards. The human being at last learned to keep some produce to share with himself and others in the future. This counteracts the selfishness which would involve keeping all of the produce for oneself, or enjoying all of it in the present. (Animals in the wild need to wolf down the whole of a carcass because they cannot take the surplus meat with them or store it for the future). The idea of sharing with someone in need leads to building up trust and mutual support between people, and it arises from an awareness that when oneself is in need in the future, the others might reciprocate in like manner. At the heart of this is the idea of caring for one's brother. Sacrificing can thus create union among people. Being generous and reliable, creates communal bonds and a flourishing community. Chaos is then banished; order and peace are established. And that is something that might please the gods, or God. The lesson is learned: successful people offer sacrifices; they generously give up something for a greater good in the future. Work undertaken in a spirit of self-sacrifice for the good of others is suffering service.

There is always an element of ritual in ancient sacrifices. Perhaps acting out the ritual might bring about the desired result. An altar is built and an animal killed, or some fruit of the earth is burnt as an offering on the altar. In ancient Israel, as a sacrifice for the forgiveness of sins, an animal was slaughtered, bearing the penalty that the offeror should have suffered, because of his or her sins – the idea that sins are taken away through the slaughtered victim. (See Job 42:7-8).

## The Sacrifice of Cain and Abel

Much of human history is a story of brother against brother. Genesis goes on to say that Adam and Eve had two sons named Cain and Abel. (Genesis 4:1-2). Like Adam and Eve, they are representatives, archetypes of humankind. Unlike Adam and Eve, who lived in Eden, they live in the world of history. In their life "East of Eden", they must struggle and work. We see the consequences of an awareness of vulnerability, of good and evil, manifested in their story.

The story of Cain and Abel reflects an age-old rivalry between pastoralists and farmers. God seems to favour shepherds over farmers. Their rivalry is more than that between siblings. It represents 'brother against brother' in a universal sense.

> Abel became a shepherd, but Cain was a farmer. After some time, Cain brought some of his harvest and gave it as an offering to the Lord. Then Abel brought the first lamb born to one of his sheep, killed it and gave the best parts of it as an offering. The Lord was pleased with Abel and his offering, but he rejected Cain

and his offering. Cain became furious and he scowled in anger. (Genesis 4:2b-5).

In contrast to Adam and Eve in paradise, Cain and Abel live East of Eden. Consequently, they must work. It is not entirely clear why the Lord was not pleased with Cain and his offering. (4:4b). The first-born was always supposed to be the more perfect of a flock or herd. It may be significant that, while Abel offered a first-born, Cain merely brought "some of his harvest" to the Lord. Rather than offering the first fruits of the earth, the quality of what Cain offered may have been poor, begrudging, half-hearted. Perhaps Abel offered in humble faith and generosity, Cain in a spirit of arrogance. In his toiling and striving with the earth, Cain had foregone the pleasures of the moment, only to find that (in a spiritual sense) all his efforts had only produced a crop of weeds and thorns. (3:17b-18). Was his resultant anger and fury (4:5) caused by frustration and disappointment? Was he angry with creation, with the earth itself, seeing his work and sacrifice as pointless? Was his "scowl" (4:6) of anger directed against God? Looking for something or someone to blame, Cain was overwhelmed with jealousy and envy of his brother, whose efforts had seemingly borne fruit. In a word, was he cursed with the knowledge (awareness) of good and evil, knowing that he could inflict the utmost evil on his brother. (Genesis 3:5).

The Lord responds that the fault is all with Cain: 'Why are you angry? If you had done the right thing, you would be smiling; but instead you have done evil, sin is crouching at your door. It wants to rule you, but you must overcome it.' (4:6-7). Embittered with God's response, and in defiance of his Creator, Cain plotted revenge.

Whatever the cause of his anger, Cain couldn't control his rage or repent. When the brothers were out in the fields, Cain killed Abel in cold blood. He killed his brother, his own ideal, Abel being everything that he, Cain wished to be. This proves that his sacrifice had been a failure; instead of creating a bond, it resulted in the ultimate separation, namely death. When God asked him as to the whereabouts of his brother, Cain replied, 'I don't know. Am I supposed to take care of my brother?' (Genesis 4:8-9). Cain lied to God, and his refusal to take responsibility for his brother was a denial of family solidarity, something which was greatly prized in Israel. Cain was not doing the "right thing" (4:6) when he murdered his brother.

God's displeasure with Cain may have been due to his moral dispositions. This means that if human beings do not do well in the way they live their lives, their worship and offerings to God become insincere and meaningless. In the later history of Israel, when people carried out their religious rituals without faith and care for the weakest of their brothers and sisters, the prophets condemned their sacrifices as worthless. The Lord says, 'Faithful love is what pleases me, not sacrifice; knowledge of God, not burnt offerings.' (Hosea 6:6, NJB; see Isaiah 1:12-20; Amos 5:21-24; Micah 6:6-8).

Sacrificing seems to have been something which human beings themselves needed to do. It is never demanded by God. What God always wants is a disposition of caring for one another, not burnt offerings. Jesus said that before we come to offer our gifts, we should first become reconciled to our brothers and sisters. (Matthew 5:23-24). Only then will our sacrificing be sincere and meaningful.

The story of Cain represents a re-enactment of the original 'fall.' As a result of his murdering, Cain was placed under a curse and sent into exile. Like Adam before him,

Cain went away from the Lord's presence and lived in a land called "Wandering", which is "East of Eden." (Genesis 4:11-12, 16). A state of 'wandering' symbolizes a culture of scattered individuals living aimless lives with no common purpose. Cain said to the Lord, 'I will be a homeless wanderer on the earth, and anyone who finds me will kill me.' (Genesis 4:14). But as was the case with the Israelites in Babylon (their 'wandering' experience), God showed mercy to Cain, promising him that no one would kill him. God did not punish Cain but promised him his protection. (4:13-15).

The fact that the first murder in the Bible follows the sin of disobedience by the first pair, may be significant. (Genesis 2:17b; 3:19b). Genesis seems to be saying that the murder by Cain may be foundational, in the sense that subsequent societies are characterized by internecine violence, founded on creating victims, brother against brother.[25] In the descendants of Cain and Abel, humanity is split in two, resulting in separation and enmity (Genesis chaps. 4-5). This is the very opposite to the hoped-for beneficial effects of self-sacrifice. In these chapters the progression of evil continues in 4:23-24 and culminates in 6:5, 11. This means that mankind had become wholly corrupt.

The prophets of Israel always taught that brotherly love (not much in evidence in the Israel of their day) was more important than temple sacrifices. (Hosea 6:6; Amos 5:21-24). Genesis does not say that Abel had any descendants.

As the sacrificial victim, Abel foreshadows Jesus, who offered himself as a perfect sacrifice to God. Out of envy and jealousy, his Jewish brothers murdered him. (Mark 14:63). The hoped-for future good that Jesus saw in his self-sacrificing was his resurrection from death. This was also a good he would share with humanity at large.

## The Flood

Genesis recounts two further 'fall' stories in which the chaos and disorder of the dark ocean return again to God's creation, as exemplified in the stories of Noah and the Flood and The Tower of Babylon. Here again, human beings are creating and building on their own, and away from partnership with God. Noah is a second Adam figure. The destruction of the flood could be a metaphor for the fall of the kingdom of Israel in 721 BC, and that of Judah in 586 BC, which resulted in the Babylonian captivity.

Stories of a great flood, sent in primeval times to destroy mankind, are common in different parts of the world. The biblical story probably originated in some ancient, limited disaster, but was then given a religious interpretation. In the Babylonian myth, *The Epic of Gilgamesh* (ANET 93-95), there is an implication that order will not always rule on earth, and disorder and chaos may, and will in fact return. Disorder does return in the story about a great flood, told as one detail in *Gilgamesh* in which the earth was drowned, and on which the biblical authors based their own story of a great flood. (Genesis, chaps. 6-9).

There is a close correspondence between the biblical flood and the flood of *Gilgamesh*.[26] In both of them, the hero is warned by God of a flood that is to come. He is

---

[25] James Alison, *The Joy of Being Wrong, Original Sin Through Easter Eyes,* (The Crossroad Publishing Company), 1991, p. 96.

[26] Lawrence Boadt, *Reading the Old Testament,* p. 101.

given detailed instructions about building a boat. He is told to take on board his family and a variety of animals. After the flood, the boat comes to rest on a mountain, and the hero releases three birds. In the course of his search for immortality, the character Gilgamesh hears the story of a great primeval flood from King Utnapishtim, who built an ark and was saved from the flood by the gods.

The story of the Flood in Genesis is the climax of a sequence that begins with the creation of the world, and ends, after almost total disaster for mankind, but with the renewal of mankind through Noah and his descendants. However, where the biblical version of the flood differs from the Babylonian myth is in its unique understanding of God. The biblical story is a further parable of human brokenness and failure. The Babylonians felt a great deal of uncertainty about what the gods wanted and what would please them. The Bible, in contrast, affirms that God is always faithful, always just and loving towards the creatures he has created. He passes judgement on moral evil and he is quick to forgive. Israel rejects the idea of a moody, petulant God, in favour of a God whose will for humanity can be known and lived – and his constant love and blessing fulfilled. (Genesis 9:13). Despite similarities of some details in the Babylonian myth and the account of the Flood in the Bible, in *Gilgamesh* there is no word of a new beginning for humanity after the flood. However, the Creator God never gives up on humanity.

> When the Lord saw how wicked everyone on earth was, and how evil their thoughts were all the time, he was sorry that he ever made them and put them on the earth. He was so filled with regret that he said, 'I will wipe out these people I have created and also the animals and the birds, because I am sorry that I made any of them.' But the Lord was pleased with Noah. (6:5-8, 11-13).

Violence spirals out of control in Genesis 6. Chaos returns once again to the earth. "But Noah did everything that the Lord commanded." (7:5). Unlike Adam, Noah was obedient. When he was asked to build the ark as the means of his salvation, Noah trusted in the Lord, while his neighbours laughed at him for building a boat on dry land. People also laughed at the prophets when they were proclaiming God's word at a time before the people were taken into exile in Babylon in 587 BC. Noah is a new Adam and father of humanity. A remnant (Noah and his family) survived the flood to begin life anew with new hope, as in a new creation. Incidentally, it was only a remnant, with the hope of a new beginning, that returned to Jerusalem at the end of the Babylonian exile in 537 BC.

Noah trusts in the word of the Lord, builds his ark and is saved from the waters that cover everything, like the original chaos of the ocean before the first creation. The flood is about destruction and new creation. The evil of the world is washed away and the empire of Babylon is now gone for ever. The chaos of exile is replaced once again by the harmony of a new beginning for God's people following the Babylonian exile and their return home. (See Isaiah chap. 40).

The flood and its recession is a story of re-creation, echoing the opening chapters of Genesis. Just as in the first creation, the wind blows (the breath of God) and dry land, birds and plants appear. (Genesis 8:14). All the creatures once again reproduce their own kind and are spread over the earth, as in the first creation. (8:17). Noah then builds an altar and makes an offering of thanks to God for new creation (Genesis 8:20). This is an echo of the Sabbath rest in Genesis 2:1-4). "The Lord said to himself, 'As long as the world exists, there will be a time for planting and a time for harvest. There will always be cold and heat, summer and winter, day and night.'" (8:22). After all the chaos, order returns to the earth again, in a new creation.

Echoing Genesis 1:28, "God blessed Noah and his sons and said, 'Have many children so that your descendants will live all over the earth.'" (9:1). God will make provision for Noah and his descendants. (9:2-3; see 1:28-29). God reminded Noah and his sons that they were made in God's image, so he wanted to have a personal relationship with them. (9:6).

God then made a covenant with Noah and his family, signified by the rainbow in the sky. "The Lord said to Noah, 'Whenever I cover the sky with clouds and a rainbow appears, I will remember the everlasting covenant between me and all living beings on earth.'" (See 9:8-17). The covenant is with the whole human race - a promise that God will never again destroy living beings with a flood. (9:11). This is a new beginning and a new chance for humanity. The covenant is an obligation that God imposes on himself, implying his protection and blessing, conditional only on Noah's obedience to God in Genesis 6:18-21, which he, Noah carried out in 6:22.

Genesis 9:18-28 follows with its implication of serious sexual misconduct and infidelity within Noah's family, a new 'fall' story and the birth of a new cycle of evil, with a return to chaos once again.

The story of the flood raises a problem for believers, namely the idea of God calling for the destruction of sinful humanity. Noah alone and his family are to be spared. There is an ambiguity about the understanding of God here. Who is God; is he a builder or a destroyer; and if he is just and merciful, how can he destroy anyone? Or is this an insight that there can be no creation without destruction coming first?

The story of the so-called destruction of humanity in a great flood is no more than the authors' crude way of speaking of God's displeasure and his judgement on evil, which will always have consequences in some kind of destruction. An example of this would be the liberation of the Jews from Babylon. In order for this to happen, the Babylonian empire had to come to an end, as if washed away in a great flood. The 'flood' is a reality all over the world, in history's story of the rise and fall of empires, in the chaos and destruction caused by enmity, hatred and war.

We must bear in mind that the stories in Genesis - and further into the Bible - are culturally conditioned; they are not God's, but Israel's stories. However, they do reveal much of who God is, if in a rather crude manner as regards some of them. The positive side of the flood story reveals God as a saviour and friend of mankind, just as he was saviour in liberating the people from terror and chaos of Babylon. In that sense, like everything in the Old Testament, the story foreshadows the creative and liberating work of Christ, in whom there is no ambiguity. It is Jesus who calms the stormy waters and creates order and peace, symbolizing the birth of his new creation. (Mark 4:35-41).

As a literary work, and as the word of God, the Bible is inspired. As we have seen in chapter 1, this does not mean that it was dictated by God in any sense. Nor should we imagine that every single sentence would have had God's approval or sanction. If the impression of a vindictive, destructive God is conveyed in the story of the flood, this is based on a primitive understanding of God who was sometimes seen as a fearsome power, always ready to punish misdeeds, rather than the loving Father of Jesus Christ. At that time, people didn't know any better; that was the stage at which their knowledge and understanding of God had reached. Sometimes they didn't expect God to be any better than themselves. There is an evolution of moral consciousness in the Old Testament. In the earliest passages, there is a tendency to project negative human characteristics on to God, such as anger and retribution. In the later writings, these tendencies are less evident. They disappear entirely in the New Testament.

The downfall of the kingdom of Judah, before the Babylonian exile, due to the infidelity of Israel, was the work of the sovereign God. But it was really Israel who had walked away from God, in the people's chasing of other gods. So the destruction of their kingdom and State may be seen as the consequence of the people's own evil ways.

## The Tower of Babel

Noah's descendants became the diverse populations of the Near East. (Genesis 10:1-32). The scene is thus set for the story of the Tower of Babel. (Genesis 11:1-9). This story describes human beings attempting to trespass into the realm of God – a seeking of God-like power, human beings usurping God. (See 3:1-24; 6:1-4). The story of the Tower is a play on the theme of exaltation and humiliation, as is the Adam and Eve story.

As time passed, some people ceased living as nomads. They learned how to make bricks and build cities. Because the ancient Hebrews were farmers and herders of flocks, they were suspicious of cities. The Bible is partial to the nomad in the semi-arid wilderness, as the place of reflection, where God can be discovered in the peace and silence of nature. The wilderness is also a metaphor for the journey of faith – from penitence to new life, to mature and responsible living.

Babel was an ancient town in the land of Babylonia. The early settlers there found that by combining their abilities and manpower, they could achieve progress. They considered themselves more technically advanced than their neighbours, and this led to pride in their self-sufficiency. The Babylonians really did build huge towers to their gods, sometimes rising two hundred feet or more, with temples on top of them.[27] Rather than a fortress, such a tower may have been a stepped structure known as a ziggurat with a temple on top in which the gods dwelt. Archaeology has uncovered such a structure from the 3rd millennium BC at the ancient city of Ur on the River Tigris, in the land of Sumer.[28]

> At first the people of the whole world had only one language. As they wandered about in the East (suggesting an aimless life East of Eden), they came to a plain in Babylonia and settled there… They said, 'Now let's build a city with a tower that reaches the sky, so that we can make a name for ourselves and not be scattered all over the earth.' (See Genesis 11:1-4).

---

[27] Don Fleming, *World's Bible Dictionary*, p. 37.

[28] *Oxford Bible Atlas*, p. 37, 70.

The next great cultural expansion in the ancient world has a negative side. Symbolically, the story of the tower represents an attempt by human ambition to wrest absolute autonomy from God once more. It is a human attempt to reverse the fall of Adam and Eve by building up to heaven. Human beings desire to ascend to God and take back control. In this case, God's action frustrates the attempt to rise above the human condition. Building a city is a normal cultural development, but again it is misdirected by the builders going it alone against the will of the Creator. Babel is an attempt to by human beings to become builders on their own. Their mission is their own, not necessarily what God intends for them. It is a rejection of God.

The Biblical author makes the point that sin and evil did not disappear with the flood. Genesis offers an interpretation of this building project. God saw it as a symbol of the people's pride, as a drive for power and self-sufficiency, a re-enactment of the 'fall.' In other words, it is an attempt to be like God. In the builders' refusal to accept their creaturely dependence, they set themselves up as gods. Instead of honouring God's name (Psalm 8:1), they build a tower to the heavens in order to make a name for themselves. The building of the tower is about self-glorification rather than giving glory to God. It is a declaration of independence from God, whom human beings no longer need as a partner. Confusion and family fragmentation again result from eating the forbidden fruit of self-exaltation, trying to outdo God.

Sin creates a false, prideful unity, hostile to God (as in the forced unity of empires). It is an attempt to create a paradise on strength, power and wealth. Mocking their claim that the Tower of Babel reaches the heavens, "the Lord came down to see the city and the tower which these men had built." (Genesis 11:5). The idea of "one language" may be symbolic of the union and harmony of life in the Garden of Eden. Once this harmony is disrupted by humans, there follows the fragmentation symbolized by different languages and aimless wandering over the earth – the scattering of humanity into tribalism. The result is rivalry, exploitation and wars. (Genesis 11:8). History has shown that when a powerful group of people thinks it has unlimited knowledge and wisdom, that group tries to impose its ideas on other people. Such a group cares more about its own infallible wisdom than it does about people. This leads to enmity, hatred and strife, to disintegration and death. Only God's way leads to unity and salvation. Only by discovering and participating in the divine plan, can human beings make any progress towards union.

Both the flood and the tower stories may have been finally edited for inclusion in the Jewish Scriptures during the Babylonian exile (587-537 BC), in order to give the people courage and hope when all seemed lost. These stories may have reminded the exiles that they once had their own schemes for salvation, arrogantly building a society that benefited only an elite, while oppressing the common people and ignoring their needs. They trusted in their own building prowess rather than working in a partnership with God who wants justice for all. They failed to create a society organised on the basis of God's covenant of love for humanity.

The Tower may also be a satire on the values of empire, and a symbol of the arrogance of the Babylonian Empire in particular, a mere human construct, which supposed that it could be an enduring enterprise, but it was built on subjugation and slavery (contrary to God's will for humanity), creating fragmentation and enmity among peoples. The empire that held God's people in exile would collapse like a falling flower, and evil would be washed away from the world, as in a great flood. (Isaiah 47:1-2). The exiles would then be rescued and prepared for a new beginning after returning to their homeland in Israel. "Yes, the grass withers and flowers fade but the word of our God endures for ever." (Isaiah 40:8). God's purpose for the world, although often thwarted by human rebellion, remains the same for ever.

## CHAPTER 3

# Abraham, Isaac and Jacob

## Faith as Trust

Genesis chapter eleven concludes the story of how God's offer of grace and blessing is continually rejected by human pride and arrogance. God then seeks a new beginning, with the call of Abraham to be the father of a family and a nation, and as the means of carrying forward his promised blessing to humanity. After all that has happened up to this point – good beginnings ending in aimless wandering and destruction - will God meet with success this time? Instead of relying on humanity as a whole, he now calls one man and his family so that they might be the bearers of the blessing of his salvation to the whole world. Like Adam before him, Abraham is an archetype of humanity.

Up to Genesis 12 the biblical story is about the failure of faith. It is about human beings trusting in their own powers, wisdom and knowledge, rather than trusting in God. From Genesis 12 onward, the biblical story is about faith, the importance of trusting in God for the salvation that he alone can give us.

The name Abraham is related to *abba*, which means "father." And so Abraham is the great forefather, the father of the Israelites, the father of their faith. Abraham is depicted in the Bible as the great man of faith. So, what is faith? "Belief without evidence," says the scientist, Richard Dawkins. An irrational belief in things that don't exist, according to rationalists. Many scientists claim that the material world is the only reality. However, there is no evidence for such a claim. If the world of science were the only reality, then we would be looking for empirical evidence for everything. Science does not explain everything. Faith embraces another reality, the invisible, the world of spirit, which is no less real for not being visible. It is bound up with wisdom, which is a form of knowledge which enables us to live well, giving us hope even in times of pain and affliction. It is through wisdom that we discover the meaning of life, what are true values, what are the most important things in life. Wisdom is subjective and interior to the person, having to do with moral and aesthetic realities, such as faith, hope, love, goodness, truth and beauty. Living a life from the standpoint of these things is what we might call wisdom.

Religion helps to free us from the greed fostered by a materialistic society. It believes that happiness is found in serving others, not in selfish hedonism. It gives people a set of moral values, as well as faith and courage in times of suffering. It fosters trust and co-operation, self-discipline and social cohesion. Above all, it offers us the hope of an eternal destiny, thus giving meaning and purpose to human life.

One may indeed refuse to believe what one cannot test or prove. But the big decisions of life cannot be subjected to proof. People can never know in advance the facts that would make their decisions the right ones. For example, the decision to marry a certain person, to start a business, to choose a career! Choosing any one of these is to embark on a creative enterprise, an adventure undertaken with trust. There is no creation without risk, no adventure without faith, courage and hope. How can we know in advance whether it is right to trust people, to befriend them, to love, to give people a second chance? We can never be certain about these matters. For this reason, faith is distinguished from certainty. The reality of life is that we face a future that is unknowable. Faith is a risk; it is the courage to take a risk. Faith is actually trust in another person because we deem him or her to be reliable and trustworthy.

Trusting another person is relational; it unites one person to the other in thinking, deciding and feeling; it is respectful of the dignity of the other; it is saying, 'you are worthy of my trust and confidence.' In trusting, we overcome our temptation to suspicion and hostility. Before we can move out to the other in trust, these negative feelings must die in us. When trust between people breaks down, the results can be tragic – separation, hatred, a scattering. Trust, on the other hand, brings people closer; it creates a union of hearts and minds. In other words, trust, which is another word for faith, leads to love, which is the one force in the world that creates peace, harmony and reconciliation. So, although there is no empirical evidence for trust, it is not an irrational leap into the dark. It does involve discernment, and by its fruit, we can know its worth. In depending on and trusting their parents, a bond of love is established between parent and child, leading eventually to independence and maturity on the part of the child. Trust can be transforming. Trusting children are gradually transformed into something much more than they were at a younger age. When we trust in God and hand ourselves over to him, he can transform us.

## Religious Faith: Trust in God

Vatican II affirms religious faith as free assent, self-commitment and obedience to the will of God who reveals himself to us; it is about following God, trusting in him, doing things his way, in obedience to his will. The Old Testament is the story of God's faithfulness to humanity and humanity's trust, or lack of it, in God. God's word can make perfect sense when it tells us the truth about the meaning of human life. When God promises an eternal destiny to human beings, his word is trustworthy. Eternal life (participation in the life of God) gives meaning and purpose to earthly life, so that every faith journey is about the means of reaching this goal. (See Romans 1:16, 5:1-2; Psalm 40:4, 71:5, 73:26). "God loved the world so much that he gave his only Son, so that everyone who believes in him may have eternal life." (John 3:16).

God's people often saw evidence for trusting in God. God keeps his promises. He always proves himself to be steadfast and trustworthy. For this reason, people were called by Moses and the prophets to trust in his word, because his word was true and good. (Exodus 14:31; 19:9; Deuteronomy 1:30-33). The prophets of Israel taught that salvation would come through trusting in God, and not in armies or military alliances (human powers). (See Isaiah 30:15-16).

The call of faith (trusting in God) is a call to mission. We are sometimes called away from a particular task, occupation or way of life, to go on a new, and perhaps, more challenging and fruitful journey, the one that God always has in mind for us. All faith journeys are about discovering the meaning and purpose of life, which is really to discover the job God has for us. But how does God speak to us? God's word usually comes to us through the image of God in other people, as they speak to us. It also comes through reading the Bible and through the events of our daily lives. God never gives up on us; it is we who may not be alert to his promptings. "Kindness and faithful love pursue me every day of my life." (Psalm 23:6, NJB). If we are to hear the voice of God, there are two requisites: we must be in a state of listening and alertness, and secondly, we must exercise discernment. (Mark 13:35-37). The latter is important, because there will be many other voices coming from our culture prompting us to take the line of least resistance, luring us away from doing things God's way. We will recognise the voice as genuinely from God when it comes as a challenge to leave some comfort behind us and embark on a journey of service.

To sum up, religious faith is an admission of human limitation – of powerlessness and self-sufficiency. Living by faith means trusting in the power of God rather than solely in our own efforts, or in material things to bring us meaning and fulfilment. Faith is trusting that only God can fulfil our deepest hungering and thirsting for life. (Psalm 18:2; 40:4; 71:1-5; 73:26; Isaiah 55:1-2; Jeremiah 2:13; John 3:16; 4:13; 6:35). Faith is a condition of salvation. (Mark 9:22-24; Romans 1:16; 5:1). Faith can be the means of doing something very difficult, although it is God who does it. (Matthew 9:22, 28, 17:19-20).

## Origins of Abraham

The story of God's chosen people begins with the call of Abraham in Genesis 12. The subsequent stories of his descendants explain the origins of the Hebrew people, stories that originated in the second millennium BC. These stories were passed down orally and didn't take their final written form until towards the end of the Babylonian exile in 537 BC.

In the Near East (the area of the Tigris and Euphrates rivers, including Canaan and Egypt), at the time Abraham was supposed to have existed, there would have been tribal chieftains living a nomadic life, moving from place to place with their flocks of sheep and goats, but with the likelihood of eventually settling in one place. At that stage, there would have been no clearly defined borders between different parts of the Near East. For instance, the migrations of groups of people across the eastern frontiers of Egypt to seek more favourable conditions of life are well attested historically. The migration of Jacob and his sons to Egypt is an example of this.[29]

Archaeology has shown that the social and cultural background to the accounts of Abraham, Isaac and Jacob may be genuine. Excavations of middle bronze age sites in

---

[29] Barton and Muddiman, *Oxford Bible Commentary*, (Oxford University Press), 2001, ANET 251, p. 47.

Mesopotamia (the land of the Tigris and Euphrates rivers) have yielded an enormous number of clay tablets giving valuable information about the political, cultural and religious life in that part of the Near East. One such example shows the protected status of a slave woman who bears her master a son in place of his wife, who couldn't have children. (Genesis 16:1-3). That example is taken from the law code of King Hammurabi (1700 BC).[30] We know that the oral will of Isaac on his deathbed in Genesis 27:28-29 was acceptable legal practice in the ancient city of Nuzi in Mesopotamia.

It is possible that the population movements of the middle bronze age were the background of the movements of the patriarchs (Abraham, Isaac and Jacob). Like many other such people, the patriarchs were chieftains of wealthy clans, owning sheep and goats, and living a nomadic life before a time of gradual resettlement in urban centres in the middle bronze age period. Trading would have been an additional part of their livelihood. The clans maintained their family ties with their original homeland. Thus, Isaac and Jacob married wives from among their own relatives in Haran (a city near the sources of the River Euphrates) in upper Mesopotamia.

This patriarchal period would have been the middle bronze age (2000–1500 BC). At the time when the story of Abraham's adventures was finally compiled and included in the Jewish Scriptures, Abraham would have been dead for at least a thousand years. This means that little can be known about him. The accounts written about him probably had their origin in legends. But legends are not lies; they are a form of poetry, bearing some resemblance to sagas. Among primitive peoples, poetry and saga were the beginnings of history. This is true of Greece, Rome, Israel and Ireland. Legends always contain a kernel of historical truth. Sagas are heroic tales about the ancestors of a well-known family. They build up the hero larger than life. When the tale comes to be written down it will have developed much beyond its original form, with new episodes added, and with different versions of the same story included in final written accounts.

Opinions about the Abrahamic stories vary among biblical scholars. One view holds that by the time of their final editing, during or after the Babylonian exile in the late sixth century BC, the stories of the patriarchs (Genesis 12 to 36) had developed into an epic of faith. This included all the traditions of Abraham until the later slavery of his descendants in Egypt. But it still owed its origins to the days when many of the stories were simply oral tales about the heroic exploits of a clan leader.[31] Much the same view holds that the stories are part of an Israelite epic (in which the stories in the Book of Exodus were a later addition), and that the traditions of the patriarchs may preserve some authentic material, though reshaped and updated before final editing.[32] A common view is that the stories of Abraham and his descendants had an oral origin and are not to be seen as accounts of the lives of historical personages. Rather than being exact historical accounts - for those who composed them - they are a revelation of the meaning of human life, as lived under the direction of God.

Recording the traditions of their ancestors would help later Israelites to

---

[30]  Ibid, p. 109).

[31]  Lawrence Boadt, *Reading the Old Testament*, p. 121.

[32]  Ibid, p. 109.

understand how they came to be as a people and a nation. The people did not want to lose touch with their historical roots and with their ancestors' memory of the God who began their formation as a people, rescued and saved them in the past, and who would continue to be with them. Thus, the greater part of Genesis, chapter 12 to the end of the book, is an account of Abraham and his descendants, explaining the origins of the Jewish people and Israel's view of life.

The story of Abraham and his descendants is thus a literary work, and it should be interpreted the same way as any work of literature, in order to discover what it can teach us about the human condition, and especially, what it reveals about God - the chief protagonist in the story - and our relationship with him. The biblical authors are writing about the journey of faith, not the biography of a historical character. Because the story of Abraham is a work of literature, we can draw on the usual interpretative tools as applicable to any literary work. So, we look for the development of character; how characters relate to one another, how they reach maturity through the guidance of God and the trials of their lives. In these accounts, God is the main protagonist and should be seen as one of the actors in the story. As we read the story, we wonder if God will accomplish his purposes.

## The Sovereignty of God

The stories of the patriarchs (Abraham, Isaac and Jacob), are a revelation of the sovereignty of God in the world. If God created the world, it is reasonable to suppose that he is in charge of the work of his hands and that he cares about his creation. There is an objection: How can God be in control of a world which is full of suffering and evil? The stories of the patriarchs reveal a God who is progressively dealing with evil, beginning with his promise of blessing and nationhood to Abraham in Genesis 12:2. God is concerned about evil. He hasn't forgotten his promise to "crush the serpent's head." (Genesis 3:15, NRSVC). The purpose of this part of Genesis is theological rather than historical; it is meant to teach religious truth: trusting in God will transform human beings through the blessing of closer union with him.

In his relationship with human beings, God knows human nature. His patience with human beings is infinite. He knows that there is no quick-fix to the troubles of the world. God is not a slave-driver, insisting on instant perfection. He respects the freedom of human beings when they go their own way. God is rather the gentle Shepherd, going ahead of us, coaxing us to trust him and calling us to follow him in *his* way. When humans walk with God and place their trust in him, he readily showers them with his blessings, making them more fully human. (See Isaiah 40:31).

From the beginning of creation, human beings were walking away from God, rejecting his blessing, and through their disobedience (Genesis 2:17b; 3:6), failing to discharge their God-given mission of stewardship. (Genesis 1:28). Deliverance from human failure and weakness can only come from God's initiative. God's plan now is to choose one man, and through this man's obedience and trust in him, to bring union, peace and harmony to all peoples, summed up in the word "blessing," promised to Abraham and his descendants. (Genesis 12:1-3). God's choice of Abraham, and his founding of the chosen people (Israel) was the first step of God's reconstruction of a united and blest human family, a society not based on the disobedience of Adam, the vengeance of Cain (Genesis 4:8), or the self-serving arrogance of Babel. (Genesis 11:4). All nations will be blest in Abraham's name. (Genesis 22:18). God has the interests of the people of all nations at heart, and not just the people of Israel. Having first been blest, Israel was then given a mission of bearing blessing to all the nations. The extent to which Israel failed or succeeded to fulfil this God-given mission is very much the story of the rest of the Old Testament.

The story of the patriarchs (Abraham, Isaac and Jacob) can be our story too. Walking with God is a challenge. It calls for faith and hope. God's plan is going nowhere unless human beings believe in what he wants and in what they themselves are doing, in compliance with his will. All through these accounts, God stakes his hope on flawed human beings like Abraham, Isaac and Jacob. No more than the rest of us, they are not saints. But God always finds ways around our wrong turnings. He does not give up on us; he sticks with us, as our Shepherd, giving us all we need (Psalm 23:1): the empowerment to stay the pace with him. We need to trust him. (See Isaiah 40:31).

## The Call of Abraham

Abram (his original name, meaning "exalted father"), was the son of a tribal chieftain and shepherd who lived by the River Euphrates in the city of Ur of the Chaldeans, one of the world's oldest cities (in modern day Iraq).[33] His father would have been the head of a wealthy clan, raising sheep and goats and living near, or in the city. The journeying of Abram started with his father Terah leaving the city of Ur in Babylonia to go to the land of Canaan, taking with him his son Abram, his grandson Lot, and his daughter-in-law Sarai, Abram's wife. The family journeyed north to the city of Haran and settled there. (This was a journey of about 750 miles). Terah died there at the age of 205 years. (Genesis 11:31-32). The ages of people are exaggerated in Genesis, a great age may have signified the blessing of God on a person.

Haran was a city located in Northern Mesopotamia, near the source of the River Euphrates, not far from the border of present-day Turkey. Haran seems to have been somewhat of a staging-post on Abram's way to Canaan (modern-day Israel and Palestine). Having spent some time in Haran, Abram may have acquired possessions and flocks of his own. Then God's call comes to him to leave everything behind him on which he depended, so that God could shower blessings on him. (See Mark 1:16-18; 10:21). The message here is that we cannot carry out a mission inspired by God if we are too wrapped up in our own concerns and schemes.

> The Lord said to Abram, 'Leave your country, your relatives, and your father's home, and go to a land that I am going to show you. I will give you many descendants, and they will become a great nation. I will bless you and make your name famous so that you will be a blessing...' Abram took his wife Sarai, his nephew Lot, and all the wealth and all the slaves they had acquired in Haran, and

---

[33] Don Fleming, *World's Bible Dictionary*, p. 451.

they started out for the land of Canaan. When they arrived in Canaan, Abram travelled through the land until he came to the sacred tree of Moreh, the holy place at Shechem (In central Canaan).[34] The Lord appeared to Abram and said to him, 'This is the country that I am going to give to your descendants.' Then Abram built an altar there to the Lord, who had appeared to him. (Genesis 12:1-2, 5-7).

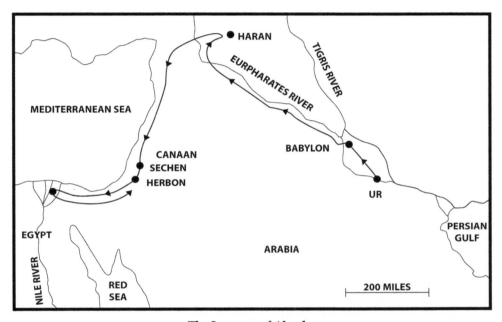

*The Journey of Abraham*

The journey from Haran to Canaan would have been about 300 miles southward. There must have been something about the ease and comforts of his life in Haran that left Abram empty, dissatisfied, unfulfilled, unchallenged. But in being thus empty, he was ready to be filled with God's fullness. Abram must have been a dreamer, his mind open to new possibilities. He may thus have wanted to explore new horizons, prompting him to undertake a journey of faith. Because of his trust in God, he was able to look beyond the here-and-now, towards a greatness that only God could give him, and through him, to his descendants. God must have seen that Abram was at heart, a searcher, a seeker of wisdom, a man with the potential for greatness. God takes delight when people are open to the new. He wants to accompany them on their journey towards newness, empowering and guiding them on their chosen path, once they trust in him and learn to depend on him. (Psalm 23:3; Isaiah 40:31). Perhaps Abram had a vision of God as guide and carer, granted to him through the experience of his own care for his flocks, and his awareness of their complete dependence on him.

---

[34] Ibid, p. 401.

Whatever the manner or shape of his experience of God, Abram felt called to leave behind everything that made him feel secure - all the things the builders of Babel sought - family, fame, culture, a name for themselves, life centred on themselves. Their project ended in a scattering – separation from one another and from God. (See Genesis 11:9). On the contrary, Abram's mission was directed towards others. It was to be the means of bringing blessing to other people, by gathering them together in a union with one another and with God. It could thus be said, that Abram's mission was to be the undoing of the Babel project. When his name was later changed to Abraham, God expanded his mission to include the blessing of the people of all nations – all because of his obedience to God. (Genesis 22:17-18). The call to leave his country came from God. It is God who would make his name famous, not Abram himself. (Genesis 12:2). This was to be a project entirely directed by the sovereign God. Abram was asked to cooperate with God as a faithful servant.

Abram's journeying may be a metaphor for growth in the Christian life - the notion of leaving everything in order to follow Jesus on his journey to Jerusalem. (See Mark 1:16-20; 10:21).

When Abram arrived at "the sacred tree of Moreh, the holy place in Shechem," which was inhabited by Canaanites, the Lord appeared to him and promised all of that country to him and his descendants. (Genesis 12:5). Abram then built an altar at this, his first staging post in Canaan. (12:7). Perhaps he wanted to convey his gratitude to God and demonstrate his dependence on the one guiding him thus far. Abraham built altars in different parts of Canaan: after God brought him home safely from Egypt (Genesis 13:4), and at Mamre, another sacred place (13:18), which will later figure significantly in his story. The altars built by Abram may be symbolic of communion between himself and God, and may indicate Abram's willingness to sacrifice himself for the sake of the long-term goal of bringing blessing to his descendants. During his faith journey, Abram made three sacrifices to God: he gave up his homeland for a new journey; he sacrificed his own flesh as a sign of his obedience to God (17:9-13), and later he was willing to sacrifice his greatest possession - his only son. (22:1-3). The altars built by Abram, and his sacrifices, foreshadow the self-sacrificial work of Christ.

## Abram's Lack of Trust in God

Having reached Canaan, Abram found the land already populated, and the local kings fighting to defend their territory. A famine soon appeared in the land, and Abram had to journey on to Egypt. (Genesis 12:10). Confronted with such obstacles, Abram must have asked himself, how could his descendants inherit the land of Canaan? It was difficult for Abram to see things God's way. Because of our limited vision, we have the same difficulty. Like ourselves Abram wants everything to go smoothly all of the time. He would have to learn to trust this mysterious God and to discover that there are no quick fixes. Life's journey is hard; there are innumerable obstacles to be surmounted; the road ahead is often obscured by darkness. It is often difficult see God mysteriously with us, guiding us, as we go through a valley of darkness. (Psalm 23:3a, 4).

Why the famine, and was Abram's journey to Egypt like the reverse of the exodus, another exile? Abram wasn't always obedient to God. God called him to leave *everything* behind him, his relatives, his nephew Lot, his entire household, his flocks, and especially his own way of seeing things. It looks as if his relatives, especially his nephew, were brought as a kind of insurance. Was he placing his trust in all of these things rather than in God? God told him he would have many descendants (12:2), but Genesis says that his wife "Sarai wasn't able to have children." (11:30). So did Abram see his nephew as a surrogate son? God promised Abram new land, but he must have wondered what good would land be to him if he had no heir? Apparently, he loved all his old crutches and still trusted in lots of things rather than in God. In other words, he had not totally surrendered himself to God. His faith journey was only beginning. He could have left Lot behind, because the latter caused him a lot of trouble. (See Genesis 13:5-13; 14:14-16). Was his trouble with Lot God's way of reminding him of his lack of trust?

The famine, which may have been due to a lack of rain, or infertility of the land, was God's way of showing Abram that he didn't really trust God to grant him an heir. Thus, his lack of faith in his own fertility is matched by God's restraint on the land's fertility.

When he went to Egypt, he tried to work out everything on his own. He lied to Pharaoh, telling him that Sarai was his sister, because of his fear that the king of Egypt would kill him in order to take her as a bride. 'Tell them you are my sister,' he said to her. (12:13). This was his deceitful scheme to save his own skin. During all this time, and perhaps because he was so obsessed with saving himself, Abram was far from God, and God was not speaking to him. God moved Pharaoh by sending him plagues to get him to release Sarai and restore her to Abram. Thus, the pagan king heard God and obeyed him, while his chosen ones did not.

Abram's journey to Egypt foreshadows the Israelites exile in Egypt. (Genesis chaps. 46-50). Having left Egypt behind him, Abram was once again back in the promised land. He then decided that he could do without one of his crutches. He gave Lot the choice of better pastures and allowed him to go his own way. With this separation, and his generosity towards Lot, Abram found that blessing would follow his generosity. God then appeared to him and promised to give him the land and countless descendants. (Genesis 13:14-17). "Then Abram moved his camp and settled near the sacred trees of Mamre at Hebron (in the south of Canaan), and there he built an altar to the Lord." (Genesis 13:18).

"Soon again, Abram had a vision and heard the Lord say to him, 'Do not be afraid, Abram. I will shield you from danger and give you a great reward.'" (Genesis 15:1). It's as if God is saying to him, 'Don't be anxious, this is not your project, it is mine, trust in me. I will give you the necessary direction and protection.' Fear is a sign of a lack of faith. Abram would have everything he needed for his journey, as long as he trusted in God. The famine and his journey to Egypt were probably God's first test of Abram's faith. The promise was enticing: land and numerous descendants. (We must bear in mind that the two most prized possessions in life for the ancient Israelites were land and progeny).

But Abram was not satisfied. He was still lacking in trust. He asked God what good would his reward be to him when he had no children. Without children, there would be no one to inherit the land promised to him by God. By now, his nephew Lot had gone his own way. Abram says to God, that perhaps one of his slaves, a girl named Eliezer, might inherit his property. (Genesis 15:2-3). Then he heard the Lord speaking to him again with further reassurance:

> 'This slave Eliezer will not inherit your property; your own son will be your heir.' The Lord took him outside his tent and said, 'Look at the sky and try to count the stars; you will have as many descendants as that.' Then Abram put his trust in the Lord, and because of this the Lord was pleased with him and accepted him. (Genesis 15:4-6).

Abram is a second Adam figure. Adam and his family were placed in the Garden of Eden, where God called them to a mission of blessing, to be "fruitful, multiply and fill the earth." (Genesis 1:28). Abram was promised the land of Canaan (a new Eden) and many descendants (filling the earth) as "numerous as the stars of heaven." (Genesis 15:5). God walked with Adam in Eden. Abram is asked to walk with God, to do God's will. Through the disobedience of Adam (his failure to discharge his particular mission), human beings lose their freedom through bondage to the self, and thus, become estranged from one another. The result is family break-up and the scattering of humanity. Abram, a second Adam figure, would be the bearer of blessing because of his trust and obedience (15:6). New Testament writers see Abram's obedience and faith as something to be imitated. (Hebrews 11:8-10; Romans 4:1-5; Galatians 3:6-9).

"Then God said to Abram, 'I am the Lord your God who led you out of Ur in Babylonia, to give you this land as your own.' But Abram asked, 'Sovereign Lord, how can I know that it will be mine?'" (Genesis 15:7-8). Abram was still not prepared to take the word of the Lord on trust. He wanted certainty, which is not faith. "Then the Lord made a covenant with Abram. The Lord said, 'I promise your descendants all this land from the borders of Egypt to the River Euphrates.'" (Genesis 15:18). The covenant was an agreement between the two parties. God would keep his promise, and in turn, he expected that Abram would trust in his word and be obedient to him.

In Genesis 15 the promise is land, in 17:6 it is a dynasty, and in chapter 22 it is a worldwide blessing for all the nations. The promises would gradually be fulfilled. In the much later Mosaic covenant (agreement between God and his people), the people were freed from Egypt to return to the promised land (see Exodus). In the Davidic covenant, the kingdom and dynasty were established. (2 Samuel 5). In the new and everlasting covenant, the blessing and salvation of the nations is definitively established by Jesus. (Mark 14:24).

## Abram's Solution to his Lack of Progeny

Abram would have to show through many more tests of his faith that he was worthy of blessing. For Abram, as for all of us, the journey involves doubt, struggle, fear of the unknown, calling for commitment and dedication.

Abram continued on his wanderings, often not knowing where he was going. His life was still one of anxiety about God's promise of blessing, which seemed to be going nowhere. How could he become the father of a great nation when his wife Sarai had not borne him any children? (Genesis 16:1). As long as Abram was crippled with anxiety over the promise, he was not a free man. But the reason for his anxiety was that he still did not trust God, but instead, placed too much reliance on his own schemes. Like all of us, he couldn't totally surrender himself to God.

Abram found the solution to becoming a father, or at least, Sarai did. She asked Abram to sleep with a slave girl of hers named Hagar. When Abram agreed to do this, she gave Hagar to him to be his concubine. (Genesis 16:3). When this girl became pregnant, she became proud and despised Sarai, as if to say: 'This is something you couldn't do.' "Then Sarai said to Abram, 'It's your fault that Hagar despises me.'" (16:5). Abram told her to do whatever she wanted with Hagar. Then Sarai treated Hagar so cruelly that she ran away into the wilderness. (16:6).

This has echoes of the blaming by family members that went on in the Garden of Eden after that other act of disobedience. Like Eve (Genesis 3:6), Sarai gives the forbidden fruit of Hagar to Abram, thus causing division, enmity, rivalry, family bitterness, and finally a journey into life East of Eden. (Genesis 3:11-13). But then the angel of the Lord met Hagar at a spring in the desert on the road to Shur (a desert region in the north of the Sinai Peninsula)[35] and told her to go back to her mistress. (16:7-9). "The angel said to her, 'I will give you so many descendants that no one will be able to count them. You are going to have a son, and you will name him Ishmael, because the Lord has heard your cry of distress.' (16:10-11). Hagar named the God who had spoken to her "A God who Sees." (16:13). Hagar returned home to Abram, bore him a son and named him Ishmael. (16:15).

According to Genesis, after taking Hagar as a concubine, and probably as a result of the family division and strife, Abram and his family heard no more from God for thirteen years. They had gone into a kind of exile away from God. But God hadn't abandoned them.

## Abraham, Father of Nations

When Abram was ninety-nine years old, the Lord appeared to him and said, 'I am the Almighty God. Obey me and always do what is right. I will make my covenant with you and give you many descendants.' Abram bowed down with his face touching the ground, and God said, 'I make this covenant with you: I promise that you will be the ancestor of many nations. Your name will no longer be Abram, but Abraham, because I am making you the ancestor of many nations... I will be your God and the God of your descendants. I will give to you and to your descendants this land in which you are now a foreigner. The whole land of Canaan will belong to your descendants for ever, and I will be their God. You also must agree to keep the covenant with me, both you and your descendants in future generations.' (Genesis 17:1-5, 7b, 8-9).

The name Abraham means 'father of Nations.' This was the name which would make Abraham famous. The builders of Babel wanted to give a name to themselves. The name

---

[35] *World's Bible Dictionary*, p. 245, 405.

was 'Fame.' It meant self-exaltation. Abraham's name signifies a creative mission directed by God, through which God would exalt Abraham.

In appointing Abraham "father of nations," God was telling him that through his faithfulness, God's blessing (salvation) would come to all the nations. It is in this sense, that Abraham would have many descendants – all people of faith. The Tower of Babel symbolized a broken and scattered human family, living with enmity and division. Faith in God creates union. The scattered nations are now to be united in faith with Abraham as their Father. God is entrusting his family (mankind) to a father who will bring blessing (salvation) to his descendants (the nations). Through Abraham, God will bring a nation (Israel) into being - God's own people - and through Israel he will bless all people. (Genesis 18:18). Israel's vocation was to share God's light with the nations, not keep it hidden under a tub. (Mark 4:21).

As we will see, Abraham and his descendants (Israel) were only partially successful in bringing blessing to the nations. Jesus saw himself and his followers as the renewed Israel, through whom salvation would eventually reach the ends of the earth.

God then makes a covenant (agreement) with Abraham: 'I will keep my promise to and your descendants in future generations, as an everlasting covenant. I will be your God and the God of your descendants.' (Genesis 17:7). God's promise is the land of Canaan to Abraham and his descendants. (17:8). God tells Abraham that keeping the covenant means that he and his descendants must be obedient to God – as his part of the agreement. (17:9). Perhaps Abraham had learned his lesson, to the extent that he would never again forget his call to obedience. As a sign that the covenant would be everlasting for Abraham's descendants, God told him that he must agree to circumcise every male among his kinsmen (himself included), and this would apply to their descendants also. (17:12-13). Was this to be Abraham's way of atoning for his sins? Obedience and faithfulness to God always involves self-sacrifice. "Then God said to Abraham, 'You must now call your wife Sarah (meaning 'mother of nations'). I will bless her and give you a son by her. She will become the mother of nations, and there will be kings among her descendants.'" (Genesis 17:15-16).

But Abraham remained sceptical, still not trusting in the Lord. He preferred his own way of doing things. He bowed down with his face touching the ground and he began to laugh when he thought, 'Can a man have a child when he is a hundred years old? Can Sarah have a child at ninety?' He asked God, 'Why not let Ishmael be my heir?' But God said, 'No, your wife Sarah will bear you a son and you will name him Isaac. I will keep my covenant with him and his descendants for ever. It is an everlasting covenant.' (Genesis 17:17-19). It's as if God is saying to Abraham, 'You are still tied to your own agenda, *your* journey; trust me, because it is not you who will do this, but me. I know what you need.'

What did this promise mean? Obeying God starts with the trust that God will grant our *needs* rather than what we might *want* in a given situation. What we want may not always be for our good. "The Lord is my shepherd; he gives me all I need." (Psalm 23:1). It is only if we accept him as our shepherd, that he *can* grant us our needs.

# Visitation of the Three Men at Mamre

Abraham must have often asked himself, and God, when was he to have a son? Then in Genesis chapter 18 there is an awesome story, a revelation of how God's creative presence can be mediated to us through people –if we can hear and recognise their voice as the voice of God. Now follows the incident at Mamre, which was located in Hebron, [36] about twenty miles to the south of the later city of Jerusalem. It was the chief town of the later tribe of Judah. In the ancient world, there were lots of local deities, and shrines to gods of particular places. Mamre was probably one of the many sacred places in Canaan where sacrifices were offered to the pagan god Baal. Abraham himself had made offerings to God at that place.

> The Lord appeared to Abraham at the sacred trees of Mamre. As Abraham was sitting at the entrance to his tent during the hottest part of the day, he looked up and saw three men standing there. As soon as he saw them, he ran out to meet them. Bowing down with his face touching the ground, he said, 'Sirs, please do not pass by my home without stopping. I am here to serve you. Let me bring some water for you to wash your feet; you can rest here beneath this tree. I will bring you some food; it will give you strength to continue your journey. You have honoured me by coming to my home, so let me serve you.' They replied, 'Thank you; we accept.' (Genesis 18:1-5; see Luke 24:13-32).).

Abraham then invited the men to stay with him for what amounted to a banquet – "bread made with the best flour and the meat of a fattened calf," to be prepared by Sarah and their servants - while he talked with the men under the trees. During the course of the meal, one of the men said to Abraham: 'Nine months from now I will come back, and your wife Sarah will have a son.' (Genesis 18:10). The three men whom Abraham treated with much kindness and generosity, and who reciprocated his generosity, represented God in disguise. (Genesis 18:6-15).

The promised son came at last with the birth of Isaac. (Genesis 21:1-3). The Genesis narrative then returns to Hagar. Sarah saw Hagar's son Ishmael playing with, or making fun of the younger Isaac. She wasn't pleased and she asked Abraham to send "this slave and her son away." This troubled Abraham very much because Ishmael was also his son. (Genesis 21:10). God said to Abraham, 'Don't be worried about the boy and your slave Hagar. I will give many children to her son, so that they too will become a nation.' (Genesis 21:11-13).

Early the next morning, Abraham gave Hagar some food and a leather bag full of water, and sent her away. She wandered about in the wilderness of Beersheba (the southern region of Palestine known as the Negeb, a semi-barren wilderness). When the water was gone, she left the child under a bush, sat down some distance away and began to cry. "God heard her crying, and from heaven an angel of God spoke to Hagar, 'Don't be afraid. God has heard the boy crying. Get up and pick him up and comfort him. I will make a great nation out of his descendants.'" Then God opened her eyes and she saw a

---

[36] *World's Bible Dictionary*, p. 272, 170.

well. She went and filled the leather bag with water and gave some of it to the boy. God was with the boy as he grew up. He lived in the wilderness of Paran (a semi-arid region to the south of Kadesh-Barnea, bordering Egypt in the Sinai Peninsula) and became a skilful hunter. His mother found an Egyptian wife for him. (Genesis 21:14-21).

Having sent Ishmael away into the wilderness, Abraham must have wondered if this son of his was now dead. Was he struck with a sense of guilt for having expelled Ishmael from the family? What was his standing before God now? Would he have to make atonement for this cruel act? In later asking Abraham to sacrifice his son Isaac, God may have been reminding him of the part he played in the loss of his son Ishmael. Was this God's way of bringing home to Abraham a sense of the abandonment suffered by Hagar? But in the end, no one would be abandoned or treated unjustly. God would spare both sons; an angel came with deliverance for each of them.

## Abraham's Sacrifice of Isaac

Child sacrifice (sacrifice of the firstborn) was practiced by natives in the land of Canaan, in which Abraham, Isaac and Jacob and their descendants lived - and sometimes even by God's people, the Israelites. The practice continued up to the time of the Babylonian exile in 587 BC. Child sacrifice was roundly condemned by the Mosaic law and the prophets. (Deuteronomy 12:31; 2 Kings 16:3; 17:31; 21:1-6; Jeremiah 7:30-32; 19:3-5; Ezekiel 16:20-21; 20:25-26).

At the time in which Abraham lived, there would have been a primitive understanding of God among peoples of the Near East. The belief in many gods was widespread – a system known as polytheism. The Canaanite gods to whom sacrifices were offered in appeasement, were variously named Baal, El or Elohim. Belief in many gods continued long after the time of Abraham. In giving the Ten Commandments to his people, God speaks as Yahweh: "I am Yahweh your God who brought you out of the land of Egypt, out of the house of slavery. You shall have no gods except me." (Exodus 20:1-3, JB), The statement "no gods except me" recognises the existence of many other gods. Abraham would have understood God, simply as one of the many gods. He may have understood God as speaking to him at different times under one or other of the above names. It was Yahweh, as God, who appeared to Moses at the burning bush (Exodus 3:1-10, JB), calling him to rescue his people (descendants of Abraham, Isaac and Jacob) from slavery in Egypt. However, ancient names for God (El, Elohim) gradually disappear in the Bible and the name "Yahweh" becomes the main one in Israel's worship. Some Bibles use the original Hebrew "Yahweh" throughout the Old Testament, e.g. The Jerusalem, and New Jerusalem Bibles. Many Bibles translate the Hebrew "Yahweh" as "the Lord."

With regard to Abraham's sacrifice of Isaac, it would appear from Genesis that it was one of the Canaanite Gods who asked him to sacrifice his son, and that Yahweh countermanded it. (See Genesis 22:11).

The Genesis narrative is mainly about Abraham's trust and obedience as he moved from a particular understanding of God, a God who demanded the sacrifice of the firstborn, to a more mature understanding of God, and being henceforth blest because of that.[37]

---

[37] James Alison, *Jesus the Forgiving Victim,* (DOERS Publishing), 2013, p. 133.

It is significant that Genesis 22:19 says that after Abraham's sacrifice on the mountain, "he went back to his servants and they then settled in Beersheba." (22:19). The text does not mention Isaac going back with them. Based on this, verse 19 would then be a trace of an earlier story in which Isaac was sacrificed.[38] Biblical commentators think that here we have a story of human sacrifice that was changed by later editors of the Scriptures when the final version of Genesis was being compiled.

> It happened sometime later that God put Abraham to the test. 'Abraham, Abraham!' he called. 'Here I am,' he replied. And Abraham answered, 'Yes, here I am!' God said, 'Take your son, your only son, your beloved Isaac, and go to the land of Moriah, where you are to offer him as a burnt offering on one of the mountains which I will point out to you.' (Genesis 22:1-2, NJB).

Abraham's faith was not yet perfect; he was still not ready to carry forward the promise of God's blessing to his descendants. Then he finally passed one last test. The story of Abraham's sacrifice is one of the most brilliantly told narratives in Genesis. All the details of the preparation for the sacrifice, the drawn-out journey, the dialogue between father and son, serve to retard the pace of the action and increase tension, reaching its greatest intensity in 22:10, and denouement in verse 22:11.

In referring to Isaac as Abraham's "only son," God may be gently telling him that his other son, Ishmael, was dead. The last time Abraham saw Ishmael, he was sending him on a death-march into the wilderness with a little bread and water. At the time of his expulsion, Ishmael would have been aged about sixteen or seventeen. Isaac would have been younger than Ishmael, but he was old enough to carry the wood for the burnt offering. (22:6a). Was God making Abraham experience what Hagar suffered? Abraham put himself entirely in God's hands.

> Early the next morning Abraham saddled his donkey and took with him two of his servants and his son Isaac. He chopped wood for the burnt offering and started on his journey to the place which God had indicated to him. On the third day of the journey Abraham saw the place in the distance...Abraham took the wood for the burnt offering, loaded it on Isaac, and carried in his own hands the fire and the knife. Then the two of them set out together. Isaac spoke to his father Abraham. 'Father?' he said 'Yes, my son,' he replied. 'Look,' he said, 'here are the fire and the wood, but where is the lamb for the burnt offering?' Abraham replied, 'My son, God himself will provide the lamb for the burnt offering.' And the two of them went on together. (22:3-4, 6-8, NJB).

The journeys of Abraham and Hagar into the wilderness begin with Abraham rising early in the morning. (21:14, 22:3). At the start of both journeys, a parent knows that the death of a beloved son is imminent. In both, an angel of the Lord comes with deliverance. God opens the eyes of Hagar and she sees a well that will bring saving water, while Abraham

---

[38] Ibid, p. 134.

lifts up his eyes and he sees a ram that will replace Isaac as a burnt offering.

At this stage, Abraham may have been wondering if he was only deluding himself into thinking that God had been speaking to him at all. Abraham now had to choose between obedience to God and his love for his son, the son of the promise. How does he feel about this new danger to God's promise? But he still chooses obedience. Can we still place our trust and hope in God as we "walk in a ravine as dark as death?" (Psalm 23:4, NJB).

> When they arrived at the place which God had indicated to him, Abraham built an altar and arranged the wood. Then he bound his son and put him on the altar on top of the wood. Abraham stretched out his hand and took the knife to kill his son. But the angel of Yahweh called to him from heaven. 'Abraham, Abraham!' he said. 'Here I am,' he replied. 'Do not raise your hand against the boy,' the angel said. 'Do not harm him, for now I know you fear God. You have not effused me your own beloved son.' Then looking up, Abraham saw a ram caught by its horns in a bush. Abraham took the ram and offered it as a burnt offering in place of his son. The angel of Yahweh called Abraham a second time from heaven. 'I swear by my own self, Yahweh declares, that because you have done this, because you have not refused me your own beloved son, I will shower blessings on you and make your descendants as numerous as the stars of heaven and the grains of sand on the seashore... All nations on earth will bless themselves by your descendants, because you have obeyed my command.' (Genesis 22:9-18, NJB).

It is thought that Mount Moriah was the site of the later Jerusalem and its temple, where a lamb would be offered up every day. The offering of burnt animals in the temple may have been a concession by God to the Israelites as a substitute for the child sacrifices of the other nations.

Is there not something arrogant about God demanding that sacrifices be offered to himself? God is not some kind of tyrant demanding that human beings should grovel before him. The later prophets often had a negative view of animal sacrifices offered in the temple, which they said were worthless without, at the same time, the practice of justice and mercy towards one's fellow men and women. The prophets emphasised fidelity of heart more than sacrifice. Fidelity to God and our neighbour is demanding; it can, in itself, be a sacrifice. God does not need our sacrifices. It is we who need to make them, as a sign and recognition of our dependency on God, and as a willingness to surrender something that is part of us, so that we can be filled with something immeasurably greater: God's grace and blessing, preparing a banquet for us and filling our cup to the brim. (Psalm 23:5). What God wants from us most of all, is obedient hearts. We are limited beings, limited in what we can achieve, limited in knowledge, power and wisdom, and inclined to selfishness. God can see the whole picture – what we can become if we are humble enough to listen to his voice, calling us to obedience.

God did eventually provide a lamb for the sacrifice. Jesus believed that his call to obey God trumped any obligation to family, race or State. Just as Abraham found a substitute victim to sacrifice (22:13), God provided a substitute (Jesus) for us, so that we might escape death. In both the case of Isaac and Jesus, there is an obedient son who willingly sacrifices himself in obedience to a father. Jesus is the obedient Son who carried the wood of his sacrifice up a hill and laid himself down on it. He is the Lamb of God, whom God provides for the sacrifice which fulfils his promises to Abraham and brings blessing to the nations, so that through his self-sacrificial obedience to his Father, his followers would become as "numerous as the stars of heaven and the grains of sand on the seashore." (Genesis 22:16-18).

## Abraham's Descendants: People of Faith

Abraham gives away everything and puts himself entirely in God's hands. In surrendering his life to God (the highest form of faith), he enters communion with God, who gives it all back to him in unimaginable blessing, his descendants being blest in his name. In allowing God to take over his life, Abraham becomes a fully free man, liberated at last from his attachment and reliance on all the props he brought with him from Haran; liberated from the long, drawn-out anxiety over God's promise of progeny, something that had weighed on him throughout his long journey. He needs to have no further anxiety about the future, which he now places in God's hands. He could at last say to God, 'It's over to you, Lord.' Because he surrenders himself to God in his heroic act of obedience, God is also free to shower his blessings on Abraham. Faith and obedience to God's will has led Abraham gradually all the way to freedom and fulfilment. He doesn't see his descendants. He doesn't see the promised land as one of his possessions. But through faith, he sees the Lord as his guide and Shepherd, with whom he now walks. He has seen all there is to see, and received all that God has to give him. "The Lord is my shepherd; he gives me all I need." (Psalm 23:1).

In their later history, the chosen people always taught that all the blessings granted to Israel were coming through the promises made to their father Abraham. However, Jesus would point out that carnal descent from Abraham did not matter, and of itself, was no guarantee of blessing. (Matthew 3:7-9). What is important is practising the virtues attributed to Abraham: obedience and trust in God. Jesus said to them: 'If you are the children of Abraham, do the works of Abraham.' (John 8:39; see James 2:21-22; Galatians 3:6-9). The promise of universal blessing (salvation) is fulfilled in Jesus – all because he surrendered himself in total obedience to God. (Mark 14:36b; see CCC 72, 422, 705, 1222, 1716, 1725, 2619).

Like Abraham, we are often put to the test. We hope that it will not be more than we can endure. We may be faced with the dilemma whether to be guided by feelings, or sacrifice something now for the sake of future benefit for ourselves and others. Jesus named this as selling everything and following him in service (Mark 10:21). It is about trusting in what God can do for us, and that God knows what is best for us.

## The Deaths of Sarah and Abraham

The reader of the Bible will observe that there is no further dialogue between Abraham and Isaac. Abraham's wife, Sarah, dies soon after the sacrifice of Isaac.

> Sarah died in Hebron in the land of Canaan, and Abraham mourned her death. He left the place where his wife's body was lying, went to the Hittites (a Canaanite tribe) and said, 'I am a foreigner living here among you; sell me some land, so that I can bury my wife.' They answered, 'Listen to us, sir. We look on you as a mighty leader; bury your wife in the best grave we have.' (Genesis 23:1-5).

The property Abraham asked from the Hittites was the Macphelah Cave. "That is how the property which had belonged to Ephron, son of Zohar, the Hittite at Machpelah, east of Mamre, became Abraham's. It included the field, the cave which was in it, and all the trees in the field." (Genesis 23:17). This was the only part of the land of Canaan that Abraham owned. There was no question of conquest. The above shows that Abraham had good relations with the local tribes.

In chapter 25 we read that Abraham died at the age of 175 years. (Genesis 25:7). His sons Isaac and Ishmael buried him in the Machpelah Cave along with his wife. (Genesis 25:7-9). "After the death of Abraham, God blessed his son, Isaac, who lived near 'The Well of the Living One Who Sees Me.'" (Genesis 25:7-11).

The purchase of the field in which to bury Sarah in the land of Canaan, was a hopeful sign to readers of the Scriptures after their return from the Babylonian exile. Although the purchase was only symbolic, it represented the first fruits of the promise that Abraham's descendants would eventually possess the whole land, which, after the Babylonian exile, was held by the Persian empire.

## Isaac in his Later Years

Genesis 24:1-67 is about the search for a wife for Isaac. The chapter is mostly reported speech. The woman's name was Rebecca. This marks a new stage in the theme of the promise. Abraham's heir is provided with a wife who, in turn, will produce a new heir. The narrative speaks of the guidance of God at every stage. In the matter of a wife for Isaac, it is Abraham who takes the initiative. Isaac's marriage to a Canaanite woman is ruled out, so Abraham sends his oldest servant, who was in charge of all that he had, back to Haran in northern Mesopotamia to find a woman from among the family of his own brother, named Laban, a man who will also feature prominently in Jacob's search for a wife. "Isaac brought Rebecca into the tent that his mother Sarah had lived in, and she became his wife. Because Isaac loved Rebecca, he was comforted for the loss of his mother." (Genesis 24:67).

There was another famine in the land similar to the earlier one. The Lord appeared to Isaac and said, "Do not go to Egypt; stay in this land. Live here and I will be with you and bless you. I am going to give all this territory to you and to your descendants. I will keep the promise I made to your father Abraham." (Genesis 26:1-3). Isaac avoided the famine by going to Gerar, the territory of the Philistines. (Genesis records at least three famines in the land of Canaan). Why were there never any famines in Egypt? Egypt was not dependant on rain for its crops. The annual floods caused by melting snow on the mountains deep in Africa ensured that there was always plenty of moisture for the growth of wheat in the Nile delta).

Isaac had good relations with the Philistines, and he continued to prosper. He had many herds of sheep and cattle and many servants. He eventually moved to Beersheba. (26:23).

> That night the Lord appeared to Isaac and said, 'I am the God of your father Abraham. Do not be afraid; I am with you. I will bless you and give you many descendants because of my promise to my servant Abraham.' Isaac built an altar there and worshiped the Lord. (Genesis 26:24-25).

The promise was renewed to Isaac. God's blessing would be passed on through his descendants. After a number of disputes with the Canaanites of Gerar over the ownership of wells, Isaac made peace with Abimelech, king of the Philistines, in which Isaac was credited with taking the initiative. (26:26-33).

Rebecca had twin sons named Esau and Jacob. Esau was the first to be born, and whose "skin was like a hairy robe." (Genesis 25:25). Even before they were born, the twins struggled with each other in their mother's womb. (25:22) The struggle continued at their birth, with Jacob grasping the heel of his twin brother (Genesis 25:26), leading to Jacob's later struggle to grasp the birthright. (The name Jacob means 'he who grasps'). When Esau was 'forty years old, he married two Canaanite women. These women made life miserable for Isaac and Rebecca. (26:34-35). Esau was a skilled hunter, a man who loved the outdoor life. Jacob was a quiet young man, who stayed at home. (25:22-27). Isaac preferred Esau, because he enjoyed eating the animals that Esau killed. (25:28). But Rebecca preferred Jacob. In the matter of awarding the birthright, it was her wish that would prevail. (27:7-10).

(In the ancient patriarchal and tribal system, there was an unwritten law that the firstborn of a tribal leader would receive a double portion of the inheritance and become the head of the tribe after the death of his father. This was known as "birthright" – a claim both to inheritance and blessing. The head of a tribe had a status and a level of authority over ordinary members of the tribe).

Because Esau was the first-born of the two sons of Isaac and Rebecca, he had a claim on his father's blessing. But because God is sovereign, he often chooses the youngest son as the leader who will best serve his purposes. (See 1 Samuel 16:11-13). The story of Rebecca's scheming to secure the birthright and Isaac's blessing for Jacob, is told in Genesis 27. Esau was wronged, in that Rebecca and Jacob tricked Isaac, who at this time, was old and blind, into giving Jacob the blessing. (27:11-27). Dressed in Esau's clothes, and with hairy skins attached to his arms and chest, Jacob the "smooth man" passed himself off on his hirsute brother. Thinking him to be Esau, Isaac spoke the words of the blessing to Jacob: 'May God give you dew from heaven and make your fields fertile! May nations be your servants, and may peoples bow down before you. May you rule over all your relatives and may your mother's descendants bow down before you.' (Genesis 27:28-29a).

69

When Esau later came home from the fields, he asked his father for the blessing. It was then he realized that Jacob had cheated him. Esau said, 'This is the second time he has cheated me. No wonder his name is Jacob.' (27:36). "Esau pleaded with his father: 'Have you only one blessing, father? Bless me too, father.' He began to cry." (27:38). Then followed the lesser "blessing" of Esau. "Isaac said to him, 'No dew from heaven for you. No fertile fields for you. You will live by your sword, but be your brother's slave. Yet when you rebel, you will break away from his control.'" (27:38-40). Both blessings reflect the later relations between the State of Israel and Edom. Esau was the ancestor of the Edomites. He established himself in Seir, later to be part of the nation Edom. (32:3; 33:14, 16). Israel will rule over Edom, but eventually Edom will "break his yoke" and achieve its independence. (See 2 Samuel 8:14; 1 Kings 11:14; 2 Chronicles 21:8-10). Although Esau was deprived of both birthright and blessing, he was rewarded in the end with material wealth (33:9-11). The later rivalry between Edom and Israel is reflected here.

Esau hated Jacob because his father had given him the blessing which was his by right. (27:30-38). Esau then threatened to kill Jacob as soon as his father died. (27:41).

In his deception of his aged father, Jacob arouses the sympathy of the reader, though the depiction of Esau's distress is intended to elicit some sympathy for him as well. This story reveals a strongly held belief that blessings and curses possessed a power that couldn't be taken back. (27:33). One of the remarkable features of this story and the events that follow is the assertive role of Rebecca, in contrast to Isaac's passivity.

God may have seen that Esau was not spiritually fit to be the vehicle of divine blessing. Esau seemed to think only of the satisfaction of his bodily needs. By nature, impetuous, he brings home the meat of a wild animal and is off out again after hastily guzzling his food – "that red stuff," as he calls it. (Genesis 25:27-34). Jacob is shrewd and calculating, quiet and reflective. Never satisfied with the here-and-now, he worries a lot about how he might shape the future. His worries are a sign that he has a lot to learn about trusting in God. Jacob is a visionary, a searcher. He is a dreamer of dreams, and as such, God can communicate with him.

## Jacob's Journey to Haran

Esau's marriage to Canaanite women did not please Rebecca at all. It was she who again took the initiative when the question of Jacob's marriage arose. She quietly told Jacob about Esau's plan to kill him. She then advised him not to marry Canaanite women, and told him of her plan to send him to her brother Laban in Haran, where he could stay for a while until it was hoped Esau's anger cooled down. Isaac also advised Jacob to go to Laban and to marry one of his daughters. (See Genesis 27:41-45 – 28:1-5).

In fleeing for his life to Haran, Jacob, in a sense, may be going into exile in a direction opposite to that taken by Abraham. In his journey away from the promised land, he may have been suffering the consequence of his treachery against Esau. How can God's promise be fulfilled if he doesn't return home safely? The story of Jacob may represent elements of a familiar ancient folk-tale in the Near East in which a young hero heads off on an adventure into the unknown, overcomes various obstacles and returns home transformed by his experiences. In the context of Genesis, Jacob's adventures are a continuation of the history of the promise made to the patriarchs.

As Jacob left his home in Beersheba in southern Canaan and set out on his own for Haran, a journey of about 500 miles northwards, he had nothing with him but his walking stick, symbol of the shepherd's staff. (Genesis 32:10, see Mark 6:7-8). The walking stick may be a sign that Jacob was being sent on a mission, with a hint from God that he, Jacob should rely more on God and less on his own meagre resources. In the Bible, it is always God who calls people to mission, so that they may participate in his creative work. (Genesis 12:1; Exodus 3:1, 7-8). And as in the case of Moses and Jesus' disciples, he only provides them with a staff (symbol of God's power) as the means of working his wonders. (Exodus 7:8-9, 14-17; 14:15-16; 17:5-6; Mark 6:8). In this instance, God's call came to Jacob through his parents. A mission involves a journey into unknown territory in order to carry out a work of liberation of some kind, and it always comes with God's assurance of help and protection. (Exodus 3:12). It is really God who is doing this work, through his chosen servants. (Exodus 3:7-10). In Jacob's case, the liberation would be from his own flaws, fears, anxieties and lack of trust in God, so that he might become the means of blessing to others.

Jacob was like a shepherd in search of a flock. God would guide him on the right path and provide for his needs. (Psalm 23:1-3). What is entailed in Jacob's mission will only become clear as the narrative progresses. At this stage Jacob was probably in the dark with regard to the details of his journey. (Psalm 23:4). On our earthly journey, and for good reason, God only reveals himself to us one step at a time, as the need arises.

"Jacob left Beersheba and started towards Haran. At sunset he came to a holy place and camped there. He lay down to sleep, resting his head on a stone." (Genesis 28:10-11). When God calls us to mission, he always wants us to move away from our comfort zone. A mission means forgetting oneself, being prepared to sacrifice oneself for the sake of future benefit to oneself and others. Jacob was now a frightened fugitive, swopping the comforts of his parents' home for a stone pillow, and trying to find rest in a place that seemed devoid of the comfort of a human presence. Jacob's discomfort may have been the direct result of his cheating and deceit. In his flight from Esau, he may have experienced abandonment. His plight may have brought home to him his vulnerability and dependency, leaving him open to what God might do for him.

Up to this time Jacob had not received any direct communication from God. In this desolate place, deprived of both physical and human comfort, Jacob would discover God as his comforter, guide and protector. "Even if I go through the deepest darkness, I will not be afraid, Lord, for you are with me. Your shepherd's rod and staff protect me." (Psalm 23:4).

But if God were to appear to Jacob, would he rebuke him because of his duplicity in deceiving his father and defrauding Esau of his birthright? Jacob had yet to face his uncle Laban, who would outsmart him in the duplicity stakes.

In his sleep, Jacob the dreamer, had a dream, a vision of God in the night. In the Bible, dreams have a religious significance. They can be occasions of God giving important messages to humans, often by way of encouragement and guidance for making a long and difficult journey. (Genesis 15:1; 31:24; 37:5-11; 40:5-8; 41:1-36; 46:2-4; 1 Kings 3:5; Matthew 1:20-24; 2:13). Such dreams can be interpreted as visions of a future free from fears and dangers. It is as if the dreamer can see into the future and visualize some kind of fulfilment, salvation and glory for oneself and others. Dreamers are open to what the future may bring, together with the hope of new and enhanced life - a 'promised land.'

> Jacob had a dream: a ladder was there, standing on the ground with its top reaching to heaven; and there were angels of God going up it and coming down. And Yahweh was there standing over him, saying, 'I am Yahweh, the God of Abraham your father, and the God of Isaac. I will give you and your descendants the land on which you are lying. Your descendants will be like the specks of dust on the ground; you shall spread to the west and the east, to the north and the south, and all the tribes of the earth will bless themselves by you and your descendants. Be sure that I am with you; I will keep you safe wherever you go and bring you back to this land, for I will not desert you before I have done all that I have promised you. Then Jacob woke from his sleep and said, 'Truly, Yahweh is in this place and I never knew it!' He was afraid and said, 'How awe-inspiring this place is! This is nothing less than a house of God; this is the gate of heaven!' (Genesis 28:12-17, JB).

(The story of the ladder may have been inspired by the existence of Babylonian ziggurats, temple towers, one of which was discovered in the ancient city of Ur, from which Abraham originated. Stairways lead from the ground upwards to a temple on the top of the structure, in which a god was supposed to dwell, and where child sacrifices may have been offered to the national god).[39]

The poetry of the above passage is equal to anything in the Bible. In some Bibles, Yahweh is the name for God. It was the name given to Moses at his burning bush experience. (See Exodus 3:2, JB). The "house of God" and the "gate of heaven" may be closer to us than we think: "Be sure that I am with you" were the same words spoken to Moses as he set out on his own journey of liberation. (Exodus 3:12; see Matthew 28:20). God would guide Jacob on the right path. (Psalm 23:3). The phrase "house of God" could suggest a place where God manifests himself on earth.

God placed an awesome responsibility on the shoulders of Jacob. As was the case with Adam and Eve and Moses, God called Jacob to a representative role, as the means of bringing God's blessing of salvation to his descendants. In the discharge of his mission, Jacob would struggle whether to rely on his own resources or place his full trust in the God, who promised to be with him and keep him safe. (Genesis 28:15; see Luke 12:22-28).

From the moment of his conception, Jacob's life was one of restless ambition – a kind of dreaming. He outsmarted his father and brother so that he could grasp everything he desired. (25:26). The image of the ladder may signify ordinary mundane ambition – the human desire to get to the top of the ladder, to realize one's dreams. Jacob's ladder may also represent the human tendency toward transcendence–a yearning for the perfect good. It may be symbolic of the natural human desire to grasp something of the

---

[39] *Oxford Bible Atlas*, p. 70.

sacred, what the infinite God alone can give us, connecting us with his eternal love, as his response to our yearning. The human being is a searcher for meaning. People are never satisfied; there is always something more for which to hope, something new to grasp. Human desire seems to be infinite. However, it an illusion to think we can ever reach the top of the ladder through our human striving. Having reached the perceived top rung, we will find the ladder still extending, as if into infinity. The unattainable good is as far away as ever. Yet, for Jacob, the ladder, with angels descending and ascending, may have been a hint that he shouldn't rely entirely on his own strength in climbing. God would be with him to lift him out of his darkness.

At the foot of the ladder, Jacob saw God "standing over him," coming to his aid, giving him a message of hope and encouragement for his mission of bringing blessing to "all the tribes of the earth." God confirmed that Jacob would be granted everything promised to his grandfather Abraham: he would inherit the promised land, that is, he would reach his destiny – the goal of his salvation. (28:13). God would strengthen Jacob for his journey and bring him home ("I am with you," verse 15), giving hope and meaning to his life. Thus, strengthened and encouraged, he could continue his journey without fear. In his dream, instead of a reprimand, Jacob received the promise of blessing. Alone, and in the dark, he was confronted with the chaotic situation of his own life, over which, he had no control. But he is given the assurance that he could leave the future in the hands of God, who promises to crown his efforts with heroic achievement. (See Psalm 8:8:5). He could trust that God would bring meaning and order out of the chaos of his life.

Through the dream of the ladder, Jacob would learn to relax, to forget himself and his own schemes. God would do for him what he himself couldn't do. God was coming down to Jacob to free him from his disabling attachments, and give him new hope and promise. The men of Babel (Genesis 11:1-9) sought meaning and salvation in trying to reach heaven by their own powers and resources. For them, it was a question of ascending to the place of God, rather than God coming down to guide them. Having grasped God-like powers, all their achievements would be due entirely to their own efforts. But this would only result in their separation from God and from one another. (See Genesis 11:1-9).

Salvation is not something we ourselves can accomplish. It is God's initiative, God coming down to us to lift us up and put us on our feet. (Isaiah 40:39-41; Mark 5:42). Salvation, lasting happiness– a promised land – is what we dream about in some shape or other. We cannot reach it on our own. Our part is to try and discover God's will for us, and then to allow ourselves to be guided on the path he has laid out for us, a path leading us on the right way. (Psalm 23:3). This relieves us from the anxiety of thinking that the attainment of a 'promised land' can be entirely due to our own efforts. The message of the Bible is that God will come more than half way to meet us in our searching and struggling to do his will, and that he will reward us with his blessing. (Luke 15:1-7, 20-24).

In his representative role, Jacob foreshadows Jesus, who fully discharged his own representative role of standing in for us before God, fully bridging the gap between heaven and earth. It is Jesus who ultimately creates a union between God and humanity. The mediator Christ came down to earth to become that ladder in order to bring us up to our promised land. (John 1:50-51; Romans 5:1-5). The dream of Jacob is fulfilled in Jesus, the one who unites us to God in a new world: the union of heaven and earth in a new creation at the end of time. (Revelation 21:1-4).

Jacob rose early in the next morning. He took the stone he had used for a pillow and set it up as a monument, naming the place Bethel, a word meaning 'house of God.' (Bethel was an important religious and administrative centre in the time of the prophet Samuel. It features prominently in 1 Kings 12:25-33).[40] Jacob would return to this place again. God would eventually ask him to live there. (Genesis 35:1). Jacob poured olive oil on the stone monument to dedicate it to God. Fearful that he might never return to the promised land, and aware of his vulnerability in strange places, he prayed for God's help. His prayer was conditional. Jacob's journey of quest may be symbolic of his quest for the God who could guide him through his troubled life. Jacob made a vow to the Lord:

> 'If you will be with me and protect me on the journey I am making and give me food and clothing, and if I return safely to my father's home, then you will be my God. This memorial stone which I have set up will be the place where you are worshiped, and I will give you a tenth of everything you give me.' (Genesis 28:20-22).

## Jacob and Laban

Jacob eventually reached Haran. His uncle Laban had two daughters, Leah and the younger Rachel. Jacob loved Rachel and wanted her for his wife. He would do anything to win her. He said to Laban, 'I will work seven years for you, if you let me marry Rachel.' (29:18-19). Laban agreed, but when the time came for Jacob to marry Rachel, Laban deceived him by sending Leah to sleep with him, thus in effect tricking him into marrying Leah. Laban then agreed to give him Rachel as well, but only after Jacob agreed to work for him for another seven years as the extra "bride-price." (In the ancient world, the custom was for the bridegroom to give some service or payment to the father of the bride as the price for the daughter he was taking from him). So Jacob ended up with two wives with whom he had children.

Jacob was confronted with further problems. When Leah and Rachel, at different times, stopped having children they gave their two "slave girls" to Jacob as his wives. These women bore Jacob three sons. (Genesis 30:2-12). In ancient Israel it was considered a matter of social shame if a wife did not have children. (Genesis 16:1; 30:1; 1 Samuel 1:10-11; Luke 1:7). According to one ancient custom, if a wife was not able to have children, she could allow her husband to produce a child by her maidservant. But all legal rights over the child belonged to the wife, not the maid. (Genesis 16:2; 30:1-8).[41] Today's reader of the Bible may be a little bemused over all of this. However, there was probably more than a grain of historical truth behind the stories of Jacob's many wives.

Genesis teaches that from the beginning, God's ideal for marriage was one man and woman living together. (Genesis 2:18-24). The union of a man and woman to become

---

[40] *World's Bible Dictionary,* p. 47.

[41] Ibid, p. 279-290.

"one" means that it excludes all others. (Genesis 2:24). However, the history of mankind is one of almost total disregard of this ideal. Polygamy - many wives at the same time - became so widespread that even God's people did not regard it as wrong. (Genesis 25:6; 2 Samuel 5:13; 1 Kings 11:1-3). Inevitably, jealousy and conflict resulted from such unions, leading people to eventually recognise that the ideal of monogamy was best. (Genesis 21:8-10; 29:21–30:24; Deuteronomy 21:15-17; Judges 8:30 – 9:6; 1 Samuel 1:4-8; 1 Kings 11:1-8). However, if a tribal chieftain was able to support more than one wife, there was nothing in social custom to prevent him from marrying more than one woman.

Jealousy and conflict were not long in coming to the family of Jacob. Due to the trickery of Laban and the distractions of his marriage relationships, Jacob may have been moving away from the guiding hand of God and trusting in his own schemes for salvation. (See Genesis 28:15). It may be of significance that he had no communication from God during his lengthy stay with Laban.

As the years progressed, Leah bore Jacob six sons and one daughter. But Leah was bitter, because she felt unloved by Jacob. (29:33-34). And because Rachel had not borne Jacob any children, she became jealous of her sister and bitter over long years of waiting for a family. Her frustration and impatience were evident in her impulsive outburst to Jacob: 'Give me children or I will die.' (Genesis 30:1). At last, God answered Rachel's prayer and she had a son whom she named Joseph. (Genesis 30:22-24). Leah's fifth son, who was named Judah, would become the ancestor of the kings of Judah (one of the kingdoms of the later Israel). But God would make Joseph's name famous for his work of feeding the hungry. (See Genesis chaps. 37 - 50).

At last Jacob felt secure; he had wives, children, flocks – everything that a tribal chieftain could hope for, as if he had reached the top of the ladder of his dreams. He would soon discover that these might not be enough to sustain him.

"Jacob discovered that Laban had not been as friendly as he had been earlier. Then the Lord said to him, 'Go back to the land of your fathers and relatives, and I will be with you.'" (Genesis 31:2-3). After twenty years of service to Laban, and fed up with being cheated of his wages, Jacob fled from Laban. He took with him his wives and eleven children (three of them by his two concubines) and all the flocks to which he felt he was entitled, as payment for his long years of service to Laban. But did his sudden and secretive flight mean that he was guilty of stealing? He got ready, and along with Rebecca and Leah and the children, he set out on the long journey back to his father and mother in the land of Canaan. (See Genesis chap. 31).

When Laban heard of Jacob's flight with his daughters and flocks, he set out in pursuit of them until he caught up with them in the hill country of Gilead, (a fertile area east of the Jordan river, and divided in two by the River Jabbok, a tributary of the Jordan, which flowed from Ammon).[42] After all the difficulties between them were resolved, Laban and Jacob agreed to part as friends. "Early the next morning Laban kissed his daughters and grandchildren goodbye and left to go back home." (Genesis 31:22-55).

---

[42] World's Bible Dictionary, p. 150.

## Jacob's Wrestling with God

Then follows the account of Jacob's effort to meet his wronged brother and to be reconciled to him - his effort at last, to heal this lingering sore of his duplicity once and for all. (Genesis 32:1-21). The brothers hadn't met for over twenty years. Jacob knew that if he was to live in peace and safety, he would have to become reconciled to Esau. But would Esau want to be reconciled with him?

By this time, Esau had established a powerful clan in the land of Edom (south east of Canaan, to the east of the Dead Sea). Thus, in a parallel role with Jacob, Esau became the father of the Edomites.

Jacob immediately sent messengers to Esau in Edom, asking for the latter's forgiveness for having cheated him of his birthright. But when the messengers told him that Esau was already on his way to meet him with a small army of four-hundred men, Jacob was terrified. (Genesis 32:6). Hoping for forgiveness and reconciliation, Jacob sent a caravan of gifts, including livestock, across the Jabbok River. With his abundance of gifts, was he trying to buy his brother's forgiveness? He then divided into two groups the people who were with him, also his flocks. He thought, 'If Esau comes and attacks the first group, the one behind might be able to escape.' (32:7-8). He may have expected that if the group of women and children at the front were attacked, he himself might escape. When the safety and protection of everyone was endangered, he seemed to care less for his wives and children than for himself.

Now physically exhausted, alone on the river bank, and with death staring him in the face, Jacob was powerless to control his fate. Thus, his faith was tested. There is something going on here which resembles the crisis Abraham faced when God asked him to sacrifice his son Isaac. Unlike Abraham, Jacob was not asked to sacrifice his wives and children, but he himself seemed willing to do just that. He seemed to be still enslaved to self-preservation. He could not see that the people whom he brought back from Haran were gifted to him by God. They represented the first part of the fulfilment of God's promise to him of numerous descendants. So if God was already fulfilling his promises, Jacob should abandon his own schemes for saving himself and place his trust in God to save everyone. Such level of trust takes a great leap of faith. (Matthew 17:19-20). As of yet, Jacob was not up to it.

Once again, feeling as vulnerable and fearful as at the outset of his journey, all Jacob could do was pray. God might come to him and show him a way out of his recurring troubles. With his vulnerability looming large before his eyes, Jacob humbled himself before God. He acknowledged his fears, his weakness and dependency. He recalled God's previous promises of land and descendants and that everything would go well for him. (Genesis 28:13-15). In his prayer, he admitted that he was afraid. This was his first time he acknowledged his dependency and the part God had played in his life.

> Jacob prayed, 'O God of my father Abraham, and God of my father Isaac, Yahweh who said to me, 'Go back to your country and family, and I will make you prosper.' I am not worthy of all the kindness and goodness you have shown your servant. I had only my staff when I crossed the Jordan here, and now I have grown

into two camps. I implore you, save me from my brother Esau's clutches, for I am afraid of him; he may come and attack me, mothers and children alike. Yet, it was you who said, 'I shall be very good to you, and make your descendants like the sand of the sea, which is too numerous to count' Then Jacob passed that night there. (Genesis 32:10-14, NJB).

With his family and his possessions on the far bank of the Jabbok river, and with his fear of Esau and four-hundred men lying in wait, Jacob wondered if God would show himself and respond to his prayer for deliverance. That night, as if the darkness and a sense of isolation had intensified his fears, he could neither rest nor sleep. Jacob had been a determined and ruthless man, but he had always remained open to a new future, to what God might have in store for him.

> On that same night, Jacob got up, took his two wives, his two concubines and his eleven children and crossed the River Jabok. After he had sent them across, he also sent across all that he owned, but he stayed behind all alone.
>      Then a man came and wrestled with him until just before daybreak. When the man saw that he was not winning the struggle, he struck Jacob on the hip, and it was thrown out of joint. The man said, 'Let me go; daylight is coming.' 'I won't, unless you bless me, Jacob answered. 'What is your name?' the man asked. 'Jacob,' he answered. The man said, 'Your name will no longer be called Jacob. You have struggled with God and with men, and you have won; so your name will be Israel.' Then the man blessed Jacob. In response, Jacob said, 'I have seen God face to face and I am still alive; so he named that place Peniel - in Hebrew, meaning the 'face of God.' (Genesis 32:22-31)

(In the ancient world, Peniel was located on the north bank of the River Jabbok, about twelve miles east of the Jordan River. Once Jacob crossed this river, he would be home in the promised land. In Hebrew, the name 'Israel' is associated with the verb 'struggle').

There are times in our lives when we face a crisis, a turning point, a moment when we suddenly become aware of self-imposed bondages and a longing to be free of them, so that we might move to a better way of life – what Genesis names as "blessing." (Verse 29 above). Such a moment may involve us in a mighty struggle.

Jacob had been in thrall to power and possessions, deception and deceit. He tried to find meaning in these things. He had built his identity on them, but he still felt uneasy and dissatisfied. Could his story take a different direction and give him new meaning and fulfilment? His life was an unending struggle between what he was and what he still could be. God at last confronted him with his assumed identity: 'You have struggled with God and with men.' (Verse 28). His life was one of restless ambition from the moment of his conception. He struggled with Esau for the birthright. His flight from home as a young man with nothing but a walking stick left him struggling with the dark and the unknown. Jacob often struggled to make sense of his experiences with his brother Esau and his uncle Laban. He had to struggle with his demons of deception and trickery. He struggled to live up to the promise that God would give him and his descendants the land on which he lay.

(Genesis 28:14). And now he struggled with his selfishness in putting his own life and safety before that of his family. As he was about to enter his homeland, he was faced with the stark reality of his wrongdoing of so many years.

After the night of struggling with the mysterious stranger, Jacob was suddenly disabled by his opponent. (32:24). Although the stranger was able to injure his hip, he still had to ask Jacob to release him. Jacob refused to let the man go unless he received a blessing from him. Jacob then knew that he had not been fighting with a mere mortal, but with a manifestation of God (described as an angel in Hosea 12:3-4). Before agreeing to bless Jacob, the angel demanded a confession from him, by asking Jacob his name. Jacob was thus forced into an admittance: 'I am Jacob.' (We recall that the name Jacob means 'grasper'). It is as if Jacob said, 'My name is grasper, duplicity, deception, I take what is not my own.' (See Genesis 27:36; 31:26-27; 31:20-21; 31:43). Thus, in a flash, Jacob realized who he had been, and he did not like what he saw. He had built his life on things that were tying him up in bondages. Throughout his life of duplicity, he had been away from his true self and from God. Without this confession of guilt, he could not have been blessed. The blessing he now received was from God, and was a new name, Israel, a name that would make him great. (See Genesis 11:4). All along, he had been seeking greatness through his own schemes and duplicitous behaviour. His greatness now was in his decision to break free from his bondages so that he might be open to what God could do for him. God's blessing would empower him for a new journey – his embodiment of the nation Israel. He had struggled with God and men and "won." (32:28).

Jacob recognised his vulnerability, his powerlessness to deal with his troubles through his own trusted schemes. All along, he struggled over allowing God to enter his life and take control over what he himself felt powerless to handle. Once he surrendered to the will of God, then God could bless him, and do for him what he himself was powerless to achieve. (See Mark 14:36). His name being changed to Israel was a sign of his transformation, and it confirmed him in his representative role for the nation Israel. (32:28). God gave him a new mission, and thus a new identity as the bearer of blessing to the nations. (See Genesis 22:18). Once freed of his former obsessions, his life henceforth would have new meaning and purpose. No longer crushed by his former bondages, Jacob found new strength and hope. Thus transformed, he could face the Esaus of life without fear or anxiety.

Following his spiritual wrestling, Jacob limped towards his reunion with Esau, with a weakened body, but with a stronger faith. God had afflicted Jacob with a debilitating injury – a dislocated hip, perhaps symbolic of his self-inflicted wounds resulting from past treacheries. (Genesis 32:25). This had the effect of making him more vulnerable to Esau. It's as if God was saying to him, 'Don't be relying on your own strength to overcome your demons.' Now, although physically weak, he felt himself strong in the Lord's blessing, which empowered him for a new journey of allowing God into his life and trusting in God to continue guiding him.

Jacob's long journey is one of a slow maturing faith in the God who rewards those who seek to do his will. In his transformation, he resembles Abraham after the sacrifice of Isaac. No longer the grasper and deceiver, he is now a fully free man, free of overweening ambition, free from the anxiety that everything was down to his own powers and struggles, free of the troubles that only disabled him, including the threat from Esau.

There is something of the character of Moses revealed in Jacob, who saw God face to face and also struggled with God and men. This night-long encounter with the mysterious stranger declared Jacob to be not only a heroic figure who struggles with God and men, but also the founder of the nation Israel.[43]

Jacob is the hero returning home transformed after a long journey. In his flaws and failings, he is everyman. We can see ourselves reflected in his failings and can thus empathise with him. His story reminds us that we also have the potential for the great and extraordinary things that God can accomplish in us, once we place our trust and hope in him. (See Romans 5:1-5).

Because we tend to remain in bondage to our demons, we struggle against God's will for us. God, in turn, struggles with us to get us to do his will, which is for our good. God wants to free us from everything that may be holding us back from being the people we could be. There can be many things disabling us: a bad pattern of behaviour, an addiction, an old resentment, greed, the lingering guilt from a past wrong, a remembrance of something that should have been done in the past. We are not free as long as such things are disabling us. In order to be freed from them we have to struggle, because we are we afraid of being wounded in some way by getting into a fight against them. Can we place them in the hands of God and say, 'Lord, let you deal with them!' Our human condition is one of woundedness, disablement. Only God can transform us, if we surrender to him, and say, 'May your will be done unto me.' (Mark 14:36; see Jeremiah 18:1-4; Psalm 130:7-8). However, such a surrender can involve a great leap of faith, as much of a struggle as moving a mountain! (Mark 11:22). Jacob was at last able to say that God had been with him all along and everywhere he had gone. (Genesis 35:3). Can we ourselves say the same thing?

Our lives were never meant to be easy. Real growth always involves struggle and pain, wrestling. God's will is always for our best. Doing his will can transform us. After Mary said to the angel, "I am the servant of the Lord, let it be done unto me according to your word," she was then ready to be filled with Jesus, the gift of God's fullness to humanity.

## Jacob's Reconciliation with Esau

The reconciliation between Jacob and Esau was accomplished. (Genesis 33:1-20). Jacob went out to meet his brother, with the empowerment and courage he received in the nocturnal encounter. God heard Jacob's prayer. (Genesis 32:11). Esau met him in forgiveness. "Jacob bowed down to the ground seven times as he approached his brother. Esau ran to meet him, threw his arms round him, and kissed him. This has echoes of the Father's meeting the returned prodigal son. (See Luke 15:20). "They were both crying" (33:3-4). Esau then enquired about the people accompanying Jacob. 'These, sir, are the children whom God has been good enough to give me,' Jacob answered. (33:5). "Then the women and children bowed down to Esau." Esau was reluctant to accept the caravan of gifts brought to him by his brother. Jacob said, 'Please, if I have gained your favour, accept

---

[43] Barton & Muddiman, *The Oxford Bible Commentary*, 2001, (OUP), p. 59.

my gift. To see your face, is for me seeing the face of God, now that you have been so friendly to me.' (33:10). In the brother whom he had injured, and who now forgives him, Jacob sees the face of the same person with whom he struggled during the night. The formerly vengeful older brother was acting like the forgiving father of the prodigal son. Jacob kept on urging Esau until he accepted the gifts. Having stripped Esau of his birthright so many years before, Jacob was desperate to make amends. Esau may have seen the gifts as a token of Jacob's regret over his former deceit, and for that reason may have been more ready to forgive his brother. In his role as the forgiving one, Esau may also have achieved heroic status.

Can we see the face of God in all those brothers with whom we may need be reconciled? If we prevail in our wrestling with God, we will receive the strength to be reconciled with our past, and with the brothers we have wronged. In this story, there are echoes of the sibling rivalry between Cain and Abel, but with the difference here that there is reconciliation between the brothers. In his forgiveness of his brother, Esau may be foreshadowing Jesus. Reconciliation between all brothers is of the will of God. Universal reconciliation was ultimately accomplished by Jesus through his forgiveness of all his brothers everywhere for the wrong they did to him. Once all the brothers learn to imitate Jesus' forgiveness, by forgiving one another, they become reconciled. The foundational murder of Cain is thus undone, as is the scattering of Babel. (See Genesis 4:8; 11:1-9).

After Esau made peace with Jacob, the brothers divided territories between them. Esau took the land of Edom. Jacob received Palestine (Canaan). Esau became the ancestor of the people of Edom. He left Canaan for Edom because the land available to them in Canaan could not support both brothers. They had so many livestock that they could not stay together.

## Jacob Moves to Bethel

On the instructions of God, Jacob went to Bethel and settled there. "Jacob said to his family, 'We are going to leave here and go to Bethel, where I will build an altar to the God who helped me in the time of my trouble, and who has been with me everywhere I have gone.'" (Genesis 35:3). God again appeared to Jacob and renewed his promise of many descendants: 'I am Almighty God. Have many children. Nations will be descended from you, and you will be the ancestor of kings.' (Genesis 35:11). Being "ancestor of kings" means that Israel would become a nation. And there is an implication that the blessings bestowed on Abraham would be shared with other nations. Thus, God confirms Jacob's new status as Israel and reaffirms the promises made to Abraham and Isaac. From now on, God frequently speaks to Jacob. (See 35:1, 9, 11).

In chapter 35 it is recorded that Jacob's beloved wife Rachel died giving birth to Benjamin (Jacob's youngest son). "When Rachel died, she was buried beside the road to Ephrath, a place now known as Bethlehem. Jacob set up a memorial stone there, and it still marks Rachel's grave to this day." (Genesis 35:19-20). Rachel had just two sons, Joseph and Benjamin, both of whom will figure prominently in the later chapters of Genesis. Jacob's twelve sons would become the patriarchs of the twelve tribes of Israel.

Up to this point Jacob had been a trickster, a cheat. He is now fitted for his role as representative of Israel and servant of God. From now on he becomes a model character, no longer Jacob "the deceiver," but he himself continues to be deceived – for example, when his sons trick him into believing that his son Joseph had been killed by a wild animal. (Genesis 37:31-35).

"Jacob went south to his father Isaac at Mamre, near Hebron. He wanted to be with the aged Isaac in his last years." (Genesis 35:27). Mamre was the place where his grandfather Abraham mysteriously encountered God who promised him that his wife Sarah would have a son within a year. (18:10). "Isaac lived to be 180 years old and died at a ripe old age, and his sons, Jacob and Esau buried him." (35:28). Jacob remained at Mamre while his sons took his flocks from place to place looking for fresh pastures. (Genesis 37-14-17).

Out of these circumstances came the sequence of events in which Jacob's older sons betrayed their young brother Joseph and lied to their father about what they did.

## The Story of Joseph and the Sovereignty of God

The story of Joseph and his brothers is told in Genesis, chapters 37-50. It is recommended for reading in its entirety. This story is a necessary addition to Genesis, in order to show how the Hebrew tribes (descendants of Abraham) in the promised land, ended up in Egypt, and eventually in captivity there, in order to prepare for the Exodus.

The story of Joseph wasn't written until hundreds of years after the events related. The story is an example of narrative wisdom literature, depicting Joseph as the ideal wise man of the ancient world. Other near eastern cultures had their own wisdom stories, which helped to define them as a people. Because King Solomon is depicted as a wise man and king, the story of Joseph may have been composed during his reign, about 900 BC. However, the time of composition is not certain. The story is another example of endangerment to God's promises to Abraham and his descendants. The wisdom of the story lies in its insight into the perplexing human condition: jealousy, rivalry, victimizing, but also piety, courage, compassion, forgiveness and reconciliation. In this story we learn how God works through human failure and betrayal in order to ultimately overcome these negative forces. God brings good out of evil. He creates light out of darkness. (Isaiah 45:7-8; John 8:12). There is much in this story that may be legendary, but that doesn't matter.

In the story of Jacob and his sons, Genesis further develops the theme of the sovereignty of God over human affairs. So the purpose of the story is in its theology – what it teaches us about God, his providence in guiding human affairs in line with his good purposes, creating redemption, union and reconciliation out of human brokenness. The story, which begins with Jacob, can be taken as a metaphor for God's restoration of a broken world. It is like an enactment of the Biblical story as a whole – a parable of humanity's fall, redemption and restoration. In our own failures and limitations, we ourselves can empathize with the characters and learn wisdom from them.

We can easily forget that God is always in the background of our lives, guiding us on the right path, even though we may not advert to that fact. We may even struggle against his will and choose to go our own way. Human beings make their choices, many of which may not be very principled. But in fulfilment of his purposes, God finds a way around such human failings, often bringing good out of the evil that human beings do to one another. So while it was his mother Rebecca who sent Jacob to Laban, it was really God who called him to go there, in order that Jacob's mission of bringing blessing to the world would bear fruit. Of Jacob's twelve sons, it is Joseph, the second youngest, whom God chooses to rule over his brothers. (Genesis 35:5-11). God finds his way around the trickery and self-interest of Laban, and seemingly frustrates Jacob's love for Rachel, in order to ensure that Leah, through her large family, would contribute significantly towards Jacob's innumerable descendants, through the foundation of the twelve tribes of Israel. However, Rachel's lesser contribution, through her sons Joseph and Benjamin, may be more significant in other respects. (Genesis 30:22-24).

Much of the suffering in the world is the result of the evil that human beings inflict on one another. The roots of suffering and death can be traced back to the disobedience of the foundational pair in the Garden of Eden, and to the foundational murder of Cain. Suffering can also have meaning, and because God is sovereign, he can use it as a path leading to redemption, thus providing deliverance from it. Jesus himself suffered injustice, and those who were responsible for his rejection and death would bear the consequences in the final day of reckoning, but his suffering and death were still part of God's plan (with which Jesus aligned himself), as God's way of bringing all suffering and death to an end once and for all, and ultimately gathering scattered humanity together into his spiritual family, as his sons and daughters, as brothers and sisters of Jesus.

The story of Joseph begins with family fragmentation – arrogance, enmity, hatred, attempted murder, betrayal, loss, abandonment, grief. How can the characters of this story – the great grandchildren of Abraham, be a channel of blessing to their descendants, enmeshed as they are in such an abyss of evil. And what does this mean for God's promises to Abraham? But God, in his hidden purposes, does not give up on the self-inflicted suffering of human beings whom he created in his image. (See Isaiah 49:13-16). Despite their flaws, the children of Jacob are gradually shaped and made fit to bear and transmit God's blessing to the world. But this will only be possible with their gradual growth in maturity, and in final forgiveness and reconciliation. In this story, we see Joseph (Jacob's second youngest son) developing, through suffering, from a spoiled arrogant child (Genesis 37:3-11) into a mature leader, and eventually becoming fully reconciled to the brothers who betrayed him.

God's plan was that Joseph would ultimately be the saviour of his people. For this to become a reality, a large number of what seemed like coincidences had to happen, all of them evil acts. Had these not happened, the characters would not have matured and found redemption in the end. Joseph would have ended up consumed by his pride – in a dream, seeing his brothers bowing down to his sheaf of corn. (Genesis 37:5-7). Were these events not to happen, the brothers would have remained bitter in their resentment of Joseph. (37:18-31). Jacob would have remained locked into his selective love for his two younger sons, causing unending anger and resentment in the hearts of his other sons. If Joseph had not been an arrogant young boy, his brothers would not have turned against him. If the brothers had not betrayed Joseph and sold him into slavery, the whole family would not have been ultimately saved from death through the abundance of food in Egypt.

All the characters make their choices and take the consequences, but God is able to bring good out of the evil they do. Joseph's exaltation is not due to his own efforts or abilities, but to the unseen action of God.

Joseph was Jacob's favourite son. (Chap. 37). He told the other brothers about dreams he had, which they interpreted as implying that he would become a ruler over them. Because they hated Joseph over this and resented their father's favouritism, the brothers initially plotted to kill him, but changed their minds sold him into Egypt as a slave for twenty pieces of silver (37:28) and then told their father that a wild animal had killed him. (37:18-28, 31-35). For a while, Joseph prospered in Egypt, but eventually he was imprisoned on a false charge. (39:1-23). He was released from prison because he was able to interpret one of Pharaoh's dreams. He told the king that there would be seven years of good harvests, to be followed by seven years of famine. Pharaoh then appointed him governor of Egypt to take charge of the collection and distribution of grain which would last during the years of famine. (41:14-49). Once the famine began in the land of Canaan, Joseph's brothers arrived in Egypt and stood before Joseph to purchase grain. Joseph knew who they were, but they did not recognise him. (See Luke 24:15-16). He began giving them a number of tests to see if they had changed their hearts from the time when they sold him into slavery. (Chap. 42f.)

Joseph asked the brothers to bring their youngest brother, Benjamin (the second child of Rachel), with them on their next visit to Egypt. However, their father did not want Benjamin to go to Egypt in case anything happened to him. At last, Jacob allowed his youngest son to go with the others. During their second visit to Egypt, things took a bad turn when Joseph accused Benjamin of stealing his silver cup. As a result of this, Joseph threatened to make Benjamin his slave. It was then that Judah intervened, offering himself as a slave in place of Benjamin.

In speaking on behalf of the other brothers, Judah, showed his change of heart from the time he and the others sold Joseph into slavery. His concern now was about the grief that would afflict his father if Benjamin did not return home. He said it would be the death of his father. Judah assumed a substitutionary role, as if he was trying to atone for his own and the brothers' sins of betrayal many years previously. He was prepared to become a slave, even to die in order that Benjamin might be saved. (Genesis 44:1-34). In his new role as representative, Judah becomes one of the heroes of the story. As to Joseph, in his mature wisdom, he saw all that had happened to him as having been ordained by God. And because of that dawning realization, he could then forgive his brothers and be reconciled with them. Joseph was no longer able to control his feelings. No one else was with him when he made himself known to his brothers. He wept so loudly that all the Egyptians heard it, and the news reached Pharaoh's palace. Joseph spoke to his brothers:

> 'I am Joseph. Is my father really still alive?' His brothers could not answer him, they were so dumbfounded at seeing him. Then Joseph said to his brothers, 'Come closer to me.' Then he said, 'I am your brother Joseph whom you sold into Egypt. But now, do not grieve, do not reproach yourselves for having sold me here, since God sent me here to preserve your lives, and to assure the survival of your race. So it was not you who sent me here, but God, and he set me up as a

father to Pharaoh, as lord of all his household and governor of the whole land of Egypt.' (Genesis 45:1-8, NJB).

When the brothers returned to Canaan, they told their father that Joseph was still alive and that the king had invited him to come to Egypt with all his family and possessions. 'Joseph is ruler of Egypt,' the brothers said to him. When Jacob recovered from the shock, he said, 'My son Joseph is still alive. This is all I could ask for! I must go and see him before I die.' (45:27-28, GNB).

As Joseph had requested (Genesis 45:9-10), Jacob took his whole family to Egypt to live there. The number of direct descendants of Jacob who went to Egypt was sixty-six. Two sons were born to Joseph in Egypt (Ephraim and Manasseh), bringing to seventy the total number of Jacob's family who went there. (46:26-27). The tribe of Ephraim was prominent in the later kingdom of Israel.

Jacob's meeting with Joseph is recorded in chapter 46:29-34. For Jacob's last request of Joseph, see 47:27-31. Jacob called his sons and spoke his last words to them. (49:1-28). "Then Jacob commanded his sons, 'Now that I am going to join my people in death, bury me with my fathers in the cave that is in the field of Ephron the Hittite at Machpelah, east of Mamre in the land of Canaan. Abraham bought this cave and field from Ephron for a burial ground.'" (49:29-30). "When Jacob had finished giving instructions to his sons, he laid down and died." (Genesis 49:33).

After the death of their father Jacob, the brothers were afraid that Joseph would wreak vengeance on them because of the way they treated him. They came and bowed down before him, as a fulfilment of his former dreams. (Genesis 37:6-10). They pleaded with him to forgive the wrong they had done to him:

> 'Here we are before you as your slaves,' they said. But Joseph said to them, 'Don't be afraid; I can't put myself in the place of God. You plotted evil against me, but God turned it into good, in order to preserve the lives of many people who are alive today because of what happened. You have nothing to fear. I will take care of you and your children.' So he reassured them with kind words that touched their hearts. (Genesis 50:18-21).

In its high theology, the above speech sums up a major theme of the first five books of the Bible: God is with his people, directing the course of events so that his promises of salvation may be fulfilled.

"When the time came for him to die, Joseph said to his brothers, 'I am about to die, but God will certainly take care of you and lead you to the land he solemnly promised to Abraham, Isaac and Jacob.' "Then Joseph asked his people to make a vow. 'Promise me,' he said, 'that when God leads you to that land, you will take my body with you.' "So Joseph died in Egypt at the age of 110. The brothers embalmed his body and put it in a coffin." (50:24-26).

One of the messages we glean from the patriarchal narratives is the importance of families and the way God blesses, guides and cares for all families, as a foretaste of the new spiritual family he will create around Jesus, with God himself as its Father.

Despite their flaws and failings, the family of Abraham eventually found union and reconciliation under the direction of God. Their union was a paradigm of the eventual union of all the Hebrew tribes in the promised land, and a foreshadowing of our union with Christ when all of humanity will have their sins forgiven and become reconciled to one another in God's new family - Jesus' Kingdom of God.

## Joseph Prefigures Christ

This story of Joseph prefigures Christ's redemptive work. It helps us to understand Jesus better. Jesus' older brothers (the religious authorities, Pharisees, scribes, the Chief Priests) resented Jesus' special claim to speak with authority on behalf of God, and as a threat to themselves and their religious system. In the Garden of Gethsemane, Jesus suffered betrayal and abandonment by his brothers (the disciples), one of whom sold him over to the Gentiles for pieces of silver, leading to his death on a cross. This was the cup of suffering handed to Jesus by his Father, but which he freely accepted as the means of saving all his brothers and sisters everywhere by forgiving the wrongs they did to him, and feeding them with his life of love. Jesus saw suffering as part of God's plan to bring good out of evil, to bring forgiveness and reconciliation to all his brothers and sisters, through being raised up in his resurrection. On the cross, he said, 'Father forgive them.' (Luke 23:34).

Like Joseph's enthronement in Egypt, Jesus was raised to God's right hand, as Lord of creation. Thus enthroned, Jesus sends his Spirit to all his brothers and sisters, in order to empower them for their earthly journey towards eternal life. The Sovereign God had the final word on evil. Had the envious ones not delivered Jesus over to death, and had Jesus not been raised to new life, the mocking crowds and the evil powers would have been victorious, and human beings would have been left starved of the hope of union with God and with one another, as their salvation.

Can we look at our own life stories and find similar patterns of uncertainty - blind alleys, pain, struggle, anxiety, loss, leading ultimately in mysterious ways to healing and transformation? God must be working things out in our own lives too, even when everything is not going our way, when the future is unclear, or when we don't immediately receive what we ask of God. However, from God's perspective, everything has a meaning, even though we cannot see it at a particular time, blind as we are to the possibility of light coming out of darkness. God sees the whole picture – the darkness and the light, the beginning and the end of every time and story. And far from glorying in our human predicament, he suffers along with us. He is dying to bring us into the light, to bring good out of the evil we may inflict on ourselves. In fact, a difficult and challenging situation may be a necessary prelude and preparation for the good that will follow. (See Psalm 23:4-5).

God's promise to Abraham that he would have many descendants, is partially fulfilled in the story of Joseph. Jacob's children became a large flourishing group in Egypt. (Genesis 47:27). But a new king arose in Egypt who knew nothing of Joseph. (Exodus 1:8). This change signalled the start of the enslavement of the Hebrews (descendants of Abraham) and their eventual rescue by Moses - the story told in the Book of Exodus. The revelation of the sovereignty of God in Genesis is the groundwork for God's rescue of his people from slavery and their creation as a people dedicated to him alone.

CHAPTER  4

# Exodus and Deuteronomy

## The Book of Exodus

The name "exodus" means 'departure.' The book deals with the most important event in Israel's history – the departure of the Hebrew tribes from Egypt where they had been slaves. The book tells how, through the guidance of their God, the Hebrew tribes became bound together as a people, then a nation, in fulfilment of God's promises to Abraham. (Genesis 22:18). Exodus presents its story as the work of the sovereign God, rescuing, saving and guiding his people, accompanying them on their journey, even at times when they are unfaithful to him.

The Book of Exodus has four main parts; (1) The rescue of the Hebrew tribes from slavery in Egypt; (2) Their journey through the wilderness towards Mount Sinai; (3) God's covenant with his people at Sinai, which gave them the laws by which they could live; (4) the building and furnishing of a place of worship for Israel – the Ark of the Covenant. God is the main character of the book. A central role is given to Moses, the man whom God chose to lead his people from Egypt. The Egyptian Pharaoh also has a role, as the main foil to God.

## The Book of Deuteronomy

The Book of Deuteronomy, as its name implies, is a second version of the law of God given through Moses. It is a long discourse purporting to come from the mouth of Moses and delivered to the people in the land of Moab before they entered the promised land.

Deuteronomy may be the book of the Law that was discovered in the Jerusalem temple at the time of the religious reforms carried out by King Josiah of Judah in 622 BC. Although the book contains some earlier material, it has many of the characteristics of the teaching of the later prophets and must have received its final shape during that period (ca. 600-500 BC). Therefore, it could not have been written by Moses. Its attribution to Moses lends it an air of authority.

The book is written in the style of a preacher and is structured on three great discourses of Moses. It is concerned with God's love for Israel, and his call to the people to imitate God's generosity to them by the way they treat one another. God chose Israel and gave its people a homeland. (Deuteronomy 7:7; 8:1; 9:4-5). He called Israel to serve him and to be obedient to him alone. (Deuteronomy 6:1-3; 10:12-13). The book commemorates the great events of the liberation from Egypt and the Sinai covenant. It explains the religious meaning of these events and appeals for fidelity to God's law.

The great theme of Deuteronomy is that God has saved and blessed his people. The people are to remember this, and are called to love and obey God in return, so that they may have life and continued blessing. God wants his people to freely obey him, not because they are forced to do so. (Deuteronomy 6:3; 5:7; 7:7-8, 11; 8:5). Deuteronomy contains the great commandment, so called by Jesus: 'Love the Lord your God with all your heart, with all your soul, and with all your strength.' (Deuteronomy 6:4).

Deuteronomy opens with God recounting all he has done for Israel (1:1-3, 39) and urging the people to be loyal to him in return. (4:1-43). The people will enjoy the riches of the promised land, which is to be their destiny. Life depends not only on the food they eat, but on spiritual qualities found only in God. (7:1-8, 20). So the people are to have purity of heart towards one another. (10:12–11:32). There should be faithfulness in worship, justice in government, respect for human life, sexual purity, and protection for the disadvantaged in society. If the people are obedient to God, they will prosper, salvation being understood in terms of the material riches of the promised land. If they fail in their obedience, they will suffer the consequences in a loss of this land. (See Deuteronomy 27:1–28:68).

The covenant between God and his people is summarized in the Song of Moses. (Deuteronomy 31:30–32:47). The book ends with the prophetic blessing of the twelve Hebrew tribes. (32:45–33:29). After viewing the promised land from Mount Nebo in the plains of Moab, Moses dies. The Lord buried him in a valley in Moab. (Deuteronomy 34: 1-6).

## Exodus as History

The sons of Jacob were the founders of the twelve Hebrew tribes of Israel. In the ancient world of the Near East, society was originally organized on a tribal basis. A tribe would have been like an extended family, descendants of a common ancestor, occupying one particular territory, and usually self-governing. In later times, tribes often coalesced into a nation, as was the case with Israel itself and the nations Ammon, Moab and Edom to the east of the Jordan River and the Dead Sea. These people were known as Ammonites, Moabites and Edomites. Before the Hebrew tribes entered the Land of Canaan (today's Israel and the Palestinian territories), following their liberation from Egypt by Moses, the land was occupied by a number of tribes known as the Canaanites. This area eventually became the nation Israel under King David in about 1,000 BC.

The people who formed the nation of Israel and others on its borders, were known as Semites; they belonged to the Semitic family of people, and all of them spoke the same type of language. The Hebrews were also known as Israelites, so named after Jacob, whose name was changed to Israel following his wrestling with God. (Genesis 32:22-32). The word "Israel" is often used to denote both the chosen people as a whole and the nation Israel.

The date of the rescue of the Israelite tribes from Egypt is not certain. Some scholars think it may have been about 1250 BC. The Book of Exodus was not finally compiled until about the 7th or 6th centuries BC, its purpose in those later times being to strengthen national feeling and to support national identity.[44] This means that Moses did not write Exodus, although some of its teaching originated with him.

It is reasonable to suppose that the basic framework of Exodus is historical–the existence of Moses, the exodus itself and the journey through Sinai. "Unless we concede that these events really happened, and that Moses is truly a figure of history, the subsequent history of Israel, its loyalty to God and its attachment to the law, will defy explanation."[45]

Biblical traditions bear a clear memory of Egyptian ancestry. The tradition remembered that Moses had an Egyptian name. All the Pharaohs (kings of Egypt) bear the name "mose," meaning "is born." The name of the Pharaoh Rameses resembles that of Moses. As regards dates and events, the Bible is not helpful, and archaeology provides no evidence of an exodus from Egypt. But dates or so-called historical evidence are not important, because the purpose of Exodus is not to relate history, but to reveal the glory of God and his sovereignty over history.

There is no evidence in Egyptian records of a large band of slaves having escaped from Egypt. Exodus says that six hundred thousand men, not counting women and children, set out from Egypt. (Exodus 12:37). The Bible often exaggerates numbers, perhaps in this instance, in order to underline the epical character of the narrative. The people's long years of wandering in the semi-arid wilderness could never have sustained such a throng. There would have been a small group that escaped from Egypt and passed on its traditions to like-minded groups in Canaan.[46] The numbers probably only amounted to some hundreds, and this may be the reason why their escape would not have been noticed by the Egyptians. Perhaps smaller groups entered the Land of Canaan at different times.

However, there can be little doubt, but that Moses was the human founder of the religion of ancient Israel, making them the people of the covenant. The claim of Exodus that God delivered Israel's ancestors from slavery in Egypt is certainly traditional. It is central to the prophecy of Hosea in the 8th century, as well as to the Book of Deuteronomy in the late 7th century. While we accept that there must have been a genuine oral history hidden in the narrative, dating from the period of Israel's growth as a nation, the stories didn't reach final written form until many centuries after the events described. There were embellishments and additions as the stories were passed down the generations. New material relevant to later times was included, before the final editing of the Pentateuch about 500 BC.

More so than history, Exodus can be characterized as narrative literature which tells a story. The book portrays the events narrated as a direct intervention of God. Although the book is largely a product of the authors' imagination, it is not a simple fiction

---

[44] *Oxford Bible Commentary*, p. 67.

[45] *Jerusalem Bible*, introduction to the Pentateuch.

[46] *Oxford Bible Commentary*. p. 68.

either. It imaginatively creates a people's past so that they may understand themselves in the present. The people reflected on their past and interpreted their history as the hand of God guiding them, and still being with them in the present. This leads them to the hope that God will do for them in the future what he did in the past. This, in turn, encourages a journey of faith and hope.

So Exodus is not history in the modern sense, but an interpretation of history from the standpoint of God's intervention and action in the world. Its purpose is to give an account of God as liberator and saviour of his people, and his desire to have a lasting relationship with them. "The historical setting is only very hastily sketched in. The writers then freely draw on legend and imagination to create the scenes which we read."[47] "Under the layers of tradition, plausibly lies a historical individual, named Moses, although one whose role was clearly enhanced as the traditions developed, all of these eventually being combined in one account."[48]

What kind of literature is Exodus? The story must be interpreted as an epic, and not strictly as history. As in all epics, we can expect much embellishment and hyperbole, the clash of heroic characters and a struggle between good and evil, the archetypes of which, are God and the Pharaoh.[49] Because of its epical character, many of the events, which are described on a grand scale, should not be interpreted literally.

In the early stages of a people's history, there is a looking back towards heroes who embody such values as courage and heroism, giving identity and meaning to a particular culture. These ideals give hope and courage to a people and bind them together in a union. Biblical commentators refer to the story of Exodus as a primal narrative. It is *the* important story of Israel. It shaped their identity as a people, their understanding of the divine human relationship, their life together as a community, and their vision of the character of God as liberator and saviour.

The biblical narrative from Exodus to the books of the kings of Israel is about a people, how they found union as a people and a nation, and how they lived up to God's purpose for them. The stories related in Exodus had a big part to play in this development. So Exodus embodies literary, historical and theological aspects. It is Israel's foundation story, their identity story, telling the people where they came from, where they were going and showing them their place in the world under God's sovereignty.[50] The message is that God's care and protection for them, and their obedience to him, would preserve them as a united people. This was an important message to convey to the people following their return from the Babylonian exile in 537 BC. The idea of one God uniting a people towards a common purpose, and their faithfulness to him was the only guarantee of their survival in the uncertainty of their return to their homeland at that time.

To sum up, we can say that Exodus is not factual in the sense of modern history, but it is true, in its insight into the human condition. It outlines what it is like for human beings to exist in the chaos of a metaphorical wilderness (this world), with all its trials

---

[47] Ibid, p. 67.

[48] Michael D. Coogan, *The Old Testament* (Oxford University Press), 2014, p. 190.

[49] Marcus J. Borg, *Reading the Bible again for the First Time*, (Harper Collins), 2002, p. 103.

[50] Ibid, p. 67.

and testing. Out of such an experience, there grows a yearning in the human heart for something better – a 'promised land.' When God appeared to Abraham, he said to him, "leave your own country and go to a land that I am going to show you." (Genesis 12:1). This new land would ever after be known as 'the promised land.' In looking ahead towards the fulfilment of God's promise, Exodus describes this land as a "country rich and broad, a country flowing with milk and honey." (Exodus 3:8, 17, NJB). The idea of milk suggests green pastures for the domestic animals. Honey means that there would be bees to pollinate the crops and fruit trees. In the course of a long journey through an arid wilderness, this promise would encourage the people not to give up, but continue on their way, because God would ultimately fulfil their hopes for a meaningful and happy existence as their destiny.

At a deeper level of interpretation, Exodus represents what is common to all human beings, what is known as transcendence – a yearning for the absolutes of goodness, truth and happiness. The message of Exodus is that it is only God who can satisfy deepest human yearning with a 'promised land' as the end-goal of all our yearning and journeying. So Exodus is a sacred story, a story which inspires us to live meaningful lives, with the promise of a goal and destiny prepared for us by God, and towards which we can journey in faith and hope. Obedience to the Ten Commandments liberates us from enslaving bondages that will cause us to stumble on the journey. The Commandments are given to guide us towards a right relationship with God and one another. The Israelites' testing journey through the wilderness is symbolic of our own struggle through life. Exodus poses a challenge to us, in its call to action, to work for justice, to feed the hungry.

In his role as liberator of God's people, Moses prefigures Jesus. Jesus is one greater than Moses. Jesus is sent by God on a mission of liberating the whole of humanity from the slavery of their mortal condition, namely death, and leading us to our inheritance in the Kingdom of God as our promised land destiny. Jesus is God's ultimate response to human transcendence and the search for meaning.

## A Story of Protest against Oppressive Power

In the story of Exodus, Egypt and the Pharaoh are a type of the way society was organised in the ancient world. This was the society in which the Hebrew tribes were in bondage in Egypt. All the wealth and power were concentrated in the hands of an urban ruling elite around the king, including an army, priesthood and government officials. These elites represented about two per cent of the population. The rest of the population was composed of agricultural workers, day labourers, fishermen and artisans. About two thirds of the wealth (mostly derived from agriculture) ended up in the hands of the ruling elites, through taxation. The vast majority of the population suffered from hunger, high infant mortality and low life expectancy. They endured economic exploitation and political oppression. And the belief was fostered that such a society was ordained by the gods.

The Bible overturns this received way of looking in the ancient world – the view that kings rule with divine authority, which in reality, was a claim to absolute sovereignty on their part. The kings create order and peace, but it is an imposed order and a fragile peace. They promote the belief that their authority cannot be challenged without provoking the anger of the gods. This means that the king can be as oppressive as he likes, but he cannot be criticised. The God of Israel is against such use of power, whatever the empire or ruler. This is actually the imperial system that is satirized in the Genesis story, The Tower of Babel. (Genesis 11:1-9). God sees a better way of organizing society.

The God of Israel, the God whom the later prophets named as the creator of heaven and earth, cannot be identified with the power of this or that nation. He created the world of the nations, so he rules over all of them, and over every Pharaoh. The message of Exodus is that this supreme power intervenes in defence of the powerless. Only God is absolutely sovereign.

As Israel's primal narrative, Exodus is a story of protest against, and liberation from an enslaving world, affirming such protest as the will of God. In point of fact, the law given by Moses (the Ten Commandments) was designed to prevent such a world from re-emerging, because the Ten Commandments encourage love of all neighbours. Nobody should be enslaved. The exodus story is about the creation of a new world of freedom, justice and peace. God's people are called to leave the world of Egypt and the ideals of empire behind them, and to live as a free people under the God who saved them and cares for them, and who calls them to care for one another.

Exodus is thus about the clash of two world views. But it is not simply political; at the heart of the narrative is the sovereign and saving God and his covenant with Israel: "I am the Lord your God, who brought you out of the land of Egypt where you were slaves. Worship no god but me." (Exodus 20:2-3). The call to worship no other god really means, "Don't go back again to deify the false gods and values of Egypt. You should leave all of that behind you for ever. Have no other God but the Lord who liberates you and gives you a goal at the end of your striving." God is in Israel's story because of the justice and mercy which he embodies – values totally at variance with those of empire, which are about the rule of the strong over the weak.

## Themes of Exodus

There are four central themes in Exodus. Firstly, is the theme of God as revealed to Moses, the kind of God he is – compassionate and concerned for the plight of his human creatures. (1:1–13:16). Second is the theme of rescue and salvation (13:17-18–18:27). Because of his compassion for his people, created in his image, he rescues and saves them from their oppressors. Thirdly, there is the Covenant (19:1–24:48; 32:1–34:35). In the Covenant, God establishes his presence among his people and brings them into obedience with himself, as the means of creating union among the Hebrew tribes.

Lastly is the overarching theme of the sovereignty of God and the celebration of his glory. (25:1–31:8; 35:1- 40:38). The theme of the sovereignty of God is carried over from the Genesis stories of Abraham, Isaac, Jacob and his sons. When empires like that of Egypt (embodiments of evil) rule the world, we can still count on God's faithfulness. God is to have the final word in history. He cannot allow evil to rule for ever. Because of God's saving action and faithfulness to his people, the honour and glory are due to him alone, and not to human beings or their schemes for self-salvation. Human beings are not able to rescue themselves from all the limitations that hold them captive. All through Exodus is the theme of human hungering for fulfilment and happiness, with God as its fulfilment – expressed in the metaphor of the promised land.

God called Abraham, Isaac and Jacob to a mission of bringing the blessing of union to all nations. In Exodus, God's plan becomes more explicit at Mount Sinai, in the covenant of love between himself and the Hebrew tribes, which was intended to bind them together as a people devoted to him alone. (Exodus 20:1-17; 19:7-8). God's choice of Israel was not for Israel alone. As the Book of Genesis teaches, he wanted the descendants of Abraham to be the means of bringing blessing to all the nations, in order to create a union of all peoples everywhere - a union not based on coercion, but on love. (See Genesis 22:18).

## The Early Life of Moses

According to the Bible, the Israelites had been living in Egypt for about 400 years, but there is no certainty about dates or the length of this period. (Genesis 15:13; Exodus 12:40-41). The Israelites grew so "numerous and strong that Egypt was filled with them." (Exodus 1:7). Then a Pharaoh arose who did not know Joseph. Because the Israelites were seen as a threat to Egypt, this new Pharaoh forced them into slave labour. (Exodus 1:9). It wasn't so much that Pharaoh didn't know about Joseph, as that he chose to ignore the significance of Joseph as saviour of the people.

"So the Egyptians put slave drivers over them to crush their spirits with hard labour. The Israelites built the cities of Pithom and Rameses to serve as supply centres for the king." (Exodus 1:11). These cities have been tentatively identified with specific sites in the eastern Nile delta, and the time of their construction coincides with the most likely dates of the Exodus.[51] There was a widespread practice in the near East in which monarchs used forced labour for their major building projects. This was a sore point with peasants, who normally worked on the land or as day labourers. But the more the Egyptians oppressed the Israelites, the more they increased in number. So the king issued a command that every new-born Hebrew boy should be thrown into the River Nile. (Exodus 1:22).

One particular boy was saved from drowning by the king's daughter, who rescued him, brought him to the king's palace and adopted him as her own son. "She said to herself, 'I saved him from the water, so I name him Moses.'" (Exodus 2:10). Although raised under the influence of Egyptian culture, the boy Moses had his own mother for a nurse, thus ensuring that he was aware of the traditions and the plight of his own people. (Exodus 2:7-9). When Moses grew up, he went to visit his people, the Hebrews and saw how they were forced to do hard labour. When he saw an Egyptian slave-driver beating a Hebrew slave to death, he killed the Egyptian and hid his body in the sand. (2:12).

"The next day Moses went back and found two Hebrew men fighting. He said to the one who was in the wrong, 'Why are you beating up a fellow-Hebrew?' The man answered, 'Who made you our ruler and judge? Are you going to kill me just as you killed the Egyptian?' "Then Moses was afraid and said to himself, 'People have found out what I have done.'" (2:13-14). When the king heard what Moses did, he tried to have him killed. As a result of his violent act, Moses fled and went to live in the land of Midian. (Exodus

---

[51] Michael D. Coogan, *The Old Testament*, p. 106.

2:11-16). The Midianites were a nomadic people descended from Abraham and his concubine Keturah. (Genesis 25:1-2). They were mainly shepherds who lived east of the Gulf of Aqaba in Arabia. Moses adopted their way of life and became a shepherd. He married one of the daughters of Jethro, their tribal chieftain. (Exodus 2:20-21).

Just as the treachery of his brothers resulted in Joseph being brought to Egypt (Genesis 37:25-28), so the threat of betrayal by a fellow Hebrew forced Moses to flee into the wilderness. Their life with strangers is the setting which prepares both Joseph and Moses for God's mission of rescue and salvation. It is often in situations of exile that God's servants experience his revelation and his call to mission.

## Moses' Call to Mission

Meanwhile, back in Egypt the Israelites were groaning under their heavy yoke and cried out for help. "Their cry went up to God, who heard their groaning and remembered his covenant with Abraham, Isaac and Jacob." (Exodus 2:23-24). It was then that Moses had his burning bush experience of God in the Arabian desert. God appeared to him in the form of fire, in a burning bush that was not burning up. (Exodus 3:2).

> God said, 'I am the God of your ancestors, the God of Abraham, Isaac and Jacob… I have seen how cruelly my people are being treated in Egypt; I have heard them cry out to be rescued from their slave-drivers. I know all about their sufferings, and so I have come down to rescue them from the Egyptians and to bring them to a land that is rich and fertile… Now I am sending you to the king of Egypt so that you can lead the people out of his country.' (Exodus 3:5-10).

As is often the case in the Bible, God chooses one person to bring his blessing to the world. It would seem that God can more easily speak to one person. The mass of humanity may not be listening to his voice.

Moses had been exiled from Egypt, but he would return to lead a great rescue operation. The burning bush in the desert, out of which God spoke to Moses, may be a metaphor for God's energy and power that never dies, especially his burning passion for justice. And like the fire of the bush which did not burn up, God is eternal. (Exodus 3:1-3). In the Bible, fire is often used as a metaphor for the empowering presence of God. (Exodus 13:21; see Acts of the Apostles 2:1-4).

> Moses said to God, 'Who am I to go to Pharaoh and bring the Israelites out of Egypt?' God said, 'I will be with you, and this is the sign by which you will know that I was the one who sent you. After you have led the people out of Egypt, you will worship God on this mountain.' Moses then said to God, 'Look, if I go to the Israelites and say to them, 'The God of your ancestors has sent me to you,' and they say to me, "What is his name?" 'what am I to say to them?' God said to Moses, 'I am he who is.' And he said, 'This is what you are to say to the Israelites, 'I am has sent me to you.' God further said to Moses, 'You are to tell the Israelites, 'Yahweh, the God of your ancestors, the God of Abraham, Isaac and Jacob, has

sent me to you.' This is my name for all time, and thus I am to be invoked for all generations to come.' (Exodus 3:11-15, NJB).

In the above words, God is acting on his promise of nationhood to Abraham. (Genesis 12:3). "I am" is the literal translation from the Hebrew YHWH, or with possible vowels included, YAHWEH - the name for God, given to Moses at the burning bush. The name "I am" is not so much an expression of self-existence. It is rather a revelation of a God who is involved in the lives of human beings. The Greek philosophers (ca. 500 B.C.) arrived at an idea of God as a self-existing being, dependent on nothing for his existence. However, the Greeks never formulated the notion of God as personal, creative and caring, as is exemplified in "I am with you," a God who empathises with human beings and comes to liberate and rescue them from their sufferings. God uses servants like Moses to accomplish his designs. Because the god of the philosophers was just an abstraction and not in any sense personal, no religion ever arose out of Greek philosophy. Having a relationship with an abstract force would be impossible. What could it do for you?

The ancient Israelites did not think much about abstract concepts of existence. What mattered to them was action, God with them, rescuing them and saving them. Thus, the first awakening of a belief in God among the Hebrew tribes was the historical event of their liberation from Egypt. It was actually this experience of rescue and salvation that gave rise to the religion of the Old Testament. God had heard the people's cries, had seen their sufferings in Egypt, and took pity on them. There is a moral character to this God. He is committed to this world, and we can know him through his saving action. He is concerned about us. He is with us with us in our trials and struggles.

The Israelites in Egypt were both physically and spiritually enslaved. Like the Egyptians, they probably worshiped many gods, with different names. In saying that he is the God of Abraham, Isaac and Jacob, God is reminding Moses that he is God of the living, not of the dead. When the phrase "I am" (3:14) is placed alongside "I will be with you" (3:12) and "the God of your ancestors" (3:13), its mysterious meaning may become a little clearer. It may suggest permanency, a personal God - forever with his people, guiding, caring, saving.

Although Moses had abandoned his compatriots for the comfortable life of a shepherd, he could not forget the oppression of the slave gang. His murder of a slave driver was his own impulsive, but violent way of dealing with slavery. It did not work. Salvation does not come by brutal power. God is now placing before Moses a better way. Liberation will be God's work; it is not an achievement of the human being on his own. Moses will be God's instrument in this work, but it will be God's project, not something dreamed up by Moses. Salvation will come through God accompanying Moses ("I am") on his journey and empowering him for his mission of liberation. (Exodus 4:1-9).

Thus, Moses, the humble shepherd in the wilderness is called by God to go on a creative mission of rescuing and liberation. God had a purpose for Moses, one that would make his life meaningful. This purpose would not be thwarted, because it would be directed by God. The shepherd Moses would become God's shepherd, leading his people through the wilderness. It is significant that Moses brought nothing with him to Egypt but a staff, or stick – the shepherd's tool. (Exodus 14:16; 17:4-6; Genesis 32:10; Mark 6:8).

God would provide Moses with all he needed. (Psalm 23:1).

In his dialogue with God, Moses protests that he is a "nobody" (3:11), that he is not a good speaker. (4:10). He thinks that everything will be down to his own capabilities. But the Lord said to him, 'Who gives man his mouth? Who makes him deaf or dumb? Who gives him the sight to make him see? It is I, the Lord. Now go! I will help you to speak; I will tell you what to say.' (4:11). Moses' weakness was the very thing which would allow God all the more to act through him. (See 2 Corinthians, 12:7-10). His empowerment would be the work of God, with whom "he spoke, face to face." (Deuteronomy 34:10). As to the feelings of unworthiness of those chosen by God for a mission, see Jeremiah 1:6, and the empowerment God would give him. (Jeremiah 1:18-19).

And the purpose of the exodus: the people would then be free to worship the God of their ancestors, Abraham, Isaac and Jacob on the mountain of God. (Exodus 3:12). Only in a situation of freedom, are people capable of doing the will of God and giving him thanks for his gifts, thus acknowledging their dependence on him. God tells Moses that the power of his word will be effective (Exodus 2:12; 3:14-22; 4:22), as if to remind him that his use of physical force in Egypt accomplished nothing. In the Bible, it is the word of God which makes things happen. (Genesis 1:3; Exodus 14:16, 26). The Lord said, 'My word is like the snow and the rain that come down from the sky to water the earth. They make the crops grow. So also will be the word that I speak – it will not fail to do what I planned for it; it will do everything I send it to do.' (Isaiah 55:10-11).

## Israel's Rescue

What can be said about the recurring miraculous events in Exodus: the crossing of the Red Sea, manna in the desert, water from the rock? Are they examples of divine intrusion into natural causation? Or should an incident like the raised walls of water to allow the Israelites passage through the Red Sea, be interpreted metaphorically? (Exodus 13:18, 14:16). If it were accepted that God intervened dramatically like this in the past, the question might arise, where is he in today's calamities? God has not changed. He has intervened through Jesus to liberate us from the greatest oppressor of all, namely death.

When Moses confronted the Pharaoh, the latter hardened his heart and refused to let the people go. (Exodus 7:8-10, 29). Then there followed the ten plagues of Egypt. (Exodus 7:14–10:29). The plagues were sent by God "to gain victory over Pharaoh, so that the Egyptians will know that I am the Lord." (Exodus 14:18). The plagues can be interpreted as a demonstration of the sovereignty of God over nature, over the nation Egypt, and over Pharaoh in particular, who arrogantly believed that he enjoyed absolute power and sovereignty, even over nature. Redemption of the slaves makes them into free people. Salvation is rescuing people from life-threatening perils. God rescues and saves people, not as isolated individuals, but as a community. This always generates opposition from oppressive outsiders - in the present instance, from the Egyptian Pharaoh, and resistance from within God's people.

But the main purpose of the plagues of Egypt is to convince Israel of God's sovereignty, the one who can overcome the gods of Egypt and rescue his people, accompany them and guide them in their journey. The plagues demonstrate that, what the Egyptians think to be true of their gods, is actually only true of the God of Abraham, Isaac and Jacob. Thus, it is the religious aspect of the plagues that is most important. In the light of the statement in Exodus 12:12 about "punishing all the gods of Egypt," the plagues may be directed against different Egyptian gods.[52]They represent a contest between the God of Abraham, Isaac and Jacob and the gods of Egypt. The natural flooding of the Nile in season, for instance, was associated with the resurrection of the Egyptian god Osiris. It was thought that Osiris was responsible for the flooding of the Nile. When the water of the river is turned into blood, Osiris is shown up as powerless. (Exodus 7:17). This might signal the death of this god rather than his resurrection. Pharaoh worshiped the sun as a god. The plague of the three days of darkness demonstrates the failure of the Egyptian god to control the forces of nature. (Exodus 10:21-23). In Egypt, Pharaoh himself was regarded as divine. As a god, he was responsible for maintaining order in the cosmos. When cosmic order goes wrong, then nature behaves strangely, as in the plagues. So despite his claim to absolute sovereignty, Pharaoh is dethroned. He is unable to control the forces of nature (the plagues). It is rather the Lord God and his servant Moses who prevail in this cosmic struggle. (Exodus 9:16). Whether God uses the natural elements or the hand of Moses to achieve his purposes, he triumphs in person over the oppressive enemies of Israel. "The real victory here is not a matter of personalities. Pharaoh and God are embodiments of opposed social policies, so that the victory of God is a victory of a no slave policy."[53]

Scientists tell us that every Egyptian plague mentioned in Exodus, from the annual locust swarms to skin diseases, can be found in north African countries like Egypt. Even if some of the miracles in Exodus can be explained by natural causes, they would have been seen as miraculous by those who witnessed them. The same is true of hot winds that can suddenly dry up marshy areas to allow safe passage to people. The miracles could be in the timing of these events. However, Biblical man does not look at reality as nature, which is subject to causation, but as a creation. In this sense, because God is sovereign over his creation, his hand is in everything, directing all things, at all times. It could be said that everything has a sacred character, that all reality is miraculous. Some modern poets view the world in the same light: "As to me, I know nothing else but miracles... The wonderfulness of the sundown, or the stars shining so bright and quiet, or the exquisite delicate thin curve of the new moon in spring; these with the rest, one and all, are to me miracles."[54] (See Job 26:5-14).

Ancient Israel believed that God worked in, with, and through natural processes. For instance, there is something miraculous about the sun when it grows crops; likewise, when the rain and snow fall. The whole world is said to be graced and dignified, because of God's presence in it through his act of creation, and his loving concern for it. As a creation, the world bears the imprint of God's hand. (Psalm 8:3, NJB). This is about looking at the world from a religious standpoint. Through discovering the causes of things, science may have contributed to the desacralization of the world. Ever since the industrial

---

[52] Bartholomew and Goheen, *The Drama of Scripture*, (SPCK), 2014, p.62, 63.

[53] *Oxford Bible Commentary*, p.74.

[54] Walt Whitman, *Miracles,* 19th century American poet.

revolution and because of the exploitation of the earth for human gain, the spirit has gone out of nature. Because the moon has been visited by human beings, has it not lost something of its awesome wonder in the night sky? God is the ultimate cause of everything. God, the Creator of life, is always with us as the one who heals diseases, who calms storms, saves his people, dries the land and provides food (his love) for the hungry.

When the king of Egypt eventually let the people go, the Lord led them in a roundabout way through the desert towards the Red Sea. (13:17-18). "The Israelites left Sukkoth and camped at Etham on the edge of the desert. During the day the Lord went in front of them in a pillar of cloud to show them the way, and during the night he went in front of them in a pillar of fire to give them light." (Exodus 13:20-21). God's leading and guiding of Israel is consistent with his promise to Moses that he would be with him on his journey. (3:12). The pillar of cloud during the day and the pillar of fire at night may be metaphors for God's guidance during different periods of Israel's journey to the promised land: the pillar of cloud, when things were going well for them, and the pillar of fire in times of metaphorical darkness, when they seemed to be lost and going nowhere.

We ourselves mirror the Israelite's passage through the wilderness to the promised land. God wants to direct our lives in the same way. We cannot do the journey on our own. God wants to lead us by the cloud of his presence and show us the way by his light. Jesus is the light who guides us as we follow him through our darkness. (John 8:12; see Psalm 23:4)

It is not long until we see resistance by God's people to God's saving action. When the Israelites reached the shores of the Red Sea (Exodus 14:9) on their escape from Egypt, they complained to Moses for bringing them to what they perceived as the edge of the abyss, giving them the feeling that they were facing death. They didn't trust Moses or God to do what they could not do under their own steam. At this stage of their journey, their faith hadn't even begun to blossom.

> When the people saw Pharaoh and his army marching against them from the rear, and the sea in front of them, they were terrified and cried out to the Lord for help They said to Moses, 'Weren't there any graves in Egypt? Did you have to bring us out here in the desert to die? Look what you have done by bringing us out of Egypt! Didn't we tell you before we left Egypt that this would happen? We told you to leave us alone and let us go on being slaves of the Egyptians. It would be better to be slaves there than to die here in the desert.' (Exodus 14:10-12).

Because they saw salvation only in terms of what they themselves could achieve, then there was no salvation, no way out of the abyss; they were lost. They were even deprived of graves to give them a final resting place. Although they cried out to God for help, they obviously didn't trust that he would come to their aid. Moses told them not to be afraid. They would soon see what the Lord would do. Their salvation would be the work of God, not their own work. (Exodus 13-14). The temptation for us who start on the journey of faith is to turn back to our former comfort zone. We prefer the easy option, the line of least resistance, the gratification of the present moment. But God wants us to leave that old country behind us. That is the challenge that leads us to mature faith. God wants to show us new lands, new and ever unfolding vistas that bring his blessing down on us. (See Genesis 12:1-2; Mark 8:35).

> The Lord said to Moses, 'Lift up your stick and hold it out over the sea. The waters will divide and the Israelites will be able to walk through the sea on dry ground'... Moses held out his hand over the sea, and the Lord drove the sea back with a strong wind. It blew all night and turned the sea into dry land. The water was divided. And the Israelites went through the sea on dry ground, with walls of water on both sides. The Egyptians pursued them and went after them into the sea with all their horses, chariots and drivers. (Exodus 14:16, 21-23).

In Exodus, the shepherd's stick or staff is a symbol of God's power to work wonders on behalf of his people. God needs the meagre resources of his human servants (in this case, Moses holding his stick over the sea) in order to accomplish his creative work, which is always miraculous.

When the wheels of the Egyptian chariots got stuck in the mud and when they admitted defeat (14:25), there at the sea the Lord fulfilled the promise which he made: 'the Egyptians will know that I am the Lord.' (14:18).

We should note that the original Hebrew text of the Old Testament has "reed sea" and not "Red Sea." As if to dramatize the narrative, the much later Greek translation of the Hebrew Bible has "Red Sea." (14:9b). In point of fact, Exodus has two accounts of the crossing over the sea. The first one (14:16, 21-23 above) speaks of the Reed Sea, which would have been a marshy area which could quickly dry up to allow safe passage on foot, but not for horses and chariots. The second account says that when Moses held up his stick the sea divided into two walls of water and when the Egyptians tried to cross, the waters closed over them. (14:26-28).

The author of Exodus implies that the event at the sea is a new creation. As in Genesis 1:2-9, and like the renewal of the earth after the Flood (Genesis 8:1, 14) the wind blew (wind, also a metaphor for God's Spirit), the waters were divided and dry land appeared. (Exodus 14:21). What is being created here by the hand of the Lord God is Israel.

The gospels have many accounts of Jesus rescuing and bringing new life to people who, like the Israelites at the Red Sea, were equally poised on the edge of disaster. (Mark 1:32-34; Matthew 8:14-17; Luke 4:38-41). Christians interpret Israel's passage through the waters of the sea as our own new creation in Christ, through the waters of baptism. In his healing miracles, all Jesus asked of the people was faith, trust in what God could do when all human powers are shown as inadequate. In other words, transformation can only take place when we trust God, cooperate with him and allow him to do what we ourselves cannot accomplish.

## God Feeds Hungers and Thirsts

Once the people came into the barren wilderness of Sinai, and despite all they had already experienced, there was more resistance and lack of trust in God's saving action.

> When the people came to the desert of Sin they all complained to Moses and

Aaron and said to them, 'We wish that the Lord had killed us in Egypt. There we could at least sit down and eat meat and as much of other food as we wanted. But you have brought us out into this desert to starve us all to death.' (Exodus 16: 1-3).

Preserving freedom is difficult. The forbidden fruit of slavery can still be attractive. There are many such testing crises in Exodus, which in reality is a journey which demands faith and hope, and the ability to let go of the past. (Exodus 7:2-3; 14:6-9, 11-12). God always calls his people to leave the past (their own country) behind them, because he knows that it is only holding them back from being the kind of people he wants them to be. (Genesis 12:1; Mark 10:21). The future they faced with Moses was unknown and bore all the signs of discomfort. This is like losing heart at the first hurdle of the journey. It is down to a lack of trust in the God who had been guiding them this far. When God rescues his people, they forfeit houses for desert tents, a settled urban life for a nomadic existence. They leave behind a productive land for an arid wilderness. But what the people had still to learn was trust in God and his power to meet their needs. God did not bring the Israelites into an arid wilderness to then abandon them to death. His name given to Moses ("I am") means that he is always with them (pillars of cloud and fire), providing them with food and drink, everything for their sustenance.

Following the people's complaint about lack of food, the Lord said to Moses, 'Now I am going to make food rain down from the sky for all of you. The people must go out every day and gather enough for that day. In this way I can test them to find out if they will follow my instructions. On the sixth day they are to bring in twice as much as usual and prepare it.' (16:4-5). Then Moses said to the people, 'It is the Lord who will give you meat to eat in the evening and as much as you want in the morning, because he has heard how much you have complained against him.' (16:8). The people were asked to gather enough manna for one day at a time, meaning that they should stop worrying about subsequent days. But they did not obey his command for a day of rest on the seventh day. (16:27-29). The message: surrender control, trust in the Lord. Don't look for security in yourself; let the Lord be your salvation. (See 14:13-14).

What was this manna which the Lord provided as food? In the Sinai Peninsula in the months of May and June, the tamarisk tree exudes a sweet substance which is gathered and eaten by the local people, who still call it "man." The amounts are small. Exodus goes beyond this natural fact, as the miracle of enough food to sustain a whole people one day at a time. (Exodus 16:1-36). "The people of Israel called this food manna. It was like a small white seed, and tasted like biscuits made with honey." (16:31).

However, there is more to the manna than meets the eye. Deuteronomy reminds the people that the provision of physical food was not the real purpose of the manna. Verse 3b in the passage below was quoted by Jesus in Matthew 4:4 and Luke 4:4 during his temptations in the desert. The word of God is more powerful than physical food. God has to teach Israel that there are higher values than the merely material. Human beings long for something more than ordinary bread, which only gives temporary satisfaction. Only God and his saving word of promise can satisfy the deepest hungering of the human heart: "I am the Lord your God who brought you out of Egypt where you were slaves. Worship no god but me." (Exodus 20:2-3). Turning to material things (bread) as gods, and bowing down to them will not work. Physical bread on its own, cannot save us; it cannot give us the satisfaction we still crave.

> Remember how the Lord your God led you on this long journey through the desert, sending hardships to test you, to see whether you would obey his commands. He made you go hungry and then gave you manna to eat. He did this to teach you that human beings must not depend on bread alone to sustain them, but on everything that God says... Remember that the Lord your God corrects and punishes you, just as a father disciplines his children. So then, do as the Lord has commanded you: live according to his laws and obey him.' (Deuteronomy 8:2-3, 5-6).

Moses tells the people that it is for their own good that God disciplines them through hardship. (Deuteronomy 8:5). Making them go hungry, humbling them, makes them learn something about themselves (that they are dependent creatures), and about God as the provider of deepest human needs. The issue here is not spiritual food (God's word in the Commandments) versus material food (manna), but placing more trust in the word of God, rather than on material things alone.

The imagery of parent and child is helpful in understanding God's relationship with his people during their wilderness journey. Bringing them out into the wilderness is God's way of showing tough love. It is a parent's instructive discipline. (Deuteronomy 8:5-6; Hosea 2:14-15). It is in the wilderness that they would discover who God is - the source of their life and of everything good, their leader and guide.

In today's world there is much emphasis on material comforts ("bread alone"), and we must play our part, in cooperation with God, in providing them. They are important but are never enough. For a true human existence, we need God's love (his word to us in the ten Commandments), empowering us to love one another - the real food to sustain us on our earthly journey and bring us to our promised land. (Deuteronomy 5:16; 8:1; 11:13-17; 30:15-20). Jesus spoke, not about physical food, but about a food which would satisfy deepest human hungering. Jesus said to them, 'The bread that God gives is he who comes down from heaven and gives life to the world... I am the bread of life. Those who come to me will never be hungry; those who believe in me will never be thirsty.' (John 6:25-59). It is faith in Jesus, who is the bread of life, that will satisfy deepest human hungering and thirsting.

When the people eventually reached the region of Mount Sinai, they were thirsty and they complained to Moses and said, 'Give us water to drink... Why did you bring us out of Egypt? To kill us and our children and our livestock with thirst?' (17:2, 3b). The Lord again reminded the people of his presence by drawing water from a rock. He instructed Moses to strike the rock at Mount Sinai with the same stick with which he struck the river Nile, and water would come out of it for the people to drink. (Exodus 17:5-6; see Isaiah 41:17-20). It is God through Jesus who satisfies human thirsting for meaningful life. Jesus is the rock from whom living water flows to satisfy our thirsting for the happiness of eternal life. (See John 4:13-14).

## The Sinai Covenant

> On the first day of the third month after the people had left Egypt, they came to
> the desert of Sinai. There they set their camp at the foot of Mount Sinai, and
> Moses went up the mountain to meet with God. The Lord called to him from
> the mountain and told him to say to the Israelites, 'You saw what I, the Lord did
> to the Egyptians and how I carried you as an eagle carries her young on her wings
> and brought you here to me. Now, if you obey me and keep my covenant, you
> will be my own people, a people dedicated to me alone, and you will serve me as
> priests.' Moses went down and told the people all that the Lord had commanded.
> Then all the people answered, 'We will do everything that the Lord has said,' and
> Moses reported this to the Lord. (Exodus 19:2-8).

The Ten Commandments represent God's covenant with his people. We have already seen
the accounts of God's covenant with Abraham (Genesis 1:25-26; 9:1-7). "A Covenant is
an agreement that God initiates to protect, sustain and bring to completion the salvation
he has begun on behalf of his people."[55] God promises to love and protect his people, both
now and for all time. They, in turn, promise to be faithful to him and not to give their
allegiance to rivals (other gods, material things for example); such things only lead them
away into a land called "Wandering." (Genesis 4:16). The people promised to do everything
that the Lord had said. (Exodus 19:8).

Through the covenant, the Lord transforms a "mixed" crowd who left Egypt into
a people dedicated to the God who rescued them, a 'kingdom of priests, a holy nation.'
(Exodus 19:6). God went into covenant with Israel at Mount Sinai, and did so again after
they broke the first agreement. (32:1).

The covenant could be described as an expression of the fundamental values of
a society. Every society lives by a system of some kind of values. The Mosaic covenant
pledges people to one another and to the common good. "It is politics rooted in a religious
vision of human dignity and equality."[56] It becomes Israel's standard for measuring
national success or failure. The covenant must be grounded on faith, hope and love.

Faith means trust in the God who rescues us from all the things which hold us
in bondage (Exodus 20:2). Hope helps us to imagine some purpose in human life. It offers
us the prospect of an ultimate "promised land" as our destiny and salvation, in order to
counteract the feeling that we may be going nowhere, just adrift in an absurd world
without meaning or purpose.

Lastly, there is love. A society can only be unified by some binding force. For
Israel and for ourselves, the binding force is God's love – to be imitated by his people.
Love is the binding force which enables a society to cohere instead of breaking up into a
million different parts and ending up in enmity and conflict. This kind of binding may be

---

[55] Michael W. Duggan, *The Consuming Fire, A Christian Guide to the Old Testament,* (Our Sunday Visitor, Inc.,
Huntington, Indiana, 2010), p. 153.

[56] Jonathan Sacks, *The Great Partnership*, (Hodder and Stoughton), 2012, p. 135, quoting Joshua Berman,
2008.

difficult to achieve in a culture of individualism, in which individuals go their own way. It was impossible in Egypt, because a system of organized slavery only creates resentment, enmity and anger. A society bound together by love can inspire people to put self-interest aside for the sake of the community, the strong protecting and caring for the weak.

Because God's love is at the heart of the Commandments, it would be a misunderstanding to see them as an imposition, which is the way they are often viewed in the modern world. The word 'commandment' may not be the best word to describe them. They are actually liberating, in that they free us from self-centred individualism. They provide the solid ground on which relationships between human beings are governed, which is mutual love. This means that freedom is equated with the Ten Commandments! That is a message which might not gain much traction in today's world. Today there is a suspicion of any authority telling people what to do or how to live their lives. This can be seen as depriving them of their freedom of choice. So there tends to be a rejection of rules or guidelines coming from any source. This is due to today's belief that morality is relative, meaning that there is no absolute right or wrong in anything. Morality and rules associated with it are just a matter of personal opinion. Thus, the only ground for morality is the whim of the individual. So thousands of years of acquired wisdom is dismissed as "oppressive," or at least no longer relevant in today's world. God never imposes anything on human beings. His word spoken to us in the Ten Commandments is a word of love. It calls, not for a slavish, but a free and loving response.

At Sinai, the covenant was formalised, the people made their promises for a second time: 'We will obey the Lord and do everything that he has commanded.' (Exodus 24:7). So, the question for the Israelites was: in creating their own society, would they reject the materialistic values of empire and embrace the values of a loving and liberating God?

One further point about the Sinai covenant. Verse 5 in the foregoing passage seems to imply that God's love is conditional, that he will love his people, only if they obey him. God's love for his people is never less than infinite, but the Israelites at Sinai were not ready or willing to hear such a good news at this particular stage of their journey. They believed that God would protect them and lead them safely into the promised land, if they obeyed the commandments. That was how they understood it. This would mean that God only loves people if they are good, and if they are bad, he will not love them at all. That would turn God into a sky policeman, keeping track of everything people do. This is not the God who revealed himself to the later prophets, and later again, to Jesus. When the people were taken into exile in Babylon, the prophets told them that God was with them in their suffering as well as in the good times. They thus discovered that God loved them even though they had forsaken him and turned the riches of the promised land into idols. The God of the prophets is a God of mercy and compassion, a forgiving and loving God. He will not be unfaithful to Israel even if she breaks her promises. He suffers along with her and goes into exile with her. And he promises to take her home when the time is ripe. (See Isaiah 40:10-11; 49:14-16). Prophetic faith is a more mature faith. It means that God loves us no matter what our circumstances.

On the morning of the third day, there was thunder and lightning, a thick cloud appeared on the mountain, and a loud trumpet blast was heard. All the people in the camp trembled with fear. Moses led them out of the camp to meet with God, and they stood at the foot of the mountain. The whole of Mount Sinai was covered with smoke, because the Lord had come down on it in fire. The smoke went up like the smoke of a furnace, and all the people trembled violently. The sound of the trumpet became louder and louder. Moses spoke, and God answered him with thunder... 'I am the Lord your God who brought you out of the land of Egypt, where you were slaves. Worship no God but me. Do not make for yourselves images of anything in heaven or on earth. Do not bow down to any idol or worship it, because I am the Lord your God and I tolerate no rivals.' (Exodus 19:16-20, 20:2-4).

The above passage is to be interpreted not simply as a historical event, but as an imaginative poetic construction. On Mount Sinai the Israelites are given an experience of God through an awakening of all their senses, especially sight and hearing: the mysteriousness of the partly veiled mountain itself, the blazing fire, the smoky furnace, the thunder and trumpet blasts, all of which suggest the transcendent splendour of God. This should be enough to capture the attention of a great throng. This great display of natural power is an attempt in human language to convey something of the awesome, mysterious and powerful God who still wants to have a close relationship with his human creatures. The idea that the gods lived on a high mountain is an old one and was common to all ancient cultures. Images like the above are found in Hebrew literature of all periods, as ways of describing the indescribable. (See Psalm 18:7-15). The metaphorical language of the account at Sinai is a revelation of the insignificance of the human being compared with the mystery, power and majesty of God. (Isaiah 40:21-22). The people had been slaves in Egypt, but now they must be prepared and fitted for a responsible life of freedom in the promised land.

The cloud is a symbol of the Lord's glory. It hovers over the wilderness, the Lord appearing as a "dazzling light." (Exodus 16:10). A cloud and a pillar of fire guided the people out of Egypt to Sinai. (Exodus 13:21-22; 14:19, 21-22). The Lord said to Moses, 'I will come to you in a thick cloud, so that the people will hear me speaking with you and will believe you from now on.' (19:9; see 19:16; 24:15-18; 34:5). The cloud signifies the Lord's presence as it covers the tent where the Lord meets with Moses. (Exodus 33:9-10; 40:34-35). The cloud fills the tabernacle containing the stone tablets of the law.

For dramatic effect, and as if to emphasise the importance of what is taking place, Exodus pulls out all the stops. Fire as a metaphor for God! In the burning bush, it was a quiet voice spoken to Moses, calling him to service. In order to get through to a band of recently liberated slaves who are still fixated on Egypt, God would speak in a more cogent voice. Although God sometimes speaks in a thundering voice, shaking heaven and earth, humans may still not hear him. "The Lord roars like a lion." (Amos 3:8). "His word is like a hammer which breaks the rock in pieces." (Jeremiah 23:28). But people can still be unmoved, unaware, deaf. Jeremiah tells God that it is pointless speaking his word to the people. "They are stubborn and refuse to listen to your message; they laugh at what you tell me to say." (Jeremiah 6:10).

Chapter 20 begins with the voice of God, delivering the Ten Commandments. (20:1-17). "I am the Lord your God who brought you out of Egypt where you were slaves. Worship no god but me" (Exodus 20:2-3). God thus introduces himself as the Israelites' liberator. The use of the phrase "I am" recalls God's name as given to Moses in the burning bush, a name not to be used for evil purposes, but a reminder of his love and care for his people. (20:7). The words "I am your God" and "slaves" serve to remind the Israelites of how they can preserve the freedom God gave them when he brought them through the sea to Mount Sinai. Turning to other gods would be a journey back to slavery. (20:3). Hence the importance of the first Commandment. The third Commandment places an emphasis on the Sabbath - worship of the God who saves. (20:8). While the first three commandments are about the relationship between God and his people, the other seven are about the relationships that should exist between human beings themselves, as a community, if they are to live the kind of lives that God wants them to live - loving God through loving their neighbour.

In the creation of union, God depends on his human partners to do his work of caring, especially caring for the weak. God is not a new coercive power replacing the one in Egypt. He called the people into a freedom which could be exercised by the people when they care for one another. Keeping the Commandments would be the guarantor of the Israelites' new life of freedom as a community. Jesus summed up the Ten Commandments as loving God and loving one's neighbour as oneself. (Matthew 22:37; Mark 12:30-31; Luke 10:27). Jesus said, 'Do this and you will live.' (Luke 10:28). In other words, love God and your neighbour and you will find life meaningful and fulfilling.

In giving the Ten Commandments to the scattered Hebrew tribes, God is carrying out his promises of blessing to Abraham and his descendants. Blessing is visible in a community unified with a common purpose. The Hebrew tribes would enter the promised land with God's blessing. Their mission would be one of creating union among themselves, through their trust in God and their obedience to the Ten Commandments. It would be some time before they would achieve nationhood in the land of Israel - the goal promised to them by God through Abraham. This would have to be the kind of nationhood that could be blessed by God.

Exodus 21-23 offers a list of practical laws for life in the promised land. In a kind of Sabbath rest, slaves are to be set free in the seventh year of their service. (Slavery was practiced everywhere in the ancient world. Most slaves were actually domestic servants). The covenant says that strangers and sojourners in the land are to be treated with compassion. Israel should now imitate the Lord and treat others as he treated them when they were strangers in the land of Egypt.

## Hammurabi's Code

There were other law codes in the Near East similar to the law of Moses but appearing long before the time of Moses. Could they have influenced the laws given in Exodus? In 1901, a black stone pillar was found in the ancient city of Susa, capital of Mesopotamia (Modern Iraq and Iran). Susa was one of the oldest cities of the ancient world, and it remained the capital of Persia throughout the era of the Persian Empire. (Ezra 4:9; Nehemiah 1:1; Esther 1:2, 5; 4:8, 8:11-14; Daniel 8:2).[57] On this monument was engraved the Code of King Hammurabi (1792-1750 BC), consisting of 282 laws. The central tenet of the Hammurabi's code was retaliatory justice. A reference to one example from this monument: "If a noble has destroyed the eyes of another noble, they shall destroy his eye." Then in Exodus 21:23-25 we read: "If a pregnant woman is injured so that she loses her child, the punishment shall be life for life, eye for eye, tooth for tooth, hand for hand, foot for foot, burn for burn, wound for wound, bruise for bruise."

Hammurabi boasts that he has written the law in order that "the strong may not oppress the weak, that justice may be dealt the orphan and the widow."[58] (See Psalm 68:5-6). The ancient near eastern nations shared with Israel an ideal of justice for their people. God was also speaking to them no less than to Israel, to the extent that they might have been open to and listening to his word. Contrasted with the Hammurabi code, the Mosaic law is more than a legal code. Coming from a sacred source, it is an expression of a covenant of love between God and humanity. Jesus rejected the notion of retaliatory justice when he turned the other cheek to the violence done to him. (See Matthew 5:38-39).

Evidence for the antiquity of the Ten Commandments (Decalogue) includes references to them in the prophets: Hosea in the eighth century BC and Jeremiah in the late seventh. (Hosea 4:1-2 and Jeremiah 7:9). In both of these texts, the words used are the same as those in the Ten Commandments.

## Israel's Apostasy

God called Moses up the mountain a second time, which means that he was away from the people for forty days. During this time, the Lord gave him two stone tablets on which the Ten Commandments were engraved, instructed him about the making of the covenant box to contain the stone tablets, and informed him concerning the rituals surrounding it, including instructions for ordaining Aaron (brother of Moses) and his sons as priests. (Exodus 24:12 f.)

Because of his long absence on the mountain, the people grew tired of ever again hearing from Moses, so the question arose: who would then lead them out of the wilderness which was offering neither life nor promise? (32:1f). The absence of Moses may have been a test of the people's obedience. If Moses had abandoned them, could they find a ready substitute for him? Perhaps they had lost faith in the invisible One, the mysterious One, the One veiled in a firey cloud on a mountain-top. If they didn't see him, how could he help them? Therefore, looking for something more tangible, before which they could bow, they prevailed on Aaron, to make a golden calf (an Egyptian or Canaanite god) as a god that might lead them. (Exodus 32:1). After they had made the bull calf they said, 'Israel, this is our God who led us out of Egypt!' (32:4). Exodus continues: "Early the next morning they brought some animals to burn as sacrifices, and others to eat. The people sat down to a feast, which turned into an orgy of drinking and sex." (32:6). The

---

[57] *World's Bible Dictionary*, p.422.

[58] ANET 178, quoted in Lawrence Boadt, *Reading the Old Testament*, p. 156.

lure of the rival materialistic god, tempting people to grasp the forbidden fruit of self-indulgence, was not long in coming!

Just as God was presenting Moses with the covenant written on stone tablets - probably signifying their permanence (31:18; 32:16) - in the valley down below, the people whom he rescued from Egypt were involved in idolatrous revelry.

The Egyptian god Apis was depicted as a bull calf. Worship of the calf (both in Egypt and Canaan) was a fertility cult which sought to achieve fertility in the crops planted in the fields. Perhaps the Israelites - confronted with a long journey in the arid wilderness - were worried about the life of their flocks, and about a future harvest and its possible failure. But once again, rather than trusting in the Lord, who promised to bring them to a land flowing with milk and honey, they turned to Egyptian idolatry in an effort to secure their needs. Getting the people out of Egypt was the easy part. Getting Egypt out of them would prove to be a more difficult task.

This kind of idolatry was a constant temptation once the people entered the promised land, and indeed throughout the whole period of the kings of Israel, right down to the time of the Babylonian exile in 587 BC. In 1 Kings 12:25-21, King Jeroboam of Israel set up two golden calves in his kingdom, as "gods who brought you out of Egypt." The account in 1 Kings may actually be the source of the one in Exodus.[59] At the basis of this worship was the belief that people can create their own gods, symbolizing materialism, as things that can give them security and happiness.

## Moses' Substitutionary Role

Why does God not abandon his people for their breach of the covenant? It is because of Moses' pleading on their behalf. (Exodus 32:11–34:9).

"On the mountain, God said to Moses, 'Go back down at once, because your people whom you led out of Egypt, have sinned and rejected me. They have already left the way that I commanded them to follow.'" (Exodus 32:7-8a).

Moses went down the mountain carrying the two stone tablets on which the Commandments were engraved. When he saw the orgy of feasting and dancing round the camp, he was furious. There near the foot of the mountain, he threw down the stone tablets and broke them, an action signifying the broken covenant. Then he took the bull calf which they had made, melted it, ground it into fine powder, mixed it with water and forced the people of Israel drink the water. (See 32:15-21).

"The Lord said to Moses, 'I know how stubborn these people are. Now, don't try to stop me. I am angry with them and I am going to destroy them. Then I will make you and your descendants a great nation.'" (Exodus 32:9-10). As if God was disowning the people, he now identified them as belonging to Moses. The offer of making him the father of a great nation must have been a tempting prospect to Moses. He rejected this temptation. Moses decided to intercede with God on behalf of his people, to stand in the breach between God and them, substituting himself for them, and taking on himself the penalty they deserved, so that they might escape retribution.

In his intercession, Moses appeals to aspects of the Lord's character and concerns,

---

[59] *Oxford Bible Commentary*, p. 88).

firstly, to the relationship between God and his chosen people. He urges God not to destroy this relationship, or bring to nought his redemptive work on their behalf. Secondly, he reminds God that the destruction of Israel would discredit him (God) in Egyptian eyes. Moses pleaded with God:

> 'Lord, why should you be so angry with your people whom you brought out of Egypt with great might and power? Why should the Egyptians say that you led your people out of Egypt, planning to kill them in the mountains and destroy them completely? Stop being angry; change your mind and do not bring this disaster on your people. Remember your servants Abraham, Isaac and Jacob. Remember the solemn promise you made to them to give them as many descendants as there are stars in the sky and to give their descendants all that land you promised would be their possession for ever.' So the Lord changed his mind and did not bring on his people the disaster he had threatened. (Exodus 32:11-14).

God's characteristics are revealed in the end as a God who changes his mind, bears with his people who have sinned grievously, and is still ready to accompany them on their journey. It appears that a prayer for mercy can change the heart of God. There may be no inconsistency in the Lord changing his mind. Moses' prayer to God is for God to act according to the divine will and purpose, as it has always been manifest – a purpose that is faithful, redemptive, forgiving and enduring, in his relationship with his people.

There may be a misconception that the God of the Old Testament is simply a God of retribution and condemnation. These revelations from Exodus should put pay to such a notion.

In his rejection of the temptation to self-aggrandisement (Exodus 32:10), in his suffering on behalf of his people, in his prayerful pleading with God, and interceding on behalf of Israel, Moses assumes the role of representative, as the saviour, under God, of his people. Thus, Moses is a mediator, not just of the divinely given laws, but also between God and a rebellious people, a rebellion that will be repeated as they continue their journey. (See the Book of Numbers, chapter 14).

The people themselves do nothing; they renew no promises. "Their mourning in Exodus 33:4 is not to be interpreted as repentance."[60] Moses puts his own life on the line for the people's sake. Moses said to them, 'You have committed a terrible sin. But now I will go up the mountain to the Lord. Perhaps I will obtain forgiveness for your sin.' Moses then returned to the Lord and said, 'These people made a god out of gold and worshiped it. Please forgive their sin; but if you won't, then remove my name from the book in which you have written the names of your people.' (Exodus 32:30-32).

It is here that Moses becomes the hero of Exodus. For months, he had been God's faithful servant, at all times giving his full assent to the will of God for the liberation of his people; at times, speaking as prophet; at times performing mighty wonders under the direction of God. Now, acting on his own initiative, he is transformed into God's suffering

---

[60] *Oxford Bible Commentary*, p. 88.

servant. The suffering servant in whose line Moses stands, is one who intercedes for transgressors (Isaiah 53:13), as are also prophets on occasion. (Amos 7:1-6, and Jeremiah). Like Amos and Isaiah's Suffering Servant, Moses prays for divine mercy for the people, and about their persistent disobedience. Amos and Moses plead for mercy, probably knowing that the mercy of God is equal to, and as intense as his judgement.

Moses cut two stone tablets like the ones which were broken, and brought them up the mountain, just as the Lord commanded. "Then the Lord came down in a cloud and pronounced his holy name. He passed in front of Moses and called out, 'I, the Lord, am a God who is full of compassion and pity, who is not easily angered and who shows great love and faithfulness. I keep my promise for thousands of generations.'" (34:1-6).

The Lord then restores the covenant with his people, promising that he will do great things in their presence, "such as have never been done anywhere on earth among any of the nations." (Exodus 34:10a). The restoration of the covenant leads to new revelations of God, as gracious and merciful, attributes essential for re-establishing the covenant with a people who violated the first commandment. Graciousness and mercy define the difference between the Lord and all the other gods – and between God and human beings. They are the qualities that Israelites will invoke in praying the psalms. (See Psalms 86:5, 15; 103:8; 145:8).

Aaron was too weak to restrain the people. Moses was strong enough to restrain God himself. God also proved strong enough in the end to bear with a people who not only had sinned, but who were likely to go on sinning, as Moses confessed. (Exodus 34:9). By standing in the breach between God and man, in his representative role, Moses saved his people from death, and took the consequences of their rebellion onto himself. In Deuteronomy, we get a glimpse of Moses as a type of later biblical figures who are God's suffering servants. (Deuteronomy 3:23-28; 4:21-22).

More so than Exodus, the Book of Deuteronomy emphasises the heroic stature of Moses, as one who, out of love and compassion for his people, is willing to die for them (so that they might escape death), taking on to his own shoulders, the responsibility for their sins, out of his loving service to them. (Deuteronomy 1:34-37). He shares their existence in all its flaws, so he must suffer with them. For Moses' role as intercessor, see Deuteronomy 9:7-29; 10:10-11; 18:9-22. For his role as prophet, see Deuteronomy 18:9-22.

Deuteronomy says that the Lord was angry with Moses, because, he, Moses had become one with his people, as their spokesperson and representative (part of the pain he endured). As a consequence of this, God told him that he would not enter the promised land along with the people. Moses spoke to the people and pleaded with God:

> At that time I earnestly prayed, 'Sovereign Lord, I know that you have shown me only the beginning of the great and wonderful things you are going to do. There is no God in heaven or on earth who can do the mighty things that you have done. Let me cross the River Jordan into the promised land, Lord, and see the fertile land on the other side, the beautiful hill country and the Lebanon mountains. But because of you people the Lord was angry with me and would not listen.' (Deuteronomy 3:23-26).

"Anger" can be interpreted as judgement on the people because of their lapses of faith and their turning to other gods. God would not listen to Moses' plea, but for his salvation, would give him a glimpse of the promised land. "The Lord said to Moses, 'Go to the peak of Mount Pisgah and look to the north and to the south, to the east and to the west. Look carefully at what you see, because you will never go across the Jordan river.'" (Deuteronomy 3:27-28). (In the ancient world, Mount Pisgah is located about twelve miles east of the most northerly part of the Dead Sea).[61] As always, Moses' concern was directed away from himself and towards his people:

> Because of you Israel, the Lord your God was angry with me and declared that I would not cross the River Jordan to enter the fertile land which he is giving you. I will die in this land and never cross the river, but you are about to go across and occupy that fertile land... When your ancestors went to Egypt, there were only seventy of them. But now the Lord your God has made you as numerous as the stars in the sky. Love the Lord your God and always obey all his laws. (Deuteronomy 4:21-22, 10:22, 11:1).

Because of his assumption of the role of representative and intercessor on behalf of his errant people, Moses has to die vicariously outside the promised land. But he delights in the fulfilment of one of God's promises to the descendants of Abraham: their numbers are as great as the stars in the sky. (Genesis 22:15-17). Moses himself bears no personal guilt at all, but as a vicarious sufferer, he bears his burden in a way that increases his heroic stature. God did not forget his faithful servant Moses, and made his name great, as saviour and liberator of the people of God. His exaltation would not be due to Moses himself, but was the work of God. Like Abraham before him, God made the name of Moses great.

> The Lord judges in favour of the oppressed
> and gives them their rights.
> He revealed his plans to Moses
> and let the people of Israel see his mighty deeds.
> Praise the Lord, all his creatures
> in all the places he rules.
> Praise the Lord, my soul. (Psalm 103:6, 7, 22).

In his role as representative, Moses helps us to understand Jesus better. Moses foreshadows Jesus in Jesus' representative and intercessory role; in Jesus' willingness to take on his shoulders the burden of the sins of the world, so that God's people everywhere might escape the slavery of death and enter their promised land. Jesus does enter the promised land, taking his redeemed people along with him.

It would seem that the assumption of a substitutionary role always involves suffering. This must be so, because the substitute feels a passionate empathy with his

---

[61] Adrian Curtis, *Oxford Bible Atlas*, p. 85.

people, to the extent that he identifies with them, becomes one with them. When they suffer for their sins, when they fail to embrace his self-sacrificing vision, the substitute suffers along with them in his compassion for them, and may be willing to die for them, so that they might escape death. After Jesus' life of suffering service, God brought him joy, in raising him to glory, a glory which he then shares with those for whom he died, thus uniting all the lost and scattered sheep into a union with himself in God's ultimate promised land.

## God still Journeying with his People

"I am" means "with you always." (Exodus 3:12). After their apostasy, as the people continued their journey to the promised land, how would God continue to be with them once they had left his sacred mountain behind them? The Lord told Moses to make a covenant box of acacia wood, lined with gold inside and out, and to place in it the two stone tablets on which the Ten Commandments were engraved. (Exodus 25:10-15). Thus, God's relationship with his people was cast in stone. This box was known as the Ark of the Covenant – Israel's most sacred object, and it was placed in a tent called a tabernacle, as the place where the Lord would dwell with his people during their desert wanderings. When the people moved camp, the Ark was carried with them on two wooden poles. They should have no more need of golden calves. This sacred object survived the conquest of the promised land and was eventually moved into Solomon's new Temple in Jerusalem about 900 BC. It was probably lost when the Temple was plundered and destroyed by the Babylonian armies in 587 BC. By that stage, the Ark had become more or less an idol (a rival god) because of the peoples' insincere worship of God, without the practice of justice and mercy.

The covenant box is a reminder that God created the earth as a kind of tabernacle, so that he would have a place where he could dwell with his people (as his images) while on their journey. The Garden of Eden symbolized this tabernacle, the place where God dwelt with his people in his first covenant with humankind. Jesus inaugurated the new covenant through the indwelling of his Spirit in us, who, along with him are the new Ark; God travelling with us as we journey to our promised land.

The forty-year journey of the Israelites was through a desert wilderness. The people remained slow of heart, not trusting in the Lord to get them home, complaining to Moses when they were hungry and thirsty, when neither food nor water could easily be found in the semi-arid wilderness. But God, through his servant Moses, always came to their rescue, following their complaints. (Exodus 15:22-25; 16:1-36). Because of their turn to idolatry, the first generation never entered the promised land. Eventually, the second generation arrived at the borders of the promised land, east of the River Jordan.

The Israelites' first attempt to approach the promised land was opposed by the Amalekites, a people who were descended from one of Esau's sons, named Amalek. They were a tribe of desert nomads, scattered in an area from the south of Canaan and across the Sinai Peninsula. "They attacked and defeated the Israelites and pursued them as far as Hormah," a town in what was later southern Judah. (Numbers 14:39-45; Deuteronomy 1:41-46). The Amalekites were a foretaste of what the Israelites would face in the promised land, even after they became fully established there. This tribe was a constant threat to Israel during the period of Judges and the early Kings. They would suddenly raid an area for booty and escape fast on their camels. (Judges 3:13; 6:3, 33; 10:12; 1 Samuel 15:2, 15; 30:1-20). Eventually, these people were absorbed into other nations and the tribe died out. (1 Chronicles 4:41-43).

## Obedience to the Word of God

"Moses said to the people, 'Obey all the laws I am giving you, and you will *live* and occupy the land which the Lord, the God of your ancestors, is giving you.'" (Deuteronomy 4:1). In order to give the people encouragement and hope for their difficult journey, the promise of a land with all the resources to sustain their lives is held up before them. In other words, the sovereign God gives them the hope that their struggling is going somewhere, thus making their journey meaningful. There is one condition: they must be obedient to the Lord. And that makes perfect sense, because they cannot make this journey solely through their own efforts and schemes, which may often be misguided, and thus against the will of God, leading them nowhere. "He gives me new strength. He guides me by the right path, as he has promised." (Psalm 23:3).

In applying that promise to ourselves, God is telling us that in following his word and way, we will come to "occupy the land," in other words, we will come to live in the destiny which God has promised and has prepared for us – our "promised land" as the only "land" that can satisfy deepest human hungering and thirsting. Deuteronomy goes on to tell the people about the promised land:

> The Lord your God is bringing you into a fertile land – a land that has rivers and springs gushing out into the valleys; a land that produces wheat and barley, grapes, figs, pomegranates, olives and honey. There you will never go hungry, or ever be in need… Make certain that you do not forget the Lord your God; do not fail to obey any of his laws I am giving you today… When your cattle and sheep, your silver and gold, and all your other possessions have increased, make sure that you do not become proud (self-exaltation) and forget the Lord your God who rescued you from Egypt, where you were slaves… So then you must never think that you have made yourselves wealthy by your own power and strength. (Deuteronomy 8:7-9,11, 13-14, 17).

The people are reminded that the physical gifts of the promised land will not be enough to fully satisfy them, and that they will remain unfulfilled (still hungry) if they forget the Lord their God and the really sustaining food of his love, given to them in the Ten Commandments. They still need the guidance of the Lord to keep them on the right path. So it is to the Lord that they owe their allegiance, and not to their own efforts or schemes. Love is the food that will enable them to create a united and just society, and to continue living in the promised land into the future.

The audience for this teaching was in the later period of the monarchy in Israel, when a turn to materialistic gods was leading the people towards death and destruction.

(Deuteronomy 8:18-20). Forgetting the God who liberated them, and turning to materialism would lead to their death as a people. It would mean individuals going their own way while ignoring the needs of others in the community. (See Isaiah 53:6a). The Prodigal Son, placing all his trust in his material inheritance, left the communion of his family and set out as a lone individual with all the freedom to do whatever he wanted. Instead of finding a "promised land" he ended up doing the work of a slave, the material things in which he had placed his trust for salvation having now deserted him – no fulfilment, nothing but starvation and death staring him. (Luke 15:13-17).

It is God who gives human beings every gift they have, including the power to acquire wealth. And if the Israelites forget this lesson, and give their allegiance to the gods of materialism, they might have to go back into the wilderness once again, in order to re-learn it. The following passage is taken from a speech of Moses, addressed to the people, reminding them that if they disobey the Lord in the promised land, they will once again be scattered among other nations in a new wilderness. But the Lord will still not abandon those who search for him:

> 'I call heaven and earth as witnesses against you today that if you disobey me you will soon disappear from the land. You will not live long in the land across the Jordan that you are about to occupy. You will be completely destroyed. The Lord will scatter you among other nations, where only a few of you will survive. There you will serve gods made by human hands, gods of wood and stone. There you will look for the Lord your God, and if you search for him with all your heart, you will find him. When you are in trouble and all these things happen to you, then you will finally turn to the Lord your God and obey him. He is a merciful God. He will not abandon you or destroy you, and he will not forget the covenant that he himself made with your ancestors.' (Deuteronomy 4:26-31).

There are close ties between Deuteronomy chapter 8 and Jesus' temptations in the wilderness: the testing theme, the wilderness setting, the theme of hunger, the forty days. In Deuteronomy, God is presented as father of the people as a whole. (Deuteronomy 1:31; 8:5). The evangelists present Jesus as Son of God. (Matthew 1:11; Mark 1:11; Luke 3:22). But this time, the child (Jesus) is obedient, trusting fully in God, and not on bread (material things) alone. God receives an unambiguous answer from Jesus to the question posed in Deuteronomy 8:2: 'Will you obey these commandments?' Jesus is the model for the faithful community. When Jesus was hungry, God sustained him, gave him life, with God's Word. When the tempter asked Jesus to turn the desert stones into bread, Jesus replied (quoting Deuteronomy 8:3), "The Scripture says, 'Human beings cannot live on bread alone, but need every word God speaks.'" (See Matthew 4:4; Luke 4:4). Jesus made his decision to obey the word of God (a word of forgiveness, peace and reconciliation). In so doing, he rejected the false gods of empire: bread, oppressive power and military might. Jesus would reach his promised land at the end of his journey.

## The Last Words of Moses

Deuteronomy, chapters 29-31 are about the Lord's covenant with Israel while the people rested in the Land of Moab before their entry to the promised land. It was here that Moses gave his farewell address to the people, reminding them of the blessings that would flow from keeping the covenant:

> The command that I am giving you today is not too difficult or beyond your reach… It is not on the other side of the ocean. You do not have to ask, 'Who will go across the ocean and bring it to us, so that we may hear it and obey it?' No, it is here with you. You know it and can quote it, so now obey it… I am now giving you the choice between life and death, between God's blessing and God's curse, and I call heaven and earth to witness the choice you have made. Choose life. Love the Lord your God, obey him and be faithful to him, and then you and your descendants will live long in the land that he promised to give your ancestors, Abraham, Isaac and Jacob. (Deuteronomy 30:11-12, 19-20).

Chapter 32 has the beautiful Song of Moses to the people, part of which follows below. The Word of God makes things happen; it is fruitful; it creates new and flourishing life. The Lord led and protected his people in the wilderness, but when they entered the promised land, they grew fat and forgot the Lord their God and his liberating word.

> Earth and sky, hear my words,
> listen closely to what I say.
> My teaching will fall like drops of rain
> and form on the earth like dew.
> My words will fall like showers on young plants,
> like gentle rain on tender grass.
> I will praise the name of the Lord,
> and his people will tell of his greatness…
> The Lord chose Jacob's descendants for himself.
> He found them wandering through the desert,
> a desolate windswept wilderness.
> He protected them and cared for them.
> Like an eagle teaching its young to fly,
> catching them safely on his spreading wings,
> the Lord kept Israel from falling.
> The Lord alone led his people
> without the help of a foreign god…
>
> Then the Lord's people grew rich, but rebellious;
> they were fat and stuffed with food.
> They abandoned God their creator
> and rejected their mighty saviour…

'I, and I alone am God; no other god is real...
As surely as I am the living God,
I raise my hand and vow
that I will sharpen my flashing sword
and see that justice is done.'
(Deuteronomy 32:1-3, 9-12, 19, 39, 41; see Isaiah 55:10-11).

"That poem is a development of monotheistic thought as reflected in the prophecy of Isaiah." (Isaiah 45:5-7).[62] "I am the Lord; there is no other god. I will give you the strength you need." (Isaiah 45:5). This is wisdom poetry. Both the poet and wisdom teacher stress the perfection of God in contrast to the waywardness of the people. Compare with Isaiah 1:2-3. "The Lord alone led his people without the help of a foreign god." (Deuteronomy 32:12). In the latter quote the existence of other gods is recognised. But that prepares the ground for the monotheism of Deuteronomy 32:39, reflecting Isaiah 44:6: 'I, and I alone, am God; no other god is real.' Israel's sin echoes prophetic warnings. (Hosea 11:1-3; 13:4-6). But the Lord will rescue his people, and will ask them, 'Where are those mighty gods you trusted?' (Deuteronomy 32:37). The Lord is in control of history; "he will see that justice is done." (Deuteronomy 32:41).

At the beginning of the Book of Deuteronomy, the obligations of the covenant are spelled out by Moses in the following inspiring passage in which there is a full statement of monotheism - "there is no other God." (4:39). These words are addressed to Israel and to all people everywhere.

Search the past, the time before you were born, all the way back to the time when God created humanity on the earth. Has anything as great as this ever happened before? Has anyone ever heard anything like this? Have any people ever lived after hearing a god speak to them from a fire, as you have? Has any god ever dared to go and take a people from another nation and make them his own, as the Lord your God did for you in Egypt? Before your very eyes, he used his great power and strength; he brought plagues and war, worked miracles and wonders, and caused terrifying things to happen. The Lord has shown you this, to prove that he alone is God and that there is no other. He let you hear his voice from heaven so that he could instruct you; and here on earth he let you see his holy fire and spoke to you from it. Because he loved your ancestors, he chose you, and by his great power he himself brought you out of Egypt... So remember today and never forget: The Lord is God in heaven and on earth. There is no other God. Obey all his laws that I have given you today, and all will go well for you and your descendants. (Deuteronomy 4:32-37, 39-40).

Then the Lord said to Moses, 'Go to the Abarim Mountains in the Land of Moab opposite the city of Jericho. Climb Mount Nebo (to the east of Jericho on the far side of the River Jordan) and look across to the land of Canaan that I am about to give to the people of

---

[62] Lawrence Boadt, *Reading the Old Testament*, p. 154.

Israel. You will die on that mountain as your brother Aaron died on Mount Hor.' (Deuteronomy 32:48-50; see the Book of Numbers 20:22-29). Moses ascended Mount Nebo, solitary as he had always been, the lone hero who shouldered the burdens of his people. The Lord spoke his word to Moses on Mount Sinai. He would now meet Moses on another mountain, and care for him at his death.

Moses' life and work are affirmed by God's presence with him at his death. He is a model for leadership and strength for subsequent generations.

How credible is the account of the death of Moses? The account may be legendary. "But legend gains authenticity by virtue of its ability to influence the shape of mores and morals in subsequent generations."[63]

In Deuteronomy chapter 33, Moses, the man of God, blesses the tribes of Israel before he dies:

> The Lord came from Mount Sinai; he rose like the sun over Edom and shone on his people from Mount Paran. Ten thousand angels were with him, a flaming fire at his right hand. The Lord loves his people and protects those who belong to him. So we bow at his feet and obey his commands... 'People of Israel, no god is like your God, riding in splendour across the sky, riding through the clouds to come to your aid. God has always been your defence; his eternal arms have been your support. So, Jacob's descendants, live in peace, secure in a land full of corn and wine, where dew from the sky waters the earth... Israel, how happy you are! There is no one like you, a nation saved by the Lord.' (Deuteronomy 33:2-3, 26-29).

(Mount Paran lies south of Kadesh-Barnea (just south of Judea) in the Sinai Peninsula). The Israelites camped there on their way from Egypt to Canaan.[64] (Genesis 21:20-21; Numbers 10:12).

> So, Moses, the Lord's servant, died there in the land of Moab, as the Lord had said he would. The Lord buried him in a valley in Moab, opposite the town of Bethpeor, but to this day, no one knows the exact place of his burial... The people of Israel mourned for him for thirty days in the plains of Moab... There has never been a prophet in Israel like Moses, whom the Lord spoke with, face to face. No other prophet has ever done miracles and wonders like those that the Lord sent Moses to perform. No other prophet has been able to do the great and terrifying things that Moses did in the sight of all Israel. (Deuteronomy 34:5-6, 8, 10-12).

Deuteronomy contains a promise of a new Moses, in the following words of his, spoken to the people: "The Lord your God will send you a prophet like me from among your own people, and you are to obey him." (Deuteronomy 18:15). What set Moses apart from other

---

[63] Duane L. Christensen, *A Song of Power and the Power of Song, Essays on the Book of Deuteronomy*, (Eisenbrauns) 1993, p. 191.

[64] *Oxford Bible Atlas*, p. 79.

prophets was that he had conversed with God "face to face." This was the foundation of his works, the source of the Law, showing Israel the path to follow.

Israel remained waiting for definitive liberation through a new Moses. Jesus would be this new prophet, one who would not only converse with God face to face but would be granted a real vision of the face of God, enabling him to speak from seeing, so that he could communicate God's will to the world, first hand – the salvation for which the world was waiting. No other prophet would do the miracles and wonders that the Lord sent Jesus to perform. What was partially true of Moses, has been fully realized in Jesus, who as Son, lives before the face of God in intimate communion with the Father.

## Exodus and the Call to Mission

"I have heard the cry of my people and now I am sending you to rescue them." (Exodus 3:9). All of the above leads to the question, is the Exodus narrative just a "once upon a time" story, or is there a message here for us today? Is God speaking to us today as he spoke to Moses and the Hebrew tribes from a firey mountain? Can he work the same miracles today? Moses had an experience of God as liberator at the burning bush, and he was then sent on a mission of liberation. How might God be calling us to mission today, and in what sense can mission be associated with liberation?

Throughout the Bible, fire is used as a metaphor for God, perhaps signifying his burning passion to create peace, justice and mercy on earth, and his desire to fill human beings with the same burning qualities, so that they can be his hands and feet in the world. (See Acts of the Apostles, chapter 2). Life has a meaning and purpose given to it by God, who acts to create justice on earth, though his will is frustrated by human beings, who often prefer to follow their own way and give their allegiance to a variety of golden calves. Responding to a call to mission can be difficult and challenging, but this is what gives meaning and purpose to our lives.

God speaks to us through his word in the Bible. It is in the Bible that we find the knowledge, wisdom and understanding of God, his passion for righteousness and justice. His inspiring word can burn through us like fire, with its power to impel us forward on the road he wants us to travel. But how does he call us to mission?

As was the case with Moses, we are called away from our comfort zone to the work of liberation. We may be in bondage to things of lesser account, what Exodus calls rival gods, to the extent that these things take over our lives and prevent us from focusing on what God wants us to do in furtherance of his creative purposes. From being overly concerned with the self, God may be calling us to free ourselves from such a bondage and undertake a journey of service to our neighbour.

The Christian journey begins with the discovery of God's will for us, what he wants us to do. This can happen through reflection, but also through our interaction with one another. How is it that God can speak to us through people? It is because we are created in God's image. Thus, it is often through seeing the image of God in one another, that we come to experience, hear and discover God, and what he wants us to do.

The Ten Commandments show that the way to love God is to love our neighbour. Israel's God was never much concerned about people offering animal sacrifices to him.

What God cares about is how human beings treat one another. An actual experience of some need in another person, may be a voice silently calling us to go to his or her aid, which might involve us in self-sacrifice. (Luke 10:25-37). Or the call might come through a spoken word, challenging us to act or to take a new direction. (Luke 19:5). It can also be the word of another person who may be completely unaware that his or her words are the voice of God to us. This means that we should be ever alert for this voice, waiting for it every moment of our lives. (Mark 13:35-37). Prayer is more about God talking to us, rather than our speaking to God, so we need to be listening. The call will not usually be to heroic missionary work, but rather in the doing of little things. For example, there are many people with whom we interact on a daily basis. The question is, do they go away as better persons for having engaged with us through word or deed? Perhaps, more often than not, the answer is no. But this should at least be our aim.

As regards relationships in the workplace, it might be just a matter of extending a helping hand to an associate - informing, affirming or encouraging a colleague, liberating a person from fears, anxieties, or a sense of inadequacy. A word briefly spoken can be like a seed planted in the earth - slowly and invisibly growing, but eventually emerging like a fruitful vine. (Mark 4:3, 8). It is about sending a person away transformed! It could sometimes mean simply listening empathetically to another person's troubled story. As was the case with Moses, this could involve us in self-sacrifice undertaken for the good of others. It could sometimes mean an extended period of commitment, as in the case with the mission of our life's journey as a whole.

Miracles don't have to be spectacular, like thunder claps above a firey mountain, or raised walls of water at the Red Sea. They are about the transformation of an ordinary experience of interaction with people, to the level of the extraordinary. When we allow God to work in, and through us, something miraculous takes place. Art (any creative endeavour) has often been described as the transfiguration of the commonplace; the art of living should be likewise.

CHAPTER 5

# ISRAEL IN THE PROMISED LAND

## The Books of Joshua and Judges

The Book of Joshua tells the story of Moses' successor, Joshua, who led the people across the River Jordan and into Canaan (modern-day Israel and Palestine), the land promised to Abraham and his descendants. The book opens with God calling Joshua to be the leader of his people, with the promise: 'I will be with you.' (Joshua 1:5). The Israelites were then faced with the problem that the land was already occupied by other tribes, so according to the Book of Joshua, a war of conquest ensued. The most significant part of the book (24:14-28) is Joshua's farewell address to the elders and leaders of the people–a passage which resembles the final address of Moses. Faithfulness (obedience) to the God of Abraham, Isaac and Jacob is the one guarantee of continual possession of the land promised by God to Abraham. "Now then," Joshua admonished, "honour the Lord and serve him sincerely and faithfully. Get rid of the gods your ancestors used to worship in Mesopotamia and in Egypt and serve only the Lord." (Joshua 24:14).

The Books of Joshua and Judges cover a period from about 1,200 BC to about 1,000 BC, when the monarchy was introduced in Israel. The Book of Joshua was not finally edited and compiled until the end of the Babylonian exile in 537 BC, about 650 years later than the events described. The story from Joshua to Kings is not history in the modern sense. The authors make use of a wide variety of sources: folklore, legends, songs and oral heroic tales. The characters are idealized and the events are exaggerated. The Books of Joshua and Judges were not intended as a chronological record of events, but as a religious interpretation of an important era in Israel's history. The authors' concern was how God was revealing himself, and how his people might discover his will through their life experiences. Thus, it is the religious meaning of those far-off events that is important: God is faithful to his promises. He will always be with his people, helping them in their time of need. He calls them to be faithful to him. Therefore, they should trust in this God alone for their salvation.

The Book of Joshua is a continuation of the Israelite epic which began with Exodus. The biblical authors probably wanted this story to end with God's decisive victory over the forces of evil, recalling its beginnings when God challenged the oppressive rule of the Egyptian Pharaoh. Therefore, the thrust of the book is about the sovereignty of

God over evil, symbolized by Canaanite culture in the promised land. In this sense the Book of Joshua foreshadows Jesus' kingdom of God proclamation – God's ultimate reign over all destructive forces. Understood in this sense, Joshua is prophetic of the ultimate conquest of death by Jesus Christ.

Interpreted as an epic, everything in Joshua is presented on a grand scale. And just as the scale of the conquests is exaggerated, so also are the accounts of killings in the captured Canaanite towns. Exaggerations abound in such narratives, and we must not interpret them literally. There was never an epic from the ancient world which did not portray violence and killing. The pagan gods of Greece, Rome and Egypt never sought to place any restraints on human murdering. In those nations' stories and epics, rival gods symbolically participated in the killings. The authors of the Bible were way ahead of the ideals of those nations, in their portrayal of a God who wanted to liberate people from murderous victimization (slavery in Egypt, for example) and guide them towards covenantal obedience to himself, so that human communities might grow and bear the fruit of peaceful union. It would be a long time yet before they would give up war and violence as the means of establishing union. The later prophets would eventually condemn militarism and murderous cruelty. (Amos chaps. 1-2; Ezekiel 32:23-30; Zechariah 9:9-10).

The wars of Joshua may have little to do with the message of Jesus, but they help us to see how people three thousand years ago struggled to make sense of their world. They had a limited understanding of God, as a tribal God fighting their battles. In the broader sense, we can interpret Joshua and Judges as revealing a message for ourselves. How we too might discover the will of God through our maturing life experiences and thus prepare ourselves for the inheritance God has in store for us (entry into our promised land) in the light of Jesus' conquest of evil and death.

Rather than due to military conquest as such, the Israelites' religious faith was probably the main reason why they gradually, but slowly rose to prominence and became the dominant nation in that region under King David, about 1000 BC.

## A Large-scale Invasion not Supported by Archaeology

What was the situation in Canaan at the time of Joshua? First of all, there was no centralized government in this part of the Near East at that time. The reality was more in the nature of a number of self-governing towns built on hill fortresses, and trading with one another.

The Israelites entered the promised land as a band of nomads, bringing with them their sheep and goats, and having little or no experience of warfare or settled farming. The native tribes which occupied the fortified towns were technically superior to them in every respect. The Israelites would initially have occupied the hill country away from the Canaanite towns.

Although there is much in Joshua about war and ethnic cleansing, the account should be interpreted not as a war of conquest at all, but more like the gradual incursion of a small tribal band of people into the land of Canaan, with perhaps other groups following them later. These groups could have joined forces with like-minded groups already in Canaan. Like the Israelites, such groups may have been living in the hill country of Canaan, having themselves previously escaped from the tyranny and enslavement of the Canaanite city States. An archaeological investigation of the ancient city of Hazor in northern Canaan reveals that it was not destroyed by war (no weapons discovered), but by burning, in about 1,250 BC. Examination of its habitations revealed that it had an upper city inhabited by elites and a lower city of slaves. Rebellion from below may have led to the burning of the city and the dispersion of its inhabitants. Such rebellions may have been fairly common. According to the most recent scholarly proposal, a peasant revolt took place throughout Canaan and the victorious lower classes came to identify themselves with the Israelites and their faith in a liberating God. (Joshua 24:1-28). Some scholars suggest that the local peoples who converted to the God of Israel made up the majority of the northern tribes of Israel. [65]

What may have united all repressed groups (including the Israelites) was the notion of a liberating God whom the Israelites discovered through Moses at the burning bush in Midian. Numbers of Canaanites and Hebrews could have been bound together in a new vision by a God who represented freedom, the freedom of people to work for themselves and keep the fruits of their labour, rather than handing most of it over to oppressive elites.

No extra-biblical historical evidence supports a large-scale invasion of the land of Canaan. Recent archaeological studies indicate that Israel never invaded Canaan from the outside, certainly not in the unified, massive way described in the Book of Joshua.[66] Chapter 8 of Joshua tells of the capture of the Canaanite town of Ai, Joshua having picked 30,000 of his best troops! Joshua never had 30,000 troops, nor 1,000 troops. His forces are reported to have burned the town and killed all its inhabitants. All of this making for a tale of epic proportions! The entry of the Israelites into Canaan would have been scarcely noticed. Any kind of a military conquest would have been out of the question.

Later in Joshua we learn that "very much of the land remains to be possessed" (Joshua 13:1), and that is confirmed in the first chapter of the later Book of Judges. It is likely that Joshua was a hero of the tribe of Ephraim and may have been involved in local skirmishes with Canaanites.[67] The fact that the Book of Joshua is not history in the modern sense is confirmed by archaeological discoveries. For example, archaeology reveals that the ruins of the city of Ai (Joshua 8:3-7) date from the third millennium BC, long before the time of Joshua. The place was unoccupied in the 13th century, at the time of Joshua. The same holds true for the capture of Jericho in chapter six, with its walls miraculously tumbling down. Archaeology shows that Jericho has left no surviving walls from the century of Joshua's attack on the town. [68] The emergence of Israel in Canaan was slow and complicated. The Book of Joshua conveys the impression of the Israelites having a

---

[65] Michael W. Duggan, *The Consuming Fire, A Christian Guide to the Old Testament*, (Our Sunday Visitor Publishing Division), Huntington, Indiana, 2010, p. 216.

[66] M. D. Coogan, *The Old Testament, A Historical and Literary Introduction to the Hebrew Scriptures* (OUP), 2014, p. 207.

[67] Ibid, p. 207.

[68] Ibid, p. 207.

large army under one leader, which swept through the region in triumph. By contrast the Book of Judges offers a picture of various tribes facing ongoing conflict with local people and even with one another. (Joshua 11:23; 7:2-5). Israelite control of the promised land was not achieved until the end of the eleventh century BC, i.e. about 1,000 BC.

Moreover, as we discover from the Books of Joshua, Judges, Samuel and Kings, most of the Israelites were not strict monotheists (believers in one God only) until much later times. Archaeological evidence supports this by the discovery, all over the land of Israel, of innumerable figurines (small statues) of pagan deities–usually fertility goddesses. Archaeology also reveals that the only kind of pottery discovered in the land of Israel is Canaanite pottery. God's chosen people were then not so much one particular race or tribe, but a people who chose to be free, and who discovered a liberating God in the process. The Hebrews' story of their escape from Egypt began to be told and passed on by word of mouth as poetry, such stories further binding all like-minded people together (including Canaanites) and giving them a new identity as the people of a liberating God.

What is striking to modern readers of the Bible, is Israel's insistence that their God fought directly for them and won all their victories, as the divine warrior. At the heart of this is the notion of the tribal, or national God. At that time, all the other nations in the Near East believed that their own particular god gave them victory on the battlefield. In this respect, Israel was no different. "The Lord fought for Israel." (Joshua 10:14, 42; 23:3, 10). The notion of the tribal God was a very limited understanding of the divine. The much later prophets refined the idea of God, in their proclamation that there existed only one God, who created the universe. (See Isaiah 40:21-31). Therefore, this God has the interests of all nations and all peoples at heart. Isaiah's revelation put paid to the idea of each nation having its own god - with all the implications of that for rivalry and strife. What we see in the Bible is the idea of God gradually revealing himself, but in a way only understandable to people at a particular time. In earlier times, people were not receptive to the full truth of who God is. Later revelation produced far more noble ideals, as when the prophets foresaw all nations eventually coming to faith in the Creator God, being joined to Israel and living in peace. (See Isaiah 2:2-4; 19:23-25; 45:22-25; Zechariah 8:22-23). The revelation of God in all its fullness only comes with Jesus Christ. (See Matthew 5:43-45).

We may interpret Joshua as a cautionary tale about what the people are not to do in order to avoid the fate of the Northern kingdom of Israel, when its people lost the promised land and were taken into exile in 721 BC by the Assyrian empire. All because they had deserted God for the gods of silver and gold - gods of power and affluence! With this scenario in mind, the Book of Joshua cannot have been written before 721 BC.

From the start of their entry to the promised land, there was a much greater threat to the Israelites than that posed by the Canaanites. At about the same time as the Israelites entered Canaan, a race of war-like sea people, known as the Philistines, took possession of a strip of land on the Mediterranean coast to the west of Canaan. The Philistines were a trading nation. They eventually formed a confederation of five cities (Gaza, Ashdod, Ashkelon, Gath and Ekron), some of which were on the coast and others further inland in Canaanite territory. Their presence in Israelite territory inevitably led to conflict between them and the Israelites. As the years progressed, it was actually the

Philistines, and not the Canaanites who continued to cause most of the trouble for the Israelites - all the way down to the time of King David. The Philistines followed the Canaanite religions – the Baal and Ashtaroth gods. (Joshua 13:2-3; Judges 3:3; 16:5, 8, 27, 30; 1 Samuel 5:11; 6:4, 12, 16-18, 7:7; 29:6-7).

Joshua ends like Exodus, with Joshua gathering all the tribes of Israel together with their elders, leaders and judges for a farewell address which took place at Shechem. They all presented themselves before God. (Joshua 24:1-1). Their promise to serve the Lord their God was the same as that given by their forebears at the foot of Mount Sinai (Exodus 24:3) – both proving to be empty promises. Then Joshua addressed the people:

> This is what the Lord, the God of Israel has to say, 'Long ago your ancestors lived on the other side of the River Euphrates and worshiped other gods... Now then, honour the Lord and serve him sincerely and faithfully. Get rid of the gods your ancestors used to worship in Mesopotamia and in Egypt, and serve only the Lord. If you are not willing to serve him, decide today whom you will serve, the gods whom your ancestors used to worship in Mesopotamia or the gods of the Amorites, in whose land you are now living. As for my family and me, we will serve the Lord.' The people replied, 'We would never leave the Lord to serve other gods. The Lord our God brought our fathers and us out of the land of Egypt, and we saw the miracles he performed. He kept us safe wherever we went among the nations through which we passed... So we will serve the Lord; he is our God.' (Joshua 24:2, 14-18; see 19-24).

## The Book of Judges

Native Canaanites continued to occupy major towns for hundreds of years after the incursion of the Israelites, and these people may eventually have given their allegiance to the God of Israel, while continuing with their traditional pagan religious practices (worship of the god Baal), even long after the time of King David.

The Book of Judges paints a more realistic picture than Joshua concerning the difficulties which the Israelites encountered in their continual struggle for survival in the promised land. (See Judges, chapters 1, 2, 5). The book can also be enjoyed as literature. For example, we can compare the characters' contrasting personalities and traits, as revealed in their words and actions.

The book is composed of stories from the lawless period of Israel's history between the entry of the Hebrew tribes to Canaan and the establishment of the monarchy about 1,000 BC. The stories are about the exploits of local or national heroes known as "judges," most of whom were local military leaders rather than judges in the legal sense. One of the better known of them was Samson. (See Chapters 13-16).

Judges 1:1–3:6 introduces the plot of the book–the setting, time and place. The reader learns that the book is going to be about the troubled relationship of the Israelites with God. The lesson of the book is that Israel's survival depends on loyalty to its God. But even when the nation is disloyal to God, and disaster follows, God is always ready to forgive and save his people when they repent and turn to him again.

The book can be divided into three parts: events up to the death of Joshua (1:1–2:10); the Judges of Israel (2:11–16:31); deterioration of life and leadership (17:1–21:25).

The tradition behind the First Book of Samuel (13:19-22, a time later than Judges) recalls the Philistines' technical superiority and political dominance over their Israelite neighbours. When the Philistines arrived in Canaan, they brought with them the secret of making iron tools and weapons. These were superior to the bronze implements of the Canaanites. It appears that they had a standing army. (1 Samuel 27:2; 28:1). Initially, Philistia was only a coastal strip, but in the second half of the 11th century, the Philistines began to extend their power inland to territories occupied by both the Israelites and the Canaanite tribes.

From then on, the struggle for dominance was between the Israelites and the Philistines, resulting in repeated armed conflict. Local struggles against the Philistines gave rise to tales of heroic military leaders, such as Samson. (Judges, chapters 13-16). The threat posed by the Philistines was so great that tales featuring an Israelite local hero, such as Samson outwitting them, became popular. Eventually, some of the local figures evolved into national heroes, Samuel for example, and Saul, who became the first king of Israel. (See 1 Samuel). Only during the reign of King David, were the Philistines finally driven back to their original territories, and peace established.

The tales of individual judges (3:7–16:31) are little "plots within the plot"–the relationship with God rising and falling, the direction being mostly downward. God's judgement works in cycles that characterize Israel's life in Judges. (1) The people sin by worshiping the Canaanite god, Baal. (2) This violates the covenant with God and provokes his anger. (3) The Lord then hands the people over to their enemies. (4) Due to distress under oppression by their enemies, the Israelites cry out for deliverance. (5) Finally, the Lord raises up a military leader, known as a Judge to deliver the people from oppression. (2:11-19). Then the cycle begins all over again.

This pattern would run its course. The level of sin worsens until the circular pattern becomes a downward spiral into chaos. The successive judges become increasingly flawed and ineffective, and as in the case of Samson, the conflict deteriorates into private feuds and vengeance. Repeatedly, Israel responds to God's gracious deliverance of the people with further misbehaviour, which is always associated with the worship of other gods. We hear the phrase repeated: "The people of Israel sinned against the Lord and began to serve the Baals." (2:11-12; also 4:1). But repentance and crying out to the Lord would bring deliverance from enemies. (10:15-16). This was also a message for the exiles in Babylon, to whom the Book of Judges was probably directed, it having been finally edited in that later time (587-537 BC).

There was also a threat to the Israelites from the Midianites to the south of Canaan. When the Israelites sinned against the Lord, these war-like people ruled over them for seven years. When the Midianites camped on their land for a period, the Israelites had to hide from them in caves and other safe places in the hills. Those raiders then destroyed their crops and took away their sheep, cattle and donkeys. (Judges 6:1-6). Then an angel of the Lord appeared to the Judge Gideon and said, 'The Lord is with you, brave and mighty man.' Gideon asked the Lord, 'How could all of this happen to the people if the Lord was with them?' What about all the wonderful things the Lord did when he brought their ancestors out of Egypt? Then the Lord sent Gideon on a mission of rescuing Israel from the Midianites. But Gideon proffered the excuse that his clan was the weakest of the tribe of Manasseh and that he himself was the least important member of his family. This resembles the excuses of Moses when he was called to a rescuing mission. (Exodus 3:11). The Lord said, 'You can do it because I will help you.' (Judges 6:12-16). The message again is to trust in the Lord to do what weak humans cannot do. God and human beings can work in unison to accomplish God's purposes. But how can such a calamity be inflicted by the Midianites on the people, if God is with them? We know from life experience that bad things do happen to good people. So we ask, where is God then? God may not grant us what we want in a given situation.

It would be difficult to accept the folktales in Judges as actual history. However, the stories reveal a good deal about the social history and worldview of Israel's early period. The Book of Judges seems to reflect accurately the egalitarian society that represented the early stages of Israel's development. There were no ruling kings and no urban elites. What we find in Judges is a loose association of small agricultural Israelite villages located in the highlands, and away from Canaanite power centres. Life was marked by insecurity, because of enemy attacks and recurring warfare. (See chapter 5, the Song of Deborah, who was one of the earliest of the judges). The Book of Judges is realistic about the dominance of the Canaanite city States. Because of the Canaanite walled cities and chariot brigades, the Israelite tribes were involved in an unequal struggle against them. (Judges 4-5). Local village elders (8:14, 16; 11:5, 11) provided day-to-day administration, but warfare demanded the leadership of talented heroes. (11:4-11). "In broad outline, at least, this picture corresponds with what archaeology reveals about early Iron Age Palestine."[69]

The problem of Judges is that native people remain in the land to tempt Israel into disobedience of the Lord. (Judges 2:3). Intermarriage leads to further disobedience. (3:1-6). Israel tends to drift into ever more serious misbehaviour. (2:19). The decline happens in relation to war, government, family life and relationships between men and women.

In his twenty years as a Judge, Samson never subdued the Philistines. (15:20). In one local victory, he is reported to have killed a thousand Philistines with the jawbone of a donkey! (15:9-20). Samson became sexually associated with a prostitute in Gaza. (16:1-3). Soon after this he fell in love with a Philistine woman named Delilah, who was the cause of his downfall. (See Judges 16). Samson was an image of the anarchy that Israel had become in the promised land. In a strange epitaph, the Book of Judges says: "Samson killed many more men when he died than while he lived." (16:30). Israel does not die, but neither is it delivered.

Apostasy at pagan religious shrines is a regular occurrence. (Judges 17:5; 8:27). Throughout the book, warnings from God are of no avail. (2:1-5; 6:7-10; 10:11-14). Israel continues doing "what was evil in the eyes of the Lord." (2:11; 3:12; 4;1; 10:6; 13:1). When the people sin against the Lord, things go bad for them. (6:1-6). The Lord is emotionally involved with Israel, in both anger and compassion. Following repentance, he is moved

---

[69] Nelson, *Interpreting Historical Texts, The Historical Books*, p. 98, quoting Lawrence Stager, *The Archaeology of the Family in Ancient Israel*, (BASOR Zob), 1985, pp.1-35.

to pity. Towards the end of the book, God's involvement with Israel drops down to zero. The people resort to pagan practices without seeking divine guidance. (Chapters 17-18). The pessimism reflected in 2:1-5, 19; 6:7-10 and 10:6-14 is heightened by the revelation that Israel will eventually be taken into exile and captivity. (18:30). National leaders who advocate destructive policies, have replaced the Judges.

The Book of Judges closes with a terrible description of the deterioration of Israel's religious, social and political life. (Chapters 17-21). There are stories of theft, kidnapping and civil war between the Israelite tribes. In private life, there is a lack of hospitality. There are accounts of rape, murder and irregular marriage arrangements. In the public arena, there is no leadership. Chapter 18 begins with the phrase, "There was no king in Israel at that time," which could mean that God had abandoned the people as their king. In chapter 19 there is a terrible description of a woman who was repeatedly raped (19:20-30), an incident which led to a civil war between the tribe of Benjamin and the other tribes. (20-21:10-12). This is the only time in Judges that all of the tribes united in warfare, not to attack an enemy that threatened them, but to punish one of their own tribes, that of Benjamin.

At this stage, the reader of the Bible may be wondering what else could God do that he hadn't done for his people. He rescued them from slavery and brought them to a land "flowing with milk and honey." Yet, all that they have experienced is dysfunctional personal lives, inter-tribal warfare and neighbouring peoples coming to oppress them. He gave them a covenant by which the tribes might live in harmony with one another, which was God's will for them. God's salvation is only effective when complemented by human obedience and commitment. Yet, the Book of Judges points to hope. Israel is challenged to repent once again and put away foreign gods. (10:16).

Does Israel need a king? Chapters 17-21 illustrate the military and ethical problems that are associated with kingship. The book closes with the phrase that began chapter 18: "There was no king in Israel at that time." This time, there is an additional phrase: "All the people did what they pleased." (21:25). The implication here, is that there will eventually be a king, one to unite them with a common purpose. The ending of Judges looks forward to Samuel, who was both a Judge and prophet, and one who would resist the Philistines and establish the monarchy.

## Baal Worship

When the Hebrew tribes entered the land of Canaan, they found a religion there, in which the forces of nature were worshiped in a variety of rites and rituals. The land of Israel was a gift from God to the Israelites. The danger always was that in taking the gift for granted, the people might forget the giver of the gift and attribute this largess to their own efforts. Would they be influenced by the Canaanite culture in which the inhabitants saw themselves under the protection of numerous fertility gods? God's people had received warnings about turning to pagan gods before they entered the land. (Deuteronomy 6:10-14).

The Canaanite tribes' view of the gods was a complete contrast to the God of Israel, who was personal, concerned about the salvation of people, with them in their struggles and calling them to live in obedience to his will in a covenant relationship. (See Exodus 24:1-3). The call to a covenant relationship means that there was a moral quality about Israel's God that was lacking in the gods of the other nations, whose people, unlike Israel, had no sense of sin, and did not see their gods as personal.

Unlike the Canaanite gods - who were personified in storms - rain, drought, heat from the sun, the growth of crops and sexual fertility - the God of Israel stood above the frailties and temptations of human beings. He was not identified with the seasons, but controlling them, and acting as sovereign over the nations and history. This God was faithful and merciful, never capricious or uncertain, but demanding strict moral standards from his people.

The Canaanites developed rituals to win the favour of the gods by maximising fertility, both for the soil, the animal and human populations. There was an anxiety about whether the gods could control fertility, because it was felt that human efforts were not enough. Failure in crops could mean starvation, and human birth rates had to remain high to offset the very high infancy mortality rates. There was an emphasis on performing sexual actions for the purpose of bringing about fertility. These practices involved ritual prostitution, both male and female, at religious sites throughout the land, and it often meant parents sacrificing and burning a child in order to appease the god Baal, or gain his favour.

Unlike the Canaanites, the Israelites were new to agriculture. The seductive attraction of Baal worship for the newcomers was that it promised fertility of the land, and thus, economic success. Furthermore, the worship of Baal offered immediate sexual gratification. All of this was roundly condemned by the later prophets when Israelites themselves resorted to child sacrifice and ritual prostitution in Baal worship. (Ezekiel 16:20; Psalm 106:36-39). For the God of Israel, sex was subordinated to marriage and the social good of families.

All of these practices were a constant temptation to the Israelites. Thus, it was not easy for ancient Israel to maintain its distinctive worship of the God of Israel alone. The prosperity of Canaan could be interpreted a as blessing from Baal. Furthermore, the loosening of ethical demands from religious practices made it easier to participate in Baal worship. "If Israel managed to save its faith against such odds, the biblical testimony is that only God's gracious fidelity brought it about."[70]

Archaeological excavations regularly turn up large numbers of small amulets and idols of pagan gods and goddesses in almost every ancient Israelite city that has been discovered by archaeology.[71] Many of these were statuettes of fertility goddesses. This shows that strict monotheism was not practised in Israel from the entry to the promised land until the time of the Babylonian exile in 587 BC. No such idols have been found after the period of the Babylonian exile. Worship of pagan gods was condemned by all of the prophets. (Hosea 4:12-13; Micah 1:7; Jeremiah 2:7-8; 2:23-24; 11:13). The people of many Canaanite towns eventually accepted Israel's faith, but they still held onto their pagan customs and beliefs. Similarly, many Israelites would have found it easy to add some pagan

---

[70] Lawrence Boadt, *Reading the Old Testament*, (Paulist Press), p. 193.

[71] Ibid, p. 183.

practices as part of their devotion to the God of Israel.

Psalm 29, which is entitled "The Voice of the Lord in the Storm," was probably a poem to the storm god Baal, taken over by Israel and applied to Israel's God, in order to emphasise that the Creator God, and not Baal, rules creation. "The voice of the Lord is heard on the seas; the glorious God thunders, and his voice echoes over the ocean... The Lord rules over the deep waters; he rules as king for ever." (Psalm 29:3, 10). It is God we should praise for his power over the storm, not a god identified with the storm. "You made the springs and fountains flow; you dried up large rivers. You created the day and the night; you set the sun and moon in their places." (Psalm 74:15-16). See also Psalms 93:3-4; 98:7-9.

As with all religions, there was some truth in Canaanite beliefs. One of the beliefs common to both Israel and the other near eastern religions was the sense of human dependence on God or the gods. On reflecting on the meaning of life, all human beings become aware of their own powerlessness and dependency, leading them to yearn for a fullness of perfection. Such yearning for the perfect leads to the question, is there any power in the world greater than what human beings can summon up out of their own resources, and if so, does this power care about us or can it come to our rescue in matters over which we ourselves don't have any control?

## Introduction to the Books of Samuel and Kings

The story of the kings of Israel and Judah can be read in First and Second Samuel, First and Second Kings and First and Second Chronicles. These books record the history of the Israelites after the Hebrew tribes established themselves under their own kings in the land of Canaan.

The First Book of Samuel records the transition in Israel from the period of the Judges to the monarchy. This change in Israel's national life revolved around three individuals: Samuel, a prophet, and the last of the Judges; Saul, Israel's first king, and the great king David.

The theme of First Samuel, like that of the other historical writings, is that faithfulness to God brings success, while disobedience brings disaster. There were mixed feelings about the establishment of the monarchy. The Lord himself was regarded as the true king of Israel, but in response to the people's request, the Lord chose a king for them. However, it was of the greatest importance that both the king and the people lived under the sovereignty and judgement of God. (1 Samuel 2:7-10). Living under God's law would ensure that the rights of all people, rich and poor alike, would be respected.

The authors of Joshua, Judges, Samuel and Kings have been called Deuteronomists, in the sense that their basic creed was derived from the Book of Deuteronomy. This creed could be summed up in the statement directed to the people:

> You and your descendants are to honour the Lord your God and obey all his laws (Ten Commandments), so that you may live in the land a long time... Israel, remember this! The Lord – and the Lord alone – is our God. Love the Lord your God with all your heart, with all your soul, and with all your strength. (Deuteronomy 6:2-5).

We note here the emphasis on the one and only God, to whom the people are called to give their whole allegiance, and the implication that such allegiance alone, will guarantee their possession of the land into the future.

The Deuteronomic historians were the founders of an intellectual movement that had great influence in the history of ancient Israel and its literature.[72] This movement formed a 'School,' probably made up of prophets and priests. It was similar to the 'School' which produced the Book of Isaiah over several centuries. It produced the Deuteronomic history (Joshua to Kings), which is an interpretive narrative of Israel's history in the promised land, based on the ideals of the Book of Deuteronomy. It also continued to revise the core text of the Book of Deuteronomy. This history continued to be revised up to the time of the Babylonian exile in 586 BC. The Deuteronomic School also edited the writings of the later prophets. The prophetic book with the closest connection to Deuteronomy is that of Jeremiah, who may have belonged to the Deuteronomic School.

The books of Samuel and Kings are a history of the people's acceptance or rejection of the Lord their God. According to the Deuteronomic historians, God's relationship with human beings is revealed in the ups and downs of history. Peoples' actions have consequences for their future well-being. The authors view their history as meaningful in the sense that it is guided by God towards a goal. In other words, life has a meaning when human beings accept and respect the sovereignty of God in their lives, and trust that he alone can guarantee their future. Rejecting God's sovereignty means turning to god substitutes (military might, political power, silver and gold), in the expectation that these will do for human beings (bring salvation), what only God himself can do. God delegates a share of his power to human beings. He alone is sovereign over the world. He created and controls the stars. 'To whom can you compare me, or who is my equal?' says the Holy One. 'Lift your eyes and look. Who made these stars, if not he who drills them like an army, calling each one by name? So mighty is his power, so great his strength, that not one fails to answer.' (Isaiah 40:25-26, JB).

The Deuteronomists name their sources and use them in their narrative, but their main purpose is theology - God and his relationship with humanity, God guiding history. This four-hundred-year history of the kings of Israel and Judah, is a revelation of the providence of God and his sovereignty over history. This is the Deuteronomists' unique interpretation of history. Thus, because history in the modern sense is not the main purpose of these narratives, "the books of Samuel and Kings must be treated as a story of salvation."[73] The ingratitude of the people and the failures of the two kingdoms of Israel seem to thwart God's purpose. But a small number of faithful people did not bow the knee to god substitutes. "This remnant of Zion (Israel) remained loyal to the covenant and guaranteed the future."[74] The Books of Kings end with the Babylonian conquerors showing favour to King Jehoiachin, Judah's last king, as if signalling the hope of future redemption. (2 Kings 25:27-30).

The later period of the kings of Israel gave rise to the writings of the prophets.

---

[72] M. D. Coogan, *The Old Testament*, (Oxford University Press) 2014, p. 186.

[73] *Jerusalem Bible*, Introduction to the *Books of Kings*.

[74] Ibid.

A number of questions confronted the prophets at this time: Is history shaped by the will of man or the will of God? If human beings seem to control affairs in defiance of God's will at a particular time, and if injustice now reigns, will the sovereign God ultimately establish justice and have the final word on history? The prophets insist that man's greatest efforts at putting the world right must fail. Only God can fulfil messianic hopes (the human desire for the perfect order of things). The insight of the prophets is that history may be a nightmare, but redemption will come, because a good God cannot allow evil to reign for ever.

## Kingship and the Reign of God

In ancient Mesopotamia (the land of the Euphrates and Tigris rivers) kings regarded themselves as representatives of the supreme god of the State. Kingship was regarded as the will of the gods and was seen as an intrinsic element of the social order. The king was believed to have special knowledge of justice, which was what the gods willed for the world. The king had the responsibility of promulgating law, establishing order and caring for the poor. As the representative of the State god, the king led the army in battles against enemies of the State. The king also played a role in religious rituals. He worshiped, honoured and placated the gods who created and maintained the universe. Human beings were servants of the gods. In an annual ritual, the king mated with the High Priestess in order to imitate the divine fertilization of the crops, flocks and people. Some of the above features were borrowed by Israel when they came to have their own kings, but not the last one!

The kings in Israel were all too human - in their departure from the covenant, and in their failure to create justice and mercy in their society. They were called by God as his shepherds to a mission of caring for all of God's people. For the most part, they and their subjects failed to live up to their calling as people whom God loved, and through whom he wanted to carry forward his blessings and spread his light into the world. As we have already seen above, one of the fears of the Book of Deuteronomy was that, instead of inspiring people with feelings of gratitude, the richness of the land given to the people by God would be the very thing to lure them away from him. (Deuteronomy 8:7-8, 13-14). In their new-found prosperity, they felt that everything they had gained, was through their own efforts, so they had no need of God. As if in a declaration of independence from God, the kings placed their reliance on a forbidden fruit (Genesis 2:16-17): the riches of the land, horses and armies and in alliances with foreign nations, as the means of their salvation. They turned these things into gods and bowed down before them.

But God used this period of failure to call his servants the prophets, in order to reveal himself as Creator of the world, and as a God of mercy and compassion, qualities he wanted exemplified among his people in their daily lives. Although we don't fully understand his ways, God still controls history; he knows how to bring good out of evil and will ultimately abolish all evil.

And so, there was much that was negative in the period of the kings. However, in a culture which produced the Books of Genesis, Exodus, Deuteronomy, Samuel and Kings, together with Psalms, the Book of Job and the writings of the prophets - the positives of this period must far outweigh the negatives. This corpus of writing must rank as an achievement, unsurpassed in world literature (ancient or modern), enlightening and inspiring people with noble ideals down the ages.

## Chronicles

The two Books of Chronicles come from a much later period than the Books of Kings. They were written after the Jews returned from the Babylonian exile, and after the time of the prophets Haggai and Zechariah. They were intended as a guide for struggling Judeans back from exile in Babylon. The Books of Chronicles add some new material to the accounts in the Books of Kings. They rarely use political explanations for events. Divine action in the world works at all times and in every situation.[75] The Books of Chronicles offer a reinterpretation of the history from the time of King David to the end of the monarchy in 587 BC. They explain the role of the kings in the past, with an emphasis on how it should have been under their rule. This means that many of the flaws and failings of the kings are not mentioned. For instance, there is nothing in Chronicles about King David's sins. In 2 Chronicles 8, there is an account of Solomon's great achievements, but nothing about his turning away from the Lord and his idolatry. Thus, Chronicles present a more idealized picture than the Books of Kings. They emphasise temple liturgy, ritual purity, loyalty, prayer and worship, and listening to the word of God in the Pentateuch. Chronicles ends with King Cyrus' proclamation in 538 BC for the rebuilding of the temple after the return of the Jewish exiles from Babylon. "The work is best seen as a celebration of the restored worship in the temple at a period when it was at the centre of Jewish life, ca. 300 BC."[76]

## Samuel: Prophet, Priest and Judge

After the entry to the promised land, and for hundreds of years, there had been a loose association of the Hebrew tribes. The basis of their union was their common faith in the God of Abraham, Isaac and Jacob. They worshiped this God at a common shrine in a place called Shiloh (about thirty miles north of Jerusalem) in the Canaanite hill country, but there were other shrines as well. Shiloh was the place where the covenant box, containing the two stone tablets of the Ten Commandments was kept in a shrine known as a tabernacle, before it was moved into Solomon's new temple. Religious festivals were held at Shiloh.[77] (Joshua 18:1, 8-10; 19:51; 22:9,12; Judges 18:31; 21:19-21; 1 Samuel 1:3, 9; 3:21; 4:3).

The First Book of Samuel opens with the woman, Hannah who, for a long time, had been childless, but prayed to the Lord for a son, whom she promised to dedicate to the Lord. Like Hannah, Israel was also producing no fruit. Thus, the Lord had departed from Israel. In a battle with the Philistines, the covenant box was captured, but later returned because of the disturbance it was causing them. (1 Samuel 4). Eventually, the

---

[75] Lawrence Boadt, p. 397.

[76] *The New Jerusalem Bible*, introduction to *Chronicles*.

[77] *World's Bible Dictionary*, p. 404.

Lord answered Hannah's prayer and she had a son whom she named Samuel. Chapter 2 has Hannah's prayer of thanksgiving for the Lord's blessing. Hannah's song must be Luke's inspiration for the Canticle of Mary. (Luke 1:46-56). Compare verses 1-2 of Hannah's prayer with Luke 1:46-49.

"As Samuel grew up, the Lord was with him and made everything that Samuel said come true. So all the people of Israel, from one end of the country to the other, knew that Samuel was indeed a prophet of the Lord... When Samuel spoke, all Israel listened." (1 Samuel 3:19-20, 21). When Samuel spoke, his words were accepted as the words of God. Samuel's words were regarded as reliable; he spoke with authority. Like Moses, he urged Israel to turn away from idols and serve the Lord God.

Samuel was the last of the Judges in Israel. He is also presented as both prophet and priest. Like Joshua, he was an important local leader who presided over the change in Israel's system of government. His authority was such that his sanction provided both Saul and David with legitimacy. For the Deuteronomic historians, he was one in a continuous line of prophets who acted as intermediaries between God and the people. But to what extent can we view Samuel as a historical character? "Samuel's idealized role may have largely obscured the historical Samuel."[78] Be that as it may, Samuel was regarded as a holy man and a local seer. (1 Samuel 9:6-20).

From the perspective of the Deuteronomic historians, Samuel was the first of many prophets in the period of the monarchy. His purpose was to enunciate the view of these historians, to point out the failure of Israel to live up to its covenant with God. Samuel passed judgement on the corrupt priesthood at Shiloh. (1 Samuel 3:11-21) and on the king (1 Samuel 15:22-29). Like the later prophets, Samuel was presented as crucial for kingship, both as king-maker and in anointing the king - first Saul and then David. Samuel is first in the line of prophets who speak the truth to kings when they abuse their power and act unjustly.

## A King for Israel?

Following the period of the Judges, and as Israel underwent a transition from its semi-nomadic existence to a more settled nation in the land of Israel, the tribal system was less able to deal with intertribal disputes and especially foreign threats. In about the 10th century BC, and under pressure from the war-like Philistines to the west,[79] it was becoming clear that the old Israelite confederation and volunteer militia could not deal with the Philistine threat. By the time of Samuel, the Philistines were making inroads into Israel and wrestling for control of Israelite territory as far east as the River Jordan. They had actually established garrisons in towns within Israel – at Geba, Michmash, Bethlehem, and as far north as Beth-shean in the Jezreel valley. Archaeological investigations confirm Philistine expansion into Israel. Large quantities of Philistine pottery have been found in towns they controlled within Israel. The Philistines thus emerged as a much greater threat to the Israelites than the native Canaanites. In point of fact, this threat may have served to unite the Canaanites and the Israelites against a common enemy. Because of these

---

[78] M. D. Coogan, *The Old Testament*, p. 239.

[79] Ibid, p. 341.

pressures, the Hebrew tribes began to see the need for a king to rule over them, like their neighbours. (1 Samuel 8:19-21).

At this time, it was the weakness of Egypt and Mesopotamia (the land of the Tigris and Euphrates) that enabled city states in the Near East to grow into nations with kings – Tyre, Damascus (Syria), Ammon, Moab and others. Therefore, Israel wanted to become a monarchy "like all the other nations." (1 Samuel 8:4-5).

However, if Israel was to be a nation of the covenant and a light to the other nations, as the later prophets suggested, it must be different from them in many respects. The request for a king was the first sign of a turning to the reliance of armies and power, rather than trusting in God who had been accepted as the people's true king.

There were two views, two separate traditions about the monarchy - the pro and anti-monarchical. Samuel presents both of them. The favourable view of the monarchy: (1 Samuel 9:15-17; 11:1-15; 2 Samuel 7:1-17). The unfavourable view: (1 Samuel 8:1-22; 10:17-27; 12:1-25). The Book of Deuteronomy mentions kingship as a possible force for good. (Deuteronomy 17:14-20). But there were warnings which say the opposite. (See 1 Samuel 12:24-25). "Make sure that the man you choose to be king is the one whom the Lord has chosen." (1 Samuel 17:15). The king is to keep a copy of the book of the law (Deuteronomy) beside him and read from it all his life, so that he will learn to honour the Lord and obey faithfully everything that is commanded in it. (17:19). And he is not to think he is better than his fellow-Israelites. (17:20).

"The Lord said to Samuel, 'I will send you a man from the tribe of Benjamin, anoint him as ruler of my people Israel, and he will rescue them from the Philistines. I have seen the suffering of my people and have heard their cries for help.'" (1 Samuel 9:15-16). That is an echo God's words to Moses at the burning bush. The Philistines were the new Pharaoh, the new oppressors of Israel. God hears human cries and he wants to send his servants to them on missions of rescue.

"Saul was head and shoulders taller than anyone else in Israel, and more handsome as well." (1 Samuel 9:2). After Samuel anointed Saul as king, he explained the "regulations for a king." (1 Samuel 10:25). For Israel to choose kingship, at least in some respects, would be a rejection of God. (1 Samuel 8:7, 10:19). But the Book of Samuel still presents the monarchy as God's choice. (10:24-26; 11:6, 13). Whether through a king or otherwise, God would continue to remain engaged with the people. Under God, the king's task is not to enhance his own royal prestige. (2 Samuel 24:3, 10), but to do God's will for the creation of a just society. The king should use his power as service. King David always consulted the Lord before taking action. (1 Samuel 23:2, 4; 30:8; 2 Samuel 2:1; 15:19, 23).

In reference to kingship, both Samuel's role and that of the later prophets is to provide a system of checks and balances. God, through Abraham, promised that Israel would become a great nation. The State has a role in creating peace and stability in the nation, and in providing for the material well-being of all the people. In the discharge of such a role, kingship is not to put the covenant at risk. The conflict between spiritual and material roles features highly in the subsequent history of Israel, down to the Babylonian exile.

An important aspect of kingship is that the Lord is the one who chooses the king, has him anointed by the prophet, and endows him with his Spirit. This means that authority in the State comes from a sacred source and is dependent on that ultimate source. Thus, the king is an underling to the Lord. He becomes the Lord's messiah - "the anointed one." (1 Samuel 2:10; 10:1; 16:13). Absolute sovereignty belongs to God, not to the human being. God is the real king of Israel. (Exodus 15:18). Many psalms make mention of God as king: (Psalms 18, 93, 95, 96, 97, 98). The king would play a role in public worship; he would offer sacrifices and pray for the nation.

Because of the kings' rejection of the covenant in the later history of Israel, God's dealings with the people would then reside in the prophets, and not in the official institutions of the State.

When the Israelites asked for a king, the prophet warned them about what would come to pass. He prayed to the Lord about their wishes. He then told them everything that the Lord had said to him. In summary, they would become slaves in their own land. The king would take their best fields, vineyards and olive groves and give them to his officials. He would take a tenth of their corn for his court officials. He would take their best cattle and donkeys and make them work for him, and they themselves would become his slaves. (1 Samuel 8:4-18). (Much of that actually came true in the Israel of later times). "The people paid no attention to Samuel, but said, 'No! We want a king, so that we will be like other nations, with our own king to rule us and to lead us out to war and to fight our battles.'" (1 Samuel 8:19-20). The purposes for which they wanted the king is revealing. "The Lord said to Samuel, 'Do what they want and give them a king.'" (8:22). But the Lord saw their request as a rejection of himself. (10:17-19). They were granted their king. But the big question was, would they then be faithful to the covenant? Samuel spoke to the people:

> Now here is the king you chose; you asked for him, and now the Lord has given him to you. All will go well with you if you honour the Lord your God, serve him, listen to him, and obey his commands, and if you and your king follow him. But if you do not listen to the Lord, but disobey his commands, he will be against you and your king. (1 Samuel 12:13-15).

This was a reminder that the king would still be subject to the authority of God, and a warning to the people that the rule of kings might not turn out to be the hoped-for blessing. The question was, would Israel remain faithful to the Lord, king or no king?

## The Reign of Saul (ca. 1025-1005 BC).

When Saul was chosen as king, all the people shouted, "Long live the king." (1 Samuel 10:24). Saul ruled a part of Canaan for twenty years. For an account of Saul, see 1 Samuel 10:17 to chapter 31. Saul's first action was to create a standing army in Israel. Among his soldiers were several sons of Jesse (the father of David), including David himself, whom Saul took to himself as his musician and armour-bearer.

Saul's first campaign was against the Ammonites, a tribe living east of the River Jordan. Why a war against Ammon? One of the Hebrew tribes, that of Manasseh, settled in Ammon. (This was long before Ammon became a nation state). The Israelites there may have formed a minority of the population, and may have been subjected to persecution. The incident which aroused the ire of Saul is recorded in I Samuel, chapter 11. The king of Ammon besieged the town of Jabesh-gilead (about eight miles east of the Jordan River), which was occupied by Israelites. The inhabitants were willing to accept the king of Ammon as their ruler, but the king told them that he would "put out everyone's eye so as to bring disgrace on all Israel." (11:2). When word of this came to Saul, "the Spirit of the Lord took control of him." (11:6). He marched into Ammon with a large army, and after a successful campaign against King Nahash, Samuel said to the people of Israel, 'Let us go to Gilgal (a town near Jericho) and once more proclaim Saul as king.' (11:14). "So they all went to Gilgal, and there at the holy place, all of Israel proclaimed Saul king." (11:14-15).

At this time, the Philistines were threatening the very existence of Israel. Much of the central highlands of Israel - as far north as the later Roman province of Galilee - was being contested by their armies. Saul felt the need to deal with this ongoing problem. "The Philistines had 30,000 war chariots, 6,000 horsemen and as many soldiers as there are grains of sand on the seashore." (1 Samuel 13:5). These forces launched a strong attack against the Israelites. Saul and his son Jonathan had only 600 men assembled at Michmash, in the hill country west of the Jordan river. On the day of battle, none of the Israelite soldiers except Saul and Jonathan had swords or spears. (13:15, 22). In order to emphasise the power of God, the Deuteronomist historian exaggerates the forces of the Philistines and minimizes those of the Israelites. Perhaps the author wanted to show that it was not human power, chariots or horses, but the Lord himself who would save Israel. (14:23). And the Lord did save Israel on that day. (See 1 Samuel 14:12-23).

Reliance on God, and not on military might, was a constant teaching of the later prophets. They taught that getting involved in militarism was not of the will of God. The people should place their trust in God, and not in horses and chariots. "Those who trust in the Lord for help will find their strength renewed." (Isaiah 40:31). "The Sovereign Lord, the Holy One of Israel says this to the people, 'You plan to escape from your enemies by riding fast horses. Come back and quietly trust in me. Then you will be strong and secure.'" (Isaiah 30:15). "Some trust in their war chariots and others in their horses, but we trust in the power of the Lord our God. Such people stumble and fall, but we will rise and stand firm." (Psalm 20:6-8).

The First Book of Samuel, chap. 14 tells of Saul's widespread victories in Israel against the Philistines and against Ammon and Moab. But these were only local victories. As long as Saul lived, he had to fight fiercely against the Philistines. (14:52).

In the Book of Exodus, we learn of the Amalekites, a group of wild desert nomads who were scattered in an area from the far south of Canaan across the Sinai Peninsula. (Genesis 36:1, 9,12; Exodus 17:8). They were constantly raiding and plundering in Israel. (Judges 3:13; 6:3, 33; 10:12). Through Samuel, God commanded Saul to destroy them. (1 Samuel 15:2, 7). But Saul spared the life of the king of the Amalekites and kept the best sheep and cattle to offer as a sacrifice to the Lord. (15:14-21). In other words, Saul didn't fully obey the Lord, and the Amalekites would still remain as a threat to Israel. Samuel said to Saul, 'Which does the Lord prefer: obedience or offerings and sacrifices?' (15:22). Samuel then told Saul that because of his disobedience, the Lord had rejected him as king. "The Lord said to Samuel, 'I am sorry that I made Saul king; he has turned away from me and disobeyed my command.'" (Samuel 15:10-11).

The Lord rejected Saul as king because of his disobedience, but the departure of God's Spirit from his life (16:14) seems not to be fully explained or justified in the accounts. However, obedience to God was one of the main concerns of the Deuteronomic historians. Offering sacrifices, as Saul did, after his victory over the Amalekites, was widespread all over Israel during the period of the kings. But of far less concern to the people, was obedience to God's law, as in the Ten Commandments. The constant teaching of the prophets was that without obedience to God and love of neighbour, sacrifices were unacceptable to God, as insincere worship.

The shepherd boy, David was then secretly anointed as king of Israel by Samuel. (Samuel 16:1-13). "Immediately the Spirit of the Lord took control of David and was with him from that day on." (16:13).

Chapter 17 has the account of David's slaying the Philistine giant, Goliath who came from the Philistine city of Gath with an army to do battle in Judah. Saul and his forces assembled for battle against them. Goliath came out from the Philistine camp and challenged one of the Israelites to fight him. When Saul and his men heard this, they were terrified. It was then that David arrived on the scene. David said to Goliath, 'You are coming against me with sword, spear and javelin, but I come against you in the name of the Lord Almighty... This very day the Lord will put you in my power... Then the whole world will know that Israel has a God, and everyone here will see that the Lord does not need swords or spears to save his people.' (1 Samuel 17:12-54).

David's killing of Goliath with a stone from a sling is told with saga-like embellishments. This story teaches that there is more about the human being than physical power. The story is symbolic of the faith that trusts in the Lord and not in one's own resources or strength, in order to gain victory over oppressive power. It is a case of allowing the Lord to take over and become one's shield and fortress. "The Lord is my protector; he is my strong fortress. My God is my protection, and with him I am safe. He protects me like a shield... In my trouble, I called to the Lord; I called to my God for help." (Psalm 18:2, 6). David had a reputation as a poet and musician. Psalm 18 is attributed to him, and it is included in 2 Samuel, chapter 22, as David's song of thanksgiving for having been saved from Saul, who at a later stage, sought to kill him.

After the slaying of Goliath, David rapidly rose to eminence in Saul's court and married Michal, one of Saul's daughters, whom Saul promised to him for having slain Goliath. (18:17). "David was successful in all the missions on which Saul sent him, with the result that Saul made him an officer in his army. This pleased all Saul's officers and men." (1 Samuel 18:5). In every battle against the Philistines, David was more successful than any of Saul's other officers. As a result, David became very famous. (1 Samuel 18:30; see 1 Samuel 29:5).

David's killing of Goliath made him popular, but it soon provoked Saul's rage and envy. Saul began to see David as a rival for the throne. (1 Samuel 18:6-9). Michal sided with David when her father repeatedly sought to kill David. Once when David was playing the harp in Saul's house, an evil spirit took control of Saul and he threw a spear at David, in an effort to pin him to the wall, but David dodged the spear. (1 Samuel 18:10). In order to get away from Saul, David went on to establish a power base for himself in southern

Judah, attacking enemies of Israel while serving ostensibly as a Philistine vassal. With his own militia, David protected the southern Israelite tribes from raids by the Amalekites and from Philistine attacks, while making his Philistine overlord think he was completely loyal to him. David was more successful against the Philistines than Saul's officers. As a result, David became ever more famous. (1 Samuel 18:30). Here we see Saul's fatal flaw (his spirit of rage and envy). Because of his enmity with David, he deprived himself of the services of a brilliant tactician who could have helped him to decisively drive out the Philistines.

The remaining chapters of 1 Samuel outline accounts of Saul's jealousy and his suspicion of David, whom he repeatedly tried to eliminate. But David still remained the king's loyal servant, even though the king wished him dead. David was forced to flee for his life, and had two chances to kill Saul, but refused to do so. (chapters 24 and 26). In contrast to his father's antagonism, Saul's son, Jonathan, was completely loyal to David. (18:1-4). When Saul told Jonathan that he planned to kill David, Jonathan reminded him that David had risked his life for him when he took his place and killed the Philistine Goliath.

Saul then made a vow that he would not kill David. (2 Samuel 19:1-7). Jonathan loved David as much as he loved himself (20:17), and once again he promised David that he would protect him from any threat to his life by his father. (2 Samuel 20:10-42). Jonathan recognised qualities in David which fitted him to be the next king. In contrast to his father Saul, Jonathan is presented as faithful and possessing great sense. (13:3; 14:15, 23; 14:16; 14:29-30). In order to strengthen his connections with different regions, David formed other marriage alliances. (2 Samuel 15:1-5). Thus, David was cunningly playing the role of the king in waiting.

However, what the reader of 1 Samuel may find difficult to understand is that, despite Saul's begging for forgiveness for his sin of disobedience, the Lord still rejected him as king. (15:35). Neither Samuel nor the Lord spoke to him anymore. He was on his own, the Philistines closing in on him. Samuel had already died. (See his farewell speech in 2 Samuel 12).

God's Spirit departs from Saul and he is inhabited by a spirit of anxiety and depression. His experience of God's silence drives him to consult a medium. Through the medium, Saul tries to speak to Samuel. (1 Samuel 28). Samuel said to him, 'Why did you make me come back?' Saul answered, 'I am in great trouble! The Philistines are at war with me. God does not answer me anymore, either by prophets or by dreams. And so I have called you, for you to tell me what I must do.' (28:15). All Saul hears is an announcement of defeat and death. Samuel said to him, 'The Lord will hand you and Israel over to the Philistines. Tomorrow you and your sons will join me, and the Lord will hand the army of Israel over to the Philistines.' (28:16-19). "At once Saul fell down and lay stretched on the ground, terrified by what Samuel had said. He was weak because he had not eaten anything all day. Neither would he eat now. (28:20).

Tomorrow wasn't long in coming. In Saul's final battle against the Philistines on Mount Gilboa in lower Galilee, many Israelites were killed, and the rest of them, including Saul and his sons, fled. But the Philistines caught up with them and killed three of Saul's sons, including Jonathan. Saul himself was hit by enemy arrows and badly wounded. He wanted the young man carrying his weapons to draw his sword and kill him, so that the Philistines couldn't take the credit for his death. The young man refused to do this. Then Saul took his own sword and fell on it. The young man and all Saul's men died that day. On hearing this news, the Israelites in nearby areas abandoned their towns and fled. The Philistines then came and occupied the towns. On finding Saul's body lying on Mount Gilboa, the Philistines cut off his head, stripped off his armour and sent messengers to Philistia with the good news of Saul's defeat and death. They put Saul's weapons in the temple of the goddess Astarte (the Philistine goddess of love), and nailed his body to the wall of the city of Beth-shean, one of their garrison towns in Israel. Mount Gilboa (near the town of Beth-shean) was relatively far north and a considerable distance from their heartlands in the coastal plains. This shows the extent of Philistine encroachment into Israel, and it illustrates the task that faced David. With the death of Saul, the Philistines were contained, but not defeated. (1 Samuel 31:1-13).

Twenty years earlier, Saul had rescued the people of Jabesh in Gilead from a cruel king. (see above). When the people of that town across the Jordan heard what the Philistines had done to Saul, the bravest men of the town set out and marched all night to Beth-shean, on the west side of the Jordan, a distance of about fifteen miles. They took down the bodies of Saul and his sons from the city wall, brought them back to Jabesh and burnt them there. Then they buried their bones under the tamarisk tree in the town and fasted for seven days. (1 Samuel 31:11-13).

When David heard of the death of Saul and Jonathan, "he tore his clothes in sorrow" (2 Samuel 1:11). He composed a lament for Saul and his friend Jonathan. In this lyrical eulogy Saul's heroism is remembered, and he is given unqualified praise by David. This represents a different tradition, which sees Saul in a more positive light to the tradition that says he was unfaithful to the Lord.

> Alas, the glory of Israel has been slain on your heights!..
> O mountains of Gilboa,
> let there be no dew or rain on you; treacherous fields,
> for there the hero's shield was dishonoured…
> Saul and Jonathan, loved and lovely,
> neither in life, nor in death divided.
> Swifter than eagles were they,
> stronger were they than lions.
> O daughters of Israel weep for Saul
> who clothed you in scarlet and linen…
> O Jonathan, in your death I am stricken,
> I am desolate for you my brother. (2 Samuel 1:17-27, JB).

Saul is a tragic figure. In the end, he was overwhelmed by events only partially under his control. God's relationship with him remains unfathomable. God's motives remain hidden from the reader, as they were from Saul. As for Saul, he failed in part, because he squandered his military resources in pursuit of David. Following the chaos that reigned during the period of the Judges, and as the first king of Israel, Saul brought a measure of unity to the Israelite tribes. He thus prepared the ground for David. He fought a defensive war for twenty years against enemies who were closing in on him on all sides, especially the Philistines. If he was defeated in the end, there was something noble and heroic about his failure, and that of his son Jonathan.

To what extent can we read these narratives as historical? The characters of Saul, Jonathan and David are vividly portrayed in the accounts. "For ancient audiences, both the characters and the times in which they lived were familiar, and so the historians could present a kind of fictionalized historical drama, somewhat like the history plays of Shakespeare, with frequent use of dialogue"[80]

# King David (ca. 1005-965 BC)

After the death of Saul, David was anointed king of Judah (southern part of Israel) and he ruled for forty years. (2 Samuel 2:4). Because the Lord gave victory to David (2 Samuel 8:6, 14), he was able to subjugate the Philistines and other nations such as the Ammonites when they threatened Israel. Like Moses, David was called away from the comfort zone of his lowly occupation as a shepherd, to become one to whom the people, ever after, looked back as the ideal king. David foreshadows Jesus whose kingdom would "reach from sea to sea, from the Euphrates River to the ends of the earth, the peoples of the desert bowing down before him." (Psalm 72:8).

David, who came from Bethlehem and the tribe of Judah, united the kingdom and extended its borders. Under David, the old Canaanite enclaves, with their walled towns, were finally absorbed into Israel. David was a gifted warrior and military tactician, and at times he could be ruthless. When he was enthroned as king, the Philistines came with an army to capture him but he defeated them, drove them back to Gezer, one of their inland cities, and forced them to pay him tribute. (2 Samuel 5:17-25; 21:15-22). He then defeated the Ammonites (2 Samuel 10:1-14) and the Moabites, making Ammon and Moab vassals of Israel for a time. The Books of Chronicles say that David's fame spread everywhere, and the Lord made every nation afraid of him. (1 Chronicles 14:17). David and his son Solomon had an alliance treaty with Hiram, king of Tyre, a small city State on the Mediterranean coast, and bordering Israel in the north. (2 Samuel 5:11; 1 Kings 9:13).

When David became king, the northern part of Israel, and Judah in the south, were at enmity. Saul's son, Ishbaal, succeeded Saul for a time in the north of Israel, until he was murdered by David's partisans. The revolt by David's son, Absalom, was backed by the men of the north. (2 Samuel, chap. 18). When David died, national unity between north and south had not been fully achieved.

When David became king, a Canaanite tribe known as the Jebusites still occupied the fortified city of Jerusalem. David attacked the city, defeated the Jebusites and made Jerusalem his capital and the political centre of a united Israel. After David's victory over the Philistines, he brought the ark of the covenant (the tabernacle containing the stone tablets of the Ten Commandments) from Shiloh to Jerusalem. The city then became the religious capital as well. David's city was very small – approximately 370 metres by 120

---

[80] Michael D. Coogan, *The Old Testament*, p. 235.

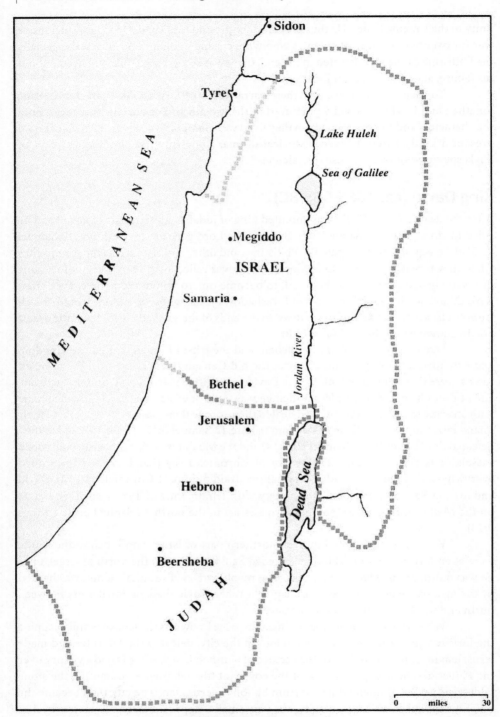

**The Kingdom of David and Solomon**

metres.[81] In order to include a space for his temple and palaces, Solomon later expanded this area considerably. Even at the time of its destruction by the Babylonians, the population of Jerusalem was only about 10,000.

After becoming king, David allowed his first wife, Michal (Saul's daughter), to be returned to him, probably to bolster his claim to the throne. Her affection for him had waned because of her long separation from him. David married many more women (1 Chronicles 3: 1-9; 14:3-7), and had seventeen sons, who were vying with one another for the succession, many of them getting killed in the process. In addition to these sons, he had sons by his concubines. (1 Chronicles 3:9).

David finally unified the Hebrew tribes and brought peace to his nation, but he didn't always live up to the trust placed in him, often following his own way rather than the way of the Lord, with disastrous consequences. Early in his reign, the Ammonite campaign provided the context for his adultery with Bathsheba. "In the spring, at the time of year when kings usually go to war, David sent out Joab, the commander of the army, with his officers and the Israelite army. They defeated the Ammonites and besieged Rabbah, the capital city of Ammon. But David himself stayed in Jerusalem." (2 Samuel 11:1). The implication here is that, whether through self-indulgence or sloth, David had failed to take his place where his duty lay.

One day late in the afternoon, David got up from a nap and went to the palace roof. There he saw a woman having a bath. She was very beautiful. David later learned that she was Bathsheba, the wife of Uriah, the Hittite, one of his commanding officers. (11:2-3). David had her brought to him and he made love to her. Later, when she found she was pregnant, she sent a message to David, telling him the news. (11:4-5). David then sent a letter to Joab, the commander of the army, ordering him to put Bathsheba's husband, Uriah in the front line where the fighting would be heaviest, and then retreat, allowing Uriah to be killed. When the enemy forces came out of Rabbah, some of David's officers were killed, and so was Uriah. (11:14-17). When Bathsheba's time of mourning was over, David sent for her to come to the palace. She became his wife and bore him a son.

The prophet Nathan pointed out to David the enormity of the crime he had committed. Through the prophet, the Lord said to David, 'Why have you disobeyed my commands? Why did you do this evil thing? You had Uriah placed in a position where he would be killed in battle, so that you could then take his wife as your wife.' (2 Samuel 12:9). Nathan told David a parable which convicted him of his sin. (2 Samuel, Chapters 11-12). Psalm 51 may have been composed by David as a prayer for mercy and forgiveness. Despite his grave sins, David believed that God still loved him. 'Be merciful to me, O God, because of your constant love. Because of your great mercy, wipe away my sins!' (Psalm 51:1). David was a murderer and an adulterer, but he repented of his sins. However, there would be consequences flowing from his evil deeds.

From that time on, David was largely at the mercy of events. The reader of 2 Samuel is reminded that there will be violence and misfortune in David's household as a result of his adultery with Bathsheba. (12:24-25; 12:10-12). In contrast to the beginning of his reign in First Samuel, he became embroiled in a narrative of sexual immorality,

---

[81] Coogan, *The Old Testament*, p. 275.

murders and tragedy in his own family. Retribution seems to have befallen him when his son by Bathsheba died. (12:15-24). David had a second son by Bathsheba and named him Solomon. David's older sons by other women were eliminated one by one. His daughter Tamar was killed by her brother Absalom. (2 Samuel 13).

Unable to control his sons, or to bring justice to the nation as a whole, David was ousted from the throne by Absalom, and forced to flee in disgrace across the Jordan. (2 Samuel chapters 15-18). Eventually David defeated Absalom and returned to Jerusalem. (Chapter 18). God's judgement reached its climax when Absalom was killed in battle. In his old age, David's other son Adonijah, desired his father's throne, but was outmanoeuvred by Solomon's supporters and eventually killed. (1 Kings 1:5). With the news of Absalom's death, David was overcome with grief. He went to his room and cried, 'O my son! My son Absalom, my son! If only I had died in your place, my son! Absalom, my son!' (2 Samuel 18:33). After this, David joined up with his army and captured Rabbah, the capital city of Ammon. (12:26-31).

## The Achievements of David

The story of David, the warrior king, the adulterer and murderer, would have encouraged despondent readers, who would have learned of God's mercy and forgiveness following the king's repentance. (2 Samuel 22:5, 17-20). David often sinned grievously, but he never forsook his loyalty to the Lord. He never established shrines to foreign gods. Echoing the covenant and promises made to Abraham, God made a covenant with David, extending down the line to all his descendants. (2 Samuel 23:5). The Davidic dynasty lasted four-hundred years, down to the conquest of Jerusalem and Judah by the Babylonian armies in 587 BC. This was the longest royal dynasty of the ancient world.

David's glory is expressed in a number of Psalms. (See Psalm 89:28-30). His dynasty is acclaimed and celebrated. (Psalm 2:7; 110:1-2). As a warrior, he brought the rule of the Lord to the surrounding nations. As a king, he received the promise of divine protection for his successors. He established Jerusalem as the centre of worship for the Lord. He composed psalms and prayers. (See 2 Samuel 22). It wasn't that he deserved divine praise, but that God used this gifted, but flawed king to accomplish his divine purposes

In the Second Book of Samuel, there is a prayer of thanksgiving to God by David for his achievements. In this prayer, David acknowledges God's sovereignty over him, and the blessings flowing from this as the work of God:

> How great you are Sovereign Lord. There is none like you; we have always known that you alone are God. There is no other nation on earth like Israel, whom you rescued from slavery to make them your own people. The great and wonderful things you did for them have spread your fame throughout the world... And now, Lord God, fulfil for all time the promises you made about me and my descendants. (2 Samuel 7:18-29; see 1 Chronicles 17:16-27).

David dreamed of building a temple to the Lord in Jerusalem, intended as a house for the covenant box which contained the two stone tablets of the Law - so that the law given to

Moses would symbolize God's presence with his people. The Lord promised to build a temple and to establish for David an everlasting dynasty through his son, Solomon. (1 Chronicles 29:1-9). David composed a prayer of thanks to God, in which he acknowledged the absolute sovereignty of God. This prayer echoes Psalm 8. Psalm 89 is a song in praise of God's promise to David and his family.

> 'Lord God of our ancestor Jacob, may you be praised for ever and ever! You are great and powerful, glorious, splendid and majestic. Everything in heaven and earth is yours, and you are king, supreme ruler over all… Now, our God, we give you thanks, and we praise your glorious name.' (See 1 Chronicles 29:10-19).

David's last words are in 2 Samuel, chapter 23: 'The Spirit of the Lord speaks through me; his message is on my lips. The God of Israel has spoken: The king who rules with justice, who rules in obedience to God, is like the sun shining on a cloudless dawn, the sun that makes the grass sparkle after rain. And that is how God will bless my descendants, because he has made an eternal covenant with me.' (2 Samuel 23:2-5).

## Royal Theology

The Davidic covenant, based on the father and son relationship, was conditional. The Lord says, 'When the king does wrong, I will punish him, as a father punishes a son, but I will not draw my support from him.' (2 Samuel 7:14-15). David and his descendants got their strength from God, something that his descendants often forgot. In the old system, the people of Israel as a whole were God's son. (Exodus 4:22). According to royal theology, the Israelite king was the essential mediator between God and the people. The Mosaic covenant was conditional: Success and prosperity depended on obedience to God's law. But the Davidic covenant was eternal and unconditional: 'I will make your kingdom last for ever. Your dynasty will never end.' (2 Samuel 7:16; see Psalm 132:11-12). The following extract from Psalm 89 foreshadows the kingship of Jesus, descendant of David (God's only Son), who inaugurated a new covenant and whose kingdom would last for ever. Jesus is the king in the line of David, who was anointed with strength as God's true Son, to become the greatest of all kings; his rule would extend over the earth and endure for ever.

> I have made my servant David king
> by anointing him with holy oil.
> My strength will always be with him,
> my power will make him strong…
> I will love him and be loyal to him;
> I will make him always victorious.
> I will extend his kingdom
> from the Mediterranean to the
> River Euphrates.
> He will say to me,
> 'You are my father and my God;

> you are my protector and saviour.'
> I will make him my firstborn son,
> the greatest of all kings.
> I will always keep my promise to him,
> and my covenant with him will last for ever.
> His dynasty will be as permanent as the sky;
> a descendant of his will always be king. (Psalm 89:20-21, 24-25-29).

The king was chosen by God, with whom he had a special relationship, described in the following passage by the metaphor of sonship.

> The Lord said to Nathan, "Tell my servant David that I, the Lord Almighty say to him, 'I took you from looking after sheep in the fields and made you the ruler of my people Israel. I have been with you wherever you have gone. I will make you as famous as the greatest leaders in the world... When you die, I will make one of your sons king, and I will make sure that his dynasty continues for ever. I will be his father and he will be my son, (2 Samuel 7:8, 12, 14; see Psalm 2; Isaiah 9:6-7).

The promise made to the house of David in the above prophecy of Nathan sustained the messianic hope in Israel for a king like David. In the New Testament, there are references to Nathan's prophecy. (Acts of the Apostles 2:29-36; Hebrews 1:4-8). Jesus is presented as a descendant of David and acknowledged as the promised Messiah in the line of David. (Matthew 1:1, 16:15; Luke 1:30-33).

A comparison can be made between David and Jesus. Jesus passes over the Kidron valley on the night before his passion. (John 18:1). David escapes across the Kidron valley and out into the wilderness while escaping from Absalom. (2 Samuel 15:23). Jesus goes up the Mount of Olives weeping and praying. (Luke 22:39). For David, see 2 Samuel 15:30). Jesus bears curses from the people. (Luke 23:35); For David, see 2 Samuel 16:5-13). Jesus' betrayer hangs himself (Matthew 27:5), as does Ahithopel. (2 Samuel 17:23). The Lord returns in glory to Jerusalem. (Revelation 21); compare with 2 Samuel 19:2-44.

## The Books of Kings

The two Books of Kings contain an outline of the history of the kingdoms of Israel and Judah from the time of Solomon in the middle of the 10th century BC, to 586 BC when the monarchy came to an end with the Babylonian conquest.

The First Book of Kings continues the history of the Israelite monarchy, begun in the Books of Samuel. First Kings can be divided into three parts: (1) the succession of Solomon as king of Israel and Judah, and the death of his father David; (2) the reign and achievements of Solomon; (3) the division of the nation into the northern and southern kingdoms, and the stories of the kings who ruled the divided nation down to the middle of the 6th century BC.

The history of the northern Kingdom of Israel (926-722 BC) is told in 1 Kings

12:2–2 Kings 17. The northern kingdom came to an end in 721 BC with the fall of its capital Samaria to the Assyrian empire. The kingdom of Judah (2 Kings, chapters 18–25) remained in existence until the destruction of Jerusalem by the Babylonians in 587 BC. Thus, the southern kingdom of Judah survived the northern kingdom by 134 years. In the later periods of both kingdoms, the prophets gradually replaced the kings as the chief protagonists. The national disasters which befell both kingdoms took place because of the unfaithfulness of both kings and people to their God. The destruction of Jerusalem and the exile of its people to Babylon was one of the great turning-points of Israelite history.

It is thought that the Books of Kings existed in some written form before the Babylonian exile, although still awaiting final editing. The authors of Kings mention three of their sources. First was the Book of the Acts of Solomon, which reported on Solomon's deeds. (1 Kings 11:41). This source contained legendary anecdotes concerning Solomon's glory and wisdom.[82] This does not mean that at least some of the legends, are not true. Two further sources are mentioned: The Annals of the Kings of Israel, and The Annals of the Kings of Judah. None of these is extant. The authors used these older sources, checked them, commented on them and added reinterpretations to them for their own purposes. "The Books of Kings represent not only stories, but also genuine history."[83] Stories about prophets in the early chapters of Second Kings may be folktales. The authors interpret history from a religious standpoint, but they also document it in the manner of all true historians.

The Books of Kings use of sources means that they have some historical value. Archaeology shows them to be correct in matters ranging from the name of the king of Moab (2 Kings 3:4) to King Hezekiah's construction of a water tunnel in Jerusalem. (2 Kings 20:20). Even kings who reigned for only a few months, are listed carefully in the books. And the authors are not afraid to document the flaws and faults of the kings and the negative effects that the monarchy had on the whole population. The major effect of the monarchy was that it gave rise to prophecy, which first emerged in the northern kingdom of Israel.

## King Solomon (ca. 965-932 BC)

Solomon ruled the whole of Israel for thirty-three years. There are accounts of his rule in First Kings chaps. 1-11 and in Second Chronicles 1-9.

Following instructions from David, his son Solomon, whose mother was Bathsheba, was enthroned as King of Israel. (1 Kings, 1:32-39). The succession did not run smoothly. One of David's other sons – Adonijah, had already made himself king. It was then that Bathsheba intervened and reminded David that he had made a solemn promise before God that her son Solomon would be king after him. (1 Kings 15). Because David was now old and senile, he was unaware of the machinations that were afoot. David told her that he would keep his promise to her. (2 Kings 1:30-40). Solomon was then anointed king by both priest and prophet. He soon secured his position by killing his rival

---

[82] Nelson, *The Historical Books*, (Westminster John Knox Press), p. 132.

[83] *Oxford Bible Commentary*, p. 234.

Adoijah and his supporters, including Joab, David's army commander. Solomon's succession story reads like a modern historical novel. (2 Samuel 13:1-19; 17:1-14; 18:19-33). The storyteller reveals to the reader that God's will is the chief causative factor behind the events, God working as best he can with flawed human beings. There was no human glory in how Solomon came to the throne - over the dead bodies of his rivals. However, under Solomon's reign, there was now a settled kingdom, with the king chosen and forgiven by God.

> When David was about to die, he called his son Solomon and gave him his last instructions: 'My time to die has come. Be confident and determined and do what the Lord your God orders you to do, obey all his laws and commands, as written in the law of Moses, so that wherever you go you may prosper in everything you do...' God replied to Solomon: 'You have made the right choice. Instead of asking for wealth or treasure or fame or the death of your enemies or even a long life for yourself, you have asked for wisdom and knowledge so that you can rule my people over whom I have made you king. I will give you wisdom and knowledge. And in addition, I will give you more wealth and fame than any king has ever had before or will ever have again.' (2 Chronicles 1:11-12; 1 Kings 2:1-4; 3:10-14).

Solomon became famous for his wisdom, and perhaps, in this way, he foreshadows Jesus. However, as we will see, Solomon did not live up to God's expectations. He outdid pagan kings in the excesses of his lifestyle. Luxury, sensuality and self-exaltation became his forte.

Jesus shows us that true wisdom is obeying the will of God, that is, following Jesus on the path that he travelled ahead of us, which means moving away from self-comforts and living a life of service. St. Paul describes Jesus as the power and the wisdom of God. "As for us, we proclaim the crucified Christ, a message that is offensive to the Jews and nonsense to the Gentiles, but for those whom God has called, this message is Christ, who is the power of God and the wisdom of God." (1 Corinthians 1:23-24).

Solomon is credited with a developed system of government for Israel. According to First Kings, Solomon was richer and wiser than any other king in the world. "Foreign kings came and consulted him to hear the wisdom that God had given him. They brought Solomon gifts – articles of silver and gold, robes, weapons, spices and horses. This continued year after year." (2 Chronicles 9:22-24). "Every year, King Solomon received almost 23,000 kilograms of gold, in addition to the taxes paid by merchants, the profits from trade, and tribute paid by Arabian kings and the governors of the Israelite districts." (1 Kings 14-15). The Queen of Sheba heard of Solomon's fame and travelled to Jerusalem. She brought him gifts of spices, jewels and a large amount of gold, and consulted him for his wisdom. (2 Chronicles 9:1-12). (Sheba was a region in south-western Arabia – in present-day Yemen. The people there were mostly merchants and traders).

"King Solomon decided to build a temple where the Lord would be worshiped. He drafted 30,000 men as forced labour from all over Israel. He had 80,000 men in the hill country quarrying stone, with 70,000 men to transport it, and he placed 3,300 foremen in charge of them to supervise their work." (1 Kings:13-18). Forced labour was a regular practice in the ancient world. Solomon supplied King Hiram of Lebanon with large quantities of wheat and olive oil to feed the workers who were logging cedar and pine wood for his new temple and palace. (1Kings 5:6, 10). The palace he built for himself was twice as large as the temple, taking into account that it would also be used for administrative purposes. Many of the people he employed in forced labour were from the Hebrew tribe of Ephraim in the northern part of the kingdom, but many more were descendants of the people of Canaan. In other words, Solomon treated these people as slaves. They included tribes such as the Hittites, Amorites and Jebusites. (2 Chronicles 8:7-8). Thus, in a sense, Solomon became a new Pharaoh. Like the Egyptian Pharaoh, he enslaved people who were not of his own tribe and race, but who were still part of his kingdom. All of this built up a resentment that would later boil over.

Solomon consolidated the achievements of his father David. He retained control over the small kingdoms east of the River Jordan – Ammon, Moab and Edom, giving his country the status of an empire. He fortified the city of Palmyra in Syria - a place in the news in recent times because of the destruction of its ancient ruins. At that time, it was a temple city. (2 Chronicles 8:3-4).

Solomon's temple was built on Mount Moriah in Jerusalem. (2 Chronicles 3:1). According to tradition, this was the mountain where Abraham was willing to sacrifice his son. All the sacrifices offered in the temple would recall a father's faithfulness and his son's obedience, and would call on God to provide a lamb for the sacrifice. Here also, God sacrificed his only Son, who was the lamb of God.

There is a description of the lavish temple in Second Chronicles 3-4: its gold and golden objects, cedar wood panelling overlaid with gold, precious stones decorations, floral motifs on the walls. The cedar-wood pillars and carvings of lions and oxen on panels were an echo of the Garden of Eden where God dwelt in fellowship with human beings. The temple would thus symbolize a mini-cosmos in which God would live with his people, and with creation, in the worship of the temple liturgy.

The temple was actually modest in size compared with similar buildings in later times. But God was concerned that his people should understand the connection between life and liturgy. He revealed to Solomon what he truly desired, which was not the temple itself, but a faithful and obedient heart. "The Lord said to Solomon, 'If you obey my laws and commands, I will do what I promised your father David. I will live among my people Israel in this temple that you are building, and I will never abandon them.'" (1 Kings 6:11-13). God will only dwell in the temple as long as the King is a good shepherd who will lead his people in the ways of God. As in the Garden of Eden, obedience to God is to be the touchstone.

The idealism of Solomon shone forth in his payer at the dedication of the temple. In the presence of the people, "Solomon went and stood in front of the altar, where he raised his arms and prayed:

'Lord, God of Israel, there is no god like you in heaven above or on earth below! You keep your covenant with your people and show them your love when they live in wholehearted obedience to you. You have kept the promise you made to my father David; today every word has been fulfilled... Lord my God, I am your servant. Listen to my prayer and grant the requests I make to you today. Watch over this temple day and night, this place where you have chosen to be worshiped. Hear my prayers and the prayers of your people when they face this place and pray. In your home in heaven hear us and forgive us." (1 Kings 8:22-24, 28-30).

Then Solomon asked God's blessing on all the people assembled in the temple: 'May the Lord our God be with us, as he was with our ancestors; may he never leave us or abandon us... May he always be merciful to the people of Israel and to their king. And so all the nations of the world will know that the Lord alone is God – and there is no other. May you, his people, always be faithful to the Lord our God, obeying all his laws and commands.' (1 Kings 8:57-61).

The city of Jerusalem and its temple are celebrated in much of Israel's poetry. "The Lord is great and is to be highly praised in the city of our God, on his sacred hill. Zion, the mountain of God, is high and beautiful; the city of the great king brings joy to the world." (Psalm 48:1-3; 99:2). Pilgrimages to Jerusalem inspired many Psalms. (See Psalms 120 - 134).

The Lord then made a covenant with Solomon in which he, the Lord, promised to protect the temple if the king obeyed the commandments of the Lord. But if Solomon was disobedient, the Lord, would remove his people from the land and abandon the temple, because the people would be walking away from the Lord their God, who brought their ancestors out of Egypt. (1 Kings 9:1-9; 2 Chronicles 2:1; see Genesis 2:16-17; 3:23).

So far, the picture is admiration for the achievements of Solomon's kingship. But the mood of First Kings soon changes. Solomon's rule was ambiguous; he did not always live up to God's expectations. From the beginning of his reign, the cracks were beginning to show, and his great wisdom was deserting him. Often, he was more concerned about self-exaltation than serving the Lord and his people. First Kings, chapter 11 shows a different side of Solomon, one that the tradition condemns, which may be closer to the real truth about him. Under Solomon, a kind of triumphalism and self-exaltation of building and making began to take over. The people saw themselves achieving things by their own power instead of relying on the power of God. The later prophets taught that trusting in oneself would lead to humiliation, but those who trusted in God would be exalted. (See Isaiah 40:31).

Solomon became a tyrant who outdid pagan kings in his sensuality and in the luxury of his lifestyle. Solomon turned away from the Lord. "He loved many foreign women." (1 Kings 11:1). At the start of his reign he married the daughter of the king of Egypt, which required him to acknowledge the deities of Egypt, as well as the God of Israel.[84] In order to please this woman, he built a shrine to the gods of Egypt on the Mount of Olives, just outside Jerusalem. Besides the daughter of the king of Egypt, he married Hittite women (from a native tribal group in Canaan), women from Sidon (a coastal city in northern Israel) and women from Moab, Ammon and Edom (kingdoms east of the River Jordan and the Dead Sea). The purpose of marriages to foreign princesses was to

---

[84] Gray & Cavins, *Walking with God, A Journey through the Bible*, (Ascension Press, West Chester, PA, 19380, USA), p. 161.

cement alliances with the nations in question. It was what all kings did in those times and was intended as a guarantor of peaceful co-existence with neighbours.

Eventually Solomon established an astonishing harem of seven hundred wives (foreign princesses) and three hundred concubines. It was not considered unethical at the time to have a harem of wives. The argument against it in Kings is religious rather than ethical. Solomon thus broke the first commandment. These women made him turn away from God and by the time he was old, they had led him into the worship of foreign gods. (1 Kings 11:1-8).

Solomon gave his foreign wives religious freedom. But he himself followed them into full-blown idolatry, even building altars to pagan gods, some of whose liturgies demanded child sacrifice, leading to Solomon's abandonment of the God of Israel. (1 Kings 11:1-8). Solomon was not faithful to the Lord, as his father David had been. He acknowledged the God of Israel and followed the instructions of his father, David, but he also offered animal sacrifices to foreign gods "at the high places," i.e. at Canaanite hilltop shrines. (1 Kings 3:2-3). Probably, because one of his wives was an Ammonite princess, Solomon built altars to Molech the god of Ammon (east of the River Jordan), whose liturgies demanded child sacrifice. (Amman is the capital city of the present-day nation of Jordan). On a mountain, east of Jerusalem, Solomon built a place to worship Chemosh, the god of Moab (a nation to the south of Ammon). The Lord was angered by Solomon's idolatry. (I Kings 11:33). Solomon thus set events in train that would destroy his kingdom.

The amassing of gold, foreign wives, horses and chariots were prohibited in the Mosaic law. (See Deuteronomy 17:14-17). "Solomon built up a force of 1,400 chariots and 12,000 cavalry horses." (2 Chronicles 1:14). This was the first sign of a reliance on militarism, armies and foreign alliances (critiqued by the later prophets), rather than trusting in the Lord. This resulted in Solomon receiving a word from God, that because of his violation of the covenant, the kingdom would be torn asunder after his reign. (1 Kings 11:11-13). The Lord appeared to Solomon and reminded him that he had broken the covenant and disobeyed the commandments of the Lord. Because of this, God would give only a part of his kingdom to his son. (1 Kings 11:9-13).

Solomon's obedience and disobedience are indications of the positive and negative possibilities of the nation's future. His new temple made it possible for Israel to obey, for the first time, the law in Deuteronomy, chapter 12 mandating the centralization of sacrifice in one place. A centralized place of worship was important, because it should have excluded the use of shrines dedicated to the gods of Canaan and foreign gods. David's last words to Solomon outlined the goal God had in mind for all succeeding reigns: Kings who obey God's law will prosper. (1 Kings 2:2-3).

Sacrifices both to the Lord and to foreign gods in places outside Jerusalem would become widespread immediately after the death of Solomon. (1 Kings 12:25-33). This practice would continue until the much later reforms of King Josiah of Judah. (2 Kings 23:8-9, 15-20). The reforms of the latter king were short-lived. The last four kings of Judah presided over a rapid slide into national catastrophe. (2 kings 23:31–25:21).

The subjugation of the neighbouring nations of Ammon, Moab and Edom by David and Solomon was only temporary. How extensive were the building works of Solomon? "To an objective observer, the building works attributable to Solomon, seem rather modest."[85] On the evidence from archaeology, Biblical scholars place a question mark on the scale of Solomon's building projects. What archaeology provides, is some evidence for customs and practices mentioned in the Bible, of which we had no previous examples.'[86]

## The Northern Kingdom of Israel

Following the death of Solomon, the country was split into two kingdoms – the northern Kingdom of Israel and the southern Kingdom of Judah - the first sign of the disunion and fragmentation that would lead to the darkness of a raging ocean further down the road. In his self-exaltation, Solomon built a Tower of Babel which, instead of cementing union, led to a scattering. (See Genesis 11:1-9). The smaller of the two kingdoms was Judah, which included only the tribes of Judah and Benjamin. The northern Kingdom of Israel would have included the area of what became in later times the Roman provinces of Samaria and Galilee, with also some additional areas north-west of the Sea of Galilee. The northern kingdom had more fertile land and became more prosperous than Judah.

In the accounts of Solomon, once again we see the story of good beginnings, loyalty to God, wisdom, idealism and splendour. But before long everything slides into arrogance, self- aggrandisement, conflict, division and family break-up (as in the family of Abraham). Exaltation leading to humiliation! There develops a trust in created things (God's rivals), idols of pleasure, silver and gold, power, wealth, status, horses and chariots - as the road to salvation, rather than trusting in the ways of the Lord, and obedience to his saving word for establishing justice on earth. Temple ceremonial then becomes insincere worship. It only gives religious legitimacy to a materialistic society, giving rise to the critique by the later prophets. The result of all of this: a move away from the covenant with God and a journey down the road into exile and death.

How did both kingdoms fare out? Firstly, a word about the northern Kingdom of Israel. In placing a heavy yoke on his people, Solomon came to be regarded as a tyrant, an oppressor of his people. As Solomon had no children by his Egyptian wife, he was succeeded by Rehoboam, whose mother was a pagan Ammonite princess.

The people of the north promised loyalty to Rehoboam if he agreed to lighten the burdens (heavy taxation and forced labour) placed on their shoulders by his father, but Rehoboam foolishly refused to do this. (1 Kings 12:4). The result was that the people in the northern part of the country (occupied by ten of the Hebrew tribes) said to Rehoboam, 'If you make these burdens lighter for us, we will be your loyal subjects.' (1 Kings 12:4). But Rehoboam promised that he would make the burdens ever heavier, telling them, 'My father beat you with a whip; I'll flog you with a horsewhip.' (12:11). Following this rebuke, the northern tribes denounced David and his family and rebelled against the rule of Rehoboam. (1 Kings 12:16-17). The result was, that all of the tribes, with the exception of the tribes of Judah and Benjamin (the two southern tribes), rejected

---

[85] *Oxford Bible Commentary*, p. 239.

[86] Lawrence Boadt, *Reading the Old Testament*, (Paulist Press, 997 Macarthur Boulevard, Mahwah, New Jersey 07430, USA), p. 49.

Rehoboam and chose Jeroboam as their king. Rehoboam then called up an army of 180,000 soldiers from the tribes of Judah and Benjamin in order to make war on the northern tribes, but was advised against this by the prophet Shemaiah, who spoke the word of the Lord to him. (1 Kings 12:21-24). Rehoboam ruled Judah for seventeen years, from his capital city Jerusalem. But he proved to have none of the wisdom or diplomatic skills of his father.

Jeroboam was the man whom Solomon had put in charge of his forced labour gangs. He had an Egyptian heritage, in that he was a descendant of Joseph's son, Ephraim. (Genesis 46:20). This was the Joseph whom his brothers sold into Egypt. (Genesis 37:21-28).

There were other reasons for the break-away of the north. (1) During the time of their incursions into Israel, the Philistines had taken a strip of land that cut Judah off from the north. (2) There were political reasons. The northern tribes envied Judah, in that the Davidic dynasty from the tribe of Judah would always rule Israel. (3) The land in the north was better. (4) There were religious reasons. When Solomon centralized worship in Jerusalem, and the country shrines were closed, local people in the north resented this for commercial reasons.

Jeroboam was afraid that cultic union might create a desire for political union with Judah. (1 Kings 12:26-27). So, he took steps to establish places of worship in his own kingdom, which became known as the Kingdom of Israel. He made two golden calves and set one up in the town of Dan in the north, and the other in Bethel in the south, marking the northern and southern boundaries of his kingdom. He then said to his people: 'It was the golden calves that brought your ancestors out of Egypt, not the God who refuses to be imaged in Jerusalem.' (1 Kings 12:28; see Exodus 32:3-4). Jeroboam also built places of worship on hilltops, and he chose priests from families who were not of the tribe of Levi. (12:31). Thus, the break with Jerusalem was not only political, but religious and liturgical as well.

The northern kingdom was often referred to as Ephraim, so named after the tribe of Ephraim, which dominated its territory. This tribe received as its inheritance, the best part of the Land of Canaan, comprising the central highland region between the Jordan River and the Mediterranean Sea. (Genesis 49:22-26; Joshua 16:1-10).

Why did Rehoboam want to continue his father's building projects, but with greater intensity? One answer may be, that he wanted to build many more temples and shrines for the worship of foreign gods. In creating a multiplicity of pagan shrines in his kingdom, Jeroboam led the people back into Egyptian idolatry, the worship of the tangible, symbolizing materialism. (1 Kings 12:31). There would be consequences for the northern kingdom. Its people would be uprooted and scattered beyond the River Euphrates. (1 Kings 14:15-16).

With internal rebellions and coups among the ten northern tribes, no one dynasty lasted in the northern kingdom. Following his death, Jeroboam's entire family was wiped out in a palace revolt by the man who wanted to succeed him as king. This led to a civil war among the tribes. In one particular year, there was rule by four different kings. This gave no stability to the northern kingdom, which meant that the Kingdom of Israel was largely a failed State. It never knew why it existed, what god to worship, or what tribe out of the ten should be dominant or providing dynastic stability. All during the reigns of Rehoboam and Jeroboam, both kings were constantly at war with each other. (1 Kings 14:30). The rest of First Kings alternates between accounts of the northern and southern kingdoms.

Trouble arose in both kingdoms once an elite grew up around the kings who held most of the wealth and treated the people unjustly, thus fulfilling the prophecy of Samuel. (See 1 Samuel 8:4-18). The kings became new Pharaohs, and materialism the new god. Because the polytheistic gods personified natural forces and were no better than the people themselves, they could make no ethical demands on human beings. It would be easier to follow these gods than the God of Israel; you could pluck as much forbidden fruit as you wanted. Thus, the people abandoned the Mosaic covenant which was a call and a challenge to responsible communal living, in which the better-off would see to the needs of the marginalized.

From the strict historical perspective, the northern kingdom of Israel was doomed because it stood in the way of Assyria's imperial ambitions. However, from the Deuteronomic perspective, it was the Lord who was ultimately responsible for the Assyrian conquest. The Book of Deuteronomy formulated what was known as "the law of the king." (17:14-20). Not all provisions of this law were observed in Israel.

## Exile in Assyria

It was to critique this situation in the northern kingdom that God called prophets. The constant transgressions of the northern kings, and their refusal to listen to the prophets (2 Kings 17:14, 40; 18:12) produced a downward spiral into disaster.

The two great prophets of the northern Kingdom of Israel were Hosea and Amos, both of whom produced books of prophecy. They were active in the period before the conquest of the northern kingdom by the Assyrian empire (the land of the Euphrates and Tigris rivers).[87] In 721 BC. King Sargon of Assyria invaded the northern kingdom, took the capital Samaria and conquered Israel. The Assyrians removed many of the surviving Israelites and scattered them among the vast Assyrian empire. (See Genesis 11:1-9).

King Omri of Israel had previously made Samaria the capital city of the northern Kingdom of Israel. (1 Kings 16:21-28). His son Ahab also made Samaria the religious centre of his kingdom when he built a temple there. (1 Kings 16:30-33). However, the religion was the corrupt religion of Baal, imported by Ahab's pagan wife, Jezebel. (See 2 Kings 16). Israel's idolatry was the reason why God allowed the northern kingdom to be destroyed in 721 BC. When the people of Samaria and many others in the area surrounding the city were deported into exile, the Assyrians replaced them with other tribes from Assyria. (2 Kings 17:1-18; Ezra 4:2-11). These Assyrian tribes brought their pagan religious practices with them and intermarried with the locals. The resulting population became known as Samaritans. There was no deportation of people north of the Samaritan area, that is, in the area which later became the Roman province of Galilee. The Galileans retained their cultic connection with Judaism and the God of Israel. It was in Galilee that Jesus grew up.

---

[87] *World's Bible Dictionary*, p. 33-34.

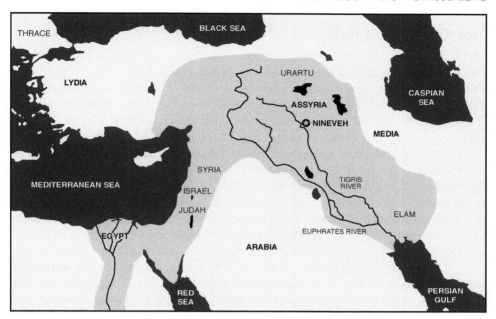

*The Assyrian Empire in the Eighth and Seventh Centuries BC*

Although the Samaritans accepted the first five books of the Bible, they still held onto many of their idolatrous customs, thus embracing a religion that was a mixture of Judaism and Baalism. (2 Kings 17:26-28). They never came to worship God in the Jerusalem temple, but built a temple for themselves on Mount Gerizim, near Shechem, in the hill country north of Jerusalem. (Deuteronomy 27:12-13; John 4:19-20). The people of the Kingdom of Judah considered the Samaritans as "half breeds" and grew to despise them. Further enmity arose when the Samaritans tried to halt the building of the walls of Jerusalem after the Judahite people returned from the Babylonian exile. (Nehemiah 6:1-14).

At the time of Jesus, there were three Roman provinces in what was then known as Palestine – Judea, Samaria, and Galilee in the far north. This meant that on a journey from Galilee to Jerusalem, Jesus and his disciples had to pass through Samaria. (See Jesus' counter cultural meeting with the Samaritan woman in chapter 4 of John's Gospel).

There is extra-biblical confirmation for the existence of some of the kings of Israel. One example comes from the time when the Assyrian empire was expanding its power and influence westwards into Israel. The Black Obelisk of King Shelmaneser III of Assyria (858-823 BC) portrays King Jehu of Israel (842-815) kneeling in homage before the Assyrian king while offering his annual tribute. This stele, which can be dated to 841 BC, indicates that the northern kingdom was a vassal of Assyria at that time.[88] There would be nine further kings in northern Israel before its fall to Assyria.

---

[88] Lawrence Boadt, *Reading the Old Testament*, p. 272.

## The Kingdom of Judah

The Kingdom of Judah had more stability than the northern kingdom. The dynasty of David continued to rule all the way down to the fall of Judah to Babylon – a period of about four-hundred years. Judah's kings tended to listen to the prophets. (1 Kings 12:24; 22:5,7). The promise to David is invoked three times to explain Judah's continued security. (1 Kings 11:36; 15:4; 2 Kings 8:19). But we learn that the wicked king Manasseh was the cause of the downfall of Judah. (2 Kings 23:26-27; 24:2-4).

Despite the flaws and failures of the kingdom of Judah, there was always a remnant who remained faithful to the Lord. The same was true of the northern kingdom. Following the fall of the northern kingdom, it is thought that some prophets and experts in the law of Moses came south to Jerusalem and brought their own traditions about Abraham and Moses with them. They combined these with the best of Judah's traditions in order to begin the creation of much of the Old Testament as we have it today. Thus, it was that the Scriptures were collected and eventually edited for inclusion in one book.

The First Book of Kings says that when Solomon's son, Rehoboam, was king of Judah, "the people of Judah sinned against the Lord." There were shrines to the god Baal at every oak tree and in every village in Canaan. The people built places of worship to false gods (Baal) on the hills and under shady trees. Perhaps because Solomon's mother was an Ammonite princess, Rehoboam wanted temples built to the god of Ammon. Worst of all, there were men and women who served as ritual prostitutes at these pagan places of worship. All of this was condemned by the prophets. (1 Kings 14:21-31; Jeremiah 3:6-10, 13:22-27; Hosea 4:7-14; Amos 2:7-8).

In the fifth year of Rehoboam's reign, the king of Egypt attacked Jerusalem and took away all the treasures in the temple and the palace. (1 Kings 14:25-26). First Kings doesn't say that the temple or palace was destroyed in this attack. They could have been, and this may be why archaeology reveals nothing of Solomon's building projects. Egypt may have been disappointed with the way affairs turned out in Israel as a whole. Perhaps Egypt could no longer see Israel as a dependable ally once the Egyptian princess whom Solomon married, failed to provide him with an heir to the throne.

The second king of Judah only ruled for three years. (1 Kings 15:1). Asa, the third king of Judah, was one of its greatest kings. (1 Kings 15:9-24; 2 Chronicles 15:16–16:6). He ruled in Jerusalem for forty-one years. This king expelled from the country all the male and female prostitutes serving at pagan places of worship and then destroyed all the pagan shrines built by Rehoboam. (1 Kings 15:9-13). Wars continued between Judah and the northern kingdom. (1 Kings 15:16).

Of the kings following Asa, there were good kings and bad kings. Some of them adopted the Canaanite practice of child sacrifice, even burning their own sons as an offering to pagan gods. (2 Kings 16:10-18). Second Kings says that King Ahaz did what was not pleasing to the Lord his God. He even sacrificed his own son as a burnt offering to idols. This king offered sacrifices and burned incense at pagan places of worship, on the hills, and under every shady tree. (2 Kings 16:1-4).

In Second Kings, chapters 18-20, there is an account of King Hezekiah who ruled Judah for twenty-nine years. Hezekiah did what was pleasing to the Lord. He destroyed the pagan places of worship and cut down the images of the goddess Asherah. It was during his reign that the Assyrian king, Shalmaneser invaded Israel, besieged Samaria and captured the city, bringing the northern kingdom of Israel to an end. Sometime later the new Assyrian king Sennacherib came and destroyed the fortified towns of Judah and laid siege to Jerusalem.

Hezekiah was succeeded by his son Manasseh who ruled in Jerusalem for fifty-five years. (2 Kings chapter 21). According to 2 Kings, Manasseh was a wicked king who sinned against the Lord. He rebuilt the pagan places of worship that his father, Hezekiah had destroyed. "Manasseh killed so many innocent people that the streets of Jerusalem were flowing with blood; he did this in addition to leading the people of Judah to worship Baal." (2 Kings 21:16). In the valley of Hinnom outside the walls of Jerusalem, Manasseh burned his sons as offerings to the god Molech, the god of the Ammonites. In later times, Hinnom became a metaphor for hell. (2 Chronicles 33:4-6). A well-known feature of the worship of Molech was the sacrifice of children by fire. As a result of this breach of the covenant and a turning to paganism and all that it symbolized, the Lord promised disaster on Jerusalem and Judah. (See 2 Kings 21:10-15; see also 2 Kings 17:17; 2 Chronicles 28:1-3; Psalm 106:38; Jeremiah 7:31; Ezekiel 16:21; 20:31; 23:39). Because Israel moved away from the covenant, God raised up prophets in both Israelite kingdoms in order to critique the society of their day.

Manasseh's grandson Josiah, was a reforming king, whom Second Kings names as having followed the example of David, strictly obeying the laws of God. (2 Kings 22-23). Josiah's reforms followed the discovery of the "Book of God's Law" in the temple. (2 Kings 22:23-24). This is thought to have been older parts of the Book of Deuteronomy. Josiah then called together the people of Judah and had this scroll read to them in the temple. The message of Deuteronomy was that the unfulfilled demands of the Mosaic law endangered the nation and was not pleasing to the Lord. (2 Kings 22:13).

Josiah was moved to reforms. "Josiah stood up in the temple and made a covenant with the Lord to obey him, to keep his laws and commands with all his heart and soul, and to put into practice the demands of the covenant, as written in the Book of Deuteronomy. All the people promised to keep the covenant." (2 Kings 22:3). Josiah extended his reforms to the former kingdom of Israel in the north. (22:15-20). He eliminated all the high places of worship. (23:8-9). He demolished the Bethel altar of Jeroboam, the place where Jeroboam had placed a bull calf image. (23:15-18). He destroyed the pagan site in the valley of Hinnom near Jerusalem, so that no one could sacrifice a son or daughter as a burnt offering to the god Molech. (23:10, 13-14). The verdict of the Deuteronomic historian on the rule of Josiah: "There had never been a king like him before, who served the Lord with all his heart, mind and strength, obeying the law of Moses; nor has there been a king like him since." (2 Kings 23:25).

However, both Josiah's life and his reforms were cut short by his untimely death. By the year 612 BC, the great Assyrian city of Nineveh had been burned to the ground by the rising Babylonians. The remnant of the Assyrian army retreated northward and assembled at Haran near the source of the rivers Euphrates and Tigris for a last stand against Babylon. The Pharaoh Neco of Egypt preferred a weak Assyria to a rising Babylonia. With this in mind, he set out with his army, marching through Israel on his way north to the aid of the Assyrians. King Josiah tried to stop him at the fortified city of Megiddo in northern Israel and was killed in the battle. (2 Kings 23:28-30). The Babylonians defeated the combined forces of Egypt and the Assyrians in 609 BC. But Neco did not leave Israel alone. He decided to control Judah as a buffer against Babylon. Thus, in its last years, the kingdom of Judah was caught up in a conflict between Egypt and Babylon, trying to play off both sides to win its freedom, but failing to do so.

Josiah was willing to obey God's law without any hope of reward. But his reforms seemed to have died with him. The influence of Manasseh was all-pervasive. Nothing would be able to divert divine judgement. (22:16-17). "The Lord said, "I will do to Judah what I have done to Israel: I will banish the people of Judah from my sight, and I will reject Jerusalem, the city I chose, and the temple, the place I said where I was to be worshiped."" (2 Kings 23:27). The religious life of this kingdom went into decline. Idolatry and other pagan practices were still tolerated, including ritual prostitution in a fertility cult of the Canaanite god Baal.

## Exile in Babylon

Babylon had been a province in the Assyrian empire. But following a rebellion which led to the overthrow of its Assyrian overlord, it became the dominant power in the Near East. Before long, it would seek to extend its power towards the land of Israel.

During the years leading up to the Babylonian exile, a succession of prophets (Isaiah, Micah, Jeremiah, Habakuk, Ezekiel and Malachi) had been warning of God's coming judgement on the nation Judah (the southern kingdom) and its people. These prophets attributed the nation's fate to the sinfulness of the people, especially the elite at the top of society, for their infidelity to the covenant, in other words, for embracing the materialistic values of empire. During the period of the kings, the biblical authors wanted to emphasise that God alone is the true king (fortress, shield, protector) of the whole of Israel (both kingdoms). The earthly king's role is to put into practice the law of God given by Moses. But the kings behaved like absolute monarchs, disregarding the Ten Commandments, ignoring the warnings of the prophets, and bringing misfortune on the people

The prophets named the kings as bad shepherds of the people, leading the people astray, but most of the kings ignored these warnings. The result was that the Kingdom of Judah came to an end in 586 BC after a siege of Jerusalem which lasted two years. The city and temple were destroyed by the Babylonian armies under King Nabuchadnezzar,[89] and the leading citizens were taken into exile in Babylon. King Zedekiah of Judah was captured, his sons put to death in his presence, the king's eyes put out, after which he himself was placed in chains and brought to Babylon, between the two great rivers, the Tigris and Euphrates. (See 2 Kings chap. 25).

The promised land was only given to Israel conditionally. If the people gave their allegiance to God by following in his ways and obeying the Ten Commandments, God would bless them and they would live long in the land he gave them. (See Deuteronomy 30:16-18). But as affairs turned out, the story was otherwise. The disobedience in the

---

[89] See *World's Bible Dictionary*, p. 37-40.

Garden of Eden led to death. This time because of the grasping the forbidden fruit of power, greed and affluence, there followed a death-like exile back in the land from which Abraham originated. But despite their desertion of him, God would not abandon the people he still loved. While away in Babylon, they might reflect on their past lives and discover that they were sent into exile because of their sins of disobedience. But that would take some time. A time would come when a remnant would return to begin a new relationship with God all over again.

After the return of the Judean exiles to Jerusalem in 539 BC, the inhabitants of Judah became known as Jews. The story of the rebuilding of the temple is told in chapters 3 and 4 of the Book of Ezra. This temple was only a shadow of the splendour of Solomon's temple. The monarchy was never restored in either Israelite kingdom.

Along with the Israelite king, the queen had a significant role in the government of the nation. In Israel, as in all other near eastern kingdoms, it was not the king's wife, but his mother (known as the queen mother) who assumed a degree of status and authority. Kings would have had many wives but there could be only one queen. People coming with petitions would approach the queen mother as their advocate with the king. This foreshadows Mary, who is our mother, queen and advocate with Jesus. When there was a crisis at a wedding, the wine running out, the servants came to Mary. Jesus' mother told the servants, 'Do whatever he tells you.' (John 2:5).

Because the Jews continued to live under imperial power after the return of the exiles from Babylon, they were left wondering when God would rescue them and bring their exile really to an end. As we will see, the prophets declared that God would truly become king of the world, the oppressive pagans would be overthrown and the people would be free at last. A later prophetic development saw God's kingdom being founded on righteousness and justice (irrespective of the political system). The hope remained that sometime in the future, God would definitively pass judgement on evil and set everything right at last.

The kingdom ideal was only fully purified when Jesus came and understood himself as Second Isaiah's Suffering Servant and the long-promised Messiah in the line of David, who would rule forever in a Kingdom extending to the ends of the earth. Through his sufferings (not by violence against the pagans, but by enduring their blows), he would liberate the whole of humanity from all the divisions, oppressions and blows that held them captive, including the captivity of death itself, and unite everyone, including the pagans in his kingdom of justice, brotherly love and peace.

## Summary of Events to Date

- The Patriarchs – beginning with Abraham (about 1850 - 1350 BC)
- Egyptian Exile (beginning sometime between 1800 - 1400 BC).
- The Founding Event: The exodus from Egypt (about 1250 BC)
- The Monarchy in Israel (1000 – 586 BC)
- The Babylonian Exile (586 – 539 BC)
- Foreign occupation (539 BC – 100 AD), first the Persians (after the exile), then in 332 BC the Greeks (following the conquests of Alexander the Great); and finally, in 63 BC the Romans). All foreign occupation was in the form of imperial domination.

CHAPTER 6

# Amos, Hosea and Isaiah

## Introduction to the Prophets

Apart from mainly Moses, all the Old Testament prophets emerged, and were active during the period of the kings of Israel and Judah, i.e. from about 900 - 587 BC. Let us recall that after the death of King Solomon, Israel was divided into two kingdoms – the northern Kingdom of Israel, with Samaria as its capital city, and the southern kingdom of Judah, with Jerusalem its capital.

First of all, there were the non-writing prophets, the most important of whom were Elijah, Elisha (1 Kings 17-19), and Samuel in the Books of Samuel. The teaching and works of these prophets were recorded and included in the Scriptures by unknown authors.

Of the prophets whose writings have survived, there were both major and minor prophets. The minor prophets were regarded as such, only because their accounts are much shorter than those of the major prophets.

In the books of the writing prophets, most of the text appears in formal poetry, in which the authors make extensive use of such images as covenant, king, shepherd and marriage in order to reveal something of God's love relationship with his people.

The prophetic message - whether from minor or major prophets - remained the same throughout the whole period of prophecy: insincere worship of God only gives legitimacy to a corrupt and materialistic society, and religious and moral corruption will lead to the fall of both Israelite kingdoms.

Amos and Hosea were two minor prophets. Amos ministered in the northern Kingdom of Israel about the middle of the eighth century BC. Hosea followed Amos and also preached in the northern kingdom during the troubled times before the fall of Samaria in 721 BC. All of the major prophets ministered in the kingdom of Judah, the first of whom was Isaiah of Jerusalem, who appeared on the scene soon after Amos. Isaiah was followed by Jeremiah, who ministered during the long period leading up to the fall of Jerusalem and the deportation of its people to Babylon in 586 BC. Then came two anonymous prophets, possibly disciples of Isaiah of Jerusalem, whose writings are included in the second and third parts of the Book of Isaiah. Ezekiel was a prophet who went to Babylon along with the first deportation in 596 BC. Prophecy came to an end soon after the Jewish exiles returned from Babylon in 537 BC. This means that the period of the writing prophets in Israel was about two-hundred years.

## The Mission of the Prophet

The primary role of the biblical prophets was to act as spokespersons for God in interpreting the meaning of historical events. The prophets were inspired to hear and listen to the word of God calling them to transmit to those in power God's words of advice and reproach. (Isaiah 50:4-5). How could the prophets be the mouthpiece of God? How did they know that their word to humanity was actually God's word, what God wanted them to say? Filled with the Spirit of God, the prophets had a deep knowledge of God. (Isaiah 61:1). They were enabled to see into the mind and heart of God, thinking and feeling like him, becoming of one mind with him, absorbing his passion for justice and mercy. Having been thus inspired by God's Spirit, the prophets were empowered to bring the good news of salvation to the poor, to all those who were denied justice and mercy in Israel. (Isaiah 61:1). "The prophet discloses divine love and disappointment, mercy and indignation."[90] He not only lives his personal life, but also has God living in him.

The prophets saw a wide gulf between the ways of man and God. (See Isaiah 6:1-5). And because of their insight that human beings had strayed so far from the God of justice and mercy, they believed that their mission was to reconcile man and God, to bring man back into obedience to the will of God. "Such reconciliation was necessary because of man's false sense of sovereignty, his abuse of freedom, his aggressive pride in his own efforts, resenting and usurping God's sovereignty in history."[91]

Having heard the voice of God, the prophets could not remain silent, ever feeling a compulsion to speak his word to the people, despite opposition and persecution. (Ezekiel 2:5-6). But like most people who speak the truth, they were met with hostility and sometimes with violence. Despite opposition and the threat of death, the prophet Jeremiah could not stop speaking the word of God, which, in his own words, had taken over his life: "I hear so many disparaging me, terror from every side! 'Denounce him! Denounce him!' "All those who used to be my friends watched for my downfall." (Jeremiah 20:10, JB; see Jeremiah 6:1-11; 15:10). What may have sustained the prophets, was their experience of the Spirit of God living in them, giving them a knowledge of the word of God and empowering them to face opposition and persecution in pursuit of God's justice.

If God's word does not take us out of our comfort zone and make demands on us, we have never heard it. If it has not called us to where we do not want to go, we have not yet heard the voice of the prophets, nor the word spoken through them. Deafness to their word and blindness to the ways of God is a constant complaint of the prophets. (See Isaiah 6:10; 42:18-20).

---

[90] Abraham J. Heschel, *The Prophets*, (HarperPerennial Modern Classics, Harper Collins Publishers), New York 10007, p. 29.

[91] Ibid, *The Prophets*, 2001, p. xxix.

# Themes of the Prophets

One of the major themes of the prophets is liberation. As was the case with Moses, the prophets were called to a mission of liberating people from their blindness and deafness to the ways of God, leaving them in bondage to things which are not of the will of God – the false gods of military power, self-aggrandisement, greed and exploitation of their fellow men and women. The message of the prophets is that those things will lead to suffering and death, and salvation will be further away than ever. The prophets envision a caring society in which social justice and mercy will prevail, no more war, peace among the vineyards. (Micah 4:3-4; Isaiah 2:4). Justice implies relationship; one cannot become just all by oneself. Justice is about acknowledging and respecting the needs and rights of everyone in society, so that the common good may be served. Justice creates peace and communal harmony, which is the will of God for the world.

Secondly is the theme of self-exaltation and humiliation. In the early stages of the monarchy, God was accepted as the true king of Israel. But before long, the Israelite kings had thrown off the protective hand of God and become politically autonomous. Rather than trusting in God, they began to rely on their own efforts and on things made by their own hands for their salvation: affluence, protective city walls, military power and alliances with other nations. Such self-exaltation would lead to humiliation. The prophets warned that the times of affluence would not last; silver and gold would melt away, horses and chariots would be ground into the dust, and salvation would be further away than ever. When human beings exalt themselves, they usurp God and his will for the world. This will always lead to unwelcome consequences.

God's sovereignty over history is one of the major prophetic themes. Because God created the world (a prophetic insight), he must be concerned about its welfare, loving it and guiding it in line with his good purposes. For the prophets, history is ultimately the work of God; it is God's justice and judgement in action in the world. Whether human beings acknowledge it or not, God is in control and present in history, even in its calamities, bringing good out of evil. Even empires can sometimes serve God's purposes in ways that can be baffling.

For the prophets, history is not just a recitation of past events. Because history is guided by God, it has a purpose; it looks towards the creation of a new and glorious future. God sees all of time in one single vision – the past, present and future. The prophets share in this vision of the whole. They look back into their past history to the time when God liberated his people from slavery in Egypt (Exodus). Having liberated them in the past, they trust and hope that he will not abandon them; he will continue to guide and help them in the future. (Exodus 3:12). And even when everything is at its darkest, when human attempts to create states of perfection only lead to chaos and destruction, the prophets still continue to hope, that, in the end, God will prevail and establish his reign over all the forces of evil. Only the Sovereign God can ultimately bring the salvation (everything put right) which humanity craves, and which, as the later prophets began to see, may only be realizable in its fullness in a newly created world beyond this time and space.

Is there not a conflict between God's direction of history and ordinary human causation? God's ways may often be obscure and hidden, but he works with his human partners and with historical causation to bring his purposes to fulfilment (just as he worked through natural causation in the creation and evolution of the universe). To take an example: Because Babylon had imperial ambitions, it wanted to control small States such as Israel in order to create a buffer against Egypt, which was also set on imperial expansion. Babylon could not tolerate rebellion by these States, so it invaded Judah and took the people into exile in 586 BC. It could be said that Babylonian aggrandisement was the proximate cause of Judah's downfall. But God had a hidden purpose in all of this, which was to use Babylon as his instrument of judgement on Judah for her failure to create a just society under God's guiding hand. The prophets thus taught that God was the ultimate cause of Judah's downfall.

The above interpretation of history is not how history is viewed in the secular world. Today, history is seen as what man, in his freedom, does with his own power. Like the prophets, secularists also see history proceeding towards the goal of a perfect society. But as against the prophets, they believe that the only driving force in history is human beings themselves. "Modern interpretations of history see history as the arena in which man reigns supreme, with the forces of nature as his only adversary."[92] However, the view that sees man as sovereign is problematic. It is a form of self-exaltation. It rejects the guiding hand of God, something which humans need, because they may misuse their power and be mistaken in their ideas of justice. The prophets repudiated human self-exaltation, as idolatrous. They warned that it would lead to the misuse of power, and ultimately to injustice and oppression. They denounced "arrogant boasting" and "haughty pride" (Isaiah 10:7-12). They denounced the kings who ruled the nations in anger, the oppressors (Isaiah 14:4-6); "these men whose power is their god." (Habakkuk 1:9-11).

In their all-encompassing vision, the prophets see God's judgement being ultimately enacted and his kingship universally established beyond this world – as voiced in a passage in Isaiah 24:17-23, which foreshadows the "coming of the Son of Man" passage in Luke 21:25-28. God's sovereignty becomes fully operative in Jesus. Human beings cannot lift themselves up out of their disabled condition solely by their own efforts. Jesus is the Good Samaritan who comes into this world and rescues and heals wounded humanity on the road of life. (Luke 10:25-37).

The modern world prizes individualism. The teaching of the prophets can be seen as sound psychology when it proposes that the less self-centred our lives become, and the more we are concerned for the welfare of others, the less likely we are to suffer from maladjustments, neuroses, depression and other modern ills.

It is a mistake to think that the prophets were people who were able to predict or foretell the future. Of course, there are times in which they can see the immediate consequences of certain actions and events, and they issue warnings. But there is no way in which they could predict the coming of a Messiah such as Jesus. It is rather, that the authors of the New Testament understand Jesus as fulfilling Old Testament prophecy. Many issues that had been left unresolved in the Old Testament were fulfilled by Jesus. He is God's definitive word to humanity.

[92] Heschel, *The Prophets*, p. 242.

## The Prophets' Critique of Domination Systems

With the establishment of the monarchy in Israel about 1,000 BC, a system developed in which the political, economic, social and religious structures were controlled by elites of power and wealth around the king, in order to serve their own interests. This system left the vast number of the population oppressed and exploited.

As we have already seen, there were two main views associated with the emergence of the monarchy in Israel: one anti-monarchical, and the other pro-monarchical.[93] As events unfolded, the monarchy would appear to have been a betrayal of God, because it led to a breach of the Sinai covenant and a rejection of the God of justice and mercy, God being the true king of Israel. The anti-monarchical tradition reflects prophetic theology. The prophet's task is to critique the flaws of the monarchical system and to call the kings to account when they depart from God's covenant (justice and mercy for everyone).

The prophets were critical of the society of their day, which did not reflect the kind of community envisioned by the Books of Deuteronomy and Exodus, in which the strong were called by God to protect the weak and in which everyone would be treated justly. (See Deuteronomy 10:17-19). During the long reign of King Uzziah of Judah (c.791-739 BC), severe social and religious problems developed in the kingdom of Judah. The people continued to offer sacrifices at pagan places of worship. Greed and injustice multiplied, and although the people maintained their religious practices, they remained ungodly in their behaviour. (2 Kings 15:1-7; 2 Chronicles 26:1-23).

## Amos

Amos was the first prophet with a book to his name. He was born and raised in the southern kingdom of Judah, but directed his prophecy mainly towards the northern kingdom of Israel. He was active in the mid eighth century BC (ca.750), towards the end of the reign of King Jeroboam II of Israel, ca.786-746 BC and King Uzziah of Judah. (2 Kings 14:23-29).

Amos would have gained the enthusiastic attention of his readers by announcing God's judgement on Israel's neighbours (Syria, Philistia, Tyre, Edom, Ammon and Moab) for their cruelty and oppression, some of which was visited on Israel. (See Amos 1:3-15). The prophet then turned his attention to Judah for its own sinfulness. Its people despised the teachings and commandments of the Lord and were led astray by false gods. Judah will not escape judgement. (Amos 2:4-5).

Amos condemned the corruption of Israel's capital city Samaria (3:9–4:3) and the refusal of the people to heed God's warnings. (4:4-13). God called for repentance (5:1-27), and warned that the nation's corruption was leading it to destruction. (6:1-14).

The eighth century BC was a period of great prosperity in the northern kingdom of Israel, but only for an elite, resulting in injustice and the oppression of the poor, especially people who worked the land. Judgement by the Creator God would follow:

---

[93]  Marcus J. Borg, *Reading the Bible Again for the First Time*, p. 128, 129.

> Israel prepare to meet your God!
> For look, he it is
> who forges the mountains, creates the wind,
> who reveals his mind to mankind,
> changes the dawn into darkness
> and strides on the heights of the world:
> Yahweh, God Sabaoth, is his name. (Amos 4:13, NJB).

Amos has an understanding of God which is close to monotheism. God has the power to pass judgement on humankind *because* he is the one who "forges the mountains and creates the wind." This is a revelation of God as the Creator of the universe, but unlike the later prophet Isaiah (Isaiah 43:10-13), Amos does not say that the Creator is the only God that exists.

Furthermore, an unjust social system went hand-in-hand with religious observance. But what God wanted more than religious ritual and festivals was a just society—people obedient to his will.

> The Lord says to the people of Israel,
> 'Come to me and you will live.
> Do not go to Beersheba to worship.
> Do not try to find me at Bethel[94] –
> Bethel will come to nothing.
> Do not go to Gilgal – her people are doomed to exile.
> Go to the Lord and you will live.
> If you do not go, he will sweep down like fire
> on the people of Israel.
> You are doomed,
> you that twist justice
> and cheat the people out of their rights…
> You people have oppressed the poor
> and robbed them of their grain.
> And so you will not live in the fine houses you build
> or drink wine from the vineyards you plant.
> You persecute good people and take bribes
> and prevent the poor from getting justice in the courts.
> Make it your aim to do what is right,
> not what is evil, so that you may live.
> Then the Lord God Almighty really will be with you,
> as you claim he is.
> Hate what is evil,
> love what is right,
> and see that justice prevails in the courts.

---

[94] Location of a pagan shrine during the time of Amos. The Ark of the Covenant was kept there before the period of the monarchy in Israel.

Perhaps God will be merciful to the people of this nation
who are still left alive…
I hate your religious festivals; I cannot stand them.
I will not accept the animals you have fattened
to bring me as offerings.
Stop your noisy songs; I do not want to listen to your harps.
Instead, let justice flow like a living stream,
and righteousness like a river that never goes dry.'
(Amos 5:4-7, 11-12,14-15; 21-24).

These prophetic warnings went unheeded in the northern kingdom. So according to Amos, the Lord God "is about to visit the nation in judgement." (See Amos 5:16-20). The metaphor of fire (5:6) may be interpreted as judgement, in that God will allow the Assyrian Empire to conquer the northern kingdom and take its people into exile.

For Amos, the God of Israel is a God who wants justice and mercy for the downtrodden and oppressed, as was the case when God delivered slaves out of Egypt and gave them a land of their own. In this context, it may be well to recall Moses' instructions and warnings in Deuteronomy before the people entered the promised land. (See Deuteronomy 8:1-20; 10:17-22; 11:8-17).

Amos ends his prophecy with a message of hope to the Kingdom of David, i.e. Judah. Its ruins will be rebuilt, restoring its glory to what it was in the past. (Amos 9:11-15). In the New Testament the kingdom of David is transformed into the Kingdom of God and rebuilt by the Messiah (Christ), who fulfilled the hopes of Amos.

## Hosea

Amos was succeeded by Hosea, who preached in the northern kingdom during the troubled times before the fall of its capital, Samaria to the Assyrian empire in 721 BC. Hosea sees his unfaithful wife (Hosea 1:2) as symbolic of the unfaithfulness of Israel to its God. His wife Gomer had repeatedly deserted him for other men. But each time God told him to take her back again. Through this experience with his unfaithful wife, Hosea had the insight into Israel's abandonment of God. God remained faithful to his people, even though they were not. God was patiently, faithfully waiting for the day when Israel would return at last to him. God still loved Israel and he would win her back again. 'How can I give you up, Israel? How can I abandon you? My heart will not let me do it. My love for you is too strong.' (Hosea 11:8; see 2:16, 23). This must have been a new revelation of God as steadfast love–still loving his people, even when they repeatedly turned away from him.

Israel, I will make you my wife;
I will be true and faithful;
I will show you constant love and mercy
and make you mine forever.
(Hosea 2:19).

Hosea is known as the prophet of divine love, of a God willing to suffer in order to win back his beloved. This prophecy of Hosea is fulfilled in Jesus, who suffered and gave his life so that the nuptial bond between God and his people might be definitively restored, through a new covenant. (See Mark 14:24).

But when tender love has been betrayed, justice can be fierce and relentless. Towards the end of his book, Hosea sees that God's beloved, namely Israel, has betrayed and abandoned her lover God, and so the prophet has no doubt about the judgement that will fall on Israel as a consequence. In the early days of her relationship with God, Israel was a faithful spouse, who was fully satisfied with everything he gave her, but then she grew proud of her own achievements in the promised land and no longer saw the guiding hand of God in her life. Although God is a caring shepherd, he can also be like a leopard ready to pounce (judgement).

> I am the Lord your God
> Since the days in the land of Egypt;
> you know no God but me,
> there is no other saviour.
> I pastured you in the wilderness;
> in the land of drought.
> I pastured them, and they were satisfied;
> once satisfied their hearts grew proud,
> and so they came to forget me.
> Very well, I will be like a lion to them,
> a leopard lurking in the way;
> Like a bear robbed of her cubs
> I will pounce on them
> and tear the flesh from their hearts. (Hosea 13:4-8, JB).

In the light of the above quotation, we may refer to some Old Testament passages, as an example of how Hosea was influenced by his tradition. (See Deuteronomy 32:8-14; 32:15-29; 14-22; Psalm 78:9-29).

Judgement would fall on the people (the northern kingdom of Israel). They turned away from their God, and all over the land they sold themselves like prostitutes to the god Baal. (Hosea 9:1). "The Lord says, 'Sound the alarm! Enemies are swooping down on my land like eagles. My people have broken the covenant I made with them and have rebelled against my teaching.'" (8:1). The prophet says, 'The Lord I serve will reject his people, because they have not listened to him. They will become wanderers among the nations.' (Hosea 9:17, see Genesis 4:16).

The prophets were the first men in history to condemn militarism as idolatrous - a reliance on horses and chariots to save them from invasion by a powerful empire. (Hosea 2:18; 10:13-14). Hosea prophesised that divine judgement would fall on the northern Kingdom of Israel, in the form of conquest by the Assyrian empire (9:3). But there remained the hope of a return to the great days of King David, who was regarded as the ideal king. (Hosea 3:5; 11:11).

Chapter 17 of the Second Book of Kings tells why the Assyrians under Tiglath Pileser, captured Samaria and took the Israelites of the northern kingdom into exile as prisoners, in 721 BC. It was because of their idolatry. "They even sacrificed their sons and daughters as burnt offerings to pagan gods." (2 Kings 17:17). It wasn't that God abandoned them; they had already walked away from the God of Israel for other gods. (See Genesis 3:8).

Hosea ends his prophecy with a note of hope. The Lord will bring his people back to himself again and love them with all his heart. (See Hosea 14:4-8).

## Introduction to the Book of Isaiah

The Book of Isaiah takes its name from the prophet Isaiah of Jerusalem. It covers three different periods in the history of the chosen people. This can only mean that there are three different prophets writing under the name Isaiah. The word 'Isaiah' means 'the Lord saves.' The book represents the prophet's dream, or vision. The book as a whole adopts a positive note - a hope in God's redemption of his people and the ultimate triumph of his rule on earth.

Chapters 1 to 39 are mostly from a prophet named Isaiah who ministered in Jerusalem during the second half of the 8th century (ca. 750-600 BC). That prophet has been named First Isaiah. The remaining chapters of the book couldn't have been written by him. He had been dead for over a hundred years. The author of Isaiah 40-55 is an anonymous prophet, whom biblical scholars refer to as Second Isaiah. This prophet was active in Babylon towards the end of the Babylonian exile, about 125 years after First Isaiah. Chapters 56-66 contain an account of Third Isaiah - also an anonymous prophet, - who ministered in Jerusalem after the Jewish exiles returned home from Babylon in 539 BC.

The early Church fathers referred to the Book of Isaiah as the Fifth Gospel. In Matthew 2:23, there is a reference to the Immanuel prophecy (Isaiah 7:14). Isaiah's Fourth Servant Song (Isaiah 52:13-15 - 53:1-12) influenced Jesus in his vocation as God's suffering servant. (See Acts 8:32-33, which is a quote from the Fourth Servant Song).

Christians see Isaiah's theme of the "new Jerusalem" (Isaiah 52:1-12; 60:1-3; 65:17-19) as a metaphor for God's people, who through Christ, are promised a glorious future. The Christian reader of Isaiah views the establishment of the "new Jerusalem" as a metaphor for God's new creation of the union of heaven and earth at the end of time, God's ultimate triumph over all the forces of evil, including death itself – a development inspired by the Book of Isaiah. (See Revelation 21:1-4).

Both Isaiah of Jerusalem and Second Isaiah are deemed to have been among the greatest poets of the ancient world. The whole book is renowned for its literary style and imagery, but mainly for its profound spiritual insights. Of all the prophets, Isaiah (including all three prophets) offers the most significant teaching about the expected Messiah. The authors of this book are more frequently quoted in the New Testament than any other prophet. Tributes to Isaiah are manifold. "Isaiah's words contain a mix of ethical insight, realistic warning of disaster, and long-range hopefulness that establish him as having the most profound vision of the Old Testament."[95] The author of the Book of Ecclesiasticus (written about 190 BC) has the following tribute to Isaiah, with the book as a whole in mind:

> In the days of Isaiah, the sun moved back;
>   he prolonged the life of the king.
> In the power of the Spirit he saw the last things,
>   he comforted the mourners of Zion,
> he revealed the future to the end of time,
>   and hidden things long before they happened. (Ecclesiasticus 48:23-25, NJB).

## Isaiah of Jerusalem (First Isaiah)

The prophecy of Isaiah of Jerusalem (chaps. 1-39) comes from a time when the Kingdom of Judah was threatened by the Assyrian empire. Isaiah saw that the real threat to the life of Judah was the people's own sins and their trust in things other than God for their salvation.

First Isaiah can be divided as follows: (1) Chapters 1-12 are concerned with the moral decline of Israel and Judah. The prophet calls the people and their leaders to a life of right living and warns that the failure to listen to the word of God will bring doom and destruction on the nation. (2) Chapters 13-23: doom will also strike the other nations for their crimes of cruelty and oppression. (3) In chapter 24, judgement is passed on the whole earth. The people have defiled the earth by their sins, and its people are paying the price for what they have done. (4) The Immanuel prophecies and the hope of the Messiah (7:14; 9:1-7; 11:1-9). (5) Chapters 25 and 26 include the promise of salvation, a hymn of praise to God for his ultimate victory over all the forces of evil and a banquet on Mount Zion to celebrate the victory. Chapter 26 has a song in praise of an ultimately renewed and purified Jerusalem. This prophecy looks ahead to the new Jerusalem in the Book of Revelation, which is a revelation of the ultimate salvation of humanity. (Revelation 21:1-2).

Isaiah of Jerusalem received his call to be a prophet about the time of the death of Uzziah, King of Judah (ca. 739 BC). This prophet ministered under the four following kings of Judah: the Jotham Ahaz co-regency (741-726 BC, 2 Kings 15:32-38 – 16:1:20); Hezekiah (726-697 BC, 2 Kings 18-20). Isaiah died during the reign of Manasseh. (2 Kings 21:1-18; 2 Chronicles 33:1-20). First Isaiah was a contemporary of the minor prophet Micah.

The greatness of Isaiah of Jerusalem rests on his vision of the transcendence of God, "the Holy One", the Mighty One who exists beyond the world, giving the world and humanity a purpose, and a destiny, as the fulfilment of history; secondly, on his insight into man's unworthiness and dependence on God. (Isaiah 6:1-5); and thirdly on his ability to see beyond the harsh reality of the Jerusalem of his day to a glorious future for the city.

It is clear that Isaiah of Jerusalem had disciples, and that he wanted them to guard and preserve his message. (See Isaiah 8:16). There may thus have been a School of Isaiah which was responsible for the composition and addition of new material (chaps. 34-35)

---

[95] Lawrence Boadt, (*Reading the Old Testament*), p. 292.

to the original text of the 8th century BC prophet (First Isaiah). These disciples continued for more than a century to work in the style and viewpoint of their founder, thus bringing to completion the Book of Isaiah.

## Isaiah's Call to be a Prophet

> In the year that King Uzziah died (ca. 742 BC), I saw the Lord. He was sitting on his throne, high and exalted, and his robe filled the whole Temple. Round him flaming creatures were standing… They were calling to each other, 'Holy, Holy, Holy! The Lord Almighty is holy! His glory fills the world.' The sound of their voices made the foundations of the Temple shake, and the Temple itself was filled with smoke. I said, 'There is no hope for me! I am doomed because every word that passes my lips is sinful, and I live among people whose every word is sinful. And yet, with my own eyes, I have seen the king, the Lord Almighty. (Isaiah 6:1-5).

An extraordinary claim – to have seen the Lord! Isaiah "saw" the Lord God. This means that his eyes were opened to God's glory and magnificence, his ears, to hear the heavenly chorus acclaim God's holiness, and his heart softened to confess his guilt and be healed. In order to convey something of his awesome experience of God, the prophet draws on a series of images. (Verse 4). This revelation of God's holiness and exaltation brought home to the prophet a deep sense of his own unworthiness and sinfulness - and the sinfulness of the people, which he saw as self-exaltation. God alone is the exalted One. This vision of the exalted God, is a major theme running through the whole of the Isaiah prophecy. The word "holy" may be a reference to the moral quality of God - the just and merciful One, who expects justice to be done on earth, and secondly to the uniqueness of God, as utterly other than the universe, God possessing the fullness (wholeness) of life and existence. The Lord's splendour and holiness permeates the prophet's whole message, and it is contrasted with man's limitations and flaws. (1:4, 5:24; 10:17, 20; 29:19, 23; 30:11, 12, 15). Isaiah would continue to proclaim that Israel owed its allegiance to this God alone.

Throughout his mission, the prophet would struggle to get people to "see" their sins. Humility means human beings seeing themselves as they really are, as having a sense of their limitations and dependency on God. When human beings exalt themselves, they violate their nature. They become proud. They usurp God and place their sole trust in their own efforts and schemes for salvation. They act in defiance of the will of God – disobedience, ultimately leading to death. (See Genesis 2:15-17; 3:6).

The prophet goes on to say that one of the flaming creatures in the vision touched his lips with a burning coal and said, 'This has touched your lips, and now your guilt is gone, and your sins are forgiven.' (6:7). The burning coal purifying the prophet's voice, is a metaphor for his empowerment to speak passionately to the people with the voice and words of God. (6:7). He has his lips purged of guilt, but as for the people themselves, not until Isaiah chapter 40 does God bring about such a remission.

In response to God's question, 'Whom shall I send?' the prophet answers, 'I will go! Send me!' (6:8). "So he told me to go and give the people this message: 'No matter how much you listen you will not understand. No matter how much you look, you will not know what is happening'" (Isaiah 6:9). Isaiah has his eyes and ears opened to who God is. His vision of the holy and exalted God would have been completely new to his audience. How is he going to deliver a message to a people whose ears are deaf and their eyes blind, both to the reality of God and to their own sins. They refuse to live as God wants them to live or obey his teachings. (See Isaiah 42:18-25). And how will the prophet communicate a new understanding of God (Isaiah 40:25-26) to a people still hooked on the notion of the tribal God, whom they see fighting battles on their behalf? There may be a touch of irony in God telling Isaiah to "make the minds of these people dull, their ears deaf and their eyes blind, so that they cannot see or hear or understand. Even if they are listening, they will have no understanding." If they did understand, they would turn to God (repent) and "be healed." (6:10).

What is the meaning of "seeing" God? (Isaiah 6:5). It has nothing to do with seeing some kind of apparition. It is about insight rather than physical seeing. The blindness of human beings consists in giving themselves glory, usurping God and setting themselves up in his place – self-exaltation. Human pride is the great obstacle to trusting in God and gaining divine wisdom. (See Isaiah 5:19, 21; 29:15). Isaiah "saw," and heard the Lord calling him to a mission of opening eyes and ears. His tragedy would be his failure to communicate his glorious vision to a blind and deaf people. Being spiritually blind, they would never be able to "see" that the unjust society, over which they presided, was not of the will of God. They would remain deaf to God's call to repent, to turn to the Lord and obey his will.

The reading of First Isaiah may prompt a question for ourselves: can we "see" ourselves and our own society today in its pages? And how should we respond to that question? At the start of his ministry, Jesus made it known that a big part of his mission would be bringing sight to the blind. (Luke 4:18c). Jesus had the same difficulty in imparting his unique vision of God, even to his closest disciples. People were neither seeing nor hearing. (See Mark 8:17-18, 31-33).

## Judgement on an Unjust Society

Under the reign of King Uzziah (ca. 783-739 BC), in fame, second only to Solomon, the kingdom of Judah reached the summit of its power - both as to its wealth and military strength. Uzziah forced the Ammonites to pay him tribute. Ammon was a country east of the Jordan River. (See 2 Chronicles 26:1-15).

Isaiah speaks out against the moral decline of the kingdom of Judah, which went hand-in-hand with its affluence. Through its armies and alliances with foreign States, Israel had declared its independence of God. The king, and the elite at the top of society, felt a sense of pride over what they had achieved by the work of their own hands. They had acquired the vast bulk of the society's wealth, all of which was produced by the peasants who didn't own the land. The great landowners who lived in the towns, gained control over the country people through heavy taxation, and often through confiscation of indebted land, leaving small farmers impoverished. (Isaiah 5:8-23; Micah 2:1-2). The rural people formed the vast majority of the population and had to make do with about one third of the wealth. Thus, some hundreds of years after the liberation from Egypt, the Israelite king and the new elites became the centre of a new domination system. They plucked and ate the forbidden fruit of greed, power and wealth, in disobedience of the will of God. (their 'fall' story). Their failure to practice justice was a breach of the Ten Commandments which they had received from Moses - a breach of the covenant. (See Deuteronomy 4:23-26; 6:10-12; 8:11-14). Throwing off the sovereignty of God was a breach of the first three commandments. Being responsible for the injustices heaped on the majority of their people was a breach of the other seven. The king became in effect, a new Egyptian Pharaoh, enslaving a large part of the population. Isaiah warned that this condition of slavery would have consequences. The threat from the Assyrian empire was looming ominously.

Chapter 1 begins with an indictment of Israel and Jerusalem's infidelity to God. God is like a parent betrayed, and Israel represents God's disobedient children. But by naming them as his children, God is saying that although he will judge them harshly, he will not withdraw his love from them, despite their infidelity. Like the dumb beasts, perhaps they know not what they do. (1:3). While the ox and ass know their owner and serve his purpose, God's human creatures should know and do better, and love and serve their creator and one another. They will not be able to escape the consequences of their actions. Judgement will fall on the country and city. "You are doomed, you sinful nation, you corrupt and evil people. Your sins drag you down! You have rejected the Lord, the holy God of Israel, and you have turned your backs on him." (1:4).

Social injustice is the reason for Judah's resistance to the word of God. The people cannot "see" that their behaviour is against the will of God, and a violation of the Mosaic covenant. (Exodus 24:7). The wealthy were intent on maximizing profit and oppressing the poor. God is offering them reformation rather than punishment: "So now listen to what the Lord Almighty is saying, 'I will take action against you. I will purify you just as metal is refined (by fire), and will remove all your impurity.' (Isaiah 1:25). In order to accomplish this, they might have to be taken into exile once again and endure a wilderness testing, as their ancestors did on their way to the promised land. There will be consequences flowing from their evil deeds. The Lord says, you will wither like a dying oak, like a garden that no one waters. Just as straw is set on fire by a spark, so powerful people will be destroyed by their own evil deeds.' (1:30-31).

## Insincere Worship

The Israelite people and nation had come into existence by rejecting the religious systems of the other nations in order to serve a God who took the side of slaves over their masters. Isaiah condemned the religious practices of the people, while at the same time, they subjected themselves to gods who support the greed of an elite (the values of Empire), who enrich themselves at the expense of the peasants, as was the case with the Egyptian Pharaoh. If the Lord had not let some of the people survive, Jerusalem would have been totally destroyed, just like the two ancient cities, Sodom and Gomorrah. (1:9). These were too ancient cities during the time of Abraham, notorious for their wickedness. (See

Genesis 19:23-26).

> Hear the word of the Lord,
> you rulers of Sodom;
> listen to the command of our God,
> you people of Gomorrah.
> What are your endless sacrifices to me?
> says the Lord God.
> I am sick of holocausts of rams
> and the fat of calves.
> The blood of bulls and goats revolts me.
> Bring me your worthless offerings no more,
> the smoke of them fills me with disgust.
> New Moons, sabbaths and assemblies -
> I cannot endure festival and solemnity...
> When you stretch out your hands
> I turn my eyes away.
> You may multiply your prayers,
> I shall not listen.
> Your hands are covered with blood;
> wash, make yourselves clean.
> Take your wrongdoing out of my sight.
> Cease to do evil.
> Learn to do good,
> search for justice,
> help the oppressed,
> be just to the orphan,
> plead for the widow...
> Zion will be redeemed by justice,
> and her penitents by integrity.
> Rebels and sinners will be shattered,
> and those who abandon the Lord God will perish.
> (Isaiah 1:10-13, 15-17, 27-28, JB).

"New Moon" was a monthly festival held in the Jerusalem temple. All the prophets, from Amos on, protest against the temptation of using temple ritual and animal sacrifices as an evasion of responsibility. The people come to the temple offering sacrifices to God, while at the same time, they ignore the widow's plea for help. Such worship only provides ideological support for an unjust social system. There would be judgement. (Verses 27-28). God rejects Israel's religious festivals, sacrifices and personal piety, because Israel has not maintained a just society. The Book of Isaiah ends as it has begun, with another critique of ritual activity. (66:24).

In their blindness, the people believed that God was pleased with their religious rituals, even though their social, political and economic life was a mockery of justice. They themselves had been oppressed and orphaned in the land of Egypt, until God came to rescue them. After they were liberated from Egypt, God spoke to them through Moses: 'Do not ill-treat or oppress a foreigner; remember that you were foreigners in Egypt. Do not ill-treat any widow or orphan. If you do, I the Lord will answer them when they cry out to me for help.' (Exodus 22:21-23).

Human beings are called to be co-creators with God, which means lifting up those among us who are "tired and weary"– something much more important than sacrificial rituals. Lifting up the weak and helpless can, in itself, be a meaningful sacrifice. The Lord God said: 'These people claim to worship me, but their words are meaningless, and their hearts are somewhere else.' (Isaiah 29:13; see Matthew 5:23-24; 15:8). Obedience to God is more important than empty ritual. "People are always rebelling against God, always lying, always refusing to listen to the Lord's teachings." (Isaiah 30:9; see Mark 7:1-8). The tragedy was that the prophet's voice was ignored except by a small number of disciples. Very few were listening.

## Trusting in Silver and Gold

> The country is full of silver and gold
> and treasures unlimited,
> the country is full of horses,
> its chariots are unlimited;
> the country is full of idols.
> They bow down
> before the work of their hands,
> before what their own fingers have made…
> Human pride will lower its eyes,
> human arrogance will be humbled,
> and the Lord alone will be exalted,
> On that day…
> When the idols all disappear,
> they will go into the caverns of the rocks
> and into the fissures of the earth
> In terror of the Lord,
> at the brilliance of his majesty,
> when he arises to make the earth quake.
> That day, people will fling to moles and bats
> the silver and golden idols
> and go into the crevices of the rocks
> and the clefts in the cliffs,
> in terror of the Lord,
> at the brilliance of his majesty,
> when he arises to make the earth quake.
> (Isaiah 2:7-8, 11, 18-21, NJB).

The "the day of the Lord" (Isaiah 2:8, 11-12) is a day of judgement. This motif is frequently used by the prophets. (Isaiah 13:6; Amos 5:18-20; Jeremiah 17:16-18; Ezekiel 30:3). The refrain "the Lord alone will be exalted on that day" (2:11, 17) sets the tone for the above poem which describes what lies ahead for Jerusalem. Judgement is coming because of sorcery, injustice and idolatry. (2:5-11). Judah cannot evade judgement, no matter what rituals may be used in an effort to placate God. Prosperity is condemned because it was achieved at the expense of the poor. The belief persisted in Israel – as in other areas of the Near east at that time – that you could appease God (get him on your side) by offering sacrifices.

An elite treating wealth as the highest value - making a god of silver and gold - was a breach of the First Commandment: "I am the Lord your God, the One, and no other." This was the situation, which according to Isaiah, would lead to the fall of the nation and exile in a far country. The elite will fall into hard times when the Lord gives a signal to a distant nation from the north. Assyria will be God's instrument of judgement on a people who call what is bad good, and good bad.

Judah's leaders will bear the primary responsibility for the ensuing chaos. The kings of Judah had taken a wrong turning, in trusting for their salvation in things made with their own hands – power, armies, affluence. They were bad shepherds (Isaiah 1:10), leading to the scattering and loss of their flock. There will be no place to hide from the consequences of their actions. The efforts to hide resembles the hiding of Adam and Eve after they plucked the forbidden fruit in the Garden of Eden. (Genesis 3:8). The forbidden fruits of silver and gold will not save them when the "day of the Lord" comes. God will pass judgement on an unjust society. So the people will be humbled. They will experience abasement in the futility of trying to find somewhere to hide from the judgement of God.

The hills and mountains and the great cedars of Lebanon - metaphors for human pride and self-exaltation – are all brought down, and the Lord alone is exalted on that day. (2:13-14, 18b). The day of judgement will come like an earthquake shaking the world. It will come in the Assyrian and Babylonian invasions and the overthrow of the kingdoms of Israel and Judah. the Book of Revelation uses that same imagery in speaking of the terrors that it sees coming at the end of time. (See Revelation 18).

"Put no more confidence in mortals" may be interpreted as ceasing to trust in human attempts at exaltation and salvation. (2:22). What human beings admire, esteem and strive for, may often be idolatrous, and not out of concern for God's justice and righteousness. Judgement is coming because of idolatry and ill-gotten prosperity for the few. "Moneylenders oppress my people and their creditors cheat them. My people, your leaders are misleading you, so that you do not know which way to turn." (Isaiah 3:12).

How are we to interpret words of Isaiah when they speak about the Lord making the "earth quake and people hiding in caverns from his anger?" (2:19). It sounds like a punishing God, one who seeks retribution for human wickedness. The main teaching of Isaiah is about a God of love and mercy, but the book also emphasises God's justice, understood in two senses. First of all, because God himself *is* justice, he calls human beings to the practice of justice by creating a just society. (3:14-15). Secondly, his justice can be equated with judgement, which will fall on those who ill-treat or oppress others. So, when we read passages in the writings of the prophets about a judgemental God, they should serve to remind us that God is not a remote sky deity, who confirms human beings in their self-indulgent ways. God is the Creator and the power of the universe, awe-inspiring, beyond all imaginings, whom we should approach with reverence and awe, and with a sense of responsibility. Judgement is not something we should self-righteously dismiss as never falling on us. God, however is not a punishing God. He does not send misfortunes to human beings because of their errant ways. The misfortunes are but the consequences of their disobedience.

The whole of chapter 3 is about God's future judgement on Jerusalem, the collapse of Jerusalem's political order, destructive social conflict and the breakdown of society. Jerusalem's leaders will bear the primary responsibility for the ensuing chaos. "Their insolent airs bear witness against them; they parade their sin like Sodom. To their own undoing, they are preparing their downfall." (3:9, JB). The Lord calls the elders and the princes of his people to judgement: "You are the ones who destroy the vineyard and conceal what you have stolen from the poor." (3:14-15, JB). "Widows of Jerusalem, your young men will fall by the sword, your heroes, in the fight. The gates will moan and mourn; you will sit on the ground, desolate." (3:25-26, JB).

Though the prophet warns Jerusalem of coming judgement, he never claims that judgement is God's last word to the city. He envisions a new city, one that God himself will create following his judgement. (See 4:2-6).

## The Song of the Vineyard

Let me sing my beloved
the song of my friend for his vineyard.
My beloved had a vineyard on a fertile hillside.
He dug it, cleared it of stones;
he planted it with red grapes.
In the middle he built a tower,
he hewed a press there too.
He expected it to yield fine grapes;
wild grapes were all it yielded.
And now citizens of Jerusalem and people of Judah,
what more could I have done
for my vineyard that I have not done?
Very well, I shall tell you
what I am going to do with my vineyard:
I shall take away its hedge, for it to be grazed on,
and knock down its wall, for it to be trampled on.
And I shall command the clouds to rain no rain on it.
Now, the vineyard of the Lord is the House of Israel,
and the people of Judah, the plant he cherished.
He expected fair judgement, but found injustice;

expected uprightness but found cries of distress.
(Isaiah 5:1-7, NJB; see Hosea 10:1; Jeremiah 2:21; Ezekiel 19:10-14; Matthew 21:33; Mark 12:1; Luke 20:10).

On the theme of the vineyard, see Hosea 10:1-2; Jeremiah 2:21; 5:10; 6:9; 12:10; Ezekiel 15:1-8; 17:3-10; 19:10-14; Mark 12:1-9).

The prophet returns to words of judgement against Jerusalem and Judah. The Song of the Vineyard is about disappointment. The Book of Genesis begins with God's work and care for his "good" creation. He appointed human beings as his stewards in order to continue his work of cultivating and caring for his Garden, and from whom he expected obedience. (Genesis 3:11). After Israel's rescue from slavery in Egypt, God gave its people a vineyard (a nation, a fertile land flowing with milk and honey, Exodus 3:8,17) so that they might produce good fruit, but the people in charge of the vineyard only produced metaphorical wild grapes. (See Genesis 3:17). They were called to create the fruits of justice and mercy, and thus, to be the means of bringing the blessing of salvation to the other nations, but because of their disobedience, they failed in their vocation. (See Genesis 12:3; 22:15-18).

They may have felt no need of the guiding and sustaining presence of God, preferring to be autonomous, and like Adam and in the first garden, they go their own way into hiding from God, so that they can do whatever they want. (Genesis 3:8). Isaiah warns that God will hand over the Judahite vineyard to those who will conquer it. The vineyard will then be abandoned and left without cultivation. By tearing down the walls, the owner (God) will stop cultivation, allowing animals to trample over the once fruitful earth. In a reversal of creation, weeds would replace the vines, in life East of Eden. (Genesis 3:18). This is what happens when human beings reject the sustaining hand of God and try cultivating on their own.

Because God created the world (vineyard), it belongs to him. He appoints human beings, created in his image as his co-workers – stewards of his good creation, with a creative mission of adding to the store of good things in God's world, i.e. producing good fruit by loving all their neighbours. All the things of the world are God's gifts, and God expects human beings to use and treat his gifts in a caring and life-enhancing way. Or do we "never have a thought for the works of the Lord, never a glance at what his hands have done.'" (Isaiah 5:10-13, JB).

After having done one thing after another in caring for his vineyard (5:2), God is left wondering what more could he have done for his beloved people. They conveniently forget that everything they have is gifted to them by God, and not made with their own hands. God will now abandon Judah to the conqueror who will come from the north and trample over his vineyard.

Will the vineyard ever be rebuilt? Jesus says that the vineyard will be taken from the original tenants and given to a people who will produce the proper fruits. (Matthew 21:33-44; Mark 12:1-12; Luke 20:9-19; see also Psalm 80:8-19; Isaiah 27:2-5). Jesus will be the one to rebuild God's vineyard. He is God's faithful gardener, God's faithful steward, working to tend God's vineyard so that once again it will produce the good fruit of righteousness. He is also the fruitful vine, giving life to all who are united to him. (John

15:1-4; 20:11-15).

After his indictment of Israel as a whole in the foregoing song, the prophet becomes more specific:

> Woe to those who add house to house
> and join field to field until everywhere belongs to them.
> The Lord God has sworn this in my hearing,
> 'Many houses will be brought to ruin,
> great and fine, but left untenanted.
> Woe to those who from early morning
> chase after strong drink,
> and stay up at night inflamed with wine.
> Never a thought for the works of the Lord God,
> never a glance for what his hands have done.
> My people will go into exile for want of perception;
> her dignitaries dying of hunger,
> her populace parched with thirst...
> Woe to those who think themselves wise
> And believe themselves cunning.
> Woe to those who for a bribe, acquit the guilty
> and cheat the good man of his due. (Isaiah 5:8-13, 21, 22, JB).

In the above passage, the prophet condemns the large estates of the wealthy which were obtained by confiscation of land from small farmers for the payment of debts. (5:8). Following their grasping and greed, they were enabled to live lives of self-indulgence, becoming "inflamed with wine." Because such large estates were turned into profitable vineyards for the export of wine, there was a shortage of grain to feed the poor. This helped to create a permanent underclass in Judah. God's gift of a land flowing with milk and honey was being exploited by an elite for the sake of greed and self-indulgence. (Isaiah 5:23). This amounted to a failure of obedience - a breach of the covenant, a new "fall" story. (Genesis 1:28; 2:15, 17; 3:6).

## The Remnant of God

Isaiah asked the Lord how long would the people persist in their blindness and deafness. The Lord told him until the cities are ruined and the houses are empty. The Lord will send them far away and make the whole land desolate. (See Isaiah 6:10-12). Isaiah then employs the theme of the surviving remnant. The few who will remain in the land will be like the stump of an oak tree that has been cut down. This means that the destruction will not be total. God will leave the shoots of fresh life (as from a tree-stump) springing up from the desolation. "The stump represents a new beginning for God's people." (6:13). This remnant will attract all nations to learn the ways of God, so as to create a new international order of peace and justice. (Isaiah 2:2-5; see Micah 4:1-5).

This remnant will be a small number, comprising of those who are left in Judah and those who will return home from the Assyrian and Babylonian captivities, having been humbled and purified through a period of slavery. "Everyone who has been left in Jerusalem, whom God has chosen for survival, will be called holy. By his power the Lord will judge and purify the nation and wash away the guilt of Jerusalem and the blood that has been shed there." (Isaiah 4:3-4). God will depend on this purified remnant to carry forward his blessing to the world.

The teaching of all the prophets is that God's purposes are fulfilled in what happened to the two Israelite kingdoms. The defeat of the Kings of Israel and Judah by the empires of Assyria and Babylon was not due to the weakness of the Lord (tribal God) compared with the gods of those nations, but to the failure of Israel to live up to their covenant with God. By way of further refinement, Isaiah said that God would appoint Assyria as his instrument to punish Judah for its crimes, leaving only a remnant who will remain faithful.

## Trusting in Foreign Alliances

The historical section of Isaiah (chapters 36-38), reproduces the material of 2 Kings 18-20. Isaiah was concerned with two political crises. The first crisis arose during the reign of King Ahaz of Judah who ruled for sixteen years, and as Isaiah says, "did not do what was pleasing to the Lord." He offered sacrifices at the pagan places of worship and even sacrificed his own son as a burnt offering to pagan gods. (2 Kings 16:2-4).

Ahaz brought trouble on himself by allying himself with Assyria. The evil that Isaiah saw in this was in Ahaz allying himself with the pagan faith of Assyria. As Isaiah saw it, Ahaz would be accepting the values of empire and moving away from the covenant with God, which was the only guarantee of his security. (See 2 Kings, chap. 16).

Isaiah tried to persuade King Ahaz that his efforts to placate Assyria was doomed to failure. He told the king that it was not the mighty Tiglath-pileser, King of Assyria, that controlled history. The world was in the hands of God. When the time came, the might of Assyria would be swept away. (Isaiah 10:24-27).

Ahaz was succeeded by his son Hezekiah, who was one of the greatest of the kings of Judah. (See 2 Kings 18:1-8). He introduced a number of religious reforms. (2 Kings 18:4-6). But in terms of foreign policy, he proved to be no different from his predecessors. This led to the second political crisis which confronted Isaiah. The prophet was concerned about the attempt of the new king to free himself from the payment of a heavy annual tribute to Assyria. Probably emboldened by troubles elsewhere in the Assyrian empire, Hezekiah revolted and declared freedom from Assyria in 705 BC. Anticipating an Assyrian assault, Hezekiah repaired the walls of Jerusalem and constructed a tunnel to bring water into the city. In 701 BC, Sennacherib, the new king of Assyria, invaded Judah and destroyed most of its fortified towns when they refused to surrender to him, including Lachish, one of its largest cities (about twenty miles south west of Jerusalem). This is the destruction to which Isaiah is referring in 1:7-8. Sennacherib then laid siege to Jerusalem. According to the Book of Isaiah, the siege ended when a miraculous plague wiped out much of the Assyrian army. Sennacherib was then forced to return home without taking Jerusalem. (See Isaiah chaps. 36 - 37).

It is thought that the siege of Jerusalem ended because Hezekiah agreed to surrender the city peacefully. In any case, Hezekiah was forced to pay a huge sum of money to Assyria and agree to vassal status in order to keep his throne. Jerusalem's escape from capture and destruction led to the belief that God would always protect the city. However, the people's joy made them forget the warnings of Isaiah about their unjust society. They believed that God would put up with anything they did. Isaiah's constant teaching was to "turn to the Lord" instead of all the other things in which they placed their trust. (See 18:1-7; 19:1-15; also 19:16-25).

Sennacherib confirms the above account in Isaiah. The king of Assyria covered a whole throne room in his palace at Nineveh with scenes of his assault on Judah's second largest city, Lachish. Archaeologists also discovered a number of relief sculptures depicting the destruction of Lachish. The king's palaces were decorated with wall reliefs and sculptures depicting his prestige and deeds, especially in battle. To the left of the depicted king, several Syrian soldiers publicly flay captured Judahites. Sennacherib also had a huge pillar of six sides inscribed with his account of his war against Hezekiah.[96] Sennacherib boasts about his destruction of Judahite cities, his capture of 200,150 prisoners of war (very likely exaggerated), young and old, male and female, from these places, his plundering of horses, donkeys, cattle and camels, and his imprisoning of Hezekiah in Jerusalem "like a bird in a cage." Sennacherib does not say anything to indicate that Jerusalem was captured. (All of these ancient remains are now on display in the British Museum).

## Oracles Against Assyria and Babylon

Once Isaiah realized the futility of speaking to Israel, he turned his attention to the oppressive empires. Isaiah saw history as the stage of God's work – empires rising and falling. They were all arrogant, setting themselves up as lords and masters of the world, doing whatever they wanted. They oppressed and enslaved the people of their conquered territories, caring not at all for justice and mercy. Isaiah taught that God is sovereign over the nations. God blesses the nations for the good things they do, but he also passes judgement on them for their arrogance and abuses.

The great Assyrian empire was the dominant force in the Near East between the tenth and seventh centuries BC. Due to the decline of Egypt during the time of Isaiah, Assyria became a great power, and posed a continuing threat to Judah from the eighth century onwards, forcing it and other small States to become vassals and pay tribute. The period of the Israelite monarchy was coming to an end.

The capital city of Assyria, Nineveh, formed a circle three miles in diameter. Its remains today are situated along the eastern bank of the Tigris River across from modern day Mosul in Iraq. Nineveh was famous for its imposing palaces and irrigation systems.

Assyria has been called the most ruthless nation in antiquity, 'like a lion killing its prey, tearing it to pieces for his mate and her cubs.'[97] (Nahum 2:12; Isaiah 10:12-14). Cutting off the heads of conquered peoples was a common practice. The kings of Assyria boasted of towns destroyed, burned, and levelled as by a hurricane, the victors taking

---

[96] The Sennacherib Prism, 111 20-40, in Lawrence Boadt, *Reading the Old Testament*, p. 287).

[97] Abraham Heschel, *The Prophets*, (Harper Perennial, 1955), p. 207).

away all the plunder they could carry. The Assyrians had the defeated monarch confined to a cage, and his eyes put out in the presence of the conquering king. (2 Kings 25:7). The wives and daughters of the captured king were carried off to the harems of the conqueror. Large numbers of the population were deported to the far ends of the empire to work on the king's building projects and the draining of swamps in the area between the Tigris and Euphrates Rivers. The small conquered nations were then forced to become allies of the conqueror, supplying soldiers and joining Assyria in the slaughter of other peoples. The king of Assyria boasted of all the lands he had conquered, the cities he had levelled and burned. (Isaiah 10:7-11; 14:17; 17:12). The empire eventually came to an end when one of its provinces (Babylon) revolted, captured Nineveh and destroyed the city. The exalted one was brought down from his high throne. After the defeat of Assyria, Babylonia then joined the madness as a destroyer. (Jeremiah 34:1).

The northern kingdom of Israel fell to Assyria in 721 BC. Isaiah insisted that Assyria would also visit Judah with devastation. The Assyrian desire for dominance in the ancient Near East was driven by Assyria herself. But whatever Assyria's own intentions were, the prophet insisted that God was using Assyria to punish Israel and Judah for "refusing justice for the poor and for robbing widows and orphans of their property." (Isaiah 10:1-2). "The Lord said, 'I use Assyria like a club to punish those with whom I am angry.'" (Isaiah 10:5). But then the Lord will deal with Assyria for its cruelty, arrogance and boasting. (See Isaiah 10:24-27; 14:24-27; 30:30-33; 31:8-9). This prediction of defeat came to pass (Isaiah 37:36) when the "angel of the Lord" wiped out an Assyrian army, as it surrounded Jerusalem. The defeat of Assyria was total when the province of Babylon revolted, captured the city of Nineveh and levelled it to the ground.

Isaiah then prophesises the destruction of Babylon and the fate of its king:

> King of Babylonia, bright morning star, you have fallen from heaven! In the past you conquered nations, but now you have been thrown to the ground. You were determined to climb up to heaven and to place your throne above the highest stars. You thought you would sit like a king on that mountain in the north where the gods assemble. You said you would climb to the tops of the clouds and be like the almighty. But instead, you have been brought down to the deepest part of the world of the dead. (Isaiah 14:12-15; see Genesis 11:1-9).

Self-exaltation ending in humiliation! Further, on the fate of the king of Babylon, see Isaiah 14:16-20.

## The New King Immanuel

The visions of Immanuel in 7:14; 9:1-7 and 11:1-9 came about because Isaiah tried to show Judah's kings that God would only stand by them if they remained faithful to him, instead of trusting in foreign alliances, military power and city fortifications. King Ahaz angrily rejected his words, and Hezekiah couldn't believe them. The prophet spoke the word of God to the kings but they disobeyed or ignored his word, and because of their disobedience, Jerusalem was doomed. There would be no salvation for the kingdom of

Judah, and its obsession with war and power politics.

Thus, in his despair over the kings of his day, Isaiah turned his hopes to a future King Immanuel, which means 'God is with us.' God is with Judah, but before Judah can experience the saving hand of God, it must experience God's judgement on its unjust social and economic system. Isaiah told King Ahaz to do nothing to save Judah, other than trusting in the Lord. He urged that king to regard the birth of a particular child (possibly Ahaz's own son) as a sign that God would protect Judah from external threats. (9:6). The only hope is for a future king Immanuel, who would be called a "Prince-of-Peace" (Isaiah 9:6, NJB; see CCC 1502).

Isaiah came to believe that King Ahaz would never listen to him. So at this time the prophet formed a group of disciples who would learn the Lord's ways. (Isaiah 8:16-20). These disciples would form a remnant of people who would keep hope alive. The child Immanuel will be a light shining in a dark world – a "Prince of Peace." A genuine son of David will come and create a reign of everlasting peace. This son will be like a light in a dark world. (See Micah 5:1-3; 2 Samuel 7:12-16; John 1:4-5; 8:12).

> The people who walked in darkness
> have seen a great light;
> on those who live in a land of deep shadow
> a light has shone.
> You have made their gladness greater,
> you have made their joy increase;
> they rejoice in your presence
> as men rejoice at harvest time,
> as men are happy when they are dividing the spoils.
> For the yoke that was weighing on him,
> the bar across his shoulders,
> the rod of his oppressor,
> these you break as on the day of Midian.
> For the footgear of battle,
> every cloak rolled in blood is burnt,
> and consumed by fire.
> For there is a child born for us,
> a son given to us!
> And dominion is laid on his shoulders;
> and this is the name they give him:
> Wonder-Counsellor, Mighty-God,
> Eternal Father, Prince of Peace.
> Wide is his dominion
> in a peace that has no end,
> for the throne of David
> and for his royal power,
> which he establishes and makes secure
> in justice and integrity.

> From this time onwards and for ever,
> the jealous love of the Lord Almighty will do this. (Isaiah 9:1-7, JB).

In the above passage, the prophet describes the rejoicing of the people who are saved from Assyrian power. (See 2 Kings 18:17; 19:32-36). He uses several metaphors to describe God's new act of gratuity to Israel. It will be like the move from darkness to light and like the harvest that brings an end to the threat of starvation. The joy it brings will remind the people of the victory of Gideon over the Midianites (See Judges 7:15-25), which was achieved without war. Israel's future rescue and salvation will be the result of a similar victory, no longer achieved by war, but by the future king turning the other cheek to the violence done to him, thus establishing a reign of peace on earth. This future king will do what Ahaz could not do. He will trust in, and obey the Lord. He will rule with integrity and justice. He will be God's representative on earth. He will bring a never-ending peace to God's people.

This prophecy was fulfilled in Jesus, who is the ideal king in the line of David, whose rule will liberate his people from their spiritual blindness and deafness and establish a new covenant between God and them. (Mark 14:24). The reign of Jesus will finally establish justice and integrity until the end of time. (Isaiah 9:7). By enduring the rod of the oppressors (Mark 15:23-25), and not by inflicting them with blows, Jesus will free humanity from all oppression. His dominion of justice and peace will be established for ever.

The evangelist Luke alludes to Isaiah 9:1-7, when he has Zechariah (father of John the Baptist) speak about what God will do for Israel. (Luke 1:78-79). Matthew 4:15-16 quotes Isaiah 9:1-2 as he describes the beginning of Jesus' ministry in Galilee. At the beginning of Luke's gospel, the angel of God tells Mary that she will give birth to a son and name him Jesus, which means 'saviour.' "He will be great and will be called the Son of the Most High God. The Lord will make him a king, as his ancestor David was, and he will be king over the descendants of Jacob for ever; his kingdom will never end." (Luke 1:31-33; see Luke 1:68-79).

The following quotation is a continuation of Isaiah's Immanuel theme. With regard to the phrase "wolves and sheep living together in peace" (11:6), Isaiah may be looking at Judah as the sheep, and Assyria as the wolf. He may also be looking ahead to a time when these two great enemies will come together in peace and reconciliation?

> The royal line of David is like a tree that has been cut down, and just as new branches sprout from a stump, so a new king will arise from among David's descendants. The Spirit of the Lord will give him wisdom, and the knowledge and skill to rule his people. He will know the Lord's will and honour him, and find pleasure in obeying him. He will judge the poor fairly and defend the rights of the helpless. He will rule his people with justice and integrity. Wolves and sheep will live together in peace, and leopards will lie down with young goats. Calves and lion cubs will feed together, and little children will take care of them... On Zion (Jerusalem), God's sacred hill, there will be nothing harmful or evil. The land will be full of the knowledge of the Lord, as the seas are full of water. A day

is coming when the new king from the royal line of David will be a symbol to the nations. They will gather in his royal city and give him honour. (Isaiah 11:1-6, 9-10; See Psalm 2).

Humanity will live in hope for this new king, whose role will be similar to that of Isaiah's disciples. These will represent a remnant - the "few who will come back to their God." From these, new life will develop in line with the will of God. (See Isaiah 10:20-22).

## God Exalts Jerusalem

The theme of exaltation and humiliation is emphasised throughout Isaiah, beginning in chapter 2, in which the prophet, for the first time, speaks about the exaltation of Jerusalem. Nineveh was a great city, basking in its self-exaltation. It had a huge army and a lust for luxury and splendour. (Genesis 10:11-12; 2 Kings 19:36). However, its pride was brought down to earth when the province of Babylon revolted and captured the city, plundered its treasures and left it in such a heap of ruins that it was never rebuilt. (See Nahum 2:1-13; 3:1-7; Zephaniah 2:13-15). The sovereign God allowed this to happen. Military and economic might don't matter to God. The fate of lowly Jerusalem will be different:

> In days to come
> the mountain where the Temple stands
> will be the highest one of all,
> towering above all the hills.
> Many nations will come streaming to it,
> and their people will say,
> "Let us go up the hill of the Lord,
> to the Temple of Israel's God.
> He will teach us what he wants to do;
> we will walk in the paths he has chosen.
> For the Lord's teaching comes from Jerusalem;
> from Zion he speaks to his people.
> He will settle disputes among great nations.
> They will hammer their swords into ploughs
> and their spears into pruning knives.
> Nations will never again go to war,
> never prepare for battle again.
> Now, descendants of Jacob,
> let us walk in the light which the Lord gives us. (Isaiah 2:1-5).

Contrasted with Nineveh, Jerusalem was a small habitation, little known in the ancient world. However, Isaiah says that the nations, eager to learn God's ways and walk in his paths, will no longer turn their eyes to Nineveh, but to Jerusalem (the seat of divine wisdom). Proud Nineveh will be humbled. Jerusalem will become great only because God will exalt her. But the exalted Jerusalem is not the city of Isaiah's day, but a metaphor for an ideal world of justice and peace in the future, which God will create when the time is right. (See 2:4 above).

Zion, the temple mountain will be towering above all others. The exaltation of Jerusalem has nothing to do with military or economic power, but is rather a reflection of the exalted God. Exalted Jerusalem is God's vision for a new world, sadly contrasted with the reality of Isaiah's time: human beings exalting themselves while trusting in swords and spears. God's vision, on the other hand, is of a new creation – a world without war, "swords hammered into ploughs and spears into pruning knives, nations never again preparing for war." (Isaiah 2:4). The nations will stream to this exalted Jerusalem to hear the teaching of the Lord (2:3), thus fulfilling God's promises to Abraham of blessing to the nations. (Genesis 12:3; 22:18).

Isaiah's vision is that Judah will not treat the nations as enemies to be defeated but people with whom Israel will live in peace – wolves (the nations) and sheep (Judah) living together - leopards lying down with young goats. (Isaiah 11:6). The enemy to be defeated is war. This vision represents something ultimate, which raises the question, was the prophet visualizing a reality beyond this world in which his glorious vision would at last be realized? For Isaiah, the new peaceful Jerusalem was a goal that should encourage and give hope to Israel and everyone else to be faithful to God in the here and now, because ultimately, God has something great in store for humanity.

The Book of Isaiah returns to the theme of the new Jerusalem several times. (11:6-9; 52:1-12; 60:1-2; 65:17-19). The new Jerusalem envisioned by Isaiah as a metaphor for God's new world at the end of time in which his prophecy will at last be fulfilled. According to the Book of Revelation, the new Jerusalem will come down from heaven, and "God will make his home with human beings." All barriers between God and his people will finally be removed. It will be like the restoration of the Garden of Eden to its original state. (See Revelation 21:2-3, 22-27).

It is Jesus who fulfils this vision of Isaiah. Jesus' birth was humble and insignificant, little noted in the wider world. There was no room for him in the "inn." (Luke 2:7b). Israel had no room for him in its heart. It rejected him, killed him and threw his body out of the vineyard. (Mark 12:8). But God raised him up to a status, towering above all hills. He is the new Jerusalem "shining like the sun." (Isaiah 60:1). He is the light of the world. (John 8:12). He is the new temple in which God dwells (Matthew 26:61; Mark 14:58; John 2:19). It is to him the nations will come streaming in order to learn his ways of justice and peace (Isaiah 2:3), and through whom their hopes for a glorious future are fulfilled. Thus, it is Jesus who fulfils God's promise to Abraham of blessing to all nations. (Genesis 12:3). Instead of making war against the nations, Jesus will turn his cheek to their violence and die in order to liberate them from their murderous ways (through forgiveness). In inviting them into his kingdom of justice and peace, he will call on them to walk the path he has chosen, which is to "hammer their swords into ploughs and their spears into pruning knives" – to become builders rather than destroyers. (See Isaiah 2:4).

The theme of exaltation and humiliation is employed in the New Testament. (Matthew 23:12; Luke 14:11; Mark 8:35, 9:35, 10:43-45). For the evangelist John, the cross, first seen as the place of weakness and humiliation, is the place of Jesus' exaltation and glorification. (John 12:32-33, 13:31-32; see Philippians 2:5-11). Jesus is exalted in his resurrection, raised up to God's right hand, as Son of God. There to lift us up along with him! "When I am lifted up from the earth, I will draw everyone to me." (John 12:32).

## Destruction and New Creation

In their message of doom and judgement, followed by victorious celebrations, Isaiah chapters 24 to 27 resemble the type of literature known as apocalyptic (dealing with the last things), and the final victory of God over the forces of evil, in which Babylon, Egypt and Moab are included. (Isaiah 15:1; 19:1).

> The earth dries up and withers; both earth and sky decay. The people have defiled the earth by breaking God's laws and by violating the covenant he made to last forever… In the city, everything is in chaos, and people lock themselves in houses for safety… Anyone who tries to escape from the terror will fall into a pit, and anyone who escapes from the pit will fall into a trap. Torrents of rain will pour from the sky, and earth's foundations will shake. The earth itself will stagger like a drunken man and sway like a hut in a storm. The world is weighed down by its sins; it will collapse and never rise again. The Lord will punish the powers above and the rulers of the earth below. God will crowd kings together like prisoners in a pit. He will shut them in prison until the time of their punishment comes. The moon will grow dark, and the sun will no longer shine, for the Lord Almighty will be king. He will rule in Jerusalem on Mount Zion, and the leaders of the people will see his glory. (Isaiah 24:4-5, 10, 18-23).

Apocalyptic in tone, the account in chapter 24 of a terrifying destruction of the earth may be a metaphor for the destruction of Jerusalem prophesied in chapter 3. What will happen will be like the end of the world. It may also be a metaphor for God's ultimate victory over evil. God's judgement is universal. It's as if all of this destruction comes together in one great cataclysm. God's covenant with the earth is put at risk because of universal disobedience. But a surviving remnant will sing for joy and be moved to praise the righteousness of God. (Isaiah 24:14-16). The city mentioned in 24:10-12 is Jerusalem, but perhaps also every city founded on injustice and oppression. "There is lamentation in the streets, no wine, joy quite gone, gladness banished from the country." (24:11). This is God's judgement on a world without justice, but his judgement is not vindictive.

As Isaiah looked around him in the world of his day, he may have seen nothing but a darkening earth. (24:23). He may have been close to despairing that justice, peace and reconciliation could ever become a reality in this world; nothing but one destructive war following the other, nation against nation; and the failure of God's chosen people to create a just and merciful society. But because of the prophet's vision of the whole, his deep insight into the holiness of God (his passion for justice and mercy) and his sovereignty over history, it is likely that he could not envisage the reign of evil continuing for ever on the earth: "The Lord Almighty will be king." (24:23). There is hope for a glorious triumph over the powers of evil, and a new world in which God's rule will be established over all creation. God will ultimately act to bring history to a conclusion in line with his good purposes.

The prophet may even have entertained the hope of a final resurrection of the dead: "Your dead shall live, their corpses shall rise. O dwellers of the dust, awake and sing for joy! For your dew is a radiant dew, and the earth will give birth to those long dead." (Isaiah 26:19, NRSVC). The Sovereign God will destroy death for ever! He will wipe away the tears from everyone's eyes and take away the disgrace his people have suffered throughout the world. The Lord himself has spoken." (Isaiah 25:8). Isaiah's glorious vision is fulfilled in the Book of Revelation. (See Revelation 21:4).

When St. Paul proclaims God's victory over death (1 Corinthians 15:51-55), he sees it as the fulfilment of Scripture. It is likely that he had Isaiah 25:8 in mind. "What is mortal must be changed into what is immortal; what will die must be changed into what cannot die, then the Scripture will come true: Death is destroyed; victory is complete." (1 Corinthians 15:53-54). "Where, death, is your victory? Where, death, is your power to hurt?" (1 Corinthians 15:55). The author of the Book of Revelation finds inspiration and hope in the assertion that God will ultimately wipe away all tears. (See Revelation 7:17, 21:3-4).

Christians see all of the above fulfilled in the Christ's victory over death, through his resurrection. Having been raised up over the oppressive powers who killed him, his rule is established over God's kingdom forever.

The darkening of the earth (Isaiah 24:23) may be a metaphor for the temporary victory of evil at the death of Jesus. (Mark 15:33). God will ultimately establish his glorious reign over darkness and chaos in a new Jerusalem. (Matthew 27:45; Mark 15:43; Luke 23:44; Revelation 21:1-4). God's glory was revealed in Jesus–in Mount Zion, but in a strange way, with Jesus hanging on a cross and the earth quaking and falling into darkness all around him. The hours of darkness at his death symbolized only a temporary victory by the dark powers which killed him. The Lord Almighty had the last word when he raised Jesus up triumphant over the darkest of dark powers, namely death itself, and made him King, to rule on God's holy mountain (Zion), all people everywhere forever seeing and sharing in his glory.

## The Eternal Banquet

The triumph of God over evil is celebrated with a banquet on Mount Zion (Jerusalem) for all the nations, who following God's judgement, are now sitting down together in peace and reconciliation. (See Revelation 18:7-8). The new creation of reconciliation follows the destruction of evil. This is the salvation for which the whole world is hungering. (25:9). Let the world rejoice and celebrate with a banquet of rich food and fine wine.

> On this mountain,
> the Lord God will prepare for all peoples
> a banquet of rich food, a banquet of fine wines,
> of food rich and juicy, of fine strained wines.

On this mountain, he will remove
the mourning veil covering all peoples,
and the shroud enwrapping all nations,
he will destroy Death for ever.
The Lord God will wipe away
the tears from every cheek;
he will take away his people's shame
everywhere on earth.
That day, it will be said: See, this is our God
in whom we hoped for salvation.
We exult and rejoice that he has saved us;
for the hand of God rests on this mountain.
(Isaiah 25:6-10, JB; see Mark 14:22-24).

In its anticipation of the feast on the holy mountain (Mount Zion in Jerusalem), the above passage can be compared with Isaiah 2:2-4, and with the expectation of salvation in chapter 12. In 26:1-6 the city is now a matter of pride–a purified Jerusalem, a symbol of redeemed humanity. In 26:7-19 there is a picture of a city under alien rule but hoping for final delivery in a resurrection of the dead. (26:19).

There was little choice of diet in the ancient world. A lavish banquet of "rich food and fine wines" is a potent symbol of God's reconciling love, his gathering together of his scattered people in forgiveness and reconciliation, through the metaphor of a great feast. Jesus' table fellowship meals are a fulfilment of the Mount Zion banquet, symbolizing as they do, reconciliation among all kinds of separated people. (Matthew 22:1-10; Luke 7:36-50; 14:15-24, 15:11-32; see Revelation 19:5-10). In the Bible, mountains are symbolic of God's presence with his people, places where he reveals his law of love to them.

There are two considerations to be deduced from the idea of the banquet. Firstly, a great feast is a metaphor for forgiveness and reconciliation. All nations will share in the feasting, because God will lift the veil of blindness that keeps them separated, through enmity, hatred and strife. (Isaiah 25:7). Secondly, with his lavish feeding, God will satisfy the deepest hungering of humanity for peace and happiness, thus making life meaningful. (See Psalm 23:5).

Isaiah's victory banquet of rich food and fine wine (25:6-10) becomes "the wedding banquet of the lamb" in Revelation 19:7-8. Jesus, the Lamb of God is coming to a great banquet celebrating his marriage to his bride (all of God's redeemed people) who are now definitively home from exile, to live with God, who is their shelter from life's storms. (Revelation 25:5).

## Exile and Rescue

Eventually, in 587 BC, when Isaiah of Jerusalem was long dead, the kingdom of Judah was invaded and its ruling elite were taken into exile in Babylon. Scholars think that these later chapters were inserted into the Book of Isaiah at a later time.

This part of the Book of Isaiah ends in a note of hope. Chapter 35 has a poem about the Lord's rescue of his people and their return from exile. (35:1-10). The people's eyes and ears are opened to the reality of what caused them to be taken away from all they held dear.

> The desert will rejoice
> and flowers will bloom in the wilderness.
> The desert will sing and shout for joy;
> it will be as beautiful as the
> Lebanon Mountains,
> as fertile as the fields of Carmel and Sharon.
> Everyone will see the Lord's splendour,
> see his greatness and power.
> The blind will be able to see
> and the deaf will hear.
> The lame will leap and dance,
> and those who cannot speak
> will shout for joy.
> Streams of water will flow through the desert;
> the burning sand will become a lake
> and the dry land will be filled with springs.
> Where jackals used to live,
> marsh grass and reeds will grow.
> There will be a highway there,
> called "The Road of Holiness."
> Those whom the Lord has rescued
> will travel along that road.
> They will reach Jerusalem with gladness,
> singing and shouting for joy.
> (Isaiah 35:1-2, 5-10; see 7:10-17, 9:1-6, 11:1-9, 28:16-17).

It is notable that the blindness and deafness which featured so prominently in the first part of the Book of Isaiah is now transformed into seeing and hearing. Before the Babylonian exile, the people were blind and deaf to the will of God and to their sins. (See Isaiah 6:9). They had created a lifeless desert east of Eden (the land of thorns and briars), but the wilderness will bloom with life-sustaining growth once again, in an abundance that will satisfy human hungering and thirsting for fullness of life. This fruitful new growth will be a reversal of the weeds and thorns in the world East of Eden. (Genesis 3:17-18). Reaching Jerusalem with gladness! A metaphor for our coming home to our promised land! "Everyone will see the Lord's splendour." (Isaiah 35:2).

The above could have been written about Jesus – the joy and gladness that followed his opening the eyes of the blind and the ears of the deaf, satisfying their desire for fullness of life. (Luke 4:18). And the joy that followed his resurrection, his triumph over the dark forces that killed him!

Isaiah differs from Amos and Hosea, in his unique, and universal vision of a glorious future for humanity. The oracles of Isaiah of Jerusalem were not forgotten. They became the basis for the prophet's later reflection on the word of God, the Holy One. His oracles provided the foundation for hope, which influenced later prophets during the time of exile in Babylon. (See Isaiah 40-55; Ezekiel 33-48). They also inspired the messianic hopes of postexilic prophets such as Haggai and Zechariah.[98]

According to Jewish tradition, Isaiah of Jerusalem was executed by King Manasseh (686-642 BC) of Judah. (2 Kings 21:1f.). Most of the prophets were persecuted in one way or another, but it is by no means certain that Manasseh had Isaiah killed. Both the Books of Kings and Chronicles say that Manasseh was a wicked king, but Chronicles says that he later repented of his sins after suffering exile in Babylon. (2 Chronicles 33:10-13). Manasseh had to pay tribute to Assyria, and perhaps, as a result, was obliged to introduce pagan worship and practices into his kingdom.

It is significant that there was no prophecy in Israel during the reign of Manasseh. Some commentators think this was because this king persecuted the prophets. But more likely, it would seem that God was loath to speak to a world mired in wickedness, a world in which no one was listening, everyone deaf to his voice.

The death of Isaiah of Jerusalem brings to an end the first part of the Book of Isaiah.

---

[98] Lawrence Boadt, Reading the Old Testament, (Paulist Press, 2012), p. 292.

CHAPTER 7

# THE PROPHET JEREMIAH

## Introduction

Having looked at chapters 1–39, we will leave the Book of Isaiah aside for the time being and continue with an account of Jeremiah, the prophet who began his ministry in the kingdom of Judah during the later years of Isaiah of Jerusalem. Jeremiah remained active as a prophet down to the fall of Jerusalem to the Babylonians in 587 BC, and for a few further years after that event. He got his call to be a prophet in the thirteenth year of the reign of King Josiah of Judah (640-609 BC).

Jeremiah came from a priestly family in the town of Anathoth, a few miles north-east of Jerusalem, where his relatives were landowners. (Jeremiah 32:6f). His prophecy comes between the years 627 and 582 BC, the longest period for any prophet. Jeremiah had close contact with Hosea's disciples and knew of the writings of that prophet. But the message he preached was his own: disaster is coming from an empire in the north because the people have forsaken God for the god Baal. (See Jeremiah chaps. 1-6). "The Lord says, 'Israel, on every hill and under every green tree you worshiped fertility gods. I planted you like a choice vine from the very best seed. But look what you have become! You are like a rotten, worthless vine.'" (Jeremiah 2:20-21; see Isaiah 5:1-6).

Jeremiah has God complaining, and he himself complains about the situation in Judah. His work reveals more of himself as an individual than any other Old Testament prophet. He evokes our sympathy for the sufferings he endured in proclaiming the word of God to a blind and deaf people. As was the case with Jeremiah (i:8), the Lord tells us not to be afraid, not to lose courage or hope, because God is with us on our journey. (See Exodus 3:12).

The main subject of the book is the fall of Jerusalem to Babylon in 587 BC, with Jeremiah either looking ahead to its fall, or lamenting its actual fall. This means that, at least some of Jeremiah's prophecy was probably intended for the exiles in Babylon, as an explanation of why the exile took place, and to encourage them with the hope of an eventual return home. His message for the exiles was that the disaster was actually a divine plan to "pluck up and to pull down" but also to "build and to plant." Plucking up and pulling down refers to the destruction of Jerusalem as God's judgement on Israel. "The city of Zion is beautiful, but it will be destroyed. Kings will camp there with their armies."

Jerusalem would suffer because of its false worship and its many sins. (5:1-11). Building and planting would mean God's work of restoration, once the people had repented. Jeremiah lived through the fall of Jerusalem in 587 BC, but he also foretold its eventual restoration and the return of the exiles.

A theological claim in this book, is that Jeremiah was sent as prophet to the nations, with the implication that God is sovereign over the nations and involved in their salvation, no less than that of Israel. (1:10). This means that Jeremiah's vision has universal significance. The God for whom he speaks, governs the rise and fall of nations and empires. (See Jeremiah 25:15-38 and chaps. 46-52). There are times when the rule of empire may be willed by God. When a number of small nations cannot live in peace with one another, an empire might establish peace between them. But the empires are then called to account when they become arrogant and exceed the authority delegated to them by God.

The lyric poetry of the many songs and laments in Jeremiah are combined with prose passages. One of the difficulties in Jeremiah is that the prophecies and stories do not appear in their chronological order. That shouldn't matter to the reader. In Jeremiah's prophecy, we can hear the voice of God speaking his word to us today, challenging us to leave the comfort zone of the self and go on a mission of following the Lord in *his* way of doing things. We should give glory to the Lord as the only one who can bring us salvation. Jeremiah is very strong on the idea that pride and self-glorification only lead to disaster for human beings. (See 13:15-16).

There are fifty-two chapters in the Book of Jeremiah, covering different periods of his life. In the first period, chapters 1-6 reflect Jeremiah's demands for conversion and reform during the reign of King Josiah of Judah.

The second period was under Josiah's son, Jehoiakim, (chapters 7 to 20), from 609 to 598 BC; and under Zedekiah. (Chaps. 21 to 34).

The third part of his ministry took place in the twelve years between the first siege of Jerusalem by the Babylonians in 598 and the final destruction of the city in 587 BC, with a short period of activity between 586 and 582 BC.

Chapters 26 to 45 are accounts about the prophet's work and sufferings, and are thought to be from the pen of his scribe, Baruch. (See Jeremiah 36:4).

Chapters 30:1–33:26 are known as the Little Book of Consolation, because of God's promise contained in them to restore his people and bring them home again.

Chapter 52 is an appendix describing the fall of Jerusalem in 587 BC.[99] The following parts of the book are recommended for reading: chapters 1-3, 7-8, 18-20, 26-29, 30-31.[100] To that list, we might add chapters 4-6 and 9-10.

Jeremiah is given a central role throughout the book, but it is really God who assumes the main role. The prophet is his mouthpiece. (Jeremiah 1:9). However, Jeremiah freely assumes his responsibility as prophet and intercessor with God on behalf of his people. In his role as intercessor, he is a new Moses to his people, shouldering the consequences of their sins. (See Deuteronomy 18:18). Because of his solidarity with a

---

[99] Lawrence Boadt, *Reading the Old Testament*, p. 316.

[100] Ibid, p. 315.

sinful people, Jeremiah experiences God's rejection along with his people. Jeremiah is thus a Christ-like figure. (See Mark 15:34). He pleads with God and complains to him. (Jeremiah 11:18–12:6).

Jeremiah's theology is rooted in the Exodus covenant - the time when God saved his people and gave them the laws which called for obedience, and by which they might live (covenant). Judgement would follow disobedience. His understanding of covenant made Jeremiah realize that God would allow Jerusalem to be destroyed. But he held out the hope of eventual restoration - a time of building up. (Jeremiah 24:4-7; 3:4; 31:1-4; 31:20-22). Just like the other prophets, Jeremiah never loses hope in the faithfulness of God and God's sovereignty over history.

Probably because the Book of Deuteronomy was receiving its final editing during the period of Jeremiah's prophecy, there are close links between the theology of Jeremiah and that of Deuteronomy. (Compare Jeremiah 21:8-10 with Deuteronomy 30:15-20). Jeremiah often refers to the mighty hand and outstretched arm of the Lord that brought Israel out of Egypt, but the same arm is now directed *against* Israel and Jerusalem. (Deuteronomy 4:34; Jeremiah 21:5; 32:21-23). In the fertile land that God gave to his people as his gift of love (Deuteronomy 12:10; Jeremiah 3:18), the people have "gone after other gods" (Deuteronomy 6:14; Jeremiah 7:6, 13:10) "under every green tree." (Deuteronomy 12:2). Judah only pretended to return to the Lord in obedience. (Jeremiah 3:10). Life or death is now the only choice facing Jerusalem. (Deuteronomy 30:15-20; Jeremiah 21:8:10).

There are also parallels between Jeremiah and the Psalms. (Psalms 7:9, 26:1-5, 42:22, compared with Jeremiah 11:19-20, 15:17-18, 20:12).

## Kings and Politics at the Time of Jeremiah

The authors of the Second Book of Kings say that King Josiah of Judah (640-609 BC) did what was pleasing to the Lord, and strictly obeyed the laws of God. He carried out reforms by closing down all the places of worship of foreign gods and worship of the stars. (2 Kings 23:5-6, 11, 12, 14; Deuteronomy 16:21; 17:3). The king abolished cultic prostitution (2 Kings 23:7; Deuteronomy 23:18); and child sacrifice (2 Kings 23:10, 24; see Deuteronomy 8:10-12).

The aim of the reforms was to restore the observance of the covenant back to the way it was thought to have been under Moses. (Deuteronomy 7:6; chaps. 12-14). It is thought that the discovery in the temple of older parts of the Book of Deuteronomy had a significant effect on the religious reforms carried out by Josiah. (2 Kings 22:8). King Manasseh may have been responsible for the hiding of Deuteronomy in the temple. Jeremiah was pleased with Josiah's reforms.

However, the reign of Josiah came to an end when the king was killed in battle at Megiddo in northern Israel, while trying to prevent an Egyptian army from going to the aid of the Assyrians, who at this time, were under pressure from the Babylonians. Josiah clearly preferred a resurgent Babylon to a powerful Egypt. The Egyptians succeeded in going to the aid of the Assyrians, but both of these powers failed in their efforts to prevent the rise of Babylon.

After the death of King Josiah, all of his reforms collapsed, and the old pagan practices were re-established. The Second Book of Kings says that all the kings who followed Josiah "sinned against the Lord." Jehoahaz, who only reigned for one year, was the first of those kings. (2 Kings 23:31-34). Then came Jehoiakim (609-598 BC), (2 Kings 23:35-37–24:1-17); and finally, Zedekiah (598-587 BC), the last king of Judah. (2 Kings 24:18 - 25:7). Chapter 25 of the Second Book of Kings is devoted to the destruction of Jerusalem by the Babylonians, followed by the deportation of large numbers of the population to Babylonia.

It seems that few people were converted under Josiah's reforms. Under the rule of Kings Jehoiakim and Zedekiah, Jeremiah despaired that anything could be done to turn back the punishment Jeremiah thought the people deserved for their sins. His message then shifted to one of doom, but he continued to maintain that God would not entirely abandon his people.

During the reign of Jehoiakim, the king of Babylon invaded Judah and Jehoiakim was forced to submit to his rule and pay him tribute. Jehoiakim was succeeded by his son, Jehoiachin who ruled for only three months. During the latter's reign, Nebuchadnezzar, King of Babylon besieged Jerusalem in 598 BC. Jehoiachin surrendered to him, but was still carried off to Babylon, together with the temple treasury, the princes and the leading men, 10,000 in all, in the first deportation. (See Jeremiah 39; 2 Kings 24:8-20).

The king of Babylon then made Jehoiachin's uncle, Zedekiah (the youngest son of Josiah) king of Judah. (2 Kings 18-20; Jeremiah chapters 36-39). After eleven years, and probably because of his heavy tribute payments to the Babylonians, Zedekiah rebelled against Babylon. This time, the Babylonians showed no mercy. They surrounded Jerusalem with an army in 588 BC in a siege that lasted one and a half years. Finally, with the people suffering from disease and famine, the king and his army fled, but the king was captured in the plains of Jericho. After being forced to witness the execution of his sons, the king had his eyes put out. He was then bound in chains and taken to Babylon as a prisoner. Jerusalem was burned to the ground. The city walls, the temple and the king's palace were all levelled, and greater numbers of the population deported to Babylon. (2 Kings 25:1-21; Jeremiah 52).

Archaeology has provided us with a first-hand account of the first siege of Jerusalem in 598 BC. This comes from the records of the Babylonian king, Nebuchadnezzar himself. It is part of the yearly list of the king's activities. It tells about the siege of Jerusalem, the city's downfall, the capture of King Zedekiah and an account of the tribute money paid to Babylon.

## Jeremiah's Call to be a Prophet

The Lord spoke to Jeremiah in the thirteenth year of the reign of King Josiah of Judah. After that the Lord spoke to him many times. In chapter 1, Jeremiah tells about his call by God to be a prophet:

> The Lord said to me, 'I chose you before I gave you life, and before you were born I selected you to be a prophet to the nations.' I answered, 'Sovereign Lord, I don't

know how to speak; I am too young.' The Lord said, 'Do not say you are too young, but go to the people I send you to, and tell them everything I command you to say. Do not be afraid of them, for I will be with you to protect you.' Then the Lord stretched out his hand, touched my lips, and said to me, 'Listen, I am giving you the words you must speak. Today I give you authority over nations and kingdoms to uproot and to pull down, to destroy and to overthrow, to build and to plant... Listen, Jeremiah! Everyone in this land – the kings of Judah, the officials, the priests and the people – will be against you. But today I am giving you the strength to resist them; you will be like a fortified city, an iron pillar and a bronze wall. They will not defeat you, for I will be with you to protect you. I, the Lord, have spoken.' (Jeremiah 1:4-10, 18-19).

On receiving his call, Jeremiah protests his unworthiness to God. (See Exodus 3:11). As was the case with Moses, God tells Jeremiah that his mission will not be all down to his own efforts. He should have no fear of anyone. God will protect him and tell him what to say to the people. The authority that God was giving to Jeremiah would weigh heavily on his shoulders (1:1-10), in the opposition he would encounter from kings and people, for proclaiming the word of God. (1:17-18).

In his life and mission, Jeremiah foreshadows Jesus, who also had to confront a whole nation and its kings, and suffer because of their opposition to him. But in being empowered by God's Spirit for his mission, Jesus overcame all the powers, including the power of the demonic.

Why do we never feel like pillars of iron or walls of bronze? (Jeremiah 1:19). Surrendering to the Lord is the highest level of faith– very difficult, because it calls us to trust him even when we feel powerless and when everything seems at its darkest! "The Lord is my shepherd; he gives me all I need." (Psalm 23:1). What he gives us is the empowerment necessary for our life's journey: faith, hope, commitment, endurance, courage, in pursuance of an ideal. Can we really believe this? Our faith is not even the size of a mustard seed. (Matthew 17:20).

## Infidelity of the People

Jeremiah's message is that calamities will follow the moral corruption of Judah, and sorrow will reign in Zion. "The Lord said to me concerning the drought, 'Judah is mourning; its cities are dying, its people lie on the ground in sorrow.'" (Jeremiah 14:1-2, see 3-9). The drought covering the land is a metaphor for the people's lack of righteousness. It's as if the whole of nature will feel the pain, because the people have forsaken their God and his law. Their disobedience is that of Adam and Eve. They seek radical freedom, preferring to go their own way, wanting to act in the drama they themselves are writing and directing. They thus reject their God-given role as responsible stewards (Genesis 2:15). In other words, they have forsaken the covenant of Sinai and given their allegiance to other gods, particularly the god Baal who was still being worshiped in Judah through ritual prostitution. (Jeremiah 2:20).

In chapters 2 and 3, Jeremiah uses the image of marriage to explain God's relationship with his people. God is the faithful husband who is rejected by a faithless wife – the people he loved and cared for ever since he rescued them from Egypt. But once settled in the promised land, they turned to "worthless idols" and abandoned the God who had saved them and still loved them. (Jeremiah 2:1–3:5; 3:19-20; 6:29:30; 5:1, 26-29; 6:13-14). Israel had become divorced from God, and acted like a prostitute. (3:1-5). From their life in an arid wilderness, God brought his people into a fertile land to enjoy its harvest, but God was deserted by the people he loved. (2:5-7). The people had defiled this beautiful land with their prostitution and vices. That was why the rains were held back. (3:2-3). That is why the Lord commanded the sky to shake with horror in judgement. (2:12). But it wasn't like that in the days of old:

> Thus, says the Lord:
> I remember how faithful you were when you were young,
> how you loved me when we were first married;
> you followed me through the desert,
> through a land that had not been sown.
> Israel, you belonged to me alone;
> you were my sacred possession.
> I sent suffering and disaster
> on everyone who hurt you…
> No other nation has ever changed its gods,
> even though they were not real.
> But my people have exchanged me,
> the God who has brought them honour,
> for gods that can do nothing for them.
> And so I have commanded the sky to shake with horror,
> to be amazed and astonished,
> for my people have committed two sins:
> they have turned away from me,
> the spring of fresh water,
> and they have dug cracked cisterns
> that can hold no water at all…
> Your own evil will punish you,
> and your turning from me will condemn you.
> You will learn how bitter and wrong it is
> to abandon me, the Lord your God,
> and no longer to remain faithful to me. (Jeremiah 2:1-3, 11-13, 19; see 3:19-20).

To satisfy their thirsting for happiness, the people looked for water in the wrong places. When they changed their gods, the new gods did not satisfy them either. All they found were dry wells and cracked cisterns, still leaving them thirsting. They will have to endure the consequences of their infidelity. (Verse 19 above).

Jeremiah next turns to the image of the parent- child relationship. "The Sovereign God says, 'Israel, long ago you rejected my authority; you refused to obey me and worship me. On every high hill and under every green tree you worshiped fertility gods (Baals). I planted you like a choice vine from the very best seed. But look what you have become! You are like a rotten worthless vine."' (2:20-21). In a reference to the idolatry of the people, the Lord reminded them that they had behaved both like an unfaithful wife and unfaithful children, but if they repent, he will take them back, heal their self-inflicted wounds and make them faithful once again. (3:1-5).

When the people refused to listen to his words, Jeremiah saw the pain of God – abandoned by the people he loved - reflected in his own anguish. Yet, the Lord called on "unfaithful Israel" to come back to him and admit her guilt, because he wanted to forgive her infidelity and to treat her again as a beloved wife. The Lord said, 'Confess that under every green tree you have given your love to foreign gods and that you have not obeyed my commands.' (3:12-13).

> The Lord says,
> 'Israel, I wanted to accept you as my child
> and give you a delightful land,
> the most beautiful land in all the world.
> I wanted you to call me father,
> and never again turn away from me.
> But like an unfaithful wife,
> you have not been faithful to me.
> I, the Lord have spoken.'
> A noise is heard on the hilltops:
> it is the people of Israel crying and pleading,
> because they have lived sinful lives
> and have forgotten the Lord their God.
> 'Return, all of you who have turned away from the Lord;
> he will heal you and make you faithful.' (Jeremiah 3:19-22).

The Lord then tells the people that if they will turn back to him, the nations will ask him to bless them, and they will praise him. (4:1-2). This a reference to Abraham's mission of blessing to the nations because of his obedience to God. (Genesis 22:18).

The people remained unfaithful because of their unjust practices. (5:1, 26-29; 6:13-14). In chapter 6, God issues a warning to rebellious Israel. But Jeremiah says that the people are stubborn and will not listen to God's message. "The Lord says, 'I am going to punish the people of this land. Everyone, great and small tries to make money dishonestly; even prophets (advisers to the king) and priests cheat the people."' (6:12b-13). And there is no sign of repentance. (6:15). Like Isaiah before him, Jeremiah condemns their religious rituals going side by side with cheating and dishonesty. (6:20). Here Jeremiah echoes Amos 5:21-24. "The Lord says, 'I gave your ancestors no commands about burnt offerings or any other kinds of sacrifices, when I brought them out of Egypt. But I did command them to obey me, so that I would be their God and they would be my people (the covenant). I told them to live as I had commanded them, so that things would go well for them."' (Jeremiah 7:22-23).

With the threat of disaster and invasion by foreign armies imminent (6:22-23), Jeremiah goes to the gate of the temple and delivers a sermon reminding the people of their breach of the Sinai covenant. Their infidelities are starkly listed in the following passage, spoken by Jeremiah.

> The Lord sent me to the gate of the temple where the people of Judah went to worship. He told me to stand there and announce what the Lord Almighty, the God of Israel, had to say to them: 'Change the way you are living and the things you are doing, and I will let you go on living here. Stop believing those deceitful words, "We are safe! This is the Lord's Temple, this is the Lord's Temple!" 'Be fair in your treatment of one another. Stop taking advantage of aliens, orphans and widows. Stop killing innocent people in this land. Stop worshiping other gods, for that will destroy you. If you change, I will let you go on living here in the land which I gave your ancestors as a permanent possession. Look, you put your trust in deceitful words. You steal, murder, commit adultery, tell lies under oath, offer sacrifices to Baal... You do all these things I hate, and then you come and stand in my presence, in my own Temple and say, "We are safe!" 'Do you think that my Temple is a hiding place for robbers? I have seen what you are doing. Go to Shiloh, the first place where I chose to be worshiped, and see what I did to it because of the sins of my people Israel.' (Jeremiah 7:1-11).

The people believed that the Lord would never allow his temple to be destroyed, and that they would find safety there, no matter about their greed, injustice and violence. In the above passage, Jeremiah warns that the temple will be destroyed. The priests seized him and demanded his death, but he said he was acting on God's command. His life was spared but he was barred from going into the temple. (7:14-15).

According to Jeremiah, the people's crimes were worse than murder. They had resorted to human sacrifice - the killing of children in order to appease local deities. (Jeremiah 2:23). During the reign of King Manasseh, the Lord complained that the people had built altars in the valley of Hinnom, "so that they can sacrifice their sons and daughters in the fire, to the god Baal," (Jeremiah 2:8; see 2 Chronicles 33:2-6). The Lord said, 'Your clothes are stained with the blood of the poor and innocent.' (2:34). 'The land will become a desert. In the cities of Judah and in the streets of Jerusalem I will put an end to the sounds of joy and gladness and to the happy sounds of wedding feasts.' (7:24). There would be no more wedding feasts, symbolizing the marriage breach between God and his people. The bride had deserted her bridegroom God.

Jeremiah's condemnation of temple ritual and the "unjust treatment of aliens, orphans and widows and the killing of innocent people" (chap.7), was to have echoes in Jesus' judgement on the same temple for its association with injustice and rebellion. (See Matthew 21:12:17; Mark 11:15-19, Luke 19:45; John 2:13-22).

## Destruction Coming from a Mighty Nation

In chapter 5 Jeremiah asks Jerusalem to look around and see if she can "find one person who does what is right and tries to be faithful to God. If you can, the Lord will forgive Jerusalem." (5:1). All of them had rejected the Lord's authority. "That is why the lions from the forest will kill them; wolves from the desert will tear them to pieces, and leopards will prowl through their towns. If those people go out, they will be torn apart because their sins are numerous, and time after time they have turned from the Lord." (4:6).

The prophet has a vision of an enemy from the north pouring destruction on the land "like a pot of boiling water." (1:13-15; see also 5:15; 6:22-23). This will be the Babylonian army on the march. The punishment will be terrible. (6:25). "Death has come in through our windows and entered our palaces; it has cut down the children in the streets and the young men in the market places." (9:21). God fills the nation with drunkenness so that the people end up destroying themselves. (13:12-14). Their enemies will take away their wealth and treasures. (17:3). Their young men will be slaughtered, leaving "more widows in your land than grains of sand by the sea." (15:8). Then they will be taken away into exile. (10:18).

"The Lord says, 'O house of Jacob, will you not tremble at my presence, who set the sands as limit to the sea, as an everlasting barrier it cannot pass: it storms, but can do nothing, its waves may roar but do not pass beyond. But these people have a rebellious, unruly heart.'" (Jeremiah 5:22, JB). The consequences of the people's rebellion will be a metaphorical storm breaking on top of them and flooding the land, resulting in chaos and destruction.

What was about to happen would be theologically, politically and socially, like the end of the world for Judah. God's anger (really anguish, disappointment) would burn like a fire because of the evil of the people and their breach of his covenant. (4:4). "Like a lion coming from its hiding place, a destroyer of nations has set out. He is coming to destroy Judah... So put on sackcloth, and weep and wail because the fierce anger of the Lord has not turned away from Judah." (4:7-8).

This is the beginning of the battle (still in the future) that will go on until the end of chapter six. The battle is lost before it begins. Lamentation and wailing are the only response to the siege of Jerusalem. The Lord is using Babylon as his instrument of judgement on Judah.

> Blow the trumpet throughout the land!
> Shout loud and clear!
> Tell the people of Judah and Jerusalem
> to run to the fortified cities.
> Run for safety! Don't delay!
> The Lord is bringing disaster
> and great destruction from the north.
> Like a lion coming from its hiding place,
> a destroyer of nations has set out.
> He is coming to destroy Judah.

Its cities will be left in ruins,
and no one will live in them...
The pain! I can't bear the pain!
My heart! My heart is beating wildly!
I can't keep quiet;
I hear the trumpets and the shouts of battle.
One disaster follows another;
the whole country is left in ruins...The Lord says,
'My people are stupid; they don't know me.
They are like foolish children;
they have no understanding...'
I looked at the earth – it was a barren waste;
at the sky – there was no light.
I looked at the mountains – they were shaking,
the hills were rocking to and fro.
I saw that there were no people;
even the birds had flown away.
The fertile land had become a desert;
its cities were in ruins because of the Lord's fierce anger...
The earth will mourn; the sky will grow dark...
At the noise of the horsemen and bowmen
everyone will run away.
Some will run to the forest,
others will climb up among the rocks.
Every town will be left empty.
Jerusalem, you are doomed!
Why do you dress in scarlet?
You are making yourself beautiful for nothing!
Your lovers have rejected you and want to kill you.
I heard a cry, like a woman in labour,
a scream like a woman bearing her first child.
It was the cry of Jerusalem gasping for breath,
stretching out her hand and saying,
'I am doomed!' (Jeremiah 4:5-7, 19-20, 23-26, 28-31).

The people would not listen to these warnings, nor change their evil ways. "They are all stubborn rebels." (6:28). It is not God who is darkening the sky and turning the earth into a barren waste. It is not God's doing. Human beings are doing this. As the prophet sees it, Israel's sins of disobedience have stripped away all the good of the land and made it desolate, producing only thorns and briars – an East of Eden wilderness. (See Genesis 3:17-19). Sin and evil bring about a reversal of God's good creation; the earth returns to a formless waste. (Verses 23-26; see Genesis 3:17-18; Isaiah 24:4-6; Matthew 24:29; Mark 15:33).

In the face of this onslaught the only course open to the people now is repentance, symbolized in sackcloth and ashes, a sign of mourning.

> The Lord says,
> 'Now a people is coming from the land of the North,
> from the far ends of the earth a mighty nation stirs:
> they are armed with bow and spear,
> they are cruel and pitiless;
> their noise is like the roaring of the sea;
> they are riding horses,
> each man equipped for war
> on you daughter of Zion!...
> Do not go out into the countryside,
> do not venture on the roads,
> for the enemy's sword is there,
> terror on every side.
> Wrap yourself in sackcloth, daughter of my people,
> roll in ashes;
> mourn as for an only son,
> a very bitter dirge.
> For on us suddenly
> the destroyer is coming.' (Jeremiah 6:22-23, 25-26, JB).

## Jeremiah's Sufferings Bound up with his Mission

The oracles in chapters 11 - 20 outline moments of Jeremiah's loneliness and despair. There are passages of deep trust in God mixed with the prophet's sense of total abandonment by God. (11:18–12:6; 15:10-21; 17:14-18; 18:18-23; 20:7-18). These passages are known as Jeremiah's confessions, soliloquies that give an insight into the prophet's psyche. His pain is in delivering a message to a people who are blind and deaf to the word of God. These are passages in which he borrows expressions from the psalms of lament and the psalms of trust. (See Psalms 44:23-26; 26:1-5; 7:9). They are full of petitions, pleas for divine help and expressions of confidence that God will come to his assistance and guard him in his proclamation of the divine word. Despite persecution, Jeremiah gives an enduring commitment to his call to be a prophet.

Unlike Second and Third Isaiah, who were shadowy figures, Jeremiah reveals a lot about his own sufferings as a result of God calling him to be a prophet. Readers are drawn into his struggles, empathising with him. His sufferings are an integral part of his prophetic vocation, which he says, he was reluctant to accept. His excuses echo those of Moses in Exodus 4:10. Like Moses he will experience rejection, and will plead with, and complain to God.

Jeremiah was persecuted by kings Jehoiakim and Zedekiah, both of whom tried to silence him. All they wanted to hear was good news, not the truth. Surrendering to God's will is costly. The load on Jeremiah's shoulders is almost unbearable. He regrets the day he was born. (20:14-15). The Lord informed him about plots on his life. But despite his sense of abandonment, the Lord would stand by him. He was the archetype of God's suffering servant – persecuted, reviled and made a laughing-stock.

> The Lord informed me of the plots that my enemies were making against me. I was like a trusting lamb led to the slaughter. And I did not know that it was against me that they devised their schemes, saying, 'Let us destroy the tree with its fruit, let us cut him off from the land of the living, let's kill him so that his name will no longer be remembered... The people of Anathoth told me they would kill me if I kept on proclaiming the Lord's message'. (Jeremiah 11:18-19, 21; see 13:10; 17:23; 20:1-2; 26:11; 38:6).

Obedience to the will of God, would cause Jeremiah much suffering. Even the people of his native village were making threats on his life. Jesus was also rejected by the people of his own village (Nazareth) for proclaiming the word of God. (Luke 4:16-30). As the lamb led to the slaughter, Jeremiah prefigures Jesus whom the Gospel of John describes as the "Lamb of God," slain, because in surrendering himself to God's will, he accepted the cup of self-sacrificial service on our behalf, as a substitute for us. (Luke 22:42).

Jeremiah is mocked and treated like a fool. (20:7). He experiences nothing but anguish while his enemies prosper. (12:1-6). He wishes God would wipe out his foes. (17:18; 18:22-23; 20:12). He longs to return to his farm and to live a quiet life, but it was not to be. (See chapter 32). But he still perseveres and endures the awful burden God had placed on him.

In the poem below, Jeremiah feels that God tricked him into calling him to be a prophet. But even in the face of failure and scepticism about his own calling, he is still able to give an almost superhuman obedience to God. In saying that God had overpowered him, he means that he has allowed God to take over his life, and in a sense, to live in him. This gives him an empowerment that has nothing to do with his own strength as a human being. (For a similar wrestling with God, see the account of Jacob in Genesis 32:22-32). The trials and tribulations of Jeremiah are vividly illustrated in the following passage.

> Lord, you have deceived me,
> and I was deceived.
> You are stronger than I am,
> and you have overpowered me.
> Everyone jeers at me;
> they mock me all day long.
> Whenever I speak, I have to cry out
> and shout, "Violence and destruction."
> Lord, I am ridiculed and scorned all the time
> because I proclaim your message.
> But when I say, "I will forget the Lord
> and no longer speak in his name,"
> then your message is like a fire

burning deep within me.
I try my best to hold it in,
but I can no longer keep it back...
Even my close friends wait for my downfall.
But you, Lord, are on my side,
strong and mighty,
and those who persecute me will fail...
A curse on the day when I was born!
Forget the day my mother gave me birth!...
Why was I born?
Was it only to have trouble and sorrow,
To end my life in disgrace. (Jeremiah 20:7-11, 14, 18).

The kings were hell-bent on war and rebellion. But their real rebellion was against God himself and his good purposes. King Zedekiah wanted to silence Jeremiah. He had him arrested and kept in prison for a period up to the fall of Jerusalem. (Jeremiah 37:12–38:13). His trials are told in great depth in Baruch's biography (chapters 30-45). The exiles in Babylon would be encouraged and strengthened in their own pain by Jeremiah's patient suffering. "In making public his anguish, he offered to the people a model for bearing exilic suffering with honesty and hope."[101]

A reading of Jeremiah should give us a fuller understanding of Jesus, whom, like Jeremiah, evil men wanted to kill, so that he would not be remembered. (Jeremiah 11:18-23; see Mark 6:1-6). Jesus also prophesised the destruction of the temple and the fall of Jerusalem. He was put on trial because of his preaching about the temple. He suffered at the hands of his own people. In his sufferings, Jeremiah is the "lamb being led to the slaughterhouse" foreshadowing the figure of Isaiah's suffering servant, whom the New Testament identifies with Jesus. (Jeremiah 11:18-19; see Isaiah 53:7, Mark 15:5). The Jewish religious authorities wanted Jesus crucified because they thought that the shame and dread associated with crucifixion would ensure that he would never be remembered.

Jeremiah questions God about matters of justice: "Why are the wicked so prosperous? Why do dishonest people succeed? Lord, they always speak well of you, yet they do not really care about you... How long will our land be dry, and the grass in every field be withered? Animals and birds are dying because of the wickedness of our people, those who say, 'God doesn't see what we are doing.' (12:1, 4).

In reference to his sufferings, the Lord told him that he hadn't seen anything yet. The Lord said, 'Jeremiah, if you get tired racing against people, how can you race against horses? If you can't stand up in open country, how will you manage in the jungle of the Jordan? Even your relatives, members of your own family, have betrayed you; they join in attacks against you.' (12:5-6). Yes, the Lord had worse punishment in store for Jeremiah. "Again, the Lord spoke to me and said, 'Do not marry or have children in a place like this. I will tell you what is going to happen to the children and their parents who are born here.

---

[101] Lawrence Boadt, *Reading the Old Testament*, p.326.

They will die of terrible diseases and no one will mourn them or bury them. Their bodies will lie like piles of manure on the ground. They will be killed in war or die of starvation, and their bodies will be food for the birds and the wild animals.'" (Jeremiah 16:1-4).

## Jeremiah's Intercessory Role

> So I prayed, 'Lord, hear what I am saying and listen to what my enemies are saying about me. Is evil the payment for good? Yet they have dug a pit for me to fall in. Remember how I came to you and spoke on their behalf, so that you would not deal with them in anger.' (Jeremiah 19:20).

No more than the Israelites after the making of the golden calf (Exodus 32), were these people prepared to repent or change their destructive ways. Perhaps Jeremiah could offer God a repentance on their behalf. Jeremiah accepted the role as intercessor and representative of his people. It was like a living death. In standing in for his people as a substitute, he accepted the penalty that should fall on them – so that they might escape judgement, in terms of destruction by a foreign power.

Moses was repeatedly able to intercede for Israel when the Lord threatened the people with destruction following their apostasy. (See Exodus 32:1-4, 6). However, Jeremiah was prohibited from trying to dissuade the Lord from his purpose. Jerusalem and its people were doomed. Pleas for mercy went unheeded. There was nothing now but judgement. The Lord said, 'When these people ask you where they should go, tell them that I have said: some are doomed to die by disease – that's where they will go! Others are doomed to die in war – that's where they will go! Some are doomed to die of starvation – that's where they will go! Others are doomed to be taken away as prisoners – that's where they will go!" (Jeremiah 15:2).

In the following divine lament, the Lord says that Jerusalem has rejected him, so there is no one left to grieve over the fate of its people.

> The Lord says,
> 'Who will pity you, people of Jerusalem,
> and who will grieve over you?
> Who will stop long enough to ask how you are?
> You people have rejected me;
> you have turned your backs on me.
> So I stretched out my hand and crushed you.
> In every town in the land
> I threw you to the wind like straw...
> There are more widows in your land
> than grains of sand by the sea...
> The mother who lost her seven children has fainted,
> gasping for breath.
> Her daylight has turned to darkness;
> She is disgraced and sick at heart.' (15:5-7a, 8-9).

Jeremiah can scarcely bear the pain of his people. In interceding with the Lord on their behalf, he becomes God's suffering servant. He identifies with his people. When they suffer, he suffers along with them, feeling the pain of their own abandonment. God stretching out his hand and crushing the people should be interpreted as Judgement rather than punishment. The people have brought this suffering down on their own heads. They have already abandoned their Garden of Eden and gone into hiding. (Genesis 3:8).

In a lament of his own, and despite his sufferings, Jeremiah says that God's word has filled his heart with joy. (15:16). Yet, his complaint to the Lord can be the complaint of all of us in the face of innocent suffering:

> A disaster for me, mother, that you bore me to be a man
> of strife and dissention for the whole country.
> I neither lend or borrow, yet all of them curse me.
> Have I not genuinely done my best to serve you, my God?
> Have I not interceded with you in time of disaster and distress?
> Lord, you understand. Remember me and take care of me...
> Remember that it is for your sake I am insulted...
> When your words came, I devoured them:
> your words were my delight
> and the joy of my heart;
> for I was called by your Name.
> I never sat in the company of scoffers, amusing myself.
> Why is my suffering continual, my wound incurable,
> refusing to be healed?
> Truly, for me you are a deceptive stream
> with uncertain waters. (Jeremiah 15:10-11, 15a, 16, 17a,18, NJB).

Jeremiah's substitutionary role in the above poem is a recurring theme. (See 5:7-9; 7:16; 7:27-28; 11:14-16; 15:1) He has emptied himself (sold everything, given up everything, his private life, his farm, not having children, keeping away from scoffers) and surrendered himself to God. This has only made his life one of danger and solitude. It's as if God has thrown him into a turbulent stream in which he may be drowned. A Christ-like figure, he is mocked and insulted for proclaiming the word of God. (See Mark 14:65; 15:17-20).

The power of the arm of the Lord is a recurring theme with the prophets. The Lord commands Jeremiah to go to the potter's house (18:1-11), where the potter performs a symbolic action (verses 1-4), which Jeremiah interprets in his sermon (18:5-11). Whenever a piece of clay turns out imperfectly, the potter destroys it and makes it anew. As the potter can crush the clay pot, so the arm of the Lord can destroy a nation or kingdom. But the Lord's threat of destruction is conditional. All that the people have to do is repent, and their obedience will induce the Lord to build and plant instead of destroying. (18: 9-11). The sermon concludes with the Lord appealing to the nation to change its evil ways (verse 11), but the people respond by saying that they will be as stubborn and as evil as they want to be. (Verse 12).

In the following poem, Jeremiah wonders if he should abandon his unfaithful people. The people are wondering if the Lord has abandoned Zion. But it is really the people themselves who have abandoned God and turned to foreign gods. Their violence and dishonesty have been their ruination.

> My sorrow cannot be healed;
> I am sick at heart.
> Listen! Throughout the land
> I hear my people crying out,
> is the Lord no longer in Zion?
> Is Zion's king no longer there?
> The Lord, their king, replies,
> 'Why have you made me angry
> by worshiping your idols
> and by bowing down to your
> useless foreign gods?'
> The people cry out,
> 'The summer is gone, the harvest is over,
> but we have not been saved.'
> My heart has been crushed
> because my people are crushed;
>  I mourn; I am completely dismayed.
> Is there no medicine in Gilead?
> Are there no doctors there?
> Why, then, have my people not been healed'?..
> I wish my head were a well of water,
> and my eyes a fountain of tears,
> so that I could cry day and night
> for my people who have been killed.
> I wish I had a place to stay in the desert
> where I could get away from my people.
> They are all unfaithful, a mob of traitors…
> They do one violent thing after another,
> and one deceitful act follows another…
> Their tongues are like deadly arrows;
> dishonesty instead of truth rules the land…
> Everyone speaks friendly words to his neighbour,
> but is really setting a trap for him.
> Will I not punish them for these things?
> The Lord says, "I will make Jerusalem a heap of ruins,
> A place where Jackals live;
> The cities of Judah will become a desert,
> A place where no one lives. (Jeremiah 8:18-22, 9:1-2, 8-9, 11).

Jeremiah's sense of abandonment along with his people foreshadows the abandonment of Jesus on the cross. (Mark 15:34; see Deuteronomy 9:25-29). Jeremiah prefigures Jesus who surrendered himself to his Father. In his substitutionary role, Jesus endured the suffering that his people deserved: mockery, scorn, insults, rejection and the threat of death. Jesus was persecuted in the cause of right. In his single mindedness, his total commitment to God's goal for him, and through the power of his faith, Jesus would also be a "pillar of iron and a wall of bronze in confronting a whole nation," both its religious and secular authorities. (Jeremiah 1:18-19).

In the lyric poem below, God has his own complaint. The people have forgotten their God, lost their way by making offerings to false gods. So is it a case that God cannot walk with them anymore? If God is turning his back on the people, thus abandoning them, is he abandoning Jeremiah too, as the one who identifies with them and intercedes with God on their behalf? When God turns his back on his people, has Jeremiah's mission come to an end?

> The Lord says this,
> 'My people have forgotten me!
> They burn their incense to a Nothing!
> They have lost their footing in their ways
> to walk in tortuous paths,
> a way unmarked.
> They will make their country desolate,
> everlastingly derided:
> Every passer-by will be appalled at it
> and shake his head.
> Like the east wind, I will scatter them
> before the enemy.
> I will turn my back to them
> and not my face
> on the day of their disaster.' (Jeremiah 18:15-17, JB).

Apart from proclaiming desolation and disaster, as above, what was the word spoken by Jeremiah that provoked such opposition from kings and people?

## The Greedy Shepherds Abandon their Flocks

The people have turned to gods of their own creation: "sumptuous palaces," greed, selfishness, militarism. Jeremiah severely criticised the king for neglecting the welfare of his people while building palaces for himself, the shepherd feeding himself rather than his flock. (See Hosea 8:14). Jeremiah sees the sumptuous palace of the king as a metaphor for a society built on greed and in disregard of the general welfare of the people. This was Jeremiah's uncompromising message to King Jehoiakim:

> The Lord says concerning Josiah's son who succeeded his father as king of Judah,
> 'He has gone away from here, never to return.
> Doomed is the man who builds his house by injustice
> and enlarges it by dishonesty;
> who makes his countrymen work for nothing,
> and does not pay their wages...
> You can only see your selfish interests;
> you kill the innocent and violently oppress your people.
> So then, the Lord says about Josiah's son, Jehoiakim, King of Judah,
> 'No one will mourn his death or say,
> How terrible, my friend, how terrible!
> No one will weep for him or cry,
> My lord! My king!
> With the funeral honours of a donkey,
> he will be dragged away
> and thrown outside Jerusalem's gates.' (Jeremiah 22:11, 13-14, 17-19).

Jeremiah sees the kings of Judah as bad shepherds whom he accuses of plundering and scattering the Lord's flock. In other words, the kings are the ones responsible for their people being taken into exile.

> The Lord, the God of Israel says, 'You have scattered my flock, you have driven them away and have not taken care of them. Right, I shall take care of you for your misdeeds. The remnant of my flock I myself will gather from all the countries where I have driven them and bring them back to their folds; they will be fruitful and increase in numbers. For them I shall raise up shepherds to shepherd them and pasture them. No fear, no terror for them anymore; not one will be lost.' (Jeremiah 23:1-4, NJB; see Ezekiel 22:23-25; 34:1-6, 11-15).

The Lord expresses his regret over having to abandon his people because they have forsaken him for their own gods:

> I have abandoned Israel; I have rejected my chosen nation. I have given the people I love into the power of their enemies. My people have turned against me; like a lion in the forest, they have roared at me... Many foreign rulers have destroyed my vineyard; they have trampled down my fields; they have turned my lovely land into a desert. My people sowed wheat but gathered weeds; they have worked hard but got nothing for it. (Jeremiah 12:7-8, 10, 13; see Genesis 3:17-18).

Household slavery was practised in Israel at this time. However, there was a Mosaic law stating that a fellow-Israelite who had been bought as a slave should be set free after seven years of service. (Exodus 21:11-2; Deuteronomy 15:12-18). King Zedekiah and the people of Jerusalem made an agreement to set free their fellow-Israelite slaves. But despite their solemn promise made in a temple ceremony, the king and the people refused to do what they promised. (Jeremiah 34:14-17). As a result, God looked on their king as an enslaving Egyptian Pharaoh who must be called to account. The Lord says, 'Very well then, I will give you freedom: the freedom to die by war, disease and starvation. I will hand over King Zedekiah of Judah and his officials to the Babylonian army. They will attack this city, capture it and burn it down.' (Jeremiah 34:18-22).

Jeremiah warned the people of Jerusalem of the coming disaster: 'You are under siege. Gather up your belongings. The Lord is going to throw you out of this land; he is going to crush you until not one of you is left.' (10:17). Jeremiah told King Zedekiah to surrender Jerusalem to the Babylonians so that their city, the lives of its citizens and the king's own life, might be spared. The king refused to do this, believing that the Lord would perform a miracle and force the King of Babylon to retreat. The peoples' pride was blinding them from seeing the Babylonian armies already descending on them. They could no more change their ways than the leopard could change its spots. The kings were bad shepherds who had abandoned their flocks. The Lord will now abandon those shepherds to the Babylonians.

Jeremiah was dissuaded from pleading with the Lord on behalf of his people. His role as an intercessor was finished. "The Lord said to me, 'Even if Moses and Samuel were standing here pleading with me, I would not show these people any mercy.'" (15:1). The lyric poem below is a plea from the heart by Jeremiah to the people of Jerusalem to give glory to the Lord and give up glorying in their own schemes for salvation.

> Give glory to the Lord your God
> before the darkness comes,
> and before your feet stumble
> on the mountains at twilight.
> You hope for light,
> but he will change it to blackness,
> dark as death.
> If you do not listen to this warning
> I shall weep in secret for your pride;
> my eyes will shed bitter tears,
> for the Lord's flock
> is being led into captivity...
> Raise your eyes, Jerusalem, and look at these
> now coming from the north...
> Where is the flock once trusted to you,
> the flock which was your pride?...
> I will scatter you like chaff
> driven by the desert wind,
> because you have forgotten me
> and put your trust in Delusion.
> This is your share, the wage of your apostasy.
> (Jeremiah 13:16-17, 20, 24-25).

The kings and people are censured for their idolatry, seeking glory for themselves through things made by their own hands: foreign alliances, horses and armies, city fortifications, silver and gold, sumptuous palaces. (See Hosea 5:13; 8:9-10; Psalm 20:7-8). Jeremiah reminds them that forsaking the Lord their God for the worship of these things (false gods) is apostacy (verse 25) – a turn to false gods. Could the elite of Jerusalem still not abandon the delusion of seeking salvation in their own schemes, and instead, give glory to the Lord their God and place their trust in his word spoken by the prophet, as the only path to their salvation? (Psalm 147:10-11).

The image of light (13:16b) is often used in the Bible to signify enlightenment – righteousness, leading to fulfilment and happiness. Darkness on the other hand, signifies chaos, destruction and death. When human beings forsake God and give all the glory to themselves, they cannot expect light. They fall into a world of darkness and their feet stumble (verse 16). To "stumble" in the Biblical sense means to fall or fail in the ways of God. Relying on one's own powers and resources, and refusing to draw one's strength from God results in stumbling. In trying to escape from his enemies, the king and the elite of Jerusalem abandon the Lord's flock and try to hide in the mountains. Jeremiah will weep (13:17) for the flock whom the Lord entrusted to the kings, but whom they now abandon to destruction. These people had put their "trust in their delusions" (13:25), in the belief that greed and affluence would be their salvation.

The prophet, weeping in secret for the pride of the people who would not listen to him, is echoed in Jesus' lament over the same Jerusalem, the rebellious city that closed its ears to his offer of salvation through peace and reconciliation. Jesus would have gathered all of its people to himself like a hen protecting her chicks under her wing, but they would not listen to his saving word. (Matthew 23:37-39; Luke 19:41-44). As in the time of Jeremiah, the day came when the people of the same Jerusalem were led into captivity, their temple and city destroyed once again, leaving them stumbling in a blackness dark as death.

In the passage below, the message is about trusting and hoping in God, something that leads to flourishing lives. It empowers people to stand up to adversity. Just as water gives life to the tree, God gives fruitful lives to those who trust and hope in him.

> A blessing on those who put their trust in God,
> with God as their hope.
> They are like a tree by the waterside
> that trusts its roots to the stream:
> When the heat comes, it feels no alarm,
> its foliage stays green;
> it has no worries in the year of drought,
> and never ceases to bear fruit. (Jeremiah 17:7-8, JB).

## Death and Destruction

The Lord said to me, 'I am the Lord, the God of the whole human race. I am going to give this city over to King Nebuchadnezzar of Babylonia and his army; they will capture it and set it on fire... From the very beginning of their history, the people of Israel and the people of Judah have displeased me and made me angry by what they have done. The people of this city have made me angry and furious from the day it was built. I have decided to destroy it because of all the evil that has been done by the people of Judah and Jerusalem, together with their kings and leaders, their priests and prophets. They turned their backs on me; and though I kept on teaching them, they would not listen and learn. They even placed their disgusting idols in the Temple built for my worship, and they have defiled it. They have built altars to Baal in the Valley of Hinnom, to sacrifice their sons and daughters to the god Molech.'[102] (Jeremiah 32:26-28, 30 -35).

The above passage is a play on the sovereignty of God, in the sense that God allows Babylon to punish Judah for its sins of disobedience. The consequence would be death. (See Genesis 2:16-17; 3:6). For the fall of Jerusalem, see Jeremiah, chapters 21, 39 and 52. "The king of Babylon took away to Babylonia the people who were left in the city... But he left in Judah some of the poorest people who owned no property, and put them to work in the vineyards and fields." (Jeremiah 52:12-13, 16). For a detailed account of the siege of Jerusalem and its aftermath, see 2 Kings 25:1-21.

In the lyric poem below, it is not clear whether the speaker is the Lord or Jeremiah, probably both. The mountains and the pastures have been turned into a desert with no life. The whole of nature is suffering because of human evil. It's like the curse pronounced on the earth after the first act of disobedience in Eden, leaving a wilderness of weeds and thorns. (Genesis 3:17-18). This lamentation is for a world that has returned to the chaos before creation. (Genesis 1:1).

I the Lord have spoken:
'I will raise a wail and lament
for the mountains,
a dirge for the desert pastures,
for they have been burnt:
no one passes there,
the sound of flocks is heard no more.
Birds in the sky and animals,
all have fled, all are gone.
I shall make Jerusalem a heap of ruins,
a lair for jackals,

---

[102] Molech was the national god of Ammon, a country east of the River Jordan, a land bordering Israel. The Valley of Hinnom was just outside the walls of Jerusalem, on the south side of the city.

and the towns of Judah
an uninhabited wasteland.
The hills are a delusion after all,
so is the tumult of the mountains...
Now listen you women
to the Lord's word.
Teach your daughters how to wail
and teach one another this dirge,
'Death has climbed in at our windows,
and made its way into our palaces;
it has cut down the children in our street,
the young people in the squares –
Speak!' The Lord declares this –
'human corpses are strewn
like dung in the open field,
like sheaves left by the reaper,
with no one to gather them.'
(Jeremiah 9:10-11, 19-21, NJB; see 4:23-28; Isaiah 24:4-12).

## The Failure of Royal Ideology

Jeremiah supported the reforms of King Josiah (2 Kings 23:1-27), but when those reforms failed, Jeremiah's message changed to one of doom. Unfortunately, Judah and its people had relied too much on the divine protection which was guaranteed by royal ideology. This was the belief that because the Lord had chosen the Davidic dynasty, neither it, its capital city or temple would ever be destroyed. The belief remained that the Lord would never abandon his own house (temple).

During the long period of Assyrian domination in the Near East (9th to 7th centuries), Jerusalem was one of the few capital cities not to be captured or destroyed by the Assyrians. But Jeremiah said that royal ideology was a lie. Judah's survival depended on obedience to God, adherence to the Sinai covenant. (Jeremiah 7:9-10).

Judah had a chance to learn from the disaster inflicted on the northern kingdom of Israel, which had fallen to the Assyrians in 721 BC, but failed to do so. In order to survive, Judah had to change its conduct. In his sermon at the temple gate, Jeremiah warned the people about their crimes, but they refused to listen. (7:5-7). What the elite of Judah were doing to the poor, Judah's neighbours would now do to them. The defeat was God's judgement on the nation, on her unjust social and economic systems. The Babylonians had their own purpose for the conquest of Judah, but Isaiah and Jeremiah believed that Babylon was really serving God's purposes. (Jeremiah 5:10-12).

## Exile in Babylon

The first deportation of exiles to Babylon took place in 578 BC, under the reign of King Jehoiachin of Judah. King Nebuchadnezzar of Babylonia and his army besieged Jerusalem.

During the siege Jehoiachin surrendered the city to the Babylonians. The city was spared but Jehoiachin was taken prisoner to Babylon together with the treasures of the temple and palace. Nebuchadnezzar also carried away as prisoners the people of Jerusalem, all the royal princes and the leading men, 10,000 or more. Judah became a vassal State of Babylon. (See 2 Kings 24:8-17).

The second deportation in 587 took place under the reign of the next king of Judah, Zedekiah. Probably because of the obligation to pay heavy taxes following the first siege, Zedekiah rebelled against the king of Babylon. The Babylonians then arrived for a second siege of Jerusalem. Because the king refused to surrender the city, despite the advice and warnings of Jeremiah, the Babylonians levelled Jerusalem and its temple and took more prisoners to Babylon. The king's sons were killed in his presence, the king had his eyes put out and was taken in chains as a prisoner to Babylon. (See 2 Kings 25).

Jeremiah had warned the king: "Submit to the king of Babylonia and you will live." (Jeremiah 27:17; see 21:3-7; 34:1-5). In other words, 'Obey the word of God spoken by his prophet.' Zedekiah refused to heed the word of the Lord spoken by Jeremiah, the Lord's prophet. Zedekiah disobeyed the Lord and went his own way, a way that led him down a pathway into death. (See Genesis 2:16-17; 3:6). The collapse of the house of David was final. In calling on Zedekiah to "submit" to the king of Babylon, Jeremiah was proclaiming Nebuchadnezzar as God's new servant who should now be obeyed.

What followed the capture of Jerusalem in 587 BC was destruction, starvation and death. (See the Book of Lamentations). Calamity fell on the king and people because they had forgotten the Lord and trusted in their delusions that salvation would come through war and foreign alliances. (See Jeremiah 13:14, 25). What followed was "blackness dark as death."

> The Lord said, 'By my great power and strength I created the world, the human race, and all the animals that live on the earth; I give it to anyone I choose. I am the one who has placed all these nations under the power of my servant, King Nebuchadnezzar of Babylonia, and I have made even the wild animals to serve him. All nations will serve him, and they will serve his son and his grandson until the time comes for his own nation to fall.' (Jeremiah 27:5-7).

In seeing King Nebuchadnezzar of Babylon as God's servant, Jeremiah remained a solitary voice. Neither king nor people would listen to such a shocking word. Jeremiah wanted to convey the message that Babylon was doing what God wanted. At this time, all the small States bordering Judah became subject to Babylon. Jeremiah's message to all of them is that God is sovereign over all States, including Babylonia. This gave hope to the exiles in Babylon, because of its revelation that the nations that had destroyed Judah were also subject to the rule of God.

On their way into exile in the land of the Tigris and Euphrates rivers, the people travelled the same road that Abraham took from Ur of the Chaldeans (ancient city on the Euphrates), but this time, each step was one further away from the promised land and closer to the place where Israel's story began with Abraham. Their fate was to become slaves in the kingdom of Babel between the two great rivers.

Once the exiles were away in Babylon, Jeremiah instructed them to pray for Babylon, to build houses and settle down, to marry and have children, and work for the good of the cities to which God made them go as prisoners. (Jeremiah 27:5-7). Only a remnant returned to Jerusalem about fifty years after the deportations. Away in Babylon, their temple in ruins, the exiles established houses of prayer that later came to be known as synagogues.

The Babylonian exile led to a religious crisis. The people of Judah had found their identity as a people through the temple, the Davidic monarchy and the land of Israel, where they believed God dwelt with them. Had the Lord now abandoned them (revoked his covenant), and his promises to them? Perhaps the Babylonian gods were more powerful than the God of Israel. In the ancient world when a nation was defeated by a foreign power, the belief was that the foreign gods were more powerful than the native gods. So why not then give one's allegiance to the foreign gods? Jeremiah understood God, not just as a tribal god standing up for one particular tribe or nation, but as sovereign over all the nations, because he created the whole world. It is not that the god of Babylon was more powerful than the God of Israel. The God of Abraham, Isaac and Jacob was using Babylon as his instrument, in order to deprive the people of Jerusalem of all the things they held dear, so that they might eventually come to their senses (be refined like metal in a fire) and repent of their sins. (See Luke 15:17-18). The sovereignty of God over all nations is developed more fully in Isaiah 40:25-31.

Much of Jeremiah's prophecy was intended for the exiles in Babylon, reminding them that they had been taken into exile because of their crimes. God had not forsaken them. It was they who had forsaken the Lord for other gods. But at the same time, Jeremiah preached a message of hope, once the people were prepared to listen and repent.

## Jeremiah's Book of Consolation

The main portion of Jeremiah is concerned with faithless Israel. But he is not all doom. In chapter 2, he looks back to his tradition, to the time when Israel was faithful to the Lord. Then in 31:31-34, he looks forward in hope to an ultimate restoration.

Chapters 30-33 are Jeremiah's Book of Consolation. They are intended to comfort the exiled people with the prospect of a renewed Israel in the future. Jeremiah's message is that God had not forgotten them. They are now in a time of testing, but there is hope for the future.

Here we find Jeremiah's idea of redemption, which was brought to fulfilment in Jesus. Unremitting doom is relieved by these comforting words. Here are gathered together Jeremiah's words of hope from different times - the hope of a new beginning for the people and a new intimacy of personal relationship and reconciliation with God. These oracles are filled with expressions of healing, visions of fruitful fields, the joy of singing – a kind of return to the happy days of David and Solomon, a reversion from the barren earth to the Garden of Eden. A new creation! Like all the other prophets, Jeremiah still hopes for redemption. The God in whom he placed his trust would have the final word on evil.

> The Lord says, 'The time is coming when I will be the God of all the tribes of Israel, and they will be my people. In the desert I showed mercy to those people who had escaped death. When the people of Israel longed for rest, I appeared to them from far away. People of Israel, I have always loved you. Once again, I will rebuild you. Once again you will take up your tambourines and dance joyfully. Once again you will plant vineyards on the hills of Samaria, and those who plant them will eat what the vineyards produce… I will bring them from the north and gather them from the ends of the earth. The blind and the lame will come with them… My people will return weeping, praying as I lead them back. I will guide them by streams of water, on a smooth road where they will not stumble… I scattered my people, but I will gather them and guard them as a shepherd guards his flock. I have set Israel's people free and have saved them from a mighty nation. They will come and sing for joy on Mount Zion and be delighted with my gifts– gifts of corn and wine and olive oil, gifts of sheep and cattle. They will be like a well-watered garden. Then the young women will dance and be happy, and the men, young and old will rejoice. I will comfort them and turn their mourning into joy, their sorrow into gladness. I, the Lord, have spoken.' (Jeremiah 31:1-5, 8a, 9-13; see also 31:23-40, thanksgiving Psalms, 118, 136).

The above verses could be said of Jesus. It is Jesus who comforts the afflicted, the poor in spirit and those who mourn. (Matthew 5:4). The kings of Israel failed in their vocation as shepherds. They had no interest in comforting the mourners, nor in raising up the afflicted. Jesus is the Good Shepherd, who gathers his ailing and scattered sheep from the ends of the earth, the blind and the lame, turning their mourning into joy, their sorrow into gladness, and leading them to streams of water where their thirst for fullness of life (happiness) is fully satisfied. (John 7:37-39; Psalm 23:2).

In the following verses, Jeremiah anticipates the defeat of the Babylonians, as well as Jerusalem's glorious restoration.

## A New Covenant

> The Lord says, 'I will make a new covenant with the people of Israel and with the people of Judah. It will not be like the old covenant I made with their ancestors when I took them out of the land of Egypt. Although I was like a husband to them, they did not keep that covenant. The new covenant will be this: I will put my law within them and write it on their hearts. I will be their God and they will be my people, and they will all know me, from the least of them to the greatest. For I will forgive their sins and no longer remember their wrongs.' (Jeremiah 31:31-34, see verse 37).

Jeremiah made that statement about the new covenant after his admonition to King Jehoiakim and the elite of Jerusalem for their pursuit of wealth, power and status, while ignoring God's commandments and his words of justice for the oppressed. Jeremiah was thus confronted with the failure of human obedience to God. Obedience was tried in

Israel over a long period and did not work. The kings and people rejected the old covenant and walked away from the God who rescued them from Egypt.

But God's pact with his people is not finished. Jeremiah says that there will be a renewal of the Mosaic covenant. (See Exodus 24:3-8; Deuteronomy 6:6, 9:9). According to Jeremiah, there is to be a change in the way the divine will is revealed to human beings. People were deaf and dumb to the preaching of the prophets. There would be no more preaching! People would not have to ask their neighbours what God wants them to do. God is now to *put his will straight into the hearts of the people, Israel*. Then they will only desire what God wills. Jeremiah is speaking of a future new person who is able to obey perfectly because of an extraordinary change in his heart. St. Paul says that the will of God (new covenant) implanted in our hearts consists of the gifts of the Holy Spirit. (See 2 Corinthians 3:6). It was Jesus' forgiveness of sins that released the power of the Holy Spirit into the world. (See John 20:21-23).

The old belief that God had fought for Israel as a warrior - in order to give the people land, temple and kings as the means of their salvation - had given way, in the face of disaster, defeat and exile, to a more difficult, but more mature faith, not in temple and land, but in God himself as saviour. All God asks for is obedience of the heart, irrespective of temple sacrifices, land, kings or political system - God coming to live in peoples' hearts so that they are empowered to remain faithful to him! In writing his covenant in human hearts, God is to bypass speaking and listening (between God and man). However, this presents a problem. Jeremiah is convinced of the incapacity of human beings to turn to God in obedience. Because of his bondage to the self, obedience to God is not in the power of any human being. (Jeremiah 13:23). Israel was not saved by the law (which was ignored), or by temple ritual, which often lacked sincerity. Neither was it saved by horses and chariots, or fortified walls round its cities. Who, or what then, would bring salvation to Israel?

The covenant written in hearts emphasises integrity and obedience of the heart rather than outward show and temple ritual, and was to have its highest expression and fulfilment in Jesus' Sermon on the Mount. 'Happy are those whose greatest desire is to do what God requires; God will satisfy them fully.' (Matthew 5:6). Satisfying them fully means fulfilling their desire for perfect happiness - salvation.

So how will the new covenant work? Where on earth is the person who can achieve this total obedience to God – as was the ideal of the old covenant? Even though the Kings of Israel and Judah had been the Lord's anointed ones - God's representatives on earth, appointed as shepherds of his flock - they failed to obey God and draw their people into obedience to him. So perhaps a new, and more enlightened king might come and succeed where the kings of old failed! Who is this king?

## Jesus, the Righteous King

Jeremiah says that human beings are in bondage to the things that draw them away from God – the destructive desires of the self, and an over reliance on things made by their own hands for salvation, treating such things as the highest treasure. (See Mark 10:22; Matthew 13:44). The bitter experience of life taught Jeremiah that human beings are spiritually powerless. Left to themselves, they are incapable of turning their hearts towards the good, the true and the beautiful. If God is to be gracious to human beings, accepting them into communion with himself, how can human beings approach God without once again coming to grief because of their hearts' opposition to him? Putting it another way, God cannot rescue human beings from self-will and bring them into communion with himself, unless they themselves freely co-operate with him by heartfully doing his will. (See Mark 3:33-35)

The revelation that Jeremiah now received, was that God himself would change the heart of the human being and turn humanity back to God in order to bring about a perfect obedience. But how will God do this? Jeremiah has the answer. "The Lord says, 'The time is coming when I will choose as king, a righteous descendant of David. That king will rule wisely and do what is right and just. When he is king, the people of Judah will be safe, and the people of Israel will live in peace. He will be called 'The Lord Our Salvation.'" (Jeremiah 23:5-6, see 33:17). This king will be the long-promised Messiah.

About this future king, the Lord says, 'I will make him come near to me, that he may walk before me; for otherwise who would risk his life to come near to me.' (Jeremiah 30:21). Coming near to God is risky. It might demand the difficult task of thinking, feeling and doing things God's way. It might involve a call to give up everything one holds most dear - "treasures" that only hold one in bondage (Mark 10:21) - in order to sacrifice one's life in obedience to his will, but in the process, finding true treasure.

This anointed king is to be God's representative on earth. As such, he shares the throne with God and has most personal converse with God. (Psalm 110:1). The anointed one will deal with God in an intimate way. He will know the will of God. Nobody else can have the same intimate communion with God. But as Jeremiah says, it will involve the king risking his own life, like losing his own life so that he can be filled with the will and life of God. Jeremiah may have come to this insight into the nature of God and humanity, through his own walking close to God, thus risking his life, i.e. suffering persecution in the cause of right.

Jeremiah's prophecy was fulfilled in the New Testament. The covenant was renewed by Jesus. (Matthew 26:27-28; Mark 14:23; Luke 22:20). Jesus is the "one who was to come," the descendant of King David. Jesus is the righteous King, the one who fully aligns his will with the will of God – in a perfect obedience. (Mark 14:36). Jesus not only risked his life in order to come near to God. He gave his life. In so doing, and as our representative, he takes us with him (in a corporate sense) and unites our human will with the will of God, bringing us into his own obedience to God. Jesus would become "The Lord our salvation." (Jeremiah 23:6; see 1 Corinthians 12:12-13, 27). In the Garden of Gethsemane on the night before he died, Jesus united his own will with the will of the Father, in a definitive act of obedience to God. "Not my will, but yours be done." (Mark 14:36). Thus, Jesus was able to do what no other human being could do–surrender himself totally to God, so that God's will (law) was written in his heart. In him, God's will is done on earth as it is in heaven.

# The Book of Lamentations

The Book of Lamentations is a collection of poems attributed to Jeremiah after the fall of Jerusalem in 586 BC., and its aftermath of ruin and exile. However, according to modern scholarship, Jeremiah is not the author of Lamentations. The reasons for this are found in the author's regret that hope placed in foreign alliances had come to nothing. (Lamentations 4:17). This would certainly be out of step with Jeremiah's thinking, in his opposition to such alliances as being contrary to the will of God. Furthermore, the practices Jeremiah condemned (Jeremiah 5:7-8; 9:1-5) are not criticised in Lamentations. This book was probably written in Jerusalem by an unknown author shortly after the downfall of the city.

There are five lamentations in the book. The desolation of Jerusalem during the siege is expressed in chapters 1 to 4. Chapter 5 seems to reflect what happened immediately after the fall of the city. The last three verses in Lamentations chapter 5 express the deep emotions felt in exile – the pain of feeling abandoned, forsaken and forgotten for ever - and the desire for restoration. (5:19-21). The people's beloved Jerusalem is like a woman deserted by her lover, God. Her false lovers had betrayed her, and are no more. When the crisis came, they failed her and ran into hiding. These poems range from weeping and mourning to still trusting in the Lord and calling him to remember his abandoned people.

Jerusalem and its temple were levelled to the ground. The world had collapsed. What its people cherished and held dear was taken away from them. In what could they now place their hopes? Perhaps the Lord sent them into a far country so that they might learn the hard lesson of trusting in him rather than in things made with their own hands. Trusting might lead to repentance and the hope of restoration. (See Luke 15:11-32). This was the same lesson which the prodigal son learned in the far country of his exile, when he came to himself and repented. Israel in exile is God's prodigal son whom he still loves. According to Lamentations, the Lord's unfailing love and mercy will continue, despite the people's past sins. (3:22). Deprived of everything they held dear, the Lord is all they now have, whose love for them is steadfast. In their enslaved condition under Gentiles, in him only can they hope.

> How deserted she sits,
> the city once thronged with people!
> Once the greatest of nations,
> she is now like a widow.
> Once the princess of states,
> she is now put to forced labour.
> All night long she is weeping,
> tears running down her cheeks.
> Not one of all her lovers
> remains to comfort her.
> Her friends have all betrayed her
> and become her enemies. (Lamentations 1:1-2, NJB).

My eyes are worn out with weeping,
my inmost being is in ferment,
My heart plummets
at the destruction of my young people,
as the children and babies grow faint
in the streets of the city.
They keep saying to their mothers,
'Where is some food,
as they faint like wounded men
in the streets of the city?
To what can I compare or liken you,
daughter of Jerusalem?
Who can rescue or comfort you,
young daughter of Zion?
For huge as the sea is your ruin;
who can heal you?...
Cry then to the Lord,
rampart of the daughter of Zion;
let your tears flow like a torrent,
day and night;
allow yourself no respite,
give your eyes no rest! (Lamentations 2: 11-13, 18, NJB).

The theological explanation for this calamity is derived from the Deuteronomic tradition of the covenant. Despite the reforms of Josiah, the disaster of the exile represented divine judgement on disobedience. (4:1).

But there was still a trust in God and ultimate hope. Lamentations chapter 3 describes the plight of a single individual abandoned by God, who recognises the justice of his suffering and believes that after repentance, he or she will be helped. In the following lamentation, the author is speaking about God, whom he sees as having led him into darkness. But he begins to realize that the Lord is all he has. He can begin to trust and hope in this God.

This lamentation foreshadows Jesus' abandonment in the far country of this world, because he bore on his shoulders the full effects of human rebellion against God. But Jesus still hopes and trusts in the Lord to deliver him from death.

I am the man familiar with misery
under the rod of his fury.
He has led and guided me
into darkness, not light.
Against none but me, does he turn his hand
again and again, all day.
He has wasted my flesh and skin away,

has broken my bones.
He has besieged me and made hardship
a circlet round my head.
He has forced me to dwell where all is dark,
like those long dead in their everlasting home.
He has walled me in so that I cannot escape;
he has weighed me down with chains;
even when I shout for help
he shuts out my prayer.
He has closed my way with blocks of stone,
he has obstructed my paths.
For me, he is a lurking bear,
a lion in hiding.
Heading me off, he has torn me apart,
leaving me shattered.
He has bent his bow
and used me as a target for his arrows...
Surely the Lord's mercies are not over,
his deeds of faithful love not exhausted;
every morning they are renewed;
great is his faithfulness!
'The Lord is all I have,' I say to myself,
and so I shall put my hope in him.
The Lord is good to those who trust him,
to all who search for him.
(Lamentations 3:1-12; 22-25, NJB).

God refusing to listen (verse 8) echoes Jesus' cry of abandonment on the cross just before he died. (Matthew 27:45). But the individual in the above passage can still say, 'The Lord is all I have, and I put my hope in him.' (3:24). When the storms of life seem to overwhelm us, can we still trust and hope in the Lord? (See Mark 4:35-39).

Finally, in chapter 5, there is a prayer for mercy. Lamentations ends with a plea from sick hearts to be reunited with God – the eternal reality of the universe. (verse 19).

Remember, O Lord, what has happened to us;
consider, and see our degradation.
Our heritage has passed to strangers,
our homes to foreigners.
We are orphans, we are fatherless;
our mothers are like widows...
Our ancestors sinned; they are no more,
and we bear the weight of their guilt...
Joy has vanished from our hearts;
our dancing has turned to mourning...

This is why our hearts are sick;
this is why our eyes are dim:
because Mount Zion is desolate;
jackals roam to and fro on it.
Yet you, Lord, rule from eternity;
your throne endures from age to age.
Why do you never remember us?
Why do you abandon us so long?
Make us come back to you, Lord, and we will come back.
Restore us as we were before!
Unless you have utterly rejected us,
in an anger that knows no limit.
(Lamentations 5:1-3, 7, 15, 17-22, NJB).

## CHAPTER 8

# EXEKIEL AND SECOND ISAIAH

## Finding Meaning and Hope in the Babylonian Exile

The biblical city of Babylon was located on the River Euphrates, some sixty miles south of present-day Bagdad. According to some modern estimates, the exiles in Babylon numbered 20,000 out of a total population of 200,000 in the kingdom of Judah. Another estimate is 80,000, representing 10 or 25 per cent of the population of Judah.[103] Those taken away to Babylon would have been the majority of the leading people of the nation, mainly the educated elite of Jerusalem, but also others from the leading towns of Judah. It is likely that the Babylonians left a sufficient number of people in Judah to produce the olives and grapes for taxation purposes.

Most of the exiles were settled near Nippur, about fifty miles from the city of Babylon, and located between the two great rivers, the Tigris and Euphrates. Some of them may have lived as tenant farmers, others being put to work digging irrigation canals. Because there was always little rainfall in this area, the growth of crops relied on irrigation. The River Chebar flowed through Nippur, and was actually an irrigation canal, near which the next prophet, Ezekiel, had his vision of God and his call to be a prophet.

As advised by Jeremiah, the exiles seemed to have settled down and made homes for themselves in Babylon. (Jeremiah 27:5-7). The length of the total exile was about sixty years for the first deportees of 593 BC, and forty-seven for those taken away in 586 BC. This means that all but a few died in Babylon. Most of their children never knew any home other than that of their exile.

The reality of settling down and having families, knowing they would die in exile, must have been the cause of great pain and unhappiness. There are a number of psalms of lament, giving expression to homesickness and dated from the time of the exile. (See Psalms 80, 85, 126, 137). "Turn to us, Almighty God! Look down from heaven at us; come and save your people! Come and save this grapevine that you planted, this young vine you made grow so strong!" (Psalm 80:14-15). "By the rivers of Babylon we sat down; there we wept when we remembered Zion. On the willows nearby we hung our harps. Those who captured us told us to sing; they told us to entertain them; 'Sing a song about Zion.' How

---

[103] Lawrence Boadt, *Reading the Old Testament*, p. 335.

can we sing a song to the Lord in a foreign land?" (Psalm 137:1-2, 3a; see Psalm 42:6-11). "A foreign land!" The "land" of Israel had a deep significance for its people. The land was regarded as sacred. This was the land promised to them by God, as their destiny. In now taking them away to Babylon, was God revoking his promise to them of a land "flowing with milk and honey," symbolic of the fruitfulness of this land? (Exodus 3:17, NJB). Did God break his promises – those made to David, for example? "I will make your kingdom last for ever. Your dynasty will never end." (2 Samuel 7:16). Reflecting on these issues may have led to a crisis of faith for the exiles.

From the exiles' standpoint, the Babylonian captivity was a humiliation. Hope could have died in Babylon. How could the people find life meaningful in the midst of slavery, loss and grief? Had they not been given a destiny – only now to be taken from them? Where was God? Had he abandoned them? Was he powerless to do anything about the evil that weighed down on them? Perhaps the Babylonian gods were more powerful than the God of Israel!

However, they had only themselves to blame for the loss of the land. The chosen people first found God in the wilderness under the summit of Mount Sinai as they journeyed from the slavery of Egypt. Soon after they entered the promised land, they lost him again by plucking the forbidden fruit of power politics, temple, city and the fruits of the land. In giving their allegiance to these things, they were rejecting the God who rescued them from Egypt. God had not abandoned them. It was they who walked away from God, for the false gods who could never save them. (Genesis 3:6, 8). In order for God to get them to turn back to himself again and obey his covenant - like a parent exercising tough love - he would have to deprive his children of the things which were only leading them astray. Their wilderness experience in Babylon would be painful. Their testing "in the fire of suffering" would be severe. (Isaiah 48:10; Zechariah 13:9; Job 23:10; Jeremiah 9:7; Psalm 66:10; 1 Peter 5:10).

From God's standpoint, the exile was providential. The Creator God allowed it to happen for a purpose. It was part of his plan for the renewal of a people who had lost their way, stumbling in the very darkness which they themselves had created. (Jeremiah 13:16). The exile was time out for reflection, a kind of Sabbath rest. It might lead to a greater understanding of the designs of the God who still loved his people and was ever ready to forgive them. (Hosea 11:8-9). In their darkness, they would struggle with God. Who really is God? Can we ever know his designs? (See Genesis 32:22-31). Although deprived of everything through which they had sought salvation - and like the prodigal son, who ended up slaving for a pig farmer in the far country (Luke 15:14-15) - they would find God anew, unexpectedly speaking to them in the wilderness of exile, just as he had spoken to their ancestors in the wilderness of Sinai. Once again, they would hear him calling them to repent of their sins and to do his will on earth (renew the covenant). And just as he responded to the plight of their ancestors in Egypt, he would again listen to their cries for liberation.

There were some compensations for this particular group of exiles. The people who were exiled from the northern kingdom of Israel in 721 BC were scattered throughout the Assyrian Empire, and thus, couldn't maintain a common purpose. They became the lost tribes of Israel. The Babylonian exiles, on the other hand, had the advantage of being assembled in one place, which meant that their identity could be secured. They struggled with their faith, supported one another in their trials, and had a prophet living among them to instruct and encourage them.

There were temptations – forbidden fruit, "beautiful" before their eyes (Genesis 3:6), which might have drawn them away from their God. Having settled just south of the city of Babylon, they lived under the spell of a magnificent city, which had been massively enlarged and beautified by its greatest king, Nebuchadnezzar (605-562 BC). For two centuries, Babylon remained the world's largest city. It had a population up to 200,000 and covered an area of about 900 hectares (2,200 acres). By way of contrast, the population of Jerusalem before the exile was only about 12,000.

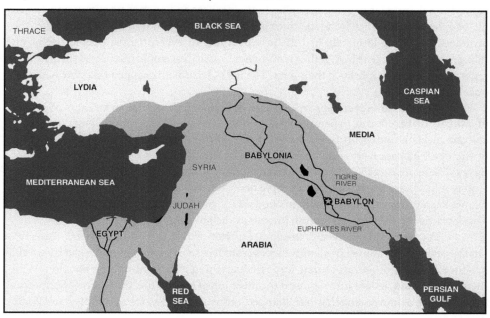

*The Babylonian Empire under King Nebuchadnezzr II (604 – 562 BC)*

Slavery existed in Babylon but the common people enjoyed basic rights, including ownership of property. Babylon's importance began in the 19th century BC under the rule of King Hammurabi who codified law and developed the city into an important administrative and economic centre. For two millennia the city was the centre of Mesopotamian culture and civilization, giving this whole area a reputation as the cradle of civilization. Babylon was responsible for developments in the arts, architecture, law and social life. It made important discoveries in mathematics, physics and astronomy. A large body of literature grew up in the Babylonian language, including a variety of wisdom writings, and the famous Epic, the *Enuma Elish*, an account of the creation of the world. In the centre of the city, and towering above every other building, was the temple in honour of the national god, Marduk, whom the Babylonians believed created and ruled heaven and earth. There were fifty other temples in the city. This was the city of the "hanging gardens" which were regarded as one of the wonders of the ancient world. The city of Babylon must have led the exiles to gaze in awe at its power and magnificence. The Israelite refugees would recall how armies of this glorious empire had destroyed Jerusalem and its temple. As a tiny minority, there was the danger of the exiles becoming absorbed into the pagan environment that surrounded them. In a sense, the Babylonians were the new Canaanites from which they must remain apart – as in the time of Joshua.

The crisis of the exile was given a religious interpretation by the prophets. In the midst of the splendour of Babylon, how could the Israelite exiles escape the temptation that the Babylonian god Marduk was the really powerful god, having recently defeated and humiliated the God of Israel? It was not that Marduk was more powerful than the God of Israel. In order to bring the exiles to their senses and open their eyes, God allowed his people to experience bondage once again, as in Egypt of old. Before the exile, the prophets (including Jeremiah) had the task of trying to overcome the people's delusion that prosperity for the few, together with temple sacrifices, would guarantee their future, regardless of how people lived their lives. The fall of Jerusalem changed this state of denial once and for all.

In order to prevent absorption into Babylonian culture, new markers of Jewish identity were introduced, as being very important for a small community living in a pagan culture: male circumcision, Sabbath observance, dietary laws and the proper celebration of the Feast of Passover, which commemorated the liberation of their ancestors from Egypt. These practices would give them an identity, and encourage them in the hope that God would again liberate them as a people dedicated to him alone. While in Babylon, the people began to meet in one another's houses for prayers and instruction in their faith. This gave rise to the later institution known as the Jewish synagogue.

For all its splendour and wisdom, Babylon would not endure. (Isaiah 21:8-10). On the other hand, a small band of refugees from Jerusalem, living lives of slavery, would produce a corpus of literature that surpassed anything ever produced by Babylon. With their wisdom and insight into God and the meaning of human life, the Hebrew Scriptures are a literary achievement that has changed the world for ever and endured for 2,500 years.

Thus, the really significant development during the exile was the creation of Israel's Scriptures as one single book, a work largely carried out by former priests of the Jerusalem temple. The prophet Ezekiel, who was a priest, was with the people in their exile. "Ezekiel's programme had an important effect on this final editing of the Pentateuch (first five books of the Bible), which placed the law of Mount Sinai at its centre point."[104] It is likely that priests and scribes brought with them to Babylon all the scrolls containing written accounts of their history and traditions. The collecting and editing of all of these would act as a further marker of the people's identity, now that they had lost the land, city and temple. In addition to the accounts of their past history, as already recorded in Joshua, Judges, Samuel and Kings, they added much new material. They composed new stories about Abraham: his call to journey towards the promised land (Genesis 12), the covenant made with Abraham (Genesis 15) and circumcision as a sign of the covenant (Genesis 17).

---

[104] Lawrence Boadt, *Reading the Old Testament*, p. 348.

The authors placed Abraham's origins in the city of Ur, just down-river from the city of Babylon. The exiles in Babylon would take comfort from their father Abraham's long journey to the promised land, a journey the prophets would encourage the exiles to undertake once the time was right. Perhaps with the same faith as their father Abraham, the exiles too would be encouraged to return to the promised land. Abraham also goes into exile in Egypt and gets back again to the promised land. (Genesis 12:10.20 - 13:1).

The above accounts helped to explain their origins as a people, how they came to be in the promised land, and the events leading up to the Babylonian exile. The exile happened because of the infidelity of the people to their God. The people had fallen into pagan practices which led them far from the ethical ideals of the Sinai covenant. Even their temple rituals were divorced from ethical demands. God did not abandon his people; it was they who walked away from him and into hiding in the far country. (Genesis 3:8). The exile was a disaster, a kind of death. God allowed it to happen, but in the most unimaginable ways, God would bring good out of this evil.

In order to lay stress on the ordered world created by God, the priests and scribes of the former temple composed a new creation story (the seven-day account in Genesis 1), which they attached to the Garden of Eden story - the older version of creation. (Genesis 2-3). The seven-day creation account would strengthen them in the belief that a God who created the universe would have the power to recreate them again as a people. This creation account ends with a Sabbath rest on the seventh day, stressing the importance of Sabbath worship in order to ensure divine protection into the future. The account is composed as a hymn of praise to God for his creation of order out of chaos, and with a promise that God will continue bringing order out of the turmoil that befalls Israel again and again. So even far away from their homeland, the people could be loyal to God and follow his commandments (covenant). Israel is called not to give up on God. From God's standpoint, the covenant endures forever.

Apart from the writings of the major prophets, which were still undergoing final editing, most of the Hebrew Bible, as we have it today, was compiled as one single book, and named the "Scriptures." In reading these writings, the people would be continually reminded of God's faithfulness. And once again, they themselves would be called to a faithfulness, which would no longer require such supports as a temple, the land of Israel and the dynasty of King David. Thus, from formerly being a religion of the shrine (temple ritual), Judaism developed into a religion of the Book. For the first time, the new Scriptures would be acknowledged as the word of God, guiding and inspiring the people into the future, their former kings having failed them as guides and shepherds. (Ezekiel 34:1-6). Their newly appointed scribes would be tasked with making copies of the Scriptures available for use in the synagogues which would spring up throughout their homeland following their return from exile.

Thus, the priestly authors emphasise history as a series of ages that had been blessed by God, stretching from the creation of the world to Mount Sinai, and from that to the period of the kings of Israel. Despite failure in each period, God promises to begin all over again calling his children to faithfulness. (Genesis 3:9). One of the greatest lessons they would learn is that God is the prime mover of history, not the people themselves, nor their former kings.

Prophecy came to an end soon after the return of the exiles from Babylon in 537 BC. The Persian empire provided a period of stability and religious freedom for the Jewish people following the exiles' return to Jerusalem. There was no need for any further prophecy. Under divine inspiration, the prophets had revealed as much about God as was possible until the coming of Jesus. The writings of Isaiah, Jeremiah, Ezekiel and those of the minor prophets were now available in the new Scriptures as God's word to guide and inspire his people.

The new reality was that Israel must become primarily a *religious* community and not a political power. The people's involvement with power politics in the promised land had proved to be a disaster. Now that the age of kings was over, God would still be with the people wherever they were. They only had to open the pages of their Scriptures to hear him speaking to them and calling them to responsible living. And because they would not be dependent on the crutches (God substitutes, temple, silver and gold) on which they had formerly relied, they would learn a new trust in God as the only one who could give them a meaningful life. (Genesis 1:27-28; Psalm 8:3-6; Isaiah 40:31; 58:10-11).

There is a message here for all of us. God is sovereign over history. God governs the rise and fall of empires and nations. God can create light out of darkness, joy out of sorrow, good out of evil. God can work his way through the chaos and calamities which he permits, though they are not of his will. (Genesis 1:3). Like the Jewish people in exile, there are times in our own lives when we become discouraged, leaving us on the verge of despair – whether because of accident, deprivation, loss, infirmity or bereavement. At such times of darkness, we might think that our world has collapsed, leaving us without hope or light. Our faith is then sorely tested. But these may be the very times when God is allowing periods of darkness in our lives, because he has something greater in store for us – a new faith journey, leading us to greater maturity, wisdom and enlightenment. Surrendering to God in times of darkness is the highest form of faith – very difficult. It is about asking God to deal with situations over which we ourselves have no control. "From the depths I call to you God: Lord, hear my cry... More than watchmen for daybreak, let Israel hope in God." (Psalm 130:1, 7, NJB). For "Israel" read family, friends, the wider community. "Even were I to walk in a ravine as dark as death, I should fear no danger, for you are at my side, your staff and your crook are there to soothe me." (Psalm 23:4, NJB).

## Ezekiel: a Message of Judgement and Promise

Ezekiel is the prophet of the early part of the Babylonian exile. He went into exile with the first deportation from Jerusalem. It is thought that the whole of the book was authored by himself. The first part of his prophecy took place between the first deportation to Babylon in 598/7 BC and the second one in 586 BC. Like the prophets before him, Ezekiel was critical of the people of Jerusalem for what he saw as their blindness to their sins, their deafness to the teaching of the prophets and their rebellion against God. (See Ezekiel 2:3-5; 13:1-2). They were blind to the reasons why God allowed them to be taken into exile, blaming God rather than themselves for the disaster that had befallen them. This means that they refused to take individual responsibility for their own sins of rebellion against God. (Ezekiel 9:9). Ezekiel must have been the first prophet to teach that personal sins, for which the individual is responsible, have consequences in death. (See Ezekiel 18:14-17, 19-20; see 33:14-16).

For Ezekiel's call to be a prophet, see chaps. 2-3. His mission was to warn the king and people, who remained in control in Jerusalem after the first deportation, against further rebellion against their Babylonian overlords, because he said that this would result in their utter destruction. (See Ezekiel 6:11-14). Because Ezekiel could see where the people back in Jerusalem were heading, the early part of his prophecy is full of doom and looming disaster. (See Ezekiel 7:5-8). God's judgement would fall on the people because of their sins, for which they showed no sign of repenting. God told Ezekiel that, despite his warnings, they would not listen to him. They would defy him, but they would at least know that a prophet was living among them. (2:5). The Lord said to Ezekiel, "You, mortal man must not be afraid of them, or of anything they say. They will defy and despise you; it will be like living among scorpions." (Ezekiel 2:6). God said to the prophet: 'I will make you as firm as a rock, as hard as a diamond. Don't be afraid of those rebels.' (See 3:7-9). These words recall those spoken to Jeremiah at his call to be a prophet. (Jeremiah 1:18-19).

The people of Jerusalem did not listen to Ezekiel. Their defiance resulted in the second siege of Jerusalem, the destruction of the city and the second deportation of more of its citizens to Babylon in 586 BC. Ezekiel then compared Jerusalem to the dead wood of the vine – doomed for the fire. (See Ezekiel 15). Because of the people's unfaithfulness, the Lord would "make the country a wilderness." (15:8). Ezekiel then prophesises against Israel's neighbours, some of whom helped the Babylonians during the siege of Jerusalem. (See chaps. 25-32).

But despite the unfaithfulness of the people, God told Ezekiel that he would still be with them in exile. (Ezekiel 11:16). Following judgement, God wants to bring his people back to obedience, in order to re-establish his relationship with them. God will "gather them from the countries where he scattered them and give the land of Israel back to them. When they return, they are to get rid of all their filthy disgusting idols." (Ezekiel 11:17-18). "The Lord says, 'I will give them a new heart and a new mind. I will take away their stubborn heart of stone and will give them an obedient heart.'" (11:19). God's covenant with Israel will then be renewed. (11:20).

## Restoration and Return

In the later part of his mission (chaps. 33-48), Ezekiel's aim is to encourage the exiles and prepare them for the return to their homeland. The promises of salvation in Ezekiel are centred around four images: (a) the shepherd and the sheep (34:1-31); (b) the new heart and mind (11:17-20; 36:23-38); (c) the raising of the dead to life (37:1-28); and the new temple and the new land (40:1–48:35).

During the exile, when the people of Judah have no king, the Lord draws nearer to them than any king ever did. Ezekiel says that the Lord will be as close to them as a shepherd to his flock. He will be their shepherd, guiding them, and once again, leading them to green pastures on the mountains of Israel. The shepherd God will restore them to their own land, feed them and heal their wounds. (See Ezekiel 34:11-15, see 24; Luke 10:33-34). The bad shepherds before the exile had been feeding themselves rather than their flock. (Jeremiah 22:13-14). "The Lord spoke to me. 'Mortal man,' he said, 'denounce the rulers of Israel. You are doomed, you shepherds of Israel! You take care of yourselves but never tend the sheep. You drink the milk, wear clothes made from the wool and kill and eat them.'" (Ezekiel 34:1-3). The rulers took no care of the weak ones, nor healed those who were sick, nor looked for those who were lost. (Ezekiel 34:1-2, 5, 10).

The kings of Israel failed in their role as shepherds. The leaders of the people will be removed from power. The monarchy will not be restored. (Ezekiel 34:1-2). The Lord himself will take charge of his flock. He himself will assume the role of shepherd. God himself will now have to take things in hand and rescue and feed his people. (Psalm 95:6-7). These images of Ezekiel will inspire Second Isaiah's vision of God restoring the exiles to their own land. (Isaiah 40:10-11).

The future Messiah will not be a militant king (like the former Israelite kings), but a Shepherd leading his flock, taking them home from exile and feeding them with new, redeemed life, as their destiny.

Down to the time of Jesus, Israel's shepherds were still failing the people. Ezekiel's Shepherd prefigures Jesus, the Good Shepherd, who loves his sheep to the extent that he is prepared to lay down his life in order to save them from the wild marauders of the wilderness. Jesus has the same intimacy with his flock as he has with God, his Father. Because he "knows" the Father he is then really the one who can rescue his flock from exile, look after them, and feed them with the food that will give them eternal life. (See John 10:7-11, 17-18). Ezekiel's parable of the shepherd is fulfilled in Jesus, who takes all of us exiles definitively home.

In Ezekiel 36, God promises new life for Israel. The exiled people will soon be coming home (36:8), their hunger for salvation will be satisfied. The temple would have an importance only when the people acknowledged that "the Lord is God," and not silver and gold, political power, or strong fortifications. (See Psalm 62:1-2, 5-7, 10; 59:16-17; 91:1-2).

Like Jeremiah, Ezekiel emphasises the necessity for the renewal of hearts and minds. Once the people return home from Babylon, the covenant with God will be written in their hearts! "The Lord says to Israel. 'I will give you a new heart and a new mind. I will take away your stubborn heart of stone and give you an obedient heart.'" (Ezekiel 36:26).

This new covenant will be fulfilled in Jesus, who represents the new Israel, and whose compassionate and obedient heart will rescue his flock from evil and restore them to obedience to God. On behalf of humanity, Jesus offers a perfect obedience to God. (See Mark 14:36). Through his obedience to the Father, and thus his willingness to die for his flock, Jesus renews the love covenant between God and humanity. (Mark 14:23-24).

The promise of God becoming the shepherd of Israel, together with his promise of new obedient hearts, would be received as encouraging words for the exiles.

## The Hope of Resurrection

Ezekiel tried to instil a sense of hope in a people who sat weeping by the rivers of Babylon, their harps hanging on the trees, their songs about their lost Jerusalem unsung. Because of their sins of disobedience in plucking all of that forbidden fruit in their homeland, they were experiencing a kind of death. (Genesis 2:17; 3:6). Could they be brought to life again and led home to their own land? For years, Ezekiel prophesied to blind and deaf Israelites; now he must do so to lifeless bones. The living people were unable to respond to him. It's as if they were dead and had shrivelled into dry bones. Can he see them returning to life as if in a resurrection?

Ezekiel experiences the hand of God and is transported in a vision to a valley filled with lifeless bones. Israel was dead – deaf and blind to the truly real, knowing nothing, only that a prophet was living among them. (Ezekiel 2:3-5). Could God open their graves and breathe new life (wisdom and understanding of the ways of God) into their lifeless bones?

> I felt the powerful presence of the Lord, and his spirit carried me away and set me down in the middle of a valley, a valley full of bones. There were vast quantities of these bones on the ground the whole length of the valley; and they were quite dried up. He said to me, 'Son of man, can these bones live?' I said, 'You know Lord God.' He said, 'Prophesy over these bones.' Say, 'Dry bones, hear the word of God.' The Lord God says this to these bones: 'I am now going to make breath enter into you, and you will live. I shall put sinews and flesh on you. I shall cover you with skin and give you breath and you will live; and you will learn that I am the Lord your God.' I prophesised as I had been ordered. Then there was a noise, a sound of clattering; and the bones joined together. I looked and saw that they were covered with sinews; flesh was growing on them and skin was covering them, but there was no breath in them. The Lord God says this: 'Come from the four winds, breath; breathe on these dead; let them live.' I prophesised as the Lord ordered me, and the breath entered them; they came to life again and stood up on their feet, a great, an immense army. (Ezekiel 37:1-10, JB).

That passage is followed with a saying by God that the bones represent the people of Israel, their hope gone, as if they were dead. "The Lord God says this: I am going to open your graves; I mean to raise you from your graves, my people, and lead you back to the soil of Israel. And then you will know that I am The Lord God." (Ezekiel 37:11-14, JB). This means that they will experience the power and love of God, and for the first time, "know" him as their saviour and redeemer. This is something that the Babylonian god Marduk could never do for them.

The image of human bodies coming to life by the breath of God (Ezekiel 37:8) recalls the second creation story in Genesis 2:7. God's restoration of Judah will thus be a new creation - something on the same scale as the original creation of human beings. God promises to bring the people from the grave of exile to new life, thus restoring them to their destiny in the promised land.

The hope for resurrection of all the dead to new life with God became more central in later Judaism. The author of the later Book of Daniel sees in Ezekiel's image, God's revelation of risen life beyond death (resurrection) for the faithful – as the true destiny of human beings. "Of those who are sleeping in the Land of Dust, many will awaken, some to everlasting life, some to shame and everlasting disgrace. Those who are wise will shine as brightly as the expanse of the heavens, and those who have instructed many in uprightness, as bright as stars for all eternity." (Daniel 12:2-3, NJB; see 2 Maccabees 7:9; Wisdom 3; Psalms 16, 10; 49:9; 73:26; Isaiah 26:19).

Jesus' disciples were dejected and without hope after his death on the cross. They were like the Jews in exile in Babylon. They were like dead things. The Gospel of John recounts Jesus, the risen Lord, "breathing" on them in order to bring them to new life in the Spirit after his resurrection. (See John 20:22-23). Compare Ezekiel 37:3-10 with 1 Corinthians 15:20-58. Those who have received the Spirit of Jesus rejoice in their hope for the destiny of eternal life. (Romans 8:11).

In his vision of the valley of dry bones, Ezekiel may have nothing more in mind than the Babylonian exile coming to an end and Israel being restored to a new liberated life. However, as Christians, we can see a deeper meaning here than perhaps Ezekiel intended. We can interpret the prophet's vision in terms of the achievement of Jesus, whom God raised from death in triumph over all the powers who exiled him from this world. Jesus not only had a vision of such a glorious future but actually realized it in his own person – a future he wants to share with all of us. (See Mark 10:33-34).

## Second Isaiah (chaps. 40-55)

Ezekiel's prophecy ended in 571 BC. Then the anonymous prophet known as Second Isaiah (very likely a disciple of First Isaiah) appears in the middle of the sixth century (about 550 BC). Speaking to the exiles in Babylon, Second Isaiah had to contend with a people who remained deaf and blind to the word of God, spoken by their previous prophet, Ezekiel. Would the people be any more disposed to listen to the word of a new prophet?

Appearing towards the end of the exile, Second Isaiah proclaimed that God would set the people free and take them home to Jerusalem in order to begin a new life. Isaiah of Jerusalem (First Isaiah) believed that the fall of the city (587 BC) was the result of divine judgement on an unfaithful people, but like Ezekiel, Second Isaiah looked forward in hope to a restoration.

Written as poetry, the words of Second Isaiah were intended to inspire his audience in Babylon, (and indeed ourselves today), to trust in the Lord for their salvation, and not in the material things on which people often place their hopes. Second Isaiah proclaimed that the magnificence of Babylon would wither away like desert grass and be no more. (Isaiah 40:8). While the oracles of First Isaiah were threatening and full of doom over the disaster facing the nation, those of Second Isaiah are inspiring and consoling. Biblical scholars are fulsome in their tributes to Second Isaiah. "The message of Second Isaiah is of no age. It is prophecy tempered with human tears, mixed with a joy that heals all scars, clearing a way for understanding the future in spite of the present. No words have ever gone further in offering comfort when the sick world cries."[105] The contemporary biblical scholar, Tom Wright considers Isaiah chaps. 40-66 to be one of the

---

[105] Abraham J. Heschel, *The Prophets*, p.185.

greatest pieces of poetic writing in all of history.[106] The language soars on long passages of metaphors for God. It is filled with descriptions of rebuilding, restoring and creating, much of it resembling the psalms of praise.

In Isaiah 40-55 there is a clash of two kingdoms (recalling the liberation from Egypt) – the Kingdom of God (liberation) and that of Babylon (domination). Israel's God once again confronts the Pharaoh of Babylon and its national gods that symbolize arrogant power. The prophet is at pains to show that the Babylonian god Marduk is powerless against the God who created the heavens and the earth and "calls the stars by name." (Isaiah 44:9; 41:26). This God has the power to do a new thing for Israel. (44:22). The humble one will be exalted and the arrogant and powerful Babylon brought down from its high throne, to "sit on the dust of the earth." (Isaiah 47:1, see 2-15).

There are two main divisions in this part of the Book of Isaiah. In chapters 40 – 48, there is an emphasis on the nation of Israel and its role under God. In chapters 49 - 55, the emphasis is on the restored Jerusalem and the glory of Zion.

## Themes of Second Isaiah

There are a number of distinct themes in Second Isaiah. (1) This is the first prophet who had a vision of God's plan of salvation extending to all the nations of the earth, because he created the whole universe. (2) The prophet visualizes God sharing his sovereignty with certain people (servants) whom he calls to act as liberators of his people. Just as Moses was called by God to liberate the exiled slaves from Egypt, Second Isaiah praises King Cyrus of Persia as the liberator of the Babylonian exiles. (44:28; 45:1-7). (3) Second Isaiah goes further than Ezekiel, with his theme of the renewed Israel being given a role in a mission to the nations. By living the kind of life God wants his people to live, the nations will be drawn to Jerusalem to worship the God of Israel. (Isaiah 49:6; 60:13). (4) The prophet introduces the theme of the Servant of God. The Suffering Servant passages in Second Isaiah mean that Israel's new missionary role will be costly; it will involve suffering service. Like First Isaiah, this prophet sees the shepherding role of the Davidic king being transferred to the nation as a whole. (See chaps. 6-9, 36-39; 55:3).

An important theme in this part of the Book of Isaiah is the sovereignty of God over history, a theme Second Isaiah shares with Jeremiah and Ezekiel, but which he himself develops more fully. Because God created the universe, he is the one in charge of the world. He is sovereign over the nations and wants to share his blessing with all of them, no less than with Israel. (Isaiah 49:6). There is a clear message for the exiles: the Creator God is superior, existing above and beyond the world, reducing national gods like Marduk to insignificance. If this God created the world, he alone is the powerful one. Moreover, he then has the power to liberate the exiles and take them home, in a new creation.

## The Good News of Liberation

Towards the end of the Babylonian exile, the task of Second Isaiah was to use every means

---

[106] Tom Wright, *Simply Jesus,* (SPCK), 36 Causton Street, London, 2011, p. 150.

– tender invitation, persuasion, theological argument and comforting words – to overcome the scepticism and lack of faith of the people. At this stage in Babylon, many of the exiles had put down roots and raised families. Apart from what they heard from their parents, most of the people of this prophet's audience would have known nothing about Jerusalem. Second Isaiah then took up where Ezekiel left off. His mission was to prepare the exiles for their return home to Jerusalem. The people may have seen their exile as a "ravine dark as death" (Psalm 23). But the prophet would encourage them in the belief that God was preparing a banquet for them under the eyes of their enemies. (Psalm 23:5). The dark ravine of exile was not the final word from God. The Creator God would welcome his dead prodigal son home as an honoured guest, and prepare a celebratory banquet for him. (Luke 15:22-23).

The prophecy authored by Second Isaiah has been called "The Book of the Consolation of Israel," because of its hopeful and comforting message to the exiles, reminding them that the day of their liberation is near. (40:1-2; see 49:13; 51:1252:7-12). Second Isaiah says that what Israel endured was more than chastisement for its sins. Its agony exceeded its guilt. (Isaiah 40:2). God's message remains the same as always. God will act for his people as he has promised, and as he has done in the past. Once they become humble enough to acknowledge their dependence on him, as the only one who can listen to their cries and save them, they are then ready for rescue. The humble ones are about to be exalted, lifted up "on wings like eagles" and carried home. (Isaiah 40:31). An important message for the exiles is that God has not abandoned his people and ignored their plight, which was what they believed. (49:14; 40:27). God's love for his human creatures does not die. Once they begin thirsting for salvation, he will respond to their cries and yearnings. "When my people in their need look for water, when their throats are dry with thirst, then I, the Lord will answer their prayer; I, The God of Israel, will never abandon them." (Isaiah 41:17).

In the opening of chapter 40, Second Isaiah receives his call to proclaim the word of the Lord to his people. (See Isaiah 6; Jeremiah 1; Ezekiel 2-3). God calls him to be the comforter of his people, to tell them that they have suffered long enough. Their sins are forgiven. (40:1).

The first verse of the following poem was set to glorious music by the German composer, George Frideric Handel, at the beginning of his oratorio, "Messiah."

> 'Comfort my people,' says our God.
> 'Comfort them!
> Encourage the people of Jerusalem.
> Tell them they have suffered long enough
> and their sins are now forgiven.'
> A voice cries out,
> 'Prepare in the wilderness a road for our God!
> Clear the way in the desert for the Lord.
> Fill every valley, level every mountain.
> The hills will become a plain,
> and the rough places made smooth.'

> Then the glory of the Lord will be revealed,
> and the whole human race will see it.
> A voice cries out,
> 'Proclaim a message that all human beings are like grass;
> they last no longer than wild flowers.
> Yes, grass withers and flowers fade,
> but the word of our God endures forever...
> The Sovereign Lord is coming to rule with power,
> bringing with him the people he has rescued.
> He will take care of his flock like a shepherd;
> he will gather the lambs together
> and carry them in his arms;
> he will gently lead their mothers.' (Isaiah 40:1-8, 19-11).

In verses 9-10 of the above poem, Jerusalem is to become a herald-prophet proclaiming the good news of God, like a victorious general, who is returning home with the exiles, the Babylonians having been defeated. God is about to prepare a road through the wilderness to make a safe passage home for his people. God is also a shepherd, gathering his flock and taking care of them. (Verse 11). This recalls Ezekiel's final gathering of the Lord's flock from the nations and bringing them home. (Ezekiel 34:11-12. The exodus from Egypt was a flight. This exodus will be a triumphal procession. Chapters 40-55 are but an elaboration of 40:1-11.

In order to encourage and empower the people, as in the above passage, Second Isaiah uses the highly charged language of creation, and as a metaphor for new creation. The valleys are to be raised up, symbolizing the exaltation of the lowly people who had endured the humiliation of exile. Here, we have a familiar theme of Isaiah: exaltation and humiliation. The mountains, symbolic of the self-exaltation of Babylon, are to be levelled, smoothing the way for the exiles. Second Isaiah wants the people to consider their plight in the broader scheme of things. Empires like Babylon will wither away like desert grass. (40:8a). The fall of Jerusalem took place because of self-exaltation. Its people were giving all the glory to themselves, through what they themselves had made with their hands. (See Jeremiah 13:16, NJB). In exile in Babylon, they were humbled, their illusions of grandeur and self- glorification shattered. The task of Second Isaiah is to give them a new vision of the Glory of God. They have to learn to place their trust in God to save them, and not in their former schemes, which only led them through a valley of death and into disaster. The prophet will struggle to get his message of salvation across to them. They simply don't believe in his words of hope. But God will rescue them anyhow and raise them up from the death of exile. This event, in itself, will be a revelation of the glory of God. The glory of Babylon will be no more. Its splendour will fade away. But the word of God which speaks of hope and salvation, will endure forever. (Isaiah 40:8).

In the New Testament, John the Baptist becomes God's new herald, crying in the wilderness, clearing a pathway, preparing the way for Jesus who is coming to bring everyone definitively home from exile in this world. (Matthew 3:3, Mark 1:2, Luke 3:4-6, John 1:23).

This same word of the Lord is spoken to us on our journey today, as God continues to bring us home to our destiny, encouraging and empowering us through his word in Scripture and the sacraments of the Church, as we do our Christian journey. "Do not be afraid, I am with you," are recurring words throughout the Bible. The Lord said to Moses, 'Yes, your journey will be difficult, impossible to do on your own, but do not be afraid, I will be with you, showing you the way and empowering you.' (Exodus 2:12; see Matthew 28:19-20, JB).

## New Revelations of God: Creator of the Universe

Who has measured the water of the sea in the hollow of his hand
and calculated the dimensions of the heavens,
gauged the whole earth to the bushel,
weighed the mountains in scales, the hills in a balance?'...
See, the nations are like a drop on the pail's rim,
they count as a grain of dust on the scales...
To whom could you liken God?
What image can you contrive of him?...
A craftsman casts the figure,
a goldsmith plates it with gold
and casts silver chains for it.
Did you not know, had you not heard?
Was it not told to you from the beginning?
Have you not understood how the earth was founded?
He lies above the circle of the earth,
its inhabitants look like grasshoppers.
He has stretched out the heavens like a cloth,
spread them like a tent for human beings to live in.
He reduces princes to nothing,
he annihilates the rulers of the world.
Scarcely has their stem taken root in the earth,
than he blows on them. Then they wither
and the storm carries them away like straw.
'To whom can you liken me,
and who could be my equal?' Says the Holy One.
'Lift up your eyes and look.
Who made these stars
if not he who drills them like an army,
calling each one by name.
So mighty is his power, so great his strength,
that not one fails to answer.
How can you insist, how can you say, Israel,
'My destiny is hidden from the Lord?'

Did you not know, have you not heard?
The Lord is the everlasting God,
he created the boundaries of the earth.
He does not grow tired or weary,
his understanding is beyond fathoming.
He gives strength to the wearied,
he strengthens the powerless.
Young men may grow tired and weary,
youths may stumble and fall,
but those who hope in the Lord
renew their strength.
They will put out wings like eagles.
They run and do not grow weary,
they walk and never tire. (Isaiah 40:12, 15, 18-19, 21-31, JB).

In the above passage, the prophet corrects and expands the idea of God, as the Creator of the universe. The Lord is not simply a tribal God who created a nation out of a band of Hebrew slaves. Neither is he simply the patron of the two former Israelite kingdoms. By a series of rhetorical questions (verses 12-14), the prophet leads the exiles to the conclusion that the Lord is the Creator of the universe. The exiles may have been tempted to give their allegiance to Marduk, the god of Babylon. The prophet tells the exiles that Marduk, cannot be compared with the Creator of the stars. (40:18). The notion of the tribal, or national God, may have persisted in Israel up the time of the Babylonian exile. In the ancient world, there was a belief that if a foreign country destroyed your country, it meant that its god was more powerful than your god. Could your god not defend his people? Then the natural thing to do was to worship the most powerful god. Away in Babylon, the exiles may thus have experienced God as absent. This may have led them to question the power of the Lord and the relevance of their faith. So why did the Babylonian exiles not turn to Marduk? It was because Isaiah gave them a totally new vision of God, as the one and the only power in the universe who can rescue them from the clutches of the Babylonians and give them a new destiny. Because this God is the creator of the whole world, he rules over Babylon and all the nations. The message of the prophet is that the exiles will not disappear into the pages of history and be forgotten for ever.

The problem with the tribal God, is that other tribes or nations can be treated as enemies to be defeated. The mistaken belief that each nation had its own gods meant that the power of any one of them was limited. War was actually a contest to see which god was the more powerful! The tribal god presides over enmity and strife, resulting in the creation of victims. This was a very limiting vision. If, as Isaiah taught, God is the One and only God, then there can be no tribal or national gods – no rivals. God is above all rivalry, enmity and strife. This was a comforting message for the exiles, because it encouraged them in the belief that the Creator God had the power to act in unimaginable ways. He rules over every land and people; he is sovereign over all creation, sovereign over Babylon. Faithfulness to him was the only hope that injustice, suffering and oppression would someday be overcome everywhere in a definitive act of liberation from all of these evils.

Second Isaiah says that the polytheistic gods are powerless to affect human affairs, to establish justice and peace. (41:21-24). Only the One who can "measure the water of the sea in the hollow of his hand" has power over the whole universe. (40:12). The prophet undercuts the belief in astral deities (the stars as gods) by his proclamation that Israel's God created the stars. (40:26). The Creator God is the One and only God, who exists above and beyond creation, and is therefore unaffected by its limitations. The prophet's purpose is to encourage the people to believe that they have a future made possible only by the Creator of the universe who controls both the stars and the destinies of the nations.

Furthermore, because God is the Creator of the universe, and is thereby concerned about all his creation, salvation must be for everyone, and not exclusively for Israel. Because God loves all people everywhere – the work of his hands - Isaiah does not speak of the nations as enemies to be defeated, but as peoples who can be won over, through Israel living the kind of life God wants its people to live – in faithfulness to the promises made to Abraham. (Genesis 22:18). It follows that other nations are also called to the practice of justice and mercy, and if they fail in this God-given mission, God will pass judgement on them too. Isaiah foresaw war as the only enemy to be defeated. (Isaiah 2:1-4). The Creator God continues his work of creation by giving strength to all those who stumble and fall. By trusting and hoping in him, he will lift them up on "wings like eagles." (40:31).

Second Isaiah's account of God as the creator of the universe represents an advancement in Old Testament theology. (See Isaiah 40:21-28; 44:24; 45:12, 18; 51:13, 16). The Lord God is beyond comparison with other gods. (40:25; 41:21; 42:7, 18; 45:16, 20; 46:5-7). Only the Creator of the universe is God. (43:8:13; 44:6-8; 45:5, 14, 21). This means that God controls the destiny of the nations. This would have been a comforting message for the exiles.

## The Redeemer of Israel and the Nations

Second Isaiah, combines the two traditions of creation and redemption; for him, they mean the same thing. (40:12-31; 43:16-21; 45:7-9; 48:12-13; 51;13-16). "I am the Lord, your saviour; I am the one who created you. I am the Lord, the Creator of all things. I alone stretched out the heavens; when I made the earth, no one helped me." (Isaiah 44:24). When Second Isaiah speaks of new creation, he is speaking primarily of a renewed human society in which God's will is done on earth, and he includes people from all nations in it. "In the Lord alone are saving justice and strength." (45:24a, NJB). Through the redemption of Israel, God will transform the world in a new creation. (41:20; 43:7; 44:24; 45:11).

In fulfilment of Isaiah's prophecy, the New Testament expands Isaiah's idea of new creation, seeing it as the transformation and glorification of humanity through sharing in the resurrection of Jesus. (Revelation 21:1).

Second Isaiah tried to get the message across to the exiles that God's love was not dependent on their ability to live up to the Ten Commandments. In the Sinai covenant, the people understood God's love as conditional on the people obeying the Ten

Commandments. The vision of Second Isaiah corrects that misunderstanding. The teaching of this prophet is that God is a God of unconditional love; his love is steadfast even though the people desert him for other gods. He still loves them and is with them without the temple rituals (sacrificial offerings) in which they could no longer participate while in exile. The Lord had not abandoned or forgotten his people, as they thought. (See Isaiah 49:14-16). Their rituals and schemes in the promised land did not, indeed, could not save them. Those practices represented a state of hiding from God. (Genesis 3:8; see Isaiah 43:22-25). God will now forgive their sins (43:25b) and give them all they need, which is to satisfy their deepest hungers and thirsts for a full and meaningful life. (Psalm 23:1-2).

> When the people in their need, look for water,
> when their throats are dry with thirst,
> then I, the Lord, will answer their prayer;
> I, the God of Israel, will never abandon them.
> I will make rivers flow among barren hills
> and springs of water run in the valleys.
> I will turn the desert into pools of water
> and the dry land into flowing springs.
> I will make cedars grow in the desert
> and acacias and myrtles and olive trees.
> Forests will grow in barren land,
> forests of pine and juniper and cypress.
> People will see this and know
> that I, the Lord have done it.
> They will come to understand
> that Israel's holy God has made it happen. (Isaiah 41:17-20).

After the Israelites' exodus from Egypt, and as they journeyed through the Sinai wilderness, the people's thirst was miraculously satisfied with water from the rock. Their hunger for food was met with manna from heaven. (See Exodus 17:3, 5-6; 16:9-14). The new exodus from Babylon proves that God still loves his people and will again liberate them and satisfy their hunger with the food of a new manna. He will satisfy their thirst for salvation by creating springs of life-giving water from their desert of desolation. In what resembles a new creation, God will satisfy human thirsting for freedom and happiness. (41:17). There will thus be something miraculous about this new creation. The new manna will come in the fruitfulness of cedars and olive trees springing up from the barren wilderness. (See 43:18-20; 48:20-21; 49:10). These are metaphors for new transformed life, resembling Ezekiel's vision of dead bones springing to new life from the earth. (Ezekiel 47:1-3). This new, abundant fruitfulness of the earth will be a reversal of the fruitless "weeds and thorns" following the first creation. (See Genesis 3:18).

In chapter 41 God calls on the nations to hear his message because they too will experience this redemption. "The nations are on trial; let them state their case." (41:1-42:9). The prophet calls them together to see who is right. "Who was it that brought the conqueror from the east, and makes him triumphant wherever he goes?" (41:2). This is a reference to Cyrus, king of Persia, whom The Lord names as "my shepherd." (44:28, NJB; see 45:1-7). Judah is insignificant, incapable of saving itself. (41:14). It is the Lord who is doing this and making Cyrus his servant to liberate his people from death-like Babylonian slavery. In this sense, Cyrus foreshadows Jesus, God's Good Shepherd who is willing to die for his flock, so that they might be rescued from death and reach fullness of life. (See John 10:11). It is God who is doing the work of liberation. King Cyrus is God's servant, appointed to a mission of shepherding. God says that Cyrus will accomplish his "entire will," by rebuilding Jerusalem. (Isaiah 44:28; see 45:1-8). The rebuilding of Jerusalem is a metaphor for the ultimate new creation of the "new Jerusalem." (See Revelation 21:2). This creative work of the Lord calls for a song of praise to him.

> Sing a new song to the Lord, sing his praise all the world!
> Praise him you who sail the sea;
> praise him all creatures of the sea.
> Sing distant lands and all who live there.
> Let the desert and its towns praise God;
> let the people of Kedar praise him![107]
> Let those who live in the city of Sela[108]
> shout for joy from the tops of the mountains!
> Let those who live in distant lands
> Give praise and glory to the Lord. (Isaiah 42:10-12).

The whole world sings in praise of the Lord for rescuing a people from the ends of the earth (See psalms 93, 96, 149). The prophet believes that the liberation of the exiles will lead all nations to acclaim the Lord as God. (42:12; see Psalms 93, 96, 149 for similar thought). The prophet visualizes a time, when instead of worshiping their own gods, which the prophet sees as useless (44:8b-9), the nations will recognise the power and the holiness of the Creator God. (Isaiah 41:14, 16, 20; 43:3, 14, 15; 49:7; 54:5). Then they will come to Jerusalem to worship this God, but only on the understanding of Jerusalem's commitment to justice and mercy. The Lord has a mission for Israel: "The Lord said to me, 'I have a greater task for you my servant. Not only will you restore to greatness the people of Israel who have survived, but I will also make you a light to the nations – so that all the world may be saved.'" (Isaiah 49:6; see also 51:4-5; 56:1-8). Israel will find its vocation as a servant who brings light to the nations. Israel itself having been liberated, its new mission is to liberate the nations from the darkness which keeps them separated from God. Second Isaiah thus sees God's promise to Abraham of bringing blessing to the nations being fulfilled by Israel. (Genesis 22:18),

In the following passage, the prophet doesn't hesitate to use feminine metaphors to speak of God as the Creator of new life. (42:14b; see 49:15).

---

[107] The people of Kadar were a nomadic tribe in northern Arabia, keeping flocks of sheep and goats.

[108] A city to the south of the Dead Sea, in northern Arabia.

God says,
'For a long time I kept silent;
I did not answer my people.
But now the time to act has come.
I cry out like a woman in labour.
I will destroy the hills and mountains
and dry up the grass and trees.
I will turn the river valleys into deserts
And dry up the pools of water.
I will lead my blind people
by roads they have never travelled.
I will turn their darkness into light
and make the rough country smooth before them.
These are my promises,
And I will keep them without fail.' (Isaiah 42:14-16).

Although the Lord accuses his people of blindness, he will still lead them to their destiny of new life. (Verse 16). In 42:18-20, he names them as his servant and says that they are both blind and deaf. The people were blind because of their illusions of self-sufficiency (self-exaltation) during their time in the promised land. They were blind to the reasons why they were taken into exile. They failed to see that religious ritual, political power, horses and chariots could never save them. They further failed to see that the loss of their state, their royal dynasty, temple and land was due to their failure to "walk in God's ways," i.e. maintain a society built on justice and mercy. And in their deafness, they failed to hear the message of the prophets who pronounced God's judgement on their society and its materialistic values.

But Isaiah believes that Judah's salvation is not dependent upon its ability to overcome its blindness and turn to the Lord. God now promises to do what his blind and deaf people, left to themselves, could never do, i.e. rescue them from their bondages. Despite its blindness and deafness, God will save Judah from its sins. This is a God of unconditional love. Perhaps the miracle of turning the land into a desert (42:15) will open the people's eyes to their disabilities and to the reality of God as saviour of Israel. Although they are blind and deaf, God will still turn their darkness into light and lead them home. (42:16).

There is a message here for all of us. We cannot rescue ourselves from our blindness and deafness to the ways of God. This is a transformation that only the Creator God can accomplish, through his Son and obedient servant, Jesus Christ.

The following passage calls on the exiles not to be afraid of the journey home. Despite their blindness and deafness, they are still God's redeemed people. God is with them, bringing their offspring home from the east and west, from the north and south. He calls them his "sons and daughters." They are his own children. He is with them. He knows them intimately.

Israel, the Lord who created you says,
'Do not be afraid, for I have redeemed you.
I have called you by name, you are mine.
Should you pass through the sea, I will be with you;
or through rivers, they will not swallow you up.
Should you walk through fire, you will not be scorched,
and the flames will not burn you.
For I am the Lord your God,
the holy one of Israel, your saviour...
Do not be afraid, for I am with you!
I will bring your offspring from the east,
and gather you from the west.
To the north I will say, 'Give them up'
and to the south, 'Do not hold them'.
Bring back my sons from far away,
and my daughters from the ends of the earth,
all those who bear my name,
whom I created for my glory,
whom I have formed, whom I have made.' (Isaiah 43:1-3, 5-7, JB).

In the above, and in recurring passages, the prophet returns to the exiles' homecoming as a new Exodus, a new terrifying passage through turbulent waters (verse 2 above; see Isaiah 42:16; 43:18-19; 49:7-12; 51:9-10; 52:7-12; 55:12-13). They should not be afraid because God will be with them (41:18), just like he was with Moses at the Red Sea. (See Exodus 14:13, 21-22). The people are not to cling to events of the past (the Exodus from Egypt). God is active in the present. As the people pass through the wilderness, God will satisfy their hungers and thirsts, just as Moses did in those far off times. He will guide them like a shepherd. (40:11; 43:16-21; 49:9-11). There will be a new Red Sea victory (51:9-10), and a new conquest of the promised land. (49:8-12).

The Lord sent Israel into exile in Babylon for its past transgressions. (Isaiah 42:18-25; 43:22-28). The Lord now grants Israel consolation, hope and forgiveness. (40:1-2; 49:13; 51:12; 52:7-12).

## Israel as God's Servant—a Model of Justice for the World

The Servant Songs in Second Isaiah derive from, and were influenced by the confessions of Jeremiah. (Jeremiah 11:18–12:6; 15:10-21; 17:14-18; 18:18-23; 20:7-18). Jeremiah's prophetic career and sufferings serve to introduce the themes of Isaiah's last three servant songs. Just as the mission of servant of God was costly to Jeremiah, it will be the same for Israel. The forgiveness of Israel's sins now enables Israel to assume the role of servant in the four Servant Songs. In naming Israel as a servant, the prophet suggests that the people are ready to serve God, and not the idols to which they formerly gave their allegiance. Thus, the word "servant" refers to the people who sinned, suffered and now turn to God as the one who will "open up rivers on barren hills and turn the desert into a lake" (41:18) for their safe passage home. Once restored to their homeland, God will then give them a new mission of bringing light to the nations. (42:6-7). Will they be obedient to this new role of service? In carrying out this mission, they are not to rely on their own strength or their former self-serving schemes before the exile. Their empowerment will come from the Creator God (verse 10 in the passage below). From the beginning of creation, God's mission for humanity was one of service, to continue his creative work on earth. (See Genesis 2:15; Psalm 8:3-8). The following is the first of the four servant songs.

> The Lord says:
> 'You Israel my servant whom I have chosen,
> descendant of Abraham my friend.
> I brought you from the ends of the earth;
> I called you from the farthest corners
> and I said to you, 'You are my servant.'
> I did not reject you, but chose you.
> Do not be afraid - I am with you!
> I am your God – let nothing terrify you!
> I will make you strong and help you;
> I will protect you and save you.' (Isaiah 41:8-10).

In the above poem, and for the first time, Israel is named as God's servant. God asks Israel not to be afraid because he will accompany his servant on his journey home - "I am with you." This recalls God's revelation to Moses: "I am," suggesting intimacy and permanency. Being with his servant is transformative: "I am your redeemer." (Isaiah 41:14, JB). This means that the servant's strength comes not from himself, but from God. And because God is "with" his servant, the latter will be empowered for his mission, the content of which is not stated until we come to the second servant song. Strengthened by God, the servant should look towards a glorious future. The prophet refers to Abraham because he wishes to emphasise the significance and the endurance of Israel's religious traditions. (41:8). There is also the hint that, like Abraham, the servant will have a mission of bringing light to the nations.

## The Second Servant Song

In the Second Servant Song, the servant's mission is stated, as bringing justice to the nations:

> The Lord says,
> 'Here is my servant whom I strengthen –
> The one I have chosen, with whom I am pleased.
> I have filled him with my Spirit,
> And he will bring justice to every nation.'
> He will not shout or raise his voice
> or make loud speeches in the streets.

> He will not break off a bent reed
> or put out a flickering lamp.
> He will bring lasting justice to all.
> He will not lose hope or courage;
> he will establish justice on the earth.
> Distant lands eagerly wait for his teaching.'
> God created the heavens and stretched them out;
> he fashioned the earth and all that lives there;
> he gave life and breath to all its people.
> And now the Lord says to his servant,
> 'I, the Lord have called you and given you power
> to see that justice is done on earth.
> Through you I will make a covenant with all peoples;
> through you I will bring light to the nations.
> You will open the eyes of the blind
> and set free those who sit in dark prisons.
> I alone am the Lord your God.
> No other God may share my glory;
> I will not let idols share my praise.' (Isaiah 42:1-8).

In being filled with God's Spirit 42:1b), the servant is linked to the promised Messiah and the latter's obedience to God's commission to create justice among the nations. (Isaiah 42:1; 11:1-10; see Ezekiel 34:23-24; 2 Samuel 8:15).

The evangelist Matthew cites Isaiah 42:1-4 in the above passage, to show that Jesus' healing ministry is fulfilled in the words of Isaiah, and that Jesus is the Servant about whom the prophet was speaking. (See Matthew 12:15-21). Jesus is both the promised Messiah and the perfect servant of God. Jesus is servant because of his perfect obedience to God. (See Mark 14:36). Jesus was filled with God's Spirit (Mark 1:10), empowering him to "bring lasting justice" to everyone. (Isaiah 42:1b above; see Luke 4:18-19). Jesus saw himself as fulfilling the mission of the Servant in Isaiah 42:6-7. In the discharge off his mission, Jesus also had to contend with blindness and deafness. (Luke 4:18; Mark 8:31-33; 10:46-52). The blindness and deafness of humanity was overcome by the power of God, through Jesus' awakening to transformed life. Jesus will establish a definitive covenant (verse 6 above) with all peoples. (Mark 14:24).

Bringing light to the nations and seeing that "justice is done on earth" mean the same thing. (See also 49:6). Israel can only be a light to the nations through the servant's own just practices. Is the servant Israel up to this task? When Jeremiah and Ezekiel admonished the people because of their unjust society, they were deaf to the word of God spoken by his prophets. Embodied and strengthened as the servant, will they listen to God now? (44:1). Israel's commission (Isaiah 42:1, 6-7) echoes the mission and life of Jeremiah. (Jeremiah 1:4–4:10). Both Jeremiah and Isaiah were called to be prophets to the nations (Jeremiah 1:5; 10; Isaiah 49:6). They both encountered opposition, and their labours seemingly being in vain. (Isaiah 49:4; Jeremiah 42:1–44:30).

Although Isaiah has hopes for his servant Israel, he still refers to him as "blind and deaf" to God's word. (42:16, 18-20, JB). "The Lord is a God who is still eager to save, so he exalted his laws and teachings and he wanted his people to honour them." (Isaiah 42:21). But they would not listen to his word, or obey the teaching he gave them. (42:24b, 25b). They could not see why they were locked up in dungeons (exile). (42:22).

Despite being blind and deaf, Israel is now called to be the servant of God's plans for the whole world. (Isaiah 42:18-19; 43:8). The empowerment ("I am with you," 41:10) for this missionary role will come from God's Spirit (42:1) and God's personal relationship with Israel (41:8-9; 44:21, 26; 45:4; 48:20). This is a power that will, at last, overcome blindness and deafness. The Lord calls Israel "my servant" both outside and within the servant songs. (41:8-9; 43:10; 44:1-2, 21; 45:4).

The prophet then has a hymn of praise to the Lord who is about to liberate the exiles and bring them home. (Isaiah 42:10-13).

## King Cyrus: God's Messiah

Second Isaiah began his prophecy at a time when a new power from the east (modern Iran) was poised, ready to invade Babylon and establish a new empire that would last until the conquests of Alexander the Great. This was the Persian Empire, and it was one of the largest in the ancient world, extending from the Indus River in India, all the way west through modern Turkey and into Macedonia in Greece, and from there southward into Egypt. Second Isaiah looked forward to the rule of King Cyrus (559 – 529 BC), the founder of the Persian Empire, because of that king's reputation for liberating captured peoples.

In 539 BC Cyrus took control of Babylon, having been welcomed into the city by its citizens. Compared with earlier kings, Cyrus was a benevolent conqueror and ruler, treating defeated people with a dignity unknown in the ancient world, leaving captured cities intact and permitting the repatriation of deported peoples. He was tolerant of local religions and permitted the Babylonians to worship their god Marduk. Cyrus issued a decree in 538 BC permitting the Jewish exiles in Babylon to return to their homeland. He sponsored and financed the rebuilding of the Jerusalem temple. The Book of Ezra quotes a proclamation made by Cyrus, which may be a Hebrew copy of the same decree. (Ezra 1:2-4; 6:3-5). Cyrus identified the God of Israel as his own God and declared that his decision to allow the return of the Jewish exiles was to please the Lord and to establish his worship in his own place, that is, in Israel. Second Isaiah says that Cyrus accomplished the will of God. (Isaiah 44:28).

Following his conquest of Babylon in 539 BC, the Persian king gradually enlarged his dominions. (Isaiah 13:17; 21:1-10; 44:28; 45:1; Jeremiah 51:11, 28). The capital city of Persia was Susa. Darius, the third King of Persia (grandson of Cyrus) invaded Greece but was defeated by the Greeks at the battle of Marathon in 490 BC. In a second Persian invasion of Greece, his son Xerxes was defeated by the Athenian fleet at the battle of Salamis in 480 BC. The empire founded by Cyrus continued in existence until the conquests of Alexander the Great in 334 BC, and as a result of which, Greek language and culture was spread throughout the former Persian empire. The empire of Alexander the Great covered the same area of the middle east as that of Persia, but with the addition of the whole of Greece.

Second Isaiah foresaw a time when King Cyrus would conquer Babylon and reveal his plans to allow the Jewish exiles home. The prophet interpreted the signs of the times, as God coming to save his people. The sovereign God is the ruler of empires and can use them as his instrument, even though they are not aware of that. God would now call Cyrus by his name and arm him to do his work of liberation. God would go before Cyrus "to level the heights and shatter the bronze gateways" (45:2 in the passage below), thus preparing a way home for the Jewish exiles.

> Thus, says the Lord to his anointed one,
> to Cyrus to whom he says,
> 'I have grasped by his right hand,
> to make the nations bow before him
> and to disarm kings,
> to open gateways before him.
> I myself shall go before you,
> I shall level the heights,
> I shall shatter the bronze gateways,
> I shall smash the iron bars.
> I shall give you secret treasures,
> and secret hoards of wealth
> so that you will know that I am the Lord,
> the God of Israel, who calls you by your name.
> It is for the sake of my servant Israel
> that I have called you by your name,
> have given you a title,
> though you do not know me.
> I am the Lord and there is no other.
> There is no other god except me.
> Though you do not know me, I have armed you,
> so that it may be known from east to west,
> that there is no one except me.
> I am the Lord, and there is no other.
> I form the light and create the darkness,
> I make well-being and I create disaster,
> I the Lord, do all these things.
> Rain down, you heavens from above,
> and let the clouds pour down saving justice,
> let the earth open up
> and blossom with salvation,
> and let justice sprout with it.
> I, the Lord God have created it. (Isaiah 45:1-8, NJB).

In the beginning of the above passage, the Lord refers to Cyrus as the "anointed" one. The kings of Israel and Judah were anointed, signifying their role as servants of God's people.

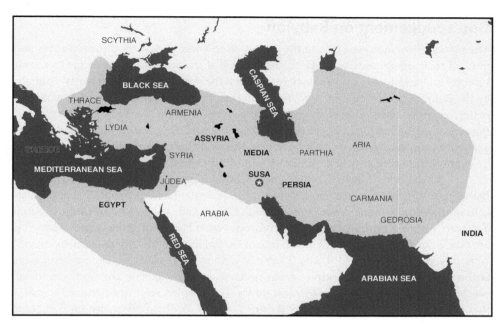

*The Persian Empire*

In his reference to Cyrus as "the Lord's anointed," the prophet implies that he, Cyrus is being given a role as Messiah. (45:1). Once Cyrus is "armed" (45:1) by God for the task of liberating God's people, everyone from east to west will learn of the uniqueness of God and of his power to create light for the exiles and darkness for Babylon. Cyrus will perform the task which was always expected of the king Messiah: make the journey to Jerusalem, liberate God's people from foreign oppression, build the temple, and assume the role of king. Cyrus has no awareness of God calling him to this mission (45:4b), but he will still be God's instrument in fulfilment of God's purposes. That Cyrus does not know God, is a sign of God's sovereignty over the nations.

The above poem continues on to verse 13. Then there is a strong assertion of God's uniqueness as Creator (45:18), who now calls people all over the world to turn to him and be saved. (45:22). "The Lord says, 'I solemnly promise by all that I am: Everyone will come and kneel before me and vow to be loyal to me.'" (Isaiah 45:23; 66:23). This is an obedience that was finally fulfilled by Jesus, who identified with all of us. (Mark 14:36).

In the appointment of Cyrus, king of the Persians, as God's Messiah, the prophet may have been controversial. How would this sound to the prophet's audience? A foreign king ruling over them! The prophet may be reminding the exiles that Judah, once returned home, will have to accept a subordinate political role; Cyrus will be their overlord. The restoration of the former monarchy is out of the question. It didn't work. The prophet may also be reminding the exiles that their idea of 'nation' may only be an idol (false god), and that trusting in the ways of God and obedience to his covenant are what really matter, irrespective of the political situation - an advice that was not heeded in later times.

## God's Judgement on Babylon

The policy of conquering kings in the ancient world was to destroy captured cities, kill most of their inhabitants and take the remainder of the population into exile as slaves. Literary and archaeological evidence reveals that the destruction and barbarity wrought by the Babylonians when they captured Jerusalem in 587 BC, left a trail of despair and suffering in its wake, almost unprecedented in the ancient world.[109] God permitted Babylon to conquer Judah because of the latter's infidelity. But in its pride and self-exaltation, and its excessive cruelty, Babylon mistook this temporary mission, believing in its absolute sovereignty and immunity to military defeat.

In chapter 47, Isaiah outlines how God's judgement will fall on self-righteous Babylon for the harsh treatment it meted out to Jerusalem and its people. Second Isaiah calls on Babylon to come down from her high throne and "sit on the dust of the ground. You were once a virgin, a city unconquered, but you are soft and delicate no longer! You are now a slave!" (47:1; see 2-15). In the face of God's judgement, self-exalted Babylon will be humbled. (See Genesis 11:4, 8-9). The skills of Babylon's priests, sages and astrologers will not be able to save its empire from collapse. (47:12-13). The city with the tower reaching to the heavens will be brought down. The prophet tries to convince the exiles that the rulers of empires are not sovereign. They delude themselves into thinking that they wield absolute power, and that their oppressive and self-serving schemes will last forever. It is only the Creator of the universe who is sovereign Lord. He rules over the empires and uses them to serve his purposes.

The time has come for God to liberate his people. But are the people prepared for this new journey to which God is calling them?

## God Loves his still Blind and Deaf People

In chapter 48, Isaiah reminds Israel that God is her teacher and leader. The Lord says to Israel, 'Long ago I predicted what would take place; then suddenly I made it happen" (the exile in Babylon, 48:3). In 48:8 the Lord again accuses Israel of being a rebel, blind and deaf to his word (disobedient) when, before the exile, he told them what would happen to their nation. God tested Israel like silver in the fire of suffering (exile), and judged her to be a "worthless" metal. (48:10). God again reminds Israel that he is the Creator of the world. "I am the first and the last, the only God. My hands made the earth's foundations and spread the heavens out. When I summon the earth and sky, they come at once and present themselves." (48:12-13). Will the people listen to their Creator? Only this God has the power to save his people. And now, despite their disobedience and failure to listen, he will summon his obedient servant Cyrus to come to their rescue. (See 48:14-15). "The Lord says to his people, 'If only you had listened to my commands, blessings would have flowed for you like a stream that never goes dry! Victory would have come to you like the waves that roll on the shore." (48:18). "Victory" in this sense means overcoming evil. Through the prophet, God reminds the people of their failure in obedience, contrasted with the obedience of their father Abraham. (Genesis 22:18). If only they had listened to

---

[109] Marcus J. Borg, *Reading the Bible again for the First Time*, (Harper Collins, 2002), p. 131.

the word of the Lord, their descendants would be "as numerous as grains of sand," and they would not have been sent into exile. (48:19).

In chapter 49, God renews Second Isaiah's call to mission. This time the Lord tells the prophet that the Creator's message is for "distant nations" and not just for Israel. The prophet says, "Before I was born, the Lord chose me and appointed me to be his servant. He made my words as sharp as a sword. With his own hand, he protected me." (49:1-2). The Lord also wants the prophet to identify himself with Israel as servant. (49:3). He tells God about his difficulties so far: "I have used my strength but have accomplished nothing. (49:4a). Jeremiah also thought his own mission had failed. (Jeremiah 15:10). The people are not listening to the prophet. Despite this, the prophet can say, 'Yet I can trust the Lord to defend my cause; he will reward me for what I do.' (49:4b). The Lord again calls him to be his servant, "to bring back the scattered people of Israel." (49:5).

God has a greater task for his prophet than simply taking the people home from exile. The Lord says to him, "It is not enough for you to be my servant, to restore the tribes of Jacob and bring back the survivors of Israel; I shall make you a light to the nations so that my salvation may reach the remotest parts of earth." (49:6, NJB). Thus, through his identification with Israel, the prophet's mission is to accomplish what God promised Abraham, that through the latter's obedience, the nations would be blest with salvation. (Genesis 12:3; 22:18). "The Lord then says to his people, 'When the time comes to save you, I will show you favour and answer your cries for help. I will guard and protect you, and through you make a covenant with all peoples. I will let you settle once again in your own land that is now laid waste.'" (49:8).

God's promise of a covenant with all peoples is, once again, a reminder to Israel of its role of bringing salvation to the wider world. (See 49:6). God then tells the people that he will make a highway across the mountains for their safe passage home. He will "comfort his people and take pity on their sufferings." (49:11-13). But the people still do not listen to this. They again complain that the Lord has abandoned them. (49:14). God then speaks through the prophet and tells them that his love for his people exceeds that of a nursing mother for her child: 'Can a woman forget her baby at the breast, feel no pity for the child she has borne? Even if these were to forget, I shall not forget you. Look, I have engraved you on the palms of my hands.' (Isaiah 49:15-16, NJB). Their names being engraved on the palms of God's hands is an image of the permanency of God's commitment to Israel and to humanity at large. The above two images are expressions of the unbreakable bond of God's love for his people. God will rescue and save his people despite their blindness and deafness and lack of faith in him. The prophet asks the exiles to look around them. People are already assembling for the journey home. (49:18).

At the beginning of chapter 50, the people are reminded that the purpose of the exile was not to end Jerusalem's relationship with God, but to discipline its people. The Lord says, 'Do you think I sent my people away like a man who divorces his wife?... No, you were sent away captive because of your sins; you were sent away because of your crimes.' (Isaiah 50:1; see Jeremiah 5:27-28; 7:5-6). "The Lord says, 'Am I too weak to save you? I can dry up the sea with a command and turn rivers into a desert, so that the fish in them die for lack of water. I can make the sky turn dark, as if it were in mourning for the dead.'" (50:2). Those words may be a reference to Babylon, for whom "the sky will turn dark" once its city and empire fall to the armies of the Persian conqueror – an event which will lead to the liberation of Israel, and leave Babylon in mourning.

## The Third Servant Song

In the Third Servant Song below, the Servant may be both the faithful remnant in the community who return to Jerusalem - i.e. those who obey the word of God - as well as the prophet who leads the community and is suffering because of the blindness of those who are still failing to respond to his mission.

> The Sovereign Lord has taught me what to say,
> so that I can strengthen the weary.
> Every morning he makes me eager
> to hear what he is going to teach me.
> The Lord has given me understanding,
> and I have not rebelled,
> or turned away from him.
> I bared my back to those who beat me.
> I did not stop when they insulted me,
> when they pulled out the hairs of my beard
> and spat in my face.
> But their insults cannot hurt me
> because the Sovereign Lord gives me help.
> I brace myself to endure them.
> I know that I will not be disgraced,
> for God is near,
> and he will prove me innocent...
> All of you who honour the Lord
> and obey the words of his servant,
> the path you walk may be dark indeed,
> but trust in the Lord, rely on your God. (Isaiah 50:4-8, 10).

Like Jeremiah when he was called to mission (Jeremiah 1:9), the Lord God has also taught Isaiah what to say, so that he may strengthen the weary. (50:4). As Jeremiah was empowered (Jeremiah 1:17-19), Isaiah too, is strengthened ("the sovereign Lord gives me help") to encounter the opposition and persecution by those opposed to him. (50:6-7).

The Third Servant Song is about the servant's submission to suffering that is endured for a purpose. He is "eager" to hear the word of God. (50:4). Like Jeremiah before him, he cannot stop proclaiming this word to a deaf people. (See Jeremiah 20:8-9). Because of his "understanding" (v. 5) of God's word (one of the gifts of God's Spirit), the prophet-servant will suffer, but he trusts that God will vindicate him. (50:7b). In saying he has not "rebelled," the prophet implies that he will obediently discharge his God-given mission. But his obedience will be costly. (50:6-7). The servant will drink the cup of suffering. (See Mark 14:36).

Jeremiah and Isaiah were commissioned to be prophets to the nations. (Isaiah

49:6; Jeremiah 1:5, 10). Both of them suffered opposition and persecution because of their proclamation of the word of God. (Isaiah 50:6; Jeremiah 20:7-13). And both were faced with the possibility that their mission might be a failure, because of opposition and the people's spiritual deafness and blindness. (Isaiah 49:4; Jeremiah 42:1–44:30).

Can the servant Israel place his trust in God and imitate the prophet by "walking the dark path?" (Isaiah 50:10; See Psalm 23:4). Trusting in the Lord will put Israel on the right path. (Psalm 23:3). At the beginning of his prophecy, God reminded Isaiah that the people would not listen to, or understand the word of God spoken by him. If they did, they might "turn to the Lord and be healed." (Isaiah 6:9-10). Second Isaiah is given "understanding" (50:5) of the word of God, but Israel is still blind and deaf to the word. (Isaiah 42:16, 18-19).

For Israel in exile, suffering was first of all a penalty. But Israel's new role as servant would mean obedience to the word of God, which would mean commitment to a mission of creating justice in its society. This would be a mission of redemptive service, but because it would be met by opposition and deafness, it would involve suffering. (See Isaiah 50:6, 10; 53:10). Part of the mission of both the prophet and Israel is to patiently endure innocent suffering in obedience to the will of God, to accept the insults and the blows inflicted by those who oppose or oppress them. (50:6-7).

For all those (including ourselves), who honour God and obey his word, the path they walk may be "dark" indeed. (Isaiah 50:10; see Psalm 23:4). But by trusting in the Lord and obeying his will, those who suffer because of their service, will be vindicated. (Isaiah 50:8a). They will not suffer in vain. Suffering endured as a service, and for a noble purpose, is redemptive. It transforms the lives of people. God will respond to innocent suffering. The God who created the heavens and earth will have the final word on suffering and evil. His "victory will be final. It will endure for all time." (Isaiah 51:3, 6-8, 15-16; see 2 Corinthians 4:8-18; 5:1).

The servant theme demonstrates the connection between God's word and personal suffering. A person whose heart is set on God will always be afflicted in a variety of ways. But this can be a means of purification, leading to a deeper hearing of the word and greater faithfulness to God. Second Isaiah's new teaching of purification through suffering contradicts the theology of retribution that views suffering as God's punishment for sin. (Genesis 3:14-19; 12:17; 42:21; Job 33:19-30). Trusting in the Lord in the midst of innocent suffering is the highest form of faith, but very difficult. Jesus has already done it on our behalf. For Jesus, his suffering is a work of service to humanity - a sacrifice of his life, bringing the blessing of salvation to the whole world.

In his servant theme, Isaiah is trying to persuade a demoralized people that God is about to do something wonderful for them, and that they have a decisive role (as servants of God) in their own restoration, and a mission to accomplish – "healing the broken-hearted and freeing captives from prisons." (Isaiah 61:1). In calling them to this mission, the prophet is offering them a reason for living a purposeful life. Serving their neighbour, although costly, will make their life meaningful and worthwhile. Jerusalem's liberation, however, did not have the effect on the nations that Isaiah hoped. The servant would continue to be blind and deaf. (Isaiah 42:16; 56:9-12, 57:3,7-9).

When the exiles finally come home, the monarchy will not be restored in Israel.

The Israelite king had been tasked with the role of servant. This role is now transferred to the nation as a whole. (42:4-6). The monarchy actually facilitated the oppression of the poor within Israel. The kings failed in their mission to be both shepherds (servants) of their people and a light to the nations. (Isaiah 1:21-23; 3:1-12; 28:14-22; 29:14-15).

## Salvation is Coming

In Chapter 51 the prophet exhorts his fellow exiles to believe in the future of Jerusalem. "Listen to me you who pursue justice," i.e. those who are committed to the establishment of a just society. He goes on to show that their dreams of a restored Jerusalem are realistic. Those who think this is impossible should remember the story of Abraham and Sarah. God's promises to them were fulfilled, although it appeared impossible for them ever to have children. The people should trust in the power of the Lord to perform another miracle by turning the ruins of Jerusalem into a garden: "like the garden I planted in Eden. Joy and gladness will be there, songs of praise and thanks to me." (51:3). If the Lord created the stars (Isaiah 40:26) and destroyed the chaotic sea monster (Genesis 1:2; Isaiah 27:1; 51:8), surely, he can recreate Jerusalem. The Lord again calls his people to listen to him. The deliverance he will bring them "will last for ever. His victory will be final." (51:6b).

Salvation will also be for the nations. "The Lord says, 'Listen to me, my people, listen to what I say. I give my teaching to the nations; my laws will bring them light.'" (Isaiah 51:4-5). Again, recalling the words of Isaiah 2:2-4, the prophet assures the exiles that all nations will recognise God's triumph of justice. The Lord will thus exalt Jerusalem so that the nations will come to it to learn the ways of God and do his will. Though the created world exhibits all the signs of permanence, it will be swept away before God's salvation for Jerusalem will fail. (51:6). The Creator of the universe will bring deliverance to all peoples - a teaching that will give them wisdom and enlightenment. God's sovereign rule will thus be established over the nations. God will have the final word on history. This will be a new creation, preceded by destruction (51:6b), which may be a metaphor for the fall of Babylon to the Persian empire. The Lord "strengthens" his people. "Why should they fear mortals (the Babylonians) who are no more enduring than desert grass?" (51:12). What God accomplished in ancient times God can do once again. (See 51:9-16). The Lord calls Jerusalem to wake up. Its people have drunk the cup of punishment. Thy have suffered devastation and starvation. (51:17). "The Lord your God defends you and says, 'I am taking away the cup that I gave you in anger. I will give it to those who oppressed you, to those who made you lie down in the streets and trampled on you as if you were dirt.'" (52:22-23). The prisoners will soon be set free. (51:14a).

In chapter 52, God again promises to rescue Jerusalem, so that "the heathen will never enter its gates again." (Isaiah 52:1). With a hint of resurrection, God calls on Jerusalem to "rise from the dust and sit on her throne." (52:2). "Break into shouts of joy, you ruins of Jerusalem! The Lord will rescue his city and comfort his people. The Lord will use his holy power, and all the world will see it." (See 52:9-16). the Book of Revelation says that the prophet's vision of the new Jerusalem (Isaiah 52:7) will be fulfilled only at the end of time with the descent of the heavenly Jerusalem to earth. (Revelation 21:27).

# The Fourth Servant Song: Jesus, Servant of God

Salvation is coming. Perhaps at this stage, Second Isaiah could see no sign of blind and deaf Israel coming to repent of its sins of blindness and deafness. What Israel as a whole could not do, Isaiah now sees being accomplished in one individual who substitutes himself for blind and deaf Israel. "The Lord says, 'My servant will succeed in his task; he will be highly honoured.'" (Isaiah 52:13). When the nations see what the servant has accomplished, they will "marvel at him, and kings will be speechless with amazement. They will see and understand something they had never known." (52:15). The kings cannot believe what they are seeing, since they had considered the servant as of no account, an object of contempt. (52:14).

It is ultimately because of the work of this servant that the sovereignty of God (a major Isaianic theme) is made fully manifest. Because God is King, Babylon and its gods are overthrown, peace is established, Israel is rescued and salvation comes to all nations. The work of the servant is also related to Ezekiel's theme of resurrection, and to the theme of the Shepherd (God), who takes the exiles back to their own land and feeds them on the mountains of Israel, the shepherds of Israel (kings) having failed in their vocation. (Ezekiel 34:1-4, 11-16; 37:1-10).

The Fourth Servant Song (Isaiah 52:13-15–53:1-12) is a development of the thought of the third song. It foreshadows Jesus and helps us to better understand his own suffering service. Jesus saw his sufferings, death and vindication in terms of Isaiah's fourth servant song. (Luke 24:25-27). Christians see the passage below fulfilled in Jesus and in his followers with whom he identified. We are all called to be servants, to participate in the service of Jesus, with all the implications of such a role. Jesus' own role as suffering servant will be the means of bringing all of us home from our exile in this world and giving us a place of "honour" along with himself at God's right hand (Isaiah 52:13), thus fulfilling our destiny of eternal life.

The Lord says,

'My servant will succeed in his task;
then he will be highly honoured.
Many people were shocked when they saw him;
he was so disfigured that he
hardly looked human.
But now many nations will marvel at him,
and kings will be speechless with amazement.
They will see and understand
something they had never known.' (Isaiah 52:13-15).

The people reply,
'Who would believe what we now report?
Who would have seen the Lord's hand in this?'
It was the will of the Lord that his servant

should grow like a plant,
taking root in dry ground.
He had no dignity or beauty
to make us take notice of him.
There was nothing attractive about him,
nothing that would draw us to him.
We despised him and rejected him;
he endured suffering and pain.
No one would even look at him –
we ignored him as if he were nothing.
But he endured the suffering that
should have been ours,
the pain that we should have borne.
All the while we thought that his suffering
was punishment sent by God.
But because of our sins he was wounded,
beaten because of the evil we did.
We are healed by the punishment he suffered,
made whole by the blows he received.
All of us were like sheep that were lost,
each one going his own way.
But the Lord made the punishment fall on him,
the punishment all of us deserved.
He was treated harshly,
but never said a word.
Like a lamb about to be
slaughtered,
like a sheep about to be sheared,
he never said a word.
He was arrested and sentenced
and led off to die,
and no one cared about his fate.
He was put to death for the sins of our people.
He was placed in a grave with the wicked,
he was buried with the rich,
even though he had never
committed a crime
or ever told a lie.' (Isaiah 53:1-9).

The Lord says,
'It was my will that he should suffer;
his death was a sacrifice to bring forgiveness.
And so he will see his descendants;
he will live a long life,

and through him my purpose will succeed.
After a life of suffering he will again have joy;
he will know that he did not suffer in vain.
My devoted servant, with whom I am pleased,
will bear the punishment of many
and for his sake I will forgive them.
And so I will give him a place of honour,
a place among the great and powerful.
He willingly gave his life
and shared the fate of evil men.
He took the place of many sinners
and prayed that they might all be forgiven.' (Isaiah 53:10-12).

The structure of the above Song consists of a three-part dialogue between God and the audience of the nations about the suffering servant. God's words at the beginning (52:13-15) and at the end (53:10-12) enclose the confessions of the nations (53:1-9) about their misunderstanding of the Servant. The middle section (53:1-9) shows that humanity does not think the same way as God about the suffering of the righteous. (See 55:8-11).

In the song's opening lines, God promises the servant vindication. (52:11). If the servant is understood as Israel, the latter will instruct people and the nations, not by persuasive words, but by the endurance of exilic suffering. (52:14-15; see 42:4; 50:4-7). It is ultimately Jesus who instructs the nations by the endurance of his sufferings during his exile from God in this world.

In the middle section, humanity confesses guilt and ignorance. (53:1-9). The nations are amazed at Israel's passage from the humiliation of exile (53:2-9) to the exaltation of being restored to Jerusalem. (53:10-11a). Living as scattered and straying sheep, the people of the nations cannot experience compassion, since they are separated from one another. (53:6; see Ezekiel 34:1-31). In contrast to this scattered flock, stands the silent lamb about to be slaughtered (53:7), in this instance, the servant, one like Jeremiah. (See Jeremiah 11:19; 1:5, 10). The nations reject the servant by imposing a death sentence on him – exile in Babylon. (53:8; see 50:8-10; Jeremiah 26:1-24). The idea of Israel being "placed in a grave" (53:9) is a metaphor for the exile, as a deathlike period. (Isaiah 53:9-10; see Ezekiel 37:1-4; Psalm 38:1; 30:3; 40:2; 147:3). Israel's silence and nonviolence signify its righteousness in contrast to the nations' guilt in oppressing Israel. (Isaiah 53:7-9; see 2-6). The nations conclude their confession by proclaiming God's vindication of the servant Israel. (Isaiah 53:12b).

In Isaiah 53:4-5 there is a suggestion of vicarious atonement - the servant acting in a substitutionary role for Israel. This is the idea that one person, in solidarity with others, can bear the consequences of their sins (namely death), so that they might escape such consequences, God using the undeserved violence against his servant to save other people – the guilty ones. "The Lord made the punishment fall on him, the punishment all of us deserved." (53:6b). Apart from the suggestion in the Book of Deuteronomy concerning the vicarious suffering of Moses (Deuteronomy 4:21-22), this is the only other instance in the Old Testament of vicarious suffering.

At the opening of his prophecy in chapter 40, Second Isaiah states that Israel in exile has suffered long enough, so its sins of disobedience in the promised land are now forgiven. (40:2). This is surprising, because there is no indication here or elsewhere in Second Isaiah that Israel repented of its sins. On the contrary, the prophet accuses Israel of persistent blindness and deafness. (42:18-20, 43:24). It is only when we come to chapter 53, that we find the meaning of verse 40:2. Israel itself never repented. Repentance came to Israel because the servant identified with Israel, substituted himself for Israel. He took the consequences of their sins of disobedience on to himself by his vicarious suffering, and thus offered God a repentance on their behalf. It was the will of God that he should suffer. (53:10a). This means, that unlike Israel, the Servant was obedient unto death. (See Mark 14:36). The Servant's sufferings were thus not in vain. They fulfilled a purpose. "His death was a sacrifice to bring forgiveness." (Isaiah 53:10a, 11b). This forgiveness was twofold. Firstly, God was able to forgive Israel of all its accumulated sins before the exile. Secondly, in seeing the servant's exaltation through suffering, the nations and their kings will be "speechless with amazement," their eyes opened to a new understanding of God as a forgiving saviour. (52:15). The poem ends as it began, with the vindication and exaltation of the servant. The Lord rewards the servant with a "place of honour, a place among the great and powerful." (53:12; see Mark 14:62; Luke 24:51).

The theme of forgiveness connects this servant song to the introduction of Second Isaiah (40:2) and to the conclusion of his prophecy in 55:7. Home from exile follows forgiveness. (Isaiah 55:12-13).

The original meaning of the Servant may be applied to Israel – humiliated by the nations (Isaiah 53:3) and suffering a death-like existence in Babylon, but then given a 'place of honour' in being brought home from exile and given a new role of bringing salvation to the nations, through its own just practices. (Isaiah 49:6; 55:5). But once restored to Jerusalem, Israel again proved to be blind and deaf to the ways of God. (Isaiah 56:10-12). Once again, the people turned to false gods, even "sacrificing their children in rocky caves and the bed of a stream." (Isaiah 57:3-5). And again, they failed to create a just society at home, so that God's promises to Abraham of bringing blessing to the nations might be fulfilled. (Isaiah 58:3-4; 59:3-4, 8, 16; Genesis 22:15-19).

Second Isaiah may have come to the conclusion that, left to itself, and its persistent blindness and lack of trust in God, Israel could not be the means of its own salvation. This would have to be the work of a servant who, through his perfect obedience to God, would, at last, bring justice to the nations.

Who then is the servant who will succeed in his task? Perhaps the prophet turned in hope of a future Messiah, who would accomplish what blind and deaf Israel failed to do. (See Isaiah 9:6-7). Jesus is this Messiah-king and suffering servant, who fulfils Isaiah 53. Jesus identifies with sinful humanity and offers himself as a substitute for Israel (Mark 1:9, 12-13), in order to do for Israel and the world what itself cannot do. As a true servant of God, Jesus offers a perfect obedience to God. (Mark 14:36). He fully obeys the will of God, which is to suffer and die, as a substitute for sinful humanity (Isaiah 53:6b, 8b; Mark 8:31; 10:45), so that God's people everywhere might be forgiven (Isaiah 53:10a) and escape the consequence of their sins of disobedience, namely death. (Genesis 2:17; 3:19). Jesus places his absolute trust in God to vindicate him and give him a place of honour. (Isaiah

52:13; 53:12a; Mark 10:34; 14:62; Luke 24:46, 50-51). Jesus' death is "a sacrifice to bring forgiveness." (Isaiah 53:10a, 11b). Because he identifies with humanity at large (Mark 1:9, 12-13), his words of forgiveness on the cross (Luke 23:34) have a universal significance. Through enduring the mockery and blows of his torturers, without retribution (Isaiah 53:7; Mark 14:61a; 15:16-19), and by forgiving those who killed him - everyone (Luke 23:34), he leaves the nations "speechless with amazement" (52:15; see Mark 15:39). Thus, through turning the other cheek to violence (Isaiah 53:7) and then forgiving his torturers, he gathers all the lost sheep together (Isaiah 53:6a) - enemies turned into friends - into his new spiritual family, in which they can participate in his own sacrificial service and obedience to God. (Mark 3:33-34). Because he identified with everyone, the whole of humanity can thus share in his vindication and glory, as their salvation. (Isaiah 53:11a, 12a).

Isaiah's servant songs are a revelation of the meaning of life. God calls all of us to be his servants. (Genesis 1:27-28; 2:15; Psalm 8:6-8). He wants us to respond to people's cries for liberation, and to the cry of the suffering earth itself. (Exodus 3:7, 9; see Isaiah 24:4-5). To the extent that we become less self-centred and orient our lives in service towards other people, to the earth and all its creatures, all the more will our lives have meaning and purpose. This can involve suffering service, because it can mean giving up many of our self-indulgent ways and following Jesus on the path taken by him, a path leading to the glory of eternal life, as our destiny. (See Mark 10:17-21; Matthew 24:34-35). This gives our lives meaning and purpose. It gives us hope as we make our earthly journey. We live in a story that is going somewhere wonderful. In speaking of his own sufferings (Matthew 16:24-25; Mark 8:35), Jesus reiterates the paradox of Isaiah 53: victory comes through defeat, exaltation through humiliation. Life comes from death.

## God's Reconciliation with Israel

The fourth Servant Song leads to a triumphant conclusion in 53:12. But the real triumph comes in the next two chapters, in which Isaiah sees the work of the suffering servant bearing fruit, in the forgiveness of Israel' sins and her reconciliation with God. Despite her blindness and deafness, Zion (Jerusalem), the childless woman is reconciled with God.

> Jerusalem, you have been like a childless woman, but now you can sing and shout for joy. Now you will have more children than a woman whose husband never left her! You will forget your unfaithfulness as a young wife... Your Creator will be a husband to you – the Lord Almighty is his name. The holy God of Israel will save you – he is the ruler of the world. (Isaiah 54:1-5).

The Lord says, 'Israel, you are like a young wife, deserted by her husband and deeply distressed. But the Lord calls you back to him and says, 'I turned away angry for one brief moment, but I will show you my love for ever ... The mountains and hills may crumble, but my love for you will never end.' (54:6-8, 10). And Jerusalem, the suffering, helpless city, with no one to comfort her, will be rebuilt - its "foundations with precious stones, its towers with rubies, its gates with stones that glow like fire, and its walls with jewels."

(54:11-12). The precious stones signify the city's permanence. But its real treasure will be the justice and righteousness of its citizens. The Lord says, 'Justice and right will make you strong. You will be safe from oppression and terror.' (54:14).

Jesus sees himself as the faithful bridegroom, feasting with his bride, his home-from-exile people (Mark 2:19), with the blessing of innumerable descendants in faith (Isaiah 54:1) flowing from him. (Matthew 9:15, 22:1-2). As "the ruler of the world" (54:5), the Creator God brings salvation to all nations, a work that was brought to completion by Jesus, thus fulfilling God's promises of blessing to Abraham.

In Isaiah 55, the Lord promises to extend his loving sovereignty to anyone anywhere who comes hungry and thirsty for the food and drink that only God can give. (55:1-2). In inviting anyone to come to him, God is once again, reminding Israel of its role as a light to the nations. God wants the whole of humanity to join him in a union in which his will is done on earth as it is in heaven – a new and lasting covenant, finally sealed by the blood of Jesus. (Mark 14:24). That is what will satisfy everyone's hunger and thirst for meaningful life and happiness.

> The Lord says,
> 'Come, everyone who is thirsty – here is water!...
> Listen to me and do what I say,
> and you will enjoy the best food of all.
> Listen now, my people, and come to me;
> come to me, and you will have life!
> I will make a lasting covenant with you
> and give you the blessings I promised to David...
> Now you will summon foreign nations;
> at one time they did not know you,
> but now they will come running to join you.' (Isaiah 55:1-3, 5).

## New Creation

> You will leave Babylon with joy;
> you will be led out of the city in peace.
> The mountains and hills will burst into singing,
> and the trees will shout for joy.
> Cypress trees will grow where now there were briars;
> myrtle trees will come up in place of thorns.
> This will be a sign that will last for ever,
> a reminder of what I, the Lord, have done. (Isaiah 55:12-13).

God leading his people out of Babylon is the first step of their journey towards the new, transformed Jerusalem, the city now rescued by God. (See Isaiah 52:8-10). The joy and happiness there signify that the people have reached their hoped-for destiny. (See Isaiah 33:20-22). This foreshadows the new Jerusalem in Revelation 21, God's definitive creation at the end of time, in which "God will make his home with human beings," as their ultimate destiny. "God will wipe away all tears from their eyes. There will be no more death, no more grief or crying or pain." (See Revelation 21:1-4). After the disobedience of Adam and Eve, God's good creation became corrupted with metaphorical "weeds and thorns" - life East of Eden. (Genesis 3:18). Human beings lose their fruitfulness once they separate themselves from God and go into hiding. (Genesis 3:8). The sprouting of the fruitful cypress and myrtle in the above passage is symbolic of the fruitful lives of human beings when they remain obedient to God. The sudden emergence of these trees from the earth is symbolic of future resurrection ("a sign that will last for ever"). This new, redeemed life is a reversal of the fruitless "weeds and thorns" of Genesis.

The obedience of Jesus (God's perfect servant) restores creation to its fruitful abundance, as in the Garden of Eden before the original act of disobedience. The risen life of Jesus is the abundant fruit he shares with all of us – into eternal life.

The hope of new creation in the foregoing passage recalls the opening of the prophecy of Second Isaiah in 40:3-5 and concludes his prophecy in 55:13.

# CHAPTER 9

# THIRD ISAIAH

(Chaps. 56-66)

The followers of Second Isaiah responded to their leader's call to return to Judah and rebuild the new Zion. (Isaiah 49:8-26; 51:1–52:12; 54:1-17; see Ezra 2:36-54; 3:2). Many of the exiles never returned to Jerusalem. Despite Second Isaiah's songs of gushing water and a desert bursting with life, the thought of a journey of 500 miles on foot, mostly through semi-desert, must have been daunting. Groups only arrived back in stages.

After the return to Jerusalem, salvation seemed as far away as ever, but the longing for better times persisted. The hope for a future Messiah remained alive, if only in the hearts of a small number of people – the remnant. (See Isaiah 11:1-4). Ezekiel, Second and Third Isaiah looked beyond the restoration of Jerusalem, (which proved to be a disappointment), to a time when God would restore his people in mysterious ways to a perfect peace and justice. (Isaiah 2:2-4). Thus, was born the longing for a future Messiah, an "anointed king."

Probably a disciple of Second Isaiah, Third Isaiah was the prophet who ministered to the returnees in Jerusalem after the end of the exile. He laboured there during the rebuilding of the temple. Third Isaiah was a contemporary of the minor prophets Haggai and Zechariah. (See Haggai chaps. 1-2; Zechariah chaps. 1-4, 9-10; Ezra chaps. 7-10; 1 Chronicles 13-16).

There are three main themes in Third Isaiah: (1) the renewal of Jerusalem which can only take place through repentance (56:1–59:21); (2) the glory of the Lord which will overshadow the people and be the source of their new life (60:1–62:12); and (3) the Lord's re-creation of Judah through judgement and promise. (63:1–66:24).

The Creator God who defeated the forces of chaos (Genesis 1:2), now in a new creation, has led the exiles back to Jerusalem, but it turned out to be a disappointment. The returnees were dogged with drought, crop failure and harassment by people from northern Israel. The rebuilt temple was only a shadow of that built by Solomon. The people of Judea had to live with the thought that the golden era of David and Solomon would never return. They would never again exercise sovereignty over their own land. The glorious restoration that would draw the nations to Zion (Jerusalem) gives way to a more realistic picture in this part of the Book of Isaiah.

The larger towns of Judah had been destroyed by the Babylonians. The population of Jerusalem was less than in pre-exilic times. Aramaic (a language similar to Hebrew) became the official language of the Persian Empire, and it would soon be the common language of Palestine itself (newly named Israel). (Ezra 4:7). Aramaic was the language spoken by Jesus. (Aram was a region to the north of Israel, also known as Syria).[110]

## The Temple and Sabbath Observance

One of the priorities after the return was for the rebuilding of the temple, a work which took twenty-three years to complete. Concern for the temple and the Sabbath (56:2-6; 58:13-14) and for devotional practices such as prayer (56:7) and fasting (58:1-12) distinguishes Third Isaiah from Isaiah 40-55. Sabbath observance would give the Jewish community an identity in their new situation after their return from Babylon. God has a vision of Israel summoning foreign nations to join its people in prayer. (Isaiah 55:5-6). On the fulfilment of certain conditions, foreigners could now become part of the Jewish community. God not only brings the exiles back to Jerusalem but also calls the nations to become part of God's people.

> The Lord says to those foreigners who become part of his people, who love him and serve him, who observe the Sabbath and faithfully keep his covenant: 'I will bring you to Zion, my sacred hill, give you joy in my house of prayer, and accept the sacrifices you offer on my altar. My temple will be called a house of prayer for the people of all nations. (Isaiah 56:6-8; see Mark 11:17).

Mention of righteous foreigners entering the temple provides the overarching theme at the beginning (56:1-7) and the end (66:19-23) of Third Isaiah. When Jesus entered the temple after arriving in Jerusalem, he quoted Isaiah 56:7b above, with the implication that this prophecy remained unfulfilled in Israel. (See Mark 11:15-17).

Third Isaiah tells the people that Sabbath observance is meaningless without the practice of justice. Once again, the clear message from the prophets is that a temple without fidelity of heart would have no power to bring God's blessing on Israel or the world. What God really wants is for his Spirit to live and reign in human hearts for their flourishing.

The word "Zion" features a lot in the Book of Isaiah. Mount Zion was the name given to one of the hills within the city walls of Jerusalem. The Canaanites had a fortress there for centuries. As the site of King Solomon's temple, Zion was regarded as a holy hill - the place where God would speak his words of salvation to the nations. Zion is often used figuratively to refer both to the temple and city. (2 Kings 19:31; Psalm 51:18, Psalm 87; Matthew 21:5). The prophets use Zion as a metaphor for God's salvation. (Isaiah 28:16-17; Psalm 20:1-2; 53:5; Micah 4:2). The Saviour (Messiah) would come from Zion and save his people from their sins. (Isaiah 59:20; Romans 11:26). New Testament writers use Zion as a symbol for universal salvation. They see it as the heavenly Jerusalem coming down to unite heaven and earth in a new creation at the end of time. (Revelation 3:12, 21:1-4).

---

[110] *World's Bible Dictionary*, p. 25.

For Second Isaiah, Zion is the climax of a great journey. Zion is an image of human beings reaching their destiny – their deepest hopes being fulfilled. The prophecy of Third Isaiah is a mixture of hope and despair, and Zion is the starting point all over again. Where Isaiah 40-55 sees Israel's sins forgiven, his successor condemns Israel once again because of its unfaithfulness to God.

## Judgement on Idolatry and Infidelity

The reality of the return was stark. The leaders of the restored community were supposed to be an example to the people. The prophet condemns them as blind. "They are like greedy dogs who never get enough. They each do as they please and seek their own advantage." (Isaiah 56:10-12). A new elite grew up who cared little for the poor. They were using their position to enrich themselves at the expense of the greater population. Most people were not listening to the prophet. Back in Jerusalem the old social divisions re-emerged, and once again, religious observance was insincere because it was not founded on the practice of justice.

Chapters 57-59 express pessimism and disappointment, and single out only the righteous few who have been faithful. The leaders only care about their own self-aggrandisement. No one pays attention to the death of just people. (57:1).

> Come here and be judged you sinners! You are no better than sorcerers, adulterers and prostitutes. Who are you making fun of? Who are you jeering at? You worship the fertility gods by having sex under those sacred trees of yours. You offer your children as sacrifices in the rocky caves near the bed of a stream. You take smooth stones from them and worship them as gods. You pour out wine as offerings to them and bring them grain offerings. Do you think I am pleased with all this? You go to the high mountains to offer sacrifices and have sex. You set up your obscene idols inside your front doors. You forsake me and take off your clothes and climb into your large beds with your lovers, whom you pay to sleep with you. And there you satisfy your lust. You put on your perfumes and ointments and go to the god Molech. (Isaiah 57:3-9a; see 2 Kings 23:10; Jeremiah 32:35).

The prophet associates an unjust social system with the worship of pagan gods. Bad leadership opens the door to recurring idolatry. In the above passage, the prophet condemns idolatry in all its guises, especially the practice of child sacrifice, and the worship of fertility gods which involved having sex under sacred trees. (57:5, 9). Despite all that had been said and had happened, the worship of the fertility god, Baal was still alive in Jerusalem.

## Fasting

Then the people resort to fasting in an effort to move God to bring about a quick renewal. The prophet reminds them that fasting is useless if at the same time, there is no willingness to create a just society. What God wants is that Judah "fast from injustice." The prophet tells them that fasting would not elicit God's mercy, nor hasten the day of complete renewal. The performance of ritual is no substitute for serving one's neighbour.

Perhaps Third Isaiah found it necessary to oppose the one-sided value given to temple ritual by prophets such as Haggai and Zechariah. (See Zechariah 8:18). God was more interested in inner faithfulness than in external rites and practices such as fasting. Only when Judah becomes a compassionate society, will the restoration proceed. Until then, the people can expect nothing but divine judgement on an unjust and uncaring society.

The evangelist Matthew 25:31-46 echoes the thoughts of Third Isaiah in the following passage.

> The people ask the Lord,
> 'Why have we fasted if you do not see,
> why mortify ourselves if you never notice?'
> The Lord says,
> 'Look, you seek your own pleasure on your fast-days
> and you exploit all your workmen;
> look, the only purpose of your fasting
> is to quarrel and squabble
> and strike viciously with your fist.
> Fasting like yours, today,
> will never make your voice heard on high.
> Is that the sort of fast that pleases me,
> a day when a person inflicts pain on himself?
> Hanging your head like a reed,
> spreading out sackcloth and ashes?
> Is not this the sort of fast that pleases me:
> to break unjust fetters,
> to undo the thongs of the yoke,
> to let the oppressed go free?
> Is it not sharing your food with the hungry
> and sheltering the homeless poor;
> and not to turn away from your own kin?
> Then your light will blaze out like the dawn
> and your wound will be quickly healed over...
> Saving justice will go ahead of you
> and the Lord's glory come behind you.' (Isaiah 58:3-8, NJB).

The Lord wants to save his people, but their evil deeds have made a gulf between him and them. Public displays of fasting do not impress the Lord, while, at the same time people exploit and oppress their workers and strike them with their "fists." (Verse 3 above). Their failure to create a just society at home means that they could not be a light to the other nations. (58:3-4; 59:4-8, 15-16). "The Lord will wear justice like a coat of armour and saving power like a helmet." (59:17). But his people will not imitate his gratuity. They will not "undo the thongs of the yoke (a metaphor for oppression) and let the oppressed go free." (Verse 6).

Clearly, there were divisions within the community between workers and their oppressive masters. What was disappointing was the lack of response to God's saving word. Because God always acts for the sake of the oppressed, his judgement would fall once again on Jerusalem. The people hoped for the light of salvation, but their deeds only created darkness. Their salvation was far away. (59:11). It's as if they were still not home from exile.

> No, the arm of the Lord is not too short to save,
> nor his ear too dull to hear,
> but your guilty deeds have made a gulf
> between you and your God.
> Your sins have made him hide his face
> so as not to hear you,
> since your hands are stained with blood
> and your fingers with guilt;
> your lips utter lies,
> your tongues murmur wickedness.
> Thus, fair judgement is remote from us
> nor can uprightness overtake us.
> We looked for light and all is darkness,
> for brightness, and we walk in gloom.
> Like the blind, we feel our way along walls,
> we grope our way like people without eyes.
> We stumble as though noon were twilight,
> among the robust we are like the dead.
> We growl, all of us like bears,
> like doves we make no sound but moaning,
> waiting for the fair judgement
> that never comes,
> for salvation, but that is far away. (59:1-4, 9-11, NJB).

It is clear from chapters 58-59 that the prophet's vision has yet to become a reality. Critical to his vision is his expectation that the people of Jerusalem will promote justice and mercy. Salvation is delayed because of wickedness. "Violence fills their hands. Their feet run to do evil; they are quick to shed innocent blood." (59:6-7). The first step in reversing this process is the community's confession of sin. People have to take responsibility for their sins of creating a society that is self-destructive, because of its internal divisions. There is something satanic about such a society. (See Mark 3:23-25). Some people do confess their sins: "Lord, our crimes against you are many. Our sins accuse us... We have oppressed others and turned away from you. Our thoughts are false; our words are lies. Justice has been driven away, and right cannot come near. Truth stumbles in the public square, and honesty finds no place there." (59:12-15).

The Lord tells his people that he will come to Jerusalem and save all those who turn away from their sins. He will make a new covenant with them and give them his power and his teachings, to be theirs for ever. He then calls for their obedience to this new covenant. (See 59:20-21).

## The Glory of the New Jerusalem (60:1–62:12)

> Arise Jerusalem and shine like the sun;
> the glory of the Lord is shining on you!
> Other nations will be covered in darkness.
> But on you the light of the Lord will shine!
> The brightness of his presence will be with you.
> Nations will be drawn to your light,
> and kings to the dawning of your new day...
> Foreigners will rebuild your walls
> and their kings will serve you...
> The descendants of those who oppressed you
> will come and bow low to show their respect.
> All those who once despised you
> will worship at your feet.
> They will call you 'The City of the Lord,
> Zion, the city of Israel's Holy God...'
> No longer will the sun be your light by day,
> or the moon be your light by night;
> the light of my glory will shine on you.
> Your days of grief will come to an end.
> I, the Lord, will be your eternal light,
> more lasting than the sun or moon.
> Your people will all do what is right,
> and possess the land forever.
> I planted them, I made them
> to reveal my greatness to all...
> When the right time comes,
> I will make this happen quickly.
> I am the Lord God. (Isaiah 60:1-3, 10a, 14, 19-22).

In chapter 60, the Lord reminds the people of who they can be. He calls them to arise and shine like the sun. With the Lord empowering them, they can become a blazing light in a world of darkness. But is it too much to expect that the nations will be drawn to their light? It must have been very difficult to convince this small band of returnees, opposed by locals (book of Ezra 4:4-5) and struggling to survive, that they reflected the glory of God. (60:2). Did they laugh at the prediction that the nations would be drawn to their light, and "kings to the dawning of their new day?" (60:3). The Lord says, 'My Temple will be called a house of prayer for the people of all nations.' (56:7b; see Mark 11:17). But how can the Lord "bring foreigners to his sacred hill and give them joy in his "house of prayer" (56:7a) while the leaders of the people are "blind" to their sins (56:10). However, the Lord promises to save all of those who turn from their sins and obey him through a renewal of the covenant. (59:20-21).

"The right time" (60:22b) comes with Jesus. It is Jesus who truly reflects the light and glory of God into the world. People everywhere are drawn to him, who is the source of new light and life. It is he who brings all "days of grief" to an end for human beings. (60:20; see Revelation 1:4).

## The Prophet is Called to Mission

In the following passage, Third Isaiah experiences his call to be a prophet and is given a commission in line with that of the servant songs. Having been filled with God's Spirit, he describes his mission in terms of bringing good news to the poor, justice to the oppressed and comfort to those who mourn - in language similar to Isaiah 42:1-4, 49:1-6, and 50:1-11.

> The Sovereign God has filled me with his Spirit.
> He has chosen me and sent me
> to bring good news to the poor,
> to heal the broken-hearted,
> to announce release of captives
> and freedom for those in prison...
> He has sent me to comfort all who mourn,
> to give to those who mourn in Zion
> joy and gladness instead of grief,
> a song of praise instead of sorrow.
> They will be like trees
> that the Lord himself has planted.
> They will all do what is right,
> And God will be praised for what he has done. (Isaiah 61:1-3).

Through his proclamation of the word of God, the prophet himself has a central role in the working out of God's plan. Filled with God's Spirit, he is given a missionary role in the transformation of Judah. Justice for the poor is a major Isaianic theme. Judah was taken into exile because of the injustice of its social and economic system. The "captives" (61:1) are those who are still in exile in Babylon, and those back in Jerusalem who are still far from God. The "broken hearted" are the victims of the corrupt leadership whom the prophet condemned in 56:9-12 and 58:1-9. God will bring good news to the poor and heal the broken-hearted, thus creating a just Judahite social system. This will not be a human achievement, but the work of God's Spirit. Salvation and restoration are the work of God – with the cooperation of human beings.

The above prophecy of 61:1-3 was fulfilled in Jesus, as the one who will definitively bring good news to the poor, heal the broken hearted, comfort the mourners and release people from the prisons of blindness to their sins. (See Luke 4:16-19). Jesus was empowered for this work of salvation by the Spirit of God living in him and confirming him as God's beloved, and obedient Servant and Son. (Mark 1:10-11; see Matthew 5:3-4, 7, 9, 21-24, 43-47).

## The People's Prayers and God's Response

The final chapters of Isaiah have much to teach us about our approach to God in prayer, and indeed, could be used as prayers. In times of darkness, we should challenge God in our prayers and call out, "Why, why, where are you?" God was always been ready to act, but the people ignored him and turned to their old self-indulgent ways. (65:1-16; see Genesis 3:8).

It would seem that the prophet still didn't give up hope in a restored Jerusalem becoming a reality in his own day. In 63:7-64:11, he has a lament, a prayer for mercy and for the restoration of Jerusalem. He tries to get God to act by reminding him of his great deeds in the past and by describing the difficulties experienced by Zion:

> The people asked, 'Where now is the Lord who saved the leaders of his people from the sea (Exodus)? Where is the Lord who gave his Spirit to Moses? Where is the Lord who by his power, did great things through Moses, dividing the sea and leading his people through the deep waters to win everlasting fame for himself? Led by the Lord, they were as surefooted as wild horses, and never stumbled.' (63:11-13).

The prophet understands salvation in terms of an intimate relationship and personal union with God, expressed in three metaphors from family life: as a mother to her nursing infant (66:12-13), as a bridegroom to his bride (62:5; 64:4-5) and in the following passage, as a father to his child. In his pleading on behalf of the people, Isaiah does not see God as a judge, but as a merciful father:

> 'Lord, look upon us from heaven where you live in your holiness and glory. Where is your concern for us? Where is your power? Where is your love and compassion? Do not ignore us. You Lord are our Father, the one who has always rescued us. Why do you let us stray from your ways? Why do you make us so stubborn that we turn away from you? Come back for the sake of those who serve you, for the sake of the people who have always been yours.' (63:15-17).

But Jerusalem continues to experience God as absent because of the people's infidelity, sinfulness and lack of prayerfulness. (64:6-7). In the failure of the restoration, the prophet does not find fault with God, but with Judah.

In the passage below, Third Isaiah continues his prayer on Judah's behalf. He reminds the people that they will experience God's presence and power, as their ancestors did in past times, only because in those far off times they continued to hope in him (64:4), and found joy in doing what is right (64:5). The prophet reminds God that his holy people were driven out by their enemies, who trampled down his sanctuary. God treats his people as though they had never been his own. (63:18-19). The prophet continues:

> 'Why don't you tear the sky apart and come down? The mountains would see you and shake with fear. They would tremble like water boiling over a hot fire. Come and reveal your power to your enemies and make the nations tremble at your presence. There was a time when you came and did terrifying things that we did not expect; the mountains saw you and shook with fear. No one has ever seen or heard a God like you, who does such deeds for those who hope in him. You welcome those who find joy in doing what is right, those who remember how you want them to live... Because of our sins, we are like leaves that wither and are blown away in the wind. No one turns to you in prayer; no one goes to you for help. You have hidden yourself from us and have abandoned us because of our sins. But you are our Father, Lord. We are like clay, and you are the potter. You created us, so do not be angry with us or hold our sins against us forever. We are your people; be merciful to us. Your sacred cities are like a desert, Jerusalem is a deserted ruin, and your Temple has been destroyed by fire... All the places we loved are in ruins. Lord, are you unmoved by all of this? Are you going to make us suffer more than we can endure?' (Isaiah 64:5a, 6b-12).

Those verses are an expression of the ever-present tension between divine and human action. Why doesn't God intervene dramatically in our lives to change numb hearts and disastrous situations? Can we expect him to intervene, while at the same time we don't cooperate with him in the furtherance of his purposes – even as we continue on the path of self-destruction?

The tearing of the sky apart in order to bring God's salvation down to earth was fulfilled in Jesus, who is the definitive bridge between heaven and earth. (See Mark 1:10-11; 15:38).

God responds to the preceding prayer. The Lord says, 'I was ready for them to find me, but they did not even try. I have always been ready to welcome my people, who stubbornly do what is wrong and go their own way.' (65:2-6). The Lord says, 'No one destroys good grapes. Neither will I destroy all my people–I will save those who serve me.' (65:8). But it will be different for those who "forsake God and worship the gods of luck and fate" – those who did not answer when the Lord called or listened when he spoke. 'You chose to disobey me and do evil.' (65:11-12). The former people 'will sing for joy,' but the latter 'will cry with a broken heart.' (65:14). God thus responds through the prophet with a word of judgement - seemingly coming with a tone of finality-for all people, the good and the bad. Here is a message of salvation for those who are faithful to the Lord, and despair for those who forsake him. There are two ways to go: one leads to life and the other to death. (65:15; see Deuteronomy 30:15-16).

# The New Jerusalem: God's New Creation

Despite the disillusionment with the return to Jerusalem, Third Isaiah does not lose hope in the Lord. He tries to comfort the small community who still held on to the faith, by telling them about the glorious future the Lord has in store for Jerusalem (60:1-3; 62:1-9). God's glory will become manifest in the restoration of Judah. Third Isaiah's image of light (God) overcoming darkness represents the climax of a central theme in the Book of Isaiah. (See Isaiah 2:5; 9:1; 42:6; 49:6; 60:1, 3, 20).

Third Isaiah sees God doing nothing less than foreshadowing a new creation to enable a new life of joy and gladness to overtake the old life of suffering and death. However, because of the recurrence of the divisions that the prophet believes led to the fall of Jerusalem in the first place, his vision for a just society is a long way from being realized, but he still hopes for it. Because of his deep insight into the nature of God as just, merciful and compassionate, he may be able to trust and hope in God's ultimate triumph over the forces of evil. But he does not know when this might happen.

The prophet then returns to a familiar Isaianic theme: the pilgrimage of the nations to Jerusalem. (66:18-23; see 60:3). The Lord says, 'I am coming to gather every nation and every language. They will come to witness my glory.' (66:18). Third Isaiah uses the image of a new Jerusalem as an expression of the triumph of God's new creation. Salvation will come about through God's transformation of Jerusalem, making it a shining new city. (60:1). As Jerusalem begins to reflect the Lord's glory, it will gain the attention of the nations, who will come to it in search of salvation for themselves. (62:1-5; 66:10-14, see Genesis 12:3). The prophet hopes that God will restore Jerusalem to its former glory – a restoration that will include all humanity, except those who have rebelled. (66:3-4).

Third Isaiah's utopian picture of a New Jerusalem (60:1-7), a place to which people from all over the world will stream in order to worship God, and populated by people who practice justice and mercy, sounds like the hopeful words of Second Isaiah. God says that he will send some of the faithful to the "distant lands who have not heard of my fame or seen my greatness or power... Among these nations, they will proclaim my greatness." (66:19). This represents God's universal offer of salvation. However, there was a growing realization that the perfectly just society might be only something to hope for, but never to be realized in this world. Would there need to be a completely new creation, a whole new world for this to take place?

The prophet finally concludes that the present world would not be the place of the ultimate triumph of God's justice. The new Jerusalem is not the city in which he lives. The triumph will come in the new world that God will bring into existence.

> The Lord says, 'I am making a new earth and new heavens. The events of the past will be completely forgotten. Be glad and rejoice for ever in what I create. The new Jerusalem I make will be full of joy, and her people will be happy. There will be no more weeping there, no calling for help. Babies will no longer die in infancy, and all people will live out their life-span... Wolves and lambs will eat together; lions will eat straw as cattle do, and snakes will no longer be dangerous.

On Zion, my sacred hill, there will be nothing harmful or evil.'
(Isaiah 65:17-20, 25).

Third Isaiah is speaking here of a new creation which will enable the new life of Joy and gladness to overtake the old life of suffering and sorrow. Second Isaiah's understanding of God as both Creator and Redeemer provides the background for Third Isaiah's announcement that the Lord is producing "new heavens and a new earth." (65:17; 66:22; see 40:26; 43:1, 7; 45:8). The renewal of Jerusalem that began with the redemption from the Babylonian exile, now becomes a sign pointing to a future new creation. (65:17; 66:22; see 43:18-19). Then Jerusalem is turned into a metaphor for the whole cosmos – a new heaven and renewed earth. Isaiah 65:25 envisions the kind of world described in the lyric poem in Isaiah 11:6-9–a utopia arising out of the disappointment experienced by the people of Jerusalem at difficult periods of their lives. New Testament texts such as 2 Peter 3:10-13 reinterpret the prophet's vision of the "new heavens and a new earth" as in the above passage. (see Revelation 21:4).

The word "Jerusalem" means 'city of peace.' But was it ever a city of peace? – "wolves and lambs eating together." (65:25). In the Israelite kingdom, Jerusalem was founded as a city of peace, divinely established, but when it turned its back on God and relied on human power and strength (Genesis 11:1-9), it only brought destruction and death down upon itself. Third Isaiah is aware of the failures of Jerusalem, but he still sees the city as a symbol of hope towards which human beings are but blindly stumbling. This stumbling is in evidence in the first eleven chapters of Genesis, where there are a number of failed human attempts to become like God, to conquer heaven, in a kind of building without God, human beings going their own way, like scattered sheep. (Isaiah 53:6). Humanity is in turmoil, enmity and antagonism leading to murder (Genesis 4:8). Human beings are in bondage to pride and self-exaltation. (Genesis 11:1-9). Every generation tries to create paradise on its own terms, but it is only by human beings trusting in God and discharging their God-given task of stewardship that any progress can be made at all. (Psalm 8:6-8).

## Fulfilment of the New Jerusalem

In the light of the persistent chaos all around him, Third Isaiah seems to have finally realized that his utopian vision of a New Jerusalem shining like the sun could never become a reality in this world. It is only the Lord's eternal light that can banish darkness from the earth. It cannot be the unaided work of human beings. Often when humans try to create light on their own terms, they only bring darkness black as death into the world. (See Jeremiah 13:15-16). We constantly hope for the best. We want things to be put right, but we are soon confronted with the limitations of our power to so act. Because of human limitation and the tendency towards evil, human beings on their own cannot achieve perfection; they cannot find fulfilment through their own efforts. This does not mean that Third Isaiah fell into despair. Above all else, the prophets were people of undying hope– a hope which they believed God alone can, and would eventually fulfil.

We must bear in mind that the Jewish people at this time had no clear idea about life after death. But that being said, was the prophet looking ahead to the possibility of life beyond this world in which his mighty dream would finally be realized? Because God was revealed to the prophets as Creator of the universe, a God of power, justice and mercy, they may have finally come to the insight that his purpose for a perfect world has to be realized, and if not in the here-and-now, then why not beyond the boundaries of this world, and only through a decisive intervention in history by God himself. Surely - as the prophets believed - the Sovereign God, the Creator of the universe, will have the final word on history, the final word on human rebellion, evil and death. If the Creator God is sovereign, as the prophets claimed, it is reasonable to suppose that he should have the power, in his own time and way, to act in history and to deal decisively with evil.

In passages about the New Jerusalem and a new heaven and earth, Isaiah is giving voice to what we all experience as natural human longing and hungering for an end to the chaos of the dark raging ocean - for a new and perfect order of peace and harmony, an end to wars, an end to domination and exploitation, an end to mourning and weeping. And there would be something incomplete in the resolution of those things, without an end to death itself. Furthermore, if human longing for justice and mercy was to be frustrated, there would be no hope of vindication for the innocent who suffer injustice. Then the evildoers and destroyers would escape judgement. Where would that leave the notion of a just and merciful God? In other words, the scales of justice would never be balanced. If the hungering placed in the human heart by God for ultimate fulfilment were to be frustrated, then life would be absurd. And instead of God having the final word on history, human beings would be left hungering for the good, the true and the beautiful, while the reign of Satan would go on for ever, as the supreme power in the universe. And so to the New Testament! It is to feed and fully satisfy the deepest desires of the human heart that Jesus came to live among us. (John 6:32-40).

Isaiah's vision of the new Jerusalem is fulfilled in the Book of Revelation, in God's end-of-time new creation, the perfect world in which God and human beings are joined together in peace and harmony. Here Jerusalem re-appears, but this time, not as a city built on a hilltop by human hands, but coming down from heaven as a gift from God. And unlike the old Jerusalem, which was but a pale reflection of God, it will be "shining with the glory of the Lord." (Revelation 21:2, 10-11). Evil, including death itself, will be defeated and Christ will reign for ever.

> Then the seventh angel blew his trumpet, and there were loud voices in heaven, calling out, 'The power to rule over the world now belongs to our God and his Messiah, and he will rule for ever and ever!' (Revelation 11:15).

With the reign of God definitively established, everything is at last put right, justice finally established. God is victorious over all the forces of evil. "There will be no more death, no more grief or crying or pain." (Revelation 21:3-4).

The first two verses of the passage below are full of hope for God's eventual new world in which God and human beings will live in perfect harmony, which was God's purpose in creating humanity in the beginning. But the Book of Isaiah ends with as negative a statement of human rebellion and disobedience of God, as is found in the Bible. (66:24).

> For as the new heavens and the new earth I am making will endure before me,
>> declares the Lord, so will your race and your name endure.
>>> From New Moon to New Moon,
>>> From Sabbath to Sabbath,
>>> All humanity will come and bow
>>> In my presence, the Lord God says.
>>> And on their way out they will see
>>> the corpses of those
>>> who rebelled against me;
>>> for their worms will never die
>>> nor their fires be put out,
>>> and they will be held in horror
>>> by all humanity.
>>> (Isaiah 66:22-24, NJB).

The Book of Isaiah ends with a familiar Isaianic theme: the pilgrimage of the nations to Jerusalem. In the above passage, there is a reference to "your race," meaning Israel. Since God's choice of Israel was not just for the sake of Israel, but with the expectation that Israel would be a light to the nations, we interpret this phrase as referring to the salvation of all humanity, except those who have rebelled. The word "endure" refers to salvation as complete and everlasting. New Moon was a Jewish monthly festival of hope, celebrated in the temple, during which mourning and fasting were not allowed. The reality of all of humanity bowing in God's presence (verse 23 above) indicates a perfect obedience to the will of God, which was fulfilled by Jesus as God's new human representative. (See Mark 14:36). This will be a completely new creation – a transformation of humanity. (See Revelation 21:1)

The words of judgement in 66:24, together with Isaiah 1:10-20, serve to frame the Book of Isaiah. But in Jewish tradition, a public reading of the Book of Isaiah always concludes with a repetition of the positive statement of verses 22-23, in order to leave the hearers with a word of hope and promise, rather than judgement.

## Apocalyptic Replacing Prophecy

Prophecy came to an end soon after the time of Third Isaiah. It was replaced by apocalyptic literature, which represents a belief that God will intervene in history and create a radically new order, replacing the old one. The conclusion of the Book of Isaiah is a continuation of the apocalyptic passages which later editors inserted into the book in response to the fall of Jerusalem. (See Isaiah 24:1–27:13). These passages illustrate that in the end of time, God will replace the old order, dominated by human power (rule of the nations) with a new order of divine life symbolized by the holy mountain of Jerusalem–God reconstructing the city where the humble will be victorious and exalted. (Isaiah

65:17-25; see 25:1-5; 26:1-6, 19). Third Isaiah picks up on the vision of all nations coming to the heavenly banquet on God's holy mountain. (66:18-21; see 25:6-9).

## God Dealing Decisively with Human Rebellion

In the beginning, in the image of the Garden of Eden, God appointed human beings to a mission of caring for the earth and its creatures, including its people. (Genesis 2:8-9, 1:28, NJB). Through their task of caring, God wanted to establish a relationship of love with his people. But the human story is otherwise. Instead of obeying his God-given task of caring for God's world, Adam (representing all of humanity), chooses the path of disobedience (Genesis 2:17; 3:6) and plucks the forbidden fruit of autonomy, leading to greed and exploitation, which, as we see today, is turning God's good earth into a new desert of "weeds and thorns" (Genesis 3:17), threatening the life of all God's creatures, and human life itself, with untimely death. (Genesis 2:17b).

Adam and Eve have two sons, named Cain and Abel (also archetypes of humanity). Instead of fulfilling his God-given mission of care, consumed with enmity and jealousy, Cain kills his brother, murder being the ultimate rejection of caring and brotherhood. (Genesis 4:8). Cain (humanity) then becomes exiled in a land called "Wandering" – a prodigal son, alone in a wilderness, without guide or direction, homeless and fearful of death. (Genesis 4:12, 14, 16, see verse 24). The lone wanderer is a recurring theme in the Bible. It signifies exile, estrangement and separation from one another and from God - scattered sheep without a shepherd – the world of individualism. (Ezekiel 34:5-6; Mark 6:34; 8:2-3). Following a downward spiral into evil, God seeks a new beginning with the character Noah. After evil is washed away in a great flood, God appoints Noah and his sons to a new mission of creating and caring. (Genesis 9:1-2). but this soon ends in drunken chaos and immorality. (Genesis 9:20-23). All the while, God is calling out to his human creatures, 'Where are you?' (Genesis 3:8-9; see Luke 15:20). This is the human condition, one of estrangement, loss and wandering–individuals going their own autonomous way, rebelliously following their own will, rather than in obedience to God. (Isaiah 53:6). Despite their wandering, God still wants an intimate relationship with his human creatures, a love relationship that will last for ever: 'I will never forget you, my people; I have carved your name on the palms of my hands'. (Isaiah 49:16). What then will God do about wandering and scattered humanity? (Genesis 11:1-8).

God next calls one man, Abraham (a new human archetype), whom he blesses and to whom he gives a mission of bearing his blessing to the world, all because of Abraham's trust and obedience to the Creator. The word "blessing" may be interpreted as a universal brotherhood, with the aim of reversing Cain's rejection of brotherhood. (Genesis 12:1-3; 22:18). But eventually the family of Abraham breaks up in enmity, jealousy, hatred and betrayal - leading to death-like exile in Egypt. (Genesis 37:12-36).

After every period of wandering, God is left picking up the pieces and starting all over again. (Exodus 3:9-10). He next forms one nation (Israel) whose people are tasked with the creation of brotherhood by practicing justice and mercy in their society, so that they may thus become shining lights to the wider world, drawing the other nations to the Creator God - a blessing promised to Abraham and his descendants. (Genesis 22:18).

Through the sovereignty he shares with the leaders of this nation (the kings of Israel and Judah), God does everything he can to guide it on the path of righteousness. But the leaders he puts in charge of his people choose the way of disobedience (again as in Adam) because of their failure to discharge their God-given mission of responsible stewardship. (Genesis 1:28; 2:15). The leaders prove to be bad shepherds, leading the people astray, greedily feeding themselves rather than their flock (Ezekiel 34:1-6, 10; Isaiah 1:22-23), and thus failing in their mission to be a light to the nations. (Genesis 12:1-3; Exodus 9:14.16; Isaiah 49:6).

God then calls insightful individuals known as prophets who are filled with God's Spirit, giving them knowledge of God, in the sense of knowing God's will for the world. The prophets preach a God of justice and mercy, a God who wants these same qualities exemplified in his people. With this purpose in mind, God calls Israel to be his servant, with the task of spreading the light of his blessing into the world. But as in the Garden of Eden, Israel proves to be a disobedient servant, blind to its sins of injustice. (Amos 2:6-8; Isaiah 6:9; 42:18-20, 24b). God pleads with his people to repent of their sins and come back to him, as the only God who can save them (Isaiah 45:22), but they give their allegiance to the false gods of affluence, materialism, power and glory - gods who can never save them. (Isaiah 46:6-7). The prophets try to communicate the anguish of God to the numbness of humanity, but their message is met with deaf ears and hardened hearts, in other words, with disobedience, leading once again to wandering and exile, this time in Babylon (another untimely death).

As the Old Testament ends, we get an inkling of unfinished business – people still like Cain, lost in the "Land of Wandering"- of a story without a satisfactory or happy ending. Although once again back home after the Babylonian exile, the people still feel like captives in their own land. (See Isaiah 56:10-11; 57:3-5). They are still metaphorically in exile, because of their failure, once again, to create a just and merciful society. Abraham's God-given mission of blessing to the nations shows no sign of being fulfilled. However, the prophets entertain the hope that some time and somehow, the Creator and sovereign God will intervene in the world in order to deal decisively with the evil resulting from human disobedience. (Isaiah 57:18-19; 60:20-22; 66:22-23). If evil is to be finally confronted, the serpent's head crushed (Genesis 3:15) and the curse of the earth reversed (Genesis 3:18), who then will God call to be his new representative on earth, his perfect obedient servant, one who can reverse the disobedience of Adam and the murdering of Cain, in order to establish a universal family of brotherhood, as his final word on history? Eventually, as a response to human disobedience, God promises that he himself will assume the task of shepherding, the old shepherds having failed in their mission. (Ezekiel 34:1-2, 11-12). God also promises to take away Israel's stubborn heart of stone and give it a new obedient heart. (Ezekiel 11:19-20).

Israel's experience echoes our own human story. We live in our God-intended home – God's good earth, but clearly all is not well. We experience evil, suffering and death as reminders that we are exiles in our own homeland. Like the Israelites of old, we hunger and thirst for a promised land in which all will be well, where there will be no more sorrow or grief, every tear wiped away. (Revelation 21:3-4). We ourselves cannot reach this land of our dreams under our own steam. God sent Moses and the prophets to perform his rescue operations. Who will God send as our own rescuer and saviour?

For a definitive intervention of God into human affairs, and the good news of a happy ending to the human story, we next turn to the New Testament for an account of the life and work of Jesus of Nazareth. Jesus is the light of the world. (John 8:12). He is the new Jerusalem who "arises and shines like the sun, the glory of the Lord shining on him." (Isaiah 60:1; Mark 9:2-3). Jesus is God's suffering servant (Isaiah 53), a servant, who through his perfect obedience to God (Mark 14:36), undoes the disobedience of Adam. Jesus does for human beings what they themselves cannot do. All of the old servants and shepherds failed in their God-given task. (Ezekiel 34:1-2). Jesus is God's Good Shepherd (John 10:11), who comes into this world and goes out in search of the bruised and beaten, the lost and wandering sheep (humanity), and having found it, places it on his shoulders and definitively carries it home from exile. (See Luke 15:1-6). Filled with God's Spirit, Jesus is God's obedient Son (Mark 1:11), who through his obedience (Mark 14:36), and in solidarity with human beings (Mark 1:9-13), redeems wandering humanity from its disobedience (Isaiah 66:23) – and thereby, from death itself, as a happy ending to the human story. (See Isaiah 9:6). Our home from exile destiny will be in a completely new creation, a new heaven and a new earth, one that will endure for ever. (Revelation 21:1).

For as the new heavens and the new earth I am making will endure before me, declares
the Lord, so will your race and your name endure.
From New Moon to New Moon,
from Sabbath to Sabbath
all humanity will bow
in my presence, says the Lord God.
(Isaiah 66:22-23, NJB).

The above two verses are prophetic of the redemptive work of Jesus Christ, and in closing the Book of Isaiah, they set the scene for a journey through the Christian gospel.

## CHAPTER 10

# PROLOGUE TO MARK'S GOSPEL

## (1:1-13)

## Four Gospels

The first parts of the New Testament are the four gospels written in Greek by Matthew, Mark, Luke and John. Their authors are referred to as evangelists. The Greek word *evangelion* is the root of the English word 'evangelize,' which means to bring 'good news' or 'joyful tidings.' The old Anglo-Saxon word 'godspel' means glad tidings, deriving from God – 'good' and 'spel' meaning 'story' or 'message,' and becoming abbreviated to gospel.

The four gospels give an account of the life, works and teaching of Jesus, written in the style of the particular evangelist, and with a particular early Christian audience in mind - though not exclusively for any one community. The evangelists' purpose is to show that, a generation after his death, Jesus could be relevant, not only to the Jews in Palestine, but to all people outside Palestine.

The gospels are unlike any other kind of literature. In many ways, they resemble ancient biographies. The contemporary biblical scholar, Tom Wright, says that the gospels do conform to the first century standard of what biographies looked like. But they are not biographies in the modern sense - as if media reporters had accompanied Jesus all through his public life, noting his every word and deed in their proper sequencing. "They are theologically reflective works, cast as theologically reflective *biographies*."[111]

Matthew's gospel is placed first in the New Testament because in the early Christian centuries it was thought to have been the first to be written, especially by St. Augustine. However, most Biblical scholars agree that the Gospel of Mark was the first one to be written, during or soon after the Jewish revolt against Rome in 69-70 AD. As the gospels are unlike any other kind of literature, the evangelist Mark is credited with the "invention" of a new literary genre known as a 'gospel,' setting a headline for Matthew and Luke, who borrowed much material from his account. Mark's is the shortest gospel. It contains no account of the infancy of Jesus, like we find in Matthew and Luke. It doesn't have Jesus' Sermon on the Mount as in Matthew, nor Luke's parables of the Good Samaritan, the Lost Sheep, the Lost Coin and the Lost (Prodigal) Son. This gospel,

---

[111] Tom Wright, *Who was Jesus?* (SPCK, London, 1992), p. 95

however, contains the whole of the Christian message within its pages.

The Scriptures of the first Christians comprised the Old Testament Bible, which was known to the Jews as the 'Hebrew Scriptures.' These Scriptures shaped the identity of the first Christians, their sense of who they were as individuals, and as a community. The four gospels were written as a continuation of those Scriptures. They present Jesus as the fulfilment of the promises made to Israel in the Old Testament. The message which the writers of the gospels wanted to transmit was that Jesus Christ was still alive as a present source of grace for believers, and that the gospels would deepen the faith of those who read them. God's dealings with his people Israel in the Old Testament find their full meaning and fulfilment in Jesus.

Jesus asked his disciples to transmit his own good news story to the succeeding generations: 'Go, then, to all peoples everywhere and make them my disciples.' (Matthew 28:19; Luke 24:47). The disciples preached and proclaimed Jesus Christ crucified and risen from the dead and passed on this good news to the next generation of Christians.

The New Testament emerged somewhat like the old, although over a much shorter time span. Firstly, there were probably oral accounts originating with the apostles and first disciples. As the years passed, those who had met and known Jesus grew fewer in number. To preserve their memories of Jesus, some people began writing down accounts of what he said and did. (Luke 1:1). Later again, others wrote more complete accounts, probably making use of earlier oral and written sources. These were transmitted to the next generation of Christians, and following further reflection on the meaning of the life and death of Jesus, the gospels took their final shape in the style and aims of the particular evangelist. The evangelists were more than mere editors of their material. Each one of them brought his own particular theological interpretation to the significance of Jesus Christ, Son of God and saviour of the world. The gospels are unique in world literature, in that they were written from the standpoint of faith in Jesus, who rose from the dead and is exalted to the throne of God, as Lord over all creation. Contemporary biblical scholars agree that the gospels were written by second generation Christians. Eventually the writings of the New Testament were accepted by the Church as part of Sacred Scripture.

Why was the New Testament written in Greek? After the Greek king, Alexander the Great conquered the Middle East in 331 BC, Greek culture and language spread everywhere in his empire. When the Roman Empire was extended eastwards in 63 BC, Greek continued as the spoken language of the eastern Roman Empire. Following his victory in the civil war, Augustus became Emperor of Rome in 31 BC. The Romans then gained control of the whole of the Middle East, but the Latin language never took hold in that area. The Romans paid their respects to a culture superior to their own.

At the time the gospels were being written, comparatively few Jews in Palestine (Galilee and Judea) had converted to Christianity. However, outside Palestine, both Jews and pagans were becoming Christian in large numbers. The commonly spoken Greek language facilitated the spread of Christianity. When St Paul went on his far-flung missionary journeys through Asia Minor (modern Turkey) and into Greece, he could speak to everyone in the one language they all understood.

How reliable are the gospels? Tom Wright, says that the four gospels present a portrait of Jesus Christ which is firmly grounded in real history. The earliest available New Testament manuscripts come from the first seven centuries, which according to Tom Wright, is many centuries earlier than the oldest surviving manuscripts of most classical authors. There are some surviving New Testament manuscripts from the third, or possibly the fourth century. In these early times, manuscripts were copied by hand. As newer copies were made, older ones might be lost.

The gospels complement one another. Mark is a storyteller who emphasises the role of the cross in the life of Jesus and his followers. Matthew is a teacher and Church leader who emphasises morality and Christian fellowship. Luke is a skilled storyteller who is concerned with the love and mercy of God, as revealed in Jesus' parables. John, the author of the fourth gospel, is a contemplative, who emphasises faith, love, and intimacy with Jesus and fellow believers.

The four gospels are followed by the Acts of the Apostles, whose author is also Luke. These give an account of the post-resurrection early Church. The first part of Acts (chapters 1 to 12) deals with the missionary work of the apostles, especially Peter. The second part is an account of the far-flung missionary journeys of St. Paul, until he arrived in Rome as a prisoner.

Next come the letters written by Paul to the first Christian communities, which he founded throughout the eastern Roman Empire. Some of Paul's letters predate the first written gospel. These letters (known as epistles, from the Greek word for a letter, *epistola*), comprise the greatest part of the New Testament. There are some minor epistles by other authors. The last book of the Bible is the Book of Revelation, a vision of the new creation at the end of time, echoing the story of the first creation in the opening chapter of Genesis, and bringing to fulfilment, God's plan of salvation for humanity and the world.

## Society in the Galilee of Jesus' Day

Before dealing with the question of Jesus and his kingdom of God proclamation, let us first consider the social situation in first century Palestine.

When Jesus came, he found the same fragmentation as of old - the official shepherds of Israel failing to look after *all* of the Lord's flock. Israel was riven by factions, which were separated from one another, and living in enmity. Because of such division, it failed in its vocation to be a light to the Gentiles – the mission given to it by God through Abraham. The Shepherd Jesus, has the task of uniting God's flock everywhere into one single sheepfold (Kingdom of God) so that original family relationships – God walking with his people, as in the Garden of Eden - would be fully restored.

The middle class of Palestine was very small, made up of landowners, shopkeepers, tradesmen and fishermen, and it included the scribes and Pharisees. The upper and ruling classes were smaller and enormously wealthy, living in great luxury. These were the Herod nobility, the lay nobility who owned most of the land, and the chief priests who lived off the temple taxes (tithes), which amounted to one tenth of people's income. This was a situation not all that different from the time of the prophets Isaiah and Jeremiah, and against which they directed their preaching!

When Jesus looked around him, he saw the majority of the population in a state of the most extreme distress. These people were mostly peasants who couldn't afford to pay the taxes to the temple priests and the Herodian nobility. Many of them had been reduced to tenancy, having been dispossessed of their lands by the Herodian and religious authorities. The latter regarded them as ritually unclean, which meant that they were not allowed to participate in the temple liturgy. Because they were illiterate, they were regarded as lawless, immoral, incapable of virtue or piety. They were taught to think of their sins as being due to their failure to observe religious laws of which they were ignorant.

These people were the poor, the hungry and "lost" ones who longed for liberation from systems of domination both within and outside Israel. They were the excluded ones who formed the overwhelming majority of the population – the crowds who followed Jesus throughout Galilee. They were afflicted by spiritual, no less than physical poverty. They were the dispirited, the poor in spirit (Matthew 5:3), people with no dignity. These were the people to whom the Pharisees ("the separated ones") referred as the "rabble who know nothing of the law – they are damned." (John 7:49, NJB).

Among the poor were many widows, the blind and the crippled, lepers, unskilled day labourers (often with no work). Among those were the men who herded flocks - hired shepherds. Widows in particular were extremely impoverished. With no man to support them, they were totally dependent on charitable donations and the temple treasury. All of these people seldom starved, but they usually had to resort to begging. They were the people for whom Pharisees waited at street corners ringing a bell so that they might dispense their charitable donations in full view of the public. The principal suffering of these people was a loss of human dignity and status in society. They were regarded as sinners because of the ingrained belief that their misfortunes were due either to their own or their parents' sins, or to their failure to observe innumerable rules and regulations. (John 9:1-11; Luke 5:17-26, 11:46).

So to be poor and a sinner was one's lot in life. There was no way out, no chance of release, no salvation. They were the lost sheep without a shepherd. They were captives, held in a prison of fatalism, predestined to inferiority, and never to be accepted into the company of the "respectable." They were also prone to disease, due to both physical and psychological states. They suffered from guilt and frustration, with the thought that God's punishment would fall on them. This wretched state of existence gave rise to the belief that demons could enter human beings and cause illness–physical sickness, psychological (madness, despair) and moral evil (alienation from God and from other people).[112] Out of his compassion for them, Jesus mixed with, and identified with these people. (Matthew 14:14; Mark 6:34). The poor were the most vulnerable, exposed to the effects of disease and dispossession of their lands, all of this leading to banditry and pillaging.[113] They were the captives whom Jesus said he came to release from their prisons, as he quoted words of Isaiah in the Nazareth synagogue at the start of his mission. (See Luke 4:16-19, Isaiah 61:1-2).

"As Jesus saw the crowds, his heart was filled with pity for them, because they

---

[112] Albert Nolan, *Jesus before Christianity*, (Orbis Books), Ch. 3

[113] Sean Freyne, *Jesus a Jewish Galilean*, (T & T Clark International), p. 134.

were worried and helpless, like sheep without a shepherd." (Matthew 9:36). He felt moved to deal with this situation. (See Luke 4:18-19). He felt called by God to fulfil the prophecy of Isaiah. (Luke 4:21; see Isaiah 61:1-2). But How would he liberate the captives? How would he deal with the powers that held these people captive to fatalism? How would he feed their deepest hungers – their hunger for peace of soul, for dignity, for respectability, for reconciliation with neighbours, for a meaningful life, for inclusion as full members of God's people? How would Jesus liberate the oppressed from their oppressors, especially since these same oppressors were numbered among the religious authorities in Jerusalem? Would a political revolution be the only way?

Jesus must have seen the religious leaders as bad shepherds, feeding themselves rather than their flocks (Ezekiel 34:1-2), treating large numbers of their people, the poor and the sick, as hopeless outcasts. The leaders were thus failing in their God-given mission of caring. Their stubborn hearts of stone left them in a state of disobedience and rebellion against God. (See Ezekiel 11:19-20).

The people with whom Jesus associated were seen as "disreputable" by the urban elites who crushed them with a triple tax - to the Romans, Herod and the temple. Unemployed and impoverished peasants often had to resort to banditry, which the Romans treated as rebellion, and which they punished with crucifixion. The two people crucified along with Jesus may have been condemned for 'banditry.' (Matthew 27:38; Luke 23:32).

About the time of Jesus' birth, and just after the death of Herod the Great, there was a massive revolt against his son and successor, Archelaus. The revolt started in the Jerusalem temple and spread all over Judea and Galilee. It was eventually suppressed by Quintilius Varus, the Roman Governor of Syria, who came south with two Roman legions, and with the help of Archelaus, ravaged the countryside, raping, killing, looting, burning and destroying everything in sight. The Greek-speaking city of Sephoris in Galilee (a few miles north of Nazareth), which had been occupied by the rebels, was burned to the ground by the Roman army. Following his victory, Varus crucified 2,000 rebels in Jerusalem, including all those who had risen up as so-called messiahs, together with their followers.

This was the atmosphere of sadness and despair in which Jesus grew up. During his early years he may have found work as a builder in the rebuilding of Sephoris. (The Greek word *tekton* can mean both a builder and carpenter). In the early part of his mission, when large crowds were following him around Galilee, he knew he would have to tread warily in case his "Kingdom of God" movement would be interpreted by the authorities as the makings of another rebellion.

## Satan, the Real Oppressor

Jesus rejected the temptation to embrace a power system similar to that of Caesar, Herod and the Jewish religious leaders. (Matthew 4:8-9). And if the Jewish religious authorities continued to lack compassion and a spirit of inclusivity, would overthrowing the Romans make Israel any more liberated than before? Following a revolution against Rome, if the Jewish religious leaders continued to live out the same worldly values of prestige, power and making outcasts, would Roman tyranny not be replaced by an equally loveless Jewish oppression? Without a change of heart (repentance) within Israel itself, liberation from oppression of any kind would be no solution. However, there were many in Israel who believed that a violent rebellion against the Romans was the only way to go. Because of the blindness of many people to their sins, Jesus actually foresaw that such a rebellion would be the outcome. Jerusalem would be surrounded by Roman armies and ground into dust.

As Jesus saw it, there was something demonic about all domination systems. Jesus intuited that Satan ruled the whole world, through its oppressive systems: people being marginalized, deprived of their dignity, enslaved, dehumanized, oppressed by civil and religious powers, and living without hope. Satan owned and ruled the kingdoms of the world and shared them with rulers, provided they worshiped him and did what he told them. (See Matthew 4:8-10). This means that the task facing Jesus was gigantic. Not only Israel, the whole world would need to be liberated from demonic oppression. His faith in the infinite goodness and mercy of God was what empowered him.

In Jesus' day, Israel, through its religious leaders, was metaphorically still in exile; it was the prodigal son in the far country, a wanderer, naked (Genesis 3:7) and alone - struggling to exist without God. (Luke 15:15-16). With God absent from Israel, and in its present state of rebellion (people doing their own will rather than the will of God), Satan had taken up residence within the chosen people. Official Israel had been disloyal to its God; it had sold out to idolatry, among which, were the gods of mammon (wealth), power, prestige and nationalism. The real enemy Jesus would confront was not Rome but the Satan hiding behind all of these oppressions. The enemy from which Israel needed rescuing was its own leadership.[114] The evil spirit and seven worse spirits were occupying the "house" - Israel. (Matthew 12:43-45; Luke 11:24-26). Jesus saw his mission as replacing the reign of Satan (oppression) with the liberating rule of God (love).

## The Kingdom of God

The idea of God as King goes back to the beginning of the Bible. First of all, God is the cosmic King in virtue of his work as Creator of the world. (See Psalms 95 to 99; 72:12-14). God is accepted as King over Israel. (Deuteronomy 33:5). God is rejected as King of Israel. (1 Samuel 8:7). God is King of the nations. (Psalm 22:27-28; 29:1-2). In the Old Testament there was the hope that God's kingdom would be restored through the King's victory over Israel's enemies, as Israel's final return from exile. As there was no sign of this happening, it turned into a hope for a future Messiah-King. In the gospels, Jesus is often referred to as "Son of David," in other words, a Messiah king in the line of David. (Mark 10:48; Luke 18:35-43).

Expectations about a liberating Kingdom (salvation) varied greatly in Jesus' day. For the Pharisees, it would come about by complete fulfilment of the law – the law understood as the only means of salvation. The Pharisees' belief that unless people observed the innumerable prescriptions of Jewish law, the Messiah would never come. For the zealots (a physical force group), salvation meant a political theocracy to be

---

[114] N. T. Wright, *Jesus and the Victory of God*, (SPCK, London), 1996, p. 461,

established through force of arms. Although they hated the Romans, the Sadducees (the priestly class) were happy enough collaborating with them, thus saving themselves through securing their status and privileges. In a general way, there was a hope for a just ruler and a temporal well-being which had never before been fulfilled historically. The kingdom over which official Israel presided was broken up into what Mark's gospel calls fighting groups, each one only concerned with its own particular agenda. Such a kingdom would fall apart. (See Mark 3:34). This divisive kingdom was not of the will of God. The thought of bringing all of their people into a union of justice and peace was far from the minds of everyone in Israel. The thinking of Jesus was revolutionary. His kingdom of God project was aimed towards creating a union among all of them which would resemble his own union with God. Mark's gospel is an explanation of how Jesus accomplished this.

The kingdom of God is not a place. A better way of expressing the idea would be to speak of 'the reign of God,' which means God's sovereignty over the world, through his power to deal decisively with evil and bring all "exiles" definitively home. When Jesus says, "the kingdom of God is near," he means that God is about to intervene in the world in order to establish his rule over evil. (Mark 1:15).

Jesus' proclamation of the Kingdom of God and its offer of hope must be seen in the context of man's search for freedom, peace, justice, reconciliation and happiness, symbolized by the idea of a "promised land" as the goal of human hoping. This represents a search for the meaning of life, for what is truly fulfilling for human beings. Life has a meaning in the sense that we are on a journey with the faith and hope that, ultimately, all will be well. The Kingdom of God sums up the yearnings of Israel, and indeed, all of our yearnings, for the full manifestation of God's authority in the world, so that everything may ultimately be put right, evil abolished – the reign of God definitively established. (Isaiah 24:21-23).

Jesus' kingdom comes in love, mercy, forgiveness of enemies and reconciliation, as God's way of changing and ruling the world. The world cannot be changed, or justice established by violence or class conflict, as revolutions try to do, or by the marginalization of certain groups in society, as was the case both in the Israel of Jesus' day and the wider world of that time. Jesus' Kingdom has nothing to do with revolution. It is like a slowly growing seed. (Mark 4:26-29). God knows and respects human freedom; he does not coerce. His way is the way of love, calling for a loving response as the only way to proceed. The Bible teaches, and indeed history shows, that human beings are incapable of creating definitive peace and justice through their own unaided efforts. Life is constantly threatened by war. Freedom is suppressed and justice imperilled. Death is above all a sign that man's attempts to deal with his tragic situation must remain only partial, and ultimately fail. Man is not King. Man is not sovereign. At best, man can only limit evil. Attempts to deal decisively with evil always end in violence and totalitarianism, and are shown up in man's powerlessness.

There is an objection that Christianity is all about the next world, while it ignores the major concerns of this life. While it is true that human beings cannot definitively establish a reign of love, justice and peace, solely by their own efforts, that doesn't mean that we don't have a mission of stewardship to accomplish in this world. The Kingdom is *for* this world. God works with his human stewards (Genesis 1:27-28) in the here and now and calls them to a creative mission of caring for his good world and all its creatures and people. (Genesis 1:28). By trusting in what only God can do, then by obeying his will and living in hope, human beings can help to make the world a little better today, so that it will be better tomorrow. "Our help is in the name of the Lord, who made heaven and earth." (Psalm 124:8).

The kingdom comes when we accept the will of God (his rule) in our lives, in our relationships with one another and with planet earth. Jesus shows us the way. The Gospel of Mark invites us to follow Jesus on Jesus' own journey, as the only way to proceed. (Mark 14:36).

## Jesus' Miracles: Signs of the Reign of God

Mark's gospel presents Jesus as both teacher and healer. His miracles are works of liberation. God is revealed in the Book of Exodus as a God of revelation and liberation. Moses is God's servant, the one he sends on a mission of rescuing his people from slavery in Egypt and revealing to them his law. Just as Moses confronted the oppressive kingdom of Pharaoh with God's mighty works, and delivered God's law on Mount Sinai, Jesus (the new Moses), both in his miracles and teaching, now challenges Satan (the new Pharaoh) as the malevolent power keeping people in bondage. Jesus' assault on Satan's kingdom that begins with his temptation in the wilderness (Mark 1:13) will proceed apace until it reaches its climax in the Garden of Gethsemane near the end of the gospel. (4:36).

Ever since the European enlightenment, there has been a tendency to dismiss the notion of miracles as a sign of the ignorance and superstition of ancient peoples. Rationalism was an ideology that arose with the enlightenment. It was founded on the belief that reason is the only true guide to truth and life, and that it can explain everything. Yes, reason and science must always assume that there is a natural cause for phenomena. But rationalists cannot prove that miracles are impossible, or that there are no other kind of causes or explanations for phenomena. To state that science proves that there are no such things as miracles (other causes), is not a finding of science. It is actually a statement of faith. Rationalism must be distinguished from reason. It is neither reasonable nor scientific. To accept the possibility of the miraculous is eminently reasonable.

If there is a Creator God, there is nothing irrational about the possibility of miracles. Human beings have always reached out beyond practical everyday concerns in order to make contact with a spiritual reality beyond what they can observe with their senses. In contrast to the closed world of rationalism, this is a world open to new and ever-unfolding possibilities – including the possibility of the miraculous.

The purpose of Jesus' miracles is not to impress or coerce. Instead, Jesus uses his power to heal the sick, to feed the hungry and raise the dead, as signs of the coming of the reign of God over evil. God did not make the world to have hunger, disease and death ruling it, and thus oppressing humanity for ever. These things are the result of human disobedience of God. They are against the will of the Creator, who created everything "good." (Genesis 1:31). Jesus came to do the work of the Sovereign God, to set the world right by inaugurating a new creation, in which the reign of malign forces would be no more. (See Romans 8:21-22). In the light of his observation of the situation in Israel, it's

281

as if he intuited, 'This is not the way God meant the world to be. God, and only God, can put it right.' It cannot be God's will that the world (God's good creation) forever remains in bondage to sickness, decay and death.

Jesus' miracles are signs that the Creator God is King, enabling his creation to be more fully itself. The miracles are signs that order can be created out of chaos, light out of darkness, as in the first creation (Genesis 1:3; Mark 4:35-39; John 8:12). Suffering and its association with evil may hold sway in the world, but God will ultimately overcome suffering and death itself, and set people free from these demonic forces. (Matthew 11:2-6; 4:8-10; Luke 11:20; 7:18-23). God created the world, so it is reasonable to suppose that he is the one in charge, whose wise rule is for human flourishing, and which will ultimately prevail over the forces of darkness. These insights were granted to Jesus through his filial relationship with God.

In their liberation from a variety of bondages (illness, demonic possession), people saw Jesus as satisfying their deepest hungering for meaningful life. Jesus' miracles are victories over Satan, and a guarantee of his final conquest of Satan when God's kingdom will reach its triumphant climax. (See Revelation 20:10). Jesus' raising of the dead foreshadows his conquest of death through his resurrection. (Matthew 11:5; 1 Corinthians 15:24-26; Revelation 21:4). His calming of the storm on the Sea of Galilee (forces of chaos, Genesis 1:2) foreshadows the new creation, the final coming to perfection of the natural creation. (Mark 4:35-41). Jesus' provision of food and wine (his table fellowship) gives a foretaste of God's great banquet in the day of the kingdom's triumph, and as prophesised by Isaiah. (Isaiah 25:6-9; John 2:1-11; Mark 6:20-44; Mark 14:25; Revelation 19:9). God's final banquet signifies the fulfilment of deepest human hungering for everlasting happiness.

In Jesus' miracles, people are being made whole again, restored to the fullness of their humanity, as a foretaste of the end-of-time wholeness when there will be no more storms at sea upsetting anyone, no more crying or weeping, every tear wiped away, and evil and death itself abolished. (Isaiah 11:6; Revelation 21:3-4).

The miracles are thus a foretaste of what the new world will eventually look like – the world we all want, and for which we hunger and thirst. It is only the Creator God who can satisfy this hungering and thirsting. (See Isaiah 55:1-2). In his healings and teaching, Jesus is actually feeding, satisfying the hungering of humanity for this new world, and calling us to help him in bringing it about. (See Mark 6:37). In the miracles, the heavens are being opened in order to release the healing and compassionate power of God into a "wilderness" world. (Mark 1:10; See Luke 10:25-35).

The miracles are not about the establishment of a social utopia, or any project with the aim of creating states of perfection in this world. They are pointers to a wholly new creation beyond this world, in which the kingdom of God will reach its fullness of perfection. Jesus did not set out with any systematic plan to improve the world. He did not heal all the sick or drive out all the demons. His healings were isolated signs offering hope for an ultimate new world at peace with itself, as foretold by the prophets. (See Isaiah 11:6-9). Jesus' message is that human beings and their world can only become fully human (fullness of life) when they have God as their Lord (King). History has shown that superhuman efforts by human beings to create the perfect society have always ended in disaster, dehumanization and death.

Expressions of faith appear in connection with the healings - an admission that when human powers and possibilities have been exhausted, people can place their trust in God to do what only God can do. With God, all things are possible. (Mark 10:27). This is not a counsel to passivity; faith leads to action; it is a call from God to cooperate with him in a partnership of bringing blessing to the world, making the world a little better today so that it will be better tomorrow.

Jesus' exorcisms, especially, signify the battle with Satan, the arch-enemy. They are signs that Jesus is winning the battle and establishing the reign of God over evil. "Jesus said to the Pharisees, 'If it is by the Spirit of God, that I cast out demons, then the kingdom of God (rule of God) has come to you.'" (Matthew 12:28, NRSVC). Because the miracles are often accompanied by the forgiveness of sin (Matthew 12:28; Mark 2:1-12; Luke 11:20), they are signs of the defeat of the enemy holding Israel and the world captive to enmity, violence and retribution.

God sent Jesus to bring good news to the 'poor,' among whom are all those in the grip of Satan. (Mark 1:25; Isaiah 61:1; 58:7). Who are the 'poor'? In a sense, everyone is poor. All human beings are held in bondage to forces which prevent them from being the kind of people God wants them to be. The human condition is one of dependency. We are continually in need of help to do what we ourselves cannot do. We are dependent on God to raise us up to new life – a life of hope and purpose. God does not leave us mired in the depths of our poverty. He has seen our poverty and has sent his Son to liberate us from our limitations. The Son dies so that we may be liberated from death – the greatest poverty of all. Jesus has promised us that the poor will be numbered among the eternally blessed. (Matthew 5:3).

The demons which Jesus exorcised are much more than symbols of the misfortunes to which human beings are prone. The Church has always taught that they are real spiritual beings, fallen angels who were created by God but became evil by their own free choice. (CCC 391-395). As created beings, their power is not infinite. As the "stronger" and greater one (Mark 1:7), the power and authority of the Son of God is superior to these forces. He eventually conquers them in his resurrection, bringing God's creation to the fullness of perfection in his own person.

We have only to look around the world today for evidence of the demonic; something much more than merely human malice is at work, seeking to destroy the image of God in human beings. Human lives can sometimes be taken over by forces, over which they have no control. The demonic is at work in the more or less hidden, but widespread human trafficking of men, women and children for the kind of slavery that is still in operation in the modern world. According to figures released by Global Slavery Index, in 2016, at any given time, an estimated 40.3 million people worldwide are held in modern slavery, including 25 million in forced labour and 15.4 million in forced marriages. Seventy per cent of these are women and children. An estimated 4.8 million people are victims of forced sexual exploitation, the vast majority of these being women and children. By comparison with that, between the 15th and 19th centuries, an estimated 13 million people were captured and sold as slaves. More people are enslaved today than at any time in history.

The miracles of Jesus free people for discipleship, fitting them for mission. (Mark 5:18-20; see Mark 6:7; Matthew 10:1; Luke 9:1). Miracles thus bring about the gathering together of God's people into his family. (See Mark 3:33-35). Through the miracles, Jesus is saying that God is carrying out his plan. God is acting in him for the salvation of the world.[115]

As members of Christ's body (1 Corinthians 6:15), we are called to continue the work of Jesus, to be his hands and feet in today's world - to bring good news to the poor: opening eyes to the 'good news', liberating people from their anxieties, offering help to distressed souls and encouragement and hope to those closest to us.

## The Gospel of Mark

In exploring the Christian message in the following chapters, we will focus on the Gospel of Mark, while also making reference to the gospels of Matthew, Luke and John, and to other parts of the New Testament.

After about 60 AD, Christianity began to spread rapidly. By 350 AD it is estimated that there were close on 40 million Christians in the Roman empire, out of an estimated population of 60 million.[116]

The main appeal of early Christianity and its rapid growth, was because it brought a revolutionary idea of salvation to the pagan Greek-speaking world, a world which had been searching for salvation but had no idea where or how to find it. (See Galatians 3:27-28; Romans 10:9-12). Christianity also created a community in which all classes of people, without distinction, could find a new dignity as brothers and sisters of the risen Jesus, and adoption into the family of God along with him. (Mark 3:33-35). For the Greek philosophers, there was much speculation about the meaning of life, of what constituted the good life, but the Greeks never did, or indeed, never could, have arrived at the idea of salvation beyond this world. Then came Christianity which offered them the hope that a God of love would answer their search for meaning, with the gratuity of eternal blessedness. (See Acts of the Apostles 17:18-34).

Mark's gospel was intended for Gentile converts to Christianity. St. Irenaeus, bishop of Lyon (b. 130 AD) and St. Clement of Alexandria (b. 150 AD) agree that this gospel was written in Rome. It was probably based on the preaching of the apostle Peter who had been in Rome at that time. This means that Mark's gospel may be the nearest we have to an eye-witness account of the life of Jesus.

Mark's gospel is often regarded as a simple narrative. However, one short sentence in Mark, even a single word, can contain a world of meaning. Modern literary critics agree that Mark writes with great skill and in a vivid style. There is a sense of urgency and fast-paced action in his narrative. The gospel is a well-structured account, with a beginning, middle and end. Mark offers the most human portrait of Jesus of all four gospels. Like any human being, Jesus becomes tired (6:31) and hungry (11:12). He feels a wide range of human emotions including anger (3:5), amazement (6:6), compassion (1:41; 6:34), discouragement (8:12), indignation (10:14), love (10:21), distress and sorrow

---

[115] Walter Kasper, *Jesus the Christ*, (T&T Clark International), 2011, p. 86).

[116] Rodney Stark, *The Rise of Christianity*, (Harper One), 1997, p. 7.

(14:34-34). Mark frequently describes the emotional reactions of Jesus' audience to his words and deeds. This is manifested in a sense of wonder (15:5), astonishment (1:27; 2:12; 10:24), fear (9:6; 10:32), and perplexity (6:20). Mark is also aware that Jesus is filled with the Spirit of God, giving him a unique relationship with God, and an identity as "Son of God" (Mark 1:1, 11). This empowers Jesus to do what God wills and what only God can do.

More than any other evangelist (perhaps due to his unique insight into human nature), Mark places great stress on the weakness and faithlessness of the disciples, including Peter. He portrays them as repeatedly failing to understand what Jesus is trying to teach them, often only seeking their own advantage. (Mark 4:35-41; 5:25-34; 6:37-38; 8:14-21, 31-33; 9: 2-6, 32). In their flaws and failings, the disciples are mirror images of ourselves. In their place, we would be no different. In the end, it took a mighty earth-shattering event to change their whole mindset, leading to their transformation.

Mark's gospel is full of the joy of the good news of Jesus Christ the Son of God, crucified and risen from the dead. For Mark, the life of Jesus of Nazareth is an event that has changed the course of world history. The gospel brings to completion all that God had been doing for his people and all that was foretold by the Old Testament prophets. Mark wants his readers to embark on the same journey that he himself and the first disciples have begun – one of meeting Jesus, gradually opening their eyes to who he really is and then committing their life to him. This turned out to be a demanding commitment, a severe test of faith. For Mark and the first disciples, following Jesus could mean rejection or disapproval from friends and family, over the perceived absurdity of following a poor manual worker from a backwater village, who had suffered a shameful death on a Roman cross. Furthermore, it could mean embarking on a new table fellowship with people one would have previously shunned: the poor and outcasts of society, with rich people and Gentiles. And for some of the first Christians it would mean arrest and persecution, even death.

## Relevance of the Gospel in Today's World

Mark's gospel presents Jesus as the "Stronger One" (1:7; 3:27) who sets human beings free from demonic control. This 'good news' is as relevant today as it was 2,000 years ago. Today, we may be held captive to different things from those experienced by people in first century Palestine, but they are still forces, over which we often seem to have little or no control (metaphorical leprosies), and from which we need to be freed – various kinds of addictions, for example.

Despite the unprecedented affluence and freedom enjoyed by people today, especially in the West (mainly Europe and North America), there are signs that all is not well in present-day society. Let us look at one example. For the human being, moderate anxiety may be a good thing; it keeps us attentive and focused. Today, however, anxiety seems to have become an epidemic. It is reported that Ireland has one of the highest rates of mental-health illness in Europe. We see reports in our media about young people feeling dissatisfied, disturbed, anxious, depressed, living without hope. After having enjoyed all the freedoms, all the choices open to people today, and having tasted all the pleasures that materialism has to offer, there still seems to be a lingering sense of disappointment and dissatisfaction. And being thus dissatisfied, there is a feeling that there is nowhere else to go, no meaningful future, nothing more for which to hope. It's like spending money (placing one's hope) in what does not satisfy. (Isaiah 55:1-2; see Mark 10:17-22). The question then is, whether there is something greater than materialism and its pleasures, something that can give us a hope that will not disappoint. Human beings cannot live without a story that is going somewhere, without hope and a sense of purpose. They cannot live without a meaningful cause for which they will feel a need to sacrifice themselves, for the sake of some future good. However, this may be a daunting prospect in a culture of individualism, in which the needs of the self are paramount.

Young people are idealistic, open to challenge. But today, there may be a sense of rootlessness - the feeling that there are no values given to us by which we can live and through which we can find meaning. The message from contemporary culture is that you yourself, as an individual, decide your own meanings and values. In this situation, young people may be left with the burden of deciding what is good and worthwhile, every day, without guidance. This can be terrible burden, and may lead to anxiety. Can we find ways to communicate the Christian story to young people and show them a cause and a goal to which they might be willing to devote themselves, something they could do, which would liberate them from self-obsessions and make a difference in the lives of other people – and in their own lives too, something to give them a sense of meaning?

Mark's gospel addresses the darkness of unbelief and despair that is so much a feature of modern life. The disturbed and anxious feelings, so much in evidence today, are symptomatic of a bondage from which Jesus can liberate us, as he calls us to "get up," taking us by the hand and lifting us up out of our darkness, and then giving us a cause for which we can live. (See Mark 1:31; 2:11; 5:41; 9:27). God gave Abraham a goal (promised land), towards which he could journey in hope, and a mission of creating blessing for his descendants of all nations. (Genesis 12:1-2; 22:18). The "good news" is that Jesus of Nazareth, as Son of God, is the one who fulfils what began in Abraham. It is Jesus who gives us a cause for which we can live and a destiny in which we can hope. By feeding us with the "bread of life," he satisfies our hungering and thirsting for a peace and happiness which will endure, when all the other things in which we often place our hopes have melted away and failed to satisfy us. (Mark 6:41-42; John 6:48-51; 7:37-38).

The particular appeal of the Gospel of Mark is in its account of the Christian life as a journey of faith, a "way" to be followed towards a goal which ends in triumph and glory. However, in Mark's account, this is a demanding journey. It is a call to mission, a call to forget our selfish concerns - *our* way - and to follow Jesus on *his* way of service. And paradoxically, Mark presents this as 'good news' for humanity; good news because it is the road to a fulfilled and meaningful life. However, in a world in which many people live only for the present moment - seeking easy options in every department of life - this may be difficult news to accept today.

Realistically, we have to face the fact that there are no easy options in life; no matter what our circumstances. Life is a mixture of darkness and light, sorrow and joy, success and failure. Much as we might think so, we cannot be in full control of our lives, as if everything was down to ourselves. Things happen to us that are completely outside our control–illness, fear, anguish, failure, loss of friends, relationship breakdown, the death of loved ones, and then the onset of old age. If we try to fight these things, as if we could magic them out of existence, and resort to short-cut solutions such as addictions, we will end up in frustration, disappointment and despair. The challenges of life are part of what it means to be human. Mark's gospel teaches us that in accepting these living realities – while praying that we will have the courage and strength to come to terms with them - we are following Jesus on his way. We can take comfort from Jesus' triumph over them, a triumph he will share with us, bringing our story to a happy ending. What if Mark's message represents the truth about life! We have little choice but to live in this world with all its pains. How we deal with suffering is what matters. Jesus gave it meaning by accepting it as a means of service to humanity, and then triumphing over it.

Mark's gospel can be divided into three main sections (three acts), with a prologue, middle section and an epilogue:

> Prologue. (1:1–13). The gospel begins in the Judean wilderness where the prophet John the Baptist was preaching and baptising, and where Jesus was baptised and tempted.

Jesus begins his ministry in Galilee, where he remains for the following seven chapters (1:14–8:30). He is the promised "Mighty One" in whom God is powerfully at work, releasing people from all that oppresses or dehumanises them. At times, Jesus travels beyond Galilee towards Gentile territory, indicating that his mission has ultimately the Gentiles in view as well.

After the Galilean section, the second half of the gospel opens with the "way" (8:27–10:52). Jesus announces his journey to Jerusalem and teaches his disciples on the" way." He begins to speak of himself as the Son of Man who must undergo great suffering and be killed, indicating that he is to be a suffering Messiah.

In 11:1 Jesus reaches Jerusalem, beginning the Jerusalem section of the gospel (11:1–15:47). These chapters are an account of his brief ministry in Jerusalem, during which he concentrates on teaching rather than healing. This intensifies his conflict with the religious leaders and leads to his passion, death and burial. He goes willingly to his death in fulfilment of his mission, trusting that God will vindicate him.

> Epilogue (16:1-8). Corresponding to the prologue at the beginning of the gospel, these last verses can be considered an epilogue. The women disciples discover an empty tomb and tell no one.

## The Beginning of the Good News (Mark 1:1)

> The beginning of the gospel about Jesus Christ the Son of God. (Mark 1:1, NJB).

The first verse of Mark's gospel is a title for the whole work. In the opening verse, the "beginning" recalls the first words of the creation story in Genesis 1:1 and suggests that the good news (gospel) that Mark is about to tell is a new beginning for humankind, a new creation by God, comparable in ways, to the creation of the universe. The news is good because it will change people's lives. For the Old Testament prophets, the good news is not a past event but a promise that God will come to liberate his people. (Isaiah 40:9-10; 52:7; 61:1). In the New Testament, the good news is that, now, in Jesus Christ, the long-promised visitation of God to his people has begun, in order to establish the reign of God on earth as it is in heaven. This news is so good that it is worth more than life itself. (Mark 8:35; 10:29-30). This is a news that fulfils the deepest hungering of the human heart for a fulfilment that only God can give. (Isaiah 55:1-3).

The content of this good news is that Jesus is the "Christ the Son of God." The name "Jesus" means "saviour." "Messiah" is a Hebrew word meaning the "anointed" one, which is translated into Greek as *Christos* and in English, to Christ. In ancient Israel, kings were crowned in a ceremony of anointing with olive oil. (1 Samuel 10:1; 1 Kings 19:16). When Israel no longer had kings of their own and lived under foreign rule, the prophets taught that God would send a new "anointed" one, descended from King David (the ideal king), a Messiah king who would end their exile and restore freedom, justice and peace to Israel, seen as the 'promised land.' (Isaiah 9:2-7; 52:7).

As interpreted in the New Testament, this king will establish the reign of God and bring the whole of humanity definitively home from its exile in this world. (Psalm 89:21-38). Thus, to say that Jesus is the Christ (Messiah) is to proclaim that he is the long promised anointed King, who will establish his reign over evil.

Jesus is King in a different way from Caesar or the rulers of the old empires, whose rule was marked by domination and exploitation, creating division and enmity. Jesus is a King whose power is equated with service to his people, rather than lording it over them. Jesus is a King who reigns in human hearts when we take from him the values by which we live.

This King would do much more than liberating Israel from foreign domination. Jesus is more than Messiah. The Israelite kings enjoyed the title 'Son of God,' probably signifying their God-given task as shepherds of God's people. The good news is that Jesus is 'Son of God' in a greater sense, meaning that the Spirit of God is working in him, empowering him to do what no Israelite king could ever do, that is, to free all of us exiles from bondage to satanic evil and bring us definitely home from our exile in this world, thus establishing the reign of God on earth as it is in heaven.

How would 'Son of God' as applied to Jesus have sounded to the first hearers of Mark's gospel? Handwritten copies of the gospel would initially have been rare. The only way to communicate its message to people would have been through a person reading it in its entirety to small groups, some of whom would probably have been Gentiles. These people would have known that "son of God" was a title claimed by the Roman emperor at that time. And the emperor's birthday was always celebrated as 'good news.' Yet, here is a man from the backward Roman province of Galilee, who suffered death by crucifixion, now being presented to people everywhere as a rival 'Son of God,' someone greater than the emperor of Rome. And this is being offered to the reader's audience as 'good news.'

The fact that Mark lays out his stall so uncompromisingly in the opening words of his story, creates a sense of anticipation and suspense. His audience will want to hear more about this man whom Mark designates as "Messiah" and "Son of God." The central theme of Mark's story is the inauguration of God's rule over all creation, over all people, over the nations and over the Roman emperor. Unlike the oppressive rule of the empires, Jesus' rule is liberating. It is equated with service. The full meaning of "Messiah" and "Son of God," as applied to Jesus, will gradually unfold in the course of Mark's narrative. (See 8:29; 15:39).

## The Precursor– Messenger (1:2-8)

Mark continues by quoting Isaiah's prophecy of a messenger appearing to the exiles in Babylon and preparing a path for the Lord, who is about to lead them home.

> It is written in the prophet Isaiah: *Look, I am going to send my messenger in front of you to prepare your way before you. A voice of one that cries in the desert: Prepare a way for the Lord, make his paths straight.* (Mark 1:2-3; NJB, see Isaiah 40:3; Malachi 3:1; Romans 1:2-4; CCC 422).

Mark quotes Isaiah 40:3 (in italics above) in order to show that the coming of Jesus was planned and prepared by God for centuries. In Isaiah's day, the road was straightened and prepared to take the exiles home from the bondage of Babylon. (Isaiah 40:4-5). Jesus will call for repentance as the clear "way" to bring all of us exiles home from the bondage of Satan.

By quoting Isaiah's prophecy, Mark asserts that John the Baptist is the fulfilment of Isaiah's voice crying in the desert. As God's new "messenger" (prophet), John is sent to prepare the "way" for the coming of Jesus. John is the one now levelling the metaphorical hills and mountains (Isaiah 40:4) - obstacles in Jesus' path, among which are Israel's blindness to its sins and its failure to repent of them. In his baptising and call to repentance, John is trying to remove these obstacles.

> So John appeared in the desert, baptising and preaching. 'Turn away from your sins and be baptised,' he told the people, 'and God will forgive your sins.' Many people from Judea and the city of Jerusalem went out to hear John. They confessed their sins and he baptised them in the River Jordan. John wore clothes made of camel's hair, with a leather belt round his waist, and his food was locusts and wild honey. (Mark 1:4-6, NJB).

John's appearance in a "desert" has a special significance. The desert is symbolic of deprivation, a place without homely comforts, a place of testing, of new beginnings. Mark's first hearers, who were Jews, would remember the desert as a place of testing where the Israelites wandered for forty years after their exodus from Egypt. Life in a desert awakens a hunger and thirst for something better. (Exodus 16:3; 17:1). In the case of the Israelites, God satisfies their hungering (Exodus 16:4) and gives them the hope of an eventual 'promised land' in which all their yearnings would be fully satisfied. (Exodus 6:7-8). With the coming of the Messiah and Son of God, Mark may have a deeper hunger and thirst in mind than that of the ancient Israelites. Thirsting for water can symbolize human yearning for the liberation that only God, through Jesus, can bring to humanity. This represents a definitive coming home from exile in the new promised land of eternal life with God. (Isaiah 41:17-18; Mark 1:21-27; 6:35-44).

Relying totally on God's provision, John brought no food with him to the desert. His dress and food may have been usual enough for desert nomads, but they signify his willingness to give up everything, to deny himself of all attachments that might come in the way of his focus on God and on the mission to which he believed God had called him. His self-denial echoes what Jesus would later ask of his own followers, but in a different way. (Mark 8:34). Locusts and wild honey also evoke Israel's wilderness experience. A plague of locusts was symbolic of God's judgement on the Egyptians for Pharaoh's refusal to let the Hebrew slaves escape. (Exodus 10:13-15). The wild honey evokes God's promise to his people of a homeland flowing with milk and honey – the promised land of Israel. (Exodus 3:8; see Psalm 119:103).

When John began his ministry, the people of his audience were still, in a sense, in exile, because they had not repented of their sins. One experience of their exile was living under the domination of the Roman empire, from which many in Israel wanted to free themselves through a violent revolution. This, in effect, would be a rebellion against God. Within Israel itself, there was a self-righteous elite which created a society of victims - a whole class of people who were denied full membership of God's people, and treated as outcasts and hopeless sinners. Treating people thus was a sin against justice, calling for repentance. Furthermore, Israel was also obsessed with itself, rather than living in obedience to its vocation of being a light to the wider world (the mission given to Abraham and his descendants. (Genesis 12:3). The self-righteousness of many in Israel (mainly the religious leaders) led them to believe that they had no need of repentance. This was a form of spiritual blindness, and was censured by the prophets. (See Isaiah 6:10; 42:18-20. They were deluding themselves (blindness) that they were already saved by their religious rituals and practices, which had become divorced from ethical demands. They were God's chosen people, but their society was not of the will of God. There were many sins of which they needed to repent before they could be brought home from exile.

Significant numbers went out to hear John in the wilderness. (Verse 5). His challenging call to repentance must have made a powerful impact on the crowds. John was a prophet, and like the prophets of old, he was calling Israel to turn to God, to undergo a change of mind and heart. This would involve an acknowledgement by people of their sinfulness and their need for a cleansing, which John was offering through his baptising in the River Jordan. (See Isaiah 55:7; Jeremiah 18:11; Zechariah 1:4).

John's baptising (Mark 1:4) echoes the exodus of the Israelites from their exile in Egypt and their journey through the wilderness until they came through the waters of the Jordan and arrived in the promised land. (See Joshua 1:1-2). A new, and greater exodus and return from exile is now being brought about by John's preaching and baptising. This exodus is not a liberation from Pharaoh, but from Satan's control of people's lives and confirming them in their sins. The people are called to come home from exile through immersion in the water of John's baptising, to leave metaphorical Egypt behind them – the world of sin in which they are living, in rebellion against God. The cleansing of John's baptising recalls the prophecy of Ezekiel – God's promise to cleanse his people of their sins. (Ezekiel 36:24-27).

John's message was for everyone, priests, scribes, Pharisees, tax collectors; all were sinners, and now called to repentance. (Matthew 3:7-10). Official Israel had been disloyal to its God; it had sold out to idolatry, among which, were the gods of mammon (wealth), power, prestige and nationalism. It had also been guilty of the injustice of marginalizing a large number of its population and making exclusions. John was counter-cultural; he didn't tell them that they were required to go to the Jerusalem temple and perform certain rituals in order to put themselves right with God. All John was looking for was a confession of sins, a change of hearts. (1:5). His call to repentance was crucial for the mission of the future Messiah. Without repentance first, there would be no "way" cleared for a return from exile. Without repentance, there could be no rescuing from the bondage of Satan. Then John made a surprising announcement. He was not the one who would accomplish this rescue operation.

> John announced to the people, 'After me is coming someone who is more powerful than me, and I am not fit to kneel down and undo the strap of his sandals. I have baptised you with water, but he will baptise you with the Holy Spirit.' (Mark 1:7-8, NJB).

John makes it plain that he is not the expected Messiah. He is not the one who will fulfil the Old Testament prophecies. The "more powerful" one is a term usually applied to God himself. (Deuteronomy 10:17; 2 Samuel 23:1; Psalm 24:8). In what way is Jesus more powerful than John? Jesus is empowered by God's Spirit, and thus has power to confront Satan and to expel demons. He portrays himself as a burglar who is able to enter the house of the "strong man" (Satan), bind him and relieve him of his goods - human beings. (Mark 3:27). Jesus is stronger than the demonic world. Only he can establish the reign of God over evil. What John is doing with water, the Messiah will do with the power of the Holy Spirit. In the exodus from Egypt, God accompanied and guided his people in the form of a pillar of cloud and fire. (Exodus 13:21-22). Now God's Spirit would come like fire and live in everyone, empowering them to turn their hearts to God, in repentance. (See Acts of the Apostles 2:1-4).

The baptism by the Holy Spirit of the "more powerful one - the Messiah (Mark 1:8) - would bring about a transformation that cleansing by water could never accomplish. It would bring a change of heart that would enable people to respond to God's love with love in return, and experience the blessing of an immersion into the life of God himself. God would then be their God, and they would be his people, obedient to him, as sons and daughters. (Isaiah 32:15-18; Ezekiel 36:24-29; see Ezekiel 37:21-25). According to Isaiah, the blossoming of nature symbolizes the transformation of the people following the outpouring of the Spirit. "The people will thrive like well-watered grass, like willows by streams of running water." (Isaiah 44:3-5). To "thrive" in this sense means to produce the fruits of righteousness. In their repentance and in their readiness to practice justice and mercy, in obedience to God, they would become new people.

The early Christians understood that the Baptist's prophecy in Mark 1:7-8 was fulfilled on the day of Pentecost. (Acts of the Apostles 2:1-18; see CCC 694, 1302).

## The Significance of Jesus' Baptism

> It was at this time that Jesus came from Nazareth in Galilee and was baptised in the Jordan by John. And at once, as he was coming out of the water, he saw the heavens torn apart and the Spirit, like a dove, descending on him. And a voice came from heaven, 'You are my Son the Beloved; my favour rests on you.' (Mark 1:9-11, NJB; see Isaiah 64:1).

Why does Jesus submit himself to a baptism of repentance? It is not because he himself needs to repent (2 Corinthians 5:21), but as a sign of his identification with sinful humanity, (represented in the crowds coming to John to be baptized). He would thus offer a perfect repentance on their behalf – as a substitute for them. The Israel of Jesus' day, symbolizing humanity at large, failed to repent of its sins and to turn wholeheartedly to God. Because Jesus identifies with sinful humanity, he suffers the consequences of our sins, which is death. (See Genesis 2:17; 3:19b). He is God's suffering Servant, who suffers on our behalf so that we may escape the consequences of our disobedience of God – namely death.

In the anointing of Jesus, there was no need for John to use oil as a symbol, because the Holy Spirit came down on him visibly through the symbol of a dove. (1:10). The Spirit's descent as a dove recalls the dove sent out by Noah to confirm the end of the flood, as a sign of peace to a renewed world. (Genesis 8:8-12). The Spirit now coming down on Jesus inaugurates a new creation, a new beginning for humanity, his justice creating peace and union. (See Isaiah 2:4; 11:2-4, 5-6; 42:1).

The heavens being "torn apart" (1:10 above) in order to release the Spirit of God into the world was prophesised by Isaiah. In calling on God to "tear the sky apart" (64:1), Isaiah says a prayer on behalf of the people, who had turned away from the Lord. (Isaiah 63:17). Isaiah pleads with the Lord to reveal himself in all his power so as to deal with the sins of his people. (Isaiah 64:5). Isaiah's prayer is now answered by God at the baptism of Jesus. God confirms Jesus as "Son, the beloved" (Mark 1:11b), suggesting a divine status for Jesus and an intimate relationship of love between the Father and Son. In his solidarity with those coming to John for baptism, Jesus embodies Israel, which was called "God's son." (Exodus 4:22; Hosea 11:1; Psalm 2:7). But because of its disobedience of God and lack of repentance, Israel could not be a true Son of God. The fact that the Father's favour "rested" on Jesus (Mark 1:11) is an indication of his filial obedience, confirming him as the obedient new Israel (comprising himself and his followers). This means that we are all drawn into Jesus' own obedience and made sons and daughters of the Father along with him. His obedience will be further confirmed in his testing in the wilderness (Mark 1:13), later again in the Garden of Gethsemane and later again on the cross. (Mark 14:36). Adam, the first human representative failed in his obedience to God. As the new Adam, the new human representative, Jesus reverses the disobedience of Adam, who succumbed to the rule of Satan. Through his filial obedience, Jesus is empowered by the Spirit of God to reject the rule of Satan and establish the reign of God, thus uniting humanity to God, as the essential part of his mission, the purpose of which is outlined in the prophecy of

Isaiah. (61:1-2; see Luke 4:18-19; see Acts of the Apostles 10:38).

In the Garden of Eden, heaven was already open to humanity, symbolizing the close relationship between God and human beings– a relationship that God wanted to continue for ever. But when human beings went their own way and into hiding from God, they themselves shut the door to heaven. (Genesis 3:8). What is happening at Jesus' baptism is a recovery of what was lost in Eden. God is now breaking through and healing our fallen world with the presence of his beloved and obedient Son. Final confirmation of the opening of heaven will take place at the death of Jesus. (See Mark 15:38). The voice from heaven at Jesus' baptism is that of a Father who loves and affirms his Son, even before the Son sets out on his mission of struggle with Satan.

The anointing of Jesus with the Holy Spirit is thus an initiating event that leads to the inauguration of the reign of God. Peter's recognition of Jesus as the anointed Messiah is a turning point between Jesus' travels around Galilee and his journey to Jerusalem. (Mark 8:29-30).

"You are my Son the Beloved." (1:11b). Because Jesus identified with us, God says these same words to all of us, both at our baptism and ever after. This is why Jesus came: to make us sons and daughters of God, through the Holy Spirit coming down on us. The New Testament proclaims that all of Jesus' followers have become children of God, as sharers in Jesus' own relationship with God the Father. This makes us brothers and sisters of Jesus. (Romans 8:15-16; 1 John 5:10). Just as Jesus was empowered by the Spirit for his future mission, our own empowerment as brothers and sisters of Jesus, makes it possible for us too, to embark on the mission of liberation to which God calls us.

Jesus' prayer life was the foundation of his union with God, giving him the authority and empowerment to fulfil his mission of self-sacrificial service to humanity. The Gospel of Luke pays specific attention to Jesus' prayer life. (Luke 3:21; 5:16; 6:12; 9:18, 28; 22:32; 22:44; 23:34, 46). We can assume that his prayer life involved him in communion with the Father about the will of God for him and for the world (the Kingdom of God), leading to his insight into God as a compassionate and loving Father.

## Jesus' Testing in the Wilderness

And the Spirit immediately drove him out into the wilderness. He was in the wilderness for forty days, tempted by Satan, and he was with the wild beasts; and the angels waited on him. (Mark 1:12-13, NRSVC; see Matthew 4:1-11; Luke 4:1:1-13; see Genesis 3:6).

The fact that the Spirit "drove" Jesus into the wilderness means that God wanted Jesus to confront the powers of darkness ("wild beasts") as the essential part of his mission. His obedience to the Father is implied in his willingness to be driven out. Here in the Judean wilderness, Jesus begins his campaign against Satan. It is here that his resolve is tested to carry out his mission in obedience to the Father's will, and to establish the reign of God.

The consequences of Jesus' decision to associate himself with sinners will now become apparent – consequences that will eventually lead to the cross. The wilderness is the realm of evil powers, symbolized by the predatory beasts (Satan) that lurk there. (Leviticus 16:10; Isaiah 35:7-9; Ezekiel 34:25). There, with the "wild beasts" in the barren wilderness beside the Dead Sea, Jesus experiences deprivation, isolation, loneliness – the starkness of the human condition, with which he associates and identifies.

Jesus' forty days testing by Satan in the Judean wilderness is a preparation for his mission. In the Old Testament, the wilderness was the place where Israel was tested for forty years, as the people journeyed from Egyptian slavery towards the promised land. Moses said to the people, 'Remember the long way that the Lord your God led you these forty years through the wilderness, in order to humble you, testing you to know what was in your heart, whether or not you would keep his commandments.' (Deuteronomy 8:2, NRSVC, see Psalm 66:10; Isaiah 48:10). Moses asked the people to do as the lord had commanded them, to live according to his laws. (Deuteronomy 8:6). But they turned away from the Lord and set up a golden calf to which they bowed down. (Exodus 32:1-7). The consequences of that was forty years of wandering in the wilderness. Mark and the other gospels present Jesus as the new and obedient Israel. Jesus endured forty days in the wilderness but proved himself obedient to God. Jesus was empowered for his mission of confronting Satan, making him the true "beloved Son," in contrast to the disobedience of Israel which failed to pass the test of obedience during its wilderness journey. So far in the Bible has been the story of humans giving in to evil. But now in the Judean wilderness, a new humanity appears, empowered by God's Spirit to confront evil.

So far in Mark we notice an alternating pattern of events. On the one hand, Jesus associates, himself with sinners (humanity, through his baptism) but then follows the heavenly opening confirming his uniqueness. In the foregoing passage, his vulnerability and humanity are again to the fore, but then angels came and "waited" on him. The tension between these two realities will form one of the themes in the rest of the gospel. It will only be resolved at the very end.

In their vision of a future Messiah, the prophets looked forward to a time when God's will would be obeyed by a king descended from David, the wild beasts tamed and living in peace with one another and with human beings, thus restoring God's good creation to its original fruitfulness and harmony. (See Isaiah 11:1-9). In the wilderness, Jesus now proves to be the obedient descendant of King David.[117] As Messiah, King and Son of God, Jesus fulfils the prophecy of Isaiah. (See Romans 1:3-4; CCC 440, 453, 547).

St. Paul portrays Jesus as the new Adam. (Romans 5:14b). The "wilderness" symbolizes the Israel of Jesus' day, and is also symbolic of the unredeemed world at large. On the promptings of Satan (Genesis 3:6), the first human representative disobeys God, which has the effect of turning the world into a metaphorical wilderness. Weeds and thorns are its only fruits. (Genesis 3:17-18). This is the world into which the Son of God is driven, as the new human representative. Through his obedience to God, Jesus rejects

---

[117] King David ruled Israel about 1,000 BC. He was the greatest of the kings of Israel – poet, musician statesman, and warrior. His full story is told in 1 Samuel chapters 17-31, 2 Samuel, 1 Kings and 2 Kings 1:1-12. God promised David that his dynasty would last forever. The people of Israel, thus looked forward to a Messiah king like David, who would liberate Israel from foreign rule. (2 Samuel 7:13). Jesus is the promised Messiah King who restores and transforms the kingdom of David, which became the Christian Church after humanity's liberation from death through his resurrection.

the temptations of Satan and restores the world wilderness to metaphorical fruitfulness, as in the Garden of Eden. (Genesis 2:8-9; see Isaiah 41:18-20).

Even at this early stage of his mission, Jesus must have known where his faithfulness to God would lead him. His wilderness experience is a foretaste of the future. The metaphorical "wild beasts" will be with him throughout his mission, intensifying his sense of isolation and loneliness. They will test him in the opposition he will encounter from official Israel – all those who will try to trip him up. (Mark 3:6). They will be with him in the guise of the Satan within his own disciples, who will object to his commitment to face rejection and execution in Jerusalem. (Mark 8:31-33). It is thus that the strength of his relationship with the Father will be tested. The wild beasts will later re-appear during his passion, when, all alone, he will be deprived of all comfort, thus reliving his Judean wilderness experience. He will be betrayed and deserted by his friends and condemned to a shameful death. But Jesus will prove himself to be God's faithful and obedient Son - Jeremiah's "pillar of iron" and "bronze wall to confront a whole nation." (Jeremiah 2:19). He will have the empowering hand of God as "angels waiting on him," in the triumph of his resurrection. (Mark 1:13; 16:5-6).

The women who followed Jesus all the way from Galilee to Calvary are one expression of the angels who were "waiting" on him. Then at the end of the gospel, at the moment when Jesus dies, Mark refers to the women at the foot of the cross and says, "They looked after him while he was in Galilee." (Mark 15:40-41).

Our life on earth is a wilderness journey, in which our trust and obedience to God are tested. (See CCC 409, 2752). We are often assailed by the wild beasts of anxiety, anger and despair – as our own wilderness experience. We need to place our trust in the power of God to overcome them and not in the quick fixes we ourselves often employ. When things are running smoothly in our lives and we are not troubled, we tend to rely on our own strength, which is of little account compared with Jesus, who is made the "powerful" one by God's Spirit. (Mark 1:7). When a troubled ("wilderness") experience is thrust on us, our faith and hope can be sorely put to the test. Will we then trust and hope in the Lord and stay the course with him? Can we trust God when we find ourselves in the throes of such innocent suffering? Such a test can come in the form of deprivation, failure, regret, disappointments, loss, illness, or bereavement. God wants an end to these things. He does not send them to oppress or torment us. They arise from our flawed and damaged nature. God actually sent his Son on earth in order to ultimately liberate us from all of them "Those who trust in the Lord for help will find their strength renewed. They will rise on wings like eagles; they will run and not grow weary; they will walk and never tire." (Isaiah 40:31; see Psalm 124:8; 23:4).

The prologue of Mark's gospel ends at this point. It summarises the work of our redemption in Christ, which Mark will spell out in greater detail throughout the rest of the gospel.

# CHAPTER 11

# Jesus' Early Galilean Ministry

(1:14-3:6)

## The Good News of the Reign of God

> After John had been put in prison (Mark 6:17), Jesus went to Galilee and preached the Good News from God. 'The right time has come,' he said, 'and the Kingdom of God is near! Turn away from your sins and believe the Good News.' (Mark 1:14-15).

As Mark is about to move into the main part of the gospel, he concludes his prologue on an ominous note – the imprisoning of John the Baptist by Herod, the tetrarch of Galilee. Mark will later provide details of John's fate. (See Mark 6:14-29). John's sufferings prefigure those of Jesus. After John's arrest, Jesus began preaching, as John had been preaching. The lesson here is that you preach the "good news" and then you are handed over to be punished. Jesus will preach the good news of the reign of God and he will be "handed over." (Mark 14:10, 18:21). His followers are warned of the same fate. (Mark 13:9-12). It becomes immediately apparent that proclaiming and living the "good news" is going to be testing and costly. Mark's shift between reminders of Jesus' heavenly identity and the ominous note of opposition to him will set the tone for the first eight chapters of the gospel.

With John the Baptist away in prison, his mission has been accomplished. The way has been prepared for the Son of God. Jesus may have taken John's absence from the scene as a signal from God that this was the time for him to break with John and go public with his own mission. With this in mind, he left the Judean wilderness and went to Galilee in order to be with its masses of people who hungered and thirsted for liberation from their bondages. Jesus will satisfy their hungering for freedom, dignity and acceptance in Israel. He has been anointed for his mission by the power of the Holy Spirit. He now begins a tour of preaching the "good news" in his native Galilee. His message is in words and deeds, revealing his power and authority to inaugurate the reign of God.

"The right time has come; the kingdom of God (his reign over evil) is near." (1:15). This means that the time has come for God's will to be done on earth, as it is in heaven. The king is now here in order to establish his just rule, replacing the divisive rule of Satan, which holds people in bondage to destructive forces and practices. Ever since Adam's disobedience, human beings have chosen to be kings themselves and to reign as individuals, like lost sheep – each one going his and her own individual way, away from one another and from God. (Isaiah 53:6). This is the way of self-centredness, what the prophets of Israel call self-exaltation. It destroys relationships. It can lead to unhealthy rivalry, breakdown of the human family, strife, wars. In its divisiveness, it represents the rule of Satan - a kingdom that will fall. (See Mark 3:25-26). The king who will do the will of God is now here. He is also the Good Shepherd who will gather and unite his flock from wherever they have been scattered. (See Ezekiel 34:11-13). This will be the undoing the divisive rule of Satan.

In what way does Jesus' message differ from John? Jesus preached the "good news." What was it about John's preaching that wasn't good news? John preached a message of repentance, but his emphasis was on punishment for sins. The God of John the Baptist was a punishing God. (See Matthew 3:7-10). The good news is that, as the 'powerful one,' and the 'beloved Son of God,' Jesus is the one who is empowered to rescue Israel and humanity at large from its sins and establish the reign of God over evil.

The really good news is that Jesus has come into the world to deal with evil and put everything right. He will do this not by calling for punishment. The God of Jesus Christ is a God of mercy, compassion and forgiveness. For Jesus, repentance is still important, but belief in the good news of the reign of God is also necessary. Believing means trusting that God can free human beings from their captivity to Satan. (Luke 4:18b). Jesus' mission was good news to the physically and spiritually poor (Luke 4:18a), the dispirited and lost sheep of Israel - people living under bad shepherds. The prophet Ezekiel foretold a time when God would melt Israel's stubborn heart of stone and give it an obedient heart. (See Ezekiel 11:19-20; 34:11-12). Jesus is the faithful remnant of Israel, the one with the compassionate and obedient heart, as foretold by Ezekiel. He is obedient to the mission of service to which God has called him. (See Luke 4:18-20). Through his mercy and compassion, Jesus transforms the lives of all those hungering for meaningful life. The poor of Israel had no trust (belief) that Israel's hard-hearted leaders would ever rescue them from their desperate plight. They were in the grip of Satan (symbolized by civil and religious rule). They hungered to be liberated from their lives of fear, anxiety, sickness and their sense of being excluded from Israel. Once they experienced the love, mercy and compassion of Jesus, their hearts were moved to trust that he alone could feed their hungers for meaningful life. (Mark 6:34). Jesus looks at human beings and 'sees' only what they can become: transformed by his mercy and compassion. The Good and compassionate Shepherd feeds them with *his* kind of life. They eat and have "enough." (See Mark 6:42a).

Jesus' good news is no less intended for the religious and political leaders and the Zealots (those who believed in coercion and violent rebellion). Jesus will try to melt their stubborn hearts of stone, by offering them a new vision of love, mercy and compassion. He will invite them to create an inclusive society in which all of its people would be loved, accepted and cherished. But their ears will remain deaf to his all-encompassing vision. Their hearts will remain stubborn to the needs of the poor in their society. Rather than trusting Jesus and listening to his good news, they had placed their trust in a number of false gods which held them in a satanic grip. Jesus will invite them to "sell everything," i.e. to give up their addiction to worldly power, possessions, honour, status and prestige, and follow him on his path of mercy. (See Mark 10:21-22). Jesus will call them to repent of their delusions and place their trust in the 'good news' of his new message of love, forgiveness, inclusivity and reconciliation, because this would be the only way of establishing the reign of God over evil. The kingdom of God cannot be established by the exercise of any kind of power, only by compassionate service. (See Isaiah 44:22; Hosea 14:1-3).

Jesus' still loved all those who rejected his message of love and mercy, and who found no room for him in the 'Inn' of their stubborn hearts (Ezekiel 11:19). Through envy and jealousy, they sought to be rid of him by hanging him up on a Roman cross. He responded to their evil act with love, mercy and forgiveness, thus loving and forgiving his enemies. (See Matthew 5:43-45). Jesus good news of love, mercy, compassion and forgiveness was also Christianity's good news to the pagan world outside Israel. It is the same message for today's world. God wants all of us to imitate the mercy, compassion and forgiveness of Jesus in our own relationships with one another.

At the beginning of Mark's story, the reign of God has arrived and the people of Israel are called to turn their lives around. (Mark 1:15). The reign of God will not come effortlessly. Not everyone will follow the 'way' of Jesus – the way of love and inclusivity. The initial responses of the people and the disciples will be positive. Almost immediately, however, the religious leaders will harden their hearts against Jesus, and his disciples will find it hard to understand him and his new "way." But despite all the obstacles, Jesus will not waver in the discharge of his mission of bringing 'good news to the poor' (Luke 4:18), a mission on which he firmly believed God had sent him, a mission which will eventually be extended way beyond the borders of Israel – to all of human beings, who still know nothing of mercy, compassion and forgiveness. (Matthew 28:18-19).

## Jesus Calls his First Disciples

As Jesus walked along the shore of the Lake of Galilee, he saw two fishermen, Simon and his brother Andrew, catching fish with a net. Jesus said to them, 'Come with me and I will teach you to catch people.' At once they left their nets and went with him. He went a little further on and saw two other brothers, James and John, the sons of Zebedee. They were at their boat getting their nets ready. As soon as Jesus saw them, he called them; they left their nets and went with him. (Mark 1:16-20).

As Jesus sets out on his mission of liberation, he needs helpers. With this in mind, he forms the nucleus of a group of people around himself, with whom he will begin to build his new family of God (Kingdom). These four will be the leading men of the twelve apostles.

He called them to accompany him on his missionary journey of establishing the reign of God - to discover his identity as Messiah and Son of God, to absorb his all-inclusive vision for the union of humanity and to prepare them to continue his mission after he has gone back to the Father. Initially, they were prepared to "sell all" and follow him. Their new role as catchers of people might transform them. It could add meaning to their lives by giving them a purpose for living. But for a long time, they would have no idea where Jesus was leading them, and in the end, they would fail to go all the way with him. Before Jesus called these four to follow him, they may already have heard him preaching the "good news" and found it attractive.

Jesus asked these men to give up everything for the sake of a new destiny. It would mean abandoning obligations to their families, something unheard of in that day. (Mark 1:20), but it would lead to the creation of a new brotherly union a "hundred times greater" than that of a natural family. (Mark 10:29-30). Following him would mean much more than as interested observers. It would mean living out his message in their daily lives, so that God could establish a new spiritual family in which his will would be obeyed. (Mark 3:33-35). Turning towards Jesus entails turning towards others in service, in order to extend God's family ("catching people," 1:17). The four fishermen might have been regarded as people of little account, but they were the men Jesus tasked with gathering God's people from among the nations. (Matthew 28:18-19). The phrase "catch people" recalls Jeremiah, in which God promised to send out many fishermen to gather in the Israelites who had been scattered in exile among the nations. (Jeremiah 16:14-16; see Mark 13:27). Just as Abraham immediately set out on a long journey when God called him, the four fishermen did not hesitate. (Genesis 12:1-4; Mark 1:20).

These four disciples, Simon (later named Peter, meaning a rock), Andrew, James and John, became Jesus' most intimate friends. (1:29; 13:3; 14:33). In his gospel, Mark does not hesitate to show their failures as disciples, i.e. as followers of Jesus. (8:32-33; 10:35-40; 14:66-72). Although Mark has already proclaimed Jesus as Son of God, at this stage the four fishermen do not have a clue about the meaning of that, or about the full implications of following him. (Incidentally, Mark does not record Jesus as having ever told his disciples about his anointing as Son of God by the Spirit, 1;11). They would not have understood the meaning of this. It is something they will have to discover for themselves, as Jesus gradually reveals his identity to them. Once their eyes become fully opened to the full identity of Jesus, their courage and faithfulness to him will lead to the gathering of the nations into the kingdom. (See Acts 2:38-41). Mark portrays the prominent role of Peter, as leader and spokesperson of Jesus' disciples, a group that did include faithful women. (Mark 3:16; 8:29; 14:37; 16:7; Matthew 16:18-19). Peter stood up on Pentecost Day and "caught" 3,000 people for Christ. (Acts 2:38-41). In living the life of Jesus, the apostle James was executed by Herod for preaching the "good news." (Acts 12:2).

Jesus wants to emphasise that discipleship will be central to his story, as he creates a new family around himself whose father is God. (Mark 3:33-35). "Follow me," he says. This means that *he* comes first. Following Jesus takes precedence over everything else. It means abandoning everything – family, career – for the sake of a new family of God. (Luke 14:26). The phrase, "I will make you" signifies a transformation that Jesus will work in his followers, but he will struggle to make his first disciples into "fishers of people." Lake Galilee is in a sense, a symbol of a world under demonic rule from which "fish" must be "caught" so that the reign of God may be established.[118]

## Jesus Begins his Work of Liberation

> Jesus and his disciples came to the town of Capernaum and on the next Sabbath Jesus went to the synagogue and began to teach. The people who heard him were amazed at the way he taught, for he wasn't like the teachers of the law; instead, he taught with authority. Just then a man with an evil spirit in him came into the synagogue and screamed, 'What do you want with us, Jesus of Nazareth? Are you here to destroy us? I know who you are – you are God's holy messenger.' Jesus ordered the spirit, 'Be quiet, and come out of the man.' The evil spirit shook the man hard, gave a loud scream and came out of him. The people were all so amazed that they started saying to one another, 'What is this? Is it some kind of new teaching? This man has authority to give orders to the evil spirits and they obey him.' And so, the news about Jesus spread quickly everywhere in the province of Galilee. (Mark 1:21-28; see Luke 4:16-19; Isaiah 61:1-2; 58:6-7).

Capernaum was located on the northern shore of Lake Galilee. It was Jesus' home base for his ministry in Galilee. He may have shared a house there with Simon and Andrew. After he later left Galilee, Jesus' ministry assumed an itinerary character. Being continuously on the road, he and his disciples may have lived in tents. But how were they supported? A number of women disciples accompanied Jesus on his long and winding journey to Jerusalem. (See Mark 15:40-41). Luke's gospel mentions Mary Magdalene, Joanna, and Susanna as women who accompanied Jesus and "used their own resources to help Jesus and his disciples." (Luke 8:1-3).

By this time most villages in Galilee would have had a synagogue where people gathered on the Sabbath day for prayer, Scripture readings and instruction in the law of Moses and the prophets. At the beginning of his mission, Jesus regularly attended synagogue services and taught in them. (Luke 4:14-15; John 6:59).

The Sabbath is the seventh day of the week, on which God "rested" after the creation of the world (Genesis 2:2-3) and commanded a day of rest for his people. (Exodus 20:10-11). Jesus respects the holiness of this day. He performs many works of liberation on the Sabbath, as signs of the restoration of human dignity that had been disfigured as a result of the disobedience of Adam and Eve. (Genesis 3:11). Days of "rest" would be given to people whom Jesus restored to new life.

In the synagogue, anyone with knowledge of the Scriptures could be invited to comment on the readings. Mark will repeatedly emphasise the amazement of Jesus' listeners at his words and deeds. (Mark 6:2; 7:37; 10:26; 11:18). In contrast to the scribes, whose teaching derived from the authority of their Scriptures, Jesus spoke as one who

---

[118] Brendan Byrne, *A Costly Freedom – a Theological Reading of Mark's Gospel*, (Liturgical Press, 2008), p. 42.

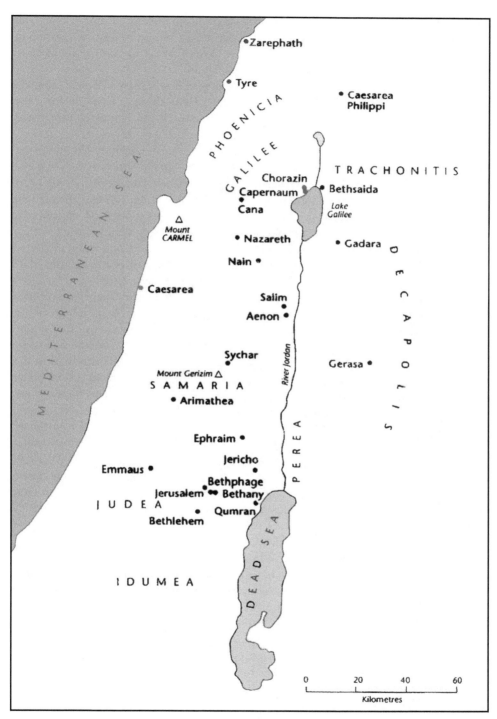

*Map of Palestine in New Testament Times*

had been anointed with the Spirit of God, and so, could speak with the authority of God himself, to reveal the definitive meaning of the Scriptures. For Jesus, it was a question of 'Now I say to you,' rather than referring to what Moses said, as the scribes would do in their own teaching. (See Matthew 5:21-22, 27-28, 33-34).

The man with the evil spirit probably had been listening to scribal teaching on every Sabbath day in the same synagogue, but that did nothing to free him from the control of the evil spirit. However, when Jesus began to teach, the demon felt threatened and cried out in alarm.

The evil spirit felt the brunt of Jesus' authority, which may have led him to see that Jesus was "God's holy messenger" and because of that, to feel threatened. (Verse 24). The phrase "God's holy messenger" is usually reserved for God (1 Samuel 2:2; Hosea 11:9), but is sometimes used for priests and prophets. (2 Kings 4:9; Psalm 106:16). Throughout his ministry, the evil spirits claim a hidden knowledge of Jesus' identity - a frequent demonic tactic. (Mark 3:11; 5:7; see Matthew 4:3). In possessing such knowledge, they demonstrate their power, a power through which they hope to control Jesus, as they have been controlling human beings. But confronted with the superior power of Jesus, they become fearful of their downfall and scream out in despair. (Mark 1:26).

Jesus' action in bringing peace and order to the man's internal chaos, echoes God's ordering of primeval chaos at the first creation. (Genesis 1:1, 6-10; Job 26:10-12; see Mark 4:39). A world of chaos is one at war with itself. Jesus is accomplishing a new creation. In his release of the man from the bondage of Satan in the foregoing passage, Jesus is banishing chaos and restoring God's world to its original harmony as in the Garden of Eden. God's promise that he would crush the serpent's head is now being fulfilled. (Genesis 3:15b). The demon's cry is one of defeat. Jesus brings new hope and joy to a troubled soul – a foretaste of resurrection. Jesus' loud cry on the cross (Mark 15:37) is an apparent triumph for the demonic, but is, in fact a moment signalling its ultimate defeat. Jesus is now taking on a role that no other human being could attempt. His teaching is new and authoritative because it is linked to his power to accomplish what it says, in fulfilment of the prophecy of Isaiah (Isaiah 55:10-11), i.e. to expose evil so that it can be expelled. As Son of God, his teaching and good works come with the authority of God himself, and with the good news of God's plan for freeing human beings from their captivity to the demonic. (See Mark 1:39; 6:12-13; CCC 391-95). This is the good news that spread "quickly everywhere in Galilee." (Mark 1:28).

Empowered by the Spirit, and following his rejection of Satan in the wilderness, Jesus is ready to begin his dethronement of Satan. The reign of God has come and is visible in the works of Jesus. Already John the Baptist's prophecy of a "more powerful one than me" (1:7, NJB) is being fulfilled before the eyes of the people in the synagogue at Capernaum. From now on in the gospel, there will be many accounts of Jesus' healings and exorcisms. Jesus has been named the "beloved" Son of God with whom the Father is "pleased." (Mark 1:11). This means that he is fully obedient to the mission of caring handed to him by the Father. Adam, the first human representative, refused this same mission and was obedient only to his own desires. But having walked away from his God-given mission (Genesis 3:8), he found himself suddenly "naked," no longer drawing his life and strength from God. (Genesis 3:7). We should see the liberating works of Jesus as signs of our rescue from destructive forces and being clothed with divine life. (See Mark 5:15). In his obedience to his mission of caring, Jesus undoes, on our behalf, the disobedience of the first human representative, who walked away into hiding, thus refusing his God-given mission. (Genesis 3:6).

> On leaving the synagogue, Jesus and his disciples, including James and John, went to the house of Simon and Andrew. Simon's mother-in-law was sick in bed with a fever. Jesus went to her, took her by the hand and helped her up. Then the fever left her and she began to serve them. (Mark 1:29-31; NRSVC).

Jesus' first exorcism in the synagogue is followed by his first physical healing - both being signs of the initiation of the Kingdom of God. In the gospels, illness is closely related to demonic possession, and as part of the fallen human condition, from which Jesus has come to liberate human beings. (See Matthew 12:22; Mark 9:20; Luke 13:20). Simon's wife is not mentioned here, but according to St. Paul, Simon Peter's wife accompanied him on at least some of his missionary journeys. (See 1 Corinthians 9:5).

Whatever the malady afflicting Simon's mother-in-law, she was unable to carry out the demands of hospitality for her honoured guest. In addition to her physical illness, she may have been upset and saddened over her inability to serve Jesus. Jesus will use the word "serve" (verse 31) to sum up his own mission and the mission of his disciples. He himself came to serve – to take people "by the hand" (verse 31) and raise them up. (Mark 10:45). Jesus would have understood the woman's feelings, and was moved by pity to "take her by the hand and help her up." Jesus' healings often involve his physical contact with the patient, demonstrating his personal and consoling approach. And he wasn't going to be bound by Jewish laws of ritual purity which held that anyone touching a sick person was made ritually "unclean." Jesus' helping her up (1:31) has echoes of being raised up, the same word used for his resurrection. (Mark 16:6). Jesus' healings and exorcisms are signs of an ultimate resurrection for all human beings. Later in the gospel, he will challenge the Jewish purity laws because they have the effect of keeping people apart and making outcasts - a divided family, a kingdom at war with itself, one that would fail. (See Mark 3:25).

The mention of service on the part of women at the beginning and the end of Mark's gospel (see 15:40-41), makes Simon's mother-in-law a model for all women disciples who are raised up for life in Jesus' kingdom, serving along with Jesus himself. In the gospel, there is always a place for the ministry of women alongside that of the male disciples. (Luke 8:1-3; John 12:2). Christians are called to rise up and serve the needs of others.

> After the sun had set and evening had come, people brought to Jesus all the sick and those who had demons. All the people of the town gathered in front of the house (that of Simon). Jesus healed many who were sick with all kinds of diseases and drove out many demons. He would not let the demons say anything, because they knew who he was. (Mark 1:32-34).

Constantly in the Galilean ministry - in the excitement generated by his healings - the press of the crowd on Jesus is a recurring theme. But Jesus doesn't want the demons to betray his messianic status at this stage of his ministry, for fear of giving the wrong impression to the civil authorities. This may have been the reason why he wants to leave Capernaum with no further delay. (1:38).

For Mark, the healings and casting out of demons make the presence of the reign of God real and perceptible. Those events are inseparably linked to the proclamation of the gospel, both for Jesus, and later on, for his disciples. (6:12-13; 16:15-18). Jesus' mission is to seek and save the lost. (Luke 19:10; see John 3:17; 12:47).

> Very early, the next morning, long before daylight, Jesus got up and left the house. He went out of the town to a lonely place where he prayed. But Simon and his companions went out searching for him, and when they found him, they said, 'Everyone is looking for you.' Jesus answered, 'We must go on to the other villages round here. I have to preach there also, because that is why I came.' So he travelled all over Galilee, preaching in the synagogues and driving out demons! (Mark 1:35-39; see Psalm 57:7-9; 92:1-2; 1 Thessalonians 5:17; Luke 4:42-43).

The above passage reminds us of Jesus' humanity. Like every other human being, Jesus seeks the guidance of God in prayer. Aware that crowds would be following him, Jesus was determined to find time for prayer and reflection. The "lonely place" recalls the wilderness in Mark 1:12-13, a place of solitude, free from distractions, where he could more easily commune with his heavenly Father. We can speculate that the subject of his prayers must have been God's will for his mission of liberation, and how it might be accomplished. He must also have prayed for his disciples. Mark mentions Jesus at prayer also in 6:46; 14:32-34.

"Searching for him!" The disciples may have begun to "see" Jesus as the one who might satisfy their deepest desires and longings. Everyone is looking for Jesus, but maybe for the wrong Jesus, or the wrong things. (Song of Songs 1:7). The disciples' "searching" has echoes of the human search for God. Human beings are searchers; we have a hunger for many things: possessions, security, comforts, status (Mark 10:17-21) - all of which may represent a distorted search for God. Our desires appear to be infinite. Because material things are finite, they can never fully satisfy the longings of the human heart for what is permanent. Only the infinite God can satisfy our deepest hungering. Only in God, can we find fulfilment through the truth, love and happiness for which we never stop searching. (CCC 27, 29). People were searching for Jesus because he could rescue them from their human limitations and give them meaningful life.

The disciples, however, would continue the search for a long time before they would really "see" Jesus as the one who would fully satisfy their deepest longings. 'Seeing' in this sense means 'understanding.' As we will later see in Mark's gospel, Jesus' understanding of God and his vision of life will prove to be vastly different from that of the disciples. Now, in his response to their searching, he reveals his aim and the task ahead, which is to fulfil the mission on which he has been "sent" by God (Mark 1:38) - possibly a decision he arrived at during his night of prayer. (1:35). The time has come for him to leave Simon's house and set out on that long road into the wider world. Without further delay, he must embark on a journey of preaching the 'good news', not only in words, but with a power that would have a dramatic effect on people. Through him, God responds to searching for release from all the disabling forces preventing human beings from attaining the fullness of their humanity.

The expulsion of a demon in the synagogue at Capernaum (1:25) is typical of a wider campaign of usurping Satan, in order to gain lives for the Kingdom of God. By saying, 'Let us go,' Jesus includes his disciples in his mission. Travelling "all over Galilee" (1:39) has implications of both time and distance. This must have been a mission lasting a number of months. (The Roman province of Galilee was about twenty-five miles from east to west and thirty-six miles from north to south).[119] The only means of travel would have been on foot, although people sometimes rode donkeys.

> A leper came to Jesus, begging him for help, and kneeling, he said to him, 'If you choose, you can make me clean.' Moved with pity, Jesus stretched out his hand and touched him and said to him, 'I do choose. Be made clean!' Immediately the leprosy left him, and he was made clean. (Mark 1:40-42, NRSVC).

In approaching Jesus, the leper violates the strictures of Jewish law, and risks the revulsion of anyone approaching him. The religious authorities would have treated the leper as ritually unclean and excluded him from the community.

Leprosy may have included a number of other skin diseases. In the society of Jesus' day, lepers were regarded as punished by God for their sins. They suffered social and religious exclusion by being compelled to live in a wilderness outside towns and villages. (See Leviticus 13:45-46). All of which, must have left people who were suffering from skin diseases in a state of despair. Regarded as ritually unclean, they were refused entry to the temple, God's holy dwelling place – confirmation of the temple's misuse of keeping people separated, as against God's will for the gathering together of humanity. Nobody had any "pity" (verse 41) for lepers, well, not until Jesus came. Jesus meets their despair with compassion and hope – God satisfying the desire of the human heart for life and happiness. Jesus is already on the road towards the fulfilment of his mission. Just like the shepherd gathering his scattered sheep, Jesus is God's new Shepherd, feeding the hungering of the 'poor' and bringing all of them home. Jesus is doing the work for which he was "sent." (See Ezekiel 34:11).

The religious leaders didn't touch lepers because they believed they would become ritually unclean as a result. But Jesus wasn't afraid to touch the man who was socially excluded. Jesus was not defiled by the leper. He removed the defilement. The man was thus restored to full membership of Israel and welcomed back into his community, thus fitting him for life in God's Kingdom.

The leper kneels before Jesus in a sign of supplication and reverence. (Psalm 22:30; 95:6). Both his kneeling and his plea "if you choose" shows his sense of dependency and his faith in the power of Jesus to make him clean. If the leper saw his ailment as the

---

[119] *Catholic Bible Dictionary*, map of Palestine of the New Testament.

consequence of his sins, then his healing would restore him, both in body and soul, to new life. This healing of the leper illustrates the difference of approach between John the Baptist and Jesus in dealing with the broken human situation. (See Mark 1:15). And it is in stark contrast to that of the religious authorities.

After healing the man of leprosy, Jesus warned him not to tell anyone. The man however, spread the news everywhere, so that Jesus could not go into a town publicly. (Mark 1:43-45). At this stage of his ministry, Jesus may have been wary of being arrested by the civil authorities as a Messiah pretender, a development that might bring a sudden end to his ministry. The cost to Jesus is not uncleanness over touching a leper. Rather, it is in the anger and hostility which his healings will provoke, an anger that will lead to enmity and jealousy on the part of the religious leaders. (See Mark 15:10). Once the people begin to follow one whom the leaders view as a rival, that person becomes a threat to their status as teachers and guardians of Israel's religious heritage. The "uncleanness" of the leper is symptomatic of the psychological state of the civil and religious powers in Israel. All of them need to be liberated from their self-righteousness. The irony is that they themselves are really the unclean ones. But in their blindness, they could only see themselves, as the 'good' people.

Jesus will soon begin to feel the pressure of the demonic in the guise of both the civil and the religious authorities. So instead of the towns, he stayed out in lonely places, and people flocked to him from everywhere. (Mark 1:45). Jesus was thus being treated as a leper. He had become as though one abandoned, a kind of outcast in the same wilderness from which he set the leper free. Such is the cost of proclaiming the good news – then and today. Jesus' costly entrance, as Son of God, into the "uncleanness" of the human situation, will climax at Calvary, with isolation and abandonment, even by his closest friends - and everyone else too. The wild beasts of the wilderness will soon begin to growl and bite in earnest. (Mark 1:13).

When we approach Jesus, especially in the sacrament of reconciliation, he is not scandalized or contaminated by any human defilement. He willingly removes it and restores us to communion with others and with God. (See CCC 1422-25).

## Scribes, Pharisees and Sadducees

The religious leaders fall into four main groups. First of all were the scribes. In the local synagogue the community came together on the sabbath day for Scripture readings and prayers. The scribes were people who made copies of the Old Testament Scriptures for use in these services, over which they themselves may have presided. Because of their familiarity with the Scriptures, they had become experts on the law of Moses, making them "teachers of the law." Some of them may also have been Pharisees.

The Sadducees belonged to the priestly class, which was hereditary. To become a priest, one had to be the son of a priest. The priests were centred in Jerusalem, although many of them would have lived outside the city. They had no official function in the synagogues. Their main duty was offering animal sacrifices in the Jerusalem temple. They were trained in Jewish law, their Scriptures being mainly the first five books of today's Bible. It is thought that they paid less heed to the writings of the prophets. They supported the status quo and did not believe in rebellion against the pagan Romans, because they owed their status and influential positions in society to Roman patronage. They lived elaborate lifestyles, while the ordinary peasant struggled to survive. Many of the priests may have been large landowners. Unlike the Pharisees, they did not believe in the general resurrection of the dead. (Mark 12:18; Acts of the Apostles 23:7-8).

Levites were of a lower order of priesthood. They performed a number of manual duties in the temple: slaughtering animals for the sacrifices, manning the gates, cleaning the temple, and possibly managing the temple taxes.

The Pharisees came from the wealthier class of people. The Jewish historian Josephus (37-100 AD) claims that there were 6,000 Pharisees in Israel at the time of Jesus. Some of them may have been large landowners. They were members of a small party, which formed a revival movement within Judaism. They practiced strict piety and regarded themselves as guardians of Jewish law as found in the first five books of the Bible. The word "Pharisee" means the "separated one." To insulate themselves from defilement from Gentiles, and from Jews whom they classed as hopeless sinners, they developed innumerable rules and regulations of their own. (See Mark 2:18; 7:1-5). The Pharisees were concerned about the safeguarding of Jewish identity, which they felt was threatened by the Greek pagan culture of the day. Towards this end, they laid great stress on external observances: food laws, Sabbath observance, what was clean and unclean. They wanted to extend to the nation as a whole the holiness and observances that had been prescribed for the temple priests. They believed that their salvation depended, not on the mercy of God, but on their own efforts to observe these rules. So for them, it was a question of self-dependency rather than trusting in God. Jesus tried to teach them that salvation depended on trust in God rather than in their own piety and their petty laws and regulations. (See Mark 8:15; 12:15; Matthew chap. 23).

The Pharisees would load the outcasts and sinners with innumerable rules and regulations – a form of oppression. Contrary to that approach, Jesus said, 'Come to me all of you who are tired from carrying heavy loads (petty laws) and I will give you rest.' (Matthew 11:28). Jesus taught that, in order to be healed of any defilement, all that people needed do was approach himself in repentance and faith. Jesus saw that the Pharisees, along with the Gentile kings, were using the law as an instrument of oppression. He criticized their ritual observances, contrasting their outward piety with their lack of inner purity. (See Mark 7:5-8; Matthew 15:8). Yet Jesus was closer to them than the other religious groups. He agreed with their teaching on the general resurrection of the dead, the existence of angels, and commended their prayers, fasting and almsgiving. (Acts of the Apostles 23:7-8).

## Five Conflict Stories

So far, Jesus' mission has all the signs of success – preaching the good news, healing the sick and casting out demons. Then comes a turning point, with the opposition and disapproval of the religious authorities, leading to conflict. Jesus will face increasing resistance, culminating in a plot to kill him. A sequence of five conflict stories in Mark's gospel brings out into the open the threat of the scribes (teachers of the law) and Pharisees to Jesus. (Mark 2:1–3:6). Each conflict story further illustrates Jesus' "new teaching with authority" (1:27) and there are further revelations of his identity.

The sequence begins with the healing of a paralyzed man, and includes Jesus' calling the tax collector Levi, to be one of his disciples. This is followed by Jesus eating a meal in the house of Levi with other tax collectors and outcasts. The conflict with the authorities ends with the healing of the man with the paralyzed hand in a synagogue on the Sabbath day. (Mark 3:1-6).

## Healing the Paralysed Man

Jesus went back to Capernaum, and the news spread that he was at home. So many people came together that there was no room left, not even out in front of the door. Jesus was preaching the message to them when four men arrived, carrying a paralyzed man to Jesus. Because of the crowd, however, they could not get the man to him. So they made a hole in the roof right above the place where Jesus was. When they had made an opening, they let the man down, lying on his mat. Seeing how much faith they had, Jesus said to the paralyzed man, 'My son, your sins are forgiven.' Some teachers of the law who were sitting there thought to themselves, 'How does he dare talk like this. This is blasphemy! God is the only one who can forgive sins.' At once Jesus knew what they were thinking, so he said to them, 'Why do you think such things? Is it easier to say to this paralysed man, 'Your sins are forgiven' or to say, 'Get up, pick up your mat and walk? I will prove to you then that the Son of Man has authority on earth to forgive sins.' So he said to the paralysed man, 'I tell you get up, pick up your mat and go home.' While they all watched, the man got up, picked up his mat and hurried away. They were all completely amazed and praised God, saying, 'We have never seen anything like this.' (Mark 2:5-12; see Psalm 51; Isaiah 43:25).

What kind of a house was this, in which a hole could easily have been made in its roof? At the time of Jesus, houses in the rural villages of Galilee were built of stone. The walls were covered with a coating of hardened clay, and whitewashed. The houses usually had one large room. The flat, slightly sloped roofs were made of strong timber trusses and covered with a lattice of wattle or straw. Laid over that was a covering of hardened clay, making the roof durable enough to spill off the light rainfall of that climate. This outer layer of the roof often needed repair. Making a hole in such a roof would be easy. There were steps on the outside of the house leading up to the roof. The family often went up there for relaxation or prayer, and perhaps, sometimes to eat. In such houses, there was a small room attached to the back of the house for the ox and the donkey. Was it in a room like this that Jesus was born, because there was "no room for him in the inn?" (Luke 2:6-7). The ox was used to pull carts and to plough the land for growing wheat. The donkey was used for light farm-work and to carry people on a journey. Sheep were kept for their meat and wool. Goats provided milk for the family.

The foregoing account is the first of five conflict stories with the religious leaders in Galilee. The first and the fifth are paired episodes about healings. The second and fourth are about eating. The central episode is about fasting. There are a number of hostile forces with which Jesus finds himself in conflict. First of all are the demons, illness and forces of nature. Second is his conflict with the religious authorities, and thirdly, with his disciples. These conflicts are about power, the misuse of power by some people, and contrasted with that, the use of power to serve.

It is the arrival of the reign of God that gives rise to all of these conflicts. God is now taking action to bring his creation into harmony with itself. But the forces of evil will be opposing him. Through the prophet Isaiah, God spoke powerful words about a future Messiah King who would "come to rule with power." (Isaiah 40:10-11). God's rule calls for a new social order, free from the oppression of the ruling powers in Israel, both civil and religious. Jesus condemns these authorities for being uncaring, destructive and oppressive. But underlying all of this, Jesus upsets the conventional idea of God and sets forth a new understanding of the merciful, compassionate and forgiving God, which the powers reject. Hence the conflict!

This first conflict story draws on the biblical theme connecting sin to illness. (See Psalm 38:2-18; 107:17; Exodus 34:6-7; Isaiah 43:25). There was a belief in Israel (probably promoted in scribal teaching) that illness could be caused by a person's own sins or those of his or her parents. It is quite possible that such a belief, strongly held, could paralyze a person both mentally and physically. Jesus sees into the paralyzed man's heart, and as a condition of freeing him from his physical paralysis, he releases the man from a burden of guilt (spiritual paralysis) that he may have borne, perhaps for years. (Mark 2:9). Although illness is contrary to God's intention, it is one of the evils which afflicts humanity, sometimes as a consequence of personal sin. This does not mean that all illness can be attributed to personal sins. The examples of Job (Book of Job) and the just man in the psalms show that innocent people also suffer. Jesus' works of healing are a revelation of his divine identity, and thus, of his power to take away sins. (Exodus 8:6; 10:2; 16:12; Isaiah 45:3).

The scribes know well that forgiveness of sins is a prerogative of God alone. (See Psalm 51; Isaiah 43:25). Their immediate reaction is to accuse Jesus of blasphemy (verse 7), the charge on which he will be condemned to death at his trial. (Mark 14:64). For the first time, Jesus refers to himself as the 'Son of Man' (2:10), a title he will use later as he speaks of his passion (8:31) The ongoing opposition by the religious authorities to Jesus will eventually lead to his death. The proof that the paralyzed man's sins were forgiven was that he got up when Jesus said, 'Get up' - the same words used in Jesus' resurrection. (See Mark 16:6). The man's healing was a kind of resurrection.

In a certain sense, the paralyzed man may be said to represent humanity in its state of paralysis (a kind of death) from which it cannot free itself. Jesus identifies with paralyzed humanity (Mark 1:9, 13), a humanity suffering the consequences (death) of its sins of disobedience. (Genesis 2:17b). With Jesus' forgiveness of sins after his resurrection (Luke 23:34), the paralysis of death is finally undone. The full implications of the forgiveness of sins will form the climax of Mark's gospel.

Thus, we see the aims of Jesus' mission on earth (Mark 1:15) already being realized in Mark's account of the healing of the paralyzed man in Capernaum. (2:1b). The reign of God over evil and death has truly come to earth.

The reaction of the crowd with amazement (2:12) may have inflamed the jealousy and resentment of the scribes with Jesus. Here was a man, who in their view, was acting as if he were God, doing only what God can do. They may thus have seen their status as the official teachers of Israel being undermined by Jesus, their status being dependent on the approval of the crowds, who were now amazed by the saving works of Jesus. (2:12).

We often rely on the faith and prayers of others (parents, teachers, friends, family members, even strangers) to "carry" us to Jesus, especially in times of spiritual darkness, illness or troubles of one kind or another. There are numerous ways in which we can help one another to "get up," one big way being forgiveness.

## The Call of Levi

> Jesus went back again to the shore of lake Galilee. A crowd came to him, and he started teaching them. As he walked along, he saw a tax collector, Levi son of Alphaeus sitting in his office. Jesus said to him, 'Follow me.' Levi got up and followed him. (Mark 2:13-14).

The second 'conflict' story is the call of the tax collector Levi to be a disciple, and its aftermath in a meal. Like the four fishermen, when they were called to leave their nets, Levi was also doing his job when he got the call to follow Jesus. The words 'follow me' changed his life. Tax collectors were despised, branded as extortionists, squeezing as much tax from the people as they could, their own income being a share of the collected tax. Levi's custom post was located on a trade route that went through Capernaum. (See Matthew 9:9).

A person collecting tax on behalf of the Roman government belonged to the class of people labelled as hopeless sinners, outcasts, untouchables. A question in the minds of the religious authorities was, 'How could Jesus invite this man into his inner circle?' (See Luke 19:2-7). Jesus' only concern was what persons could become, not their present state. Levi may have heard some of Jesus' teachings or witnessed his wonderful works. This may have left him open to what Jesus might do for him. Like the fishermen, his response to Jesus was immediate. (See Luke 19:2-7). Matthew's gospel names this tax collector as Matthew, who became one of the twelve apostles. (Matthew 9:9).

Levi may have felt a free man at last, Jesus having given him a way out of the bondage in which he may have felt imprisoned. (See Luke 19:1-10). Probably for this reason, large numbers of tax collectors were drawn to Jesus. (Luke 15:1-4). Mark confirms this in what follows next:

> Later on, Jesus was having a meal in Levi's house. A large number of tax collectors and other outcasts were following Jesus, and many of them joined him and his own disciples at the table. Some teachers of the law, who were Pharisees, saw that Jesus was eating with these outcasts and tax collectors, so they asked Jesus' disciples, 'Why does he eat with such people?' Jesus heard them and answered,

'People who are well do not need a doctor, but only those who are sick. I have not come to call respectable people, but outcasts.' (Mark 2:15-17).

Classed as sinners and outcasts, tax collectors may indeed have seen themselves in need of a doctor, while the Pharisees and teachers of the law looked on themselves as self-righteous and perfectly healthy, in a spiritual sense. They belonged to the class of 'good' people, who, in their own eyes, had no need of repentance, while they labelled everyone else as "such" people. (See Luke 18:9-14). On the other hand, because some tax collectors and sinners recognized their spiritual poverty, they were open to what God, through Jesus might do for them.

In Jewish culture, there was no greater way to cement a relationship than to share a common meal. (Genesis 26:30; 31:54; 1 Samuel 9:24). Israel's covenant relationship of love was celebrated by a meal. (Exodus 24:11; Deuteronomy 12:7). The hope of a future Messiah coming to save his people is often expressed in terms of the rich banquet which God would provide to celebrate the occasion. (Isaiah 25:6; 55:1-2; see Luke 15:27, 32). Jesus is this Messiah. Levi's new relationship with Jesus is followed by what would be regarded as its natural consequence: table fellowship, a sign of forgiveness and reconciliation – home from exile. In Levi's invitation of Jesus to a meal in his house (2:15a; see Luke 5:29), there is an implication that he has something to celebrate. The meal symbolizes a transformation from his old life to a whole new outlook - a sense of being forgiven, loved and accepted into the Israelite family, from which he had been excluded as an outcast. Levi's meal is thus, a celebration of renewed covenant relationship – God the Shepherd gathering his lost sheep, uniting them to himself and carrying them home to a celebratory feast with the neighbours. (See Luke 15:32).

In eating with sinners and accepting some of them as his disciples, Jesus demonstrates that he has the power to lead people to repentance and to forgive sins – to free people from the rule of Satan. The reign of God is thus being established. (Mark 1:15). Jesus' forgiveness of sins is the beginning of a new union of humanity (kingdom of God) being created around himself. Thus, we see the gradual unfolding of Jesus' divine status, and its effect on human beings. The religious leaders are scandalized by his claims and by Jesus' association with those whom they name as 'undesirables.' All they can do is demand an explanation from his disciples. (2:16b). In his saying that the sick need a doctor, Jesus is assuming the role of God as physician (Exodus 15:26), whose messianic mission is to heal and restore people to the fullness of their humanity and to fellowship with one another and with God. (John 10:10). Sin is a rebellion against God, a refusal to do his will. Through the sharing of a meal, Jesus rescues people from this state of rebellion and brings them into a new covenantal relationship with God. (See Jeremiah 3:22; Hosea 14:4-5).

Jesus did not want to exclude the scribes and Pharisees (the self-righteous) from his table fellowship. As St. Paul says, "no one is righteous." (Romans 3:9-18; see Psalm 14:1-3). All are sinners. Some admit to their lack of righteousness and repent, and some (like the Pharisees) do not, and then refuse Jesus' invitation. (See Matthew 22:1-3). Jesus' mission is an offer of healing to all.

This meal in the house of Levi is the first of several meals in Mark's gospel (see 6:41-42; 8:6-8; 14:3), leading up to the Last Supper – Jesus and his disciples celebrating the new covenant of love to be brought about by his death - God's definitive gathering of his people to a new relationship with himself and with one another. (Mark 14:22-24; see 16:14).

## The Bridegroom and the New Wine

On one occasion the followers of John the Baptist and the Pharisees were fasting. Some people came to Jesus and asked him, 'Why is it that the disciples of John the Baptist and the disciples of the Pharisees fast, but yours do not? Jesus answered, 'Do you expect the guests at a wedding party to go without food? Of course not! As long as the bridegroom is with them, they will not fast. But the day will come when the bridegroom will be taken away from them, and then they will fast.' (Mark 2:18-20).

Fasting was one of the three basic practices of Jewish piety. (Matthew 6:3, 6, 16). Although Jewish law only required fasting once a year, on the Day of Atonement[120] (Leviticus 16:29-34), the Pharisees – always outdoing everyone else in piety - fasted twice a week. Jesus and his disciples are observed to be not only feasting with sinners, but also failing to observe days of fasting. (See Matthew 11:11:18-19).

In the Old Testament, God's covenant of love was described in terms of a marriage between God and his people. God is the bridegroom, his people being the unfaithful bride. A wedding feast (banquet) is a metaphor for the Kingdom of God, with its implications of celebration, because of the two becoming joined together as "one" (Genesis 2:24), God united with his people. In the Old Testament, God revealed his love for his chosen people as a spousal love, even as they were unfaithful to him. "Your Creator will be like a husband to you – the Lord Almighty is his name. The holy God of Israel will save you – he is the ruler of the world." (See Isaiah 54:4-8). If God is often imaged as a bridegroom, and his people Israel as a bride, Israel behaved like an unfaithful bride. "Israel, like an unfaithful wife, you have not been faithful to me." (Jeremiah 3:20). God would do everything he could to win back his bride, promising to take her into the desert once again and woo her with words of love. Then, as prophesised, she would respond to him as she did in her young days after he rescued her and brought her out of Egypt. (See Hosea 2:14-23).

God's promise to make Israel his true and faithful wife and show her love and mercy for ever (Hosea 2:19) was not fulfilled in the Old Testament. Israel remained unfaithful and disobedient to God, refusing to do his will. "They are always rebelling against God, always lying, always refusing to listen to the Lord's teachings." (Isaiah 30:9). Israel remained blind and deaf to God's pleadings to come back to him. (Isaiah 42:18-19). The prophets were critical of Israel's failure to repent, but they looked ahead to a future messianic banquet (Isaiah 25:6-9), celebrating the bridegroom's marriage to his people, his new bride having been rescued from her disobedience. Up to the coming of Jesus, there had never been such a restoration. In the works of Jesus, the nuptial bond between

---

[120] *World's Bible Dictionary*, p. 90.

God and his people is now being restored through his feasting with his restored people.

Jesus' reply to the question of fasting in the foregoing passage reveals that he is now assuming the role of God, as the bridegroom. In his meals with outcasts and tax collectors (2:15), Jesus is already fulfilling Isaiah's prophecy of a messianic banquet. (See Isaiah 25:6-9). The meal in the house of Levi, who symbolically represents repentant Israel, can be interpreted as the feast prepared by God the Father for the wedding of his Son (the new bridegroom) to his bride, who has now repented of her sins of disobedience. (See Matthew 22:1-10). However, the self-righteous Pharisees and teachers of the law ('elder brothers') are unrepentant of their sins of exclusion ('why do you eat with such people?'), and have chosen to remain outside God's celebratory feasting, despite God's pleading. (See Luke 15:28; Matthew 5:20; 21:31). Jesus is the bridegroom, and Levi and other repentant and forgiven sinners represent the new Israel, God's new faithful bride – united with the bridegroom.

Jesus' table fellowship, his works of mercy and healings of the "sick" are signs that Israel's infidelities and infirmities are being washed away (sins forgiven), and that the wedding covenant is being renewed once and for all – God united with his people who are now home from exile. This represents a huge step in the formation of Jesus' new family–kingdom of God. It is forgiveness that brings about this united and reconciled family. As a sign of mourning, fasting - symbolizing life in exile from God - is out of place in this new situation. By continuing to fast, John's disciples and the scribes and Pharisees are still living in an old era that is now overtaken by the 'good news' of God: salvation (union with God) is for everyone – no exclusions. (Mark 1:14-15). For Jesus, the time of fasting is over. The bridegroom (Jesus) is now here. There remains one blot on this celebrating: the bridegroom will be taken away and killed. (Mark 2:20 above; see Isaiah 53:7-8). However, on the cross, the bridegroom will freely give his life for his bride (now encompassing the whole of humanity), with a love stronger than death. Through Jesus' sacrificial death, everyone is forgiven and thus reconciled to God. (Isaiah 53:10).

When Jesus is no longer visibly present on earth, his disciples will resume the practice of fasting, as a way of preparing for the full joy of the messianic banquet at the end of time, when Jesus will return in glory to definitively celebrate with his redeemed people, who are gathered with him – the shepherd definitively uniting his scattered sheep. (Matthew 25:3e; Revelation 19:5-8).

Mark concludes this section with two images which further symbolize the futile attempt to deal with a totally new reality by clinging to the outworn practices of Judaism. Jesus tells them:

> No one uses a piece of new cloth to patch up an old coat, because the new patch will shrink and tear off some of the old cloth, making an even bigger hole. Nor does anyone pour new wine into used wineskins, because the wine will burst the skins, and both the wine and the skins will be ruined. Instead, new wine must be poured into fresh wineskins. (Mark 2:21-22).

Old cloaks and old wineskins had completed their role in the Judaism of Jesus' day. Jesus didn't come merely to confirm his people in their outward devotional practices and man-made rules, such as fasting and dietary laws. These were never going to transform the human situation. To continue with them would be like patching an old worn garment, or putting new wine into old wine containers. Those outworn practices had been an attempt to gain salvation through human effort. In this, they could never succeed, no matter how hard the striving. Only God can transform humanity by creating a kingdom in which his will is done on earth as it is in heaven. (See Mark 3:33-35). Obedience of the heart is then more important than outward show or ritual. Jesus calls for fresh skins and new wine – a new vision, new ways of thinking and behaving, new ways of understanding God and what God wants. But the guardians of the old wine skins were finding the new wine of Jesus' ministry disturbing, and they would reject it. Jesus himself is the new wine, the best wine kept until last. The wine being served at the wedding feast of Jesus' ministry has a newness that takes people by surprise. (John 2:10; see Isaiah 25:6-8). This wine puts a new Spirit into people, making them appear as if drunk, giving them a new vision and empowering them to act with passion and enthusiasm for the good news. (See Acts of the Apostles 2:15-21).

## Lord of the Sabbath

The fourth conflict story involves a meal on the go. (Mark 2:23-28). Jesus and his disciples are so busy ministering to the crowds that they often have no time to eat. (3:20; 6:31; 8:1). Here, on their way to a new part of the country, the hungry disciples take advantage of their route along by a wheat field to pluck some grains of raw wheat. But a group of Pharisees are watching nearby to see if they can entrap Jesus. They accuse Jesus of breaking the Sabbath by doing forbidden work on that day: plucking grain. (2:24). The law of Moses prohibits reaping on the Sabbath. (Exodus 20:8-11). But they interpret hand-plucking to ease one's hunger on the road, as reaping, and therefore, as work forbidden on the Sabbath day.

Drawing a comparison between himself and King David, Jesus declares that the requirements of his messianic mission take precedence over the letter of the law. (Mark 2:25-26; see 1 Samuel 21:2-7). Jesus likens himself to David, and the disciples to David's loyal soldiers who were pursued by King Saul (1 Samuel 21), until David eventually took up his throne. Like David, Jesus is the Lord's anointed one, the Lord's Messiah, who is being persecuted by the leaders of Israel until he takes up his throne. The disciples, who share in his mission are doing God's work and are therefore granted a dispensation from the Sabbath regulations.

"And Jesus concluded, 'The Sabbath was made for the good of human beings; they were not made for the Sabbath. So the Son of Man is Lord even of the Sabbath.'" (2:27-28). In a veiled way, Jesus is pointing to his divinity, by assuming the authority that belongs to God alone, who instituted the Sabbath. (Genesis 2:2-3). The Sabbath was intended to bring human beings into closer union with God, a mission that will now be fulfilled in the work of Jesus. Why does Jesus heal on the Sabbath? It is because the 'Son of Man is Lord of the Sabbath.' The Hebrew word 'Sabbath' means 'rest,' because on that day God rested from his work of creation; his work was finished, and he was satisfied. Jesus *is* the Sabbath; it is he, who through his works of liberation, gives humanity rest, peace and fulfilment. On the cross, Jesus said, "It is finished." Then he could rest. We can rest too in the knowledge of what he has done for us.

## The Man with the Withered Hand

> Again he entered the synagogue, and a man was there who had a withered hand. They watched him if he would cure him on the Sabbath, so that they might accuse him. He said to the man with the withered hand, 'Get up and stand in the middle!' And he said to the man who had the withered hand, 'Come forward.' Then he said to them, 'Is it lawful to do good or to do harm on the Sabbath, to save life or to kill?' But they were silent. He Looked around at them with anger; he was grieved at their hardness of heart and said to the man, 'Stretch out your hand.' He stretched it out and his hand was restored. The Pharisees went out and immediately conspired with the Herodians against him, how to destroy him. (Mark 3:1-6, NRSVC).

This is the fifth conflict story. Many of Jesus' healings take place on the Sabbath day, the day of rest. On other days, the sick themselves or their relatives or friends approach Jesus for healing.

The whole point of the Sabbath commandment had to do with celebrating God's creation and redemption, past, present and future. In order to observe the Sabbath, the Mosaic law appointed the seventh day as a day of rest, free from work. (Exodus 20:8). But this had been lost sight of in a plethora of man-made rules defining what was, and was not "work."

The Pharisees' cold, hardness of heart is contrasted with Jesus' mercy. Instead of feeling compassion for the man with the withered hand, they use Jesus' healing as an opportunity to bring a legal charge against him, even though they would have known that the Mosaic law always allowed for action to preserve life on the Sabbath day. The man probably needed the use of his hand to do his daily work. Why wait any longer to restore it? The word "anger" (verse 5), used here by Jesus, is often used in the Old Testament to describe God's indignation in the face of human rebellion. (Exodus 32:10; Isaiah 60:10).

Jesus' phrase "come forward" is the same one used for his resurrection. (Mark 16:6; see John 11:43). Mark often uses that phrase in healing stories (1:3; 2:9-12; 5:41; 10:49), to indicate that Jesus is not only doing physical healings, but foreshadowing the definitive transformation of human life that would result from his resurrection – God's ultimate victory over suffering and death itself.

However, even if the Pharisees saw Jesus' healing as a forbidden "work" on the Sabbath day, this could hardly have been the sole reason why they formed a conspiracy to kill him. (Verse 6). So what was it that really angered them? There is more to this story than a simple account of a miracle. The key is Jesus' interpretation of Moses. Jesus could see that the Pharisees were using the man with the withered hand as a means of testing him, to see if he would fit into their idea of goodness. He would turn this incident into a teaching opportunity.

In his question to the Pharisees (verse 4), Jesus implies that obeying God's commandments means pursuing life and what is good (leading to blessing), and disobeying means pursuing death and evil. In other words, he is asking them if they are really celebrating the Sabbath according to Moses. (See Deuteronomy 30:15-16, 19-20). If they are, they should want him to choose life and good, by healing the man with the withered hand. So how could they accuse him of disobeying the law of Moses? What Moses meant, runs counter to their way of interpreting Moses. They could say nothing to Jesus' question. Jesus was grieved at their hardness of heart (verse 5), which signifies a stubborn refusal to be open to Gods saving word. (Jeremiah 11:8; Ezekiel 3:7; Ephesians 4:18). This is a stubbornness that, at times, will characterise even Jesus' disciples. (Mark 6:52; 8:17).

Jesus goes further in his interpretation of the Old testament for the Pharisees. The one person in the Old Testament who, more than anyone else, suffered from hardness of heart was the Egyptian Pharaoh. "Then the Lord said to Moses, 'Pharaoh's heart is hardened; he refuses to let the people go.'" (Exodus 7:14, NRSVC). Jesus is revealed here as the new Moses, looking at the new Pharaoh (the Pharisees and their "hardness of heart", v.5), refusing to "let one of God's people go." In this story, the man with the withered hand stands for the people of Israel – "withered," crushed, despised, marginalized by a plethora of man-made laws, from which official Israel, represented by the Pharisees, would not liberate them, would not "let them go." So as well as accusing them of misinterpreting Moses, Jesus also reproaches them for being a new enslaving Pharaoh. But he had even more than that to say to them.

Jesus then says to the man, 'Stretch out your hand.' This really angers them, because they know to what he is referring. He has made the man a symbol of Israel, now rescued by God from a new Pharaoh (the Pharisees). Jesus not only interprets Moses for the people in the synagogue; he assumes the role of God, who on several occasions during the build-up to the exodus from Egypt, says to Moses, 'Stretch out your hand,' which Moses often does, to good effect (Exodus 9:22; 10: 12, 21; 14:26), bringing confusion to the Egyptians; and especially at the Red Sea where the people were finally freed from the power of the Pharaoh. (Exodus 14:21-22; See Deuteronomy 4:34, NRSVC).

Jesus is revealing to the Pharisees that he, through the power of God, is fulfilling God's work of freeing Israel from its withered state - its disabling g man-made rules (7:1-23), which have the effect of dividing people into the "good" (Pharisees) and the "sinners" whom they regard as outcasts, represented in the synagogue by the man with the withered hand. The Pharisees' rules contravene the real good, the life-giving prescriptions of the Ten Commandments, which serve to unite people, as distinct from creating hostile groups.

The Pharisees would have well understood Jesus' references to the Old Testament Scriptures. In their own eyes, they were the spiritual heirs of Moses. On the contrary, Jesus reveals to them who they really are: acting like the Egyptian Pharaoh, as new oppressors. With Jesus having revealed himself both as the new liberating Moses, and assuming the role of God, it is little wonder that the Pharisees went out to form a plot to destroy him. (Mark 3:6). Ironically, the "good" they chose to do on the Sabbath was actually evil–to destroy life by conspiring to put Jesus to death, in a breach of fifth Commandment. (Exodus 20:13; See Mark 12:13). Jesus' fate is thus linked with that of John the Baptist, who will be killed by Herod. (Mark 6:14-29). This conspiracy is the first hint of the bridegroom being taken away and killed.

"Herodians" (verse 6 above) would not have meant officials in the court of Herod Antipas, tetrarch of Galilee, but politically minded Jews actively supporting his dynasty and enjoying his favour.[121] The unofficial leaders of Jewish opinion (the Pharisees) conspire with their natural enemies in an attempt to kill Jesus. On their own, the Pharisees did not have the authority to do away with Jesus. In the end, that would be a matter for those with real power, the chief priests and the Roman governor.

If we see ourselves as Pharisees, what in the above story might move us to anger? It might be a sudden revelation as to how wrong we were about something. Can we then accept the healing of forgiveness?

---

[121] *Jerusalem Bible* footnote to Mark 3:7.

CHAPTER 12

# THE LATER GALILEAN MINISTRY

(3:7-6:6a)

In the previous chapter, the conflict between Jesus and the Pharisees has reached a point where they begin to plot his death. (Mark 3:6). In response, Jesus withdraws to the sea and countryside. From this point on he avoids the synagogues and travels back and forth across the lake, often at night. He continues his ministry of teaching and healing in Galilee. While opposition to him will be mounting, his popularity with ordinary people will increase. People will flock to him from every quarter, from both Jewish and Gentile lands.

In the healing of the man with the withered hand, Jesus tried to open the eyes of the religious leaders to the truth about themselves and about God. He tried to show them that their perceived 'goodness' was an illusion. They wanted to build a kingdom of God around their own exclusive group – seen as "good" by comparison with other marginalized groups in their society, whom they regarded as bad, despised outcasts. As the story of the man with the withered hand in the synagogue reveals, they were intent in turning Jesus himself into an excluded one, even into a murdered victim. Their thoughts were not God's thoughts. (Isaiah 55:8-9). They had got it all wrong about God. The God who created the universe is a universal God (Isaiah 40:28), who does not favour any one group, race or state over others, but wants to establish a kingdom which will include everyone, even the Gentiles. This God cares for everyone. He "strengthens those who are weak and tired" – those whom the Pharisees despised. (Isaiah 40:29). Those who trust (faith) in this God "for help will find their strength renewed." (Isaiah 40:31).

Probably influenced by the prophecy of Isaiah, and knowing the mind of God, Jesus takes steps to do something new, something the scribes and Pharisees never dreamed of, i.e. to establish a new Israel, a new family of God around himself. (See Mark 3:13-15). There would be no obstacles to membership of this family. It would include all of those who had been "weak and tired," but who through their faith in Jesus, are now strengthened with new life. The messianic banquet proceeds apace. Satan, who presides over a divided kingdom (Mark 3:26), would remain as the one major obstacle to the creation of Jesus' new spiritual family.

## Jesus Chooses Twelve Apostles– Nucleus of the New Israel

> Jesus and his disciples went away to Lake Galilee, and a large crowd followed him. They had come from Galilee, from Judea, from Jerusalem and the territory of Idumea, from the territory on the east side of the Jordan, and from the region round the cities of Tyre and Sidon. All these people came to Jesus because they heard the things he was doing. The crowds were so large that Jesus asked his disciples to get a boat ready for him, so that the people would not crush him. He had healed many people, and all those who were ill kept pushing their way to him in order to touch him. And whenever the people who had evil spirits in them saw him, they would fall down before him and shout, 'You are the Son of God.' Jesus sternly ordered the evil spirits not to tell anyone who he was. (Mark 3:7-12; see Zechariah 8:23).

Idumea was more than two hundred miles to the south of Galilee. The cities of Tyre and Sidon were far north on the coast of present-day Lebanon. The territories on the east side of the Jordan river were other Gentile lands. All of these territories foreshadow the gospel's later outreach to the Gentile world.

Mark uses the words "went away." Jesus may have wanted to move away from conspiring Pharisees and from those in Galilee who might see his work as the makings of a rebellion against the Romans. He may have also sought some time for prayer and for instructing his disciples in private. (See 1:35; 3:13; 6:31-32). As was usual, the opposite took place. The Sea of Galilee will be the background in the scenes that follow.

Unlike the religious authorities or the crowds, the evil spirits had clear and certain knowledge of who Jesus was. Their prostration before him was not a sign of worship, but of obeisance, yielding to the superior authority and power of Jesus. (Mark 3:11, see Matthew 4:3). The crowds following Jesus were getting bigger. He was treading on dangerous ground. Herod and the Romans would not be impressed by rumours of any kingdom other than the one over which they themselves reigned.

The crowds were mainly interested in Jesus because of what he could do for them, hoping against hope for relief from debilitating illnesses. However, Jesus' conquest of Satan which began in the desert, was unstoppable. (Mark 1:13, 25-26, 34).

> Then Jesus went up a hill and called to himself the men he wanted. They came to him, and he chose twelve whom he named apostles. 'I have chosen you to be with me,' he told them. 'I will also send you out to preach, and you will have authority to drive out demons.' (Mark 3:13-15).

It now becomes clear that Jesus does not intend to carry out his mission on his own, but to form a chosen company to assist him, and to continue his work after he, the bridegroom has been "taken away" from them. (Mark 2:20). Mark highlights the solemnity of this act by stating that Jesus went up a hill. Moses went up Mount Sinai (Exodus 19:3) and under the direction of God, formed the original people of God, who were bound together as a people by the Ten Commandments – the old covenant. (Exodus 19:3; 24:1-4). The number twelve recalls the twelve tribes of Israel, descendants of the twelve sons of Jacob. This is an indication that the group Jesus is forming around himself - doing the will of God (Mark 3:35) - will constitute a new and renewed Israel.

Jesus must have intuited that the Pharisees, with their limited vision, represented old Israel. In choosing the twelve apostles, Jesus was establishing a new leadership for a new Israel, comprising himself and his followers. The word 'apostle' (from the Greek *apostolos*) means 'one who is sent out.' The call of the twelve is different from the earlier call of the disciples. (Mark 1:16-20; 2:14). The apostles are a special group chosen from among the disciples to participate in Jesus' mission in a unique way. (See Mark 6:7). Their names are given in Mark 3:16-19. In being sent out, they are to assist Jesus in his liberating mission of preaching and healing. (See Romans 10:15). Jesus calls the twelve to be "with" him, to listen to his teaching, to learn of his inclusive vision for the union of humanity, to support him in difficult times and not to let him down. (Mark 3:14). One of the apostles is named Judas, the man who will betray him.

In calling and forming the new people of God, the new Israel, Jesus is once again assuming the role of God, as prophet, shepherd and king. As the ancient Israelites were rescued by Moses from slavery in Egypt, the members of this new Israel would be liberated from their particular captivities to the new Pharaoh, namely the Satan lurking behind the oppressive powers. Jesus is the shepherd gathering his scattered sheep into his new family. His role as messianic King is evidenced in his fulfilment of Old Testament prophecies, which looked forward to a new King-Messiah who will rescue the new Israel, which represents the whole of humanity, and bring them definitively home from exile. (Isaiah 2:2,4; 9:6-7).

The call to discipleship is a universal call to follow Jesus, who sends all of us "out" on the very same mission as the apostles. Following him means participating in his mission. (Mark 2:15; 3:7; see Matthew 11:28-29). Each and every member of the Church, through its missionary vocation, is likewise called to mission. (Matthew 28:18-20; see CCC 849, 858).

## Jesus' Spiritual Family

Then Jesus went home. Again, such a crowd gathered that Jesus and his disciples had no time to eat. When his family heard about it, they set out to take charge of him, because people were saying, 'He's gone mad!' Some teachers of the Law who had come from Jerusalem were saying, 'He has Beelzebul in him! It is the chief of the demons who give him the power to drive them out.' So Jesus called them to him and spoke to them in parables. 'How can Satan drive out Satan? If a country divides itself into groups which fight each other, that country will fall apart. And if a family divides itself into groups which fight each other, that family will fall apart. So if Satan's kingdom divides into groups, it cannot last, but will fall apart and come to an end. No one can break into a strong man's house and take away his belongings unless he has first tied up the strong man; then can he plunder his house.' (Mark 3:20-27; see Mark 6:1-3 with reference to the names of Jesus' relatives).

In reference to Mark 3:20-21 above, perhaps Jesus' natural family may have been concerned about the opposition he was encountering, worried over the accusation levelled against him of working through the power of the devil (3:22), uneasy over his challenging of the official wisdom of Israel, and perhaps fearful of the trouble his mission might bring down on him and on themselves too.

Between Jesus' return home (3:20) and his family later coming to see him (3:31), Mark inserts an account of a group of scribes, who, for the first time in the gospel, came all the way from Jerusalem to confront Jesus. (Mark 3:22-30; see also 7:1-23). These scribes may have been people with greater expertise in the Mosaic law than the Pharisees of Galilee, who were Jesus' fiercest opponents. (Mark 7:1, 5; 10:33; 11:18, 27; 14:1). Having probably been sent by a higher authority, they arrived in Galilee spreading false rumours about Jesus, telling people, 'He has Beelzebul (the chief of devils) in him!' (3:22). This was a more serious misunderstanding of Jesus than that entertained by his family, who simply wanted to "take charge of him." (Verse 21). His family may have been fearful and taken aback by the rumours being spread by the scribes. The scribes' accusation amounted to a charge of practicing sorcery, which was a capital offence.

In order to refute the allegations of the scribes, Jesus called them to him and spoke to them in parables. He demonstrated the absurdity of Satan driving out Satan, of Satan being at war with himself. (3:23f). As John the Baptist had already announced: Jesus is the "more powerful one" (Mark 1:7, NJB), who, with the power of God's Spirit (Mark 1:10), has come to bind Satan, the "strong man" (Mark 3:27) guarding his house (Israel under the power of Satan). Jesus came to rescue Satan's belongings (human beings), in order to liberate them from his tyrannical rule. No one can release people from such captivity without first "tying up" the strong man. (3:27, see Isaiah 49:24-25). Jesus' exorcisms have a significance greater than everyday events. They reveal the ultimate overthrow of Satan and his power over human beings. Satan's divisive kingdom will "fall apart and come to an end." In 3:24-27 above, Mark implies that the end-time has arrived. Jesus (the stronger man) has won the final victory over Satan.

Since it is by the power of God's Spirit that Jesus expels demons, to accuse him of doing so through the chief of demons is the same as identifying the Spirit of God with the demonic world —a charge of blasphemy. Jesus warns the scribes that they will find themselves under the severe judgement of God unless they open their hearts to the Spirit of God and repent of their charges of attributing evil to the good works he is doing. They "call evil good and call good evil." (See Isaiah 5:20). This incident is the first sign of what may be in store for Jesus once he reaches Jerusalem at the end of his journey. Incidents like this are a continual reminder of the fate of the bridegroom.

As their journey from Jerusalem to Galilee suggests, the real concern of the official teachers of Israel may have been about Jesus' threat to their power and status. Any compassion for suffering humanity, or thoughts of freeing a fellow-Israelite from an oppression may not have occurred to them at all. For the scribes, such a man belonged to the class of outcasts and sinners - people to be shunned. In the Beelzebul story, Jesus may be casting the scribes in the role of the oppressor Pharaoh, who refused to set God's people free from Egypt. (Exodus 5:1-2).

Jesus' main purpose here may be to teach that Satan's kingdom, a country (Israel) cannot last, because it is divided into 'fighting groups.' (3:26 above; see Luke 10:18). Satan's kingdom tries to create social cohesion by the exclusion and victimization of undesirables (sinners, ritually unclean ones, lepers, tax collectors, disabled people, those possessed by demons). This makes the victimizers feel better about themselves by comparison with the undesirables. Such casting out, expelling some people or groups, as unworthy of membership of the people of God is a recipe for creating "groups which fight each other" (3:24 in the foregoing passage), because it creates enmity, resentment and hatred, a scattering of humanity and self-destruction. (Verse 25b). Israel, represented by its official teachers, was actually a kingdom divided against itself. (3:26). Jesus contrasts that kind of kingdom with the Kingdom of God, which is the undoing of the Satanic social structure based on exclusions. The Kingdom of God is founded on the self-giving service and care of Jesus for everyone, a kingdom which consists of a new and inclusive family, created by God through Jesus. (See Mark 3:33-35).

Jesus could "see" that a system of exclusions was against the will of the Creator God, who, because he created the world and everyone in it, loves everyone in Israel and beyond the boundaries of Israel. God does not exclude or forget anyone. (Isaiah 49:16). This was God's inclusive vision of "family" when he promised his blessing to Abraham, and through Abraham to the people of all nations. (Genesis 12:3, 22:18). Time and again, this vision was proclaimed by Israel's prophets, only to be met with deaf ears and hardened hearts. The Israel of Jesus' day also chose to ignore the teaching of its own prophets: "All the ends of the earth shall see the salvation of our God." (Isaiah 52:10, JB; see Isaiah 2:2-3). God cannot be the kind of God who backs up one nation or one group against some other group or nation. As the above episode with the Jerusalem scribes demonstrates, official Israel did not know God, and was showing no willingness to repent of its sins of victimization. In 70 AD the "fighting groups" rose in rebellion against Rome, resulting in the 'fall' of their kingdom and State.

Jesus himself was excluded and cast out by the official teachers of Israel. They could see no room for him in "the inn," i.e. in their kind of Israel (Luke 2:87; see Mark 12:6-8). They regarded him as a threat to their whole social system, based, as it was, on exclusions, with an elite of supposedly 'good' people oppressing those whom they regarded as hopeless sinners. As Jesus saw it, such a society could not be willed by God, and therefore, would "fall apart and come to an end." (Mark 3:25-26). The kingdom of Satan would collapse. The Kingdom of God will last forever, because it is founded on the will of God, who is justice, mercy and compassion.

Perhaps, in order to contrast Satan's divisive kingdom with Jesus' universal Kingdom of God, Mark places the Beelzebul incident alongside the following passage, in which Jesus graphically illustrates what God's kingdom looks like: everybody doing the will of God in order that God may create a universal union of brotherhood, with Jesus as brother of everyone.

Jesus' mother and brothers arrived, and standing outside, sent in a message asking for him. A crowd was sitting round him at the time the message was passed to him, 'Your mother and your brothers and sisters are outside asking for you.' He replied, 'Who are my mother and my brothers?' And looking round at those sitting in a circle about him, he said, 'Here are my mother and my brothers. Anyone who does the will of God, that person is my brother and sister and mother.' (Mark 3:32-35, JB).

Like the religious leaders, Jesus' natural family are seeking to divert him from his mission. (Mark 3:20-21). For Jesus, even close family relationships are of lesser importance than discipleship, symbolized in the circle sitting round him and listening to his teaching. (3:32). Jesus challenges not only the traditional notion of kingdom systems (founded on division and oppression), but also the long-held symbols of family, in order to create a new spiritual family (Kingdom of God) around himself. (Mark 3:31-35, see Matthew 12:46-50, Luke 8:19-21).

In terms of the culture of his day, what Jesus was saying and doing was scandalous. In Israel, the family bond was long-lasting. It was normal for children to live close to their parents and to work in the same occupation. Loyalty to the family was the local outworking of loyalty to Israel and to God. To break this link would have been unthinkable. In the closely-knit communities of that time, not only parents, but the whole neighbourhood could become quite outspoken over a young man challenging the established order. (See Luke 4:25-30).

The Jewish historian Flavius Josephus (37-100 AD) says that there were about 240 small villages in Galilee at the time of Jesus, with an average population of anything from 100 to 250. Josephus was not certain about the total population, as nothing in the way of a census was ever taken. The inhabitants of a village worked the land, tended their flocks and plied their trades. Jesus' natural family lived in one of these villages - a community probably having little contact with people in neighbouring villages and knowing little of the outside world. Their horizon would thus have been limited by the boundaries of their village. By way of contrast, Jesus' vision was universal; it embraced all of humanity. The whole world was his village. Jesus will later challenge many other restrictive symbols of Jewish identity, for example, food laws and purity laws. (See Mark 7:1-23).

Jesus was not rejecting his natural family (3:33 in the foregoing passage). What he had in mind was a new spiritual family. He wanted to widen the idea of family to include everyone everywhere, who place their trust in God, and "do the will of God." (3:35). In his obedience to the Father, Jesus is our model in obeying the will of God. His first concern from an early age was to obey the will of the Father. (Luke 2:49; Mark 14:36; Matthew 7:21; John 4:34; 8:29). Doing the will of God is the perfect expression of the covenant relationship between God and humans. (See Exodus 24:7-8; Psalm 40:9; 143:10). Despite its promise of obedience (Exodus 24:7), Israel of old failed in its obedience to God. Doing the will of God creates a union of people and brings the love and blessing of God into the world. To do God's will, one must learn what his will is by gathering round Jesus and listening to him, as the crowd was doing in Mark 3:32. Listening to Jesus leads to faith, to trusting in his word. Faith makes it easier to do God's will, which means doing the works of Jesus: feeding all who are hungry for fullness of life (Mark 6:30-44), in effect, freeing people from various kinds of bondages. (Mark 1:25, 41-42; 2:11; 3:5). Mark 3:33-35 is related to the first two petitions in the Lord's Prayer: "Thy kingdom come; thy will be done on earth as it is in heaven." (Matthew 6:10).

The works of Jesus are but the foundation of his creation of the all-inclusive brotherly union of peoples and nations, which was willed by God from the time of Abraham, whose obedience to the will of God was based on his faith. (Genesis 22:16-18). In his vision of a new universal family (Mark 3:35), Jesus is now acting to fulfil God's promises to Abraham, the Israel of his day having failed in its obedience to God by presiding over a divided society. In order for God to create his new all-inclusive family, based on the brotherly care of Jesus, he calls us to imitate Jesus by taking care of our brothers and sisters – so that a completely new social order (family of God) may be brought to birth, undoing the one based on exclusions and 'fighting groups' - the divided kingdom of Beelzebul. (Mark 3:22).

The members of this new family of God – first announced in Mark 1:15) - are united to Jesus in bonds of loyalty and love, greater than any blood relationship, making them his spiritual brothers and sisters. (See John 1:12; Romans 8:28-30; Ephesians 2:19; Hebrews 2:11-12). The members of this new community share one Father (God) with Jesus. See Exodus 24:7; Psalm 143:9-10).

Jesus is going to Jerusalem where he will definitively overcome the power of Beelzebul, through surrendering his life in obedience to God (Mark 14:36). The Shepherd will lay down his life so that his flock may be rescued from division and exclusions, and through forgiveness, definitively gathered into his new united family. Mark 3:33-35 provides a thread that runs through the rest of his gospel. It implies forgiveness, because there can be no union without forgiveness of one another. But this was something completely foreign to the thinking of the religious leaders of Jesus' day. The statement in Mark 3:33-35 will become central towards the end of the gospel. These verses represent the beginning of God's unfolding plan for the definitive establishment of his universal family (kingdom), a work now initiated by Jesus with his appointment of the twelve apostles.

Jesus is becoming increasingly isolated. The opposition from the scribes and Pharisees, and the attempt by Jesus' relatives to "take charge of him" (3:20), must have brought home to him the weight of the cross he is already carrying. But despite the obstacles on his path, he will complete his journey alone, misunderstood, and abandoned by his friends - ruled as they still are by the power of the divided kingdom (8:33) - with the exception a few loyal women disciples, who will follow him all the way to the end. (Mark 15:40). Very few are prepared to embrace his glorious vision for the union of all peoples.

What made Jesus stand out from the society of his day was his insight into the heart of God. Jesus could "see" God, while even his disciples, and especially those opposed to him, were afflicted in varying degrees with blindness, a blindness to their sins. (See Isaiah 42:18-29, 23-24). Jesus "sees" God, sees that God is on his side. (Job 19:25-27a, NRSV). Enlightened by God's Spirit, Jesus has a vision of God's will for himself and the world, a vision he struggles to share with everyone else. He will be prepared to give his life so that his glorious vision of a universal family, gathered together by God, will be definitively established.

We may note that obeying the will of God (care, acceptance, mutual forgiveness) is probably being offered by Jesus as a model for relationships also within natural families.

## Mary: Mother of God's Family

For the time being, Jesus' relatives have to stand "outside the crowd sitting round him" (3:32). Their eyes will be opened and they will "see" the full significance of his glorious vision at a later stage, when they will join the apostles Peter and Paul in making his name known to the wider world. (See 1 Corinthians 9:5; Galatians 1:18-19). Jesus' brothers did eventually accept the reality of kinship with Jesus in the early Church. (See Acts of the Apostles 1:14). The most famous of Jesus' brothers was James (not the apostle James), to whom Jesus appeared after the resurrection. (See 1 Corinthians 15:7). James became the great leader of the Jerusalem Church, while Peter and Paul were off on their far-flung missionary journeys. (See Acts of the Apostles 15:13-19; Galatians 1:18-19).

However, at this stage of Jesus' ministry, the role of his mother is to remain "outside the house" (Mark 3:31), and away from Jesus' "business with the Father." (Luke 2:48-49). Her role is to misunderstand him (Luke 2:50), to endure a sorrow that would break her heart (Luke 2:35), which must have been really heart-breaking as she witnessed, what to her at the time, was her son's shameful death on the cross, (John 19:25). That was Mary's cross. But in thus standing apart, her faith could grow towards her greater role in the new spiritual family which Jesus was creating, i.e. the Church. According to John's gospel, just before Jesus died on the cross, "he saw his mother and the disciple he loved standing there." Then he said to the disciple, 'She is your mother.' (John 19:26-27). Jesus' words on the cross confirmed his beloved disciple in a role of representing all people of faith, and his mother Mary as mother of the family of believers. Thus, Mary's role as mother continues in the Church. As mother of Jesus the Redeemer, she is thereby mother of all the members of his body, the Church. Her role in the Church is to give spiritual birth to believers, so that Christ's body may continue to grow and flourish. (See CCC 963-72). [122]

We do not worship Mary. We honour her and pray to her. Through her assumption into heaven, Mary is exalted by God as Queen of heaven and earth, where she acts as our advocate with Jesus, who is King. (CCC 966, 969). Mary's role as queen and advocate has biblical roots. In ancient Israel, the person who acted as queen was always the king's mother, her role being that of advocate with the king on behalf of people coming to him with their petitions. The king's wife couldn't assume the role of queen because the king usually had many wives. "Turn then, most gracious advocate, your eyes of mercy towards us." (Salve Regina). Everything Mary does for us is through her advocacy with Jesus. When, as servants of Jesus, we approach Mary in our prayers, she will probably tell us to do what Jesus asks us to do. (See John 2:5). Mary was exalted by God for fulfilling, in complete obedience to God, her role of giving Jesus to the world. (See Luke 1:46-55). We can join her in her prayer when she accepted this role: 'I am the servant of the Lord,

---

[122] Pope Benedict XVI, *Spe Salvi,* see sections 49- 50 on Mary.

let it be done to me according to your word.' (Luke 1:38). In this prayer, Mary is shown as a model disciple, in that she illustrates by example the ideal response of the Christian to the word of God, which is a readiness to do the will of God, no matter what the cost. We can be servants of the Lord in small things, but there are circumstances in which totally accepting God's will may demand faith of a high order, and is very difficult. Jesus totally surrendered himself to God, to the extent of giving up his life in service to humanity. (Matthew 26:42; Mark 14:36; Luke 22:42; John 17:4).

## The Conception of Jesus, his 'Brothers'

With reference to the "brothers" of Jesus, (see above Mark 3:31), there may be an ambiguity. The gospels were written in Greek, and the Greek word *adelphos* for 'brother' could sometimes mean 'cousin.' In Mark 6:3 and Matthew 13:55, the brothers of Jesus are named, including James, also that Jesus had sisters. Perhaps, in the context of near family relatives (Jesus' mother, as above), *adelphos* is used to mean a true brother or sister. The Greek word *exadelphos* is sometimes used for cousin. In the context of Jesus' wider spiritual family, "brothers" are his followers in faith. (See Matthew 18:15, 21; Acts of the Apostles 9:17, 30; 1 Thessalonians 5:25-27). "Brothers," in this sense also, should become forgiving and loving of one another.

If Jesus had true brothers and sisters, there arises the question about the virginal conception of Jesus. Matthew's gospel says that Mary "was found to be with child through the Holy Spirit." (Matthew 1:18, NJB). However, Mary's virginity has nothing to do with physicality, but should be understood in a spiritual sense. This is how the modern Irish theologian, Fr. Enda Lyons, sees the conception of Jesus: "The Christian community does not see God as taking the place of the human father in Jesus' case, in such a way as to be 'himself' the physical biological father of Jesus."[123] In other words, Jesus was not conceived of a human mother and divine father. The phrase "with child through the Holy Spirit" means that the Holy Spirit was with Mary in order to empower her in her role of giving of Jesus to the world. The above phrase in Matthew's gospel may be a reference to the biblical theme of the interplay between divine and human causality. If God is truly sovereign, and as the author of nature and its laws, it is he who causes all things to be, including the conception of children. While the rain and sun make the crops grow, ultimately, this is caused by the Creator God. Jesus is not half divine and half human. He is one hundred per cent a human being. When Jesus accepted the role of saviour, which was handed to him by God, he was filled with the Holy Spirit, confirming him as Son and empowering him for his mission on earth. (Mark 1:10-11).

Fr. Lyons also refers to Cardinal Ratzinger (later Pope Benedict XVI), who says that the conception of Jesus is to be understood as "new creation, not begetting by God. God does not become the biological father of Jesus."[124] In the creation account "there was darkness over the deep, and God's Spirit hovered over the waters." (Genesis 1:2b, JB). Then in Luke's gospel, the angel says to Mary: "The Holy Spirit will come upon you and the

---

[123] Enda Lyons, *Jesus: Self-Portrait by God*, (The Columba Press), 2004, p. 95.

[124] Joseph Cardinal Ratzinger, *Introduction to Christianity*, (Ignatius Press), 1968, 2000, p. 274.

power of the Most High will cover you with its shadow. And so the child will be holy and will be called Son of God." (Luke 1:35, JB). God's Spirit is the power behind the first creation, bringing order out of chaos. (Genesis 1:2). Through the Spirit of God, living beings are created. (Psalm 104:30). So what is happening with Mary is the beginning of a new creation. The God who, in the beginning, created living beings out of nothing, now through the Son of God, makes a new beginning for humanity. With the birth of Jesus, God creates a new world order out of its chaotic darkness. (See John 1:1-5).

What are the implications in this for Jesus' divine sonship? For an understanding of his divine sonship, see the account of his baptism (Mark 1:9-11) and his transfiguration (Mark 9:2-8, especially verse 7). The gospels of Mark and John and the letters of St. Paul make no references to the virginal conception of Jesus. His divine sonship does not depend on that. It would be a mistake to think that Mary's sexual relations with her husband Joseph would have made her less holy. Marital sex is willed and blessed by God, so Jesus being conceived in the same way as everyone else, may add a further element of dignity to marital sex.

Mark's less than positive view of Jesus' family may reflect the situation of his readers in the early Church, when commitment to the gospel required sacrificing family attachments, or when followers of Jesus did not have the support of family members. (See Mark 10:28-31; 13:12-13).

## Parables of the Kingdom

Jesus' healings always reveal something about God and the reign of God. So far in Mark's gospel - apart from the Beelzebul incident and his proclamation of a new family of God - there is little about Jesus' formal teaching, only that he "taught with authority" in the synagogues. Now through the medium of parables, Jesus gives an extended discourse in which he casts further light on the meaning of the reign of God, whose arrival he has proclaimed. (Mark 1:15). The key word during this discourse is "hear." (4:9). Essentially, what Jesus is teaching and revealing is a continuation and further elucidation of his family of God proclamation in Mark 3:33-35 - how this family differs from the kingdom of Satan, and how it will grow and flourish. The parables are a warning against placing one's hope in kingdoms founded on exclusions or oppression. They are a direct follow-up on the previous section about the crowd sitting in a circle round Jesus, listening to his teaching. (3:32).

A parable is a short story or image drawn from nature or daily life that expresses profound religious truths. In his parables, Jesus shows how the wisdom of God shines through the material realities of this world. The visible can become a window into the invisible. For example, the idea of a seed falling to the earth and dying, but rising again to produce an abundance of fruit, opens a window into God: Jesus dies and rises again, in order to share the fruit of his abundant life with us. The image of the shepherd, for example, can give an insight into the nature of God, who he is and what he does in rescuing us from our scattering and feeding us with his love, so that we might have life in all its fullness. (John 10:11-12, 10b, 15c). Because of their metaphorical character, Jesus' parables reveal hidden depths of meaning that only come to light on thoughtful reflection. Because the reign of God is a divine reality, it can only be spoken of by using analogies - word pictures that encourage listeners to think of deeper meanings.

The God revealed in Mark's gospel is no longer hidden behind the smoke of a firey mountain, evoking fear and trembling. (Exodus 19:16-18). In Jesus, the veil separating human beings from their God is pulled back for all to see. (Mark 1:10; 15:38). In his teaching, Jesus reveals a God who is here on earth, close to people wherever they are in their daily tasks, guiding and encouraging them towards his good purposes.

Jesus' parables may be regarded as Mark's "Sermon on the Sea."[125] (For Jesus' Sermon on the Mount, see Matthew 5-7, and his Sermon on the Plain, Luke 6:17-49). Sitting down (4:1) was always Jesus' posture for teaching.

## The Parable of the Sower

> Again, Jesus began to teach beside Lake Galilee. The crowd that gathered round him was so large that he got into a boat and sat in it. The boat was out in the water, while the crowd stood on the shore at the water's edge. He used parables to teach them many things, saying to them: 'Listen! Once there was a man who went out to sow corn. As he scattered the seed in the field, some of it fell along the path, and the birds came and ate it up. Some of it fell on rocky ground, where there was little soil. The seeds soon sprouted, because the soil wasn't deep. Then, when the sun came up, it burnt the young plants; because the roots hadn't grown deep enough, the plants soon dried up. Some of the seed fell among thorn bushes, which grew up and choked the plants, and they didn't produce any corn. But some seeds fell in good soil, and the plants sprouted, grew and produced corn; some had thirty grains, others sixty, and others a hundred.' And Jesus concluded, 'Listen then, if you have ears.' When Jesus was alone with his disciples some of those who heard him came to him with the twelve disciples and asked him to explain the parables. 'You have been given the secret of the kingdom of God. But the others, who are on the outside, hear all things by means of parables, so that *they may look and look, yet not see; they may listen and listen, yet not understand. For if they did, they would turn to God, and he would forgive them.*' (Mark 4:1-12, quoting Isaiah 6:9-10 in italics; see CCC 546).

In the Old Testament, "secret" (Mark 4:11) refers to God's plans that are hidden, yet revealed to the prophets, for the sake of God's people. (Daniel 2:19, 28; Amos 3:7). God's plans can only be known by God speaking to humans who are receptive to his word (i.e. those who "hear"). God's plan of salvation is fully revealed in Jesus. (Romans 16:25-26; 1 Corinthians 2:7; Ephesians 3:3-9). The disciples are especially privileged; to them the Kingdom of God is revealed through the person and teaching of Jesus. (Mark 4:10).

In his words about people on the "outside" (verse 11 above), Jesus does not mean that he wants to exclude some people from his kingdom family. It is rather that the kingdom is not obvious to the naked eye of people who remain unchallenged by it - the

---

[125] Mary Healy, *The Gospel of Mark,* p. 81, (Baker Academic), 2008.

unconverted men and women who are spiritually blind. Jesus describes their predicament with his quotation from Isaiah. (Verse 12 in italics above). In the time of Isaiah, the Lord proclaimed his word to the people time and again, but they deliberately rejected it. His servant Israel remained blind and deaf to his sins. (Isaiah 42:18-20; see Psalm 81:10, 11a, 13, 16; Matthew 23:37). If they had turned to the Lord, he would have forgiven them. (Verse 12). Like the Pharaoh in Exodus, it is as if God is hardening people's hearts as an act of Judgement on their failure to listen to him. (Exodus 4:21; 7:3; 14:4). So to the "outsiders," the parables remain a puzzle; they have the effect of further blinding and deafening them. (Mark 4:12, Jeremiah 5:21; 6:10-12; 7:13-14). The prophets were looking for "fruit," which is what the unsuccessful seeds fail to produce (as if Satan was carrying away the word that was sown in people). Jesus was aware of the disciples' incomprehension:

> He said to them, 'Don't you understand this parable? Then how will you understand any of the parables? What the sower is sowing is the word. Those on the edge of the path where the word is sown are people who have no sooner heard it that Satan at once comes and carries away the word that was sown in them.' (4:13-15, NJB).

The sower is God. The seed is his word. (Mark 4:14). In sowing seeds, Jesus assumes the role of God. He is sowing seeds among us so that we may bear fruit. In order to hear what God is saying to us, we must try to "see," i.e. understand the meaning of the life, death and resurrection of Jesus, and be willing to participate in his Kingdom-of-God project, which is about creating a union of brothers and sisters who do the will of God. (Mark 3:33-35). At this stage, the disciples would have been blind to all of this.

In the Old Testament, God spoke his comforting word (seeds) to the exiles in Babylon about their rescue and homecoming to Israel. (Isaiah chap. 40). But in Jesus' day, Israel was metaphorically still in exile. But as in the time of Isaiah (42:18-19; 48:18), they were still deaf to God's word and blind to their sins, among which were their sins of exclusion, and making victims. (Mark 3:6). So it's as if the seed was falling on stony ground and among thorn bushes (Mark 3:6; 4:17), and producing no fruit. In telling this parable, Jesus is reminding his hearers that the exile is now over; God's final rescue operation of opening blind eyes and deaf ears has begun. (See Luke 4:18).

The farmer sowing seed is a picture of God (through Jesus) sowing Israel again, making Israel fruitful again, replacing the weeds and thorns which symbolized fruitless life away from God (Genesis 3:18). It's as if the Garden of Eden is now being restored to its original fruitful state. (Genesis 2:8-9). This is Jesus' good news of rescue and salvation. The Kingdom is here; God is really King, and through Jesus, he is preparing a road to liberate all "captives," and definitively take them home. (Isaiah 40:1-11, especially verse 8; see also Isaiah 55:10-13). Through Jesus, God's word will not fail to fulfil its purpose. (Isaiah 55:11). Jesus fulfils the prophecy of Isaiah. Jesus is sowing a crop that defies weeds and thorns. (Genesis 3:18). The kingdom (liberated Israel) is coming in a strange hidden way, not visibly in a sudden upheaval, as many people expected, or wanted.

When Jesus reproached his disciples for their failure to understand the parable

(4:13), perhaps he saw them as representing blind and deaf Israel. They didn't understand the parable because they were focused on an old and different story. They couldn't hear his new story. The prophets spoke of a descendant of David (Messiah) who would come and restore the fortunes of Israel and bring justice and peace. The great misunderstanding among the people in Jesus' day was that the Messiah would come to their rescue in some visible and dramatic way, by a quick fix political revolution (the disciples' old story). Jesus said no to that particular hope. The people of Israel would be rescued and would live in safety, but in a different way – Jesus' new story. (Jeremiah 33:14-16). So far, in Israel, no one had any idea how or when this would happen.

Jesus has a clear vision of how and when God's rescue operation will be accomplished. (the new story). For him, the rescue of Israel will come like a farmer sowing seed (his word), much of it going to waste because the soil is poor; the people are not receptive to it. (4:13-20). Held captive in their own agendas, they either don't hear the word, or they reject it. They are spending their money on a useless food: nationalism, elitist power, creating victims and outcasts in their society. (Mark 1:14; 3:6). That kind of "food" will not satisfy their hunger for meaningful life (Isaiah 55:2), and as a result, they will still be hungry. (Isaiah 55:1). The expected Messiah is here. The kingdom is coming, but not in the way the people of Jesus' day imagined or hoped. They are not prepared to hear Jesus' word of peace, inclusivity and reconciliation–God's seemingly slow and patient way of inviting humanity to follow him in *his* way of creating brotherhood. Jesus' telling of this story comes as a warning and invitation. Israel will not be affirmed as it now stands - spending its money on the wrong food (Isaiah 55:2), nationalism, etc, as listed above - when her God acts, as he is now doing, in order to establish his Kingdom.

As the parable of the Sower reveals, Jesus' Kingdom will be established, not by revolution but in the hidden and unexpected way of suffering (the seed falling in the earth and dying). It will come by the persecution of the powers of this world (then and today), by setbacks and seeming failure, culminating in Calvary. About the time Jesus was born, violent revolution had been tried in Israel, but it ended in misery, death and destruction. Jesus' parable comes as a warning against violence. By turning the other cheek in forgiveness to the violence done to him, Jesus sows a seed which can change a world of retribution into a world of forgiveness, peace and union. His word will not fail to do what he plans for it. It will make the seeds and crops produce the abundant food of peace and reconciliation – a food which will fully satisfy the hungering hearts of human beings. (Isaiah 55:1-2, 10-11). A cry from the heart of God is calling us to listen to his word and obey it, in a sense, to eat it (Ezekiel 3:1-2), because it will satisfy our deepest hungering. This was Jesus' way of challenging and defeating the powers of evil, who through violence, only create victims and division. His sowing will bring all exiles definitively home and gather them together round himself in a new family, like a shepherd gathering and caring for his flock. (See Isaiah 40:9-11). With the defeat of the evil powers in his resurrection, the fruitful reign of God will be established. But the world does not always hear and may often ignore this word, and go the way of enmity and war.

Once the seed is sown in us, what can *we* do? The farmer God sows the seed, and like the farmer, we have our work (cultivating, weeding, tending) to do, but it is not all down to us. God is secretly at work in our lives when we try to do his will. Our lives can then bear the brotherly fruit of reconciliation. But just as the farmer cannot harvest in winter or speed up the growth of the seeds, we cannot create or hasten the arrival of the kingdom by our own efforts. (1 Corinthians 3:6-7). Jesus himself is the one who secretly sows the seed of God's word in our lives, giving us time to bear fruit. We can reflect on the dangers (weeds) in our lives that threaten the fruitfulness of the word. What kind of soil am I? If there are obstacles in terms of a parched earth, do I call on God to help me to remove them?

The kingdom of God is a way of life. Whenever we live like God wants us to live (hearing him and doing his will), the Kingdom of God is present there, and its good fruits are visible in obedience to his will. (Mark 3:33-35; 1 Peter 1:23). In the Garden of Eden, Adam followed his own will (Genesis 3:6), and as a consequence, God told him that, despite his hard work, the ground East of Eden would only produce weeds and thorns. (Genesis 3:18).

The sower is also anyone who spreads the good news of the gospel in today's world. Sowing the seed of the word is a work of service. We are all called to be sowers of the word – at home in our families, in the workplace and in the wider society. It can be a word of comfort, gratitude, appreciation, encouragement; it can be a creative experience shared with others, raising someone up from an anxiety, responding to a call for help, sharing a meal with family or friends, sharing our time and talents with others. In other words, it satisfies the needs of others – feeding the hungry, giving a drink to the thirsty. (In this context see Mark 4:35-41; 5:1-42; 6:30-44). We may not always instantly know whether our spoken word or deed will bear fruit, but we have the Lord's assurance that it will often fall on good soil, and that sooner or later, it will produce a harvest.

When has the plant and its slowly maturing seed fulfilled its purpose? The seed slowly ripens, the flower stops blooming and then gives up its seed to the earth, in which it dies. The plant has then fulfilled its purpose; all is accomplished. Jesus is both the sower and the seed itself dying in the earth. At what stage of his life had he accomplished all? When had he given everything? It was the moment before his death when he had given up his power to teach and heal, when he had lost his disciples and friends – even his God. (Mark 15:34). When he was nailed to a cross, robbed of all human dignity, he knew that he had reached the fullness of his life, of what he could accomplish, and then said, 'It is fulfilled,' (John 19:30, NJB). That was when he gave off the seed of his self-giving life, allowed himself to fall into the earth and die, so that he could rise again to the fruitfulness of eternal life. Calvary is the prelude to the seed rising up from the earth to produce a hundredfold yield, feeding the hunger of humanity for both a life of fulfilment on earth and eternal life with God. (Mark 4:20).

In this parable, Jesus teaches that the Kingdom of God is a divine work, not a human achievement. God plants the seeds and brings about their growth, which can often be hidden from eyes. The parable is an encouragement to those who think their efforts for the Kingdom may be fruitless, and a warning to those who think they can bring about the Kingdom (considered as a state of perfection in this world) by what they name as "progress," or by ways clearly contrary to the will of God.

Perhaps Jesus was especially saddened by the failure of his own people to listen to his word. But he still knew that the word would slowly spread everywhere, and it would bring rejoicing and fulfilment: "People will come from the east and the west, from north and the south, and sit down at the feast of the kingdom of God." (Luke 13:29; see Matthew 8:5, 11; 22:1-10; Isaiah 66:22-23). The parable of the sower points to the worldwide reach of the kingdom of God. (Matthew 28:19-20).

Are we aware of ways in which we may be spiritually blind and deaf in today's world? Do we sow seeds that will bear fruit in the lives of other people?

## The Lamp under a Bowl

Jesus continued: 'Does anyone ever bring in a lamp and put it under a bowl or under the bed? Don't people put it on a lampstand? Whatever is hidden away will be brought out into the open, and whatever is covered up will be uncovered. Listen, then, if you have ears.' (Mark 4:21-25; see Matthew 5:15; 10:26; Luke 8:16-17; 11:33; 12:2; 19:26)

It is reasonable to suppose that God would not light the lamp of his kingdom, and then keep it covered up forever. The lamp is Jesus who has come into the world to bring humanity the light of the word of God, opening people's eyes to see their sins and to see God as their saviour and eternal Father. Jesus himself is the "light of the world," overcoming its satanic darkness. (John 1:9; 8:12; see Luke 2:32). If we do not focus our eyes on him, we are lost. We are left walking in darkness, without guidance or direction. Jesus does not want to hide the Kingdom, but to make it known to everyone. With his light, he searches the house (this world) for the lost coin (humanity). He is happy when he finds it, and then calls for a celebration. (Luke 15:8-10).

Israel's God was not going to keep the lamp permanently hidden under a bowl, as Israel itself was doing – hiding God's light from many in Israel and from the Gentiles. The divine plan, the mystery of God's kingdom is being revealed in Jesus' visible life and work - in his parables and healings. (Mark 6:3; 2:7; 3:6, 21-22). Although the light should be plain to all, it still remains a mystery (puzzle) to most people, and in effect, remains hidden through the opposition Jesus encounters (Mark 2:7; 3:6, 21-22), but hidden only for a time. Jesus' mission on earth is to make the good news of his kingdom visible (like a bright lamp) to all, provided they are receptive (repentance and faith) - their eyes focused on him and their hearts open to him. In a world of darkness, light is attractive.

The full light of Jesus will be revealed in his triumph over death in his resurrection. At that stage, his followers - their eyes fully opened to his messianic identity– are charged with a mission of bringing his light to the whole world. (Mark 13:10; Matthew 5:14; 28:19). How can we share our light with others?

On another level, the kingdom is still hidden in the trials and setbacks of the Church's mission. But in the end, God will fully reveal all.

# The Mustard Seed

'What shall we say the kingdom of God is like?' asked Jesus. 'It is like this. A man takes a mustard seed, the smallest seed in the world, and plants it in the ground. After a while it grows up and becomes the biggest of all plants. It puts out large branches that the birds come and make their nests in its shade.' (Mark 4:30-32).

In mentioning large branches that give shelter to many birds, Jesus is evoking the Old Testament image of a large, shady tree, symbolizing an empire that gives protection to people of different races (Ezekiel 17:23; 31:6) – as Jesus' extended family would later do, but in a different way from an empire

In Jesus' mustard seed parable, the emphasis is on the seed's smallness. From its humble beginnings in Galilee, the kingdom of God will grow to a large tree in which the Gentiles will find a home. Instead of a small seed, Jesus' listeners might have preferred to hear of a large conquering army as the means of bringing in the kingdom. His Kingdom is not going to come in the one fell swoop; neither is it an ideology to be forced on people against their will. No, it will begin like a mustard seed. And its growth will be due to God's hidden power. Because the patience of God is infinite, and because of his understanding of human nature, his kingdom will be an evolution, not a revolution, neither in Israel nor anywhere else. The kingdom is a divine work, not a human achievement. We cooperate with God, but we cannot control or hasten the growth of the Kingdom by our own efforts.

The Kingdom is hidden in the trials and failures of the Church's mission of evangelization. It will be established and will grow in a hidden and unexpected way, through suffering, setbacks and seeming failure – culminating in the cross - for his followers no less than for Jesus himself. But in God's good time, the Kingdom will grow into a mighty tree, offering shade and a home to people of the whole world. (Mark 13:26-27; Matthew 25:31-32). Jesus thus speaks with assurance about the future success of the Kingdom, encouraging his disciples to persevere with hope and patience. People's lives will be transformed by Jesus' teaching, by his life, death and resurrection, aided in these latter times by the power of the Spirit, with his disciples participating in his work of gathering people into the Kingdom. Jesus is assured of the future success of the Kingdom and urges his disciples to persevere with faith and hope.

In 4:33-34, Mark gives the sense that the crowd, for the time being at least, is left in darkness, while the disciples have been "given the secret of the kingdom of God." (4:11). However, the following scenes will reveal just how far the disciples have yet to travel on the journey of opening their eyes and fully understanding the Kingdom.

After Jesus' teaching in parables, Mark narrates a number of miracle stories that reveal Jesus' power over nature and death - his power to accomplish what he has already taught as his word. These mighty deeds are part of the apostles' eye-opening to Jesus' identity and training for their mission. (6:7). By the end of this section they will have experienced Jesus' authority over all threatening powers, although they will not understand that, in Jesus, the sovereign God is acting to set everything right and to bring his creation to its fullness of perfection–no more overwhelming storms threatening human life.

In the following section, Jesus' mission will expand into Gentile territory. The word he is sowing is also for the Gentiles.

## Jesus' Power over Nature, Demons and Death

On the evening of that same day Jesus said to his disciples, 'Let us go across to the other side of the lake. So they left the crowd; the disciples got into the boat in which Jesus was already sitting, and they took him with them. Other boats were there too. Suddenly a strong wind blew up, and the waves began to spill over into the boat, so that it was about to fill with water. Jesus was in the back of the boat, sleeping with his head on a pillow. The disciples woke him and said, 'Master, don't you care that we are about to die?' Jesus woke up and rebuked the wind. 'Be quiet!' And he said to the waves, 'Be still!' And the wind died down, and there was a great calm. Then Jesus said to his disciples, 'Why are you frightened? Have you no faith?' But they were terribly afraid and said to one another. 'Who is this man? Even the wind and the waves obey him.' Then Jesus said to his disciples, 'Why are you frightened? Have you still no faith?' But they were terribly afraid and said to one another, 'Who is this man? Even the wind and the waves obey him!' (Mark 4:37-41).

Jesus has been teaching the crowds in parables from a boat anchored near the shore of Lake Galilee. After concluding his "Sermon on the Sea," and as evening approaches, he asks his disciples to cross to the eastern side of the lake, which was predominantly a Gentile area. The purpose of the crossing may have been partly to get away from the crowds, but it is likely that Jesus also wanted to extend his mission to the Gentiles, later repeated in Mark 6:45; 7:31; 8:13, 22-26.

Alone, of the evangelists, Mark says that "other boats were with them." (v. 36). In Mark's gospel, to be "with Jesus" is a technical phrase for discipleship. (see 3:14; 5:18). The other boats may indicate the presence of an extended group of disciples beyond the Twelve. Can we place ourselves in these "other boats?"

Jesus' rescue of the disciples from their old thinking about the coming of the Kingdom in the parable of the Sower is comparable to their rescue from a storm in the Sea of Galilee. The former expresses in word pictures, what the latter expresses in concrete terms. Jesus has the power to accomplish both kinds of rescuing. God's sovereign power is being unleashed in the world. This is the power which created the world. It is the power now present in Jesus. The prophet Daniel speaks about a "human being surrounded by clouds who was given authority, honour and royal power, so that the people of all nations, races and languages would serve him. His authority would last forever, and his kingdom would never end." (Daniel 7:13-14). Jesus has that authority and power. He is that king. His Kingdom, his rule over Satan is being established. Beelzebul's divisive kingdom will fall. The calming of the storm on the Sea of Galilee is but a further revelation of Jesus' divine status.

The Old Testament reveals that sovereignty over the unruly and powerful forces of nature belongs only to the Creator of the world. (Psalm 65:7-9; 77:16; 106:9-10; 107:23-30; Job 9:8; 26:6-13; 38:6-11; Isaiah 51:9-11). Psalm 107: 23-30 may have been an inspiration for the story of the calming of the storm in Mark 4:35-41. (See also Exodus 14:15, Psalm 89:8-10, 95:1-5). In the Old Testament, the sea is a symbol of chaos and the habitation of evil powers. (Psalm 74:13-14; Isaiah 27:1). But God's creative power is sovereign - bringing the natural world into harmony with itself. Jesus confronts the adverse forces of nature with the same authority with which he frees human beings from demonic possession.

It was after the disobedience and flight from the Garden of Eden that nature became chaotic and fruitless. (Genesis 3:17-18). Through his obedience to the will of God (Mark 3:35), Jesus is now establishing his authority over a chaotic world and creating a universal family of brotherhood, thus undoing the flight and scattering from Eden. (Genesis 3:8).

Jesus' authority and power over the raging waters recalls the first creation (Genesis 1:2; Psalm 104:5-9) and is suggestive of a new creation, a new order and peace for the world and humanity, brought about by the life, death and resurrection of Jesus. (Revelation 21:1). St. Paul speaks of nature itself being set free from its turmoil and "slavery to decay," as are human beings. (Romans 8:21-22).

Jesus' authority over the turbulent sea (4:39) is the same divine power that gets a great catch of fish for weary fishermen (Luke 5:1-11); and is revealed in Jesus' power over death. (Mark 5:21-43; John 11; Luke 7:11-15). The message here is that human beings are not slaves to physical or metaphorical storms, to decay, strife, destruction and death. They are not slaves to the universe and its laws. As King and Lord of nature, Jesus liberates us from domination by its destructive forces.

The Lake (Sea) of Galilee is well known for the violent storms that can arise without warning. In the Old Testament, the image of uncontrolled water symbolizes a weight of trouble over a person. The way to respond to that is by hoping and trusting in the Lord. (See Psalm 42:5-11). Although crushed by the insults of his enemies, the psalmist still hopes in the Lord. God is with us in the storms that threaten to overwhelm us. (Isaiah 43:2).

Jesus asleep in the boat displays a confidence that the forces of chaos will not overwhelm the sovereign King and his new family. (4:38). It is a confidence not shared by the disciples. Jesus exemplifies the trust in God that is often signified in Scripture by a peaceful and untroubled sleep. (See Job 11:18-19; Psalm 4:9; 65:5-8; Proverbs 3:24). In the Book of Psalms, the psalmist often calls on God to awake from sleep and rescue his people from their troubles. (Psalm 35:23; 44:23; 59:3-4). So far in Mark's gospel, the forces of evil surrounding Jesus have been angry and threatening, but Jesus is so trusting in God's power that he can fall asleep on a pillow in the midst of all.

"We are about to die." (4:38). What can be more frightening than the fear and prospect of immediate death? This story is symbolic of Jesus' eventual triumph over death, which represents his calming of the greatest storm of all. "Jesus woke up." (Verse 39). This is a phrase suggesting resurrection. In his resurrection, Jesus is fully revealed to all as Lord of nature, life and death, having brought order out of the chaos of human existence. (Psalm

65:5-8; Isaiah 25:8). Jesus "rebukes" the wind and waves and orders them to be "quiet." These words recall Jesus' exorcisms, suggesting that hidden within the chaotic natural forces of the lake, lies the evil of the demonic world, but, as he had done in exorcising the demons from people, only Jesus can reduce the lake to silence and obedience. (See Mark 1:25; 3:12; 9:25). The raging sea may be symbolic of the much greater threat to Jesus. There are the shrieking demons asserting their power in the synagogues. Shrieking and violent men are plotting his death, until they eventually get him hung on a cross. But on the third day he will be awoken from his sleep of death and will stand up in order to bring to birth a new world of calm and peace for all humanity.

God is sovereign, for otherwise, everything in the world would be random, without meaning or purpose, signifying a reign of chaos. God is king. As his final word on history, he will ultimately calm our greatest storms, which are caused by the fear of death, thus definitively establishing his sovereign rule. Jesus will calm all storms. He will destroy destruction, kill death – but only by himself dying and allowing the storm to overwhelm him.

"The disciples were overcome with awe." (4:41, NJB). Fear and awe are signs of an experience of God in Scripture. (Exodus 19:16-19). The disciples' reaction to the power of Jesus epitomizes human powerlessness in the face of adverse forces. The disciples learn the lesson that human beings are vulnerable, limited and dependent, and should have the humility to accept that. The disciples are witness to an exercise of divine power which fills them with awe, and prompts them to ask, "Who is this man that even the winds and the sea obey him?" (4:41; see 16:8). Despite Jesus' demonstration of his power, the disciples are still uncomprehending. They do not see that his authority over the forces of nature is a further revelation of his divine status.

Jesus was teaching a band of followers who would need faith as the prerequisite for their earthly mission of bringing the peace and authority of the kingdom of God into all the troubles of humanity. He called them to accompany him on a mission to the far side of the lake. Would he have done so only to let them perish beneath the waves? From the Exodus on, God's control of the sea has signified his tender care for his people. (Exodus 15; Isaiah 51:9-10). The disciples' question, "Who then is this man?" is a question that all readers of the gospel are meant to ask. (See Mark 8:29).

It is not that the disciples had no trust in Jesus. They had been following him faithfully up to this point. Facing death on the lake, however, presented an extreme test of their faith. How do we ourselves respond when we are almost overwhelmed, sorely tested by a sea of troubles? It is one thing to know that Jesus, the Christ, has absolute authority over the cosmos and its unruly forces. It is quite something else to trust that, somehow, he will calm our personal storms, which can sometimes be overwhelming. Can we still hope and trust in him if the storms are not immediately calmed? It is in hope that we pray for calm. But hope does not mean that things will suddenly get better. Such calming may not come immediately, or in the way we want it, but hope means that we can trust in God to grant us calm in ways, and at a time he knows is best for us. We may not immediately be liberated from a sea of troubles, but only from being dominated by them. Our great hope is for the ultimate calm of being raised up from death along with Jesus. The compassionate Lord walks with us in our troubles, giving us the courage and strength to see us through them. (Psalm 23:4). "Lead us not into temptation" means "do not test us beyond our capacity to endure." That is why we need to pray, "deliver us from evil." Jesus himself willingly went through the storm of death, sacrificing his life for the future good of humanity.

The boat bearing the disciples and the sleeping Jesus is an image of the Church. The struggling members of the early Church - storm-tossed on the seas of the great Roman Empire - must have often wondered why their Lord was asleep in the stern, seemingly unconcerned about their troubles. But the Lord's mastery over the turbulent forces is without limit, so that nothing can overcome those who trust in him.

In order to fulfil its mission - even if the Lord seems asleep - the Church must go out upon the sea that is the world and fearlessly proclaim the good news, no matter what the storms or forces that seek to overwhelm it, whether in the form of extreme secularism or materialism. The corona virus is the natural storm that threatens human existence in these times. God does not send such storms to punish us. But he may use them to bring good out of evil. Such storms might open our eyes to some of our destructive ways, to our vulnerability and dependence. We are not kings, doing whatever we want, without accountability.

As members of the Church we must trust that somehow, the Lord will bring order out of the chaos which sometimes descends on itself and the world. We pray that he will give the Church the humility, courage and authority to fearlessly discharge its mission. (Ephesians 4:14-15; see Mark 6:7; Matthew 28:18-20; CCC 849, 851).

## Liberation of the Man with the Legion of Demons

The following story represents in graphic form what has already happened on the lake. Jesus' miracles on behalf of Gentiles are signs that the turbulence afflicting them will also be addressed. They too will be liberated from their particular storms and welcomed into God's Kingdom. (Matthew 8:5-13, 15:21-28, 7:24-30; Luke 7:1-10; Mark 6:45; 7:31; 8:13).

This first excursion of Jesus' into Gentile territory was to a place east of the River Jordan, known as the Decapolis, because of the ten Greek-speaking towns (*deca polis*) located there. This visit underlines his mission to the Gentiles. Jesus' healing of the man with the legion of demons is a hopeful sign for them too. (Mark 5:1-20; see Deuteronomy 14:8; Mark 6:45-52; 7:31; 8:13). God's generosity has no limits; it is not bound by borders or by any taboos. The message here is that nobody anywhere is to be treated as an outcast or excluded from the love, compassion and mercy of God.

(It is not clear whether Jesus went to the area near the town of Gadara, a few miles southeast of the Sea of Galilee, or Gerasa, which was about thirty miles southeast of the lake. Mark's knowledge of local geography may have let him down as to the true location of this incident. He probably had in mind a place much closer to the lake, such as Gadara).

The area on the east bank of the Jordan was marked by a series of caves, many of which were used to bury the dead. The people there may thus have viewed the tombs as a haunt for demons. For the Jews, graveyards were regarded as unclean places, and were to be avoided. Contact with the dead, or with graves made one unclean and untouchable.

Pig farming seemed to have been the mainstay of the economy of this non-Jewish area. For the Jews, this was another reason why the place should be avoided. Jewish dietary laws forbade the eating of pigs' flesh, which was regarded as unclean. And the inhabitants in this area did not observe Jewish moral laws. This means, that as far as Jews were concerned, this whole territory, including the people and their food, was regarded as unclean – and should not be touched. All of this may serve to indicate how far Israel was from bringing God's blessing to the Gentiles. Israel of old was called to be a light to the Gentiles, so that, in the words of God, "my salvation may reach the remotest parts of the earth." (Isaiah 49:6, NJB). But the Israel of Jesus' day, still in bondage to injustice, was deaf to this word of God.

A century or so before Jesus' time, the area had been conquered by the Roman legions, probably leading its inhabitants to see their continued dominance as an enemy. This may help to explain the "legion" of demons inhabiting the man Jesus was about to heal.

> They reached the territory of the Gerasenes on the other side of Lake Galilee. And when Jesus disembarked, a man with an unclean spirit at once came out from the tombs towards him. The man lived in the tombs, and no one could secure him anymore, even with a chain, because he had often been secured with fetters and chains but had snapped the chains and broken the fetters, and no one had the strength to control him. All night and all day, among the tombs and the mountains, he would howl and gash himself with stones. Catching sight of Jesus from a distance, he ran up and fell at his feet and shouted at the top of his voice, 'What do you want with me, Jesus, son of the Most High God? In God's name, do not torture me!' For Jesus had been saying to him, 'Come out of the man, unclean spirit.' Then he asked, 'What is your name?' He answered, 'My name is legion, for there are many of us.' And he begged him earnestly not to send them out of the district. Now on the mountainside there was a great herd of pigs feeding, and the unclean spirit begged him, 'Send us to the pigs, let us go into them.' So he gave them leave. With that, the unclean spirits came out and went into the pigs, and the herd of about two thousand pigs charged down the cliff into the lake, and they were drowned. (Mark 5:1-13, NJB; see 1:21-27; Genesis 1:1-3).

This is the longest exorcism account in Mark's gospel. It offers a model of Jesus' mission to rescue human lives from destructive forces in order to prepare them for inclusion in the family of God (Kingdom of God).

So far, Jesus has been liberating the excluded and marginalized of Israel: the "poor," the outcasts, the "unclean" ones, tax collectors, the paralyzed, lepers, the blind, the deaf, those suffering from demonic possession. Immediately on entering the Gentile world, Jesus is challenged by the demonic powers inhabiting the place, as if they are jealous of their territorial rights. Jesus begins the same way as in his ministry among the Jews– with a decisive victory over evil. Jesus alone was strong enough to bind Satan and set the man free. This recalls Jesus' image of Satan as a "strong man" who can only be bound by a "stronger one." (Mark 1:7; 3:27).

Satan has acquired a certain domination over human beings. (Romans 5:12-19, John 8:34; CCC 407). Demonic influence distorts and destroys the image of God in people. The possessed man was unclothed (5:15), symbolizing his loss of human dignity and separation from God. (Genesis 3:10). Jesus had just calmed the destructive powers of nature. (Mark 4:35-41). His power is now revealed over the forces of chaos within the human person – isolation, self-hatred, despair, self-destruction – the man "wandering among the tombs and through the hills, screaming and cutting himself with stones." (5:5). In the Bible, the theme of wandering always symbolizes situations of loss, separation, alienation - life being lived far away from God, without meaning or purpose.

The man's plight may have been due to his oppressive treatment by the people of the local town. They had him bound in chains, which he duly broke. (5:3-4). The people there may have thought that they could solve their problem with a troublesome man in their midst, by tying him up. Victimizing him may have resulted in themselves feeling more safe and secure. His badness may have united them in a feeling of their own goodness, by comparison. Perhaps their eventual solution was to banish him to the caves outside the town and let him fend for himself, a fate similar to what lepers endured in Israel. Back in Galilee, Jesus had already challenged the same marginalization of the poor and outcasts, leading to conflict with the self-righteous – the scribes and Pharisees.

The man's expectation that Jesus was coming to "torture" him, may be a hint as to how he had already been treated by his own people. The prospect of further torture may have terrified him. He gave his name as "Legion," indicating the push and pull of an internal conflict, from which no one could free him – not until he met Jesus. The demonic world had occupied him, much like the legions of Rome had occupied and controlled this whole area. (A Roman legion was a regiment of about six thousand soldiers). In calling themselves "Legion," the demons may have been trying to impress Jesus with a show of power.

The demons tried to bargain with Jesus not to expel them from the territory. They asked to be sent into the pigs, but they couldn't control their new hosts. The pigs were seemingly driven mad, leading to their headlong rush down the cliff and into the underworld of the lake, the land being thus cleansed of demonic presence. (5:13). The sea is often portrayed in Scripture as the abode of evil. (Daniel 7:3; Mark 4:39; Revelation 13:1; 21:1).

> The men looking after the pigs ran off and told their story in the city and in the country round about; and the people came to see what had really happened. They came to Jesus and saw the demoniac – the man who had the legion in him – properly dressed and in his full senses, and they were afraid. (5:14-15, NJB).

When the people arrived, what they saw was a human being totally transformed - no more chains, howling and gashing himself with stones. Being "properly dressed" signifies the restoration of his human dignity and a new relationship with God and his fellow humans. His transformation recalls the "great calm" which Jesus created in the previous scene when he rebuked the raging sea. (4:39). The people's fear (5:15) resembles that of the disciples after Jesus calmed the waters of the lake. Fear can be a symptom of something totally unexpected, as if it couldn't happen. Fear is a sign of a lack of faith in new possibilities. In this instance, it comes from the realization that what the people are seeing could only have been brought about by a power greater than the human, greater than the people's powerful "chains."

The "properly dressed" man (5:15) may signify the transformation to be wrought by the resurrection, when human beings will become fully clothed with divine life. St Paul speaks about being clothed in Christ and that we should "put on Christ." This is about being clothed in the virtues which reflect our identity as children of God: "compassion, kindness, humility, patience, and forgiveness." (Galatians 3:26-29; Colossians 3:12-15). 'Putting on Christ' also involves a transformation of our wounded bodies. (1 Corinthians 15:51-54).

The reaction of the people to the man's restoration says something about their treatment of him. Instead of enquiring about Jesus, who had come among them with such surprising effects, they asked him to leave the territory. (5:17). They were seemingly more comfortable with having a demon-possessed man at a safe distance outside their town than one among them (Jesus), who could transform a broken life and restore such a man to his community. Their concern for their animals outweighed their compassion for an unfortunate human being.

They were not angry with Jesus. They just didn't want to have him there, turning their familiar world of insiders and outsiders upside down. Jesus understood them; he didn't chide them. Unlike the people of Galilee, they didn't have the background of the law and the prophets to prepare them for what Jesus was doing. Jesus then signalled that he was about to leave the place. (Verse 18).

> As Jesus was getting into the boat, the man who had been possessed begged to be allowed to stay with him. Jesus would not let him, but said to him, 'Go home to your people and tell them all that the Lord, in his mercy has done for you.' So the man went off and proceeded to proclaim in the Decapolis all that Jesus had done for him. And everyone was amazed. (5:18-20, NJB).

It is surprising that Jesus wouldn't let him "stay with" him. Jesus usually says, 'Come, follow me.' But he may have had a bigger task for his restored and fully-dressed man, which would, in a sense, mean the man staying with him. Jesus commissions him to share with his own people the good news of what the Lord had done for him. (5:19). The fact that Jesus asks him to go on a mission to his own people implies that he has something to share with them which they don't have. What they didn't have was the ability to create an all-inclusive society. In order to make them feel good in their self-righteousness, they were creating an outcast. They were accustomed to having good and bad, insiders and outsiders among them, in other words, a divided family. What the man wanted to share with them was his all-inclusive vision: a family united in their acceptance and care for one another

In Mark's Gospel, the expression 'staying with' Jesus means following him as a disciple. (Mark 3:14). Being "properly dressed," in a metaphorical sense, the man was thus prepared for mission. It doesn't appear that he was in the least worried about going back and facing his former torturers. Having been clothed with new life (see Genesis 3:21), he was encouraged and empowered to fearlessly proclaim the good news of his transformation. He didn't go back to his town in order wreak retribution, but in a spirit of forgiveness to the people for making him a victim. His forgiveness might melt their hearts of stone (Ezekiel 36:26-27), lead them to repent of their victimizing and form an inclusive society. The man is a model disciple – and evangelist. Transformed lives cannot hide under a tub the good news of what God has done for them. There is a compulsion to share it. (Mark 4:21; Acts of the Apostles 2:1-4, 14; see Jeremiah 20:9; 23:9).

According to Mark, the man's mission was a success. This unnamed man, raised to new life by Jesus, became the first apostle to the Gentiles. And he had a bigger mission in mind than that suggested to him by Jesus. (5:19). Not only did he go back to the people of his own town, "he went all through the Ten Towns, telling what Jesus had done for him. And all who heard it were amazed." (5:20). Their amazement might provoke questions that could lead to their conversion. In calling him to mission, Jesus gave the man who had been possessed by demons a new meaning and purpose to his life, thus empowering him to live life to the full. Bringing the good news of the forgiveness of sins to the Gentiles is the same mission that Jesus will propose to his disciples after his resurrection. (See Luke 23:46-47). The transformation of the man who had the legion of demons is a sign pointing to our resurrection.

In a certain sense, Jesus himself is the outcast who was consigned to a tomb. The powers of the world will put him in chains and cast him out of their 'town' as a victim, seeing him as possessed by malevolent forces. (Mark 3:22). But the demons are ultimately controlled by Jesus' turning the other cheek to the demonic inspired violence done to him, and by his hanging naked on a cross, his flesh cut (Mark 5:5) by Roman lashes and spears. But God will raise him from the tomb, and then, "clothed' with new life," he will come back again to their town in order to free them from their murderous victimizing by forgiving them. And according to Mark, that is ultimately how our own healing from "gashing with stones" takes place.

The story of the man in the tombs may be a revelation of the human condition. Separated from God, symbolized by nakedness (Genesis 3:10), human beings are in a situation of going their own way, lost and incapable of rescuing themselves. We may sometimes find ourselves living "among the tombs," chained up by self-destructive anxieties, fears, terrors, addictions - bondages of one kind or another, from which we cannot free ourselves. When human power runs up against its limitations, God does not leave us alone and abandoned to 'tombs.' He sent his Son to rescue us and do for us what we, as chained-up individuals, could never do. Jesus is the Good Samaritan, who came and paid the price of rescuing all of us wounded on the road of life, thus raising us up from our tombs. (See Luke 10:30-35; 15:1-6).

The story of the man in the tombs is a challenge to Christians. Like the restored demoniac who was raised to new life, Jesus is calling us too, to spread the good news of our liberation and to proclaim what God, in his love and mercy, has done for us. (Mark 4:21; see Genesis 3:8; Matthew 28:19).

The foregoing incident is a hint that the door was open for the mission of the Church to the Gentiles. As Jesus died on the cross, the Roman centurion, who was present at his crucifixion, would be the first Gentile to acknowledge him as "Son of God." (Mark 15:39; see Acts of the Apostles chap. 10).

> Jesus went back across to the other side of the lake. There at the lakeside a large crowd gathered round him. Jairus, an official of the synagogue, arrived, and when he saw Jesus, he threw himself down at his feet and begged him earnestly, 'My daughter is very ill. Please come and lay your hands on her, so that she will get well and live.' Then Jesus started off with him. So many people were going along with Jesus, that they were crowding him from every side. (Mark 5:21-24, as in Mark 2:13; 3:9; 4:1).

Like the man from the tombs, Jairus also throws himself at the feet of Jesus. (5:21). Kneeling is a deep expression of human need. When all earthly powers and remedies run up against limits, are we not confronted with the question, "Is there a power in the universe in charge of the world, or is suffering, illness and death to remain forever as part of the human story?" If that were so, then God is not sovereign, and Satan is the powerful one. It is he who will reign forever. No Kingdom of God! The result would be despair, a sense of the futility of human life, our desire for ultimate meaning unfulfilled. But yet, there continues the natural human hungering that everything should, and hopefully, will be put right. If that natural longing and hoping were to be frustrated, then life would indeed be meaningless.

As an official of the local synagogue, if Jairus had been concerned about religious controversy, he would now forget his pride and fears, as his daughter lay dying. Similar to the man with the legion of demons, resurrection is also the theme of the story of Jairus and his daughter.

On his way to the house of Jairus, Jesus healed a woman who had been suffering from severe bleeding for twelve years. In her faith, the woman touched Jesus' cloak and her bleeding stopped at once. She had the feeling within herself that she was healed of her trouble. (5:25-29). "Jesus said to her, 'My daughter, your faith has made you well. Go in peace and be healed of your trouble.'" (5:34).

While Jesus was saying this, some messengers arrived with the news that Jairus' daughter had died.

> Jesus paid no attention to what they said, but told them, 'Don't be afraid, only believe.' He went in and said to them, 'Why all this confusion? Why are you crying? The child is not dead – she is only sleeping.' They laughed at him, so he put them all out, took the child's father and mother and his three disciples (Peter, James and John), and went into the room where the child was lying. He took her by the hand and said to her, 'Little girl, I tell you to get up.' She got up at once and started walking around. (She was twelve years old). When this happened, they were all amazed. But Jesus gave them strict orders not to tell anyone, and he said, 'Give her something to eat.' (Mark 5:35-43; see Matthew 9:18-19; Luke 8:40-42; John 11:25-26).

Jesus' raising of this one girl to life is symbolic of a deeper raising up. He himself suffered physical death, but God raised him up – offering us the consolation and hope that physical death is not the end of the human story, just a temporary phase from which all will be awakened at the final resurrection. Jesus will confront death itself, the main obstacle threatening God's good creation (Genesis 3:19; 1:31), and defeat it. And this time, there will be no commands to silence. (Mark 5:43). Instead, the message will be, 'Go, tell everyone the 'good news.' (Mark 16:7).

For the believer, despair and terror over the thought of death are no longer an inevitable part of human life. (See Hebrews 2:14-15; 1 Corinthians 15:51-55; Isaiah 25:8). Jesus is Lord of nature, Lord of storms, Lord of demons, Lord of life and death. Satan's reign is being usurped. The reign of God is here. These are new revelations of God, which at this stage, his disciples fail to understand. However, seeds are being sown which will bear fruit in the growth of God's new family. (Mark 3:33-35). The nuptial bond between God and his people is being restored. This was the hope of the prophet Isaiah (See Isaiah 54:5, 62:4-5).

Despite some opposition from the religious authorities, the advance of the reign of God seems unstoppable. Crowds of people have experienced the liberation and compassion of Jesus. But at the beginning of chapter six of Mark, this activity comes to a halt. The mighty works that demons, disease and death could not stop, are blocked by a greater obstacle, namely unbelief.

## Rejected in his Home Town

> Jesus left that place and went back to his home town, followed by his disciples. On the Sabbath day he began to teach in the synagogue. Many people were there, and when they heard him, they were all amazed. 'Where did he get this,' they asked. 'What wisdom is this that has been given him? How does he perform miracles? Isn't he the carpenter (builder), the son of Mary, and the brother of James, Joseph, Judas and Simon? Aren't his sisters living here?' And so they rejected him. (Mark 6:1-3).

Jesus has just performed two miracles in the context of faith. Then for the second time in the gospel, he returns to Nazareth where he grew up, and he is met with complete scepticism. (See 3:20-21).

Mark designates Jesus as "son of Mary." The normal practice was to identify a person through the father, even if he were dead. (Matthew 16:17; Mark 10:35). This may be Mark's way of hinting at the virginal conception of Jesus, which is treated in more detail in the infancy narratives of Matthew and Luke.[126]

The idea that their hometown craftsman could be inaugurating the reign of God is scandalous to the people of Nazareth. It does not conform to their preconceived notions about how God could and would act to liberate Israel. So what Jesus is doing is an obstacle to their faith. Like the "outsiders" in the parable of the sower, they "look but do not

---

[126] Brendan Byrne, 2008, p.104.

perceive, and hear but do not understand." (Mark 4:12).

Although amazed by Jesus' wisdom and miracles (verse 2), the people still cannot accept ("see") that through them, the attributes of the Creator God are revealed. (Jeremiah 10:12; 51:15; Daniel 2:20-21). In their minds, his works cannot be from God, especially since Jesus is just an ordinary young man, one of themselves, a local craftsman, and from a place of no importance. Jesus' response to them is about a prophet being "respected everywhere except in his hometown." (verse 4). By referring to himself as a prophet, Jesus links his destiny to the Old Testament prophets, who suffered rejection or violence because of unbelief or the unpopularity of their message. (Jeremiah 20:1-2, 8, 10; 23:9; 26:7-9; 37:36:14-16; 37:4-6). However, Mark's readers know that the source of Jesus' wisdom and power derives from his being empowered as Son of God by the Spirit of God. (Mark 1:9-11).

> He was not able to perform any miracles there, except that he placed his hands on a few sick people and healed them. He was greatly surprised, because the people did not have faith. Then Jesus went to the villages round there, teaching the people. (Mark 6:5-6).

Jesus' reception in his home town shows that this is not the first time the works of God have caused people to stumble in their faith. (Judges 6:14-15; see Isaiah 53:2). The people of Nazareth were afflicted with the usual deafness and blindness which we have witnessed so far in the gospel. They could not see God in the craftsman and builder they knew from his youth, even though he was already building a whole new world before their eyes – the family of God. (See Luke 4:16-30). Jesus' experience in Nazareth was an example of a small community, first of all, having no faith in their own potential, and then failing to see the works of God being revealed in one of their own.

The kind of kingdom Jesus was proclaiming was not the kingdom his contemporaries wanted. Jesus' rejection in Nazareth is a pointer to his final rejection when, as Messiah he will come "home" to his town and temple, but this time, with fatal consequences for himself. In his account of Jesus' rejection by his own people in Nazareth, Mark is pointing us to where the story will ultimately climax.

CHAPTER 13

# Jesus Shares and Extends his Ministry

(6:7-8:21)

## The Mission of the Twelve

Then he went about among the villages teaching. He called the twelve and began to send them out two by two, and gave them authority over the unclean spirits. He ordered them to take nothing for their journey except a staff: no bread, no bag, no money in their belts; but to wear sandals and not to put on two tunics. He also said to them, 'Wherever you enter a house, stay there until you leave the place. If any place will not welcome you or they refuse to hear you, as you leave, shake off the dust that is on your feet as a testimony against them.' So they went out and proclaimed that all should repent. They cast out many demons and anointed with oil many who were sick and cured them. (Mark 6:6-13, NRSVC; see Matthew 10:5-15; Luke 9:1-6; James 5:14-15).

The disappointment resulting from Jesus' mission to his hometown will be outweighed by the fruits of the mission on which he now sends his apostles. Their sowing of seeds will result in abundant fruit. The apostles will bring healing, freedom and new life to many people. The word "apostle" means "one who is sent."

The first phase of the training of the twelve is complete, and they are ready to participate in Jesus' mission. They have been instructed in the secrets of the kingdom (Mark 4:1-34) and taught to become "fishers of people." (1:17). They have been with Jesus for some time and have seen his measured response to opposition (3:21-30; 6:1-6). They have been shown his power and authority over demons, over the turbulent sea, and over death itself (4:35-5:43). Their task as apostles is "to be with him" (3:14), and to be "sent out." When Jesus called Simon, his brother Andrew, and James and John, "at once they left their nets and boats and followed him." (Mark 1:16-17, 19-20). Being apostles means giving up everything on which they formerly relied for security and sustenance (fishing nets, boats, livelihoods).

Jesus now extends his ministry by sharing it with the twelve, and later, by moving more and more in the direction of Gentile territory (7:24-37).

A "staff" (verse 8 above) was always carried by a shepherd and used to protect, guide and gather his sheep together. It is a biblical symbol of divine authority and protection, a sign of God's leadership and guidance. (Exodus 4:20, see Psalm 23:4b). A staff is also symbolic of meagre human resources, in contrast to the power granted to human beings by God, in carrying out a mission. (See Exodus 7:9; 14:13-16; 17:6-7; Genesis 32:9-10). The lack of a sack and money means that the apostles have to rely, not on their own resources, but on God's provision. (Philippians 4:11-13; see Acts of the Apostles 3:6).

The mission of the apostles resembles the role of the shepherd, which is to feed God's people, heal their wounds and gather them together into God's new family - the Kingdom of God, centred on Jesus as Shepherd. (See Mark 3:33-35; John 11:52). In the mission of the twelve apostles, there is a strong emphasis on expelling evil spirits. When Jesus earlier chose the twelve, as well as giving them authority to drive out demons, he gave them a role of preaching the word. (Mark 3:14-15). Calling people to repent of their sins and expelling demons are the only tasks mentioned in Mark 6:7-9. Jesus shares his own authority and power with the Twelve so that that they too may be enabled to discharge their mission.

Shaking the dust off their feet (verse 11) is meant as a gesture of judgement and a reminder not to be discouraged by a hostile reception. There are always those who prefer to remain sick rather than face the challenge of a new way of life, a new beginning. The apostles' task is to faithfully and fearlessly carry out their mission of sowing seeds, and leave their fruitfulness in the hands of God, regardless of who might or might not be listening or opposing them. (Jeremiah 2:17-19).

Mark wants to emphasise that it is God who is sowing the seeds, with human beings as his instruments. It is God who rescues humanity from evil powers and gathers them together in his family. (Mark 3:33-35). Freed from worry about their physical needs and strengthened by God's Spirit, the apostles are able to focus wholly on their task. (2 Corinthians 12:9-11; see Genesis 28:20-21). Through their lack of physical resources, they make it known that they are preaching the gospel out of conviction rather than for material reward. (Acts 3:6; see Genesis 18:1-8; 19:1-3; Job 31:32). Furthermore, their need for food and shelter would call forth hospitality in those to whom they ministered. God would supply them with their daily requirement of manna. (6:10; see Exodus 16:4-5). In the Jewish tradition of hospitality, it was common for travellers to be welcomed into homes and given a meal. (See Genesis 18:1-5). The welcome for the apostles would signify an acceptance of their message. (Mark 6:10; see Genesis 18:1-8; 19:13; Job 31:32).

Jesus made it plain at the start of his ministry that he himself was sent on a liberating mission, resembling that of Moses in Egypt. His first task after calling the four fishermen (Mark 1:14-20) was to liberate a man from an evil spirit in the Nazareth synagogue. (1:21-28). According to Luke's gospel, it was in the Nazareth synagogue that he made his mission statement when he announced to those present that God's Spirit had empowered him to "bring good news to the poor and to proclaim liberty to captives, to set free the oppressed." (Luke 4:18-19). And this liberating work would be the visible sign of God bringing salvation to his people.

All of us are called to mission, which can take a variety of forms, depending on our circumstances. (See Mark 10:1-31). Our mission may not mean going to the ends of the earth. It can be carried out within our families. The call to mission comes from God. It is carried out in obedience to the will of God, and it always involves service to others.

The mission of the twelve foreshadows that of the Church. In its preaching of the gospel, together with the healing ministry of the sacraments, the Church keeps an eye on circumstances in today's world which may be holding people in chains.

## The Death of John the Baptist

While the twelve apostles are away on their mission, Mark goes into considerable detail in his account of the death of John the Baptist. (Mark 6:14-29).

With the title of tetrarch (the Romans refusing him the title of king), Herod Antipas ruled Galilee. His brother, Philip ruled the territory to the north and east of the Sea of Galilee. As a ruler, Philip proved to be one of the better of the sons of Herod the Great. Philip's wife, Herodias, left her husband, took her daughter Salome with her to Galilee and then married Herod Antipas. "John the Baptist kept telling Herod: 'It isn't right for you to be married to your brother's wife.'" (Mark 6:18, see Leviticus 20:21-22).

John's baptism of repentance (Mark 1:4) was a call to the whole population, including those in power, to turn away from their sins. As a prophet, John would have understood that the behaviour of leaders can impact on the morals of the community. Like the prophets of old, John was willing to risk his life for his message. "Herod himself had ordered John's arrest and he had him chained and put in prison. Herod did this because of Herodias, whom he had married, even though she was the wife of his brother Philip." (6:17). At this point Herod had no plans for putting John to death. However, that soon changed.

"Herodias held a grudge against John and wanted to kill him, but she could not because of Herod. Herod was afraid of John because he knew that John was a good and holy man, and so he kept him safe. He liked to listen to him, even though he became greatly disturbed every time he heard him." (6:19-20).

Herodias' grudge against John was because of his criticism of her marriage. Her opportunity came during a banquet to celebrate Herod's birthday, to which he invited "the chief government officials, the military commanders and the leading citizens of Galilee." (6:21). Represented in the latter group were Jewish supporters of Herod, known as Herodians. (See Mark 3:6; 12:13). Salome, the daughter of Herodias, came to the feast and gave a display of erotic dancing for Herod and his officials which so pleased Herod that he rashly offered to give her anything she asked, even half his kingdom. (The Romans would not allow him to do this). Prompted by her mother, the girl asked for the "head of John the Baptist on a dish." (6:23-24). "This made Herod very sad, but he could not refuse her because of the vows he had made in front of his guests." (6:26). As he delivered on his rash promise, Herod valued the admiration of his guests more than an innocent man's life.

"When John's disciples heard about his death, they came and took away his body, and buried it." (Mark 6:29).

When Herod later heard about the miracles and preaching of Jesus in Galilee, he said, 'He is John the Baptist! I had his head cut off, but he has come back to life.' (6:16).

The banquet to which Herod invited his courtiers, officials, military officers and leading men of Galilee, is contrasted with the life-enhancing banquets of Jesus for crowds who were like sheep without a shepherd. (6:30-43). Herod had pretentions to be a real "King of the Jews," but could not, because he was a bad shepherd. Jesus' meals with outcasts and sinners are signs that he is the true Shepherd and King, the one who is already liberating God's people from their sickness and creating a kingdom of peace and reconciliation. This is in stark contrast to the kingdoms of this world which glory in oppressive power and use violence as a means of holding on to power. (Matthew 4:8).

The death of John the Baptist foreshadows that of Jesus. The precursor John prepared the way that Jesus would go. Jesus would soon begin speaking about a similar fate awaiting himself – and his disciples. All the characters, from Herod to his guests, behaved in a way similar to those who will be complicit in the death of Jesus. Out of cowardice and the need to preserve their reputations, both Herod and Pilate condemned a good man to death whom they knew to be innocent of any crime. Neither did the officials or leading men in either case protest against unlawful killings. (See Luke 7:18-28). Both Herod and Pilate were ruled by the "crowd." (Mark 15:8-14). Jesus preached the word of God all over Galilee, but his word, no less than that of John, fell on stony ground as far as Herod was concerned; it was fruitless, because it did not take root in him.

John preached a message of repentance (1:4-8, 6:18) and he was arrested. In a number of ways, the fate of John prefigures that of Jesus (Mark 3:19; 9:31; 10:33; 14:10, 11, 18, 21, 41, 42, 44; 15:1, 10, 15), and that of his disciples. (13:9, 11, 12). Winning people for God's Kingdom will not proceed without cost. John, like Jesus, was willing to give his life for his message.

Luke's Gospel records Jesus' glowing tribute to John the Baptist. "Jesus said to them, 'I tell you, of all the children born to women, there is no one greater than John the Baptist; yet the least in the Kingdom of God is greater than he.'" (Luke 7:28, NJB).

Why was John not in the kingdom of God? John worked from within the old prophetic expectations for the liberation of Israel. John's call to repentance was not enough, because Israel remained in the grip of Satan. As the new Pharaoh, Satan would have to be confronted with a power greater than that of John, if Israel and the world were to be set free from Satanic powers. John's baptism prepared people for the further demands of the reign of God, which would involve great suffering, because Satan would not yield to the superior power of God without striking a fatal blow. (Genesis 3:15b). For John, the blow was death. It would be the same for Jesus.

## The Return of the Twelve

The apostles returned and met with Jesus and told him all they had done and taught. There were so many people coming and going that Jesus and his disciples didn't have time to eat. So he said to them, 'Let us go off by ourselves to some place where we will be alone and you can rest for a while.' So they started out in a boat by themselves for a lonely place. (Mark 6:30-32).

More crowds are now coming to Jesus as a result of the mission of the apostles. The twelve are with Jesus again, from whom they will renew and draw their strength by trusting in what he can do for them. (John 15:1-8; 1 Peter 4:11; see Isaiah 40:31).

It would seem that the apostles' preaching of repentance and casting out of demons had been successful, but it might have left them exhausted (6:31), or perhaps in a mood of self-congratulation. It is notable that Jesus does not respond positively to their enthusiasm, which he may have wanted to dampen down. So he took them away to a "lonely place." (Mark 6:31b-32; see Mark 1:35). Jesus knew that the real test had yet to come; there will be more frightening obstacles to surmount, and once the crunch comes and reality dawns, enthusiasm can easily wane. Jesus had seen what happened to John the Baptist as a result of what John "taught." The disciples had yet much to "see" and learn about the full implications of Jesus' ministry and their own mission of sowing the word of God. They will soon learn how costly preaching and doing the works of God would be.

The "lonely place" (verse 32) represents the trial symbolized by the desert wilderness. It has implications of reflection, testing and preparation for new challenges. (See Mark 1:13). Jesus' desire to give his disciples "rest" evokes the rest that God promised to give his people in the promised land. (Exodus 33:14; Deuteronomy 12:10; see Hebrews 4:9-11). We can imagine Jesus taking time to listen to the apostles' stories of success and failure during their mission, and directing and encouraging them where necessary. But as we will see later, the lonely place will turn out not to be deserted at all.

## Understanding the Bread of Life

Israel had a long tradition of the sacred role of table fellowship. It was associated with worship of God, and signified communion with God. (Exodus 18:12, 24:11; 1 Kings 3:15). Eating together established social bonds, but in the Israel of Jesus' day, certain types of people - Gentiles, outcasts and sinners, were regarded as unclean, and therefore, unacceptable as dinner guests. The belief was that the sacred character of the meal was incompatible with evil, so the pious person could not sit down at table with the sinner or outcast. This attitude represents a kind of blindness. The pious person could not see what the sinner and outcast could become. Jesus met a man who had been living in tombs and cutting himself with stones, and saw the man's potential as an evangelist. The Creator God is not so much concerned about where we are, but how we can be led to a better place.

In his table fellowship with all classes of people, Jesus subverted the old beliefs and customs, and challenged the sacred order associated with them.[127] For Jesus, there was indeed something sacred and symbolic about eating at table. It symbolized God's forgiveness of sinners – the shepherd gathering together of his lost and scattered flock and bringing them home, then satisfying their deepest hungers by feeding them in a great

---

[127] Ben F. Meyer, *The Aims of Jesus*, (Pickwick Publications), 2002, p. 159

feast, as celebration and confirmation of their transformation. (See Luke 15:20-24). For Jesus, table fellowship symbolized the union created when all classes of people come together in mutual forgiveness, each one respecting the dignity of the other.

The kings of Israel were reproached by the prophets for their bad shepherding. They failed to provide good leadership, they were negligent, often corrupt rulers, feeding themselves rather than their flock (Ezekiel 34:1-4, 7-10; 2 Chronicles 18:16; Zechariah 10:2). Because of their failures, God eventually says that he himself must do the shepherding. God himself must rescue the lost sheep and feed them. (Ezekiel 34:11-13; Jeremiah 31:10). Jesus is fulfilling what God promised in the Old Testament. In his table fellowship and feedings in the wilderness, he is assuming a shepherding role that God had reserved for himself in the Old Testament. The Good Shepherd goes out into the 'wilderness' of this world and searches for the lost sheep - humanity. (Luke 15:1-6). He loves his sheep to the extent that he is willing to die in order to rescue them from the bondages that are keeping them apart in enmity. (John 10:7-16).

Jesus is also assuming the role of God as King. The King (God) called his servants to go out into the streets and invite as many people as they could find to the feast – the good and the bad alike. The banqueting hall was filled with people for the wedding of his son to his redeemed people. (Matthew 22:1-10). The end-of-time banquet – the wedding feast of the Lamb - will be the greatest celebration of all, when God will definitively gather his people from farthest ends of the earth and satisfy their deepest hungering for eternal life. (Matthew 25:31-32; Revelation 19:5-8; see Isaiah 25:6-9).

Under the system of the day, if the poor of Galilee sought repentance, the only course open to them was an eighty-mile journey on foot to the Jerusalem temple where they would offer sacrifices for forgiveness. Only then would they be accepted into communion with everyone else. As Jesus must have seen it, this process was placing an intolerable yoke on people who were afflicted in ways not of their own doing. At that time Jesus said, "Come to me, all of you who are tired carrying heavy loads, and I will give you rest. Take my yoke and put it on you, and learn from me, because I am gentle and humble in spirit, and you will find rest." (Matthew 11:30).

John the Baptist maintained the customary approach in Israel to repentance: conversion first and communion second. (Matthew 3:7-10). Jesus turned the traditional approach on its head; for him, communion comes first and then conversion, and it could all take place while seated round a table.

All were sinners, even the pious Pharisees, who regarded everyone else as unclean, and thought of themselves as in no need of repentance or of God's mercy. The God of Jesus is a God of mercy, standing in solidarity with all of his people, always ready to forgive, to rescue them from their burdens and bring them together as members of his family. All he asks is that they turn their hearts in obedience to the will of God, which is that all people may become united with one another and with himself (kingdom of God). (See Mark 3:33-35). God said to Moses, 'I have heard the cries of my people to be rescued from their oppressors, and I have come down to rescue them.' (Exodus 3:7-8).

A lot of rescuing, a lot of mercy and forgiving, was needed within Israel, if all the scattered sheep were to be brought home from 'exile' and gathered into one family. Jesus saw the healing of divisions (between clean and unclean, between the self-righteous and sinners) within Israel as the will of God, and his actions showed that no barriers should be placed in the way of such healing and reconciliation. Nobody should be excluded from the mercy of God, for any reason. To this end, he initiated his table fellowship with anyone who wanted to join in. But his initiative was misconstrued and resented by the official upholders of that which they saw as something sacred - namely sharing a meal. (Mark 2:16; Matthew 11:19, 25-30; Luke 19:6-7; 15:25-28). "The Pharisees and teachers of the law (scribes) started grumbling, 'This man welcomes outcasts and eats with them.'" (Luke 15:2).

Jesus' celebratory meals are the equivalent in real life of the homecoming party after return from exile. (Isaiah 40:1-2, 10-11). Jesus is claiming that when he participates in these banquets, Israel's God is doing it through him – bypassing the temple system in his welcoming home of sinners from exile. This is who God is: The Father welcoming the prodigal son home, celebrating his return and satisfying his hunger for love and forgiveness with a great feast for the whole village – the family reunited. (Luke 15:23-24). But there is another ending to that story. The elder brother of the prodigal son (representing Israel – scribes, Pharisees) refused to come in and join in the feasting, despite the pleas of his father. (Luke 15:28).

By accepting sinners as his equals at table, Jesus takes away their shame and guilt, gives them back their dignity and thus releases them from their burdens, in a new "exodus." (See Exodus 3:9-10). But this was resented by the official teachers of Israel. "And Jesus said to the woman who came in during a meal, with Jesus as guest, in the house of Simon the Pharisee, 'Your sins are forgiven.'" (Luke 7:36-39, 48). Jesus welcomed the woman. Simon resented her presence. Because Jesus was regarded as a man of God, his fellowship with sinners would be seen as God's approval of them. He wanted to be a "friend of tax collectors and sinners." (Matthew 11:19; see Mark 2:15). The people's limitations (shame, guilt, the sense of being excluded) are overlooked, so their sins are forgiven; there is no rejection, no punishment from God. (Mark 2:1-12; see John 8:3-6-7, 10-11). Jesus' welcome to all was a sign of resurrection - forgiveness, restoration, and return from "exile."

These meals are signs that the kingdom of God is being established through the forgiveness and reconciliation of all kinds of people, thus creating a new family union. (Mark 3:33-35). Sharing a common meal means a readiness to share one another's burdens, to comfort and encourage the downhearted. It means helping whenever help is needed. This is the new forgiven and reconciled world that Jesus is creating, a world for which Israel still waited. But according to those opposed to him (the Pharisees and teachers of the law), he is the wrong person (not a rabbi or priest) to be doing it, and he is doing it all the wrong way (bypassing the temple system of forgiveness), and with the wrong people (the outcasts and sinners). The Jewish leaders object to Jesus' renewal of Israel through his table fellowship. But those objecting to this new "exodus" are cast in the mould of the Pharaoh of old in Egypt - as oppressor.

The reign of God and the renewal of the covenant (communion with God) was all happening under the noses of the elder brothers, the self-appointed guardians of the Father's house (Luke 15:28) and the tenants of the vineyard, who killed the owner's son. (Mark 12:8; Luke 20:9-15).

Jesus had a house in Capernaum, probably shared with Simon and Andrew, so that he could reside there on occasion and entertain people. (Mark 1:35, 2:1-12; Matthew 4:13). The meals would not have been expensive. The company and conversation would be what mattered. Jesus invited Pharisees and they sometimes invited him to their houses. (Luke 7:36, 11:37, 14:1). Perhaps the parable of the Wedding Feast (Matthew 22:1-13) was based on an actual event in which Pharisees refused to sit down with sinners. And Jesus may have had to invite himself to the houses of sinners. Because of their sense of always being excluded from such events, it wouldn't have occurred to them to invite him. (See Luke 19:1-10). The tax collectors and sinners sought out his company (Luke 15:1).

There are a number of meals in the gospels of Mark and Luke. (Mark 6:41-42; 8:6-8; 14:3). There is the banquet in Levi's house, following Jesus' call to the tax collector Levi (Matthew) to become a disciple of his (Mark 2:15-16; Luke 5:27-32). There is also the meal at the house of Zacchaeus (another one of the hated tax collectors), his sins forgiven by bypassing the temple system (Luke 19:1-10). There is Jesus' meal at Emmaus with the two disciples – forgiveness and reconciliation, transforming the two disciples who had been in despair over the death of Jesus – a true return from exile story (Luke 24:28-33). Finally, the Last Supper, in which the New Covenant of God's love relationship with humanity is definitively established. (Luke 22:14-38).

## The Shepherd Feeds his Flock in the Wilderness

The story of Jesus' feeding the hungry crowd in the wilderness is told six times in all four gospels. (Mark 6:30-43; Matthew 14:13-21; Luke 9:12-17; John 6:5-13; see Mark 14:22; see Numbers 11:13, 22; Isaiah 55:1-3; 2 Kings 4:42-44; Revelation 21:6-7; CCC 1335).

Mark places the wilderness feeding just after his account of the killing of John the Baptist. (6:25). According to Luke's gospel Jesus was a cousin of John. (Luke 1:36). Before Jesus called his disciples, John may have been one of his best friends. Jesus must have been shaken by the death of John. He would have recalled that the Herodians and the Pharisees had conspired to kill himself too. (Mark 3:6). Because of the death of John, he may have wanted to cross the Sea of Galilee to a lonely place (wilderness) with his disciples. (Mark 6:32).

This crossing recalls the Israelite's escape from Egypt across the Red Sea. (Exodus 14:21-22). Moses leads his people Israel, newly liberated from the Egyptian Pharaoh, through the desert wilderness on their way to the promised land. There, in the wilderness, he feeds them with bread from heaven to sustain them for their journey. (Exodus 16; Psalm 78:24-25). Jesus is the new Moses. As he begins his journey to Jerusalem, the place of ultimate liberation, he leads his people into the wilderness, where he will feed their hunger with a bread that will give them more than physical satisfaction. This new bread will feed their spiritual hunger for eternal life (life with God). "Not on bread alone does man live, but on every word that comes from the mouth of God." (Deuteronomy 8:3; see Isaiah 55:1-2).

As Jesus begins his journey with his disciples (the nucleus of the new Israel), he will be confronted by a new Pharaoh (the scribes and Pharisees), who, like the Pharaoh of old, will try to prevent the liberation of his new people Israel. (Exodus 6:13; Mark 7:1-23; 8:14-15).

Mark's account of the feeding in the wilderness prepares the reader of the gospel for an understanding of the eucharistic banquet at the end of his gospel, which is a celebration of the passion and glory of the Son of Man who will give his life for us as a spiritual food. (Mark 14:22). This will fulfil the prophecy of Isaiah's banquet of the "richest food and finest wine" for the people of all nations who have been rescued from evil. (Isaiah 25:6-9).

The banquet in the wilderness transcends Jesus' earlier simple table fellowship. The story of the wilderness feedings must have been a tradition of some significance in the early Church, for what it reveals about Jesus himself and about God's love and care for humanity. In contrast to the lavish Herodian banquet which ended in a death (Mark 6:25), here Jesus feeds ordinary people with simple food, leading to life.

> Many people from all the towns, saw them leaving in the boat and they set out on foot and arrived at the place ahead of Jesus and his disciples. When Jesus got out of the boat, he saw the large crowd and his heart was filled with pity for them, because they were like sheep without a shepherd. So he began to teach them many things. When it was getting late, his disciples came to him and said, 'It is already very late, and this is a lonely place. Send the people away, and let them go to the nearby farms and villages in order to buy themselves something to eat'... Jesus told his disciples to make the people divide into groups and sit down on the green grass. So the people sat down in rows, in groups of a hundred and groups of fifty. Then Jesus took the five loaves and the two fish, looked up to heaven, and gave thanks to God. He broke the loaves and gave them to his disciples to distribute to the people. He also divided the two fish among them all. Everyone ate and had enough. Then the disciples took up twelve baskets full of what was left of the bread and fish. The number of men who were fed was 5,000. (Mark 6:33-36, 39-44; see Isaiah 30:19).

The towns from which the people set out were probably those on the northern shore of Lake Galilee - Capernaum, Chorazin, and Bethsaida. Jesus and his disciples were then in Gentile territory on the east side of the lake. Unless the boat was proceeding very slowly, it is difficult to see how the crowds on foot could have arrived at the place ahead of Jesus. Be that as it may, Jesus wanted to withdraw to a lonely place, but he was once again confronted with a crowd. Many of these people may have been the same ones who were crowding around Jesus and his disciples, following the mission of the Twelve. (Mark 6:7-13).

When Jesus saw the crowd, his heart was filled with pity for them. (6:34, NRSVC). Another word for 'pity' is 'compassion,' one of the attributes of God. The word 'compassion' comes from the Latin *compatio,* meaning to 'suffer with.' The suffering of a loved-one calls forth compassion in us. The suffering of someone else can thus become one's own suffering. For example, when someone close to us suffers a family bereavement, we suffer along with him or her. By sharing in the suffering of others, we may help to lighten their burden in a number of ways. The suffering of humanity draws down the infinite compassion of God into the world, through Jesus. Because Jesus identifies with all of us (Mark 1:9), his compassion is universal. God sent his Son to live among us, to suffer with us, to take on board our pain, even to die for us, in order to rescue us from the pain of our human limitations and from death itself. Jesus' compassion for the crowd (symbolic of the whole of humanity) must have been of an intensity, something way beyond anything we ourselves can conceive or experience. His heart went out to suffering human beings. His mission on earth was about rescuing humanity from death, the greatest suffering of all. The significance of the wilderness banquet is that Jesus feeds our hungering for a life beyond death - eternal life. (See Psalm 23:5).

The compassion of God for human beings is a theme running through the whole Bible. (See Exodus 33:19; Isaiah 30:18; 49:10, 13; 54:10; Psalm 51:1; 86:15; 116:5; Matthew 20:34; Luke 7:12-15). We are all called to be compassionate, just as God is compassionate. Compassion is the power that draws us into feeding the hungry. (Luke 6:36; Colossians 3:12; 2 Corinthians 1:3-4; Ephesians 4:32).

In the foregoing passage, Mark says that the people were like "sheep without a shepherd" (verse 34) – signifying that the leaders of the nation (the religious authorities, Herod and his supporters) had not taken care of God's people. The leaders were lacking in compassion, caring only for themselves, feeding themselves by safeguarding their status and privileges at all costs. (See Ezekiel 34:1-2, 11). "My sheep wandered over the high hills and mountains. They were scattered over the face of the earth, and no one looked for them or fed them," (Ezekiel 34:6). Ezekiel prophesised that God himself would come and do the shepherding. (Ezekiel 34:11-12; see Psalm 23 :1-2; Isaiah 40:10-11; Jeremiah 31:8-9; Luke 15:1-6; CCC 754). Jesus is now God's shepherd, coming to gather and unite the sheep who have been scattered ever since the flight from the Garden of Eden. (Genesis 3:8). It is only God himself who can properly rescue his people from bad shepherds (systems of domination) and satisfy their deepest hungering for fullness of life in his eternal kingdom. The sheep are hungering for a food that only God can provide. In fulfilment of the psalms and prophets, the time has come for Jesus to provide this food.

Jesus began feeding the people, firstly by teaching (Mark 6:34b). Jesus' teaching is a kind of feeding, because it is liberating; it opens people's eyes to new ways of life, to new values by which they can live, values more enduring than the merely material. After teaching, he then feeds them with the bread of life – he himself being that bread - thus satisfying their spiritual hunger for meaningful life. (Mark 6:41-42; see John 6:35). Jesus will do this out of pity (compassion) for all who are lost or wandering. (Mark 6:34a; see Psalm 86:15; Isaiah 54:7-8; Hosea 11: 8). Jesus' feeding of the multitude in the wilderness is a sign of giving up his life for his flock (John 10:11), so that they might have a share in his own fullness of life, as an answer to their deepest hungering. "This is my body which is given for you." (Luke 21:19, NJB, NRSVC). God's way of ruling the world is with compassion and service unto death.

The disciples refer to a "lonely place" as a place with no resources. So they ask Jesus to send the people away to nearby villages in order to buy something to eat. They are suggesting that Jesus should let the sheep fend for themselves. (6:35-36). They don't understand that they themselves might have a role to play in feeding the hungry crowd. Neither do they understand that Jesus is fulfilling God's promise in the Old Testament to provide a food that no money can buy. (Isaiah 55:1-3). The disciples couldn't visualize the lonely wilderness being transformed into a place of life and strength. (v. 35; see Psalm 23:1-3). Jesus wanted his disciples to participate in his own shepherding – caring, comforting the Lord's flock. (See Matthew 25:35, 40). So he said to his disciples, 'You yourselves give them something to eat.' (6:37).

The disciples receive from Jesus the power to provide for the people's needs in a way that human beings themselves cannot do. They had already received from Jesus the power to teach and expel demons. (Mark 6:7-13). Now they receive the power to feed the Lord's flock (called to be shepherds themselves), and to do so from the crowd's own meagre resources ('five loaves and two fish,' verse 38), multiplied beyond all imagining by the power of God. (Matthew 14:21; see also Mark 8:1-10). As the King-Messiah promised to Israel, Jesus is hosting a messianic banquet in the wilderness, as foretold by Isaiah. (Isaiah 25:6-8; 55:1-2).

The significance of the words "green grass" (6:39) may be easily overlooked. The green grass evokes the prophetic promise that God would transform the desert into a place of life-sustaining growth for his people. (Isaiah 35:1-2; Ezekiel 34:13-15; see Psalm 23:2a). Mark is saying that this transformation is now being fulfilled in the words and actions of Jesus. It is the transformation that takes place in us when we are fed with the food that sustains us into eternity – both through word and sacrament. The division of the people into "groups" (6:39) recalls the ordered arrangement for the tribes of Israel as they camped in the desert after the exodus from Egypt. (Exodus 18:21-25). It may signify the new order of peace and reconciliation which Jesus is now creating. Mark's gospel suggests that what is happening here in the wilderness, not only recalls the exodus by Moses and his leading the people to the promised land. This is a new and definitive exodus – God feeding his people with a new "bread from heaven," a bread bringing them eternal life as their promised land (destiny). (See Mark 1:2-3; Isaiah 40:3).

The issue in Mark 6:30-44 is the people's hunger for more than physical bread, which can only satisfy an immediate need. This can still leave a person hungering for the saving word of God, which satisfies deepest hungers. (Deuteronomy 8:3; Matthew 4:4). Human beings often hunger for happiness in material things, but in a deeper sense they also have a spiritual hunger for the love and happiness that only God can satisfy. Because we are partly spiritual beings, physical food (material things) does not give us full or lasting satisfaction. To be truly fed means listening to the word of God and doing what God says. That brings us close to God. He can then share his own life and blessing with us. (Isaiah 55:1-3; Mark 2:15-17; 14:23-24).

"Everyone ate and had enough. Then the disciples took up twelve baskets full of what was left of the bread and the fish." (6:42-43). This is a bread which gives more than enough to satisfy the spiritual hunger of everyone. (See Exodus 16:15).

For the disciples, this episode in the wilderness was a new learning experience. Jesus was calling them to a shepherding role, as if to remind them that their future missionary work must involve something more than just providing for the physical needs of people. They could now begin to see Jesus in a new light, as God's Good Shepherd, doing only what God himself can do. But as events will unfold, (and like ourselves), they will be slow to open their eyes to this new reality. (See 6:52; 8:17-18).

The feeding in the wilderness anticipates the Last Supper and the final banquet of the kingdom at the end of time when "all tears will be wiped away." (Revelation 19:5-8; 21:4). The bread signifies the passion and glory of the Son of Man who will give his life as a spiritual food. The verbs that Mark uses in the feeding of the five thousand foreshadow the last supper – "took, blessed, broke" and "gave." (Mark 14:22). This is the meal by which Jesus wants to be remembered by his followers, a meal that symbolizes his suffering service through which humanity would be definitively gathered together and brought home from exile, into a new life in the family of God. (1 Corinthians 11:24).

Mark portrays Jesus as both teacher and as the one who provides food for the people – feeding them through word and sacrament, prefiguring the later ministry of the Church. (CCC 1335). The Eucharistic liturgy follows the same pattern as the feeding of the loaves in the lonely place. Firstly, comes the nourishing Word through the Scripture readings and the homily that opens peoples' ears to their meaning. Then in the Liturgy of the Eucharist, we bring our meagre gifts, representing ourselves, to the Lord, for him to transform them (us) into his own body, the Bread of Life, given up for us, making us Christ-like, empowering us to live like him and share in his resurrected life. Having shared in the Bread of Life, we are then called to be sharers with our friends and families, and all those in need. God blesses the little that we can share (a few loaves) and multiplies it beyond all imagining, so that the spiritual hungers of many may be satisfied.

## Jesus Walks on the Sea

> At once, after the miracle of the loaves, Jesus made his disciples get into the boat and go ahead of him to Bethsaida (on the northern shore of the lake, just east of the River Jordan), while he sent the crowd away. Then he went up a hill to pray. (Mark 6:45-46).

The words "at once" and "made" suggest Jesus' concern to remove his disciples as quickly as possible from the dangerous enthusiasm of the crowds. What was this danger? After the miracle of the loaves, John's Gospel says that Jesus knew that the crowds were about to "come and seize him and make him king by force." (John 6:14-15).

The crowd in the wilderness must have been awe-stricken over Jesus' multiplication of bread. Once again Jesus rejected the temptation of turning "stones into bread"– in a spectacular show of power - as the means of becoming the Messiah-king. (See Matthew 4:1-4). Jesus' purpose in his feeding the people, is not to display his power for its own sake, but to fulfil his mission as Shepherd of God's people – a role God had reserved for himself in the Old Testament.

It is notable that Jesus "sent the crowd away." (6:45b). So far in the gospel, we see crowds rushing to Jesus. First of all, there were the crowds coming to him from all over Galilee. (1:28, 39). Later, they were coming to him from Judea, Jerusalem, Idumea, Tyre and Sidon. (3:7-8). They flocked to the lakeshore. (Mark 3:7, see also 6:45, 54). The crowds responded to him in wonder, but not in belief. He had compassion on them like a shepherd, but they never recognised him as a shepherd. (6:34). They were willing to recognise him as John the Baptist risen from the dead, or as a prophet. (Mark 6:14-15;

8:28). But no one recognised him as Son of God or Messiah.

Mark mentions Jesus alone at prayer three times. (See also 1:35; 14:32-42). In the Bible, mountains are places of encounter with God. Jesus going alone up a hill to pray recalls Moses going to Mount Sinai to receive the Ten Commandments from God. (Exodus 3:1-2, 19:3; 24:15-18; see Psalms 3:5; 68:17, Mark 3:13; 9:2; 13:3; 14:26). Presumably. in his prayer, Jesus sought an ever deeper understanding of God's will for his mission, and for the empowerment to obey God's will, even though he already must have known how costly this would be. He must have often prayed for his disciples too.

> When evening came, the boat was in the middle of the lake, and Jesus was alone on the land. He saw that his disciples were straining at the oars because they were rowing against a strong wind. Sometime between three and six o'clock in the morning he came to them, walking on the water. He was going to pass them by, but they saw him walking in the water. 'It's a ghost!' they thought, and screamed. They were all terrified when they saw him. Jesus spoke to them and said, 'Courage, it is I! Don't be afraid!' Then he got into the boat with them, and the wind died down. The disciples were completely amazed because they had not understood the real meaning of the feeding of the 5,000; their minds could not grasp it. (Mark 6:47-52; see Exodus 20:18).

The difficulty of the disciples' rowing against a strong wind may be a metaphor for their struggle to "see" Jesus' role as God's Good Shepherd who can satisfy the hungers of his flock. Instead, they "saw" him only as a ghost. In other words, despite the miracle of the loaves, they didn't really "see" Jesus. (6:51). They were terrified, signifying their lack of faith and understanding of him as embodying the power of God, a power which they witnessed in the multiplication of the loaves. In the Old Testament, there is a recurring injunction not to be afraid (verse 49 above) when encountering the divine. God is not a threat to human beings. God said to Abraham, 'Do not be afraid, I am your shield.' (Genesis 15:1, 18; see Genesis 26:24; 43:6; Isaiah 41:10; 43:1-5; Jeremiah 1:7-8, 17-19; 42:11; Mark 4:40; 5:36; Luke 8:50).

Jesus said, 'It is I' (6:50). this can also mean 'I am,' the divine name revealed to Moses at the burning bush. (Exodus 3:14). 'I am' means God *with* his people in their troubles, as Jesus is with his disciples who were rowing against the wind in a boat on the Sea of Galilee.

Confronted once again by a demonstration of Jesus' power, the disciples are terrified. (Exodus 20:18; Job 23:15; Luke 2:9). They are still confused as to his identity. (See Mark 2:12; 5:42). Why were they confused? It was because "their minds could not grasp it." (6:52). In other words, they had closed minds. A closed mind involves a failure to listen and hear something which is completely foreign to one's own cherished outlook, as if an alternative vision were not only untrue, but could not be true. To have an open mind, on the other hand, means really listening and hearing. It means a readiness, at least, to examine a different vision for what it might offer; to be prepared to see where a new faith journey might be leading. The disciples' minds were not open to the new reality confronting them. This left them in a state of confusion. They were rowing all night and had made little headway, as if they were unable to see that Jesus is a revelation of the power of God, who is "with them" in their terrors, shielding them (as with Abraham) from destruction. All of this is a far-cry from their enthusiasm and exhilaration after they came back from their mission. Their mission was but an introduction to the terrors which would later assail them, but which might lead them to a deeper faith and a new maturity. They were still in the "lonely place of testing," and not standing up too well.

Like Moses on Mount Sinai, Jesus came down from the hill where he had been praying. (Verse 46). His appearance to the disciples walking on the sea, signifies a status far beyond that of Moses. In the Old Testament, God's power to walk on the sea – to subdue and trample on the forces of chaos and destruction - is a prerogative of God, "who alone stretched out the heavens and trampled the waves of the Sea." (Job 9:8, NRSVC, see Job 38:16; Psalm 77:19). To trample the waves of the sea is a sign of God's sovereignty over creation. The disciples couldn't "see" Jesus assuming the role of God. As of yet, they don't even see him as the Messiah promised to Israel.

"Wake up Lord and help us! Use your power and save us; use it as you did in ancient times. It was you who cut the sea monster Rehab[128] to pieces." (Isaiah 51:9; see Job 9:1-10, 38:8-11, Psalm 77:13-20; 107:1-9). What the disciples in their boat didn't see - thinking it to be a ghost - was a revelation of the God who created order out of the primeval watery chaos (Genesis 1:2-3), the same God who saved Israel by controlling and parting the waters of the Red Sea. (Exodus 14:15-16). For the disciples to "see" Jesus' divine status, symbolized in his walking on the sea, would have involved a leap of faith on their part, which would have been difficult at this stage of their journey with Jesus. The final element of revelation in the foregoing passage comes with Jesus' assurance to them: "Courage, It is I! Don't be afraid." (Verse 50d). The presence of the divine is encouraging and saving. (Deuteronomy 39a; Isaiah 43:10; 41:4).

Jesus' presence in the boat with his disciples was enough to make the wind die down, confirming Jesus' mastery of the hostile elements of nature. If they had understood about the loaves, they would have seen Jesus as God's Shepherd and King, with the power to feed and rule his flock with compassion. Then they would not have been so fearful and surprised by this further manifestation of Jesus' divine authority and status – his trampling the waves of the sea. The disciples' failure to "see" will be one of the main obstacles confronting Jesus as he and they make their journey to Jerusalem, beginning in Mark 8:27. (See Psalm 51:10).

One of the lessons of the above episode is that human beings are dependent on a power greater than anything they themselves can summon up. "Rowing against a strong wind" in the dark and under our own steam doesn't work. It is a revelation of our human limitations and our dependency. "Our help comes from the Lord who made heaven and earth." (Psalm 124:8). It is only after Jesus gets into the boat that the disciples begin to make headway against the adverse forces holding them in bondage to fear, discouragement, spiritual weakness and misunderstanding. Jesus was on land the far side of the lake. He hadn't forgotten his disciples. He was compassionately aware of their struggling and suffering in the boat. Not even the watery depths of the sea would deter

---

[128] Rehab: a legendary sea monster, representing the forces of chaos and evil, and sometimes used as a symbol of Egypt under the Pharaoh, when the Israelites were oppressed.

him from coming to their rescue. Once he is "with them" (as their shield), they are relieved (if not liberated) from the negative forces that had left them immobilized and in fear. "Moses said to God," 'I am nobody. How can I go to the king and bring the Israelites out of Egypt?" God answered, 'I will be with you.' (Exodus 3:11-12a).

In some ways, the disciples resemble the people whom Jesus had been healing: powerless, dispirited humans. In their weakness and dependency, perhaps they represent all of us, as we face the headwinds of life's troubles. With the power of Jesus' presence with them, the disciples' fears are relieved and they are given the gift of courage, so that they can journey with new hope and trust in him. We need faith and courage to face the hostile forces which often assail us. In the light of Jesus' previous healings, the disciples should have been helped to answer the question, "Who is this Man?"

## Touching the Edge of his Cloak

Mark earlier noted that the disciples were supposed to cross towards Bethsaida on the northeast corner of the lake, but they came to land at Gennesaret, a region of fertile plains along the western shore of the lake. (6:53).

> The people there recognised Jesus at once. So they ran throughout the whole region. And wherever they heard he was, they brought him sick people lying on their mats. Everywhere Jesus went, to villages, towns or farms, people would take those who were ill to the market places and beg him to let them touch the edge of his cloak; and all who touched it were made well. (Mark 6:53-56; Matthew 14:34-36; see CCC 1503-5).

The above passage must be referring to an extended mission. This summary of Jesus' healing activity illustrates, once again, his compassion for the sick, as he responds to their "begging." (6:56). He enters every area of Galilean society – villages, towns and the countryside. By their faith, the people are made well, fed anew with the sustaining Bread of Life. Being "made well," they are encouraged and given new hope. Again, these healings are anticipatory signs of salvation in the fullest sense – God's compassion coming to meet human dependency and need, and satisfying human hungering and hope for a permanent healing. The same Greek verb can mean to 'heal' or 'save.' God searches in the darkness of our world for his lost coin, his treasured possession - humanity. (Luke 15:8-9). No obstacles are placed in the way of Jesus' healings. The mere touch of the edge of his cloak is enough. (6:56).

As the following episode shows, the turbulent waters of the sea will appear in a group of Pharisees who came from Jerusalem to confront Jesus. (See Mark 3:22).

## Clean Hands, Far Away Hearts

> Some Pharisees and teachers of the law who had come from Jerusalem, gathered round Jesus. They noticed that some of the disciples were eating their food with

hands that were ritually unclean – that is, they had not washed them in the way the Pharisees said people should. (For the Pharisees as well as the rest of the Jews, follow the teaching they received from their ancestors: they do not eat unless they wash their hands in the proper way; nor do they eat anything that comes from the market unless they wash it first. And they follow many other rules which they have received, such as the proper way to wash cups, pots, copper bowls and beds). So the Pharisees and teachers of the law asked Jesus, 'Why is it that your disciples do not follow the teaching handed down by our ancestors, but instead eat with ritually unclean hands?' Jesus answered them, 'How right Isaiah was when he prophesied about you. You are hypocrites, just as he wrote: *'These people,' says God, 'honour me with their words, but their heart is far away from me. It is no use for them to worship me, because they teach human rules as though they were God's laws.* You put aside God's command and obey human teachings.' (Mark 7:1-8; Isaiah 29:13 in italics).

Because of their obsession with ritual "cleanness," the Pharisees and scribes would never touch, or allow themselves to be touched, by those whom they regarded as unclean (sick people, sinners, for example). Certain foods were avoided because their laws said they would make people ritually unclean. This was a question of ritual purity rather than hygiene. Jesus' followers were accused of eating with "ritually unclean," i.e. with unwashed hands. Sitting at table with the ritually unclean would also render the self-righteous person unclean.

Mark explains the background of these Jewish practices for the benefit of his Gentile readers. (7:3-4 above). The law of Moses prescribed purity rules for priests, including washing their hands before offering animal sacrifices, and before eating their share of a sacrifice. (Exodus 13:17-21; Book of Numbers 18:11-13). These rules only applied to temple priests at the altar, but the oral tradition developed by the Pharisees had extended their application (along with many other such rules and rituals) to all Jews. (See Acts of the Apostles 10:9-15). Not all Jews observed this oral tradition, but those who failed to do so were labelled the "accursed," and despised by the scribes and Pharisees. This label was totally undeserved, as these were just ordinary people who were ignorant of these innumerable laws. (See John 7:49). This means that the religious leaders of Israel treated most ordinary country people as outcasts and sinners, thus victimizing them.

In quoting Isaiah 29:13 in the foregoing passage (in italics) about people honouring God, only by their words, while their hearts are far away from him, Jesus implies that the scribes and Pharisees are hard-hearted. Isaiah was speaking to Israelites who had lost a true relationship with God because of their emphasis on temple ritual (paying lip service) devoid of real love. Jesus rebukes his listeners for teaching human rules as though they were God's laws, while ignoring God's call to reach out and touch their neighbours (whether clean, or unclean) with healing love. Jesus said to them, 'You put aside God's command and obey human teachings.' (7:8, see 7-23).

The heart represents what is fundamental to the person; it is where a person responds to God or resists him. Biblically, the heart was seen as the seat of emotions such as love, desire, joy, grief and anxiety. The heart was also the source of thought, will and conscience. Purity of heart is about setting one's heart on God, and not on some God substitute, e.g. human rules and rituals, which only serve to keep people apart, creating enmity. Rules then become more important than people. God is not hard-hearted, but a God of compassion and mercy, and he wants these same qualities exemplified in all his people. In the Old Testament, he promises to give his people new hearts. (See Ezekiel 11:19-20). Jesus says that purity rules are incapable of creating a compassionate heart, which is what God truly desires for his people in their relationships. Compassion is of the will of God; it provides the foundation for his new spiritual family united in love. (See Mark 3:33-35). Trusting in God and doing his will enables us to "see God." It makes us children of God and brothers and sisters of Jesus – leading to a peaceful world. (See Matthew 5:8-9).

What was the real purpose of these rules? Through their rules and practices, the Pharisees defined themselves; safeguarded their identity over against all those outside their group, including many Jews (the outcasts and sinners) and all Gentiles. In all likelihood, Jesus would have observed that the Jewish religious leaders did not know God at all. The God to whom they gave their allegiance being merely a God exclusively for their own group–a false god. Wherever a group (e.g. the scribes and Pharisees) creates a "we" (insiders) at the expense of a "they" (unclean outsiders), often regarded as a wicked "they" and turned into victims, this is a matter of "group building against excluded others, and is a kind of atheism."[129] This gives the insider group a feeling of goodness (self-righteousness) by comparison with the wicked outsiders. But rather than creating a unified family (which is the will of God), it sets the scene for enmity and hatred, leading to family division and collapse. (See Mark 3:24). The universal and transcendent God who created the world and everyone in it, and loving everyone equally, cannot be a God who backs up one group in society against some other group. Seemingly, the scribes and Pharisees didn't know the true God. Jesus brought a whole new dispensation, a release from crippling burdens and man-made rules, which served to keep people apart, creating a whole class of victims, branded as outcasts and sinners. (See Mark 3:24).

It was in like manner that the hard-hearted religious leaders victimized Jesus too. At his birth, there was "no room for him in the inn" (Luke 2:7), which means that official Israel had no room for him in their hearts. They treated him as an outcast and made him a victim by killing him, thinking that God backed them up by so doing. "He came to his own country, but his own people did not receive him. Some, however did receive him, and believed in him; so he gave them the right to become God's children." (John 1:11-12). God raised Jesus from the dead as the forgiving victim, with the power to create a new Israel without barriers or frontiers, in which everyone could be included (even those who condemned him). Everyone would be invited to sit around the same table of forgiveness. By trusting in this God and doing his will, all people receive a new identity, as children of God, making them into a brotherly union along with Jesus. By merely touching Jesus' cloak (Mark 6:56), people in dire need are united with him in heart and mind, their dignity restored, placing them on the same level with everyone in the communion of the kingdom of God.

---

[129] James Alison, *Undergoing God*, (The Continuum International Publishing Group Inc), 2006. P. 21.

What is happening in Jesus' kingdom of God proclamation is the fulfilment of the old covenant – the full flowering of God's relationship of love with humanity. While they may have served their purpose as markers of Jewish identity, the rules of the scribes and Pharisees were not needed anymore. Purity laws did not touch the real human problem. Ritual purity had a value as a symbol pointing beyond itself to purity of heart, but it had become an end in itself.

Further, in his reply to the Pharisees and teachers of the law, Jesus said to them, 'You have a clever way of rejecting God's law in order to uphold your own teaching.' (7:9). As an example of this, Jesus referred to a custom whereby a person could vow to set aside a sum of money as a deferred gift to the temple treasury. This was known as "corban," meaning "belonging to God." (Mark 7:11). If a person made this vow when his parents were still alive, the money thus dedicated could not be used to support them in old age. According to the Pharisee's teaching, the vow was considered binding, even when it conflicted with the obligation of the fourth commandment to love and care for one's parents. (Exodus 20:12; Deuteronomy 5:16). In much of their teaching, the Pharisees ignored the Ten Commandments, in favour of their man-made rules. Jesus said to them, 'In this way, the teaching you pass on to others cancels out the word of God. And there are many other things like this that you do.' (Mark 7:13).

The "corban" practice was not an isolated example, for they "do many such things," including things arising from their Sabbath interpretations earlier in the gospel. (2:24; 3:24). They even have murder in their hearts – a violation of the fifth commandment. (See Mark 3:6). In the light of his final word to the religious leaders, it looks as if Jesus concluded that they would never repent of their limited vision and begin listening to him, as the authentic voice of God. (Mark 9:8, 13).

> Then Jesus called the crowd to him once more and said to them, 'Listen to me all of you and understand. There is nothing that goes into a person from the outside which can make him unclean. Rather, it is what comes out of a person that makes him unclean.' When he left the crowd and went into the house, the disciples asked him to explain this saying. 'You are no more intelligent than the others,' he said to them. 'Don't you understand? Nothing that goes into a person from the outside makes him unclean. It is what comes out of a person that makes him unclean… For from the inside, from people's hearts, come the evil ideas that lead them to do immoral things, to rob, kill, commit adultery, to be greedy, and do all sorts of evil things; deceit, indecency, jealousy, slander, pride and folly – all these evil things come from inside people and make them unclean.' (7:14-18, 21-23).

When the disciples were away from the crowds and inside the house, they asked Jesus to explain what he said to the Pharisees. He admonished them for their incomprehension. (See 4:13; 6:52). They still had no more understanding than the Pharisees. If people are not heartened by God, they will have hard hearts. They will lack compassion and a sense of care for their neighbour. From this, will flow a number of vices, listed by Jesus in 7:21-23.

Mark was writing his gospel for the early Church, where the question was asked:

are Christians who were Gentiles obliged to follow the laws and traditions of the Jews? (See Acts of the Apostles, chap. 5). Through the power of the Holy Spirit, the question was answered in line with Jesus' teaching. Jesus established an important principle for the future of Christianity. And because of it, Christianity would not become a branch of Judaism, whose members would be obliged to keep all the prescriptions of Jewish law (the Old Law). Jesus' universal vision, first articulated in Mark 3:33-35, was his new way of bringing all human beings into communion with God and with one another. It opened the door to the Gentiles, putting them on the same footing as everyone else. (See Galatians 3:26-28; Romans 10:11-12). Jesus clearly hoped that his own people would embrace his glorious and universal vision and become part of his following – as indeed many did. (See Acts of the Apostles 6:7).

In the sacraments of the Church, the risen Christ continues to "touch" us in order to heal our fears, misunderstandings, our spiritual poverty, our deafness to God's saving word, our failure to reach out to our neighbour, who often needs but the simple touch of our cloak, as our helping hand. (CCC 1504, 1421).

The following section continues with Mark's theme of the widening of the family of God. Here, God's promise to Abraham of blessing to the nations is being fulfilled by Jesus. (Genesis 12:3; 22:17).

## God Feeds the Hunger of the Gentiles

> Then Jesus left and went away to the territory near the city of Tyre. He went into a house and did not want anyone to know he was there, but he could not stay hidden. A woman, whose daughter had an evil spirit in her, heard about Jesus and came to him at once and fell at his feet. The woman was a Gentile, born in the region of Phoenicia in Syria. She begged Jesus to drive the demon out of her daughter. But Jesus answered, 'Let us first feed the children. It isn't right to take the children's food and throw it to the dogs.' 'Sir,' she answered, 'even the dogs under the table eat the children's leftovers!' So Jesus said to her, 'Because of that answer, go back home where you will find that the demon has gone out of your daughter.' She went home and found the child lying on the bed; the demon had indeed gone out of her. (Mark 7:24-30).

Tyre was located up the Mediterranean coast from Galilee. From God's call of Abraham, down to the time of the prophets, Israel's election as God's people was never intended for the exclusive benefit of Israel alone. Israel's vocation was to be God's instrument of bringing his salvation to all nations. "The Lord said to his servant Israel, 'I have a greater task for you, my servant. Not only will you restore to greatness the people of Israel who have survived, but I will make you a light to the nations – so that all the world may be saved.'" (Isaiah 49:6; see 52:10). That was the mission Abraham received from God.

This task of being a "light to the nations" had not been accomplished in the Israel of Jesus' day. Gentiles were still seen as unclean and enemies to be defeated (the Romans). Jesus is now the "light of the world" (John 8:12). Jesus and his followers, constitute the new Israel, which fulfils the prophecy of Isaiah in 49:6, thus satisfying the hunger of the Gentiles for salvation.

By referring to his works of healing as "food" (7:27), Jesus indicates that there is a deeper symbolic meaning to the bread he has provided in the desert. As Shepherd-Messiah of his people, he provides the bread of a new healed life: liberation from the demonic kingdom which divides into "fighting groups," leading to enmity and hatred - Jews against Gentiles. (Mark 3:25-26). Soon after this incident, Jesus will feed the Gentiles, not with "leftovers" for the dogs, but with an abundance of bread, more than enough to satisfy their deepest hungering. (Mark 8:1-10). The Gentile woman's faith in the foregoing passage has opened the way for this feeding. She is a model of Christian faith.

In his humorous reference to dogs in the foregoing passage, Jesus may have been giving voice, rather than approval, to a Jewish prejudice. Perhaps some Jews regarded the Gentiles as dogs. At the time of Jesus, dogs were not the cuddly domestic pets we know today. They were loathed by the Jews. Most of them were wild, savage, disease-ridden animals that roamed the streets and literally fed on "scraps from the table." They were the refuse collectors of the day. (See Psalm 22:16; 59:6; Matthew 7:6; Luke 16:21).

The woman from Tyre in the foregoing passage opens the way to a mission to the Gentiles. Jesus believed, as was prophesised in the Old Testament, that when Israel came under the reign of God, that would be the time for the rest of the world to experience the love and mercy of the Creator God. That time had now come. What Jesus did for the woman was a sign that he meant what he said about cleanness and uncleanness and the food laws. The old barriers keeping human beings apart and separated from God and from one another were being swept away. Jesus was on an outreach to the Gentiles. He knew that imposing Jewish rules and practices on them would be setting up a barrier between them and the Kingdom of God. For entering the kingdom of God, all that is required is trusting in Jesus and doing the will of God. (Mark 3:33-35).

The Gentiles would soon cease to be "dogs" under the table, simply waiting for the leftover scraps. (7:28). They would share the food round the table with everyone else, as brothers and sisters of Jesus (Mark 3:33-35), thus becoming children of the one Father. As Jesus died on the hill of Calvary, the Roman centurion in charge of the execution was the first Gentile to affirm his divine sonship. (Mark 15:39). The centurion must have sensed that the nobility and dignified fortitude of this man on the cross represented a transformation of humanity. The centurion's confession of faith signified that the time was ripe for the entry of the Gentiles into God's Kingdom. This would also bring an end to the Jewish food laws and other crippling regulations. Gentiles could not be expected to adhere to them. Burdened with such restrictions, they would be excluded from receiving the Bread of Life, and would be forever left (like dogs) with the scraps falling from the table.

God's new Shepherd would feed the Gentiles with more than scraps. He would sow in their hearts the seed of the love and compassion of God – a food which would sustain them into eternity. The King of the Jews would become the universal King. (See Galatians 3:26-29; Ephesians 3:6). The early Church preached the gospel always to the Jews first, before moving on to Gentiles. (Acts of the Apostles 13:46; 18:6; Romans 1:16).

As a prelude to his journey to Jerusalem, Jesus and his disciples left the area round

Tyre and went south to the region east of the Jordan (the Ten Towns - Decapolis), as a further sign of the outreach of the gospel to the Gentiles. (Mark 7:31).

After healing the demoniac in Gerasa, the people asked Jesus to leave the area. (Mark 5:16-17). On this occasion however, Jesus is met with a good reception from the people there. Perhaps his way had been prepared by the mission of the man who had been liberated from life in the tombs. (Mark 5:1-20). According to Mark, Jesus travelled in a wide circle. The inhabitants of the area recognised him as a worker of mighty deeds.

> Some people brought him a man who was deaf and could hardly speak, and they begged Jesus to place his hands on him. So Jesus took him all alone, away from the crowds, and put his fingers on the man's ears, spat and touched the man's tongue. Then Jesus looked up to heaven, gave a deep groan, and said to the man, 'Open up.' At once the man was able to hear, his speech impediment was removed and he began to talk without any trouble. (Mark 7:32).

The prophets of Israel saw blindness, deafness and speech impediments being overcome with the return home of the people from exile in Babylon in 537 BC. "The blind will be able to see, and the deaf will hear. The lame will leap and dance, and those who cannot speak will shout for joy... They will reach Jerusalem with gladness, singing and shouting for joy. They will be happy forever, free from sorrow and grief." (Isaiah 35:5-6, 10). Isaiah is referring to spiritual blindness and deafness. In establishing the reign of God over these negative forces, Jesus is fulfilling this prophecy of Isaiah. The Gentiles, no less than Israel, are heirs to this promise of salvation. They too are being brought home from exile, and their eyes and ears opened to the truth of the compassionate and loving God. Previously living in metaphorical tombs (Mark 5:3), blind and deaf to God's mighty deeds, but now in response to Jesus' healings, they are able to sing his praises and hear his voice proclaiming the good news of liberation to all of them. "And all who heard were completely amazed. 'How well he does everything,' they exclaimed. 'He even causes the deaf to hear and the dumb to speak.'" (Mark 7:37).

After the healing of the deaf mute, Jesus ordered the people not to speak of it to anyone. (7:36). Why would Jesus not want anyone to spread this news? Probably because the real meaning of his messiahship would be obscured. His miracles are only part of the revelation of his messianic identity. The full truth of what it means to be Messiah will only be revealed in the course of his journey to Jerusalem.

The deaf mute may be symbolic of the human failure to see, hear and relate to God. Our interior faculties are disabled by the bondages to which human beings are prone, causing a communication block between us and God. All of Jesus' healings are signs of the restoration of human beings to the fullness of their human capacities, which had been wounded by sin and separation from God. Through the mighty works of Jesus, we are enabled to hear God's voice speaking in our hearts, while we acknowledge that it is he who can empower us to see him as he is, hear him calling us to follow him and participate in his mission of opening eyes and ears.

As Jesus proceeds through the Decapolis region, he repeats the miracle of the feeding of four thousand people in the wilderness, perhaps for the benefit of the Gentile inhabitants of the region, as a sign that God would satisfy their own hungering for fullness of life. Jesus has compassion on the people for their want of food.

> He called his disciples to him and said, 'I feel sorry for these people, because they have been with me for three days and now have nothing to eat. If I send them home without feeding them, they will faint as they go, because some of them have come a long way.' (Mark 8:2-3).

The word "faint" in the New Testament is used for losing heart, or getting discouraged because of the struggles of the Christian life. (Galatians 6:9; Hebrews 12:3, 5). Jesus is challenging his disciples and their successors to respond to the needs of God's people when they feel hungry and discouraged. Our faith may be too weak to understand that Jesus is the bread, and that he is able to multiply whatever we offer him from our own meagre resources and give it back to us in abundance. The bread we bring to the altar symbolizes our meagre resources, but which is transformed into the Bread of Life for our spiritual sustenance.

The only food the disciples had in the wilderness was seven loaves. (Mark 8:5). From these meagre resources, everybody was fed. "Everybody ate and had enough - there were about 4,000 people. Then the disciples took up seven baskets full of pieces left over." (8:8-9).

No less than the chosen people, Jesus more than satisfies the deepest hungers of the Gentiles– leading once again to the question, "Who is this among us?" In his movement into Gentile territory, Jesus wants to show all and sundry that the new Israel gathered around himself will be outward looking, and not hidebound by human rules. The Gentiles are also people in need of liberation and inclusion in the family of God.

## The Yeast of the Pharisees and the Yeast of Herod

> Some Pharisees came to Jesus and started to argue with him. They wanted to trap him, so they asked him to perform a miracle (a sign from heaven) to show that God approved of him. But Jesus gave a deep groan and said, 'Why do the people of this day ask for a miracle? No, I tell you! No such proof will be given to these people!' He left them, got back into the boat, and started across to the other side of the lake. (Mark 8:11-13).

The Pharisees' unwillingness to believe, in spite of so many signs already given to them, recalls the Israelites' rebellion in the desert. "The Lord said to Moses, 'How long will this people spurn me? How long will they refuse to believe in me, despite all the signs I have performed among them? (Book of Numbers 14:11, 22; Deuteronomy 29:1-3; see Psalm 95:8-11). The Israelites tested the Lord and disbelieved. (Exodus 17:2, 7). Because of the Pharisees' hardness of heart, Jesus' miracles - revealing God's love and compassion for humanity - are not enough. (See Matthew 16:4).

The Pharisees' request for a sign (8:11) seems to have indicated to Jesus that "the people of this day," i.e. most people in Israel, were determined not to listen to his liberating reign of God message or see his works of mercy for what they were. They had a different kind of kingdom in mind – one based on exclusions, a kingdom which Jesus has already prophesised will fall apart. (Mark 3:23-26). It's as if the Pharisees were asking Jesus to do something that would force them to believe in him, but that would not be faith at all. Jesus' deeds of mercy invite faith, but they do not compel it. The Pharisees' demand is a presumption that they can impose their own criteria on how God should act. And by seeking to "test" Jesus, they play the role of Satan. (Matthew 4:5). They are tempting Jesus to turn away from his messianic mission of the slow, gradual process of sowing seeds in people's hearts. Instead, they want him to win their esteem by a dazzling display of power, as if to confirm them in their kind of kingdom, which is one of oppressive power. Jesus does not want to dominate people, while those opposed to him will use force in order to get rid of him. For Jesus, the kingdom of God would not come by force of any description. Both in his teaching and in his mighty works, he has repeatedly demonstrated the power of God for everyone to hear and see, but because of their self-righteousness, insincerity and ill will, the Pharisees closed their eyes and deafened their ears to Jesus' great signs of compassion, which revealed the kind of kingdom he had in mind. This clearly demonstrated their hardness of heart towards the suffering people whom they regarded as outcasts and sinners. Jesus' healing works were not to draw attention to himself, but to reveal his identity as God's compassionate shepherd.

The foregoing exchange with the Pharisees is a point of departure in Mark's gospel. It signals the end of Jesus' ministry in Galilee. It seems that Jesus sees the futility of trying to get his message through to official Israel. Mark then says, "Jesus left them, got into the boat, and started across to the other side of the lake." (8:13). This was a symbolic walking away from the teaching authority of Israel. From now on, Jesus will continue teaching his disciples and will focus on his sufferings. This represents his slow process of sowing the seeds of his kingdom of God message, and patiently waiting for them to ripen.

The question of Jesus being in a boat with the Pharisees (8:13) never arose; they would not have wanted it. In their self-righteousness, they felt no dependence on God, no need for enlightenment, no need of repentance, no need for the mercy of God. In their own eyes, their piety and good works were sufficient for putting them right with God. (See Luke 18:11-12). This does not mean that God would cast them out into exterior darkness. There is no limit to the love and mercy of God. God is always out on the road looking and hoping for the return of his prodigal sons and daughters. (Luke 15:20; see Genesis 3:8).

> The disciples had forgotten to bring enough bread and had only one loaf with them in the boat. 'Take care,' "Jesus warned them, 'and be on your guard against the yeast of the Pharisees and the yeast of Herod. They started discussing among themselves: 'He says this because we haven't any bread.' Jesus knew what they were saying, so he asked them, 'Why are you discussing about not having any bread? Are your minds so dull? You have *eyes – can't you see? You have ears – can't you hear?* Don't you remember when I broke the five loaves for the five thousand people? How many baskets full of leftover pieces did you take up?' 'Twelve,' they

answered. 'And when I broke the seven loaves for the four thousand people,' asked Jesus, 'how many baskets full of leftover pieces did you take up?' 'Seven,' they answered. 'And you still don't understand?' he asked them. (Mark 8:14-21; Isaiah 6:9b, 43:8-11; Ezekiel 12:2 in italics).

The disciples were feeling uneasy because they forgot to bring enough bread. (8:14). They were concerned about ordinary bread, thinking only of their physical needs. As God's Good Shepherd, Jesus' whole concern is feeding other people. He himself is the bread, which the disciples had seen him give away in abundance to the multitudes in the wilderness, as a sign of God satisfying the deepest hungering of humanity for meaningful life. What they don't see is that Jesus himself is the bread with them in the boat - "the living bread that came down from heaven," giving them true life. (John 6:51). They are still asking, 'Who is this man?' Has he not been rescuing them from the terrors of life's storms?

The word "yeast" in the above passage may be suggestive of the strongly held views of people, what people find meaningful and significant in their lives, in other words, the values by which they live and through which they seek fulfilment. In using the word "yeast," Jesus is referring to the fake goodness, blindness, hypocrisy and ill-will that the Pharisees (3:6; 7:5-13; 8:11:13) and the supporters of Herod (3:6; 6:14-29) have shown towards him and his proclamation of the reign of God.

Because of their strongly held beliefs, the Pharisees refused to acknowledge that, with the coming of Jesus' kingdom, restrictive barriers of the old era between sinners and the just (2:15-17); between fasting and celebration (2:18-22); between Sabbath obligation and human need (2:23-28; 3:1-6); between clean and unclean (7:1-5) had been abolished, as simply not needed anymore, and especially so in the context of Jesus' outreach to the Gentiles.

The Pharisees wanted God to set up a kingdom exclusively for Jews who would observe the strict obligations of the law, and not for the benefit of the universal community which Jesus had in mind - everybody everywhere doing the will of God. (Mark 3:33-35). Satan's kingdom is based on exclusions and the selfish solidarity of groups, whereas God's kingdom is based on the all-inclusive solidarity of the human race. Those who could not bear to have so-called sinners, outcasts, tax collectors, lepers, former prostitutes, servants, women and children treated as their equals; who could not live without feeling superior, would not be at home in the Kingdom of God. The scribes and Pharisees were inward-looking, whereas Isaiah prophesised that Israel would be a light to the other nations so as to include them also in its worship of God. (Isaiah 49:6). Embodying the new Israel, Jesus fulfils what Isaiah prophesised for Israel.

In his reference to "eyes" and "ears" (8:18), Jesus is quoting two of the major prophets of Israel–Jeremiah and Ezekiel (words in italics in the foregoing passage). According to the prophets, official Israel had always closed its eyes and ears to God's message and to who God really is. "Pay attention you stupid and foolish people, who have eyes but cannot see, and have ears but cannot hear." (Jeremiah 5:20-22, see Isaiah 42:18-20; Ezekiel 12:1-2). The people turned their eyes away from the Creator of the world who "placed the sand as a boundary of the sea" (Jeremiah 5:22), and away from the God who "created the stars and leads them out like an army." (Isaiah 40:26a).

Turning eyes away from the Creator of the universe implies a turning to other gods for salvation: food laws, ritual purity, the crowds, for example. The Pharisees had their eyes and ears focused on those things, rather than on the mission of compassionate service to which God calls his people. Increasingly in the gospel, Jesus calls his disciples to become servants (shepherds) of others. But the Pharisees couldn't "sell all they had and give to the poor." (See Mark 10:21). They were too preoccupied with their rules and rituals and the esteem they received from the crowds. In other words, they were self-obsessive. Thus, their hearts could not reach out in love towards the unclean: people whom they despised as inferior to themselves. If the Pharisees were to ditch their purity regulations, "sell all and give to the poor," i.e. prioritize love of neighbour, their power, status and prestige would be undermined. This they could not allow to happen.

"The yeast of Herod" and his supporters (Herodians) amounted to prestige, worldly power and glory (Mark 3:6; 6:14-29), contrary to the path Jesus was taking as the true messianic King, who would use his power as service. Herod and his supporters wanted God to establish their royal family as the true kings of Israel. Herod could never become a true king of the Jews. The disciples - still partly governed by the "yeast of Herod," may have been hoping for a king of the Jews like Herod, but one freed from his oppressive rule.

In the foregoing quotation from Mark, "yeast," or leaven, is also an image for sinful attitudes which can corrupt the Christian community. (See 1 Corinthians 5:6-8; Galatians 5:9). The word "yeast" recalls the hasty exodus of the people from Egypt, which meant that the refugees had to eat unleavened bread, which quickly baked without the essential ingredient of yeast. (Exodus 12:14-20).

Jesus was now about to set out on his journey to Jerusalem with all its implications for himself and his disciples. The confrontation between Jesus' kingdom mission and its rivals was coming fast, and the disciples did not understand what was happening. Their eyes were closed to the reality confronting them. To an extent, they were the "people of this day" (7:12), still hooked on the "yeast of the Pharisees and the yeast of Herod." Jesus wanted them to wake up to what he was doing, because the time was coming when they would be called to come "with" Jesus on his journey to Jerusalem, which would involve much more than feeding themselves with ordinary bread.

As was already becoming clear, Jesus' journey to Jerusalem would challenge the whole system and the values by which Israel lived. The disciples would only be able to follow him if they opened their eyes to the fact that he was not just a healer, not just a prophet, but one who would turn the world upside down, so that those who had always put themselves in the first place at the table would end up last. (Mark 10:29-31; Matthew 19:30). The vineyard would be taken from the original owners (official Israel) and handed over to others who would produce good fruit. (Mark 12:9). As Jesus saw it, many in Israel were caught up in their own concerns and blind to the injustice and wickedness in their society: the yeast of the Pharisees. The disciples themselves would continue to see Jesus' kingdom proclamation in terms of worldly power and prestige. (See Mark 9:34; 10:37). But the fact that they were still following Jesus implies their openness to further teaching and enlightenment.

Jesus gets into the boat with us too (Mark 8:13), enlightening us to the reality of our own flaws and failings, and giving us hope and strength for our journey, as we row all night against the hostile headwinds of life. For the disciples, seeing and understanding will eventually come. Their spiritual blindness and deafness – up until this point reserved for Jesus' adversaries (Mark 3:5; 4:11-12) - will be a major theme in the central section of the gospel.

## Healing the Blind Man at Bethsaida

When Jesus and his disciples came ashore at Bethsaida, some people brought a blind man to him and begged him to touch him. (Mark 8:22-26). Jesus' healing of the deaf-mute man (7:31-37) and now the blind man, signifies that God can overcome spiritual blindness and deafness and open eyes to his liberating work and teaching. The deaf mute and the blind man may signify the deafness and blindness of God's servant Israel–its failure to listen to the word of God and obey it. (See Isaiah 42:18-19; 48:12, 18). But a servant has come who will succeed in his task of opening blind eyes and deaf ears. (Isaiah 52:13). Jesus is that servant.

Jesus comes in contact with the blind man at Bethsaida by taking him by the hand and leading him out of the village (8:23), recalling the Old Testament idea of God leading his people by the hand and showing them the way. (Isaiah 41:13, NJB; Jeremiah 31:32). This scene invites us to imagine Jesus taking us by the hand and leading us to a place where he can enlighten us as to his true identity, thus enabling us to follow him to where he is going.

Mark places the healing of the blind man here to conclude the second part of the Bread section, just as he concluded the first part with the healing of the deaf-mute man. (7:31-37). These two healings signify the gradual opening of the disciples' eyes to faith and understanding of Jesus. So far in the gospel, despite the disciples being with Jesus, they have been blind to his divine status. They lose faith in him in the stormy sea. They think he is a ghost when he comes to them walking on the water. There is an element of tragedy in their failure to open their eyes to him, even though they share in his ministry, witness his raising of the daughter of Jairus from the dead and experience his glorious transfiguration on the mountain. They are contrasted with the blind man at Bethsaida, who "sees." The disciples will soon arrive at a partial vision of Jesus' identity (Mark 8:29), but will see no further than that until the end of the story.

The healing of the blind man at Bethsaida will be followed by a confession of faith that will mark a turning point of the gospel. (Mark 8:27-30). For the first time, the eyes of the disciples will be partly opened to see that Jesus is the promised Messiah (8:29), but their understanding of his kind of messiahship will leave them blind and confused as to its true meaning. It will take a much greater enlightenment for them to recognise that his messiahship is linked to a man hanging from a wooden cross on a hill named Calvary outside the walls of Jerusalem. That the disciples themselves would be called to follow and remain with this man on that journey, was a thought that wouldn't have entered their minds at all at this stage. Even the mere hint of it will soon terrify them.

## CHAPTER 14

# THE "WAY" TO JERUSALEM

(8:27-10:52)

From the very start of his public ministry, Jesus was facing opposition from the religious authorities. It was difficult for some people to see how an unknown rabbi (Jesus), a few uneducated disciples, a band of tax collectors, women and sinners, could remotely be expected to set out on a course of changing the world.

In terms of expectations in Israel, what was the task of the King-Messiah? Jesus does not affirm Israel as it then was. How could the people of his day expect their king to go to Jerusalem and take charge of Israel as then constituted? Jesus saw his last journey to Jerusalem as the symbol of the Messiah's return to Zion (Jerusalem) with his liberated exiles (Isaiah 40:1-5), and his enthronement as king there. Always in the past, it was expected of a king-Messiah that he would go to Jerusalem, defeat the enemies of Israel and cleanse the temple of pagan contamination. (See Isaiah chaps, 40-55). Jesus' journey was an acted narrative of the prophecies of Isaiah.[130]

Jesus would interpret and fulfil those aims and prophecies in his own way - God's way. He would call his disciples to follow him on that way – the way of the cross rather than the way of power. Jesus' journey to Jerusalem should be seen in terms of God, the owner of the vineyard, coming back to gather the grapes that his servants (official Israel) were expected to produce (Isaiah 5:1-4). But, as in the case of the fig tree (Mark 12:1-2), he would find no fruit there (Mark 11:12-14) – nothing but the weeds and thorns (Genesis 3:18) of enmity, exclusion, victimization, violence and death. (Mark 3:6; 12:3-8; 14:64). A society founded on the murdering of Cain! (Genesis 4:8).

After Jesus' work of teaching in Galilee and the surrounding areas, he then begins his journey to Jerusalem, knowing full well that it will lead to the events which will bring about his death. There will be significant episodes at a number of places along the way. (8:27; 9:33-34; 10:17, 32, 46, 52). As the disciples follow him, they will learn about the "way" of Christian discipleship, announced at the beginning of the gospel. (Mark 1:2-3). Recalling the last three servant songs of Isaiah, three times Jesus will prophesy his passion, with increasing detail. (8:31; 9:31; 10:33-34). Each prediction will be followed by incomprehension and an unsatisfactory response on the part of the disciples. This will be followed by further teaching.

---

[130] N. T. Wright, *Jesus and the Victory of God*, p. 639.

## The "Way" to Jerusalem

Jesus was now moving further away from Galilee. Perhaps this was because he had done as much as he could there by way of teaching and healing. Much of his work was met by incomprehension and blindness from the crowds and the people of his hometown. The hostile attitude of the religious leaders showed that they were not prepared to accept his unique and universal vision of God for humanity. (Mark 3:33-35). But he also wanted to be alone with his disciples in order to teach them. The disciples had yet to "see" that, because of its association with service (giving up his body to feed others), his feeding of the crowds anticipated his passion. His life of feeding service would prove to be costly because it would eventually lead to a final and deadly confrontation with official Israel. In the second half of the gospel, the implications of his self-giving life of service will become central. With regard to the disciples, their mindset at this point may not have been very far removed from that of the crowds, who wanted to make Jesus a political king after his feeding of the five thousand. (See John 6:14-15). The disciples were still governed by the "yeast" of the Pharisees and the "yeast" of Herod. (Mark 8:14-21). They were still hooked on power, status, prestige (Mark 10:37) and the desire to be honoured by the crowds (the reign of Satan), rather than the reign of God, which is all about service – satisfying the deepest hungers of humanity by feeding them with more than ordinary bread. (Mark 8:17-21).

Jesus wanted to get away from the crowds, so he headed north with his disciples towards the Gentile city of Caesarea Philippi – named after the Roman emperor Caesar and Philip, (brother of Herod Antipas). Philip and Antipas were two sons of Herod the Great. Their rule was subject to the authority of Rome. Caesarea Philippi was a Greek-speaking city about twenty-five miles north of the Sea of Galilee.

Then begins the travel narrative in Mark's gospel, known as "The Way." (Mark 8:27 – 10:52). "The Way" became the first name for Christianity in the early Church. It is a metaphor for the Christian life. (See Acts 9:2; 18:25-26). Jesus was on a journey to Calvary, in a sense, already carrying his cross.

Taking up the cross had a real and painful meaning for Mark's first readers, some of whose fellow Christians had been burned at the stake, thrown to the wild beasts or crucified under the persecution of the Emperor Nero in Rome.

With the theme of "The Way," Mark evokes the Old Testament in order to shed light on the meaning of Jesus' actions. God, through Moses, liberated his people from the oppression of Egypt and led them on the 'way' to the promised land. (Exodus 13:21-22). In the Exodus journey, the people discovered God as a shepherd (Exodus 13:21-22), leading and feeding his people in the wilderness with bread from heaven (Exodus 16:12). In order to prepare them for life in their promised land destiny, he gave them the food of his Word in the Ten Commandments. In later times, at the end of the Babylonian exile, Isaiah envisioned God preparing a "way" through the wilderness for the return home of his people from the oppression of Babylon. (Isaiah 40:3-4). Along the "way" there would be rejoicing, because their hungering for their homeland (destiny) would be satisfied. (Isaiah 41:17-20). God would lead his blind people home, thus forgiving their sins. (Isaiah 35:10; 42:16; 43:1-2; 44:23). On their way home, there would be a transformation of the wilderness into new and sustaining life (recalling the manna in the wilderness journey from Egypt), and symbolizing the new transformed life of the redeemed people. (Isaiah 41:18-19). In both the journey from Egyptian slavery and that from Babylon, the people discovered who God is: liberator, shepherd, merciful, forgiving, making and renewing his covenant relationship with his people. (Exodus 24:7; Isaiah 40:1-2, 10-11; Jeremiah 31:31-34; Ezekiel 11:19-20).

Similarly, Jesus' "way" to Jerusalem is both a geographical and a spiritual journey. It is Jesus' "way," through which he liberates human beings from the oppressions which prevent them from living a full and meaningful life, so that he can take all of us exiles definitively home to an eternal destiny in our promised land. How is Jesus doing this?

Up to this point, Jesus has been fulfilling a feeding role as God's Good Shepherd (Mark 6:41-42). His exorcisms have liberated people from demonic oppression, clothing them for new life in his kingdom. (Mark 5:1-13). His healings have rescued people from physical and spiritual disablement (Mark 2:10-11), thus satisfying their hungering for meaningful life, and metaphorically bringing them home from exile. On reaching Jerusalem, Jesus will make a new and everlasting covenant, which will be sealed with his self-sacrificial blood. (Mark 14:24). He will confirm this covenant on behalf of humanity, through his total obedience to God, taking all of us into his own obedience. (Mark 14:36). Jesus' final act of service will be his death on the cross, through which he will liberate all humans from the greatest oppressor of all, namely death itself. He will come back again in order to forgive all who had a hand in his death, forgiveness being the only to bring all of humanity into union with one another and with God. By sharing his risen life with us, he will bring us home from exile to our destiny of eternal life with God.

Although there will be further healings on the way to Jerusalem, Jesus' priority from here on will be the significance of his journey and the teaching of his disciples. But because of their spiritual blindness, he will experience their resistance to the direction in which he is leading them. In their blindness, the disciples will struggle to discover Jesus' true identity. As at the beginning, so also at the end of the journey there will be another healing of a blind man (10:46-52). With these two works of restoring sight, Mark forms a frame around Jesus' journey to Jerusalem, symbolizing the disciples' gradual growth in enlightenment.

## Peter's Confession of Faith

> Then Jesus and his disciples went away to the villages near Caesarea Philippi. On the way he asked them, 'Tell me, who do people say I am?' 'Some say you are John the Baptist. Others say you are Elijah, while others say you are one of the prophets.' 'What about you?' he asked them. 'Who do you say I am?' Peter answered, 'You are the Messiah' Then Jesus ordered them, 'Do not tell anyone about me.' (Mark 8:27-30; see CCC 439-40).

The reader of Mark may ask, 'What is the source of Jesus' power and authority?' (See Deuteronomy 8:15-18; Matthew 16:13-20; Luke 9:18-21). Who is Jesus? Already he has spoken of himself as the bridegroom of God's people (Mark 2:19), Lord of the Sabbath (2:28), physician (2:17) and the founder of a new Israel (3:14). His actions have provoked amazement (1:27; 2:7; 4:41; 6:2). He has been met with misunderstanding and resistance by the religious authorities (3:6), by his own family (3:21), by his own townspeople (6:3) and by his own disciples when he warned them against the "yeast of the Pharisees and the yeast of Herod." (8:14-21).

According to the response of the disciples in the foregoing passage, the ordinary people think Jesus is John the Baptist. Others say he is Elijah or one of the Old Testament prophets. (8:28). They do not go so far as to consider Jesus *the* prophet promised by Moses, who would speak God's definitive word. (Deuteronomy 8:15-18). Those who see Jesus only as a prophet are expecting the same message as of old, not something radically new.

Peter gives a more satisfactory answer to the question of Jesus' identity than the ordinary people. (8:29b). Like the healing of the deaf man, and the blind man at Bethsaida, Peter's eyes and ears are beginning to be opened to Jesus' identity, and to the meaning of all that he has said and done so far. It was expected that the coming Messiah would be a king, so what did Peter mean? Probably, that Jesus was the Messiah King, the one through whom God would accomplish for Israel all he had promised, which according to the common expectation, included gaining a victory over the foreign occupiers and establishing a political kingdom. The Jews clung to the promise of a future anointed king, a descendant of David, who would reign on the throne of Israel for ever. (2 Samuel 7:12-14). Like the blind man, Peter is not aware of the full implications of the meaning of Messiah. Jesus will interpret 2 Samuel 7 in a new way. He will be a different kind of king than the warrior David, and he will reign for ever in a different kind of kingdom. The readers of Mark all know that his kingship will not involve a violent confrontation with the Romans, but rather suffering *their* violence against him. Jesus is a Messiah who will outdo and confound all Jewish expectations.

Following Pater's confession of faith, Jesus enjoins silence about his messiahship. (8:30). The misguided idea that he might assume a political role as the leader of a messianic uprising (John 6:15) could derail his whole mission as he approaches Jerusalem. The understanding of Messiah needed to be purged of its human triumphalism before its full meaning could be proclaimed openly to the world. Jesus is not commanding silence because his disciples know who he is, but rather, because they *don't* know who he is. Jesus' idea of messiahship is so new, that nobody understood its true meaning up to this point.

As will soon be apparent, Peter still did not know Jesus very well. Getting to really know Jesus can be a long journey with many twists and turns - for all of us. The disciples were a very long way from the point of expecting a divine redeemer. As indicated by Peter's response to Jesus' question ('who do you say I am?'), they were longing for a king, and they thought they had found one who would upstage imposters such as Herod Antipas. They were still clinging to the idea that there would be a political role of some kind or other for Jesus once he reached Jerusalem in triumph, and that he would then reward his disciples with positions of power and honour. (See Mark 10:36-37). In their blindness, they could not connect all he had been saying and doing - which confirmed his divine status - with their preconceived notions about the political liberation of Israel. Jesus had in mind a new 'way' of being God's anointed king. Rather than a political upheaval, his 'way' was the slowly growing seed (Mark 4:3, 26-29) of a new family of God around himself. (Mark 3:33-35). The shocking newness of that way, with all its implications, would only be gradually revealed and begin to dawn on the disciples on the road to Jerusalem.

The full content of "Messiah" would not become clear to the disciples until their eyes fully opened to the reality of Jesus after the resurrection. "Messiah" in its fullness includes (1) Jesus' divine Sonship (Mark 1:11; 9:7); (2) his creation of a new Israel around himself, the Israel of old having failed in its God-given task of bringing blessing to the nations (Isaiah 48:6), first promised to Abraham and through his descendants; (3) Jesus' universal kingship - the anointed Messiah coming to put everything right and establish the reign of God over evil and death, through his resurrection (Isaiah 11:14; Mark 13:26-27); (4) his redemptive suffering and glorification by God (Isaiah 53:11-12; Mark 8:31, 38; 14:45); (5) and his gift of eternal life to all of us – his universal act of service, Israel having failed to be a true servant of God, because of its blindness to its sins and its deafness to the word of God. (Isaiah 42:18-20; Mark 10:29-30).

So far in his mission, Jesus has been showing all and sundry that his kingship and the reign of God is a work of liberation - a coming home from the bondage of exile. And although it was arousing the ire of the religious leaders, it was not concerned with toppling either them or the civil authority from power. His kingship is all about sowing a new, fruitful seed in Israel. It means opening blind eyes to God's new kind of liberation: raising people up from disabled states to newness of life. (Mark 2:10-11; Luke 10:33-34). While the crowds are merely hungry for ordinary bread, which only represents a hunger for status and political power, Jesus has in mind a much deeper hungering: the hunger for a life of meaning and purpose, for a truly fulfilling life, a life which has as its goal an eternal destiny with God. Jesus' bread is really all we need. (Psalm 23:1, 5-6).

Being fully aware of the mindset of his followers, Jesus now wants to enlighten them as to his true identity and destiny.

## Jesus' First Prophecy of his Passion

> Then he began to teach them that the Son of Man was destined to suffer grievously, to be rejected by the elders, the chief priests, and the scribes, and to be put to death, and after three days to rise again; and he said all this quite openly. Then, taking him aside, Peter tried to rebuke him. But, turning and seeing his disciples, he rebuked Peter and said to him, 'Get behind me, Satan! You are thinking not as God thinks, but as human beings do.' (Mark 8:31-33, NJB; see Luke 24:26-27; Isaiah 52:13–53:12; Acts of the Apostles 2:23; 1 Corinthians 1:18-25).

Immediately following Peter's confession of faith (8:29), Jesus abandons his method of teaching in parables, and now speaks openly about what it means for him to be the Messiah. It would only slowly dawn on the disciples that the Messiah would not be a conquering hero going to Jerusalem to defeat his enemies, but rather, a suffering servant laying down his life for these same enemies, and then rising up in forgiveness of them. Jesus' unique and universal vision was something utterly beyond the comprehension of his contemporaries.

Jesus wants to broaden the idea of Messiah. He now speaks about what it means for him to be the Messiah, and for his followers to be identified with him (God's way). For Jesus, Messiah means being put to death, which he associates with his glorification (rising again in three days (v. 31b). From here on, the cross and resurrection will be the major themes of Mark. Now that the disciples have begun to understand Jesus' messianic identity, he can fully reveal what messiahship means both for himself and his followers. The Messiah will be the suffering servant of Isaiah 52:13–53:12, not a conquering hero scattering his enemies.

Peter's rebuke to Jesus (8:31) revealed how little he, Peter understood the idea of Messiah in his confession of faith at Caesarea Philippi. (8:29). In Peter's view, how could God allow his Messiah to suffer and die? Never before in Israel had anyone connected suffering with the future Messiah. Nobody had associated the suffering servant of Isaiah 43, 44 and 53 with the hope of a Messiah. The Messiah was supposed to defeat the enemies of Israel. How could he rescue Israel from foreign rule if he were to die?

Jesus will indeed defeat the real enemies of humankind, namely evil and injustice, but in a way utterly unimaginable to his contemporaries. The outcome will be the triumph of his vindication and glory, which he will announce on three occasions. (Mark 8:38; 13:26; 14:62). This plan was established long ago and foretold by the prophet Isaiah. It is Jesus' destiny to suffer and die (Mark 8:31; see Isaiah chaps.40–55). The fact that God's plan appears in the Old Testament should have been a reassurance to the disciples that nothing that takes place will be a tragic mishap. It was all intended by the Sovereign God from the beginning. Paradoxically, Jesus' mission would not end in humiliation and defeat but in glorious victory, achieved through suffering. (Isaiah 53:11-12). Jesus *must* undergo these sufferings because it is the will of the Father, although this course will be freely chosen by himself. Jesus is obedient unto death. (Mark 14:36; 9:12; 14:21, 27, 49; see Mark 3:33-35).

Here for the first time, Jesus gives himself the title "Son of Man." (8:31). At one level this title means a member of the human race. But Jesus may be referring to the prophet Daniel, in which Daniel speaks about a royal figure who represents the people of Israel, who have suffered persecution, but whom God would vindicate in the end: "I gazed into the visions of the night, and I saw coming on the clouds of heaven, one like a son of man. On him was conferred sovereignty, glory and kingship, and people of all nations became his servants." (Daniel 7:13-14, JB). Jesus may have viewed this prophecy as applicable to himself.

Jesus can now tell the disciples what messiahship implies for his destiny: his role is to suffer, die and rise again. This is why he came. His intention was to die. As "Son of Man," i.e. representing his people, he must suffer persecution and death, but in the end, he will be vindicated by God, and all people will see his glory and accept his sovereign rule, as prophesised by Daniel. (Daniel 7:14). This is Jesus' glorious vision of his role and destiny – contrasted with the view of the people of his hometown, who saw him only as the local craftsman. (Mark 6:2-3).

Jesus' knowledge of the Old Testament scriptures taught him that obedience to God was the only way of undoing the universal act of disobedience in the Garden of Eden. But he knew that his obedience would be costly. It would not be accomplished without Satan striking a fatal blow. (Genesis 3:14-15). This means that it would involve suffering. The prophet Daniel said that an "anointed one" (Messiah) would be "cut down." (Daniel 9:26; see also Isaiah 53:3-5). Jesus' filial obedience was based on his absolute trust in God to vindicate him. Many psalms depict a man who suffers greatly, but still trusts in God to deliver him. (Psalm 22; 55; 69; 88). Jesus' mission would end, not in humiliating defeat, but in glorious victory. (Isaiah 53:12). The prophet Hosea speaks about the people of Israel in exile being healed of their wounds and revived in "two or three days" following their turning to the Lord in obedience. (Hosea 6:1-2). Hosea is looking forward in hope that God will raise Israel to new life after its death-like exile. By applying the words of Hosea to himself, Jesus implies that the destiny of Israel will be summed up in himself.

Jesus wasn't seeking suffering and death for their own sake. But he knew that the opposition to his mission would reach such a climax. He was on a journey to Jerusalem, which had always been the place of enthronement of the king; only this King would suffer a murderous death if he was to be faithful to his vocation, faithful to God, who wants an end to suffering and death and whose plan is ultimately a glorified humanity in union with Jesus.

Jesus now sees Peter as the Satan trying to strike a fatal blow (Mark 8:33), and coming once again to deflect him from his mission of service to humanity, as Satan had tried to do earlier in the desert wilderness. (Mark 1:12-13; see Matthew 4:1-11). Peter and the other disciples may not have thought of Jesus as a military leader, but they certainly did not envision him deliberately going to his death. What could that mean but defeat? And worse, was he inviting them to accept defeat along with himself? We may note that, so far, Jesus does not associate his suffering and death with a Roman cross.

In the foregoing passage, Peter receives the sharpest reprimand in the gospels. (8:32). Peter's task is to lead the other disciples and strengthen them. Does Jesus now see the others being led astray by the Satan lurking within Peter? In telling Peter to get "behind" him (8:33), Jesus is commanding Peter to follow him, not to presume to lead him. (8:34). Only if Peter is a follower of Jesus, will he, Peter be able to lead the other disciples. Peter may have been anxious to preserve his best friend from suffering, so he couldn't come to terms at all with Jesus being rejected and put to death in Jerusalem. He must have thought that this would spell the end of Jesus' ministry of teaching and healing. Despite the prophecy of Isaiah 53, the prevailing belief was that the Messiah should not be suffering and dying. Was the King-Messiah not on his way to Jerusalem to take his seat on the throne of Israel? Jesus would indeed take his throne, but a different kind of throne. Jesus is the promised Messiah-King. But this king came, not to dominate with coercive power. His power is equated with service – suffering service. And that is precisely how he will defeat all oppressive powers.

The prophet Isaiah censured Israel for its blindness and deafness to the word of God. (Isaiah 6:9-10; 42:18-19; 43:8). As personified in the disciples, Israel is still blind and deaf to the words and truth of God's Messiah. Like God's people of old, they have their eyes focused on other gods for their salvation – prestige, silver and gold, political power, earthly glory, rules and ritual. "God says, 'Summon my people to court. They have eyes but they are blind; they have ears but they are deaf... Besides me there is no other god; there never was and never will be. I alone am the Lord, the only one who can save you." (Isaiah 43:8, 10c, 11). Peter had his eyes on another kind of god for his salvation – possibly a conquering hero. Like Israel, he was blind to the true God.

At this stage of his ministry, Jesus of Nazareth must already be feeling the full weight of the cross. Our experience of life tells us how hard it is to listen to, or to take on board someone else's vision when it cuts across our own deeply-entrenched thinking. In the case of Jesus, it is not just that he already feels the physicality of the cross. What may be weighing on him more heavily is the rejection by everyone of his glorious vision of the true meaning of life. Jesus' thoughts are God's thoughts. (Isaiah 55:8-9; Mark 8:33). His wisdom, knowledge and understanding encompass the whole of reality from time to eternity, while the visionless thinking of everyone else sees no further than the quick fix of the present moment. Jesus is misunderstood by everyone: his own family, the crowds, the religious authorities and his closest disciples. But it is worse than misunderstanding. In order to misunderstand something, one first needs to actually hear it. But the religious leaders and the disciples are so focused on their own particular mindset (gods) that they have never even heard him.

Peter's misunderstanding of Jesus' messiahship (8:32) was a replay of the disciples' recurring lack of understanding. (Mark 4:13; 6:52; 7:18; 8;17-21). We cannot afford to be too hard on Peter. It is natural to wish to preserve those whom we love from suffering. We all do badly at suffering. However, each new trial that comes our way may be a test, challenging us to embrace a more enlightened and courageous following of Jesus.

Why was it so difficult for the disciples to accept the notion of a suffering Messiah? Up to this point they had been faithfully following Jesus. Apart from some minor rumblings and threats by the religious leaders, the mission of Jesus and his disciples had, so far, been a success. The good news was preached, Satan was being usurped. The disciples themselves had successfully participated in Jesus' mission. (Mark 6:7-13; Luke 9:1-6; 10:1-12). They must have thought that everything was going well, so their hearts were full of joy; they had found their mission in life, their reason for living. As far as they were concerned, there seemed to be no reason why things shouldn't proceed along this same tranquil route, so why this talk of suffering and death?

According to human wisdom and reasoning, suffering is something to be avoided as much as possible. What could come out of defeat, humiliation and death? (1 Corinthians 1:18-25). Jesus' followers are called to repentance, to an inner conversion, so that they might begin to think like God and obey his will. "Do not conform yourselves to the standards of this world, but let God transform you inwardly by a complete change of your mind. Then you will be able to know the will of God – what is good and pleasing to him and is perfect." (Romans 12:2; see Ephesians 4:23-24; Mark 4:13; 6:52; 8:17-21).

Jesus' rescue of the world from demonic control must challenge many of the human views and values that actually reveal a captivity to the demonic. His response to Peter about the latter's limited vision warns us about this. Unlike God, our vision is limited; we live for what the present moment can give us. We don't want to hear about waiting for the good the future might bring. We do not want to sacrifice now so that some future good may accrue. We know about global warming, for example, but we cannot even begin to make the sacrifices now which would avert future catastrophe. In Psalm 8 the psalmist addresses the Creator God: 'You have made him (humanity) lord over the work of your hands, set all things under his feet, sheep and oxen, all these, yes, wild animals too, birds in the air, fish in the sea travelling the paths of the ocean.' (Psalm 8:6-8, JB). In these verses, God is calling human beings to a mission of caring for everything and everyone in his creation ("set all things under his feet"), but instead of obediently discharging our mission of stewardship and exercising responsible stewardship over God's earth and all his creatures, we are literally trampling them under our feet. (See also Genesis 2:15).

## Suffering Service

> Then Jesus called the crowd and his disciples to him. 'If anyone wants to come with me,' he told them, 'they must forget self, carry their cross, and follow me. For those who want to save their life will lose it, but those who lose their life for me and for the gospel will save it. Do people gain anything if they win the whole world but lose their life? Of course not!' (Mark 8:34-36; Matthew 16:24-25; Luke 9:23-24; 14:25-27.

Jesus now openly tells both his disciples and the crowd (all of us) about the implications of following him. This is the first time he mentions the cross. No more than himself, neither can anyone else (the crowd) escape suffering (save their lives), because that is exactly what is involved in living the gospel and bringing the good news to the world. (8:35). They must "lose" their old thinking, forget their preconceived notions about earthly power, glory and prestige – "winning the whole world." (See Matthew 4:8). They should "lose" all of that life, and be prepared to take up their cross and follow Jesus on his way of service. The losing of one's old life is the saving of it. (Mark 8:35a).

Jesus' message must have sounded shocking to his disciples and to the ears of the "crowd." In the first prediction of his passion, he spoke only about his own sufferings at the hands of the religious leaders in Jerusalem. Now, for the first time, he calls all and sundry to imitate his own suffering service (8:35), if they are to be true disciples of his. To the ears of his listeners, the "cross" (8:34) meant nothing less than death by crucifixion at the hands of the hated Romans. The cross was also regarded as a symbol of shame. It was what the Romans did to rebels and bandits. And yet, here is Jesus commending the cross as the true way of discipleship. Jesus wants the "crowd" - everyone (8:34), no less than his disciples to hear this message because he knows that many of them are following him for the wrong reasons. Jesus' message is for everyone, and for all time. The cost of discipleship will be the theme which dominates the rest of Jesus' journey to Jerusalem.

For Jesus, discipleship involves the cross, because he saw the value of sacrificing in the present for the sake of the future good of everyone (thinking God's way), as the only way of liberating humanity from captivity to the lure of the present moment. Our desires are captive to the here-and-now. In order to satisfy our every whim, we literally want to have stones turned into bread (Matthew 4:3), as a short-cut to what we perceive as 'good' for us. We thus reject God's way and we reach out and grasp a forbidden fruit, which appears "beautiful" to our eyes, but its veneer of beauty is only an illusion. (Genesis 3:6a). On the other hand, surrendering ourselves to God - obedience to his will, doing things his way - is difficult; it is costly; it involves pain. But the reality is that it represents the true meaning of life. It is what works best in the end.

Thus, the Christian paradox about losing one's life in order to save it! (8:35b). What does this mean? Forgetting self (8:34) means giving up selfish desires in order to make sacrifices which will create future good. It is sowing seeds now which will later come to fruition as goodness in ourselves and the lives of other people. (Mark 4:8). It can thus amount to costly service to our neighbour. Losing one's life means giving up the self-regard that would stand in the way of making a full commitment to some ideal or mission in life. It means giving up (losing) all the habits that can hold one in bondage to self-serving tendencies. "Winning the whole world" could mean being ruled by the drive for ego-promotion, possessions, reputation and status, while altruistic values are rejected, or as having lesser priority. Jesus' words about forgetting self may be a stumbling block for many in today's world of individualism, in which the individual's desires, needs and rights are prized above all else. Yet, Jesus implies that we cannot "come" with him unless we are prepared to forget oneself (8:34), as the way to meaningful life.

Suffering service can be costly. But it liberates us from bondage to the ego and sets us free to express our true humanity - by making a difference in the lives of others. It is what gives life meaning and purpose. Serving others is bringing 'good news' (8:35b) to them. It involves feeding the hungry, giving a drink to the thirsty. (See Matthew 25:35-36). Love hurts. Trying to love our neighbour can mean forgetting oneself, out of compassion for the just needs, rights and feelings of other people. As was the case with Jesus, the more compassion and concern one has for others, the more it can hurt. Jesus' sharing in the universal compassion of God must have cost him in a way we cannot even begin to imagine. This was why he had compassion on the crowds (symbolic of humanity at large) and wanted to feed their deepest hungers (Mark 6:34), however costly to himself that was going to be in the end. Love is a sacrifice made for the sake of others. But it is the true, and only road to resurrection (8:31b) – the saving of one's life. (8:35b).

It is only when we find and pursue what God wants us to do, that we will find fulfilment and true happiness - and eternal life: the saving of our life. (See Mark 10:21). Service to others creates the inclusive union which Jesus has in mind as the kingdom of God – a union which leads also to union with God. (Mark 3:33-35). Jesus is calling us to accept some short-term losses, to deny ourselves of some comforts or pleasures for a greater long-term good. (See Mark 9:35; 10:35-38). Thus, the Christian paradox that death to self is the way to fullness of life. In the throes of his life of suffering service, Jesus is stirred, empowered and motivated by his vision of a glorious future revealed to him and promised to him (and to humanity) by his heavenly Father. This is the 'good news' of a happy ending to the human story, in the gathering together of all God's people "from one end of the world to the other." (Mark 13:26-27; Matthew 24:31, 25:31-32).

Jesus does not say that suffering and death should be viewed as good in themselves. In point of fact, he saw these as evils, which his mission on earth was to overcome and ultimately abolish. But he also wanted to show that suffering can have a positive value, especially when it is undertaken as part of a life of service. At the end of the gospel he will assume the role of Isaiah's suffering servant. (Isaiah 52:13-15 - 53:1-12). So it was now time for his role and identity to come to the fore in the minds and hearts of his disciples. At the beginning, when he called them to follow him, he asked them to be 'with him.' The issue now is, will they stay with him once the awful challenge and full significance of his messiahship becomes plain to them? His call to stay with him is also addressed to all of us, and may be seriously testing of our faith (Mark 14:36), once we come to realize the full implications of following him.

In his 'kingdom of God' proclamation, Jesus wanted to create a new Israel (family of God, doing the will of God) around himself and his followers. (Mark 3:34-35). The Israel of his day –especially exemplified in its religious leaders - had failed in its obedience to God. Instead, it had plucked the forbidden fruit of power, self-aggrandisement and prestige. It chose to blindly go its own way, excluding many groups regarded as unworthy of membership of what it saw as the true Israel. (Mark 7:5-8).

What God wanted of official Israel was for its people to love *all* their neighbours, which would include everyone within Israel, rich and poor, outcasts and sinners, and for the Gentiles no longer to be to be treated as "dogs under the table" (Mark 7:27-28), but to be invited into Jesus' table fellowship and given a seat in the Kingdom of God. (Matthew 5:43-45). But Israel was still God's blind and disobedient servant. Both John the Baptist and Jesus called Israel to repent of their lack of love, their failure to lose the comforting things, such as status, power and their sense of superiority. These things were holding them in a Satanic grip, so they could not come into Jesus' kingdom, which would create a new unity in Israel - a unity not based on exclusion or separation, but founded on the self-giving and forgiveness of Jesus. But like the man of many possessions, who approached Jesus (Mark 10:17-22), they refused the invitation, because it would involve turning their secure and comfortable world upside down. To have accepted Jesus' invitation would mean sacrificing themselves, which would actually have given meaning to their temple sacrifices. Without such obedient love, their animal sacrifices were meaningless. (See Hosea 6:6).

The disciples had little understanding of Jesus until after the resurrection. Then Jesus became a living presence among them, the foundation stone (Mark 12:10) of the new Israel of reconciled humanity, which they then set about constructing through the power of his Spirit. (See Acts of the Apostles, chaps. 1-12, especially chapter 10).

## The Transfiguration

Six days later, Jesus took with him Peter, James and John and led them up a high mountain on their own by themselves. There in their presence he was transfigured: his clothes became brilliantly white, whiter than any earthly bleach could make them. Elijah appeared to them with Moses; and they were talking to Jesus. Then Peter spoke to Jesus, 'Rabbi,' he said, 'It is wonderful for us to be here; so let us make three shelters, one for you, one for Moses and one for Elijah.' He did not know what to say; they were so frightened. And a cloud came, covering them in shadow; and from the cloud there came a voice, 'This is my Son, the beloved. Listen to him.' Then suddenly, when they looked round, they saw no one with them anymore but only Jesus. (Mark 9:2-8, NJB).

Mountains are key settings for events in the life of Jesus, (Mark 3:13-15; 13:3; 14:26). In the Old Testament, mountains are places of encounter with God, and symbolic of his presence. Moses communed with God on Mount Sinai and received the Ten Commandments there. (Exodus 19:3). On the mountain of transfiguration, Jesus is revealed as the new Moses through whom God definitively speaks his new law, which is a call to humanity to listen to his Son (9:7).

Coming soon after the announcement of his passion and his invitation to suffering service, the transfiguration is an anticipation of what Jesus has just revealed about his resurrection. (Mark 9:2-13; see Exodus 24:15-16; 1 Kings 8:10-12; 2 Peter 1:16-18).

Jesus' transfiguration recalls God's presence in a cloud which covered Mount Sinai for six days before God spoke to Moses and established the old law (Ten Commandments). "The Lord said to Moses, 'I will come to you in a thick cloud, so that people will hear me speaking with you and will believe me from now on.'" (Exodus 19:9; see 24:16-17; 33:11; 34:35; Deuteronomy 34:10; Mark 9:7). A cloud had great significance in the Journey of the Israelites through the wilderness on their way to the promised land. The cloud manifested the glory of God and his mysterious presence to the people. (Exodus 13:21; see 24:15-16). With the coming of Jesus, God is no longer hidden in a cloud. He is visibly revealed in the life, death and resurrection of Jesus. Heaven and earth, God and humanity are joined together in Jesus.

For a brief time on a "high mountain" the veil hiding Jesus' divine status from his humanity is lifted, and his three foremost disciples receive a glimpse of his glory. He may have wanted to encourage them to remain with him by revealing to them, that not suffering and death, but glory and triumph would be God's final word to humanity, as a happy ending to the human story. This must have been a highly significant event, because it remained alive in the memory of the three apostles. (See 2 Peter 1:16-18).

Up to this point, Jesus has tried to open the disciples' eyes to the meaning of his suffering service. On the mountain he reveals to them another dimension of who he is. Yes, there is suffering service, but the human story does not end with that. The goal (destiny) of humanity is a glorious future in which it will be "good for everyone to be here." (Mark 9:5). The transfiguration is a revelation of Jesus' full identity as God's Messiah, because it reveals his eventual triumph in glory, following his suffering service. In contrast to our way of thinking, God's thoughts are future orientated. All along, God's plan is ultimately to abolish suffering and death, and thereby to create the new glorified humanity, thus fulfilling Psalm 8:5.

These three disciples have seen Jesus' power over nature on the Sea of Galilee. (4:35-39). They have witnessed his power over death in the raising of the daughter of Jairus. (5:37). They will later be present at his anguished wrestling with the "cup" in Gethsemane. (14:33). They now experience an awe-inspiring revelation on the mountain of transfiguration, but they don't understand it.

Peter, James and John would later have prominent roles in the early Church. (See Acts of the Apostles chaps. 3-4; 12:2). In order to be able to lead the other disciples, they needed to get a full picture of Jesus and thus be strengthened in their faith and hope. So Jesus led the three apostles up a "high mountain," the Sinai of the new covenant. (Exodus 19:16-25; 24:12-18). As in Exodus, there is a mountain and a cloud. And Moses appears, hidden in the cloud.

The three apostles saw Elijah, the wonder-working prophet (1 Kings 17; 19:1-12) and Moses (prophet and law-giver) talking to Jesus. (9:4). As the Son (Mark 1:11; 9:7), Jesus has a status far exceeding that of Moses and of Elijah and the latter's wonderful works. (See Deuteronomy 18:15). The heavenly voice ("this is my Son") raises Jesus above the two prophets and shows him to be "more than a prophet like Moses." (Deuteronomy 18:15; 18-19).

In this vision, Jesus receives confirmation from the Father, of his own wonderful works and the truth he has been teaching (his new commandments), encouraging him to remain on his chosen path to the cross. Jesus is both God's wonder-worker (his miracles) and prophet (13:26). But as Son of God, Jesus is greater than the one who brought God's people home from exile in Egypt. (Deuteronomy 34:10-12). Twice in Mark's gospel, Jesus is revealed as Son of God in words spoken by the Father: at his baptism (Mark 1:11), and now at his transfiguration (9:7). At his death on the cross he is revealed as Son in words spoken by the Roman centurion who crucified him. (Mark 15:39). Only as Son of God and the new Moses, could Jesus accomplish what no other human being could do – liberate us exiles and take us home from our exile in a definitive exodus.

Jesus has many times called on his disciples to listen to him. Now the voice of the Father from the cloud (9:7) identifies Jesus as his "beloved Son" and that is precisely why the disciples should open their ears and listen to him. (9:7b). A short time previously they had been deaf to his teaching of his messianic role and the suffering it would entail. Now they are called to "listen" to him as God's Son in all his glory, delivering the same message. Can they not open their eyes to his glorious destiny, now that they have been given a glimpse of it on the mountain of transfiguration? He has called them to come with him, with the implication that his future glory will be shared with them. This should encourage them to stay with him. They are instructed to listen to what he is saying and to what he will continue to say. But they will still not understand that Jesus' destiny is first to suffer and die and then rise again on the third day. (8:31; 9:31-32; 10:32-34). If they struggle to understand how Jesus, as Messiah and God's beloved Son, is destined to suffer and die, then the idea of rising from the dead can have no meaning at all for them.

The transfiguration is a mystery at the core of the gospel. It reveals God's costly involvement in the evil of the world. In obedience to the Father, the Son enters into the pain and suffering of the world in order to free the world and humanity from suffering and from the greatest pain of all, namely death, through his resurrection. (Mark 10:45; see Philippians 2:5-11). This should encourage the disciples, and by extension, us too, that no matter the troubles we endure, we have a glorious destiny awaiting us.

"His clothes became brilliantly white." In the Bible, a shining light is always a symbol of God's enlightenment of human beings. The transfiguration of Jesus foreshadows our own transformation. We are all called to be lights, to plant seeds of enlightenment in the hearts of others, so that they may grow and flourish. (See Mark 4:21; Matthew 5:15-16). In the Old Testament, enlightenment is equated with wisdom. "Those who are wise shall shine like the brightness of the sky, and those who lead many to righteousness, like the stars for ever and ever." (Daniel 12:3, NRSVC). Jesus fulfils the prophecy of Daniel, as the one who will lead the whole of humanity to the light of righteousness.

Peter's reaction to the vision is expressed in his word, "wonderful" – a word denoting consolation in the presence of the divine. Through the symbol of three "shelters" (verse 5, denoting God's presence), Peter seemingly wants to hold on to this wonderful experience, as if he had never "heard" Jesus' instruction about a costly "way" and a "cup" in which he and the other disciples must first participate. (Mark 10:38). Peter cannot "see" that the way of the cross must come first, the way of a life lived in service, as the only path to glory.

The apostles then find themselves alone with Jesus, who must now complete his Father's plan (promised in the Old Testament) by going to the cross alone. Only he can accomplish the will of his heavenly Father. Both in his suffering and in his triumph over it, Jesus fulfils the role of Isaiah's Suffering Servant. "The Lord says, 'My Servant will succeed in his task; he will be highly honoured... After a life of suffering, he will again have joy; he will know that he did not suffer in vain... And so I will give him a place of honour, a place among the great and powerful.'" (Isaiah 52:13; 53:11-12). Jesus' transfiguration is a foreshadowing of resurrected humanity – a glimpse of a happy ending to the human story.

"As they came down from the mountain, Jesus ordered them, 'Don't tell anyone what you have seen until the Son of Man has risen from death.' They obeyed his order, but among themselves, they started discussing the question, 'What does this rising from death mean?'" (Mark 9:9-10). The transformation of his human nature, foreshadowed in the transfiguration, cannot take place, nor be understood properly until after Jesus' passion. Jesus becomes the exalted risen Son of God only by first passing through death. Then his glory will be fully revealed, and the disciples will be given the task of openly proclaiming it to all, while they themselves will be enlightened, making them shine "like stars lighting up the sky" in a sinful world. (Philippians 2:14-15).

As Jesus, James and John were re-joining the disciples, they saw a large crowd round them and some scribes arguing with them. At once when they saw him, the whole crowd were struck with amazement and ran to greet him. And he asked them, 'What are you arguing about with them?' A man answered from the crowd, 'Master, I brought my son to you; there is a spirit of dumbness in him, and when it takes hold of him it throws him to the ground, and he foams at the mouth and grinds his teeth and goes rigid. And I asked your disciples to drive it out and they were unable to do so.' In reply he said to them, 'Faithless generation, how much longer must I be among you? How much longer must I put up with you? Bring him to me.' They brought the boy to him, and at once the spirit of dumbness threw the boy into convulsions, and he fell to the ground and lay writhing there, foaming at the mouth. (9:14-20, NJB).

The father of the boy told Jesus that this had been happening from the boy's childhood. He said to Jesus, 'If you can do anything, have pity on us and help us.' (9:21-23).

> 'If you can?' Retorted Jesus. 'Everything is possible for one who has faith.' At once the father of the boy cried out, 'I have faith, but not enough. Help my lack of faith!' And when Jesus saw that a crowd was gathering, so he rebuked the unclean spirit. 'Deaf and dumb spirit,' he said, 'I command you: come out of him and never enter him again.' Then it threw the boy into violent convulsions and came out shouting, and the boy lay there so like a corpse that most of them said, 'He is dead.' But Jesus took him by the hand and helped him up, and he was able to stand. (9:24-27, NJB; see Mark 16:6, 9, 14; Acts of the Apostles 3:15; 10:40-43).

The disciples had previously been able to cast out demons in Jesus' name but this one had them beaten. There may be some demons who are harder to deal with than others. Jesus may have returned from the mountain with heightened power. He later told the disciples that they needed prayer to drive out that particular demon. (9:29). They didn't see how weak they were when confronted by the forces of evil. (See Mark 4:40-41). They should have been newly empowered after the vision of Jesus' future glory. The father of the boy does acknowledge his weakness, and his son is healed. What we need to do is to acknowledge our dependence on God. This is a matter of faith. Without faith, we remain closed to the possibility of making all things new. (See Mark 11:23-24). The whole of humanity is often unbelieving (verse 14) in the face of God's mercy. Jesus is hinting that his time with this "faithless generation" is short, and that the sufferings he will endure are the result of unbelief.

Having participated in Jesus' mission of healing, having seen his mighty works; having been given a foretaste of his future glory on the mountain of Transfiguration, the disciples no less than the crowds, are still unbelieving. It's as if Jesus was hinting that his mission so far may have been a failure. The deaf and dumb boy symbolizes the spiritual deafness of the disciples and humanity at large. (See Mark 9:7b). Jesus' second prophecy of his passion will soon follow, which once again, will be met with incomprehension on the part of the disciples. The upshot seems to be that the disciples will be helpless to play their part in "exorcising" the evil of the world – unless they come to terms with following Jesus on his road of suffering service. Jesus himself is not going to deal with the world's evil as a triumphal messiah. He is already overcoming evil by compassionately identifying with suffering humanity. This is God's way, the way of service. The disciples are reluctant to follow him on that same path, because of their failure to listen to, and hear the Son, as they were told on the mountain of transfiguration. They are like the boy who was afflicted by the "deaf and dumb spirit." (Mark 9:25b).

"Jesus took the boy by the hand and helped him to rise" out of his death-like state, and "he stood up." (Mark 9:27). These are words used for the resurrection of Jesus, both in Mark 16:6, 9, 14 and in Acts of the Apostles 3:15; 10:41. They also presage humanity's future resurrection. This exorcism symbolically reveals the deliverance of humanity from the power of Satan through Jesus' victory over all evil spirits – a work which will be accomplished in his resurrection.

Jesus returned from his transfiguration on the mountain with a new vision and renewed power of what God would accomplish in him. His appearance caused amazement in the crowd when they saw him. (9:15). Amazement is the usual human reaction to an experience of the divine. The healing of a dumb boy is the last exorcism performed by Jesus in Mark's gospel. It symbolizes the transformation of humanity through the raising up of Jesus into glory.

Meanwhile, the disciples will be asked to climb ever harder mountains of faith and understanding as they journey on the road. Jesus' mission is to heal spiritual deafness and dumbness, which cause people to be separated from God, leaving them in the grip of Satan. (Mark 7:33-35, 37; Luke 7:22). In this he will succeed, thus fulfilling many Old Testament prophecies about the work of the future Messiah. (See Isaiah 35:5; 29:18-19; 42:18). Jesus' healings of deafness and dumbness are both signs and a foretaste of his ultimate opening of eyes and ears to the fullness of the reign of God over evil in his resurrection, when all humanity ("a corpse," 9:26), will be "taken by the hand and raised up." But at this stage, the disciples will remain deaf and dumb to the full significance of Jesus' life-giving teaching and works. As Mark will now show, they will continue on *their* way, captive to their own dreams and illusions, until the shocking truth dawns.

## Jesus' Second Prophecy of his Passion

> Jesus and his disciples left that place and went on through Galilee. Jesus did not want anyone to know where he was, because he was teaching his disciples: 'The Son of man will be handed over to those who will kill him. Three days later, however, he will rise to life.' But they did not understand what this teaching meant, and they were afraid to ask him. (Mark 9:30-32; see Isaiah 53:12; Romans 4:25; 8:32).

Jesus moves away from being surrounded by crowds bringing him the afflicted, because he wants to enlighten his disciples. The journey south towards Jerusalem and Calvary now begins. "God did not spare his beloved Son but handed him over for us all." (Romans 8:32). Just as the Suffering Servant willingly gave his life (Isaiah 53:12), in a mysterious way, the Father himself sent Jesus at the start of the *handing over*. (9:32). Jesus freely hands himself over in obedience to the Father's plan. As Son of God, he has power from the Father to accomplish the work of redemption "for us all." But at the same time, he could not take us home from our exile unless he was fully a human being, one who could stand in solidarity with us, and like ourselves, with the capacity to suffer and die. As Son of Man, he identified with humanity, thus sharing our enfeebled state, and suffering the effects of our flaws and frailty.

This time Peter and the others voice no protest to Jesus' passion prediction, as they did in 8:32. They do not understand, nor could they come to terms with the idea of a suffering Messiah. And they are afraid to ask him what he means by rising from the dead. (9:32). Like many Jews at that time, they probably believed in a general resurrection of the dead, but the idea of one man rising from the dead may have been just too much for them. Their fear and misunderstanding signify their lack of trust in Jesus and his word spoken to them. They are not listening to him, as instructed at the Transfiguration. Their fear to act courageously in the face of loss and threat will be a stumbling block as they continue their journey to Jerusalem. (10:32). They will continue to follow Jesus, but will not be with him in spirit.

Are we not also filled with fear and lack of faith when confronted with a heavy cross in our lives? We ask, 'How could this be part of God's plan?' Where is the goodness of God? What good can come from innocent suffering? What we don't understand is God himself, who takes a long-term view of human existence. The cross does lead to glory and fruitfulness. (See Genesis chaps.37-50). But this can be testing of our faith, simply because we are lacking in vision. We cannot see beyond the present reality of suffering. We are blind to future glory. And although ultimate glory is God's final word to us, we find it hard to believe him.

> They came to Capernaum, and after going indoors, Jesus asked his disciples, 'What were you arguing about on the road?' But they would not answer him, because on the road they had been arguing among themselves about who was the greatest. Jesus sat down, called the twelve disciples and said to them, 'Whoever wants to be the first must place himself last of all and be the servant of all.' (Mark 9:33-35).

The second time Jesus told his disciples about the suffering and death that awaited him, they didn't understand him. (9:32). The proof of that is that they soon became involved in an argument over which one of them is "the greatest." (9:34). They have just heard Jesus speaking of willingly handing himself over to rejection and death, because he saw this as the inevitable outcome of his mission of teaching and healing, with the implication that humiliation is the only road to becoming "the greatest." (9:31). Their way of coping with Jesus' talk about death is to cling to their own hopes and values. They already understand that Jesus is the Messiah long promised to Israel, but they are stymied by their belief that he will be a conquering Messiah, and then rewarding the "greatest" of them with the top jobs in his glorious kingdom. All that concerns them is competing with one another for honour and glory - with no thought at all about how they might share in his mission of service, about which he has been teaching them. He has already told them that if they want to be his disciples, they must forget self and be willing to carry their cross (8:34), and now he tells them that the way to be "first" is not to be set up in power and status, but to be the "servant of all." (9:35).

In telling them this, Jesus was radically at odds with the culture of the ancient world, where humility was not viewed as a virtue, but as a sign of weakness. Nobody in their right mind would aspire to be a servant in that culture, in which servants were usually regarded as slaves. The early Church's adoption of this new ethic of service was part of what made Christianity so attractive, in that it put all kinds of people on the same level of dignity – no distinctions or differences in God's kingdom. Those who had been treated as of no account in society could be exalted through their work of service. "Whoever humbles himself will be exalted." (Matthew 23:11-12; see Philippians 2:3-9; 1 Peter 5:2-4; Isaiah14:12-15; Ezekiel 28:2).

We shouldn't judge the disciples harshly. Jesus does not condemn the innate desire in the human heart for grandiosity. In a desire for grandeur, the human tendency is to seek its own advantage, even if that involves selfish rivalry with others, as is the case with the disciples. (9:34). This again represents the lure of the present moment, the attraction of the beautiful fruit, which we cannot resist grasping (Genesis 3:6). Such a forbidden fruit may be worthless. It will not feed the longings of the human heart for peace and fulfilment, simply because it can lead to a divisive family. (Mark 3:25-26). Trying to grasp such a fruit may be a sign of the reign of Satan, the malevolent power trying to sow seeds of division and strife. Jesus wants to reorient our desires towards the reign of God, to what can truly fulfil our deepest hungering. Paradoxically, the way to be first, the only way to fulfil the desire for true honour and glory, is through service. This can involve the cross. Selfless service did not come easy to Jesus' first disciples, nor does it come easily to us. It is costly. It runs counter to the lure of the present moment. It is like a slowly growing seed (Mark 4:3) for which we have to wait until its abundant and life-enhancing fruit appears.

Jesus may have seen the disciples as still living under the reign of Satan. In order to demonstrate to them how the reign of God works, he performed a symbolic action: "He took a child and made him stand in front of them. He put his arms around him and said to them, 'Whoever welcomes in my name one of these children, welcomes me; and whoever welcomes me also welcomes the one who sent me.' (Mark 9:36-37).

In ancient society children were regarded as non-persons, without legal rights or status of their own. In this context, they stand for all who are hungry, those without esteem, or who are downtrodden in any way – slaves. Jesus teaches his disciples to have a whole new esteem for children and all those who are seen as most helpless and of little account in society - lowly servants. The word for "child" in Greek can also mean a servant. Jesus himself comes into this world in the guise of a child (Son of God) who serves. He identifies so much with all servants (including children), that he is present in them. "Welcoming" (accepting, embracing) a child is accepting him or her and their values of service. (See Matthew 25:40). Jesus is turning the values of the world upside down. He is telling his disciples that the way for them to become great is to become like little children, to become lowly servants, to become like himself, to imitate him in his service of feeding the hungry. (Mark 6:34, 41; 5:40-42). Selfless service is a sign of life lived under the reign of God.

Jesus wants to emphasise that the kingdom of God is a society in which there will be no prestige and no division of people into inferior and superior, no unclean ones, no one excluded. (Mark 7:15). God loves and respects everyone, not because of their education, wealth, possessions, authority, status, virtue or age, but because of their dignity as his children. He calls us to imitate his gratuity. Everyone is equal in God's family. (Mark 3:33-35). So the poor and little ones are not promised status or privileges, but full recognition of their dignity as human beings and as people loved by God. Those who could not live without feeling superior and dominant, would not be at home in the kingdom of God; they would want to exclude themselves from it.

Our treatment of the lowly is a measure of our relationship with God, and is linked to our own mission as disciples: feeding the hungry. (Matthew 25:35). Here, Jesus is saying that little children – through their dependency - have much to teach us about our own dependency on God, our relationship with him. Followers of Jesus can only accept the kingdom, i.e. accept God's rule (his will) in their lives, if they become like children. Little children are models of the kingdom, because of their child-like trust and absolute dependence on their parents for everything they receive. Our trust in God should be like this, acknowledging that the blessings we receive (being made children of God) comes as unmerited gift. In the Old Testament, God revealed his love for the lowly, who were often oppressed by the powerful. (Deuteronomy 10:18, Psalm 146:9; Isaiah 29:19).

## God's Plan for Marriage

The passage below and the episodes that follows it may serve to illustrate the difficulty of following Jesus on the way of the cross. Up to this point, Jesus has been making clear to his disciples the cost of discipleship. (8:31-32, 34-35; 9:31, 35). He now dwells on some of the practical implications of following him. What does discipleship entail in ordinary life – for those called by God to marry, to raise children, for the single life, running a business or owning an estate?

> When Jesus left that place, he went to the province of Judea, and crossed the river Jordan. Crowds came flocking to him again, and he taught them as he always did. Some Pharisees approached him and asked, 'Is it lawful for a man to divorce his wife?' They were putting him to the test. He answered them, 'What did Moses command you?' They replied, 'Moses allowed us to draw up a writ of dismissal in cases of divorce.' Then Jesus said to them, 'It was because you were so hard-hearted that he wrote this commandment for you. But from the beginning of creation *he made them male and female. This is why a man leaves his father and mother, and the two become one flesh.* They are no longer two, therefore, but one flesh. So then what God has united, human beings must not divide.' (Mark 10:2-9, NJB; Genesis 1:27 and 2:24 in italics).

The place which Jesus left was presumably Capernaum on the northern shore of the lake. Jesus was now in Judea for the first time since his baptism by John. He will not set foot in Galilee again until after his resurrection. It is likely that the Pharisees are trying to get Jesus to make the same statement about divorce and re-marriage that resulted in the death of John the Baptist, who was killed by Herod. Suspense increases by recalling the fate of John.

Divorce was widely accepted in the Jewish society of Jesus' day, despite the biblical teaching that God hates divorce. (See Malachi 2:16). The Pharisees asked this question while knowing that the law of Moses did permit divorce. But, just what kind of divorce was permitted? According to Mosaic law, a man who becomes displeased with his wife could write her a bill of divorce, give it to her and send her away from his home. There was no provision in Jewish law for a woman to divorce her husband. (Deuteronomy

24:1-3).

The Pharisees asked Jesus about divorce, but he replied by focusing on marriage. Jesus explained the reason for the law in Deuteronomy which permitted divorce. 'It was because of hard-heartedness.' (Mark 10:5). We may understand hardness of heart as a lack of compassion and due consideration for the feelings of another person. The Pharisees quote Moses, who doesn't command or encourage divorce. Moses made provision for a divorced wife on account of the hard-heartedness that led men to dissolve their marriages and dismiss their wives from their homes. In Jesus' day, women may have been suffering because of divorce.

Israel is often chastised in the Old Testament for being hard-hearted. (Deuteronomy 10:15-16; 2 Kings 17:13-14; Psalm 95:8; Isaiah 63:15-17). Hard-heartedness amounts to the plucking of a forbidden fruit (Genesis 3:6). It is obedience to one's own will and a refusal to obey the will of God, a refusal of his just rule which creates a communion of persons and is for the good of everyone. Hard-heartedness is based on self-will, what the self wants at all costs. This creates division, separation, enmity. It is a blindness to the truth of how the world works for the best, and for which Jesus has already chided the Pharisees and even his disciples. (Mark 3:5; 6:52; 8:17).

Jesus now draws attention to *the* commandment, which is found in the first book of the Bible, in Genesis 1:27 and 2:24. For a husband and wife to become "one flesh" is an expression of the deepest union. Jesus links the two quotations from Genesis in the above passage, to indicate that God's ultimate purpose in creating human beings in his image was to create a communion of love between a husband and wife, resembling the love within the triune God. God himself is a communion of persons, an eternal exchange of love, and he has destined us to share in that exchange. The creation of the bodily differences of "male and female" are designed for a union that will last into eternity. By referring to humanity before the fall of Adam and Eve, Jesus implies that from now on, God's original intention is the standard for marriage, and indeed, for all human relationships.

Moses' concession in Deuteronomy no longer applies, because in Jesus' kingdom of God, humanity is no longer in bondage to hardness of heart, which can lead to disunion and family breakdown, but is empowered by God's Spirit to live out what God intended from the beginning. The union of husband and wife is no mere human convention, but a sacred bond made by God himself. (See Malachi 2:14-16; Luke 16:19; 1 Corinthians 7:10-11; CCC 1601-17, 1638-54, 2360-2400). Jesus has not been trapped into setting aside the Mosaic law. Rather, he has interpreted it according to the original will of the Creator God, as set forth in the Book of Genesis.

We know that not all marriages reflect the ideal that Jesus places before us. In many cases, people will be living in circumstances beyond what they are able to endure, and may separate or dissolve their marriages. The Church does not see these people excluded from the love and mercy of God. They are still God's children. Although Jesus presented God's vision for human relationships within marriage - so that the union of husband and wife could be a living reflection of his own love for humanity - he did not condemn those who fall short of that ideal. All of us are called to love one another as God loves us, and we all fail in various ways to respond positively to that call. But when we approach the Lord with a childlike heart, in our weakness and dependency, we are then open to the grace of the Lord's love, empowering us to never cease reaching out towards the goal, the ideal that Jesus puts before us.

Jesus' further pronouncement about children and his blessing of them, immediately follows his teaching about marriage. (Mark 10:13-16). Because marriage between a man and woman is a tried and tested way in which children can grow and be loved and provided with stability and security, no other way has proved better for the nourishing of children and bringing them to the blessing of fruitful maturity. (See Genesis 48:14-16). Hard-heartedness between parents can adversely affect children. This is a question of justice. Faced with the prospect of separation, for whatever reason, spouses should be aware of how this may affect their children.

As Mark has stated, the obstacle of heartlessness should not be placed in the way of children coming to Jesus for his blessing, a blessing which can be mediated through parents themselves when they remain faithful to their children. (Mark 10:13-14). In their vocation as sowers of the word (Mark 4:14), parents assume the role of Jesus in sharing with their children the blessing flowing from their own lives of service to each other, so that children may develop and grow to maturity. This will mean sacrificing one's egotistic desires for the sake of devotion and service to those little ones who hunger and thirst for love and care. In feeding their hungers and thirsts, parents are serving Jesus himself, who, in his second coming, as king and judge, will reward all faithful servants with the blessing of his Father "in the kingdom prepared for them since the foundation of the world." (Matthew 25:37, 40, 34, NJB).

The above teachings have implications for discipleship. Marriage is a vocation in which the spouses are called by God to sacrifice themselves for one another and for their children. In entering marriage, spouses give up many freedoms in order to be free to devote themselves to each other and to their children. Marriage is a call to mission. It is the journey to Jerusalem of Mark's gospel. It is a call from God to leave behind the comforts of individualism, to leave our own country and our father's home (Genesis 2:24) and undertake a journey to a "new land." (Genesis 12:1). The new land is the God-given goal towards which we journey in hope: the creation of a new communion, known as a family.

In sending us on our marriage mission, God does not leave us alone and adrift. When Moses was called by God for his mission of liberation and the creation of union among the Hebrew tribes, he was conscious of his weakness; he protested his inadequacy. (Exodus 3:11). But God said to him, 'I will be with you.' (Exodus 13:12). When Jesus called his apostles, he wanted them to be with him, so that they could learn from his own self-sacrificing love. (Mark 3:13). A mission is always costly, but we have God's promise that he will be with us, in his power to guide, help and encourage us. We have Jesus' promise that people who leave behind a life centred on the self, for a life of following him (e.g. in marriage) will receive rewards both in this life and in the hereafter. (Mark 10:21, 29-30). Marriage vows may be summed up in the phrase which each spouse makes to the other: 'I will be with you,' meaning that they become as God, to, and for each other.

Like the disciples, we begin the journey of marriage full of joy, hope and enthusiasm. Like the disciples on their journey, initial enthusiasm may wane, misunderstandings and failings may emerge, until the reality dawns (an opening of eyes) that love is self-sacrificial rather than self-serving. It was only after the resurrection that the eyes of the disciples were opened to how wrong they had been in their previous relationship with Jesus: seeking glory for themselves, blind to the purpose of the mission to which Jesus had called them. (Mark 9:34; 10:37). In the new maturity and greater self-awareness of later life, our own eyes may be opened to the inadequacies and shortcomings of our relationships, and we may then be prepared to adopt a more mature outlook of caring and service. This may be the dawning of a new wisdom, revealing that true love is not dependent on emotions and feelings. If emotions fade away, it does not mean that love has died. We see true love in God's unconditional love for us, in all our flaws and failings. God even sacrifices himself for us. The highest form of love puts the other person first. It means willing the good of the other, so we can say that this love is a decision to fully commit to the other person. We then put the other person's just needs before our own.

All of us are revisionists with regard to our own history. There may be very few people, who in later life, would tell their story the same way as they might have done earlier. The hope is that the later story may be an improvement on the former.

Marriage spouses are like the sower going out to plant seeds in each other and in their children, with the faith and hope that such seeds will come to fruition in their own maturity and the maturity and independence of their children. Jesus gave up his body for his followers. Along with Jesus, spouses are called to say to each other: 'Take it and eat it, this is my body.' (Mark 14:22). What is married love like? St. Paul tells it like this:

> Love is always patient and kind; love is never jealous; love is not boastful or conceited, it is never rude and never seeks its own advantage, it does not take offence or store up grievances. Love does not rejoice at wrongdoing, but finds its joy in the truth. It is always ready to make allowances, to trust, to hope and endure whatever comes. (1 Corinthians 13:4-7, NJB).

God is love, speaking to us in those words, which could be summed up as follows: 'I want to draw you into my life of eternal love, freely given to you. (See John 3:16; 1 John 4:8-9). This is a love that comes to you whether you are good or bad.' In looking at us with his love, God is patient with our failures. Despite our waywardness, he is kind. Neither is he jealous, because he is above all jealousy. He is not arrogant, so we don't feel diminished or put down. We can be sure of his delight when we get things right. His love does not insist on its own way, as if he had a strictly rigid path laid out for us. He wants to join us in discovering our true way, then aiding us on that way. His love does not rejoice or take pleasure when we get things wrong. It makes allowances for our failures as we travel the long, hard road to true love. And he is ready to forgive, no matter what comes. Love helps us to trust, to hope and endure. This the model for our own loving – the ideal which Jesus places before us.

It is in reaching out to others altruistically, that we become more aware of being loved by God. It is especially in marriage and family life that the love of God can be made manifest in our lives. Jesus gives us the Bread of Life to strengthen us on our marriage journey, filling every valley and levelling every obstacle on our path. (Isaiah 40:4; see Acts of the Apostles 1:8; CCC 1615, 1624, 1641-42).

What of the single life? Christian baptism is a universal call to service and holiness. It is a call to follow Jesus on his way. All Christians, whether married or single, can find joy in serving Christ in their everyday circumstances. Some people are called to a single-life journey. The single life may leave people free to do many good things which they would be unable to do in the married state. By remaining open to God and his will, the single person will be alert to his promptings for opportunities to give of oneself in service to others. (See CCC 1658).

## The Man of Many Possessions

Then there were questions about the meaning of life. What are the highest values by which people live, what works best for human flourishing? Can human beings find meaning and fulfilment in material things alone, or are they not still left hungering for something more or better? Can the ephemeral nature of possessions bring true and lasting fulfilment? The human being is a searcher for meaning. Being unhappy with possessions may be a signal from God to continue the search for true fulfilment: "Ask (continue searching) and you will receive, seek and you will find, knock and the door will be opened to you." (Matthew 7:7). Doors may open, leading to new venturing, to new and unimaginable vistas. The following episode wrestles with these questions.

> As Jesus was setting out on a journey, a man ran up, knelt before him, and asked him, 'Good Teacher, what must I do to inherit eternal life?' Jesus said to him, 'Why do you call me good? No one is good but God alone. You know the commandments: 'You shall not murder; you shall not commit adultery; you shall not steal; you shall not bear false witness; you shall not defraud; honour your father and mother.' He said to him, 'Teacher, I have kept all these since my youth.' Jesus looking at him, loved him and said, 'You lack only one thing; go, sell what you own, and give the money to the poor, and you will have treasure in heaven; then come, follow me.' When he heard this, he went away grieving, for he had many possessions. (Mark 10:17-22, NRSVC; see also Luke 12:13-20; compare with Luke 19:1-10).

There is something odd about the man's question to Jesus - and about Jesus' response. Why did he call Jesus a "good teacher?" In Israel, teachers were people with expertise in the Law of Moses and were named as scribes. Perhaps the man thought Jesus was one of those people. In his response, 'why do you call me good,' Jesus may have understood him in that sense. The one class of people who regarded themselves as 'good' were the scribes and Pharisees. Jesus chided them for their self-righteousness. Adherence to innumerable rules and rituals made them 'good' in their own eyes, while they disregarded more important parts of the Ten Commandments. (Mark 7:1, 3-4, 6). So they may have been deceiving themselves about their goodness. Many of them may also have been men of many possessions, this giving them a high status in society. Jesus reminds this man, and indeed, all of us, that no one is good but God, and this may be why he referred the man to the really important aspects of the law, namely the Ten Commandments. These are the standard by which we should measure our goodness and judge ourselves. (Mark 10:18-19). But was Jesus himself not "good?" At his baptism by John, Jesus identified with sinful humanity – all the 'not good' people everywhere. Because of his solidarity with us, he can take us with him to where he is going, back to the Father, and to true happiness.

What was it that troubled the man of many possessions? Human beings give themselves an identity through the values by which they live. An identity means a sense of being distinct, being valuable, having something to live for, as if to say, 'This is who I am.' Such an identity can give meaning and purpose to a person's life. This man may have tried to find meaning and fulfilment in his "many possessions." But the fact that he came to Jesus with his question indicated that he still was not satisfied.

The human tendency is to turn good things - possessions, family, relationships, work, career, social status, money, house, sport, leisure pursuits - into ultimate things, in the expectation that they will give us enduring happiness. When we make any, or all of them our sole reason for living, we can end up disappointed and dissatisfied. They are never enough. Possessions, for example, are never enough. We always want more. The above 'good' things can collapse through human weakness, loss, failure, or by proving to be disappointing in some way. (Matthew 6:19-21). Then having staked all on them, there can be a loss of a sense of meaning, a feeling of failure, of being let down, with nothing more to live for - and like the above man, we may "go away grieving." (10:22). In other words, we may end up in deep anxiety. (See the Book of Ecclesiastes 2:4-9, 11, 17; the Book of Wisdom 7:7-9).

The human being cannot live without a story that is leading somewhere. Becoming dissatisfied with possessions, as if these were the ultimate, is a matter of coming to a dead end, with nothing more for which to hope. Dissatisfaction should prompt us to continue the search for ultimate meaning. So we ask if our lives as a whole have a meaning and purpose. If our lives as a whole are to have meaning, such meaning can only come from outside ourselves, as gift. It is really only God who can ultimately fulfil our search for meaning, by giving us a meaning that transcends all earthly meanings. We were created to build our identity on trusting and hoping in God for the fulfilment that he alone can give us, and not totally on the 'good' things of this world.

The man's question to Jesus about inheriting eternal life doesn't mean, 'What must I do to go to heaven?' Eternal life is the life of God, which is infinite happiness. That is where our story is going. That is our hope. The man's possessions could have left him stuck in a groove. His question to Jesus could have meant, 'What can I really do in order to make my life happy and meaningful?' True happiness is a sharing in the life of God, which is available to us even in this life, through our relationship with Jesus and with one another. Such a life can give us the values by which we can live: love, truth and a sense of responsibility towards others. Contrary to that, the man seemed to have been completely preoccupied with himself.

Having many possessions, the man would have understood the word "inherit." He may have inherited his father's property. Jesus offered him an inheritance from a heavenly Father – a sharing in the life of God, through which he could assume a completely new identity as a child of God. Jesus' message is that peace and happiness come from within the individual, and less so from the externals to which we cling. People can easily become disillusioned with the material side of life. An over-attachment to possessions can leave one completely self-preoccupied. Happiness is relational, i.e. bound up with family and community; it is about serving others. What Jesus was offering the man was the security of a brotherly existence through serving his neighbours in some way, some of whom may have been both spiritually and materially "poor." (10:21). Then he would have a goal towards which he could aim, a purpose by which he could live. And his "reward" (fulfilment, satisfaction) would arise from the difference he could make in the lives of other people. (Matthew 10:42; Genesis 12:1; Exodus 3:10). But he wasn't prepared to sacrifice the values (treasures) which he held dear for an enduring "heavenly treasure," one that would give him satisfaction even in the here-and-now. He wanted to save his life, but would only lose it. (Mark 8:35; Matthew 6:19-21; 10:39).

Jesus invited this man to sacrifice something of lesser value, for an enduring long-term gain. But he couldn't move away from his attachment and follow Jesus, even with the promise of the goal of eternal life. He couldn't leave his own country for a promised land – a land that would bring him many blessings. (See Genesis 12:1-2). Jesus' invitation to him may not have been a call to go on an itinerant mission, but simply to change his outlook and re-orient his life. There was still something missing in his life, a hole in his heart, which he himself could not fill. Staying where he was, was only making him miserable. He went away "grieving." (12:20). Jesus offered him freedom, but he chose to remain in bondage to grief and to his own "treasure," a god that was still not satisfying him. Grieving is what people do when they lose something or someone precious. Jesus called the man to heroic faith, and the goal of new journey of service - giving to the "poor" (Matthew 25:38-40). But he couldn't make the leap of faith in Jesus that would carry him forward in hope and empower him to enter a new, transforming life.

The man wanted to save his life, but would only lose it, lose real happiness, and remain in bondage to grief. The man was a searcher. Jesus offered him the freedom of the liberating kingdom, but he denied himself the "joy" experienced by the woman who, after much searching in her house, found her lost coin, symbolizing a "treasure in heaven," true happiness. (Luke 15:8-10; see Matthew 13:44-46).

Jesus listed the Commandments as the first essential. (10:19). He did not mention the first Commandment - the call to reject false gods and focus his life on the Creator God alone. But the first Commandment is implied in Jesus' phrase, "Come, follow me," which is an invitation to reject his false gods and give his allegiance to the Creator God, through Jesus. (10:14). "Jesus looked straight at him with love" (Mark 10:21), but he did not "look" at Jesus, in the sense of fully understanding or trusting in what Jesus could do for him. Jesus sowed a seed in the man's heart, but it appears to have fallen on stony ground. Jesus does not condemn the man. Jesus' deep faith in God led him to trust that God ultimately overcomes misunderstanding, human blindness and grief. (Mark 10:27).

The episode with the man of many possessions may also be interpreted as a metaphor for the religious leaders, whose sole focus was on their "possessions" - their positions of power, status and honour, the attachment to which, they could not "sell." For this reason, they had closed their eyes and ears to the teaching of Jesus. The scribes and

Pharisees were thinking only of themselves; living only from the esteem and regard of other people was their glory and grandeur. On that, they depended, rather than on God. There is evidence that at least, some scribes and Pharisees had come into the possession of large estates, making them men of many possessions.

In the modern affluent West, many people seem to have no need of God. The fruits of the work of their own hands seemingly gives them all the satisfaction they need. In this society, consumerism can be treated as the highest value, thus leaving people with no room for God. "In a godless universe, life has no meaning or purpose beyond the goals each person sets for himself or herself."[131] At the same time, there is a lot of grieving in today's world. It comes in many shapes and under a number of guises.

It is important to note that Jesus does not denounce wealth or possessions as bad in themselves. We are partly material beings and we live in a material world. We need material things and they give us a measure of comfort. Many of Jesus' sayings and parables affirm the value of ownership, business, trade and investment. Rather it is the over-attachment to possessions, persons, places or things - as if these were the highest or only values - that can entrap people in a kind of bondage (grief) from which they may be unable to free themselves.

> Jesus looked round at his disciples and said to them, 'How hard it will be for rich people to enter the kingdom of God.' The disciples were shocked at these words, but Jesus went on to say, 'My children, how hard it is to enter the Kingdom of God. It is much harder for a rich person to enter the kingdom of God than for a camel to go through the eye of a needle.' At this the disciples were completely amazed and said to one another, 'Who then can be saved?' Jesus looked straight at them and answered, 'This is impossible for human beings, but for God, everything is possible.' Then Peter spoke up, 'Look, we have left everything and followed you.' 'Yes,' Jesus said to them, 'and I tell you that anyone who leaves home or brothers or sisters or mother or father or children or fields for me and for the gospel, will receive much more in the present age. He or she will receive a hundred times more houses, brothers, sisters, mothers, children and fields – and persecutions as well, and in the age to come will receive eternal life. But many who now are first, will be last, and many who now are last, will be first.' (Mark 10:23-31).

In Old Testament times, before an understanding of life after death had fully developed, wealth and prosperity were considered a mark of God's favour. They were seen as salvation. (Deuteronomy 28:1-14; Psalm 25:12-13). The fertile land promised by God to the Israelites after their liberation from Egypt was understood as the goal of all their hoping, as their destiny. Yet there were many warnings of the danger of riches, of turning

---

[131] Jean Paul Sartre, 20th century French philosopher. Sartre's first premise was that human beings simply exist and that there is no God to grant any goals or purposes to them. Sartre is the apostle of individualism. He claimed that man must count on no one but himself. He is alone, abandoned on earth, without help, with no other aim than the one he sets himself, with no other destiny than the one he forges for himself on this earth. Sartre held that individuals are free to create their own meanings and purposes in any way they like.

riches into a god. (Deuteronomy 32:15; Psalm 49; 52:9; Proverbs 11:28).

As always in Mark, we understand "Kingdom of God" (10:24) as the new universal family of God that is being established by Jesus (Mark 3:34-35). In entering the kingdom, we begin to trust in God as our guide and shepherd, as the one who rescues us from destructive attachments and leads us on the road to fulfilment and happiness, in this world and in the life to come, when the Kingdom will be fully established. The kingdom is entirely the work of God. Our part is trusting in what only God can do for us and obediently following Jesus.

Jesus addresses his disciples as children (10:24), perhaps as a reminder of his earlier words about inheriting (Mark 10:17) and his words about receiving the kingdom as a child. (10:15, 17-22). In a flash of hyperbole, he drives home the point about the difficulty of a rich person entering the kingdom in terms of a camel going through the eye of a needle. The disciples again react in amazement and in an almost despairing attitude towards Jesus' teaching. Jesus recognises their puzzlement in face of the challenge placed before them, and reminds then that, for God, all things are possible. Being "saved" (10:30) means entering the kingdom and inheriting eternal life.

The man of many possessions asked Jesus, 'What can I do?' (10:17). Human beings cannot save themselves; they look for happiness in the wrong things; they are slow to learn wisdom, slow to understand what is of real value in life. (Book of Wisdom 7:7-9). Seeking salvation in material things is as hard as a camel going through the eye of a needle. Salvation is the work of God. Entering into eternal life is about trusting in the grace of God. When the Lord calls us, he does not leave us to our own abilities or strengths. In calling us, he empowers us to do his will. (Mark 3:35, see Exodus 3:11-12, Jeremiah 1:6, 18-19). The more we empty ourselves of attachments that don't give us fulfilment, all the more can God fill us with his grace and empowerment. What we need is faith and hope. (Isaiah 40:31).

The words of Jesus in Mark 10:29 reflect the experience of the early Christians, many of whom gave up their properties for the care of the needy (Acts of the Apostles 2:45; 4:32-37), and some of whom may have been disowned by their families (persecutions, Mark 10:30b) because of their allegiance to Jesus.

The disciples have indeed given up much, yet their squabbling for positions of honour (9:34; 10:40) and their aversion to the prospect of suffering (8:32), serves to show that they have not interiorly given up all (sold everything) and fully resolved to follow Jesus on the way he himself is going, even though he told them that his "way" would end in ultimate triumph. (8:31b; 9:31b). But they didn't understand what he meant. (Mark 9:32).

The promise for following Jesus is a hundredfold recompense (10:30), like the seed which bears abundant fruit (Mark 4:8, 20), not only in the age to come (in eternity), but in the present age. Those who give up all for Jesus will experience rewards and hospitality. (Acts of the Apostles 16:15; 28:2, 7; 2 Corinthians 8:1-4). They will experience bonds of brotherhood and sisterhood with other members of the faithful. (Galatians 6:10; see Romans 16:13). Even persecutions, which can come in the form of mockery, or other trials, are not worthy to be compared with eternal life – the life for which the man of "many possessions" so yearned (10:17).

The "age to come" (10:30) is a reference to God's new creation at the end of time, the new heaven and new earth in which every tear will be wiped away and death abolished, God making his home with human beings – the reign of God over evil fully established. (Revelation 21:1,3, 4).

## Jesus' Third Prophecy of his Passion

Jesus and his disciples were now on the road going up to Jerusalem. Jesus was going ahead of his disciples, who were filled with alarm; the people who followed behind were afraid. Once again Jesus took the twelve disciples aside and spoke of the things that were going to happen to him. 'Listen,' he told them, 'we are going up to Jerusalem where the Son of man will be handed over to the chief priests and the teachers of the law. They will condemn him to death and then hand him over to the Gentiles, who will mock him, spit on him, whip him, and kill him; but three days later he will rise to life.' (10:32-34).

As if intended as a commentary on his words in Mark 10:23-30, with their call to "sell everything," Jesus predicts his passion for the third time, but with the detail this time that he will be handed over to both the religious and Gentile leaders, who will kill him.

No matter what the road taken, in Jewish idiom, one always goes "up" to Jerusalem. (Verse 32; see Ezra 7:13; Zechariah 14:17). While it is literally a steep climb, metaphorically, it means the assumption of suffering. As against the other gospels, Mark only mentions Jesus going "up" to Jerusalem this one time, perhaps in order to emphasise the implications of the 'going up.'

In order to underline the urgency of the "way," Jesus was "going ahead of the disciples" (the shepherd leading his flock). This signifies his resolve to fulfil the will of the Father and his destiny as the suffering Messiah. His going ahead of them may also imply their reluctance to follow him. "They were filled with alarm." (10:32). Perhaps they were being tested more than they could endure. This was the same fear and lack of faith that alarmed them so much when they were in the boat with him on the Sea of Galilee, the stormy waters raging all round them. (Mark 4:35-41; see also 6:45-52).

Jerusalem has always been the real centre of hostility to Jesus throughout his ministry, and that is the storm into which he is now headed. Jesus takes his disciples away from the crowd and privately informs them in the most detailed and explicit way, of what will happen to him in Jerusalem. If that doesn't terrify them, what could? Would they themselves meet the same fate by association with him? He tries to soften the blow by saying that he will rise to new life. But that goes completely over their heads.

In the foregoing passage, and now, for the first time, Jesus informs his disciples that he will be handed over to the Gentiles, and that he will be mocked, whipped and killed. The storm continues unabated (Mark 4:35-38); the wild beasts are poised for attack. (Mark 1:13). The thought must have struck the disciples: why is he so steadfastly heading towards Jerusalem if his enemies there are waiting for him (the chief priests and teachers of the law, and the Gentiles), as he had kept reminding them. (Mark 3:22; 7:1, 5). The disciples can "see" just enough to be afraid. Jesus is leading them where they would rather not go. Thy cannot "see" the meaning or purpose of this. What is the sense of heading off to Jerusalem - and to death? Would this not spell the end of his mission, and theirs - and perhaps, lead to their own deaths too? It was only recently he told them that because they had given up everything for the "way" they would receive much more (fulfilment) in this life, and after that, eternal life. (10:29-30). Yet, they remained uncomprehending, fearful and alarmed. (Mark 4:40).

Jesus again uses the verb "hand over" which expresses the human treachery of Judas and the religious authorities, but also God's loving, redemptive purpose in handing over his Son to sinful humanity. (See 9:31; Romans 8:32). His passion will end in a glorious victory over death itself. To establish the reign of God over evil and death is ultimately the purpose of the "going up" and the "handing over."

Immediately following the third prediction of his passion, it appears that the disciples have not even begun to listen to Jesus.

## The Request of James and John

Then James and John, the sons of Zebedee came to Jesus. 'Teacher,' they said, 'there is something we want you to do for us.' 'What is it?' 'Jesus asked them? They answered, 'When you sit on your throne in your glorious kingdom, we want you to let us to sit with you, one at your right and the other at your left.' Jesus said to them, 'You don't know what you are asking. Can you drink the cup of suffering I must drink? Can you be baptized in the way I must be baptized?' 'We can,' they answered. Jesus said to them, 'You will indeed drink the cup I must drink, and be baptised in the way I must be baptised. But I do not have the right to choose who will sit at my right and my left. It is God who will give these places to those for whom he has prepared them.' (Mark 10:35-40, see Isaiah 51:17-23; Jeremiah 49:12).

Despite all that Jesus has said to his disciples about the true meaning and cost of discipleship, James and John want him to seat them next to himself in his "glorious kingdom." The kingdom they have in mind probably recalls that that of King David, with themselves sharing the throne with the new messianic warrior king. Whatever their expectations, they want all the gain, but none of the pain. In their preoccupation with self-promotion, the brothers think they can skip the cross and take a short cut to glory, forgetting that the only way to greatness is through service. (Mark 9:34-35; see 1 Corinthians 9:19; 2 Corinthians 4:5). The two disciples are obsessed with earthly power and glory–the "yeast of the Pharisees and Herod." For Jesus, power is equated with service. What the two disciples fail to see, is that, the path to true messianic glory must run through suffering and death, and only then, to resurrection, a matter about which Jesus had just been speaking. (10:33-34).

Jesus then asks the disciples if they can "drink the cup" he himself must drink. (10:38). In Biblical imagery, the "cup" refers to the fate that lies ahead for a suffering person. (Jeremiah 49:12). For Jesus, drinking the "cup" means accepting the full brunt of God's judgement on sin and evil, so that humanity may escape the consequences of such judgement. (Mark 14:36; see John 18:11). Jesus will drink the "cup." He then asks his disciples if they are willing to be united with him in his redemptive suffering by drinking the same cup. (See Colossians 1:24). The cup of his blood becomes the source of salvation to all who receive it. The "baptism" (immersion in water) mentioned in verse 38b is a metaphor for undergoing trials and dangers, as if passing through stormy, turbulent waters. (Psalm 42:8; 88:17-18; Isaiah 43:2).

The early Church understood Christian baptism as union with Christ in his death, by which believers die to their old self and begin a new life of union with him and in him. (Romans 6:4; Colossians 2:12). Thus, baptism and the Eucharist are the means through which Jesus' followers can be made worthy to share in his future glory.

Without realizing what they are letting themselves in for, James and John express a readiness to share in Jesus' fate. (v. 39a). Their desire for honour and glory is so great that the two disciples are actually willing to suffer along with Jesus – *if* Jesus will give them places to sit on his "right and left" in the kind of kingdom they think he will establish. The disciples are like the religious leaders and the civil power. The difference is that the latter people *have* honour, power, status, privilege and wealth and they want to keep them and use them to dominate others, while the disciples do not have these things and want to acquire them. They think that these will be the means of their salvation. Yet, these are the very things that represent the kind of life Jesus is asking James and John and the others to "lose" if they are to become true disciples of his. (Mark 10:21). The kind of life the disciples want is to gain the glory and honour that the world gives. (See Matthew 4:8-9). But they don't realize that this would be short-lived glory, whereas the glory God gives is eternal.

Jesus struggles to get the disciples to "see" that he himself is on a mission of service in order to oppose domination systems (rule of Satan), as his way to usher in the liberating reign of God. He is not seeking security for himself, but is willing to lose his life in confrontation with those who use power to dominate and oppress. How will he do this? The disciples, like most people of that time, can only "see" oppressive powers being successfully opposed by violence. Jesus, on the other hand, will oppose the powers by turning the other cheek to their violence, in other words, by loving and forgiving them. (See Matthew 5:39, 43).

As John the Baptist was handed over, Jesus too will be handed over to the powers. The disciples are not prepared to lose their lives in the face of persecution and death at the hands of the powers. Will they learn from this failure and resolve to follow Jesus after his death?

The "cup" is one of martyrdom. For the apostle James, this promise of drinking the same cup as Jesus will be fulfilled literally. But that was after the resurrection, when the disciples had received the enlightenment from God that honour and glory are the fruits of suffering service. (See Acts of the Apostles 12:2; John 13:14).

When the other ten disciples heard about this, they became angry with James and John. So Jesus called them all together to him and said, 'You know that among the pagans, their rulers lord it over (oppress) their people. This, however is not the way it is among you. If one of you wants to be great, he or she must be the servant of all the rest. The Son of Man did not come to be served, but to serve and to give his life to ransom many people.' (Mark 10:41-45; Matthew 20:17-28; Luke 24:21; see Philippians 2:3-4).

The seeking of human beings for honour and glory can lead to unhealthy rivalry. There will always be someone else who will want to deprive you of the glory you seek or have. This was the case among the disciples, because straight away, the others "became angry with James and John." (10:41). Seeking glory seats only leads to rivalry, enmity, division and strife – a kingdom divided into "fighting groups that will fall apart." The rule of Satan! (Mark 3:24). The alternative to that is the rule of God – Jesus' universal family, united through mutual service - the only true path to honour and glory. Jesus then talks about how the Gentiles operate - oppressing one another in their rivalry for glory. He reminds his disciples that this is not to be the way with them. Human beings should patiently wait for the honour and glory that only God can give them, which comes to them as they discharge their mission of stewardship. (Psalm 8:5-8). When Jesus is at the actual moment of his greatest glory, there will be people on his "right and left" – two criminals. Jesus' crowning honour and glory is at God's right hand, but only after his suffering service. (Acts of the Apostles 1:9). Then he shares that honour and glory with all those who follow him on his own "way" of service. (See Isaiah 53:11-12; Romans 8:32; Matthew 25:34-35).

In speaking of the rulers of the world lording it over their people (10:42), Jesus condemns the Roman emperor and the Jewish religious leaders. Instead of serving others, they use power and the threat of violence to secure and aggrandise themselves. Jesus was teaching his closest disciples, preparing them for their later role of leadership in his Kingdom. They still had to learn that true leaders do not indulge in the kind of rivalry which is evident in the Kingdom of Satan. The role of a leader, on the other hand, is to serve, because that is what unites people as in a family (kingdom of God). 'If one of you wants to be great, he or she must be the servant of all.' (10:44; see 9:35). True leadership is about using one's power like house servants or slaves, to serve without regard for status or rewards. It is the service of the shepherd who cares for everyone, especially the most vulnerable. It thus helps and empowers others. This is the kind of leadership and service the disciples have already witnessed in Jesus. (John 13:12-16; Philippians 2:2-9). St Paul looked on his apostleship as being a "slave" for his Christians. (1 Corinthians 9:19; 2 Corinthians 4:5). An unselfish life of service gives one a sense of meaning and purpose, through making a difference in the lives of other people.

In the foregoing passage, Jesus has given a full answer to the man of many possessions. (10:17-22).

## A Ransom for Many

> For even the Son of man himself came not to be served but to serve, and to give his life as a ransom for many. (Mark 10:45, NJB).

The "cup" Jesus will drink will be costly. It is a cup of service, i.e. giving his life "to ransom many people." (Mark 10:45). The word "many" is a translation of the Latin *multis*, meaning a great throng. In this context, it means everyone. Here, Jesus is now telling his disciples, not only that he will die, but *why* he will die. What does it mean to "ransom?" It was said that God ransomed his people from slavery in Egypt and in Babylon. Originally, to 'ransom' meant to buy the freedom of a slave or prisoner. It involved paying a price so that the slave might go free. (Leviticus 25:47-50; Deuteronomy 7:8; Isaiah 35:10). In the Old Testament, the hope persisted that God would definitively ransom his people from sin and evil. (Isaiah 25:8-9, 59:20; Psalm 33:24; 130:7-8).

Only in the passion of God's Son does it become clear how costly this is for God, who, through Jesus, pays the price for our rescue from the slavery of sin and death. In his explanation of the meaning of Jesus' passion, St. Paul equates "ransom" with being "set free." (See Romans 3:24; 1 Corinthians 7:23; Galatians 3:13; I Timothy 2:5-6). Jesus' "ransom for many" saying refers to the Suffering Servant in Isaiah's Fourth Servant Song. (52:13–53:12). In this passage, the suffering of an individual functions in a substitutionary sense, on behalf of "many," so that the "many" might escape the fate of the individual. "My servant will justify many by taking their guilt on himself (as a substitute). Hence, I shall give him a portion with the many... for having exposed himself to death and for being counted as one of the rebellious, whereas he was bearing the sins of the many and interceding for the rebellious." (Isaiah 53:10-12).

We must be clear that God is not demanding a blood sacrifice of his Son for the release of humanity from the slavery of evil and death. On the contrary, God himself is paying the price through the sufferings of his Son. Like Isaiah's suffering servant, he takes on board the guilt of rebellious humanity so that the "many" may be "justified," i.e. saved, made perfect. He dies as a substitute for them so that they might escape death. Why did Jesus have to be a ransom? Why did he have to die? It was God's way of showing his infinite love for humanity, loving us, not because we are good, but because we are sinners.

Jesus had to die because all true love is substitutionary sacrifice. For example, it costs nothing to love a person when everything is going smoothly and the person has no great needs. Substitutionary sacrifice is different. By all accounts, parents, for example, sacrifice themselves, through their love for a child who has serious health problems, or who may be incapacitated in some way. They love the child with a love greater than if the child was normal and healthy. The neediness of the child calls forth their deepest compassion. They sacrifice themselves so that every possible future good may accrue to their child. They substitute themselves through suffering service so that the suffering of the needy one might be alleviated. Parents, generally, sacrifice their time and freedom (as the price paid) so that their children may grow to responsible maturity. A failure to do so would mean that the children would grow up emotionally needy, vulnerable and dependent. So if the parent doesn't make the costly sacrifice at an early stage, the child will later suffer. Either the parent suffers temporarily in a redemptive way, or the child will suffer all of his or her life through emotional immaturity, and may become anti-social in a destructive way.

All life-changing love is a substitutionary sacrifice. It involves a person taking the pain now so that the other may escape, perhaps a worse pain later. It is human need and incapacity that call down the compassion of God into the world. (Mark 2:11; 6:34). God is infinitely more loving and compassionate than human beings. So in order for God to rescue humanity from suffering and death, he would need to make a substitutionary sacrifice. Through the death of Jesus on the cross, God takes on the pain, (pays the price), so that human beings may ultimately be rescued from the greatest pain of all, namely death itself. This represents Jesus' costly service to humanity. He is God's suffering servant. (See Isaiah 53).

It is human beings, through their disobedience of God, who bring untimely death into the world. (Genesis 2:16-17; 4:8). As God's Messiah, Jesus came to live among us in order to offer a perfect obedience to God. In obedience to the Father, Jesus willingly gives his life as an innocent victim. God then raises his faithful Son in triumph over death. Death, which is the consequence of disobedience, is thus destroyed. And because Jesus identifies with humanity (Mark 1:9), he takes us with him (ransom) through sharing with us his glorious victory over death, so that we would escape death and gain eternal life. God is thus revealed to human beings as love. He comes to live among us sinners and offers himself as a victim in order to liberate us (ransom) from our victimizing practices that lead to death. (Genesis 4:8).

The usual expectation in Israel was that you inflict death on your enemies in order to be liberated from them. Jesus said no to that particular delusion, a delusion from which people had to be ransomed. He would die for them so that they might be liberated from their death-dealing ways. At this stage of their journey, his disciples understood none of this.

Jesus is going up to Jerusalem to discharge his messianic role, something not in accord with the usual expectations, to which the disciples still cling, but according to a role outlined in Israel's Scriptures, especially in the suffering service songs of Isaiah. (Isaiah 41:8-10; 42:1-7; 50:4-10; 52:13-15 – 53). If James and John and the other disciples - and indeed all disciples everywhere – wish to enter and share in Jesus' glory, the only 'way' is to follow the Good Shepherd (John 10:11) and Suffering Servant, who lays down his life in service to humanity – so that he will "make many righteous." (Isaiah 53:11b, NRSVC).

## The Healing of Blind Bartimaeus

They came to Jericho, and as Jesus was leaving with his disciples and a large crowd, a blind beggar named Bartimaeus, son of Timaeus was sitting by the road. When he heard that it was Jesus of Nazareth, he began to shout, 'Jesus! Son of David! Take pity on me.' Many people scolded him and told him to be quiet. But he shouted even more loudly, 'Son of David, take pity on me.' Jesus stopped and said, 'Call him.' So they called the blind man. 'Cheer up,' they said. 'Get up,' he is calling you.' He threw off his cloak, jumped up and came to Jesus. 'What do you want me to do for you?' Jesus asked him. 'Teacher,' the blind man answered, 'I want to see again.' 'Go,' Jesus told him, 'your faith has made you well.' At once he was able to see and followed Jesus on the road. (Mark 10:46-52; see Isaiah 29:18-19, 35:5).

Jericho was an ancient city located about fifteen miles northeast of Jerusalem. Archaeologists have discovered settlements there dating back to 9,000 BC. Its population today is about 20,000.

Jesus was accompanied by his disciples and a large crowd, all of them heading towards Jerusalem for the feast of the Passover. (See Luke 19:1-10). The beginning of the journey was preceded by the healing of the blind man at Bethsaida. (Mark 8:22-28). Now at the end of the journey Jesus heals a blind man at Jericho. Positioned at the beginning and end of the journey, the two healings of blindness play a symbolic role, indicating Jesus' attempt to overcome the spiritual blindness of the disciples with respect to his true identity and mission.

In the Psalms, there is often a plea to God for "pity" – verse 47 above. (See Psalm 6:3; 25:16; 51:3; 86:16). The call to God for pity is a recognition of human need and inadequacy, because it is only God who can rescue us from spiritual blindness and bring us into his kingdom. (See Colossians 1:13; Revelation 21:4). Spiritual blindness is a block on faith. It prevents us from "seeing" Jesus and then faithfully following him on the road. (See Isaiah 42:18-20).

One of the promises associated with the coming of the Messiah was opening the eyes of the blind. (Isaiah 29:18; 35:5; see Luke 4:18). Blind Bartimaeus "sees" much more than the others accompanying Jesus, including his disciples. He could see who Jesus was ("Son of David") with the eye of faith, as the one whose need for "pity" would be met. (Isaiah 42:16). When Jesus will enter Jerusalem, the crowds will hail him as a royal "Son of David," i.e. as Messiah

This is the first time in Mark's gospel that the title "Son of David" has been applied to Jesus. Elsewhere, the New Testament affirms Jesus' descent from the line of David. (Matthew 1:1; Acts of the Apostles 3:20; Romans 1:3). As "Son of David," Jesus is the heir of God's promises to restore the kingdom of David and rule Israel forever. (2 Samuel 7:12-16; Psalm 89). However, the disciples could still only see the "Son of David" as a political Messiah. Jesus has already reminded them that this is a Satanic temptation. (Mark 8:33; see Matthew 4:8). Jesus interprets the prophecy of Samuel by connecting his messiahship with suffering service. (Mark 8:31; 9:30-32). Jesus will fulfil the prophecy of Samuel and "restore the kingdom of David" through his sufferings and death, as the only way to create a new universal Israel (kingdom of God) built around himself and his followers. He will rule over this kingdom forever, all the powers of darkness having been defeated.

The blind man threw off his cloak. (Verse 50). This can symbolize giving up everything he had, selling all for a life of following Jesus. He knew he had found all he needed. (Psalm 23:1). His faith was his new cloak, clothing him in the love, mercy and compassion of God. (See Mark 5:15). In following Jesus on the "road," he is contrasted with the man of many possessions, who could not throw away his comforting 'cloak' for the new inheritance promised to him by Jesus. (Mark 10:21; Romans 13:12; Ephesians 4:22; Colossians 3:8-9; Hebrews 12:1).

"What do you want me to do for you?" (Verse 51). That was the same question that Jesus asked James and John in the preceding episode. (Verse 36). Their answer (verse 37) revealed a self-centred ambition, indicating their spiritual blindness. Bartimaeus' request to "see again" highlights what the disciples so badly needed, but for which they failed to ask. The blind man's answer to Jesus revealed a very different outlook. He had no hidden agenda; he was open to the best that God could do for him, without being concerned about what that might be. He was prepared to follow Jesus in trust and hope. When the man of many possessions approached Jesus, he asked him what he himself could do. He didn't have the faith that God could give him all he needed, i.e. free him from his grieving and make him happy. (Mark 10:22).

Jesus said to the blind man, "Your faith has saved you." (10:52, NJB). His faith was the one thing that enabled the man to "see" who Jesus really was. Faith also leads to hope in God's power to do signs and wonders through Jesus. God's power could not work for the man of many possessions because he didn't have the faith to give up everything for a journey with Jesus. The Greek verb "save" can mean both to "heal" and "save," and recalls the eternal life Jesus has been revealing along the way. (Mark 8:35; 10:26, 30). The opening of the man's sight to the enlightenment of the truth of Jesus may have been of more significance for him than the healing of his physical sight.

After Bartimaeus was healed, he began to "follow Jesus on the road," suggesting that he may have become a disciple, and was probably known in the early Church. (Mark 10:52). The granting of physical sight to him symbolizes the true insight which is necessary for a disciple. The formerly blind man is following Jesus on the road, while his chosen disciples are stumbling, never having thrown of their old "cloaks."

In his healing of the blind man, Jesus may be issuing a challenge to the disciples concerning their own blindness. He has so far failed to get them to open their eyes, so that they might begin to see him as the true heir to the Davidic promises, and to follow him more faithfully. They have left all to follow him, but they are still attached to the human values of saving and serving themselves – "the yeast of the Pharisees." (Mark 8:14-21). They are still blind to Jesus' vision – his call to "sell all," to accept the role of being "least" and devote their lives to the service of bringing spiritual insight to others, in imitation of the "pity" of Jesus. (9:35). He will soon ask them to keep "watch," to wake up to the self-serving "yeast of the Pharisees and the yeast of Herod." They are struggling to open their eyes to the necessity of Jesus' suffering service and their own part in it as disciples. (Mark 13:23, 35-37; 14:37-38, 40). Jesus will soon tell them that following God's way will entail persecution. (Mark 13:9).

We could take the blind man as a model for our faith journey. Can we become like him: blind beggars who need to keep shouting (10:47) to the Lord for help as Jesus passes by, so that we may see him more clearly and follow him more faithfully? Faith helps us to see life, not as self-serving (9:34; 10:37), but with the eyes of God (8:34-35) - as costly service. Following Jesus on the road to Jerusalem is a call to live like him and to do what he himself is doing.

CHAPTER 1 5

# THE LORD COMES TO HIS TEMPLE

## The King-Messiah Enters his City

The blind man, Bartimaeus was able to see Jesus as the Messiah promised to Israel. The Messiah now enters his city in order to accomplish his role as Messiah. With Jesus' entry to Jerusalem, the final events of his life take place, compressed into one week in Mark's gospel, thus giving rise to the Christian liturgical tradition of Holy Week.

This part of Mark's gospel has the character of a denouement, in all its aspects. We now begin to get a glimpse of where the story is going. Jesus' messianic visitation of the city heralds an end to temple sacrifice and its teaching authority. The royal visitor who comes riding a donkey (Mark 11:7) is one who manifests an authority greater than the temple, one who prophesises its destruction. (13:2). This is followed by the announcement of the universal mission of the gospel (13:10), the end of the world (13:25), and the coming of the Son of Man in glory to "gather God's chosen people from one end of the world to the other." (13:27).

In the time of Jesus, the population of Jerusalem was about 40,000. But during the great annual festivals, especially the Passover, there was a tripling of the normal population. This means that there were large crowds of Jews from the diaspora in Jerusalem when Jesus entered the city.[132]

It is a long hard climb from Jericho to Jerusalem. (Mark 10:46) Jericho is the lowest city on earth, over 800 feet below sea level. Jerusalem, which is only about twelve miles distant, is nearly 3,000 feet above sea level. The road goes through hot, dry desert all the way to the top of the Mount of Olives, at which point, one suddenly gets the first glimpse of the temple and city. Pilgrims from Galilee would be coming along with Jesus to the place where God had chosen to live with his people, assuring Israel of fellowship with himself and forgiveness through the daily temple sacrifices. Coming now to celebrate the feast of the Passover, this was freedom time, recalling the liberation of the Israelites from Egyptian slavery. There would be singing, prayers, feasting. For the followers of Jesus, this would also be Kingdom time. God's sovereign presence in the temple would be revealed in a new way, and the focus would be on Jesus himself as the King, now coming to liberate the whole of humanity from the slavery of sin and death.

---

[132] Mary Healy, *The Gospel of Mark*, (Baker Academic, Grand Rapids, Michigan), 2008, p. 221.

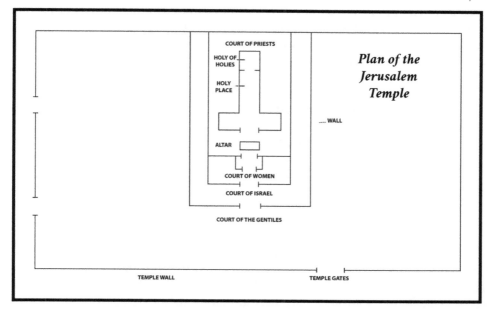

Before the time of King Herod the Great, the Jerusalem temple was the small temple which was built after the Jews returned from the Babylonian exile in 537 BC. Shortly before the birth of Jesus, Herod began the task of enlarging it to an area of 35 acres, most of it comprising open-air courtyards. The sanctuary, which was only entered by the priests, was small, but highly decorated. The retaining walls of the temple plaza rested on blocks of limestone so large that archaeologists are unable to explain how they were moved into place. The eastern wall of the platform, built up from the bottom of the hill, towered more than 300 ft. in height. Few things on earth looked more permanent and indestructible than the Jerusalem temple. The sanctuary was surrounded by a series of courts, each with strict rules of access. One of the smaller inner courts surrounding the sanctuary building was reserved for Jewish women, the other for Jewish men. The much larger outer court was reserved for Gentiles, who were not allowed into the inner courts. It was in the outer court that currency was exchanged and animals bought and sold for the temple sacrifices. Jews from the diaspora would have had to exchange Greek or Roman currency into Jewish coins. Part of the outer court was reserved for teaching. This large outer court was part of the temple and was intended as a place of prayer for Gentiles. (Isaiah 56:7). The different courts symbolized separation – priests from people, men from women, Jews from Gentiles. As far as Jesus was concerned, the money-changers and merchants were profaning the temple, which had become a marketplace for material gain, from which the temple authorities benefited. (See John 2:16).

It was always expected of a would-be Messiah-King, that he would go to Jerusalem, fight the battle against the forces of evil and get enthroned as the rightful king of Israel, and then take charge of the temple. But for Jesus, it would be a different kind of battle, a different throne and a different kind of king.[133] Both John the Baptist and Jesus

---

[133] N. T. Wright, *Jesus and the Victory of God,* (SPCK), 1996, p. 539.

had offered a baptism of forgiveness independently of the temple, while Jesus probably saw the temple as symbolic of the marginalization and exclusion of the poor, rather than the all-embracing union he wanted to create.

> Rejoice heart and soul, daughter of Zion!
> Shout with gladness, daughter of Jerusalem!
> See now, your king comes to you;
> he is victorious, he is triumphant,
> humble and riding on a donkey.
> He will banish war chariots from Israel
> and horses from Jerusalem;
> the bow of war will be banished.
> He will proclaim peace for the nations.
> His empire will stretch from sea to sea,
> from the River to the ends of the earth. (Zechariah 9:9-10, JB)

Pilgrims heading for Jerusalem always walked. But when a king of Israel was about to be crowned, he always rode a donkey in procession into Jerusalem. He thus entered his capital city to take possession of it. Jesus' triumphal entry to Jerusalem as a king riding a colt (Mark 11:7) fulfils the above prophecy of Zedekiah, the donkey or colt symbolizing his inclusive kingdom of Justice and peace. In thus entering Jerusalem, Jesus must have been conscious of the messianic claim to the city and its temple. He must have seen his entry as laying claim to David's throne - symbolizing God returning to become king of the nations. He is a King coming in peace, not as a warrior mounted on a war horse and leading a rebellion against Rome – as some people expected, or wanted. (See 1 Kings 1:32-34, 44). This King defies all expectation, He is coming to accept his crown of thorns and enthronement on a cross. That would be *his* way of bringing peace to the nations and establishing his rule to the ends of the earth. (Verse 10 above; Matthew 21:1-11; Luke 19:28-40; John 12:12-29).

To spread cloaks and lay down branches on the road was a gesture of homage to a newly-crowned king. (Mark 11:8; See 2 Kings 9:13). "The people in the front and those who followed were all shouting, 'Hosanna! Blessed is he who comes in the name of the Lord! Blessed is the coming kingdom of David our father. Hosanna in the highest heavens!'" (Mark 11:9-10, NJB). The Hosannas (in Hebrew, meaning "save us," chanted by the crowd are from Psalm 118:25-26. Jesus must have known that the acclaim of the crowds, their palm branches and their hosannas, only signalled their misunderstanding of the kind of king he had in mind: a suffering servant, a shepherd laying down his life for his flock in order to rescue and save them.

Jesus comes to Jerusalem in God's name to accomplish a salvation greater than that celebrated by the Passover festival, which recalled the freeing of the Hebrew tribes from Egypt. As the fulfilment of the ancient Passover, Jesus has a universal salvation in mind – "from the River to the ends of the earth." He will perfectly accomplish the will of the Father that all people will be liberated from the power of Satan, no longer putting their trust in war chariots and bows and arrows. (Zechariah 9:10 above; see Isaiah 11:5-

7). In Jesus, we find majesty combined with humility, sovereignty with submission, trust and dependence on God.

"They shall reach Jerusalem with gladness, singing and shouting for joy. They will be happy for ever, for ever free from sorrow and grief." (Isaiah 35:10). God, in the person of Jesus, has now returned to Jerusalem as King, in fulfilment of Isaiah's prophecy. Jesus' triumphal entry to the city with his liberated people presages the permanent return of humanity from exile, and it would ultimately bring a happiness that would last for ever, the end of crying and grief. (Revelation 21:4). Therefore, this was a time for rejoicing and feasting (a new Passover), to celebrate the marriage of the King's son to his people (Matthew 22:1-13), symbolizing renewal of the Covenant, forgiveness of sins and union with God.

The procession of entry ended with nothing happening–or not just yet. "Jesus entered Jerusalem, went into the temple and looked round at everything. But since it was already late in the day, he went out to Bethany with the disciples." (Mark 11:11). Bethany was situated on the Mount of Olives, on the east side of Jerusalem, where Jesus and his disciples may have lodged during the days leading up to the festival of the Passover.

In looking round at everything in the temple, it is unlikely that Jesus was impressed by its great stones and buildings. It might be a magnificent monument, but what of its use? What was it meant to symbolize? And was it living up to what God expected of it? It is likely that Jesus saw it as symbolizing all that was wrong in Israel. God promised his blessing of peace and union to all nations, through Abraham and his descendants, but this promise remained unfulfilled in an Israel of separations and exclusions a house "divided into fighting groups." (See Mark 3:24-25). The way in which the temple was being used made a mockery of its purpose as a prayerful place to draw the Gentiles to the worship of God.

The Jewish historian Josephus tells us that in the Passover week of one particular year, 255,000 lambs were bought, sold and sacrificed in the outer courtyard of the temple. Yet, this area was the place which was supposed to have been a house of prayer for the Gentiles, but in fact, was given over to commercial activity and profiteering. All of the temple courtyards symbolized separation – official Israel separated from the ordinary people, many of whom were classed as outcasts and sinners and who were not allowed into the temple, because they were regarded as 'unclean.' Jesus came to the temple to see if it was bearing the fruit of God's love and blessing. He would pass judgement on it appropriately. Such a visitation in judgement was foretold by the prophet Malachi. "And suddenly there will come to the temple the Lord whom you seek… But who will endure the day of his coming? And who can stand when he appears? For he is like the refiner's fire." (Malachi 3:1-2).

For the moment, Mark leaves us in suspense as to what will happen when this King makes his presence felt in his city and house of prayer. In Mark chapter 10, Jesus redefines kingship, revealing the kind of king he would be – a suffering servant. This would not be the kind of royalty to which Israel or the rest of the world were accustomed. How could they possibly see their king as a suffering servant?

## The Cleansing of the Temple

> The next day as they were coming back from Bethany, Jesus was hungry. He saw in the distance a fig tree covered with leaves, so he went to see if he could find any figs on it. But when he came to it, he found only leaves, because it was not the right time for figs. Jesus said to the fig tree, 'No one shall ever eat figs from you again!' And his disciples heard him. (Mark 11:12-14; Matthew 21:18-19).

There are passages from the Old Testament which speak of God looking to fruit trees for fruitfulness, but not finding it. (Isaiah 5:1-7). In the writings of the prophets, Israel is often symbolized by figs or a fig tree, with the God-given task of producing the fruit of righteousness and justice. (Jeremiah 24:1-8; 29:17; Hosea 9:10). "I wanted to gather my people, as a farmer gathers a harvest; but they are like a vine with no grapes, like a fig tree with no figs. Even the leaves have withered. Therefore, I have allowed outsiders to take over the land." (Jeremiah 8:13; see Matthew 23:37-38). The fig tree incident may be a metaphor for the fruit of righteousness, justice and mercy, which God expected from his people Israel, but did not find it. So judgement would follow. (Verse 14 above).

The fruitless fig tree represents the Israel which should have repented of its sins – as requested by John the Baptist, and have welcomed its Messiah when he came among them (Luke 2:7). But instead, the leading people saw Jesus as a threat to their status and privileges and their whole way of life. They had no room for him in the inn of their hearts. They cast him out of their vineyard as a victim. (See Mark 12:8). Jesus' words to the fruitless fig tree may be an acted parable of God's judgement on Israel and the temple for their unjust practices–producing only metaphorical weeds and thorns. (Genesis 3:18; Jeremiah 8:13; Hosea 2:14). The fig tree's lack of fruit signifies the absence of faith and prayer that Jesus finds in the temple. (Mark 11:17-18). When Jesus comes to the heart of Israel's life, he is rejected. So judgement would fall on Israel. The phrase, "no one shall ever eat figs from you again" was a prophecy that Israel's sacrifices and fruitless temple worship would come to an end. The parable of the fig tree serves to explain the meaning of what Jesus will do in the temple when he returns there from his first night in Bethany.

According to the prophet Isaiah, the temple was supposed to be a place where God would teach the nations about his will, "no longer doing what their stubborn hearts tell them." (Jeremiah 3:17; see Psalm 105:1; Isaiah 2:2-3; 56:6-7). Ever since the time of the prophets, Israel however, had failed in its God-given mission to do the will of God and be a light to the nations. (Isaiah 42:6; 49:6; 60:3). Israel had not been obedient to its God-given mission. It was "hiding its light under a tub." (Mark 4:21; Matthew 5:14-15, Luke 11:33, JB). The mission given to Israel would be fulfilled by the death of the Messiah, who would offer God a perfect obedience. The temple was supposed to be a place of reverence and awe before God – filled with the singing of psalms of praise and the teaching of God's word. (Nehemiah 8:1; Psalm 27:4; 48;10; 100:4). Instead of being a light to the nations, it symbolized separation, cutting Israel off from her neighbours, viewing the neighbour as an enemy. So the temple couldn't be a house of prayer for all peoples (11:17), even if purged by Jesus. He would soon foretell its destruction (13:2), which actually happened in 70 AD, a fact already known to Mark's readers.

> So they reached Jerusalem and he went into the Temple and began to drive out the men selling and buying there; he upset the tables of the money-changers and the seats of the dove sellers. Nor would he allow anyone to carry anything through the Temple. And he taught them and said, 'Does not scripture say: that God said, *'My house will be called a house of prayer for all peoples?* But you have turned into a *bandit's den.'* This came to the ears of the chief priests and the scribes, and they tried to find some way of doing away with him; they were afraid of him because the people were carried away by his teaching. And when evening came, he went out of the city. (Mark 11:15-19, NJB; Matthew 21:12-17; Luke 19:45-48, John 2:13-22).

The first quotation (in italics) in the above passage comes from Isaiah 56:7. It forms the climax of a sequence in which the Lord promises to bring foreigners to "my sacred hill and give them joy in my house of prayer." The second part of the quotation comes from Jeremiah 7:1-15, in which the prophet names the corrupt temple of his day a "den of bandits" because of the social injustice and idolatry practiced by the people. In quoting the prophets, Jesus states God's intention for the temple from the beginning, but the religious authorities have frustrated the divine intent, first of all by allowing commercial activity to ruin the court of the Gentiles, and secondly, because of the division of the house of God into an inner section for the "holy" (Israel) and an outer for the "unholy" (Gentiles). Elsewhere in Mark's gospel we have seen Jesus' overcoming of the "holy/unholy" barrier along with his casting out of demons, suggesting that such divisions have something of the demonic in them. For the same reason, he criticises the food laws and clean/unclean, as markers of separation. (Mark 7:14-15).

Jesus' cleansing of the temple was symbolic, and it had royal connotations. King David planned the original temple. His successor, King Solomon built it. The king was always the one who had authority over the temple. It was to him was granted the task of builder and reformer. Kings Hezekiah and Josiah of Judah cleansed the temple of their day of pagan worship. (2 Kings 18:4; 23:4). Jesus' driving out the money changers and sellers of doves and animals echoes the driving out of demons in Mark's Gospel. (1:12, 34, 39; 3:15, 22, 23; 6:13; 7:26; 9:18).

In his action of cleansing and speaking out against the corruption of the temple, Jesus was being true to his prophetic tradition, especially that of Jeremiah. What did Jesus have in mind? "Jesus was offering a sign of forthcoming destruction, and the present corruption of the temple served as warrant for this."[134] In other words, his action in the temple was an acted parable of its destruction. Jesus would have seen himself as a prophet like the prophets of old who pronounced judgement on the temple of their day, i.e. before the Babylonian exile. (Jeremiah 19:1-11; Isaiah 20:1-6; Ezekiel 4:1-17). Unless Israel repented of its sins, the temple would be destroyed by the pagans. Rome would be the agent of God's judgement, because of the failure of Israel to enact justice within its society

---

[134] N. T. Wright, *Jesus and the Victory of God*, p. 414.

and within the temple system itself. Jesus' action of driving out the money changers and those involved in the sale of animals, had the effect of temporarily disrupting the sacrificial system, prefiguring the temple's demise. (Mark 11:15). Here, Jesus is clearing the temple *for* foreigners. The prophets were critical of temple sacrifices as insincere as long as official Israel presided over an unjust and corrupt society, ignoring and disobeying their God-given mission of caring. God liberated them from Egypt and instituted his covenant of love, to which they promised obedience. But they only offered lip-service to God. Time and again, the prophets told them that obedience to the will of God was more important than animal sacrifices in the temple. (Hosea 5:5-7; Amos 5:21-24; Isaiah 1:11-16; Jeremiah 7:21-26).

When Jesus came back to the temple on his second day in Jerusalem, he probably brought a crowd of supporters with him in order to carry out what he had already planned to do. Upsetting the tables of the money changers (11:15) was a symbolic commentary on economic exploitation - the profiteering on donations, taxes, currency exchange rates and the sale of animals for the temple sacrifices. All of this activity was controlled by the chief priests who lived lives of luxury. The priestly aristocracy owned large estates on which they raised animals to be sold for the temple sacrifices. Archaeological investigations have revealed the chief priests' luxurious residences ("mansions" in the words of the archaeologists who uncovered them in the 1970s), showing how elegant their lifestyles had become.[135] Having been placed in charge of the temple by their Roman overlords, these people enjoyed considerable benefits from the booming pilgrim offerings and temple revenues. It was different for the members of the priestly families who lived in the countryside and served their weekly stints of temple duty. These latter enjoyed none of the luxury of the chief priests, however much they may have envied their lifestyle. Because the chief priests were seen as agents of imperial Rome, they could never lead Israel to a renewal of life. Roman officials could appoint them to office or depose them at will.

These people were behaving like the past kings of Israel, feeding themselves rather than their flock. Israel, through its leadership, was faltering in its mission to lead the world in the worship of God. (See Psalm 105:1; Isaiah 2:2-3; Jeremiah 3:17). The temple had sold out to Mammon (the god of money), and to Mars (the god of war), it having become a "bandit's den" (Mark 11:17). The Greek word *lestes*, translated 'bandit,' denotes a freedom fighter, or a rebel against Rome. Jesus was critical of the use of the temple as a final hiding place for rebels fighting against Rome – as was the case in 70 AD.

Israel had failed in its vocation to be a light to the nations. (Genesis 12:3). Jesus himself, as the new Israel of God, would fulfil what Israel of old had failed to do. As the renewed Israel (himself and his followers), he would truly be a light to the nations. (John 8:12). He would fulfil God's promises of blessing to all nations through Abraham. (Genesis 22:18). As the renewed Israel and new temple, Jesus would be the place where people everywhere could henceforth come to their God in prayer, and receive forgiveness and reconciliation, which was the original role of the temple. (John 2:21; Hebrews 9:11). Jesus' new "house of prayer for all peoples" will comprise the communities of believers from all nations. Through Jesus, the forgiving victim, God has washed away their unholiness and

---

[135] Horsley & Silberman, *The Message of the Kingdom,* (Fortress Press), p. 78.

made them one united people by the cleansing power of the Spirit. St. Paul says that our bodies are temples of the Holy Spirit who lives in us by the grace of God. (1 Corinthians 6:19-20). But our hearts may be cluttered with pursuits and practices that distract us from pursuing our mission to be a light to the nations. Like the temple, we may need cleansing.

Jesus' action in the temple represents his final challenge to official Israel, bringing into focus the question of his authority, and setting in motion the events that would lead to his trial and execution. (Mark 14:58). Because it was such a sensational event, Jesus' action drew large crowds to the outer temple courtyard, anxious to hear every word of his teaching, a fact which further inflamed the jealousy and resentment of the religious leaders. These were the crowds, who by their presence around Jesus, prevented the authorities from arresting him, until a better opportunity arose. (Mark 14:2).

> When evening came, Jesus and his disciples left the city. Early the next morning, as they walked along the road, they saw the same fig tree. It was dead all the way down to its roots. Peter remembered what had happened and said to Jesus, 'Look, Teacher, the fig tree you cursed has died!' Jesus answered them, 'Have faith in God. I assure you that whoever tells this hill to get up and throw itself in the sea, and does not doubt in his heart, but believes that what he says will happen, it will be done for him.' (Mark 11:19-23).

In placing the cleansing of the temple account between the first and second fig tree episodes, Mark wants to associate the barren fig tree with the temple.

Why was Jesus expecting fruit on a fig tree in springtime? There are two kinds of fruit on some species of fig trees. As the leaves start to come in spring, the branches can bear little nodules which are good to eat. If a fig tree has leaves, but none of these nodules, it is a sign that the tree is diseased or dying. With the temple in mind, Jesus uses this as a parable of false and dying worship. Like the fig tree, the temple would meet its fate in death. Another more fruitful tree must take its place. The cross is that fruitful tree, producing a fruit that gives us life into eternity. The prophet Ezekiel had a vision of the new temple (built after the return of the Jewish exiles from Babylon), from which flowed a river with trees along its banks, bearing fruit all year round. (Ezekiel 47:1-12; see Mark 11:13). Ezekiel's fruitful temple is fulfilled in Jesus.

## Jesus' Teaching on Prayer

Jesus wants to reassure his disciples, who were shaken by his judgement on the temple. So he responds to them with a short teaching on faith, prayer and forgiveness. (Mark 11:22-25). He wants to deepen their faith so that they may learn to trust in God's sovereignty over events in this world. God can deal with the tragedy of the barren temple, symbolized by the withered fig tree. God can raise up metaphorical withered trees (ourselves) and bring them to newness of life again. (See Ezekiel 17:22-24).

In responding to their shock over the dead fig tree, "Jesus answered them, 'Have faith in God. I assure you that whoever tells this hill to get up and throw itself in the sea, and does not doubt in his heart, but believes that what he says will happen, it will be done for him.'" (Mark 11:22-23). In asking his disciples to have faith, Jesus is reminding them that petitionary prayer can only be effective in the context of faith, which is about having a trusting relationship with God, believing that our prayers become aligned with the good he desires for us. We often want instant fixes to our woes. We want God to move our troublesome "hills into the sea," and when that doesn't happen, we may lose faith in the goodness of God. That we should expect God to respond to us with miracles every time we are in deep trouble, shows how little faith we have. Our earthly journey is a time of testing and waiting for God to act in his own good time, to give us what we *need*. (Psalm 23:1). Faith means trusting that God will ultimately put everything right, which is something we ourselves cannot do, no more than we can move hills into the sea. The transformation wrought in humanity by the life, death and resurrection of Jesus may be comparable to moving a hill into the sea. (Mark 11:23). Jesus reveals a God who wants an end to all kinds of pain and suffering. God's promises, are fulfilled in Jesus. We are like the barren, lifeless fig tree. God gives us new life by raising Jesus from death, with the promise of our own resurrection too. The hill of death is thus removed and thrown into the sea. That, above all, is what we need. (Psalm 23:1). That is what fills us with hope. God may want to test and strengthen our faith when we are sorely troubled. "Be glad about this, even though it may be necessary for you to be sad for a while, because of the many kinds of trials you suffer. The purpose of these is to prove that your faith is genuine." (The First Letter of Peter, verses 3-9).

Our life in this world is bound up with the cross, which we are called to carry along with Jesus. But along with him, we will be raised to the fullness of life in which there will be no more tears, and death itself abolished. Waiting for this fullness is a serious challenge to our faith and hope. But if we don't believe in the sovereignty of God, i.e. a God who can, and will, ultimately put everything right, then we must ask ourselves if we believe in God at all. Yes, praying with this long-term faith and hope is very difficult. Our best approach to prayer when faced with innocent suffering in ourselves or in our loved ones, is to leave in God's hands, events over which we have no control, and allow him to deal with them in his own time and wisdom. And then, so that we don't fall into despair, we should pray for the courage and strength to face our troubles with hope. (Psalm 23:4). Our faith may not be even as big as a mustard seed. (Matthew 17:20, 21:21-22). This shows how little we ourselves can do compared with what God can accomplish in us. It is God who moves the metaphorical hills into the sea, in his own way and time. Jesus asks his disciples to pray like children, trusting that the Father hears them and will answer their prayers. Jesus himself is the model for prayer that is answered, because of his total surrender to his Father's will. (Mark 14:36; Luke 22:42; Matthew 6:8-10; 26:39; 1 John 3:22; 5:14-15).

The failure to forgive may be an obstacle to prayer. "And when you stand and pray, forgive anything you may have against anyone, so that your Father in heaven will forgive the wrongs you have done." (Mark 11:25; See CCC 2734-2737).

In his instruction on prayer, Jesus reminds his disciples that all the functions of the temple – faith, prayer and forgiveness, are to be carried out in relationships between people themselves, wherever they are, temple or no temple. The purpose of prayer is to draw us closer to God. Through our prayer - inspired by Scripture, and our willingness to forgive one another - Jesus is drawing us to himself, to his love, to his own trust in God, to his forgiveness of us who turned him into a victim, so that, like him, we may be empowered to walk the same path as himself. He hands himself over to us, so that, over time, we can become more like him.

## God's Vineyard Handed over to Other Tenants

With his arrival in Jerusalem, Jesus would have seen his ministry coming to a climax. He is therefore no longer concerned about the consequences of his actions, or with hiding the meaning of his teaching from the religious authorities. He thus speaks openly to the scribes, Pharisees and the chief priests.

Following their observation of the dead fig tree, Jesus and his disciples are once again back in the temple. Then a new round of conflict with the religious authorities takes place, focused on Jesus' authority, and arising from his action in the temple.

> They came to Jerusalem again, and as Jesus was walking in the temple, the chief priests, the scribes and the elders came to him and they said to him, 'What authority have you for acting like this. Or who gave you authority to act like this?' (Mark 11:27-28, NJB).

These are the three groups Jesus had prophesied would kill him. (Mark 8:31). Now they challenge his authority. They try to force him to admit that they had not authorized his actions.

In the early chapters of the gospel, Jesus' authority was what most impressed people in Galilee. (Mark 1:22, 27; 2:10; 3:15). Now the authority with which he taught and healed has turned into authority over the temple, the highest institution in Israel. (See Mark 14:55-64). Jesus has already provided the answer to the above groups: he is the beloved Son sent by the Father (Mark 1:11; 9:7, 37). He came into this world, only to find that those to whom God had given authority, had abused that authority. He is King and Messiah in the line of David. The King has authority over Israel and the temple. He is the "master of the house" (Mark 13:35), i.e. the temple.

The questioning of Jesus regarding his authority prompts a number of discussions within the temple, which take place in a single day. (Mark 11:27–13:1). These conflicts further unveil Jesus' identity and the source of his authority. He now returns to teaching through a parable.

In the parable of the Tenants in the Vineyard Jesus speaks directly to the chief priests, reminding them of the manner in which they have behaved as tenants of the Lord's vineyard. (Mark 12:1-9; Matthew 21:33-46; Luke 20:9-19). The parable of the Tenants is foreshadowed in Isaiah's Song of the Vineyard. (Isaiah 5:1-7). Isaiah composed what he called a love song about God planting Israel like a vineyard, watching over it, hoping it would produce good fruit, but eventually discovering only metaphorical sour grapes.

As a background to this parable, Jesus may have had in mind the social situation in the Israel of his day. In the time of Jesus, the Herodians and the priestly aristocracy in Jerusalem had become great landowners through confiscation of indebted property, which once belonged to people in the rural villages. This had reduced the former owners to the status of sharecroppers, i.e. paying part of their crops as rent to the owners.[136] It often led to violence between the tenants and the collecting agents of the absentee landlords. Thus, a situation was created which resulted in oppression, division and enmity – a society that would eventually collapse. (See Mark 3:24-26). In this parable, Jesus pointedly reminds the great landowners (embodying official Israel) that they are only "tenants." God is the only true proprietor of the vineyard (the land of Israel). It is he who planted it. (Mark 12:1). and he will call to account those who lay claim to its ownership, and who see themselves as accountable only to themselves. They have rejected God and decided to cultivate on their own, in any way they like. (See Genesis 3:6).

God rented his vineyard out to Israel, in the expectation that Israel would produce the good fruits of justice, forgiveness and reconciliation in its society. (Mark 12:1; see Genesis 2:15; Isaiah 5:1-7). But the leaders whom God put in charge of his vineyard only produced "sour grapes." (See Isaiah 5:4). Jesus' critique of the religious leaders concerns the way they were falling short of what they should have been from the beginning of the foundation of Israel. God called Israel out of Egypt so that its people might build the kind of nation that God wanted (Deuteronomy 10:18-19). This would be a nation that did not victimize anyone, that cared for widows and orphans, that did not create outcasts or marginalize people, the effects of which were visible in enmity and disunion. (See Exodus 21:22-24; Zechariah 7:10; Isaiah 1:16-17). The disunity within Israel was a sign of its disobedience of God. It was a refusal of its mission of caring. (Genesis 2:15). This means that Israel could not be a model for the universal union of humanity, which was its vocation from the time of Abraham, the man of obedience. (Genesis 22:18). The current leaders of Israel had constructed a society based on exclusions and the casting out of victims. This was in the tradition of their forefathers, who killed the prophets whom God sent to them to warn them about their failure to create a just, merciful and all-inclusive society. (Mark 12:5).

When the time came to gather the grapes, the owner of the vineyard sent his servants (the prophets) to receive his share of the harvest (good fruits), i.e. to see if the tenants had discharged their vocation of caring stewardship. (Mark 12:2). But the tenants turned deaf ears to his servants. They seized the servants, beat one, killed another, and stoned another. Others who were sent again were treated the same way. (Mark 12:1-5; see Isaiah 5:7b).

> The owner of the vineyard still had someone left: his beloved Son. He sent him to them last of all, thinking, 'They will respect my Son.' But those tenants said to each other, 'This is the heir. Come on, let us kill him and the inheritance will be ours!' So they seized him and killed him and threw him out of the vineyard. Now what will the owner of the vineyard do? He will come and make an end of the tenants and give the vineyard to others. 'Have you not read this text of Scripture: *The stone which the builders rejected has become the cornerstone; this is the Lord's doing, and we marvel at it?'* And they would have liked to arrest him, because they

---

[136] Horsley & Silberman, *The Message of the Kingdom*, (Fortress Press), p. 28-29).

realized that the parable was directed at them. But they were afraid of the crowds. So they left him and went away. (Mark 12:6:12, NJB; see Matthew 23:29-36). The sentence in italics is a quote from Psalm 118:22-23.

In the Old Testament, the prophets whom God sent to Israel were repeatedly ignored. (2 Kings 17:13-14; Jeremiah 7:25-26; 25:4-5). They were mistreated and persecuted (2 Chronicles 36:15-16) and killed (1 Kings 19:10; Luke 13:34-35). The prophet Zechariah was stoned in the temple courts. (2 Chronicles 24:20-22; see Matthew 29:35). Jeremiah was scourged and put in the stocks (Jeremiah 20:2). Who then will God send to these tenants? As a prophet, Jesus would be killed, but he is more than a prophet. He is the beloved Son whom God sent to the tenants last of all. Mark's readers know what this means: Jesus is the Messiah, the Son of God, proclaimed as such in his baptism (1:11), at his transfiguration (9:7) and confirmed as such in Gethsemane. (Mark 14:36).

The Parable of the Tenants expresses the reckless love of the Father. God remains merciful in face of human disobedience and defiance. He is willing to trust human beings with the work of his hands, expecting that they will faithfully discharge their mission of stewardship of creating and caring. (Genesis 1:28; 2:15). "They will respect my son" – the foolishness of divine love!

The phrase, "last of all" is a reminder that the coming of Jesus signifies the fullness of time (see Mark 1:15), the time of the accomplishment of God's plan of salvation. "Come let us kill him" echoes the plan of the sons of Jacob to kill their brother Joseph. (Genesis 37:20). Like them, the religious leaders are plotting against Jesus, their own brother Jew. (Mark 3:6; 11:18; see Genesis 4:8).

The parable depicts Jesus as the heir to the vineyard of Israel, and the religious leaders as the usurpers who have abused their stewardship and greedily taken control of the vineyard for their own gain. The religious leaders have betrayed their sacred task of building God's kingdom. And they were deluding themselves about their involvement in violence, seeing that they will soon seize the Son and kill him. (Mark 12:8). Jesus' criticism of the religious leaders is made out of pain, ending in his great cry: 'Jerusalem, Jerusalem! You kill the prophets and stone the messengers God has sent to you! How many times have I wanted to put my arms around all your people, just as a hen gathers her chicks under her wings, but you would not let me! And so your temple will be abandoned and empty.' (Matthew 23:37-38). The heirs of Moses should have known the terrible way in which human societies work - basing their social order on victimization. They had betrayed their God-given task of constructing the kingdom of God. They were unfaithful to the covenant. They had become like the oppressive rulers of empires. They presided over a divided kingdom, one based on exclusions. This was a kingdom that would fall. (Mark 3:24-26).

Their ancestors rejected the prophets, and the tenants are now about to reject the Son. 'What then will the owner of the vineyard do?' asked Jesus. The vineyard will be taken from them and given to other tenants (the apostles and the Gentiles), who will give the Lord his share of the harvest, in terms of works of justice and mercy. (Luke 22:28-30; Mark 3:14). Isaiah 5:1-7 is fulfilled in Mark 12:1-9. The "tenants" will bear the brunt of God's judgement in 70 AD. Their city and State will be destroyed by the army of Rome –

a case of the wild animals once again trampling over the vineyard. (See Isaiah 5:5).

Jesus explains the parable with a quotation (in italics) from Psalm 118:22 about the stone (Jesus) which the builders (official Israel) rejected as worthless. But this stone will now become the foundation stone of a new temple, not built by hands (Mark 12:10; see 14:58), which Jesus will construct around himself and his followers. St. Paul says that Jesus is the one who holds the whole building together and makes it grow. In union with him, "we are being built together with all the others into a place where God lives and accepts us as his children, thus uniting us to God (the original purpose of the temple) through his Spirit." (Ephesians 2:20-22; see 1 Peter 2:5). Psalm 118 was often quoted by the early Church in interpreting Jesus' passion. (See Matthew 21:44; Luke 29:17; Acts 4:11; 1 Peter 2:7). Psalm 118 was a pilgrimage hymn sung by people entering the temple. It was the psalm sung at Jesus' own procession to the temple as he entered Jerusalem. (Mark 11:9-10).

When the beloved Son is Jesus, the parable becomes a further prophecy of his passion and glorification. Although thrown out of the vineyard, the Son triumphed over human rejection and murder, because he trusted in the help of God rather than in human beings. (Psalm 118:5-9, 12-14, 23-24; Mark 12:11). In his triumph, he achieved what is "marvellous in our eyes." (Psalm 118:22-24; see Isaiah 52:15). The brutal death of the son, with his body being thrown out of the vineyard in disgrace is not God's last word. God will raise up his murdered Son and make him heir to the vineyard, the one now in charge. And as brothers and sisters of his, all of us, who do the will of God, will receive the same inheritance. (Mark 3:33-35; 10:21).

The religious leaders realize that the parable is aimed at them, but because of their blindness and hardness of heart, they fail to accept it as a summons to repentance and conversion, which was Jesus' main purpose in telling the parable. (Mark 1:15; 3:5). In running their vineyard on the basis of exclusions and making victims of God's servants, his prophets and Son, they are frustrating God's promise to Abraham (Genesis 12:3; 22; 22:18), which is about the creation of an all-inclusive society, blessed by God, one not based on creating victims, whom, in their blindness, they cast out and kill.

The descendants of Moses should have understood the terrible way in which all human societies are organized – basing their social order on victimization. Israel's society, based on the victim people who escaped from Egypt, should not have been like the other nations. (Deuteronomy 10:18; 15:12-15; 24:17-18). The Mosaic law (Ten Commandments) was meant to create a society in which there would be no victims or victimizers, where widows, orphans, the sick, the poor and foreigners would be accepted as brothers and sisters, treated justly. (Deuteronomy 10:18-20). But instead, the law had been reduced to innumerable man-made rules, while the fundamentals of the law about loving all their neighbours were set aside. (Mark 7:6-8). In their blindness and hardness of heart, the religious leaders had created a society of outcasts and victims, and deluded themselves about their own goodness and their involvement in violence. They were now intent on using violence against Jesus. The casting out of the Son means that it is God himself who is the rejected victim. Societies based on exclusions and the casting out of victims, are based on the exclusion of God, because God, through Jesus, identifies with all victims.

Far from accepting the parable as an invitation to repentance and conversion, the religious leaders renewed their determination to kill Jesus, but because of his popularity with the crowds, they were afraid to arrest him. (Mark 12:12). The last thing they wanted was a riot, bearing in mind that the Roman authorities held them responsible for keeping order in Jerusalem. However, they will soon find an opportunity to throw Jesus's body outside the city walls, thus fulfilling the Parable of the Tenants. (Mark 12:8).

The Parable of the Tenants may be interpreted in a universal sense. The vineyard may be a metaphor for God's "good" earth (Genesis 1:31, NJB), which belongs to him, he having created it. (See Psalm 24:1-2). He then gives his blessing to human beings and appoints them stewards over the work of his hands, in the expectation that they will discharge their mission of caring for everything in the earth and for one another. (Genesis 1:28; 2:15 NJB). But like the tenants of the vineyard, human beings have claimed ownership of the earth, to do with it whatever they like. They want to take over from God, but their desire to be like God is a rebellion against the Creator, and it only leads to ruination. (Genesis 3:17-19). Most of the death-dealing wars of history have been fought over claims to different patches of God's good earth. And having claimed ownership, humans then set out to exploit the earth, treating it as a commodity for monetary gain, rather than respecting it as a gift from the Creator, something to fill us with wonder and awe. Instead of acting as good stewards, they deface the work of his hands, producing only "sour grapes." (Isaiah 5:4). Isaiah's sour grapes may be a metaphor for a new desert of "weeds and thorns," appearing today as pollution of the earth, climate change and the extinction of species. (Genesis 3:18). The reckless use of the earth today may be making human beings sick, due to pollution of the atmosphere, the irresponsible disposal of waste and the use of pesticides on human food. A case, once again of rebellion against God, leading to death. According to Pope Francis, there is an ethical dimension to all of this. It may be disrupting, not only our harmony with nature, but also with one another.[137]

## The Religious Leaders Try to Ensnare Jesus

> Next they sent to him some Pharisees and some Herodians to catch him out in what he said. These came and said to him, 'Master, we know that you are an honest man, that you are not afraid of anyone, because human rank means nothing to you, and that you teach the way of God in all honesty. 'Is it permissible to pay taxes to Caesar or not?' Recognising their hypocrisy, he said to them, 'Why are you putting me to the test? Hand me a denarius and let me see it.' They handed him one and he said to them, 'Whose image is this?' They said to him, 'Caesar's.' Jesus said to them, 'Pay Caesar what belongs to Caesar – and God what belongs to God.' (Mark 12:13, 14c, NJB).

If Jesus supports paying taxes to the Romans, he will be discredited in the eyes of the ordinary people, and if he opposes such payments, he can be denounced to the civil authorities as a rebel. Jesus' reply to the Pharisees affirms the State's right to collect taxes, and he distances himself from the zealots and Jewish nationalists who were opposed to

---

[137] Pope Francis, *Let Us Dream: The Path to a Better Future.* (Simon and Schuster).

paying such taxes. To oppose paying taxes to Caesar might signal a violent revolution. Jesus' kingdom movement was opposing a deeper evil than pagan rule.

Jesus saw that the opposition to Roman oppression was hypocritical. (12:15). The people had to suffer far more, due to religious oppression and economic exploitation by the scribes, Pharisees, the priestly aristocracy and Herodians. Jesus saw that the root cause of all oppression was humanity's hard-heartedness and lack of compassion. Those who resented Roman oppression (paying taxes), but overlooked their own oppression of the poor, were lacking in compassion. Compassion was not something expected from the pagan Romans. God's people, however, should have known better. They had the teaching of the prophets calling them to imitate God's compassion for them when they themselves were living under oppression. (Psalm 145:8-9; 86:15; 107:1-3; Hosea 11:1-4, 8-12). Their prayers lacked sincerity and they were not faithful to the covenant made with God by their ancestors. In seeking honour, power and glory for themselves, they had turned their backs on God. (Psalm 78:35-39).

What is it that "belongs to God?" (12:17). Jesus' listeners know that he is alluding to Genesis 1:27, which speaks of human beings being created in God's image. Being made in God's image, human beings owe God more than a piece of metal. God lays claim to their whole being – mind, heart, soul and strength. In this context, a teacher of the law (scribe) came to Jesus with a question: 'Which commandment is the most important of all?' Jesus said to him, 'The most important one is this: *Listen Israel! The Lord our God is the only Lord. Love the Lord your God with all your heart, with all your soul, with all your mind, and with all your strength.*' (Mark 12:28b-30). The above text in italics is a quote from Deuteronomy 6:4-5.

We owe God our unconditional allegiance and devotion. To give our whole allegiance to anything which is other than God, would be treating that thing as our god. Then quoting the Book of Leviticus, Jesus said, 'The second most important commandment is this: *love your neighbour as yourself.*' There is no other commandment more important than these two.' (Mark 12:31). Jesus thus brought these two commandments together in a way that had never been done before. Jesus criticized the scribes and Pharisees because they accorded too much importance to what was merely peripheral in the Jewish tradition (food laws, for example, and what made a person unclean), and not to what was central to it – love of God and their neighbour. (See Luke 10:25-37).

What is common to both commandments is the word 'love.' In loving our neighbour, we love God, because God's image is planted in our neighbour. This is the image to which we owe our allegiance, not the god of Mammon, symbolized by the image of Caesar stamped on a coin. (12:16).

Other New Testament writings affirm Christians' duty to respect civil authority. (Romans 13:1-7; 1 Timothy 2:1-7; Titus 3:1-2; 1 Peter 2:13-17). But our overriding allegiance is to God, whenever the civil power oversteps its bounds or imposes laws contrary to the moral law. (Acts 5:29; Revelation 13:1-18; see CCC 2238, 2240). The coming of God's kingdom is not about imposing a tyranny, but rather about confronting dehumanizing tyrannies with the news of a God whose justice aims to restore genuine humanness. (See John 19; 1 Corinthians 2; Colossians 2).

The Sadducees (the priestly aristocracy) were next in line to question Jesus. (Mark 12:18-27). They were of limited influence with the ordinary people. They recognised the written law of Moses only, and may have payed scant attention to the writings of the prophets, probably because they would have found these writings critical of many of their beliefs and practices. Unlike the Pharisees they did not believe in the resurrection of the dead, holding instead, that the soul dies along with the body at death. (Mark 12:18; see Acts of the Apostles 23:7-8). For them, salvation was about being prosperous and comfortable in this life. Their belief was that when they died, their children would perpetuate their name.

The Sadducees' question to Jesus was designed to show that the resurrection made no sense. The question was: whose wife would a woman be on the day of resurrection, if she had married seven brothers in turn, each of whom had died, she herself being the last to die? (Mark 12:18-23).

> Jesus answered them, 'How wrong you are! And do you know why? It is because you don't know the scriptures or the power of God. For when the dead rise to life, they will be like the angels in heaven and will not marry. Now as for the dead being raised: haven't you ever read in the Book of Moses the passage about the burning bush? There it is written that God said to Moses, *I am the God of Abraham, the God of Isaac and the God of Jacob.* 'He is the God of the living, not of the dead. You are completely wrong.' (Mark 12:24-27).

In the above quotation, Jesus tells the Sadducees that they are wrong on two counts. First of all, they do not understand the God who is revealed in the Scriptures, exemplified in the above quote in italics. (Exodus 3:6, 15-16). The implication here is that Abraham, Isaac and Jacob are still alive. So God is not just the God of dead heroes of the past. He does not cease to be their God in their death. For God to continue his relationship of love with human beings, they must continue to live beyond death. God saves human beings from death because he wants to love them for all eternity. So he is the God of the living.

Secondly, the Sadducees do not know the "power of God" because they fail to recognise that God has the power to restore the dead to life and to give human beings a new and transformed existence of communion with himself forever. Moreover, resurrected life will not simply be a continuation of earthly life. So the question, whose wife will the woman be after death is irrelevant, since marriage will have fulfilled its purpose in this life. (12:23). This is not to deny that a unique relationship may remain in the next life between those who were loving spouses on earth. In the Old Testament, there was no clear concept of life after death. The psalms speak only of a limbo-like existence after death. Isaiah, however, has a clearer statement: "Your dead shall come back to life, your corpses will rise again. Wake up and sing, you dwellers in the dust, for your dew will be a radiant dew, but the earth will give birth to the shades." (Isaiah 26:19, NJB; see also Daniel 12:2f; Wisdom 3:1-12; 2 Maccabees 7:29, 36).

Because human beings are embodied, salvation from death is impossible without the body. St. Paul explains that our resurrected bodies are not simply resuscitated corpses. They will have a spiritual character, radiant with divine glory – somewhat like the angels.

(1 Corinthians 15:42-44; See Romans 8:18-23). In the First Epistle of John, the author affirms that we will be like God, "for we shall see him as he is." (1 John 3:2). We will share in the life of God, in the love within the Trinity – as our inheritance. (2 Peter 1:4).

The scribes and the chief priests represented the people who were now planning the destruction of Jesus. In a society in which the Law of Moses regulated all aspects of life, their expertise gave them great power and influence over others. Jesus was critical of their expertise, which should have been directed to the honour and glory of God, but instead, was a means of drawing honour and glory to themselves. (See Matthew 23:1-12). Everything Jesus said to them was a call to repent of their pride and hypocrisy, but their ears were closed to his invitation to join him in his creation of God's new universal family. As a concluding comment to his disputations with the religious authorities, Jesus issued a warning to the scribes:

> A large crowd was listening to Jesus gladly. As he taught them, he said, 'Watch out for the teachers of the law, who like to walk about in long robes, to be greeted with respect in the market place, who choose the reserved seats in the synagogues and the best places at feasts. They take advantage of widows and rob them of their homes, and then make a show of saying long prayers. Their punishment will be all the worse.' (Mark 12:38-40).

In asking the people to "watch out for" the scribes (verse 38 above), Jesus advises the people not to be led by them. The scribes wanted the best seats at banquets as proof of their high status in society. Their long linen robes were intended for ceremonial purposes but they chose to walk about in them so as to be highly regarded by the people. And in an empty show of piety, they recited long prayers in public. (12:40). Their prayers were thus aimed at human beings rather than at God. Having forfeited eternal reward from God (12:40), they were already receiving their reward in human praise and admiration. They were serving (worshiping) themselves rather than God. Here, once again, Jesus' emphasis is on sincere inner dispositions rather than outward show with the aim of gaining the admiration of people.

It is natural to desire and seek human approval. Jesus advises us to turn our minds and hearts to God - as the one who can guide and protect us - and away from approving eyes, so that we can be open and empowered to what God wants us to desire and to do, instead of just seeking human approval. (Matthew 6:5-6).

There is a suggestion in verse 40 above, that at least some scribes had become wealthy landowners by acting as trustees of confiscated lands, and that they took more than their fair share of profits as rent.[138] When a husband died, the widow might not be able to continue paying rents to these landowners. This could lead to confiscation of the property of a widow's deceased husband by scribes. Such financial abuse recalls Jesus' denunciation of the temple because the religious authorities had "turned it into a hideout for thieves." (Mark 11:17; see Isaiah 56:6-7; Jeremiah 7:11). After the death of their husbands, widows could claim no inheritance rights in Israel. They might then be left

---

[138] *The Oxford Bible Commentary*, p. 912.

with the burden of raising children while depending on charity or male relatives. A childless widow was given the option of marrying the brother of her deceased husband. (Deuteronomy 25:5-10). If the brother chose not to marry her, she returned to her paternal home. (Leviticus 22:13).

In being forced to give up all they had, widows would be left impoverished, and dependent on God's provision. The prophets called for their just treatment. (Isaiah 1:17; see Deuteronomy 10:18). Because of their vulnerable position in society, widows were among those most deserving of care and support, and both the Mosaic law and New Testament call for their protection and support. (Deuteronomy 24:17-21; James 1:27). Though often oppressed by the powerful, they were promised vindication and protection by God. (Psalm 68:6; 72:4; Jeremiah 49:11). The Old Testament often condemns the exploitation of widows. (Isaiah 10:1-2; Jeremiah 7:6, 22:3; Ezekiel 22:7; Zechariah 7:10).

## The Widow's Offering

> As Jesus sat near the Temple treasury, he watched the people as they dropped in their money. Many rich people dropped in a lot of money; then a poor widow came along and dropped in two little copper coins, worth about a penny. He called his disciples together and said to them, 'I tell you that this poor widow put more in the offering box than all the others. For the others put in what they had to spare of their riches; but she, poor as she is, put in all she had – she gave all she had to live on.' (Mark 12:41-44).

The temple treasury did contribute in part towards the maintenance of widows and orphans. All the money was in metal coinage, and large sums donated by the rich (many of them probably scribes and Pharisees) would have rattled loudly in the money boxes, thus drawing attention to themselves. The effect would be similar to the ostentation of the scribes described above. (12:30-41). Jesus has already questioned the sincerity of the scribes' prayers while apparently, they treated widows unjustly. He accused them of self-exaltation and contrasts their haughty pride with the humility of the widow, who in her spirit of self-sacrifice, gave everything she had (verse 44) for the benefit of people as poor as herself. In selling all she had (See Mark 10:21), and because of her spirit of service and her trust and dependency on God to provide for her future needs, Jesus sees the widow as a model of discipleship. (See Mark 6:8). The poor widow is contrasted with the haughty scribes and with the disciples, who, for their part, are not yet prepared to give up everything.

The chief priests and scribes were more concerned about temple sacrifices, man-made rules and their own privileges and status, than creating justice for widows and orphans. Insincere worship was a constant theme of the prophets. "The Lord says, 'Do you think I want all these sacrifices you keep offering to me? I have had more than enough of the sheep you burn as sacrifices... Stop all this evil you are doing and learn to do right. See that justice is done – help those who are oppressed, give orphans their rights, defend widows.'" (Isaiah 1:11, 16-17, see Hosea 6:4-6).

The widow's offering of all she had exemplified the attitude of trusting in God that Jesus had been commending to his disciples. He himself would show in his passion and death that he was prepared to give up everything he had. He would give his whole life in surrender to God, in order to liberate widows and everyone else from all kinds of oppression.

Mark often uses women as role models of how true disciples should behave, i.e. being dependent on God and giving their life in service to others. (Mark 1:29-31; 14:3). The selfless widow, giving her all, is the one who truly loves God and her neighbour. Her offering represented her complete trust and abandonment of herself to God, the protector of widows and orphans. It is with this poor woman Jesus identifies, and not with those who draw attention and honour to themselves by "walking around in long robes and taking the best seats in synagogues." (Mark 12:38). For the scribes, the practice of religion was all external show, designed not to give honour to God but to attract it to themselves. For Jesus, love comes from within the heart of the human being, and is expressed in the service rendered to others. It is a question of serving others, not of oneself being honoured by others.

In all of the above discussions, Jesus emphasises one central issue: that of being liberated from self-exaltation and ego promotion, and instead, loving God and one's neighbour in a practical way, with one's heart and soul. This is more important than insincere religious practices and temple sacrifices. When people pay less attention to ego-promotion and give their lives in service to their neighbour, that in itself, is a sacrifice.

Following his struggle with the religious leaders, Jesus left the temple. His words of praise for an impoverished widow were his last words spoken there.

## Jesus' Farewell Discourse

As Jesus was leaving the Temple, one of his disciples said to him, 'Master, look at the size of those stones! Look at the size of those buildings!' And Jesus said to him, 'You see these great buildings? Not a single stone will be left on another; everything will be pulled down.' (Mark 13:1-2, NJB; see 1 Kings 9:6-9; Matthew 24:1-3; Luke 21:5-7).

This prophecy recalls what was already implied by the withered fig tree. (11:20). Jesus is echoing Old Testament prophecies of doom pronounced over the first temple before it was destroyed in 587 BC, as God's judgement on insincere worship and corrupt leadership. (Micah 3:9-12; see Jeremiah 4:13-14, 23-31; 26:18).

Despite its reputation as the most imposing and beautiful building in the world, Jesus now predicts that the temple of his day will be demolished, echoing his action earlier in the week when he temporarily stopped its sacrificial system from functioning. In one way, the magnificence of the temple resembles the haughtiness of the scribes walking about in their long robes – both of them symbolizing arrogance and self-exaltation. (See Isaiah 47:1, 10-11; Genesis 11:1-4).

Then they went out of the city to the Mount of Olives, located a few hundred yards from the still visible temple. Jesus was sitting on the Mount of Olives across from the temple, when Peter, James, John and Andrew came to him in private. 'Tell us, when this will be,' they said, 'and tell us what will happen to show that the time has come for all of these things to take place.' (Mark 13:3-4).

It was then that Jesus began his farewell discourse to his disciples (Mark 13:5-37, Matthew 24:3-14; Luke 21:7-19), part of which includes a reference to the destruction of the temple. Farewell discourses by prominent people are common throughout the Bible. Just before his own death, Moses delivered his farewell discourse to the Israelites. (Deuteronomy chaps. 29–30; see Joshua 23; Matthew 24; Luke 21:7-32). The Gospel of John has its own farewell discourse by Jesus. (John chaps. 14–16).

In order to understand Mark's discourse, we must view it as a type of literature known as apocalyptic. This type of literature is highly charged poetic language, with lots of imagery, and so, it should not be interpreted literally. We have already seen apocalyptic language in Isaiah chapters 24 and 29, in Jeremiah 51:45-49 and Ezekiel 5:11-12. The whole of the Book of Revelation is apocalyptic.

Not only is apocalyptic writing concerned about the future, but a future in which upheavals and calamities are described on a cosmic scale. There is a pessimism about the present state of affairs, and a sharp conflict between the forces of good and evil. Sin is pervasive, and there is a hope for divine intervention and a renewal of the world amounting to a new creation.

The purpose of apocalyptic literature is to give encouragement to the faithful who are suffering from wars, persecution or other evils. God's judgement will ultimately fall on the wicked, and there will be vindication and reward for the faithful, in a final day of judgement. There is hope of freedom from captivity, a homecoming across the desert (Isaiah 40:3), with miracles greater than the Exodus from Egypt. And the good news of the Kingdom of God being finally established at the end of time! (See Isaiah 40:9; 52:7). As his discourse continues, Jesus focuses on near events lying within a generation, and again on far events to come at an unknown time. The former events may help to understand the latter. The discourse marks the transition from the former age to the new and definitive stage of God's dealings with humanity – the stage that will come to an end at Jesus' second coming in glory at the end of time. (See Matthew 25:31-46).

Jesus begins his discourse by warning the disciples about false prophets speaking in his name and deceiving many. (13:5-6). Some of these may be messiah pretenders or zealots calling for rebellion against Rome. He tells his disciples not to be troubled by the news of battles and wars. Countries will fight each other; nation will rise against nation, kingdom against kingdom. There will be earthquakes and famines. (See Isaiah 24). These things "must" happen. (Verses 7-8). Natural disasters were often foretold by the prophets as signs of God's judgement on human wickedness. (Isaiah 29:6; Jeremiah 11:12; Ezekiel 5:12; 38:19-20). But Jesus interprets these events in a different way: as the birth-pangs of a new creation, so there is no need to panic. (Verse 8). Everything will take place according to God's sovereign plan. God wants to bring a new world to birth - an age to come in which justice, peace and mercy will at last prevail and flourish. Jesus believed that his kingdom' message was the divinely appointed means of bringing this new world to birth. (See John 16:21-22). He continues the discourse with a warning about the cost of discipleship:

> 'You yourselves must be on guard. You will be arrested and taken to court. You
> will be beaten in the synagogues; you will stand before rulers and kings for my
> sake to tell them the Good News. But before the end comes, the gospel must be
> preached to all peoples. And when you are arrested and taken to court, do not
> worry beforehand about what you are going to say. For the words you speak will
> not be yours; they will come from the Holy Spirit. Men will hand over their own
> brothers to be put to death. Fathers will do the same to their children. Children
> will turn against their parents and have them put to death. Everyone will hate
> you because of me. But whoever is faithful to the end will be saved.' (Mark 13:9-
> 13).

In the above passage, the discourse foresees the 'passion of the disciples.' In his discourse,
Jesus warns four of his disciples of all that may befall them. He refers to the trials his new
community will endure. They will be defendants on trial because of their faithfulness to
the gospel. Their sufferings will resemble Jesus' passion. Like Jesus, they will be "handed
over." (See Daniel 2:36-45; 9:26; 11:40). Jesus' first disciples will experience being "arrested
and taken to court." There will be division within families, some remaining faithful to
Jesus, others not. The courts were the Sanhedrins – local Jewish tribunals which had
authority to carry out beatings and scourging. The apostle Paul inflicted such punishments
on Christians before his conversion, and endured the same punishments afterwards. (Acts
of the Apostles 26:11; 2 Corinthians 11:24-25; see Acts 23-25). Peter, and James ("the
brother of the Lord") were martyred, and the others persecuted in a variety of ways. (Acts
12:1-5; 5:17-33; 7:54-60). John the Baptist was arrested and put to death by Herod. (Mark
6:14-29; 13:10). In these verses, the discourse reaches out to our own time, referring to
believers of all times.

In the act of being arrested and "handed over," Jesus calls all disciples to stand
before rulers and kings, and fearlessly tell them the 'good news.' (See Jeremiah 1:17-19).
Jesus warns his followers that they cannot expect to be applauded by a hostile world. On
the contrary, he says, 'Everyone will hate you because of me. But whoever holds out to
the end will be saved.' (13:13; see John 15:18-19). In God's providence, such trials will be
the means of spreading the gospel. (See Acts 8:1-5; 20:24; Philippians 1:12-14).

By way of encouragement to his disciples, Jesus calls on them to rely on the help
of the Holy Spirit. (13:11; see John 15:26-27; see CCC 675-77, 1816). The Old Testament
promise (Genesis 22:18; Isaiah 56:6-8; 66:18-23) that the people of the nations would
come to faith in God was being fulfilled in the early Church.

Then Jesus returns again to the immediate future - the destruction of Jerusalem.
(13:14-27). Up to this point, the disciples are asked to stand firm despite persecution. But
then something will happen which will tell them it is time to abandon the city and "run
away to the hills." (13:14). Jesus is talking about a time when Roman armies will desecrate
the temple, signifying its immediate destruction. This will be the ultimate outrage - the
"awful horror standing in the place where it should not be," precisely in the temple
sanctuary, the holy place where God is worshiped. (Verse 14; see 1 Maccabees 1:31, 54-

59; Daniel 9:27; 11:31; 9:26-27; 11:31; 12:11; 1 Thessalonians 4:16-18; 1 Peter 2:1). The desecration of the temple in 70 AD by the pagan armies of Rome under Titus, would lead to its destruction, reducing it to a pile of rubble, and permanently ending old covenant sacrifices, and the priesthood. The only way of describing such a calamity is through apocalyptic language, also used in Isaiah 13:10-11 and 34:1-4.

According to the prophet Daniel, both the sacrilege in the holy place and the destruction itself, although carried out by wicked men, are but a consequence of the sins of God's people. (Daniel 9:24). God allows these disasters so that his people can be "refined, and purified." (Daniel 12:10). Jesus then continues:

> 'How terrible it will be in those days for women who are pregnant and for mothers with little babies! Pray to God that these things will not happen in the winter. For the trouble of those days will be worse than any the world has ever known from the very beginning when God created the world until the present time. Nor will there ever be anything like it again.' (13:17-19).

For the Jews, the destruction of Jerusalem and its temple would be the end of their world, the end of a way of life that had failed: injustice towards people within Israel and revolutionary violence towards those outside - a refusal to repent of these sins and obey God's call to be a shining light to the wider world.

Continuing his discourse, Jesus then urges his disciples not to believe in false prophets or impostors making false messianic claims. His final coming will be unmistakable. (Verses 21-23). He then shifts his focus to the end of time:

> 'In the days after that time of trouble, the sun will grow dark, the moon will no longer shine, the stars will fall from heaven, and the powers in space will be driven from their courses. Then the Son of Man will appear, coming in the clouds with great power and glory. He will send his angels out to the four corners of the earth to gather God's chosen people from one end of the world to the other... Heaven and earth will pass away, but my words will never pass away.' (13:24-27, 31; Matthew 24:29-31; see Isaiah 24:23; Daniel 7:13).

In the above context, the word "heaven" refers to the sun, moon and stars. The phrase "the Son of Man coming in the clouds with great power and glory" is a quote from Daniel 7:13-14. Jesus' words about the darkening of the sun were fulfilled at his crucifixion, symbolizing the death of the old world, as a prelude to the birth of the new. (Mark 15:33). The discourse reaches its climax with the coming of the Son of Man (Jesus) again, this time, not as a vulnerable baby, looking for "room in the inn" (Luke 2:7), but as a King in all his power and glory, to judge the nations and definitively establish his kingdom - formed of "God's chosen people from one end of the world to the other." The word "gather" suggests that he is more than a king; he is also God's Shepherd definitively gathering and uniting his scattered sheep and taking them home for an eternal pasturing, in fulfilment of the prophecy of Ezekiel. (Ezekiel 34:11-25).

The idea of the Son of Man - who suffered and died, and through his resurrection, broke the power of evil and death - coming again in power and glory to judge and reward his people - gives hope and meaning to the life of Jesus and to the lives of all who follow him in discipleship and suffering service. A glorious future is held up to us, a goal encouraging us along the road. After the suffering of disciples and ongoing evils, God's victory over evil in the resurrection of Jesus, will ultimately and definitively be accomplished. As to when these things will happen, Jesus said to them:

> 'No one knows when that day or hour will come – neither the angels in heaven, nor the Son; only the Father knows… Be on guard, then, because you do not know when the master of the house is coming – it might be in the evening or at midnight or before dawn or at sunrise. If he comes suddenly, he must not find you asleep. What I say to you, then, I say to all, watch.' (Mark 13:32, 35-36).

What was Jesus' purpose in this discourse? Jesus had made a number of predictions about his death and future glory. But in the light of his prediction of a triumph over the powers of darkness in his own person, perhaps he wanted to dampen down expectations of a quick-fix of the problems of evil and suffering in the world. He wanted to remind his disciples that the trials and sufferings of his first followers would be replicated throughout history. In asking them to be faithful to him ("watch"), he was offering them the consolation and the hope of ultimately sharing in his own vindication and glory.

## The Plot against Jesus

Immediately following the "end-of-time" discourse, there is a sudden change of tone in the narrative.

> It was two days before the festival of Passover. The chief priests and teachers of the law were looking for a way to arrest Jesus secretly and put him to death. 'We must not do it during the festival,' they said, 'or the people might riot.' (Mark 14:1-2).

Mark briefly refers to the plotting of the chief priests and scribes against Jesus. Their plan was to arrest him when the crowds had disappeared from Jerusalem after the Passover festival. But as events unfold, they will find a way of doing their evil deed before that. (Mark 14:1-2). Jesus has prophesised that they would "hand him over" and condemn him to death. (8:31; 10:33). They had long been plotting his demise (3:6; 11:18; 12:12), but they would do it by treachery so as to avoid a confrontation with his supporters. This is a replay of the plotting of Israel's leaders of old against the prophet Jeremiah. (Jeremiah 18:18-20; 20:10). Treachery was one of the evils which Jesus said would defile a person from within. (Mark 7:21-23).

At the Last Supper Jesus will associate the festival of the Passover with the meaning of his mission on earth. His death during the festival will highlight the fact that everything is taking place according to God' plan.

CHAPTER 16

# JESUS' PASSION AND DEATH

(14:1-15:47)

## Jesus is Anointed at Bethany

After leaving the temple, Jesus once again went to Bethany outside Jerusalem, where he was at dinner in the "house of Simon the Leper." (Mark 14:3-9; Matthew 26:6-13; John 12:1-8). This Simon may have been healed by Jesus and become a disciple or friend of his. The anointing of Jesus took place in Bethany where he and his disciples were lodging during their stay in Jerusalem. (11:11).

> Jesus was at Bethany in the house of Simon the Leper; he was at dinner when a woman came in with an alabaster jar of very costly ointment, pure nard. She broke the jar and poured the perfume on his head. Some who were there said to one another indignantly, 'Why this waste of ointment? Ointment like this could have been sold for over three hundred denarii and the money given to the poor;' and they were angry with her. But Jesus said, 'Leave her alone. Why are you upsetting her? What she has done for me is one of the good works. You have the poor with you always, and you can be kind to them whenever you wish, but you will not always have me. She has done for me what was in her power to do: she has anointed my body beforehand for its burial. I tell you solemnly, wherever throughout the world the Good News is proclaimed, what she has done will be told also, in remembrance of her.' (14:3-9, JB).

Anointing of the head was a gracious and hospitable gesture and was the way to crown an Israelite king, who was regarded as the Lord's anointed, signifying blessing and strength for the discharge of his office. (See Psalm 23:5, NJB). The word "Messiah" means the anointed one. Much of the passion account will be dominated by the idea that Jesus is a King-Messiah. He entered Jerusalem in royal fashion. (Mark 11:1-10). He will be mocked as a king, condemned as a king and crucified as a royal pretender. In her anointing, was the woman saying to Jesus, 'You are the true King-Messiah?' Jesus said that the "good work" done by her would be an essential part of the proclamation of the gospel. (14:9). Earlier at Caesarea Philippi Peter confessed Jesus as the Messiah. The title is now symbolically conferred on him in the anointing by the woman at Bethany.[139]

---

[139] Michael Mullins, *The Gospel of Matthew*, (The Columba Press, Dublin), 2007.

The woman may have experienced Jesus' healing forgiveness and wanted to express her love in return. (The cost of the ointment, at three hundred denarii would have amounted to a year's wages, a denarius being a day's wages). John's Gospel says that it was Judas who criticized the woman, saying that the money for the ointment should be given to the poor. "He said this, not because he cared for the poor, but because he was a thief. He carried the money bag (the disciples' common fund) and would help himself from it." (John 12:4-6).

But there were other disciples who objected to the woman's action. (14:5). Jesus reprimanded the disciples for their blindness to the significance of the woman's gesture. He reminded them that the woman's anointing was a prophetic gesture, anticipating his death and burial. (14:8). The anointing of his body after his death by the other women disciples was not successful. (Mark 16:1). This woman succeeded, because she did it beforehand. She did what the male disciples failed to do for him after his death. After he was arrested, they left him and fled.

The woman came into the house and braved the criticism of those present, to perform for Jesus an action of love and appreciation for what he was about to undergo. She may have been one of those who had been listening to his teaching in the temple and observed the hostility of the religious authorities towards him. In her case, a word spoken by him might have fallen like a seed on fertile ground and awoken in her a desire to perform this act of service in recognition of his heroic stance in braving the opposition and the death which was looming over him. Her boldness contrasted with the scheming and stealth of the chief priests (Mark 14:1) and the objections of those in Simon's house (male disciples?). The woman recognised the cost to Jesus, of the service he was performing for everyone. (Mark 10:45).

Peter was placing an obstacle in the 'way' of Jesus, when he tried to dissuade him from his messianic mission, evoking a response from Jesus, 'Get behind me Satan.' (Mark 8:32). But this woman prophetically affirmed his mission, as if, like John the Baptist at the beginning of the gospel, she was showing Jesus the 'way' ahead, now that he had come almost to the end of his journey.

Jesus responded in love and gratitude to the woman for her act of doing "everything in her power" for him, giving all she had, because she knew that he was giving his all. In contrast to the male disciples who were about to abandon him, and Judas, who was so concerned about money that he would betray him, she didn't count the cost of her service to him. Through her act of love and honour, Jesus may be confirming the woman as a disciple because of her unpopular and fearless action in standing out from the crowd, and a model of discipleship. Other than Jesus himself, she is the first person in Mark to have intuitively understood the meaning of his passion, while the male disciples remained blind to its significance until the very end.

Previously, Jesus had equated "good works" (14:5) with his own work of liberation. When John the Baptist sent messengers to him enquiring if he was the Messiah, Jesus said to them, 'Go back and tell John what you have seen and heard: the blind can see, the lame can walk, those who suffer from skin diseases are made clean, the deaf can hear, the dead are raised to life, and the good news is preached to the poor.' (Luke 7:22, see also Luke 4:18-19; Matthew 25:35-36).

Christians are called to do all in their power for Jesus, in the sense of serving the needs of all those with whom he identifies (Mark 1:9): opening the eyes of the blind, lifting up the lame and spreading the good news – thus anointing Jesus' body. Anointing sick people with oil was one of the tasks of the twelve apostles when Jesus sent them on their mission. (Mark 6:13; see CCC 1511, 1520).

Mark tells the stories of two women, first, the story of the widow's offering in the temple, and her generous gift of all she had, (12:41-44), and then the woman who came to the house of Simon the Leper and anointed Jesus. (14:3-9). Both of them gave all they had, in a way, surrendering their whole lives to God. These two women may be representative of the faithful women disciples who followed Jesus from Galilee to Calvary, serving him and fearlessly standing by him as he hung on the cross, while the men abandoned him and ran away in fright. (Mark 15:40-41; John 19:25-26).

We may suppose that Judas was present during Jesus' confrontation with the religious leaders in the temple, and knew that they wanted him dead. And it may have been the incident in the house of Simon the Leper which finally convinced him to betray Jesus.

> Then Judas Iscariot, one of the twelve disciples, went to the chief priests in order to betray Jesus to them. They were pleased to hear what he had to say and promised to give him money. So Judas started looking for a good chance to hand over Jesus to them. (Mark 14:10-11, see Psalm 55:12-14).

In the interplay between divine and human causality which we find all throughout the Bible, Judas and the chief priests are making their own plans, but God is ultimately in control of Jesus' destiny. It was the will of God that Jesus would give himself up to death, as a "ransom for many." (Mark 10:45; 14:36). Jesus' firmness of purpose is echoed in Psalms 22 and 69, in which the sufferings of the messianic Son' and 'Lord' are foreseen. (Mark 12:35-37).

The chief priests were pleased with Judas' offer. They had been hampered so far by Jesus' popularity with the crowds who had been surrounding him (11:15-18; 12:1-12; 14:2). Judas would enable them to arrest Jesus quietly and privately. Mark says that Judas was "one of the twelve" (14:10, 20, 43), and that he was chosen by Jesus. (3:14-15).

Thus, between these two accounts of plotting and betrayal, Mark inserts the Bethany incident - a narrative pointing in the opposite direction: one of affirmation, encouragement and support.

## The Last Supper (New Passover)

In the passion narrative, the four gospels come closer to one another in their wording and chronology. Prophecies of Jesus' passion come in four great poems of Isaiah, depicting a Servant of God whose heart is totally set on God's will, even though, for the servant, this proves to be costly. (Isaiah 41:8-10; 42:1-9; 50:4-11; 52:13–53:12). These poems are prophetic of the obedient Servant whom God will send to humanity in the future. Like the other evangelists, Mark interprets the passion of Jesus, especially in the light of the

Suffering Servant Song of Isaiah 52:13–53:12 and the Psalms of the suffering just man. (Psalms 31:10-13; 62, 64; see Jeremiah 20:7-11). The servant poems portray the Servant's vocation: to assume the role of a substitute for sinners and to suffer vicariously for them, so that they might escape the consequences of their sins and be forgiven (Isaiah 53:6b, 10a, 12b). Following a life of suffering, the Servant is vindicated by God and given a place of honour. (Isaiah 53:12a; see 1 Peter 1:10-12). Jesus reveals himself as this Suffering Servant. (Mark 8:31; 9:31; 10:33-34, 45). The early Church recognised in Isaiah's poems a prophecy of Jesus' passage from death to life and sought in them a deeper understanding of the mystery of Jesus' passion. (See Matthew 12:15-21; Acts 8:32-35; 1 Corinthians 15:3-7).

Jesus does not go to his death as a passive victim. He aligned his own will with the will of the Father and saw every step of his journey directed towards the fulfilment of the will of God. This is evident in the predictions of his passion and in his final decision to go to the cross. (Mark 14:36).

> On the first day of the meal of Unleavened Bread, the day the lambs for the Passover are killed, Jesus' disciples asked him, 'Where do you want us to go and get the Passover meal ready for you?' (Mark 14:12).

We read in Mark 11:3 that Jesus has hidden friends who are ready to attend to his needs and offer him what they can from their resources, in this instance, a large room in which he could celebrate the Passover with his new spiritual 'family.' (Mark 14:13-16; see 3:33-35; Exodus 12:1-8; 1 Corinthians 5:7-8).

As a commemoration of the liberation of their forefathers from Egypt, each Jewish family sacrificed a lamb for the special meal known as Passover. This meal celebrated the Passover of the Israelites from the slavery of Egypt to their freedom as a people dedicated to God. (Exodus 1:11-14; 12:1-14). As a prelude to the escape from Egypt, the blood of the sacrificed lamb was sprinkled on Israelite doorposts, marking them out as God's people, the ones to be saved from the death sentence imposed on them by the Egyptians. (Exodus 1:11, 22; 12:3, 6-8, 13). This is what gave rise to the notion of salvation from death through the blood of the lamb. On the annual day of Atonement in the Jerusalem temple, the High Priest sprinkled the blood of a sacrificed lamb on the assembled people, signifying liberation from their sins. The Jewish Passover was also a celebration of the bonding together of a people dedicated to the God who saved them.

It is notable that there is no mention of a lamb at Jesus' Passover meal. Jesus himself is the true paschal lamb about to be sacrificed (Isaiah 53:7), the unleavened bread (Exodus 12:15) about to be given up, and by whose sacrificial blood humanity is saved from death. (Mark 14:22). In Jesus, the Passover of Israel is fulfilled. In the sacrifice of his life, he liberates humanity from death and establishes a new, universal family whose members do the will of God (Mark 3:33-35) - a greater family than that formed by the Sinai covenant (Exodus 24:3).

Passover time was the occasion Jesus chose for the final show-down with the temple authorities, the final conflict between his freedom movement and the new 'Pharaohs' - the forces of pagan rule and temple misrule. For Jesus, this would be a new

Passover, a celebration of a liberation greater than that from Egypt of old. He would go, as one greater than Moses, leading the twelve apostles (the new Israel) through a terror greater than the walls of water of the Red Sea, with Pharaoh in pursuit of the twelve tribes of Israel. (Exodus 14:13-18). Jesus is pursued by the army of a new "Pharaoh," but he leads the world in a new exodus to freedom from a much greater bondage than that of the Israelites under the Egyptian Pharaoh – the freeing of the whole of humanity from death.

> When it was evening, Jesus came with the twelve disciples. While they were at the table eating, Jesus said to them, 'I tell you that one of you will betray me – one who is eating with me.' The disciples were upset and began to ask him, one after the other, 'Surely you don't mean me, do you?' Jesus answered, 'It will be one of you twelve, the one who dips his bread in the dish with me. The Son of man will die as the scriptures say he will; but how terrible for that man who betrays the Son of Man! It would be better for that man if he had never been born.' (Mark 14:17-21).

In one particular verse, Mark quotes Jesus as mentioning his "disciples" eating the paschal meal with him. (14:14). However, as they assemble for the supper, Mark speaks of "twelve disciples" (verse 17 above). In the Passover context, Mark may want to hold on to the number twelve, which recalls the twelve tribes of Israel, because it signifies the new Israel, the new universal family which Jesus is founding. There is every reason to suppose that women disciples were present at this meal, especially the faithful women who followed Jesus all the way from Galilee, and perhaps many other women disciples. (See Mark 15:41).

Jesus does not name Judas as the betrayer. He may have been inviting all of them to examine their conscience. (1 Corinthians 11:28). His simple announcement of betrayal gives Judas a chance to abandon his plans and repent, without the others having to know about his secret plotting. Jesus appeals to Judas by warning him of the consequences of his act. (14:21). Jesus is the suffering Messiah whose vocation is to die, but this does not excuse Judas of his own responsibility for his treachery. Jesus' word "terrible" can be interpreted as a cry of sorrow, rather than implying eternal separation from God for Judas. (14:21). It recalls the warnings of the prophets and Jesus' censure of the scribes and Pharisees. (Hosea 7:12-14; Amos 5:17-19; 6:3-5; Isaiah 5:7-23; 28:1-2). Unwittingly, in handing Jesus over to death, Judas is fulfilling God's purpose as outlined in the Scriptures. (Verse 21a above).

For the Jews, meals were sacred occasions. But the Passover meal was of special significance. Not only did it recall a past saving event, it was a reminder that God would continue to guide and protect his liberated people. Yet during this most sacred of meals, symbolizing intimate family union, one of those present was plotting to betray the head of the family.

The gospels don't say why Judas betrayed Jesus. Perhaps he was disappointed that Jesus was not establishing the kingdom by some kind of a miracle, or by political means. The family which Judas may have wanted would be one divided against itself, fighting groups – a kingdom that would fall. (See Mark 3:22-26). Because the anointing at Bethany pointed out a different path for Jesus, Judas may have finally made his decision in the light of that incident. Judas was setting himself up as the leader of Jesus, determining Jesus' destiny. As was the case with Peter at an earlier stage (Mark 8:31-33), Judas was the Satan standing in the path of Jesus, trying to dissuade him from accomplishing his mission.

## Jesus, the Obedient Servant of God

> While they were eating, Jesus took a piece of bread, gave a prayer of thanks, broke it and gave it to his disciples. 'Take it,' he said, 'this is my body.' Then he took a cup, gave thanks to God and handed it to them; and they all drank from it. "Jesus said, 'This is my blood which is poured out for many, my blood which seals God's covenant. I tell you, I will never drink this wine until the day I drink the new wine in the Kingdom of God.' Then they sang a hymn and went out to the Mount of Olives. (Mark 14:22-26).

Like the head of all Jewish families, and as the head of his new spiritual family (Mark 3:33-34), Jesus would have told the Passover story from the Book of Exodus. He would have blessed the herbs and the unleavened bread (made without yeast)—symbolic reminders of various aspects of Israel's deliverance from Egyptian bondage. (Exodus 12:8, 39). However, he departs from the ancient script at one crucial point. His new words about giving up his body for the disciples (verse 14 above) look ahead to his death, as bringing about the new exodus from the bondage of death, through his resurrection, and the definitive establishment of the reign of God over all malign forces. This act of service to humanity is accomplished by the giving up of his body as a sacrifice (Mark 14:22; see Isaiah 53:6b, 10a, 12b), and it recalls his earlier words about his death being a "ransom for many." (Mark 10:45). The family gathered around him at the table will form the core of his new universal family, bonded to one another and to himself by their sharing in this same Eucharistic bread, recalling the purpose of his earlier table fellowship.

All through his ministry, the disciples shared many meals with Jesus, signifying the breaking of barriers, the forgiveness of sins and the reconciliation of all classes of people. These meals were signs of the establishment of his universal family. The people thus forgiven and united, learned that Jesus is the messianic shepherd gathering his scattered flock and feeding them to their fullest satisfaction with his new risen life. (Mark 6:42-43; Ezekiel 34:11-16).

Following their liberation from Egypt, the revelation of the Ten Commandments represented God's plan for binding his people together in a covenantal relationship with himself, to which God expected obedience from his people. (Exodus 4:3, 6-7; Deuteronomy 8:11-14). The people promised to obey the covenant (Exodus 24:3, 7). But as their subsequent history showed, this turned out to be an empty promise. (See Isaiah 1:2, 4; 2:7-8; 2 Chronicles 36:13-16; Jeremiah 2:5-8; 5:1; 11:7-8; 22:21). Thus because of the servant Israel's failure of obedience, the old covenant remained broken.

God repeatedly called Israel to be his obedient servant, whose vocation was to open its blind eyes and deaf ears to its sins of disobedience and to create a just society in the promised land, so that it could fulfil its God-given task of being a light to the other nations. (Isaiah 42:1, 6-7; 49:3). Because Israel failed to create a just society at home, it could not carry forward God's promise to Abraham of blessing to the nations, so that the whole world might be saved. (Genesis 22:18; Isaiah 48:18-19). Although tasked with the role of servant, Israel remained deaf to the word of God and blind to its sins. (Isaiah 42:18-20; 56:9-12; Ezekiel 12:2). The servant Israel proved to be a bad shepherd, feeding itself rather than its flock. (Ezekiel 34:1-2). God loved Israel, but Israel turned its back on God and went into hiding from God. (Genesis 3:8; Hosea 4:1-2). Israel was the unfaithful spouse who had deserted her bridegroom God. (Hosea 2:2). God revealed himself to Israel as the carer of the widow, the orphan and the homeless. (Psalm 146:7-9; 82:3-4; 68:5; 82:3; Exodus 22:21-24; Deuteronomy 27:19; Zechariah 7:9-10). God releases prisoners from their bondage. (Exodus 3:7; Isaiah 40:1-2). God provides for the poor. (Psalm 68:5, 10). He is passionate about justice. (Exodus 23:6-9). But God's own people Israel did not imitate his gratuity. They created an Israel with an identity founded on the murdering of Cain (Genesis 4:8), the casting out of victims (Mark 12:8) and the marginalisation of people who, according to the Pharisees, were "under God's curse" because of their ignorance of the law. (John 7:49; see Mark 3:6; 5:1-5; 6:27, 7:6-8; 12:1-8).

Obedience was tried in Israel over a long period but it did not work. The prophet Ezekiel reminded Israel of old of its breach of the covenant. The people had ignored their promise of obedience and turned their back on God. (See Ezekiel 16:59). So because of Israel's disobedience, its deafness to God and blindness to its sins, is God not able to fulfil the promises he made to Abraham, and through Abraham to Israel, of blessing to the nations? (Genesis 22:15-18). The sovereign God does not give up on disobedient Israel. He will fulfil his promises. (Isaiah 42:6b-7). "The Lord says to Israel, 'I will honour the covenant I made with you when you were young, and I will make a covenant with you that will last for ever.'" (Ezekiel 16:60; see Isaiah 59:21; Jeremiah 31:31-34; 32:39-40; Ezekiel 36:26). The promises of these prophets are fulfilled by Jesus at the Last Supper. As well as foretelling the coming of a future Messiah, the prophets also said that only a remnant of Israel would remain faithful to God. (Isaiah 10:20-21, 11:16). Jesus is that remnant. He represents the renewed Israel. Because of Jesus' faithfulness and obedience, God can make "a new covenant with all peoples and bring light to the nations." (Isaiah 42:6). This is the new covenant which God, through Jesus, establishes at the Last Supper. There is a permanency about this covenant; it is "sealed with his blood." (See Mark 14:24 in the foregoing passage). Having thus being sealed, it will "last for ever." (Ezekiel 16:60). (An ancient covenant was usually sealed with the blood of both partners, probably signifying that they would be willing to give their lives for it). Because Jesus identifies with all of us, there is now a covenant (a lasting bond) between God and his people that can never be broken. Jesus' new covenant undoes the scattering of the lost sheep of Israel (Isaiah 53:6a) and unites them with the Shepherd, who feeds them anew (Ezekiel 34:11-13; Mark 14:22). It is to Jesus God has given the power to see that justice is done on earth. (Isaiah 42:6a; see Luke 4:18-19). Justice creates the new spiritual family prophesised by Jesus in Mark 3:33-35).

Because Jesus is also the new Adam, the new human representative (Romans 5:14; 1 Corinthians 15:22), all of us are drawn into his own obedience to God, thus restoring our relationship with God – a love relationship that will last for ever, because love never

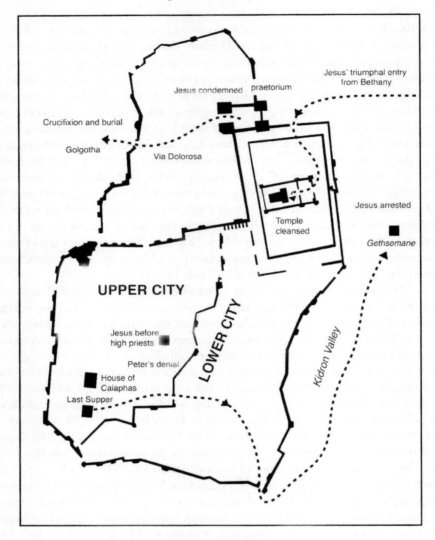

***Jerusalem in Passion Week***

dies. (See Romans 8:38-39). Through the achievement of Jesus, Israel (reconstituted) can once again become the faithful spouse of God, and God will be her husband "for ever." (Hosea 2:19-20; see Mark 2:18-19; Ezekiel 11:19-20; 37:26a). Through his perfect obedience to the Father, Jesus fulfils the prophecy of Hosea, Isaiah and Ezekiel.

Mark concludes the foregoing passage with a message of hope for human beings. (14:25). A glorious destiny awaits us. Old Testament hopes for a 'promised land' will be fulfilled. Here, Jesus reminds his disciples about one of the most fundamental aims of his mission on earth, which is to triumph over suffering and death as God's good news to humanity. The reign of God over evil and death is definitively established through Jesus' resurrection. (Isaiah 53:12a). So the Last Supper anticipates the ultimate banquet ("the new wine," Mark 14:25) which Jesus will celebrate with the members of his universal family, once they are definitively gathered into his Kingdom. This is the meal which will fulfil Isaiah's banquet of the richest food and finest wine. (See Isaiah 25:6-9). As a celebration of the end to human sorrows and the destruction of death for ever, this banquet will be full of joy. (Isaiah 53:11a). "God will wipe all tears from their eyes. There will be no more death, no more grief or crying or pain." (Revelation 21:3-4).

Eating the bread and drinking the "cup" can have a significant effect on our lives in the here-and-now. The bread and wine are more than a celebration. They represent a challenge to us. This meal signifies a new responsibility being placed on our shoulders. It is an invitation to participate in the mission of the one who came not to be served, but to serve and "give his life as a ransom for many." (Mark 10:45). Jesus has already asked his disciples if they can "drink from his own "cup." (Mark 10:38). In other words, can they participate in his own sacrifice, join him in doing what he himself is doing? Sacrificial service is costly; it is body-breaking. (Mark 14:22). Can we ourselves allow our bodies to be "broken" and given up in service to others? At the last Supper, this is the mission to which Jesus is calling us when he says, 'Do this in memory of me.' (Luke 22:19c). Service creates union; through serving others, all people are gathered into the blessedness of union in the Kingdom of God. (Mark 3:33-35; Matthew 25:34-36; see CCC 610-11; 1337-44; 1402-5).

## Jesus in Gethsemane: The Obedient Son

The hymns sung at the end of the Supper (Mark 14:26) were probably Psalms 113-118. Psalms 113 and 117 are songs in praise of God who raises us up from our troubles. Psalm 114 is a Passover song, celebrating God's miraculous rescuing of his people. Psalm 115 is a song of praise of the one true God, the helper and rescuer. Psalm 116 is a song of praise of God by someone saved from death. Psalm 118 is a prayer of thanks for victory.

"Then they went to the Mount of Olives." (Mark 14:26). The implication here is that all of the disciples accompanied Jesus to the Mount of Olives after the Last Supper. The Mount of Olives was the setting for Jesus' 'end-of-time' discourse. (Mark 13:3-37). Just as Jesus has already prophesised his betrayal by one disciple (14:18), he now prophesises his immediate abandonment by all of them.

> Jesus said to them, 'All of you will run away and leave me, for the Scripture says, *'God will kill the shepherd, and the sheep will all be scattered.* But after I am raised to life, I will go to Galilee ahead of you.' Peter answered, 'I will never leave you, even though all the rest do!' Jesus said to Peter, 'I tell you that before the cock crows twice tonight, you will say three times that you do not know me.' Peter answered, even more strongly, 'I will never say that, even if I have to die with you!' And the other disciples said the same thing. (Mark 14:27-31; Matthew 26:31-35; Luke 22:31-34; John 13:36-38).

The words in italics in the above passage are from the prophet Zechariah 13:7. In order to rescue the world from the demonic, God will "kill the shepherd," i.e. allow him to be given over to death, so that God's purposes of blessing for the world may be fulfilled. Although all the human actors are playing their part in bringing about the death of Jesus, God is still in charge of these events. In that sense, it is God who "kills the shepherd." This is costly for God. (See Genesis 22:1-2).

With the shepherd about to be killed, the sheep will scatter. (Mark 14:27). After Jesus' celebration of family union at the Last Supper, this scattering – "each one going his own way," like lost sheep (Isaiah 53:6a) - represents a break-up of Jesus' new family. It is a failure of discipleship. Such disunity represents a captivity to the demonic. (See Mark 3:26). Despite all Jesus has revealed about family union to the disciples at the Last Supper, their immediate response is now to scatter and go their own way. So does Jesus give up on them at this stage? This scattering will not be the end of the story. God will raise up the Shepherd, and he, the Shepherd will go "ahead" of them (in the same way that shepherds lead their flocks), to Galilee (Mark 14:28; Matthew 26:32). Once back with them in Galilee, Jesus will forgive them and gather them together once again into a new and reconciled family, thus fulfilling his words in Mark 3:33-35. God never gives up on humanity. (See Isaiah 49:16).

As happened once before (Mark 8:32), Peter contradicts his Lord (verse 31 above). The ever-impulsive and weak Peter is relying too much on his own human capacity to remain faithful to Jesus. The other disciples follow Peter's pledge of loyalty, stating that they too, are ready to die with him. But Jesus knows the weakness of their hearts. Betrayal, denial and desertion! (see John 16:32).

The idea of the Shepherd once again gathering his scattered flock is an assurance to the readers of Mark that forgiveness and reconciliation are available to all those who desert Jesus or deny him because of opposition or fear of persecution. God's Spirit will later descend upon Peter and the others. The Spirit will heal the sickness of their weakness and give them a new empowerment for their own role of gathering the Lord's flock. (See Acts of the Apostles 2:4). Jesus' work will end where it began, in Galilee. It was in Galilee he called them to be with him, to learn the meaning of discipleship. There in Galilee he will commission them to bring the liberating gospel to the ends of the earth. (Mark 16:15; Matthew 28:16-20; Luke 24:45-48).

> They came to a place called Gethsemane, and Jesus said to his disciples, 'Sit here while I pray.' He took Peter, James and John with him. Distress and anguish came over him, and he said to them, 'The sorrow in my heart is so great that it almost crushes me. Stay here and keep watch. He went a little further on, threw himself on the ground, and prayed that, if possible, he might not have to go through that time of suffering. 'Father,' he prayed, 'My Father! All things are possible for you. Take this cup of suffering away from me. Yet not what I want, but what you want.' (Mark 14:32-36; see Genesis 32:22-28).

This is the third time Mark has shown Jesus at prayer. (See 14:33b; see 1:35; 6:46). The above three disciples (Peter, James and John) have witnessed Jesus' divine glory in the raising of the daughter of Jairus (Mark 5:37). They were witnesses to the Transfiguration

(9:2), where they heard the voice of God calling them to "listen" to his Son. (Mark 9:7). Presently they will see his human frailty. All three have pledged to share in his sufferings. (Mark 14:29-31). But will they now listen to the Son?

Gethsemane was a garden on the western slope of the Mount of Olives. As the garden of obedience, Gethsemane recalls the first garden (Eden) in which humanity was tempted, turned away from God, scattered and went its own way in disobedience of his will. (Genesis 3:8; see Isaiah 53:6a).

Jesus moved away from his disciples to be with his Father and to face the cup of suffering all alone. His sorrow threatened his life (verse 34), recalling Psalm 43:5, but he still hoped in God. His appeal to God: 'Take this cup away' recalls his temptation to be a conquering Messiah. (Mark 1:13; Matthew 4:8). The disciples tried to deflect him from his mission of suffering service, tempting him to go for the quick fix, establish the political kingdom and reign in Jerusalem as an earthly king of the Jews. (Mark 8:11, 32). Now he is tempted to abandon his mission of being a suffering Messiah.

Jesus' temptation came to a head after his hour-long struggle (verse 37) in Gethsemane. Jesus was torn between the desire to escape the horror that faced him and faithfulness to the mission handed to him by the Father. (Isaiah 53:10a). Here we see the humanity of Jesus (Son of Man) as he struggles with temptation. Could the Father possibly take the "cup" away from him and rearrange his plan in order to spare his Son this suffering? (Mark 14:35). But he *must* drink this "cup" (Mark 10:38), because of his substitutionary role (Isaiah 53:4, 6b) of standing in the place of people who abandon God and go their own way. Jesus must drink this "cup," so that all who really deserve the "cup" might be forgiven for their "wandering." (Genesis 4:16; Isaiah 53:6a, 12c). With those few simple words ("not what I want, but what you want") addressed to his heavenly Father, Jesus definitively commits himself to total obedience to the will of God. He is willing to drink the "cup," even unto death. His own prayer is thus fulfilled: "Thy will be done on earth as it is in heaven." (Matthew 6:10).

Jesus' faith is not shaken despite his suffering. Through him, "God's purpose is fulfilled." (Isaiah 53:10c). He trusted in his Father to vindicate him - to "give him a place of honour" (Isaiah 53:12a). Both as the "beloved" Son (Mark 1:11; 14:36, NJB) and suffering Servant of Isaiah (53:8), Jesus hands his suffering over to God, allowing God to deal with it as God wills and knows best.

Jesus is empowered by the Spirit of God (Mark 1:10) to do what Israel of old failed to do. In the Old Testament, God called Israel to be his son. Like any true son, God expected obedience from Israel. (Exodus 4:22; Jeremiah 30:9c; 31:20; Hosea 11:1). But because of its disobedience and blindness to its sins, Israel could not be a true son of God. (Hosea 11:2-4; Isaiah 42:18-20). Jesus is the beloved (Mark 1:11) and obedient Son in the Garden of Gethsemane ("my Father... what you want," Mark 14:36). And as the new human representative, Jesus undoes the disobedience of Adam - the first human representative in the Garden of Eden. (See Romans 5:18-19; 1 Corinthians 15:21-22). Death was the consequence of the original disobedience. (Genesis 2:17b; 3:19b). This means that, in Jesus' obedience as the new Adam, death is undone. And then, because Jesus identifies with humanity (Mark 1:9, 13), he takes us with him into his own triumph over death. Through Jesus' filial obedience, God has "destroyed death for ever" - for everyone

(Isaiah 25:8). By identifying with us and thus rescuing us from death, Jesus the obedient Son, makes all of us sons and daughters of God. Once freed from the bondage of death, we are made partakers in Jesus' own eternal life – his place of "joy" with God. (Isaiah 53:11a). Jesus' redemptive suffering was not in vain. (Isaiah 53:11b). Through him, God's purpose has succeeded. (Isaiah 53:10c).

It took God himself to die a death - in solidarity with us in our own death - in order that death might be conquered, the death-dealing reign of Satan defeated (Genesis 3:15; Mark 5:37-41) and humanity gathered together as a family under the fatherhood of God, with Jesus as our shepherd, feeding us with eternal life in "the mountains and streams of Israel" – a metaphor for *our* promised land. (Ezekiel 34:11:14; see Matthew 25:30-31).

In his agony, Jesus recites a number of psalms, applying them to himself. (See Psalms 31:10-13; 42:6-7, 11; Psalm 42, 43). By placing his hope and trust in God, and aligning his will with the will of the Father, Jesus fulfils the prayer of Israel, the hope of Israel. (Mark 14:32b). His prayer is an acknowledgement that the Father is in control during the entire passion (verse 36), but there is a cost to the Father, in the sense that he "hands over" his beloved Son to those who will kill him. We should be clear about one thing: God does not demand the death of his innocent and beloved Son in order to satisfy his wrath with sinners. God is not punishing his Son for the sins of humanity. God is actually coming benevolently towards us sinners, as a victim. (Romans 8:31-32). God is not indifferent to the fate of his Son. The Father suffers along with the Son. The Son absorbs the pain, violence and evil of the world onto himself (as a human substitute), so that, ultimately, human beings would be freed from all pain and violence. (Isaiah 53:6). In thus handing over his beloved Son to those who will kill him, God is revealed to us as love. It is love that turns the other cheek to violence (Isaiah 53:7) and thereby loves and forgives the victimizer, no less than the righteous. (1 John 8b-10; see Isaiah 53:10a,11b). The God revealed in Jesus Christ is a God of love, a forgiving and reconciling God, not a punishing God.

Jesus' surrender to God, his absolute trust in his Father, points the way for Christians when faced with suffering, over which they have no control. The life, death and resurrection of Jesus reveals to us that God is truly sovereign; he can, and will, deal with suffering and evil, but in a way and time he knows best for human beings. Our part is to pray for the faith and strength to face our pain, and, like Jesus, to leave its resolution in God's hands. (Mark 14:36). To surrender control to God, and to say the prayer, 'not my will but yours' is very difficult. God may not be able to take away from us the pain resulting from our human frailty and mortality. But as the Son, he comes to live among us, suffering with us, empathising with us, sharing our pain even unto death – substituting his suffering for ours, so that we might escape the suffering of death. Suffering and death are not the end of the human story. We can live in hope. The good news is that God raises us up along with Jesus so that we might share in his eternal life.

Surrendering to God is liberating, because it releases us from the burden of thinking that we ourselves should always be in control of events. Such a feeling can lead to anxiety and disillusionment, and might prove to be an intolerable burden on a person's shoulders. If we can surrender control to God, allow him to take over our lives, he will make us God-like, and we will find rest and peace. This surrendering is very difficult. It is as hard as "moving a mountain into the sea." (Mark 11:22-23). It is the highest form of faith, of which, in reality, we possess very little. (Matthew 17:19-20; Luke 17:5-6). We should take heart that Jesus has already surrendered himself for us, in a substitutionary sense. (Mark 14:36). He has lightened our burdens. (See Matthew 11:28).

Jesus' sacrifice leads to resurrection. (Mark 8:31; 9:31; 10:34). Because of Jesus' trusting obedience of God in sacrificing his life for humanity, it would be inconsistent of a God of love, indeed, inconceivable, that God would abandon his beloved and faithful Son to death, or indeed, any of the beloved sons and daughters of his new family. On the contrary, God raises Jesus to a place of honour (Isaiah 53:12a) at God's right hand. (See Acts of the Apostles 7:55-56; Romans 8:34; Ephesians 1:20-21). St. Paul tells his Christians that they have been raised up to the same life as Christ. (Colossians 3:1). They have been drawn into God's family as brothers and sisters of Jesus, thus fulfilling Jesus' own words in Mark's gospel. (Mark 3:33-35). Redemption can be understood as a restoration. God is restoring humanity to what was his glorious vision from the beginning, which is expressed in terms of his walking in close companionship with humanity in the Garden of Eden (this world). (See Genesis 2:8, 15, 22).

## The Sleeping Disciples

Then Jesus returned and found the three disciples asleep. He said to Peter,' Simon, are you asleep? Weren't you able to stay awake even for one hour?' And he said to them, 'Keep watch and pray that you do not fall into temptation. The spirit is willing but the flesh is weak.' He went away once more and prayed, saying the same words. Then he came back to the disciples and found them asleep; they could not keep their eyes open. And they did not know what to say to him. When he came back the third time, he said to them, 'Are you still sleeping and resting? Enough! The hour has come! Look, the Son of man is being handed over to the power of sinners. Get up, let us go. Look, here is the man who is betraying me!' (Mark 14:37-42; John 18:1).

The three disciples fell asleep in the garden, blind to the drama taking place beside them, and signalling their future scattering. Throughout the whole of their journey to Jerusalem, they were asleep to Jesus' teaching about suffering service. Now in the garden, they couldn't stay awake even for one hour. To Peter (his future representative on earth) Jesus said, 'Simon, are you asleep?' (14:37). It is significant that he addresses Peter as Simon, his former name. Peter is no longer the rock of faith (*Petrus*) on whom Jesus can rely for support. To be watchful was the same admonition which he gave them at the end-of-time discourse. (Mark 13:34-37; see Matthew 26:36-46; Luke 22:39-46; Psalms 55:3-6; 88:3-4; 116:3-4; Hebrews 5:7-9).

The apostles' closed eyes (verse 37) is a metaphor for the blindness that afflicted them during Jesus' repeated attempts to teach them. (Mark 8:31-33). Jesus called them to be "with" him. (Mark 3:14). If they had so far been with him in Spirit, they should have been able to "watch," to actually "see" the significance of his works of liberation, and to hear his repeated predictions of his death and resurrection. But they acted as if they had never seen or heard them. James and John assured him that they would "drink the cup" he would drink. (Mark 10:8-9). Now in his agony, and with his closest disciples beside him, their failure to "watch" is a failure of obedience. It is a failure to support Jesus, to empathise with him in his suffering, to stay the course with him. The disciples desired to be faithful to Jesus, but because they couldn't "see" that his messiahship necessarily involved suffering service, they were not able to "drink the cup" and go all the way "with" him. Their failure may be symptomatic of general human blindness to the full implications of Jesus' messiahship. We are all represented in the sleeping disciples. We may want a Messiah who makes no demands on us, one who leaves us in our comfort zone, rather than calling us to self-sacrificial service.

Jesus went away again and prayed, but once again, they did not know what to say when he found them asleep a second time. (Verse 40). Three times Jesus asked them to watch with him (verses 34,37,38). Their failure to do so portents Peter's later threefold denial. This will humble them and teach them to rely on God's power in prayer, and not on their own bluster and bravado. They were still asleep when he came back to them a third time. (Verse 41a). His first remark to them ("are you sleeping and resting") may indicate his disappointment with them. (14:41). In the midst of all of this, Jesus was aware that one of them was already on his way to betray him.

The phrase "get up" (14:42) recalls Jesus' repeated call to disabled or dead people to come from death to life, and in the present context, it is a reminder to the disciples that they are, in a sense, dead. Discipleship involves us in getting up and going with Jesus on the "way." But we often find the cross too heavy, and like the man of many possessions (Mark 10:17-22), we may walk away, or like the disciples, run away, in an evasion of responsibility. Our spirit may be willing but our flesh is weak. (Mark 14:38b). Jesus' remark, 'Let us go' signals his determination to face his tormenters and drink the bitter "cup" to the full.

## Betrayal and Arrest

Jesus was still speaking to the three disciples when Judas, one of the twelve apostles, arrived in the garden. With him was a crowd, sent by the chief priests, the scribes and the elders, armed with swords and clubs. The traitor had given the crowd a signal: 'The man I kiss is the one you want. Arrest him and take him away under guard.' As soon as Judas arrived, he went up to Jesus and said, 'Teacher!' and kissed him. So they arrested Jesus and held him tight. But one of those standing there drew his sword and struck the High Priest's servant, cutting off his ear. Then Jesus spoke up and said to them, 'Did you have to come with swords and clubs to capture me as though I were an outlaw? Day after day I was with you teaching in the Temple, and you did not arrest me, but the Scriptures must come true.' Then the disciples left him and ran away. A certain young man, dressed only in a linen cloth, was following Jesus. They tried to arrest him, but he ran away naked, leaving the cloth behind. (Mark 14:43-52).

Jesus allows himself to be handed over to the physical power of his enemies, their work being facilitated by Judas, "one of the twelve." (V. 43). Judas had inside knowledge about where Jesus might be found and arrested without commotion. He is now part of the "crowd" (Chief Priests, scribes, Pharisees and elders), members of the Sanhedrin, who have come to arrest Jesus by stealth. The people with swords and clubs were members of the temple guard in the employ of the High Priest.

Judas' kiss – normally an act of affection, is turned into an act of betrayal. Jesus taught with authority in the temple. Now. with swords and clubs in their hands, the temple authorities treat the Lord of the temple as if he were an outlaw. A real outlaw, Barabbas, will be released instead of him (15:15), and he himself will be crucified between two outlaws. He will be condemned on a trumped-up charge of being an outlaw. (Mark 15:27).

John's Gospel tells us that the disciple who cut off the ear of the High Priest's servant was Peter. (John 18:10). Peter's first impulse is to pull out the sword and strike, as if to signal that this might be the way of fulfilling Jesus' messiahship. This recalls Jesus' former remark to Peter ("get behind me Satan") when he wanted to turn Jesus away from the path of suffering service. (Mark 8:33).

The "swords and clubs" (verse 48) were unnecessary. They implied that Jesus was the kind of revolutionary messiah he steadfastly refused to be. The irony is that Judas may have wanted that kind of messiah. Jesus said to them that if they came with swords and clubs, they must have thought that he would retaliate with the sword. The kingdoms of this world are established by overthrowing the social order with swords and clubs. But the reign of God is different; it doesn't use money, politics or military might to establish itself. Jesus is going to sacrifice himself for others. He is going to turn the other cheek to violence. He will overcome swords and clubs with love and forgiveness. Jesus' revolution does not come with any kind of weapons, but in weakness, suffering and rejection. It is the first true revolution. (See Isaiah 2:4; Micah 4:3).

The crowd with swords and clubs represented the very group of people who unsuccessfully opposed and challenged Jesus as he "taught daily in the temple." (Mark 14:49). These were the people at whom he aimed his parable of the wicked tenants. (12:1-11). Instead of repentance and conversion, their response to Jesus' parable of the Tenants now comes in the form of a violent arrest as darkness covers the earth, (Genesis 1:2). They were intent on killing the Son and throwing his body out of the vineyard. (Mark 12:8). This scene in Gethsemane was far removed from the temple, where other crowds supported Jesus in the full light of day, and observed the lack of authority of the High Priest's crowd when they confronted him.

"Then the disciples left him and ran away." (14:50). Mark's short sentence says much. It is a pointer to the disobedience and flight from Eden. (See Genesis 3:8). The disciples now go into hiding. This is the last time we encounter Jesus' male disciples until after the resurrection. Jesus goes to the cross without them being "with" him, which was his original purpose in calling them to discipleship. (Mark 1:17). True discipleship means following Jesus to the bitter end.

What Jesus does for humanity, he must now do alone. Only he can liberate humanity from the bondages which disable them. (Mark 2:10-11; Luke 10:33-34; 15:22-23). When the disciples are finally confronted with the full implications of Jesus' mission and its meaning for their own lives, they desert him. Peter, James and John were privy to

443

many of Jesus' mighty works, including his farewell address to them on the Mount of Olives. Yet, they let Jesus down more than the other disciples, because they were the ones whom he asked to keep watch with him. They were the same three whom God asked to listen to his Son on the Mountain of Transfiguration. (Mark 9:7). Despite all that was said and done, the disciples separated themselves from Jesus and went their separate ways. (Mark 14:50; see Isaiah 53:6). Their flight into hiding fulfils Jesus' prophecy in Mark 14:27. It represents all human flight from God, recalling as it does, the foundational flight and hiding of humanity in the Garden of Eden. (Genesis 3:8). Once the shepherd is killed, the sheep scatter.

Peter holds out a little longer than the others, but eventually his denials are greater than their flight. (Mark 14:66-72). Jesus never gives up on them. The message that goes out from the empty tomb is that Jesus has not abandoned those who abandoned him. He wants them back. (Mark 14:28; 16:7). Time and again, God wants to gather his scattered flock together and feed them with his love. (See Ezekiel 34:11-12; Psalm 23:2).

Mark then has the detail about a young man dressed in linen and escaping naked. (14:51-52). Nakedness is a symbol of separation from God. This recalls another garden where people were tested, failed in their obedience and then fled naked. (Genesis 3:7-8, 10). But in the Garden of Gethsemane, there is a person who is passing a test by losing his life, while others are saving their lives by flight, others again trusting in swords and clubs. Jesus would be saving his life – and ours too – by losing it.

Jesus sees his own predictions and the prophecies of the Old Testament being fulfilled in himself, indicating that everything that takes place is God's will. "The Scriptures must come true." (Mark 14:49b, see Psalm 31:12-13; 38:12). Jesus fulfils the scriptures in which many Old Testament figures suffered for their fidelity to God. (Jeremiah 20:7-9; 26:7-9; 37:13-16; 38:4-5).

## Two Trials

Jesus undergoes two trials. The first one is conducted by the Sanhedrin in the house of Caiaphas, the High Priest (Mark 14:53-72), and after that, before the Roman governor. (Mark 15:2-15; see Psalm 35:11-15; Isaiah 50:5-9; 53:7-8).

The Sanhedrin was a Jewish council, composed of the High Priest, chief priests and possibly some scribes and pharisees. It has already decided that Jesus must die. (Mark 11:18; 14:1). They brought false witnesses against him, who did not agree with one another. (14:59). Like the suffering just man in the psalms, Jesus was surrounded by people bent on his destruction. (See Psalm 35:11-12; 27:11-12). These witnesses had no difficulty in swearing falsely, in violation of the eighth commandment. (See Exodus 20:16, Mark 10:19). Some witnesses accused Jesus of saying, 'I will tear down this temple which men have made, and after three days I will build one that is not made by men.' (14:58). Jesus never said that he would tear down the temple. He did however predict its destruction. (Mark 13:2). Jesus' disputes with the authorities in Mark 11 and 12 arose out of his cleansing of the temple. That action was seen as a challenge to the authority of the High Priest, but it served as a warning that the temple was under God's judgement (11:13, 20) and would be destroyed. (11:15; 13:2). Jesus' action of cleansing the temple was the main reason for his arrest.

The destruction of the temple was imminent. This would be a greater cataclysm than the Sanhedrin could ever have imagined. It would bring an end to old covenant worship, its rituals and sacrificial system, and its priesthood. God allows the consequences of sin to take their toll so that he can bring a new world to birth. Jesus will raise up a new temple, "not made with hands," a temple that God had intended all along – the temple of his own body, of which all his followers would be members – joined to him in a spiritual union. (See John 2:19-21; Ephesians 2:19-22).

The High Priest said to Jesus, 'Have you no answer to the accusations they bring against you?' (14:60). Jesus' silence (verse 61) evokes the Suffering Servant in Isaiah. "He was treated harshly but endured it humbly; he never said a word. Like a lamb about to be slaughtered, he never said a word." (Isaiah 53:7). Jesus did not respond in kind to the violence done to him. Turning the other cheek to it implied his forgiveness.

"Again, the High Priest questioned Jesus, 'Are you the Messiah, the Son of the blessed God?' 'I am,' answered Jesus, 'and you will see the Son of Man seated on the right of the Almighty and coming in the clouds of heaven.'" (14:61-62). The "clouds of heaven" symbolize God's presence. Jesus thus further amplifies the meaning of 'Messiah' and his divine sonship, by saying that he will be seated at the right hand of God, symbolizing his power to judge humanity at the appointed time. Psalm 110:1 speaks of the Messiah's enthronement at the right side of God. The prophet Daniel speaks of a "son of man coming before God's throne with the clouds of heaven, and being given dominion, glory and a kingdom." (Daniel 7:9-14). Jesus interprets these two prophecies as referring to his own coming in judgement at the end of time. (Mark 8:38b; 13:26-27; see Matthew 24:30). The members of the Sanhedrin know who the son of man is in the Book of Daniel. The Son of Man now before the High Priest will come from the throne of God to judge the world, and by implication, the High Priest and the other members of the Sanhedrin. These people, mostly comprising the chief priests, did not believe in the resurrection of the dead. Therefore, they didn't see that God had the power to raise and judge the dead. And not believing in the resurrection, they therefore could not see any ultimate judgement falling on themselves.

There was no longer any need for strict silence concerning Jesus' messiahship. His messianic vocation to lay down his life as a "ransom for many," was about to be fulfilled. (Mark 10:45). Jesus might now be a helpless prisoner being judged by the leaders of Israel, but he reminds them that they will ultimately see him in the fullness of his divine majesty when it will be he who will sit in judgement on them. (Matthew 25:31-36). Jesus' vindication as King and Judge means that God will prove him right, and the High Priest's court wrong. (On Jesus' divine sonship see CCC 441-45; Jesus at God's right hand CCC 659-64; Jesus as the temple, 583-86.)

The High Priest remained unfazed by the revelation of coming judgement. In response to Jesus' explicit claim to divine sonship, "he tore his robes" and said, 'We don't need any more witnesses! You have heard the blasphemy. What is your decision?' They all voted against him: he was guilty and should be put to death. Some of them began to spit on him, and they blindfolded him and hit him. 'Guess who hit you,' they said. "And the guards took him and slapped him." (Mark 14:63-65; see Isaiah 50:5-8; 53:7).

It is ironic that the ones who couldn't "see" Jesus, were the very ones who put blindfolds on him, who was the one who could see into their minds and hearts, and into the heart of God. Jesus was subjected to the physical abuse and mockery that proclaimed him a prophet, (14:65, and a king, 15:16-20). The religious authorities could now present Jesus to Pilate as a rebel king, and to the Jewish people as a blaspheming false prophet, leading Israel astray.

After Jesus' arrest - and desiring to be a loyal disciple, while still keeping himself at a safe distance - Peter followed Jesus into the courtyard of the High Priest. (Mark 14:54). Peter wanted to be loyal but was unable to do so. He did not really know Jesus, because he had yet to understand and accept God's plan for a suffering Messiah, and his own part in that plan. (Mark 8:31-32). Mark twice mentions Peter warming himself at a fire. (14:54, 67). Like his sleep in the garden, Peter was providing for his own comforts while his Lord and Master was being deprived of all human comfort and enduring the insults and blows of his enemies. Peter was saving his own life while Jesus was losing his. While Jesus was proclaiming his true identity as "Son of God" in the house of Caiaphas (14:61-62), his closest disciple and friend was outside denying his allegiance to him (as Jesus predicted), not once, but three times, even cursing and swearing (perjury) that he did not know him. At his third denial the cock crowed, reminding Peter of Jesus' prophecy. Then in repentance for his sin, Peter broke down and wept. (See Mark 14:66-72). Peter will be forgiven for his denial and reinstated as the Lord's chief shepherd. (See John 21:15-17).

Peter himself must have been the source of the story of his denial, which is recorded in all four gospels. At the time Mark's gospel was being read to the first Christians, Peter was the leader of the Church and Jesus' successor on earth. (See Acts of the Apostles, chaps. 1-12). Peter would later go to heroic martyrdom for the love of his Lord and saviour. For the first Christians, some of whom may have failed Jesus under persecution, Peter's failure, and then his repentance and restoration would have brought them a message of consolation, hope and forgiveness.

Mark's detailed description of Peter's failure highlights the solitary journey of Jesus. Betrayed by one disciple, abandoned by ten more, and now bitterly renounced by his closest friend and chief apostle, Jesus stands alone, defenceless before the Jewish court, and before everyone else too. Mark wants to emphasise that what Jesus has to do now, he must do alone. He alone can give his life as a "ransom for many." No one else can liberate humanity from its bondage to self-will.

Echoed in Peter's denials and downfall are our own choices of the safe, easy path of self-interest, over the hard reality of truth and uprightness. We try to save our life, but in effect, we lose it. (Mark 8:34-35). Thinking only of all those whom he was about to ransom, Jesus will lose his life, while trusting that his heavenly Father will save it.

"Early in the morning the chief priests met hurriedly with the elders, the scribes and the whole council, and made their plans. They put Jesus in chains (see Mark 5:3), brought him away and handed him over to Pilate, the Roman Governor." (Mark 15:1; see 5:4). In being tied up in chains, Jesus substitutes himself for all of us, so that we might be freed from all the metaphorical chains that bind and disable us. Jesus being tied in chains recalls his liberation from chains of the man with the legion of demons. (See Mark 5:3). The chief priests and the other religious leaders—no less than Jesus' own disciples – are prepared to sacrifice Jesus and hand him over to death, for the perceived good of safeguarding their own power, status, privileges and safety - what they see as the saving of their lives. Jesus is condemned by the leaders of the Jews and will now be sentenced to death by a leader of the Gentiles. It is important to note that the Jewish people were not collectively responsible for Jesus' death. (CCC 597).

The chief priests "hand over" Jesus, as Judas handed him over, further fulfilling Jesus' passion predictions. (Mark 9:31; 10:33). The chief priests must now persuade Pilate that Jesus is deserving of death. They know that the charge of blasphemy will mean nothing to Pilate. Instead, they plan to use Jesus' admission that he is the Messiah king (14:62), and will make this appear as a threat to Roman rule. 'Are you the king of the Jews,' Pilate asks Jesus? (15:2). Without affirming or denying this, Jesus answers, 'So you say.' Jesus had claimed to be the promised Messiah, which was a royal title. (14:61-62). The claim to be a king would have been considered treason, punishable with death. (See John 19:12). Jesus proclaimed himself King of the Jews, but not in the sense that Pilate understood it–as a threat to Rome. (John 15:9, 12, 18, 26).

Pilate was reluctant to condemn Jesus because he knew that the chief priests handed him over to him because of their envy. (Mark 15:10). He tried to find a way of setting Jesus free without alienating the crowd, and without putting himself on the wrong side of the emperor Caesar. (14:6-15). Possibly representing humanity in its victimizing practices, Pilate, like all the other characters in this drama, was willing to sacrifice Jesus and hand him over to death for the perceived good of saving his own skin. Thus, both the chief priests, and the Roman governor, sacrifice Jesus, because he is seen as a threat to their status and their very existence. The inconvenient victim must be killed and his body "thrown out of the vineyard." (Mark 12:8). Brother continues to murder brother out of self-protection, envy and jealousy (Genesis 4:8b), and to secure them in their power. However, because God is in control of this whole drama, Pilate unwittingly stands for God, as the human being who enables God to hand over his Son to wrathful humans in order to assuage *their* vengeance-seeking wrath.[140] Mark sees all humanity represented in Pilate and the chief priests, all of whom are thus implicated in the mockery, mistreatment and condemnation of the Son of God.

There is irony in the dialogue between Jesus and Pilate. Jesus is the beloved Son of God (Mark 1:11; 9:7), who is destined to reign over the whole world. (Mark 14:62, Daniel 7:13-14). As he stands before the ruler of a small province in the Roman Empire, it is Pilate who questions and judges Jesus.

> At every Passover festival Pilate was in the habit of setting free any one prisoner the people asked for. At that time a man named Barabbas was in prison with rebels who had committed murder in the riot. When the crowd gathered and began to ask Pilate for the usual favour, he asked them, 'Do you want me to set free for you the king of the Jews?' He knew very well that the Chief Priests had handed over Jesus to him because they were jealous. But the chief priests stirred up the crowd to ask, instead, for Pilate to set Barabbas free. Pilate said, 'What do

---

[140] James Alison, *Jesus the Forgiving Victim*, p. 270.

you want me to do with the one you call king of the Jews?' They shouted back, 'Crucify him!' 'But what crime has he committed,' Pilate asked? They shouted all the louder, 'Crucify him.' Pilate wanted to please the crowd, so he set Barabbas free for them. Then he had Jesus whipped and handed him over to be crucified. (15:6-15).

Perhaps some of the people in the "crowd" before Pilate were the very ones who hailed Jesus during his messianic entry to Jerusalem (11:7-10). They may have believed that he was coming to establish a political kingdom. Those people were mostly Passover pilgrims arriving from Galilee and elsewhere. But it is more likely, that most of the "the crowd" before Pilate was made up of the chief priests and their guards, as well as Jewish nationalists who may have been there to lobby Pilate for the release of a prisoner. (14:43).

The leaders of Israel manoeuvred the crowd into choosing a "Barabbas," whose name means "son of the father," and who was implicated in rebellion and bloodshed, while rejecting "Bar Abba," the beloved Son of their God, who turned the other cheek to the blows of his torturers. This Son died a victim, rejecting all violence, in order to bring to their nation, the kind of unity which could only be established by peace and forgiveness, and never by violence or making victims. Jesus gave his life in suffering service, while the self-serving religious leaders and the Roman governor sought to preserve their lives and status. They killed the Son and threw his body out of the vineyard, claiming the vineyard as their own, as a way of serving their selfish interests. (Mark 12:8).

God had done everything he could for his vineyard, but his tenants had only produced bitter grapes. (See Isaiah 5:1-7; Psalm 80:9, 12-16, 19-20). They rejected the Son and his message of peace, forgiveness and reconciliation, as the only means of freeing everyone from the slaveries of violence, enmity, hatred, retribution and death itself. But ironically, in their rejection of the Son of God, they were actually establishing the reign of God. In 70 AD, following their rebellion against Rome, the hedge and wall surrounding their city would be taken away and trampled by "wild animals" (Isaiah 5:5), represented in the legions of the Roman army. (See Isaiah 5:5). And they themselves would be bound in chains and taken into slavery. God would then hand over his vineyard to other tenants, who would give him his share of the harvest. (Mark 12:2).

Pilate was puzzled by Jesus' reluctance to say anything in his defence. Jesus' silence again evokes the suffering servant who remained silent in the face of his persecutors. (Isaiah 53:7a). Mark conveys a sense of awe with the phrase "Pilate was amazed." (Mark 15:5; see 5:20). Isaiah's Servant had the same effect of amazement on kings when they witnessed his patient endurance of suffering. (Isaiah 52:15). Pilate couldn't escape responsibility for condemning Jesus. Like Herod in the case of John the Baptist (Mark 6:17-29), he had been led, against his better judgement, for fear of offending a crowd (6:26; 14:15), to pass a death sentence on Jesus, whom he knew to be innocent. Mark himself may also be in awe over his own awareness that it was for this crowd who callously rejected him, that Jesus was about to lay down his life, in forgiveness of them.

The prelude to a Roman execution was scourging (Mark 15:15) - perhaps in order that the victim would be so weakened, he would soon die on the cross. The condemned person was stripped naked, bound to a pillar and beaten until his flesh hung in shreds.

The instrument of torture was a whip made of rawhide and braided with bone or metal. There was no limit to the number of strokes meted out by the soldiers. It was not unusual for the victim to collapse and die from this torture alone. Jesus survived this torture.

> Then the soldiers led him away to the inner part of the palace, that is, the Praetorium, and called the whole cohort together. They dressed him up in purple, twisted some thorns into a crown and put it on him. And they began saluting him, 'Hail, king of the Jews!' They struck his head with a reed and spat on him; and they went down on their knees to do him honour. And when they had finished making fun of him, they took off the purple cloak and dressed him in his own clothes. They led him out to crucify him. They enlisted a passer-by, Simon of Cyrene, father of Alexander and Rufus, who was coming in from the country, to carry his cross. (Mark 15:16-21, NJB; see Isaiah 50:6-7; 53:3-5).

The Praetorium was a large courtyard surrounded by living quarters. This was Pilate's temporary headquarters in Jerusalem. He preferred the greater comforts of the coastal city of Caesarea, where he normally resided. A Roman cohort was a detachment of about six hundred soldiers, one tenth of a legion. The "whole cohort" simply means those members who were on duty at that particular time.

After the scourging, and for a second time during his passion, Jesus is mocked - a humiliation that will be repeated while he is dying on the cross. (Isaiah 50:6-7; 53:3-5). Now the Gentile soldiers under Pilate's command mock him as "king of the Jews," with a crown of thorns on his head. The soldiers ironically kneel before him in mock homage. Mark's readers know that Jesus is worthy of all homage. It is in his suffering and humiliation that Jesus is crowned "King of kings and Lord of Lords." (Revelation 19:16).

Once again, Isaiah's Suffering Servant is in the background of Mark's account. "I bared my back to those who beat me. I did not stop them when they insulted me, when they pulled out the hairs of my beard and spat in my face. But their insults cannot hurt me because the Sovereign Lord gives me help. I braced myself to endure them. I know that I will not be disgraced." (Isaiah 50:6-7). The words 'not disgraced' refers to the vindication of the servant.

A person condemned to death was forced to parade naked through the streets of Jerusalem while he was being flogged by the soldiers. The victim was also forced to carry the crossbeam. This was the piece of wood to which his hands were later nailed or tied. The upright post of the cross would have already been set in the ground at the place of execution.

Probably because Jesus had been weakened by the scourging, the soldiers forced a man named Simon of Cyrene (then a Roman city in present-day Libya) to carry his cross. (Mark 15:21). This man would have been a member of the Jewish diaspora and very likely in Jerusalem for the Passover festival. Mark hints that his action may have changed the man's life. The fact that Mark names Simon's two sons as Alexander and Rufus, means that they were probably known as Christians in the early Church. (See Romans 16:13). The man named Simon Peter, however, is nowhere to be seen. Jesus had described the essence of discipleship as taking up the cross along with him. (Mark 8:34).

## Crucifixion

Crucifixion was the Roman punishment for slaves, violent criminals and rebels against Rome. It was forbidden to crucify Roman citizens. This was a form of execution designed not only to inflict maximum physical pain, but also to humiliate and shame the victim. It was intended to obliterate the victim's memory and eliminate any possible following he may have gathered in life. After the scourging, the condemned person was led to the place of death through the crowds, who would further humiliate him. In a Roman crucifixion, the victim was stripped naked, his outstretched arms nailed through the wrist, or tied to the wooden crossbeam. Then the beam was lifted up with the body and fastened to the upright stake. The victim's feet would be either nailed or tied to the upright. A crucified man might linger in agony for days, eventually dying from asphyxiation or thirst.

The crucifixion of Jesus is given its true meaning in Old Testament prophecies of the just man who suffers, but who is finally vindicated by God - especially the figure of the just man in the Psalms and Isaiah. (See Psalms 22, 69; Isaiah 52:13-53:12). In the Old Testament, those who were crucified were seen as being cursed by God. "God's curse rests on him who hangs on a tree." (Deuteronomy 21:22-23). But for the early Church, Jesus' crucifixion was redemptive: "Christ himself carried our sins in his body to the cross, so that we might die to sin and live for righteousness. "It is by his wounds that you have been healed. You were like sheep that had lost their way, but now you have been brought back to follow the shepherd and keeper of your souls." (1 Peter 2:24-25; see Isaiah 53:5-6). The quote from 1 Peter evokes Jesus' substitutionary role of identifying with us sinners.

Crucifixion, according to St. Paul, was a "stumbling block to the Jews and foolishness to the Gentiles." (1 Corinthians 1:23). And yet, ironically, the cross of Jesus remains a potent and inspiring symbol of Christian life down the ages. The memory of this man on the cross will never be erased.

They took Jesus to the place called Golgotha, which means the "Place of the Skull." There they tried to give him wine mixed with a drug called myrrh, but Jesus would not drink it. Then they crucified him and divided his clothing among themselves, throwing dice to see who would get which piece of clothing. It was none o'clock in the morning when they crucified him. The notice of the accusation against him said: "The King of the Jews." They also crucified two bandits with Jesus, one on his right and the other on his left. People passing by shook their heads and hurled insults at Jesus: 'Aha! You were going to tear down the Temple and build it again in three days. Now come down from the cross and save yourself.' In the same way, the chief priests and teachers of the law jeered at Jesus, saying to each other, 'He saved others, but he cannot save himself. Let us see the Messiah, the king of Israel, come down from the cross now, and we will believe in him.' And the two who were crucified with Jesus insulted him also. (Mark 15:22-32; see Psalm 22:16-18, 24-25; Galatians 3:13-14; 1 Peter 2:24; Isaiah 53:12).

The soldiers' offer of cheap wine to Jesus may have been intended as a continuation of the mockery that had already taken place. The wine mixed with myrrh may be a reference to Psalm 69:21. In this psalm, the just person cries out for help in the face of torture. Jesus refuses this cup. The "cup" he drinks at the Last Supper is the last one he will drink until the messianic banquet at the end of time.

Jesus was left hanging naked on the cross. In the Scriptures, nakedness always symbolizes separation from God, a refusal to obey him. (Genesis 3:9-10). Jesus identifies with us in our sins of disobedience, which leave us separated from God.

The notice on the cross (Mark 15:26) was a sarcastic warning by the Roman authorities that this is how messianic pretenders end their days. Pilate may also have intended it as a jab at the Jewish leaders who had brought the charge of messiahship against Jesus. (Mark 14:61-62). What Pilate and the Jewish leaders did not know was that Jesus was indeed the Messiah King whom God intended for Israel. He was enthroned on the cross, because it is there that he exercised dominion over evil by turning the other cheek to Satanic violence, thus establishing the reign of God over evil.

In reference to the two bandits crucified along with Jesus (Mark 15:27), the Greek word for 'bandit' can also mean a political insurgent. These two may have committed murder during an uprising and may have been imprisoned with Barabbas. (15:7). At his arrest in the garden, Jesus protested that the temple guards had come out against him as though he were an outlaw (bandit). (14:48). Now he hangs on a cross as a bandit between two bandits, thus identifying himself with all bandits (everyone) so that he might turn their stubborn hearts to repentance and save them. The two bandits represented the false understanding of messiahship (violent revolution) that Jesus had continually rejected in favour of a Messiah who would be a suffering servant. (Isaiah 53:12). He was dying the death, which under Roman law, belonged to the two who were crucified beside him. Mark says that both of the men who were crucified along with Jesus joined the other mockers in insulting him. (Mark 15:32). According to Luke's gospel (23:40), one of the men did not do so, giving rise to the phrase of the "good" thief (bandit). In Mark's usual bleak account, nobody is good. All are sinners. All are victimizers. Jesus' association with sinners (rebels against God) which began with his baptism (1:9), now reaches its climax, as he places himself beside those who are separated from God because of their sins. (Isaiah 59:2; see 5 3:12). Jesus experiences only scorn and rejection by those whom he came to save, represented by the two bandits who were crucified with him. He is the just man who is abused and insulted by the wicked, but who still trusts in God to vindicate him. (Psalm 22:12-17, 27-31; Isaiah 53:5). He will come back again to forgive all of them.

Ironically, the right and left positions beside Jesus were the places of royal honour that James and John had requested of him. (See Mark 10:37-39). But the kind of royal honour they had in mind was in terms of a conquering king. Discipleship means being beside Jesus at every stage of his life. Being close to Jesus is now graphically displayed as "drinking the cup" of suffering along with him, something that hadn't entered the minds of James and John when they sought places of honour beside him in his kingdom.

Passers-by joined in the insulting and mocking of Jesus, challenging him to come down from the cross and save himself. If he could tear down the temple, as they said, and then build it up, surely, he could save himself! (15:29-30). At his trial and on the cross,

Jesus' mockers could not imagine an anointed one (Messiah) who would not choose to save himself. Weakness of any kind was despised in the ancient world. Losing your life, refusing the power you have to save yourself is alien to the thinking of those who readily use their power to save and promote themselves, even though it may be at the expense of others.

It is by staying on the cross that Jesus establishes himself as the true King and saviour. Jesus trusted in God to vindicate him (Isaiah 53:12), and not in words spoken in malice by mockers. By not coming down from the cross Jesus is bringing an end to the earthly temple (Mark 15:38) and building a new temple, "not made by hands," (14:58), but on the cornerstone of his crucified and risen body – a temple that will truly be a "house of prayer for all nations." (Mark 11:17).

In the same way the chief priests and scribes jeered at Jesus about not being able to save himself, saying that they would believe in him if he came down from the cross. (15:31-32; see Psalm 22:8). These people were demanding a miracle which they thought would enable them to believe in him. For Mark, faith can never be based on miracles. Miracles can only occur in the context of already existing faith. (See Mark 8:11-12). The religious leaders demand for a miraculous sign recalls the same demand by the Pharisees earlier. (Mark 8:11).

The above demand by the chief priests is the culmination of the testing that began with Satan in the desert. (Mark 1:13). It is the temptation to be a Messiah who gains followers through stunning displays of power in order to defeat his enemies and thus gain "all the kingdoms of the world." (Matthew 4:8). On the contrary, Jesus' way of gaining the whole world is by turning the other cheek to violence and forgiving his torturers, because he knew that this was the only way to establish a universal kingdom of brotherly love and peace. (See Isaiah 2:4; 9:7; 11:5-7). Jesus rejects the oppressive power and rivalry employed by the rulers of empires. (Mark 10:41-42). *His* power is exercised through suffering service (Mark 10:43-45), i.e. through forgiveness, leading to reconciliation, as the only way to establish the new covenant of love between human beings themselves and between them and God. (Mark 14:24; 14:36; see Isaiah 53:10a). Jesus refuses to "save himself." In obedience to the Father's plan he refuses to meet violence with retribution (Isaiah 53:7). Only by giving himself up to death will he be raised to new life by the Father. That is how Jesus saves himself and all those with whom he associates - everyone. By staying on the cross in obedience to the Father, Jesus creates God's new family of brotherhood. (See Mark 3:33-35, Romans 5:5-8; Galatians 2:20).

## The Death of Jesus

At noon the whole country was covered with darkness, which lasted for three hours. At three o'clock Jesus cried out with a loud shout, *'My God, my God, why did you abandon me?'* Some of the people who were there thought he was calling on Elijah. One of them ran up with a sponge, soaked it in cheap wine and put it on the end of a stick. Then he held it up to Jesus' lips and said, 'Wait! Let us see if Elijah is coming to bring him down from the cross.' With a loud cry Jesus died.

The curtain hanging in the Temple was torn from top to bottom. (Mark 15:33-38). The words in italics above are from Psalm 22:1a).

Mark has shown a progressive increase in Jesus' sense of isolation and abandonment. He is the stone rejected by the builders. He is killed by the tenants of the vineyard, who represent all of us. (Mark 12:8). He is abandoned by his closest friends, culminating in his sense of abandonment by God, whose will he is still obeying by remaining hung on the cross. (15:34). Although Jesus experiences separation from God by identifying with us sinners, his words are not a cry of despair. In quoting the first verse of Psalm 22 (15:34, in italics above), Jesus addresses the Father, not with the familiar words 'my Father,' but as 'my God,' as if he identifies with those who address God out of a sense of being abandoned in their troubles. He confesses his filial trust that the Father will, somehow, have the final word on all the injustice and suffering in the world.

The prophet Isaiah uses the image of the darkening of the earth as signalling that the "day of the Lord" has come. This is a day when God's judgement will fall on Babylon, bringing that empire to an end. God will then liberate the people of Israel from its slavery. (Isaiah 13:9-10; 14:3). Three days of darkness preceded the liberation of the Israelites from Egypt. (Exodus 10:21-23; see Amos 8:9-10; Mark 13:24). The "darkness" at the death of Jesus may be a prelude to the liberation of all of us from the darkness of our death - exile in this world.

The three hours of darkness may also be symbolic of the chaos in the rejection, mockery and killing of the Son of Man. It's as if God allowed creation to slide back into the chaos and darkness that reigned before the first creation. (Genesis 1:1). Mark's gospel reveals that this darkness is only the prelude to a new creation, which will come with a light that no darkness will ever again extinguish: the glorious vindication of the Son of Man - his rising from the darkness of the tomb to the new light of Easter morning. (Mark 16:6; see John 1:4-5; 20:1; Isaiah 53:11-12).

In the darkness of the cross, Jesus looks to the Father and asks why. It is the question of Job – why do the innocent suffer? (See Job 1:6-12; 2:23-26). For Jesus, no answer to his cry will come from God until after he has shared the full lot of human beings in death. "Christ was without sin, but for our sake God sent him on a mission of sharing our sin (our death in sin) in order that in union with him, we might share the righteousness of God." (2 Corinthians 5:21; see Philippians 2:8). The "righteousness of God" can be understood as the eternal love-life of God, which we inherit through the obedience of his Son.

The first verse of Psalm 22 quoted by Jesus is a cry of abandonment by God and a feeling of despair over help that does not come to the sufferer. This psalm ends with an expression of hope and vindication for the sufferer, which Mark sees as fulfilled in the resurrection of Jesus, when a few women disciples are told to proclaim God's victory to the other disciples. (Mark 16:7; see John 20:17). The sovereign God listens to cries of desperation. God has the final word on suffering, evil and death, thus opening the way to eternal life for humanity. Deepest human hungering for life will be fully satisfied: "the poor (everyone) will have as much to eat as they want... The Lord is King and rules the nations." (Psalm 22:26a, 28). Jesus' feeding of the multitudes in the wilderness is fulfilled, thus satisfying humanity's hunger for fullness of life. "People not yet born will be told, 'The Lord saved his people.'" (Psalm 22:31).

In his cry of abandonment, God's beloved Son screams out with the agony of all human hearts in the face of innocent suffering, as they are unable to fathom the mind of God in all its darkness and obscurity. But as was the case with Jesus, God always finds a way out for human beings who are enveloped in darkness. The God in whom we believe, is sovereign over history. Trusting in this God means believing that he can, and will, deal with human darkness and abandonment, and bring good out of evil, not perhaps in the way we want at a given time, but in a way and time that may be best for us. This kind of trusting in God is the highest form of faith, but very difficult! As the darkness and chaos surrounding Jesus on the cross disappeared in the new creation of his resurrection, for us also, an experience of darkness may be the prelude to new hope, a new journey to which God may be calling us, leading to the light of new creation. God always brings good out of evil. We may be walking in a death-like darkness (Psalm 23:4), but he prepares a table before us and welcomes us home as honoured guests. (Psalm 23:5).

The reference to the tearing of the temple curtain in the foregoing passage (15:38) is to a large curtain which was hung at the entrance to the inner sanctuary of the temple (the place where God was supposed to dwell), and beyond which, only the High Priest could go on the annual Day of Atonement. (See Leviticus 16). This curtain symbolized a barrier between people and their God. In the Old Testament, there was a persistent longing for God to definitively reveal himself and come to the aid of human beings in their darkness. "Why don't you tear the sky apart and come down? The mountains would see you and shake with fear. Come and reveal your power to your enemies." (Isaiah 64:1-2).

The first sign of the divine silence being broken at the death of Jesus is the collapse of the temple curtain, signalling both the end of old covenant worship and the role of the High priest in offering temple sacrifices. The members of God's earthly family, the Jewish leaders, Jesus' disciples, and the Gentiles, had been living in darkness, blind and deaf to who God is, disobedient to his covenant. (Isaiah 42:18-20; 64:6-7). In the old covenant, God was hidden behind a metaphorical curtain. In Jesus, we see who God is, a God of love coming to live among us in order to rescue us and take us home - and suffering for us in the process. The barrier between heaven and earth has come down. Jacob's dream of the ladder stretching to heaven is fulfilled. (Genesis 28:12). The tearing of the temple curtain is an eye-opener, revealing Jesus as the power of God in the world, and shining a light "on those who live in the dark land of death." (Matthew 4:16; John 1:4-5; see Isaiah 9:2-7). The human weakness of Jesus on the cross reveals a God, who can turn darkness into light and death into resurrection. (See 2 Corinthians 12:9-10). With the curtain of the temple torn down, God can be seen most clearly in the isolation, abandonment, and powerlessness of the just man crucified on the hill of Calvary. Jesus' weakness is actually a revelation of his strength – losing his life in order to save it - dying in order to rise into glory - and to raise up everyone else too. (Isaiah 53:11a, 12).

The tearing of the temple curtain also foreshadows the destruction of the temple, which will occur a generation later, as Jesus himself predicted. (13:1-2). The earthly temple will be replaced by a new temple, "not made with hands" (Mark 14:58), with Jesus himself as the foundation stone. (Mark 12:10). This new temple of the Christian community will be a true "house of prayer for all nations" (Mark 11:17), giving both Jews and Gentiles immediate access to God through Jesus. By his obedient death, Jesus enters God's presence as High Priest on behalf of all humanity, opening access to the Father for everyone. (See Ephesians 2:18; Hebrews 10:19-22). The tearing of the temple curtain recalls the first tearing of the heavens that occurred at Jesus' baptism, with the announcement of God's pleasure in his beloved Son, and its implied revelation that everyone else would be made sons and daughters of God, through their brotherly relationship with Jesus. (Mark 1:10-11; 3:33-35).

The curtain of death still lies across the path of every human being. But Jesus has opened a way, leading us through the curtain, to eternal life, once we place our trust in him and remain united to him (obedient to the covenant). The victory is in him, and not in the powers of darkness. "The light shines in the darkness, and the darkness could not overpower it." (John 1:5, NJB). Jesus is that light. As we make our earthly journey, all of us face the experience of Jesus' sense of abandonment, suffering and death. But because we believe that Jesus was not abandoned by God, we are given the courage and hope to face the fears of suffering and death that might otherwise paralyze us. We are thus empowered, not so much to *believe* something about Jesus – the one faithful person in Mark's story - but to imitate his self-sacrificial service, in faithfulness and obedience to God. The example of Jesus' life for others in the face of death helps to free us from self-centredness, so that we may live for others (fearlessly spread the gospel, Mark 16:6-7), even in the face of opposition and misunderstanding.

After the death of Jesus on the cross, and his reference to the tearing of the temple curtain, Mark shifts his focus to the Roman centurion who was in charge of the crucifixion of Jesus. The tearing of the temple curtain may also symbolize the opening of the eyes of the Gentiles to the reality of God, as seen in Jesus, the just man dying on a Roman cross.

## The Centurion's Confession of Faith

The army officer (centurion) standing there in front of the cross saw how Jesus had died. 'This man was really the Son of God,' he said. (Mark 15:39).

In contrast to the mockers who demanded that Jesus come down from the cross, the Roman centurion in charge of Jesus' execution responds to his death with a confession of faith. At Jesus' baptism the Father bore witness to his "beloved Son." (Mark 1:11). Now, for the first time, a human being - who is a Gentile – "saw" how Jesus died and confesses him as "Son of God." His seeing "how" Jesus died implies that, for him, Jesus' death was unlike any of the other deaths he had ever witnessed. As a Roman citizen, the centurion would have acknowledged his emperor's claim to be a son of God. Is he now giving his allegiance to the man on the cross as the true Son of God? This man may be more deserving of the title, 'Son of God,' than the emperor of Rome. In contrast to the disciples who remained blind to Jesus' sonship, and the mockers who demanded to see Jesus come down from the cross, the Roman centurion "saw" Jesus embracing insults and mockery, enduring and accepting the blows of his torturers and freely giving up his life in a cry of abandonment. (Mark 15:34). Such a thing had never been seen before. The Roman

455

centurion who was in charge at the execution of Jesus would have been a man whose heart was hardened by bloodshed and killing. But as he must have seen it, a man who dies with such dignity, and without crying out against his killers (Isaiah 53:7), must have something of God in him. The Roman centurion, whose cohort mocked Jesus as king of the Jews with royal apparel and imperial salute, has his eyes opened to the fact that in killing Jesus, he may have been killing the Son of God. The prophet Ezekiel says that when God demonstrates to the Gentiles who he really is "they will know that I am the Lord." (Ezekiel 36:23). The temple curtain is torn down, showing the Gentiles who God is.

On the hill of Calvary, God demonstrates who he really is—a suffering servant, willingly dying while accepting the blows of those who killed him. Standing at the foot of the cross, the Roman centurion may be said to represent the Gentile nations, thus fulfilling the prophecy of Isaiah: "Now many nations will marvel at him, and kings will be speechless with amazement. They will see and understand something they had never known." (Isaiah 52:15; 66:23). Through the words of the Roman centurion, Mark may be speaking to his possible Gentile audience, asking if more of them can imitate the centurion, and confess Jesus as Son of God. The centurion is the first fruit of Jesus' sacrifice. He represents the beginning of the gathering of the Gentiles prophesied in the Old Testament (Genesis 12:3, 22:18; Isaiah 42:6; 45:22-23), and announced by Jesus himself. (Mark 13:10, 27).

In the confession of the Roman centurion, Mark is sending a signal to the whole world that the reign of God has come, that a new age is being born. God has done something, the good news of which, will spread round the world.

At the beginning of Mark's gospel - and before the disciples appeared on the scene - the heavenly voice proclaims Jesus as 'my Son, the Beloved.' (Mark 1:11, NJB). Apart from Jesus himself, it is only the readers of the gospel who are aware of this revelation. It's as if Jesus wants his disciples to discover his divine sonship for themselves, through their experience of his mighty works and teachings. Midway through the gospel, Peter recognizes Jesus as no more than the Messiah promised to Israel. (Mark 8:29). On the mountain of Transfiguration, Peter, James and John hear the voice of God, with the words, 'This is my Son the Beloved. Listen to him.' (Mark 9:7, NJB). But that revelation, together with its call to "listen" to the Son, may have completely gone over the heads of the three disciples. In Gethsemane, the same three were asleep when Jesus spoke the words, 'My Father,' signalling his obedience to the Father's will. Throughout his ministry, Jesus cast out demons, forgave sins and worked extraordinary wonders. But although the disciples were witnesses to these works of Jesus, the revelation of his divine sonship still remained hidden from their eyes. It is Jesus' filial obedience unto death on the cross, above all, that confirms him as Son of the Father. Because of their scattering, the disciples were not present in Calvary to witness Jesus' self-sacrificial death, which means that they had denied themselves the opportunity of receiving this revelation at that time. However, Jesus will give them another chance to open their eyes and really "see" him.

The revelation of Jesus as "Son of God" is the foundational tenet of the Christian gospel. (See Romans 1:1-4; Galatians 1:16; John 1:14; 3:16; 17:1, 20:30-31; the First Letter of John 5:5, 10, 13).

Mark brings his account of the passion of Jesus to a conclusion with his reference to the "many" faithful women disciples who followed Jesus from Galilee to Calvary.

## Jesus' Women Disciples

> Some women were there, looking on from a distance. Among them were Mary
> Magdalene, Mary the mother of the younger James and of Joseph, and Salome.
> They had followed Jesus while he was in Galilee and helped him. Many other
> women who had come to Jerusalem with him were there also. (Mark 15:40-41).

For the first time Mark speaks of the women who had been accompanying Jesus during
his public ministry. In contrast to the male disciples, they stayed "with" him all the way to
Calvary. "They helped him out of their own resources" (Luke 8:1-3) - carrying out his
exhortation that a disciple must be "the servant of all." (Mark 9:35; 10:43). In Gethsemane,
Jesus asked the male disciples to stay awake, to keep watch with him, but they fell asleep,
failing in their obedience. (14:37-38). In contrast to the male disciples, who could not keep
"watch," the women were present in Calvary "looking on from a distance." (15:40). They
may have wanted to stand under the cross and close to Jesus, but the soldiers who crucified
him may have kept them at a distance. Their "looking" at Jesus may suggest that the women
disciples had a fuller understanding of Jesus' messiahship than the men. By using the
phrase "many other women" in the above passage, Mark also suggests that Jesus' women
disciples formed a faithful crowd (v. 41), in contrast to the crowd who called for his
crucifixion and who mocked and abused him, and the crowd of male disciples who ran
away.

The presence of the women disciples in the gospel fulfils an important function.
Because of their watching, they were witnesses to the death of Jesus, to his burial and to
the empty tomb. (Mark 16:4-5).

## The Burial of Jesus

First century Jews buried their dead in family tombs dug out of hillsides or solid rock.
According to ancient tradition, Jesus' tomb was dug into a hillside just outside the western
wall of the city. In the fourth century, a basilica was built on this site.

Crucified criminals were usually left hanging on the cross until their bodies
decayed or were eaten by wild animals. In contrast to those, Jesus was given a reverent
burial. This was because Jesus had a secret disciple. Mark says that a man named Joseph
of Arimathea was a "respected member of the Council (the Sanhedrin), who was waiting
for the kingdom of God." (15:42). This means that he was present at the night session in
the High Priest's house and that he was witness to the accusations and condemnation of
Jesus. Mark leaves open the question whether he gave his consent to the condemnation
of Jesus. Luke's gospel says he did not give his consent to this. (Luke 23:51). Both Matthew
and John say that Joseph of Arimathea was a disciple of Jesus, and Matthew also says that
he was a rich man. (Matthew 27:57; John 19:38; see Isaiah 53:9). Joseph's courage of openly
associating himself with Jesus is contrasted with the fear of Peter.

Risking the ire of the Sanhedrin, Joseph boldly went to Pilate and asked for the
body of Jesus. Pilate was surprised to hear that Jesus was already dead. He verified the
death by summoning the centurion who had witnessed the death. (See Mark 15:42-44).

After hearing the officer's report, Pilate told Joseph that he could have the body. Joseph bought a linen sheet, took the body down, wrapped it in the sheet and placed it in a tomb which had been dug out of solid rock. Then he rolled a large stone across the entrance to the tomb. Mary Magdalene and Mary the mother of Joseph were watching and saw where the body of Jesus was placed. (15: 45-47).

The Mary referred to above was not the mother of Joseph of Arimathea. The latter may have owned the tomb in which he placed the body of Jesus. The burial recalls the Suffering Servant who was given a "tomb with the rich." (Isaiah 53:9, JB). The large stone rolled against the entrance to the tomb was for the protection of the body from scavenging animals.

Mark continues with the theme of "watching" by the women disciples. Now they watch his burial, which is a confirmation of his death. Later the same women will watch at the empty tomb, leading to their mission to announce Jesus' resurrection to the world.

CHAPTER 17

# RESURRECTION AND NEW CREATION

## The Empty Tomb - Good News for the Disciples

Just like the male disciples, as far as the women knew, Jesus' life and mission had come to a tragic end. There was nothing left but to show their respect for his remains. Jesus' prophecies of his resurrection (8:31; 9:9, 31; 10:34) had eluded the women's grasp, just as they had for the male disciples. The women's reason for coming to the tomb was to anoint the body of Jesus. It was customary at that time to prepare bodies for burial by anointing them with aromatic spices.

> After the Sabbath was over, Mary Magdalene, Mary the mother of James, and Salome bought spices to go and anoint the body of Jesus. Very early on Sunday morning, at sunrise, they went to the tomb. On the way they said to one another, 'Who will roll away the stone for us from the entrance to the tomb?' (It was a very large stone). Then they looked up and saw that the stone had already been rolled back. So they entered the tomb, where they saw a young man sitting on the right, wearing a white robe – and they were alarmed. 'Don't be alarmed,' he said. 'I know that you are looking for Jesus of Nazareth, who was crucified. He is not here – he has been raised! Look, here is the place where they put him. (Mark 16:1-6; see Matthew 28:1-6; Job 19:25-26; Psalm 16:9-11; Hosea 6:1-3; CCC 638-58, 992-1004).

All four gospels say that Mary Magdalene was among the women who were the first witnesses to the resurrection. The Gospel of John says that Mary Magdalene was the first person to whom Jesus appeared. (John 20:11-17). Luke names her as a woman out of whom Jesus had driven seven demons. (Luke 8:2). The watchfulness, courage and faithfulness of the women disciples is in marked contrast to the faithlessness of Peter and the Twelve (Mark 14:50, 66-72), all of whom had gone into hiding, and are only watching out for themselves.

Mark's mention of the "sunrise" is the first hint that the darkness accompanying the death of Jesus (15:33) - symbolizing the temporary triumph of evil - had been overcome. Sunday morning was also the first day of the week, the day when God created light out of darkness (Genesis 1:3-5), but now it signifies the first day of the new creation, a new beginning for humankind.

The fact that the tomb was already open may have completely disorientated the women. They expected to find death in the tomb, but they were left grappling with the reality of an unseen, but new world, which Mark can only describe in terms of a visit by an angel. Confronted with death, the human being is utterly powerless. Human beings cannot open their graves. They might not believe that God himself would have the power to do so. The women were "distressed, terrified" (16:5), as if overwhelmed by an experience of the mysterious, of a divine power beyond the ability of human beings to grasp or speak about. (See Mark 10:27; 11:22-24). The mysterious presence in the tomb of a young man is suggestive of another world beyond this. The barrier between the divine and human worlds had broken down momentarily after Jesus' baptism (Mark 1:10) and at his transfiguration. (9:7). God wants to permanently remove all barriers separating humanity from himself. Out of love for humanity, he has entered history and opened the grave, and will open all graves, so that transformed human beings can live in close relationship with him in their "promised land" – a metaphor for their eternal destiny. "When I open the graves where my people are buried and bring them out, they will know that I am the Lord. I will put my breath in them, bring them back to life, and let them live in their own land. I have promised that I would do this – and I will. I, the Lord have spoken." (Ezekiel 37:13-14; see Genesis 2:7b). Ezekiel's prophecy is fulfilled in Jesus. Because of his conquest of death, we now "know" that Jesus is Lord. He is now the one in charge. His kingdom has come.

The phrase "has been raised" means that it is God who raised Jesus. Jesus' agonized cry of abandonment on the cross has received an answer from God. (Mark 15:34). Jesus trusted and hoped that God would deliver him from the powers who killed him. (Isaiah 53:11). The resurrection is God's triumph over death, and his victory over the powers who use death as a weapon of enslavement and oppression. Jesus' prophecy has come true. He is the stone rejected by the former builders, who has become the foundation stone of God's new temple – God's new created world. (Mark 12:10-11; 14:58; 15:29). God has not abandoned his beloved Son, but vindicated him with an everlasting triumph over death. God has raised his "devoted servant and gave him a place of honour." (Isaiah 53:12). And because Jesus is the devoted servant whom God raised, then God will raise all those servants with whom Jesus identified and who associate with him, by living for the good news, as he did. (See 1 Corinthians 15:12-20, 22-23). The way Jesus lived is the way for all humans to live – as servants, liberated from status and power, and other harmful attachments, in order to do the will of God, so that God's kingdom may fully come on earth. (Mark 3:33-35).

And because God raised Jesus, God has the last word on Jesus' conflict with the authorities, both civil and religious. Jesus' victory over the powers is God's victory. The powers that put Jesus to death are disarmed. However, they still continue to function after the resurrection, but only under the authority of God, who appoints them to bring a measure of order to his world. With God's victory over death, the human authorities are robbed of their pretention to absolute authority when they put Jesus on the cross. The reign of God has been established, and its sign is not a gilded throne but a wooden cross. (See 1 Colossians 1:18; 1 Corinthians 2:6-8). Having been appointed by God, the rulers of the world are to be obeyed, although they may sometimes abuse the power entrusted to them and resort to greed, glory-seeking and injustice, thus becoming instruments of evil. This is the Adam and Eve temptation for the powers. Giving free reign to social and cultural feeling (the spirit of the age) is no way to administer unchanging justice. God is sovereign, and his reign requires that the State acknowledges its responsibility to reflect the justice of God into society. (See Romans 13:1-4). Furthermore, the State can never create the perfect society or eliminate evil from the earth. It is only in the second coming of the Son of Man that God will put the world right and deal definitively with evil and death.

Jesus has been raised from death. (16:6). It is human disobedience that brings death into the world. (Genesis 2:16-17, 3:6-7; see John 8:44; Romans 5:12; 6:22-23; 1 Corinthians 15:20-22; Book of Wisdom 2:23-24, NJB; CCC 1006-9). Jesus' death was not due to his own disobedience, because he was obedient unto death, but was to ransom others from their sins of disobedience that lead to death. (Mark 10:45, NJB). Jesus is the living proof that death is not part of God's creation of human beings. (See the Book of Wisdom 11:24). How could God create the evil known as death? God does not know death. Because Jesus was the beloved and obedient Son, and thus without sin, death could have no power over him. (Romans 6:8-9). Death is not willed by God. It is a biological reality, but it is not something natural. If death were part of human nature, it could not be redeemed. Human death is a fallen reality, and only as such, can it be redeemed by Christ.[141] Redemption does not change human nature; it restores human beings to the fullness of their humanity, which is what God wanted from the beginning, when he walked with them in his garden called Eden. (Genesis 2:8-9, 3:8a).

## Back again to Galilee

After the angel showed the women the place in the tomb where Jesus had been laid, he then appointed them to the mission of bringing the good news of Jesus' resurrection to the world:

> Now go and give this message to his disciples, including Peter: 'He is going to Galilee ahead of you; there you will see him, just as he told you.' So they went out and ran from the tomb, distressed and terrified. They said nothing to anyone, because they were afraid. (Mark 16:7-8).

The women were told to confirm with their own eyes what the early Christians would later affirm – that God raised Jesus from death. (Acts 13:30-35; Romans 10:9; 1 Peter 1:21). The reference to Peter makes it likely that Peter's "seeing" Jesus will be a resurrection experience for him, in which, for the first time, "seeing" would mean enlightenment and understanding. (Luke 24:34; see 1 Corinthians 15:3-5). The words "going to Galilee *ahead of you*" (as a shepherd leads his flock) recall Jesus' prediction in Mark 14:28. The suggestion here is that Jesus is fulfilling a role God had reserved for himself in the Old

---

[141] James Alison, *The Joy of Being Wrong, Original Sin Through Easter Eyes*, (The Crossroad Publishing Company), p. 272.

Testament – that of Good Shepherd - of gathering his scattered sheep and feeding them with new life in their promised land destiny. (See Ezekiel 34:11-15). "All of us were like sheep that were lost, each one going his own way." (Isaiah 53:6a). But we are now represented in this gathering of the disciples. Our promised land destiny is eternal life with God.

Having been given a commission to proclaim the resurrection to the other disciples, the women "said nothing to anyone, because they were distressed and terrified." (Mark 16:7-8). In Mark's gospel, fear is a sign of a lack of faith. (See Mark 4:40). Fear and lack of faith lead people to "save" their lives rather than "lose" them for the sake of the good news. (Mark 8:34-35). Mark sees fear as a bondage to self-interest and self-protection. It was fear for their own skins and lack of faith in Jesus that sent the disciples into flight when he was arrested. (Mark 14:50). No more than the men disciples, the women did not believe in the power of God to raise Jesus from death.

Fear may be a stumbling block preventing us from discharging our mission to proclaim the resurrection of Jesus to the world. Placing our faith in Jesus, who is "the power of God and the wisdom of God" (1 Corinthians 1:24), can free us from these negative tendencies. Then we may be prepared to go back again to Galilee to be led by him on the way he has gone before us. There in Galilee we are commissioned to become shepherds ourselves. (Matthew 28:16-20; Mark 16:14-18; Luke 24:36-49).

The disciples' desertion of Jesus was a failure of obedience, a failure to follow him and stay awake with him to the end, as he had asked them to do. (Mark 14:33b, 37-38; see Mark 1:16-17, 19-20). Their flight into hiding resembles the hiding of Adam and Eve from God in the Garden of Eden, following *their* act of disobedience. (Genesis 3:8). The fact that the young man in the tomb announced that Jesus would "see" the disciples again in Galilee, "just as he had told them" (14:28; 16:7) implies that their flight and desertion of him would be forgiven. The Good Shepherd Jesus rescues his lost sheep and gathers them together once again in forgiveness, leading to their reconciliation with him and one another. (See Mark 14:28). We are all represented in this gathering of the disciples, which means that we are all forgiven for going our own way like lost sheep. God's new family (Kingdom of God) is thus established, fulfilling Jesus words in Mark 3:33-35.

Because the women say nothing to anyone (also a failure of obedience), the restoration of the disciples with Jesus will have to depend on their recollection of Jesus' words to them at the Last Supper (Mark 14:28), and on their own willingness to return to Galilee. (See Matthew 28:16-20; John 21:1-3f).

Mark's gospel ends (16:8) with the flight of the women from the tomb in terror. Their failure to proclaim the resurrection, as ordered by the young man in the tomb (16:7), confirms the pattern of divine command and human disobedience, which continues here in Mark's account of the resurrection. The women disciples in Mark act as correctives to the disobedience of the male disciples: "remain here and keep awake" (14:34). But in the end, they too are shown up as failing in obedience to the word of God. Mark appears to be saying that human disobedience (represented in Adam) is all-pervasive. It is contrasted with Jesus' total surrender and obedience to God. As the new human representative, Jesus reverses the disobedience of Adam and restores humanity to a filial relationship with God – union with God.

Although Jesus unites us to his own obedience, this does not mean that we will always do the will of God. We pray for this: "Thy will be done on earth as it is in heaven." (Matthew 6:10). Just like the disciples (they represent us), we continue to fail in our obedience. What Jesus has done on our behalf represents a new power in the world, which works in us through his Spirit. We can access this power by imitating his own obedience to the Father. Because of our tendency to follow our own will, obedience is difficult and costly. It is like a journey to Calvary. Jesus calls us to follow him on his own journey, as we discharge our earthly mission. Like the disciples we often fail to remain with him, and we follow our own will, chasing other gods. But he still remains faithful to us, calling us to go back to Galilee again and again.

## The Question of the Ending of Mark's Gospel

The oldest manuscripts of the Gospel of Mark end at verse 16:8 in the foregoing passage, and they record no appearances of the risen Jesus to his disciples. The longer ending (verses 9–20) does not appear in the earliest manuscripts of the gospel. There is agreement among scholars that verses 9-20 are a second century addition to Mark, comprising a brief summary of Jesus' appearances, as recorded in the other three gospels. The Church, however, accepts the later addition to the gospel as part of the canon of inspired Scripture. "The inspiration of the Holy Spirit encompasses each biblical book in its final edited form."[142] Some scholars think that Mark himself wrote a longer ending to the gospel, but that it became detached from the earliest manuscripts and was lost.[143] After Jesus' ascension into heaven, the longer ending of Mark's gospel ends with the news of the disciples preaching everywhere and the Lord working with them, proving that their preaching was true by the miracles that they performed. (Mark 16:19-20; Acts of the Apostles 1:8; 2:43; 5:12; 6:8; 14:3).

However, evidence for the ending of the gospel at 16:8 may be found in Mark's sparse literary style, leaving us with the need to use our imagination and to read between the lines in his gospel. (See Mark 1:12-13; 16:7, 8). By referring to appearances in Galilee (14:28; 16:7), Mark makes it clear that he is aware of stories of such appearances. But his restraint here is very effective. At the beginning of the gospel, Mark introduces the fundamental question of forgiveness. (2:1-12). His gospel ends with Jesus' invitation to the disciples to a new beginning in Galilee, where they would "see him again" and by implication, receive his forgiveness. There is also the suggestion in Mark that the disciples represent humanity as a whole, meaning that everyone's sins are forgiven. Thus, it may be said that Mark's gospel climaxes with the forgiveness of sins, fulfilling Jesus' purpose in coming to live among us. (Mark 1:15). As we will see below, the other evangelists deal more explicitly with the questions of repentance and forgiveness.

As Mark concludes his story, he may want his readers to place themselves in the position of the disciples and come to a decision about what they *themselves* will now do. Mark's ending may be posing the question: have we, like the disciples, failed to understand the gospel of the cross and to faithfully follow and stay with Jesus? And are we too, like

---

[142] Mary Healy, *The Gospel of Mark*, (Baker Academic, Michigan), p. 330.

[143] Tom Wright, *Mark for Everyone*, (SPCK) 2001, p. 224.

the women, refusing to obey the divine command (16:7a) to tell the world about the resurrection of Jesus, but instead, run away, "terrified and say nothing to anyone?" (16:8). And have we learned, that in order to follow Jesus on his way, we need to give up our hungering for status, power, prestige and attachment to possessions (the yeast of the Pharisees and Herod, 8:15), and rather choose the path of service and self-sacrifice? (Mark 8:18). The disciples did eventually wake up to the mission Jesus had in mind for them. We ourselves need to be "awake" to the reality that not only will Jesus be handed over and persecuted, but that we too, like the disciples, must be prepared for opposition in its many guises. But we are assured, that whatever our flight and terror and silence might be, Jesus will still be there, giving us new strength and guiding us on the right path. (Psalm 23:3). Although we often fail and stumble, we are invited to a new beginning–back to the beginning of the story, back to Galilee, to begin again the task of following Jesus, as our mission in life, while being aware that our relationship with him is sustained by *his* faithfulness to us, not ours to him. (See Isaiah 49:14-15).

## The Resurrection: An Objective Reality

The first accounts of the empty tomb and the appearances of Jesus are recorded, not in the gospels, but in the letters of St. Paul, which were written between fifteen and twenty years after the death of Jesus. The Gospel of Mark was not written until about 70 AD. The apostle Paul says that Jesus appeared to all twelve apostles and to more than 500 of Jesus' disciples at the same time, "most of whom are still with us." (1 Corinthians 15:3-7, NJB). Paul implies that anyone denying the reality of the resurrection had only to check with any of those who were still alive to whom Jesus appeared.

Today, there are some who hold that the resurrection was merely a subjective experience in the minds and hearts of the disciples. In other words, sometime after Jesus' death, the disciples had a feeling that Jesus, was in some way, alive to them through faith. But faith always needs to be grounded in some reality - in this case, both the empty tomb and the appearances! There could be no faith unless the resurrection had already really happened. The early Christians did not invent the empty tomb and the meetings or sightings of the risen Jesus in order to explain a faith they already had. They developed that faith because of the occurrence and convergence of these two phenomena.[144]

Without the empty tomb and the appearances taken together, it is doubtful if the disciples could have embarked on a mission of proclaiming the "good news" of the resurrection of Jesus to the world. Without the resurrection as an objective reality, there would have been no Church, no "good news" about the forgiveness of sins and the liberation of humanity from death, and therefore, no good news that could be brought to the wider world.

To see Jesus again after his death was something the disciples never expected, in their wildest dreams. (See Mark 16:1-6). So in what way did they experience him as alive? Certainly not as a ghost, nor as a resuscitated corpse! They saw him bodily – they touched him, he ate with them, he talked to them. (Luke 24:13-30, 36-39, 42). He appeared to them as embodied, but also with hitherto unimaginable properties. For instance, he could appear

---

[144] N. T. Wright, *The Resurrection of the Son of God*, (Fortress Press, Minneapolis, p. 696).

through closed doors, and suddenly appear and disappear anywhere. He could move through space without taking time to do it. (Luke 24:31; John 20:26-27). This means that he was equally at home both in the earthly and heavenly dimensions (heaven being God's dimension).

The empty tomb and the appearances, in themselves, are not a proof of the resurrection, but signs that can lead to faith. (Acts 13:30-35; Romans 10:9; 1 Peter 1:21). God answered Jesus' cry of abandonment on the cross by raising his trusting, beloved Son to new and imperishable life, a triumph that neither his enemies nor the disciples themselves could ever have imagined.

## The Disciples "See" Jesus for the First Time

No less than the crowds, the disciples completely misunderstood Jesus on their journey with him to Jerusalem. This is so, because human knowledge is always shrouded in self-deception.[145] We don't know ourselves. We are often lacking in self-awareness. For example, we can be deceiving ourselves about our goodness. Eventually, when we come to understanding, and our self- awareness increases, we find that our whole way of looking has profoundly changed. Before the resurrection, the mindset of the disciples was one of self-serving preservation and seeking short cuts to power and glory. In their blindness, they had mistaken views about the liberation of Israel and their own role in it. After the resurrection, their eyes were opened in a profound way. It was only then they discovered that they were not good people. Jesus coming back to them as the forgiving victim upset their previous sense of self-serving goodness and gave them a longing for another kind of goodness. This goodness would come to them, not through their own efforts, but as gift from the Spirit of Jesus (Luke 24:49), which would empower them to see the truth about themselves (blind, misunderstanding deserters, victimizers), and their need for forgiveness. Jesus knew and understood the disciples all along. He wasn't overly concerned about who they were, but what they could become. God knows us. He is not concerned by how little good we are. He wants to lead us to a better place – a place where we sense the need for forgiveness. It is only people who are not good, in their own eyes, who can allow themselves to be forgiven. Because the Pharisees saw themselves as "good," they felt no need of forgiveness. The good news is that we are loved by God, forgiven and rescued from our delusions.

In Luke's gospel, the first appearance of Jesus to his disciples is on the first day of the new creation, the day of resurrection. (Luke 24:1). As Luke's gospel recounts it, two of the disciples were on a journey from Jerusalem to the village of Emmaus (their flight into hiding) when the resurrected Jesus appeared to them on the road. (Luke 24:13-35). They did not recognise him, probably because they could still only "see" him as the Messiah to "set Israel free," which they understood simply as freedom from Roman rule. (24:21). And did not his shameful death on a Roman cross show him up as a failed messiah - in their eyes? "Jesus said to them, 'What are you talking about to each other, as you walk along?'" (24:17). One of them asked him, 'Are you the only visitor in Jerusalem who doesn't know the things that have been happening there these last few days?' 24:18). 'What things,'

---

[145] James Alison, *Knowing Jesus*, (SPCK, 1993), p. 40.

he asked. 'The things that happened to Jesus of Nazareth,' they answered. 'How the chief priests handed him over to be crucified. And we had hoped he would be the one to set Israel free.' (24:20-21). There is irony in their accusation of Jesus as being the only visitor to Jerusalem who does not know what happened there.

Then in response to their blindness (failure to "watch," Mark 13:33), Jesus interpreted the Old Testament Scriptures for them as never before understood in Israel. He told them that everything that was written about Moses, and by the prophets, was all about himself. (Luke 24:27). He wanted to show them that what seemed like a shameful and purposeless death was but the necessary fulfilment of prophecy, and that it was God's plan that his future Messiah would be a suffering servant, so that Israel and the whole world would be freed from the tyranny of death – a much greater liberation than that from Roman rule. He said to them, 'How foolish you are, how slow you are to believe everything the prophets said! Was it not necessary for the Messiah to suffer these things and then to enter his glory?' (24:25-26). The latter quotation from Luke recalls the passage in Isaiah 53:7-12. Up to this point, no one had connected the future Messiah with suffering and death. The belief was that Messianic status did not fit with suffering, humiliation and death. Hence the disillusion and the shattering of hopes when it actually happened. Jesus had repeatedly forewarned them about the reception that awaited him in Jerusalem. But because of their lack of self-awareness, it all escaped their understanding.

Here for the first time, Jesus is revealed to the disciples as the Messiah who is also God's Suffering Servant. And far from dying a shameful death, "after a life of suffering he will again have joy; he will know that he did not die in vain" (Isaiah 53:11a). His joy is due to his being raised up in victory over the oppressive powers who killed him, and then entering his glory (Luke 24:26; Isaiah 53:12a). And that is precisely how he has the power to "set Israel" and the whole world "free" (Luke 24:21) from the greatest oppressor of all, namely death itself. The disciples deserted and abandoned Jesus. The religious authorities and the Roman power killed him. The fact that he has come back again in a spirit of friendship to these two disciples on the road implies that he forgives them for their blindness, desertion and flight. Having suffered a shameful death on a cross, the crucified Jesus comes back again in love and forgiveness of all deserters and killers – all of us. He died so that he could rise again in forgiveness of everyone. (Isaiah 53:10a). The awesome and shocking truth that made the disciples' hearts "burn within them on the road," was that they were forgiven and thus freed from their former blindness and lack of understanding – a kind of death. With death and its attendant evils destroyed through the rising of Jesus from death, sins of disobedience are then forgiven, death being the consequence of such sins. (Genesis 2:17; 3:6; Isaiah 53:11; see Romans 5:12-15; I Corinthians 15:3-4; Acts 3:18-19; CCC 661-667).

The journey to Emmaus ends in the home of the two disciples, and with a meal apparently hosted by Jesus himself. They still do not recognise him at the table. But the symbolism of the shared meal would not have been lost on them. This meal recalls Jesus' table fellowship and his feeding of the crowds during his earthly ministry, all of these meals symbolizing forgiveness and reconciliation. The meal at Emmaus also recalls the first meal of the old creation in the garden of Eden (Genesis 3:6), a meal associated with disobedience, leading to the scattering of humanity (3:8) and death (3:19b). Here Luke describes the first meal of the new creation, thus fulfilling the prophecy of Ezekiel about the Shepherd God gathering and feeding his sheep. (See Ezekiel 34:13). This meal follows the conquest of death, by which disobedience and human scattering is undone, thus reconciling humanity in obedience to God, through Jesus' obedience in the new garden (Gethsemane, Mark 14:36). In their disobedience (Mark 14:32, 37, 40), flight and desertion of Jesus (14:50, 71), the disciples represent scattered humanity. The meal at Emmaus is symbolic of God's ultimate gathering together of his scattered sheep in forgiveness.

"Now while he was with them at table, he took the bread and said the blessing; then he broke it and handed it to them. And their eyes were opened and they recognised him; but he had vanished from their sight." (Luke 24:30-31. NJB). This is the beginning of God's new creation, new transformed life, celebrated with the first meal of the new creation – a reconciling meal. In the sharing of this bread, Jesus will be with the disciples always (and us too), feeding them with courage and enlightenment, and strengthening them for their own role of feeding the hungers of the Lord's flock: the mission to which all of us are called. (See John 21:15b, NJB). They could at last "see" Jesus as Isaiah's suffering Messiah, the servant whose broken body is giving new life to them: wisdom, understanding, courage, self-knowledge, and filling them with awe over the gratuity of God. (See Mark 6:41-42; 8:31; 9:31; 10:33-34; 14:22).

Jesus has led lost humanity out of the slavery (Exodus 3:7-8; Isaiah 40:1-2) resulting from going its "own way." (Isaiah 53:6a). He now invites all of us to accompany him on the journey to *our* promised land, where he will provide a "table" before us. (Psalm 23:5, NJB). On our journey, Jesus will be walking the road with us, and with all the sufferers of the world, listening to our sad stories (Luke 24:17), and strengthening us for our journey with the Eucharistic bread – his body broken, and given to us to eat, as a spiritual food.

## Universal Forgiveness Establishes God's family

After receiving the broken bread in Emmaus, the two disciples "got up" (words symbolic of resurrection) and went back to Jerusalem. Their flight from Jerusalem was a kind of hiding from God, each one going his and her own way, and away from the other disciples. (Genesis 3:8). Their journey back there again to join the other disciples, may be symbolic of their desire for union and reconciliation.

Back in Jerusalem, they found the "eleven disciples now gathered together with the others, who were saying, 'the Lord is risen indeed and has appeared to Simon' (Peter). (Luke 24:33-34). While the two were telling the others the good news of what had happened on the road to Emmaus and how they recognised him when he broke the bread, Jesus suddenly stood among them and said to them, 'Peace be with you' (Luke 24:35-36; see John 20:19). Jesus had appeared to two of the disciples on the road. He now appears to all of them in a locked room and gives them a message of peace. Hiding away in a house in Jerusalem, and fearful for their lives, the disciples were not at peace with themselves. (Genesis 3:8, 17). Their hearts must have been in turmoil over their guilt in having abandoned Jesus and handing him over to death. In thus deserting him, they may have seen themselves as complicit in his death. In offering them peace, Jesus calms their disturbed hearts. He still loves them. He has not come back in retribution. If Jesus had not been raised from death, he couldn't have come back in forgiveness of all those who killed him. "The Lord says, 'It was my will that he should suffer. His death was a sacrifice to bring forgiveness.'" (Isaiah 53:10a). His offer of peace to the disciples implies forgiveness for their failure to stay awake and remain with him during his moment of great "sorrow," as he had asked them to do. (Mark 14:33). Jesus' forgiveness of his disciples implies universal forgiveness. Why is this so? Jesus called twelve disciples to be his closest friends. He named them "apostles," meaning 'those who are sent.' The number twelve recalls the twelve tribes of ancient Israel. Jesus understood these twelve, together with his followers, as constituting the new Israel, even the new humanity. Thus, as the disciples may be said to represent humanity as a whole (blind, sleepers, deserters, victimizers), their forgiveness has implications of universal forgiveness.

Jesus then told them that everything written about himself in the prophets and the psalms had come true. (See Luke 24:36-45). He showed them the wounds in his hands and feet, as if to remind them that he was not a ghost. He wanted to meet their disbelief with the full physicality of his presence, both as crucified and risen. His wounds attested that he was the crucified victim, now coming back to them in forgiveness. Only as the crucified one, can Jesus forgive the sins of his victimizers. We must bear in mind that Jesus rose from death as a human being, a fact which is confirmed in the events with his disciples in this house in Jerusalem and in other appearances. (See John 21). For instance, he asked them if they had anything to eat. They gave him a piece of cooked fish, which he took and ate in their presence. Because even in his risen state, Jesus was fully human, he had to ascend to his heavenly Father (the hope of all Christians), where he would be confirmed in his power and glory with a "seat at God's right hand" – a metaphor for his vindication and honouring by God. (Isaiah 53:12a; see Luke 24:50-51).

Furthermore, Jesus has a mission for them. Just as their own sins had been forgiven, he now commissions them to go and tell the people of all nations the good news of what the Lord had done for them (See Mark 5:19), and for everyone else too – everyone's sins are forgiven. Forgiveness of sins would indeed be universal. "He said to them, 'This is what is written: The Messiah must suffer and must rise from death three days later, and in his name the message about repentance and God's forgiveness of sins must be preached to all nations, beginning in Jerusalem.'" (Luke 24:44-47; see John 20:21; Acts of the Apostles 10:42-43, 2:38; Matthew 28:19-20). Here, the events concerning Jesus are placed within a wider divine plan reaching out beyond Israel to bring salvation to the whole world. In summary, the disciples' experience of resurrection was (a) as gift to themselves, (b) forgiveness, (c) mission.

Jesus' emphasis on universal forgiveness means that this is to be the fundamental message of the gospel, as it goes out to the nations. Universal forgiveness has huge implications. It is founded on Jesus' rising from death and coming back to forgive of all those who killed him. Death came into the world because of the sins of disobedience of one man (Adam). But in the obedience of one man (Jesus), death is conquered. (Romans 5:12, 18-19; 1 Corinthians 15:21-22). Jesus is alive in order to forgive everyone's sins. Had Jesus not risen from dearth, human beings would be still in their sins: retribution, an eye for an eye, victimizing, murdering, death. Because sins are forgiven, death, which was the consequence of sin (Genesis 2:17; 3:19b), is "destroyed for ever." (Isaiah 25:8). So there is a twofold message for the nations: their sins are forgiven and they are liberated from death. (See 1 Corinthians 51-52, 55). All barriers between God and humanity are broken down – barriers which were created by human beings themselves. (Mark 15:38). God can then "make his home with human beings. He will be with them and they shall be his people." Revelation 21:3). It will be like the restoration of the Garden of Eden before the 'fall.' (Genesis2:8-9). The preaching of this good news to the Gentiles will be the fulfilment of God's promise to Abraham, of the blessing of salvation to the nations, because of Abraham's obedience, now fulfilled in the perfect obedience of Jesus. (Genesis 22:17-18).

Because there was no experience of sin in the ancient pagan world outside Israel, forgiveness was unknown in that world. Retribution was the order of the day, brother against brother, an eye for an eye. (Genesis 4:8). In the Old Testament, God was revealed as a God who forgives out of love for humanity. God's forgiveness was freely available to people when they failed to observe the Mosaic Law (Ten Commandments), and to individuals or groups who had been guilty of apostasy (turning to other gods for their salvation). However, even within Israel, retaliatory justice was still part of the Mosaic code. (See Exodus 21:23-24).

How can Jesus' forgiveness be universal? Was it not just the Roman governor and a few religious leaders who killed him? God's forgiveness through Jesus is of an entirely different order from that of the Old Testament. Why is this so? It is because the whole of humanity - represented in the Roman emperor and the Jewish leaders - is complicit in the death of the Son of God. In a reference to all of those who were responsible for his death, before he died on the cross, Jesus said, 'Father forgive them! They don't know what they are doing.' (Luke 23:34). All of those who had a direct hand in the death of Jesus, represent humanity as a whole, but they did not know what they were doing. (See Luke 23:34). In all their murdering down the ages, brother against brother, they did not know that they had been, in effect, killing the Son of God. Humanity had thus been blind to its sins – a constant observation of the prophets, a blindness that Jesus came to heal. (Isaiah 6:9-10; 42:18-20; Isaiah 61:1; Luke 4:18b).

Human society has always been a violent place. The history of the world shows that murderous victimizing, brother against brother, has gone on in all societies down the ages, such societies having been founded on the murdering of Cain. (Genesis 4:8; See Mark 12:7-8). Not only in Israel, making victims has been going on among individuals and in every society. Because Jesus identifies with all of his brothers and sisters in a universal sense (Mark 1:9 12-13; 14:36), all acts of killing are thereby, the killing of him. To paraphrase Matthew: "As long as you did it to the least of my brothers you did it to me." (Matthew 25:40; see Genesis 4:8; Acts of the Apostles 9:1-2, 4-5). God is on the side of the "least" ones, those who are victimized. He identifies with them (the hungry and thirsty ones, the naked, the excluded stranger, the spiritually and physically sick, the spiritually imprisoned, the homeless, the victims of human trafficking, slaves, refugees), in a sense – everyone. (See Matthew 25:35-36).

On the day of Pentecost, human eyes were at last opened to the kind of people they were and to what they had been doing. (Luke 4:18c). Having been enlightened and empowered by the Holy Spirit (Acts of the Apostles 2:4), Peter stood up before the assembled crowds in Jerusalem and plainly told them that they "killed" Jesus. (Acts of the Apostles 2:23). Most of the people in that crowd were Jews, but they had come from all over the Mediterranean world, and from as far east as Arabia and Mesopotamia. (See Acts 2:9-11). It may be said that they represented humanity at large. The now fearless Peter told them that the Jesus whom they killed had been raised to the right-hand side of God, his Father. God had made him "Lord and Messiah." (Acts 2:23-24, 33, 36). Peter thus opened their eyes to the fact that, in killing Jesus, they had killed the Son of God. He then told them that God was not seeking retribution for what they did. They should turn away from their victimizing sins and they would be forgiven through the power of the Holy Spirit. (Acts 2:38). The age of retribution is no more. The Son of God has come back from the dead in a spirit of universal forgiveness of all those, who formerly, didn't "know what they were doing." (Luke 23:34).

Jesus' identification with the whole of humanity is also revealed in the conversion of St. Paul. Before his conversion, the man Saul (his name changed to Paul after his conversion) had been persecuting the first Christians. (Acts 7:58-60; 8:1-3;). But as always, God was only concerned about what Saul could become. In his conversion on the road to Damascus, Jesus appeared to Saul as the victim whom he, Saul had been persecuting. "As Saul approached the city, suddenly a light from the sky flashed round him. He fell to the ground and heard a voice saying to him, 'Saul, Saul! Why do you persecute me? I am Jesus whom you persecute.' (Acts 9:3-5). Saul's eyes were thus opened to the reality of what he had been doing: killing Jesus. Because Jesus identifies with his followers, persecuting them is the same as persecuting him. All victims of oppression are embodied in Jesus. (See 1 Corinthians 12:27).

Saul discovered that, instead of honouring God, he had been killing God himself. That revelation changed his life. It transformed him into Paul, apostle to the Gentiles. His new mission would be about telling everyone the good news of what God had done for him. (See Mark 5:19). His temporary physical blindness after this event may have been symbolic of his former spiritual blindness to his sins. (Acts 9:8). He did not know what he had been doing. The changing of his name to Paul was symbolic of his forgiveness, and of the new job God had for him. So not only does Jesus' forgiveness embrace the disciples and those who were directly responsible for his death, it is extended to all persecutors and victimizers everywhere. In identifying with all victims and forgiving their persecutors, Jesus' forgiveness is thus on a cosmic scale. Its full meaning, and the depth of God's love is made manifest in the gratuity of God in sending his Son into the midst of violent humans who would treat him as a human victim and kill him.[146] (See Mark 12:1-8). In coming back again as the crucified victim risen from the dead, he forgives his disciples and executioners, and through them, everyone else, everywhere.

In his infinite compassion and mercy, God looks on victimizers and sees only what they can become. The awesome truth is that God loves victimizers. Jesus' forgiveness of his 'brothers' (see Genesis 45:3-4), who sold and killed him melts their stony hearts, reconciles them with one another and turns their hearts to God in a new covenant of love. (See Mark 14:24; Matthew 26:28; Jeremiah 31:31-34; Ezekiel 11:19-20; 36:26-27; Letter

---

[146] James Alison, *The Joy of Being Wrong, Original Sin through Easter Eyes*, (Crossroad), p. 108.

to the Hebrews 8:10-12). The prophecies of Ezekiel and Jeremiah are fulfilled in Jesus. Once 'brothers' everywhere learn to imitate Jesus' forgiveness, by forgiving one another, they become reconciled to one another. In a society reconciled, and free of retribution, everyone can then go out into the world and resume their God-given mission of caring for the earth and one another – a mission that was disrupted in the Garden of Eden. (See Genesis 1:28; 2:15; 3:6). Obedience to our God-given mission of caring represents the first steps of our journey towards eternal life. (See Matthew 25:34-36). Forgiveness of brothers and feeding the hungry create the union and reconciliation which are of the will of God. Both as the obedient Son and as the new human representative in the new garden, Jesus restores humanity to a filial relationship and union with God, as originally in the Garden of Eden before the 'fall.' (Genesis 2:8, 15). This is the union for which Jesus prayed shortly before his death. (John 17:20-21; see also 12:32).

Universal forgiveness is liberating. God's forgiveness through Jesus, has the effect of freeing human beings from their tendency towards retribution and tit-for-tat violence. God has a purpose in giving up his beloved Son to victimizers. It took God to allow us to kill him for him to be able to free (forgive) us from this Satanic bondage.[147] When human beings learn from Jesus to forgive one another's victimizing sins (John 20:23) – as God has forgiven them - the "good news" has at last emerged that there can be an end to the eye-for-an-eye, tit-for-tat rivalry and violence (whether in personal relationships or between groups or States, which has caused wars and plagued humanity down the ages. Jesus turns the other cheek to violence (Matthew 5:39) and forgives his torturers (humanity) on the cross (Luke 24:34). As the new representative of humanity (through his identification with us), Jesus breaks the terrible circle of retribution and unites the human family in a spirit of peace and harmony – all through his forgiveness.

In offering forgiveness to everyone, Jesus is saying to us, 'Do not get involved in retribution, because if you do, you remain on the same level as the person who persecutes or victimizes you. Turn the other cheek to the victimizer. This will set you free from being locked into endless cycles of retribution. It will free you from death.' Jesus' universal forgiveness is thus foundational. It undoes the foundational murdering of Cain when he, Cain, put the definitive separation between himself and his brother. (Genesis 4:5b, 8). Forgiveness thus creates a brotherly union out of cycles of endless retribution. It is of the will of God. And It fulfils Jesus' words about family union (the Kingdom of God) in Mark's gospel. (Mark 3:33-35; see Isaiah 2:4; 9:3-7; 11:5-7). Repentance is the first step for the victimizer, in order to get into good terms with his or her victim. All of this is the good news that is to be preached to the nations. (Luke 24:46-47). Forgiveness leading to reconciliation thus makes available to humanity the possibility of forming a new human society which maintains its unity in a completely different way from all human societies, that is, by not making victims, because victimizing results in "fighting groups," a divided and broken family. (See Mark 3:25).

The freedom to turn the other cheek to violence is the mark of the followers of Jesus, and it prepares and frees them to face persecution. It thus lays bare the workings of human society, a society that reacts to such freedom with persecution. By imitating his

---

[147] Ibid, p. 98.

own forgiveness, Jesus implies that his disciples are to forgive those who will persecute them in the course of their mission to the nations. (John 20:23). Imitating him (being "with" him, "seeing" him) is to be the true test of discipleship. Now that the stumbling block of the fear of death has been removed, through the promise of resurrection to the disciples also (1 Corinthians 15:51-55; Isaiah 25:8; Hosea 13:14; Revelation 21:3-5), they will, at last, be able to fully imitate him and remain with him, when they are faced with the kind of persecution and martyrdom which he prophesised when delivering his farewell message to them shortly before his death. "Jesus said to them, 'You yourselves must be on your guard (awake to the gratuity of God). You will be arrested and taken to court. You will be beaten in the synagogues; you will stand before rulers and kings for my sake to tell them the good news... Everyone will hate you because of me. But whoever holds out to the end will be saved.'" (Mark 13:9, 13). Being on their "guard," with eyes newly opened, the disciples are empowered to follow Jesus all the way to death, while forgiving those who kill them. (See Mark 14:50). Because of their new understanding after the resurrection, and with the fear of death removed, this prophecy of Jesus was fulfilled by some of the first Christians in the early Church. The disciples would be empowered by the Holy Spirit to "stand before rulers and kings" and forgive their persecutors. (See John 20:22-23; Acts of the Apostles, 5:17-18, 40-41; 7:54-60; 12:1-5).

## Jesus Sends the Holy Spirit to his Followers

In Mark's gospel there are a number of openings of heaven in order to release God's Spirit into the world: at Jesus' baptism, at his transfiguration and at the tearing of the temple curtain after his death. It is only Jesus' enthronement at God's right hand after his last words to his disciples (Matthew 28:18-20) that gives him the authority to send his Spirit down on everyone. (Acts of the Apostles 1:8-9). This is why Jesus told his disciples that he would have to depart from them before his Spirit could come to them. (See John 16:7). At the end of his last earthly meeting with them (Luke 24:36-48), he said to them, 'And I myself will send upon you what my Father has promised. But you must wait in the city until the power from above comes down upon you.' (Luke 24:40).

Jesus thus implies that the disciples are still lacking in one thing. Just as the Spirit of God had empowered Jesus at the start of his mission (Mark 1:10), before the disciples could go out into the world with the good news, they too, needed encouragement, enlightening and strengthening for their mission. (Luke 24:48-49). They obeyed Jesus by staying together in Jerusalem, waiting for the coming of the Spirit. (Luke 24:47). "When the day of Pentecost came, all the disciples were gathered together in one place." (Acts of the Apostles 2:1). The Spirit of Jesus suddenly appeared to them in the form of "tongues of fire." (Acts 2:3). In being created in the image of God, there is a heavenly "fire" within us that can give us a hunger and thirst for grandiosity and self-glorification. The "fire" coming down on the disciples replaces that negative fire with a hunger and thirst for union with God, the true source of human glory. (Psalm 8:5). The symbolism of fire appearing as "tongues" is a sign of the gift of speech that would empower the disciples for their future mission to the nations, making the gospel persuasive and credible to people of different languages and nations. (Acts 2:11; see Matthew 28:19; Luke 24:44-47).

The transformation wrought by the Holy Spirit was immediately evident in the courageous and fearless action of the disciples, as they burst forth from the house like a "violent wind" (Acts 2:2, NJB), symbolizing the power of the Spirit to move them to action and fill them with wisdom, understanding, courage, and the awesomeness of God's gratuity to undeserving human beings. (See Acts 6:3; 8:29; 11:28; 13:9; CCC 1830-32).

The apostles were thus enlightened and empowered by the Spirit of Jesus to continue the work of his earthly ministry. (Acts 3:15-16; 4:9-10; see John 14:12-18). Despite persecution, they continued speaking the good news of the forgiveness of sins, so that "the number of believers grew to about 5,000." (Acts 4:1-4; see 5:17-18, 27-32; 7:54-57; 12:1-5). Persecution only caused the number of believers to grow. Jesus' prophecy - when he delivered his farewell address to the disciples (Mark 13:9) - was already being fulfilled in the early Church. These disciples were the former deserters and deniers who could not stay awake and remain with Jesus as he faced execution. They were now prepared to go all the way with him to death. Having been encouraged and strengthened by the power of the Holy Spirit, they could not stop delivering the good news. (Mark 13:11). Jesus' last words to his disciples were that he would be with them always, and with us too as we discharge our own mission in life. (See Matthew 28:19-20; Exodus 3:11-12). This was but the beginning of the growth of God's new universal family. God's promises of blessedness to the nations, through Abraham's faithfulness, and his promise to definitively gather his scattered people together from one end of the earth to the other, are already being fulfilled. (Deuteronomy 30:3-4; Jeremiah 31:10; Ezekiel 11:17, 28:25; 34:11-15).

"The Lord says, 'I am coming to gather the people of all the nations. When they come together, they will see what my power can do.'" (Isaiah 66:18; see 66:22-23; Genesis 12:3; 22:17-18; Matthew 28:19-20). The "coming together" of the unity of Babel was false (Genesis 11:4), based, as it was, on human pride and grandiosity, humans obedient to their own will. It resulted in division and separation – a scattering of humanity, each one going his and her own way. (Genesis 11:8). The unity of God's universal family is based on doing the will of God (Mark 3:33-35), thus undoing the disobedience and scattering of Adam and Eve, Cain and Babel. (Genesis 3:8; 11:7; 4:16).

The preaching of the apostles made it clear that Jesus' offer to the people of Israel still stood after the resurrection. God's forgiveness and reconciliation would always be open to them. The offer was largely rejected by Israel, but God's project of creating a new universal brotherhood was now launched anyway. The centre of the project would eventually move, with the apostles Peter and Paul, from Jerusalem to Rome, and from there to the ends of the earth (Matthew 28:19). Isaiah's "banquet of the richest food and the finest wine" (Isaiah 25:6-8) would take place, celebrating God's rescue of his people from their slavery to victimizing, bringing them joy and happiness, thus establishing a brotherhood even greater than any that had been lost in the murdering of Cain or the scattering of Babel. (See Isaiah 25:6-9; see Luke 14:15-24).

With the coming of the Holy Spirit at Pentecost, no longer does God rely on one people Israel to bring the blessedness of his salvation to the world. This is now the task of the new Israel, founded on the forgiveness of the self-giving victim, who is God himself. All peoples can become part of this new Israel, God's universal family. All can receive this forgiveness, and even small groups coming together and doing the will of God can begin to form God's family, in imitation of the crucified victim's self-giving service and forgiveness.

In today's culture of individualism, the message of God's universal family, founded on Jesus' self-giving and forgiveness, may be a difficult one to get across to people. Individualism has implications of rivalry; it can lead to making exclusions - some people being treated as outsiders, victims. Individuals may not want to be part of anything bigger than themselves. The lone individual seeks what he understands as salvation through his own efforts and schemes, and not through the empowerment of the Spirit. Individualism is based on the notion that one can create one's own meaning, look after oneself, while believing that others should do the same. On the contrary, Jesus has made present a new reconciled humanity through mutual forgiveness. We receive our unity from the forgiving victim, as a new way of living together. We are thus saved as a community, not as individuals - each one going his and her own way. (Isaiah 53:6a).

## The Mission of the Church: God's Family on Earth

Believing in God's new family implies belief in Jesus' founding one universal Church whose members form their unity from the forgiving victim - forgiving one another, as they have been forgiven. This new Israel of God has, as its foundation, the self-giving of Jesus. St. Paul says that the members of the Church form a body, with Christ as its head, who is the source of the body's life. (Colossians 1:18; see 2:6). The Church's task is the same as that of the Good Shepherd. Its mission is to unite scattered humanity into a union resembling that of a family, by feeding them through word and sacrament - as the hungry multitudes were fed in the wilderness, as the blind were raised to sight - in order to satisfy their hunger for a full and meaningful life (eternal life). (Mark 6:34, 37, 42; 10:46, 51-52; see CCC 845, 850, 851). No less than the leaders of the Church, the mission of all the faithful is also feeding the hungry - in whom Jesus himself is represented - taking their cue from his own self-sacrificial service. (Matthew 25:40).

Just as Jesus always accompanied his preaching with works of healing (1:34; 3:10), the Church is called to do the same: healing anxious and troubled souls through the sacraments and its proclamation of the gospel of hope. (See Acts 16:16-18; 19:13-16; Mark 16:17; John 15:16, CCC 434). The preaching of the gospel is a demonstration of God's power. (See Acts 14:3; 1 Corinthians 2:4-5; 2 Corinthians 12:12; Hebrews 2:4). For the early Church, healings were a major part of evangelization, and were a sign that sins were forgiven. (Acts 3:1-10; 5:15-16; 8:7; 9:33-34; 14:8-10; 20:9-12; 28:8-9).

## Jesus is Lord of Creation

"After the Lord Jesus had talked with them, he was taken up to heaven and sat at the right hand of God." (Mark 16:19; see Acts 2:33-36; Ephesians 4:8-10; Hebrews 1:3; 12:2; 1 Peter 3:22). The "right hand of God" is a metaphor for Jesus' power and authority – his vindication and honouring by God, following his faithful suffering service. (Isaiah 53:12, see Philippians 2:5-11; Ephesians 4:10; Acts of the Apostles 1:1-11). In sending his Spirit down on the disciples (us), his presence will continue on earth in order to empower everyone for their own mission. Jesus disarmed the evil powers who killed him. His turning the other cheek to their violence was the means of overcoming them and making him Lord over them, through his rising from death. His resurrection reveals his divine sovereignty, his victory over death-dealing evil, and it is confirmed in his seat at the "right hand of God." This fulfils Jesus' prophecy to the high priest when he was brought before the Sanhedrin on the night before his death. (Mark 14:62). The seat of highest honour, assigned to the king, belongs to Jesus who is enthroned as king and Lord of the whole creation. (See Psalms 110 and 111). It was through his obedience to the Father and his rejection of Satan and Satan's divisive kingdom (Mark 3:24, 26), that Jesus definitively established the reign of God. Jesus is Lord, and Caesar and the dark powers behind him have been dethroned. Jesus is now the one in charge, the only human being to fully do God's will on earth, so that in being joined corporately to him, all of us may realize the fullness of our humanity in a new relationship of union with God and with one another. Jesus thus fulfils his vision of family, proclaimed earlier in the gospel. (Mark 3:33-35). He is seated at the right hand of God until his unveiling in all his glory on the last day, when he will come again to call the world to account and gather together his human family from all over the world. (Mark 14:62; Matthew 25:31). Jesus is now called "Lord," the Old Testament title for God himself.

For Jesus, personally, the victory over evil is complete, through his exaltation in glory. God is sovereign over his creation. In the resurrection of Jesus, God has restored creation to its good purposes. In this new creation, the power of brute force has been challenged by the power of love - the only power that can change the world, because love creates forgiveness and reconciliation. God's good creation is renewed, the night of exile is over, a new day has dawned. The Lord says, "On Zion, my sacred hill, I have installed my king." (Psalm 2:6). With the king installed, Satan is dethroned.

But despite all of that, is the world not still in a mess? The question is asked: 'If evil is defeated in Christ, how is it that it still seems to rule the earth?' Is Satan not as powerful as ever? The sovereignty of God may be obscured in a world in which retribution, rivalry, enmity and victimizing (Satan's divisive kingdom, Mark 3:33-35) still takes place. The daily news is full of reports of murders, human trafficking, and people in the third world now literally dying because of climate change. People still refusing to care for the earth and one another! There is little sign of God's universal family being definitively established. (Mark 3:33-35). Isaiah's vision of new creation has not yet been realized: metaphorical "wolves and sheep living together in peace; on Zion, God's sacred hill, nothing harmful or evil." (See Isaiah 11:2-9).

Be that as it may, as a created being, Satan is not all-powerful. Jesus is the "powerful" one. (Mark 1:7, 23-27). Jesus' reign over evil is a reality, but it is not complete. The "last enemy," namely death, remains as of yet, still powerful, though overcome in principle through Jesus' resurrection. Although Jesus is the powerful one, that hasn't stopped human beings claiming absolute power. Despite the many efforts by humans in the modern world to create the perfect society, no utopia has suddenly arrived. History seems to take two steps backward for every one going forward. God is patient with his human creatures. God doesn't know time, which is as much the measure of decay as it is of creative achievement. But God's good purposes will, in the end, be realized. As Jesus said, 'No one knows when that day or hour will come – neither the angels in heaven, nor the Son; only the Father knows.' (Mark 13:32). Jesus' "heart is still crushed with sorrow" (Mark 14:34a) under the weight of human greed, folly and destructiveness. Jesus asks us to keep watch, i.e. to imitate him by doing the will of the Father (Mark 14:34b). The God revealed in Jesus still suffers along with human beings, walks with them, and in his own time, will take away the burden of evil weighing down on their shoulders too. Can human beings trust in the God whose kingdom will fully come - and do his will on earth as it is done in heaven?

The kingdom of God (the reign of God) is like a slowly growing seed. (Mark 4:30-32). Jesus' enthronement over the powers of darkness who killed him is the beginning of something new that will be completed one day. God's rule on earth may not yet be fully established, but Jesus' triumph over death has dealt the rule of Satan a fatal blow. The completion of Jesus' work will not happen until the coming of the Son of Man in glory to judge the world, as Jesus himself prophesised. (Mark 13:24-27).

Because of the resurrection of Jesus, the final and decisive phase of the history of God's relations with his people has arrived. Because Jesus represented human beings before God, our destiny is bound up with him. Human beings have been given a new dignity; they can now understand themselves, who they can become, and where they are going, in relation to Jesus, through being united to him. And this can make a difference to how we live our lives. There are now ways of living together that need not be anxious or fearful, vengeful or violent. Even the fear of death has been removed. We can relax in the knowledge that God is in charge. God can rule now; the kingdom is here. His will can be done on earth as it is in heaven. Doing his will means bringing his forgiveness into our relationships so that he can create a reconciled humanity, meaning that evil will ultimately be abolished. So we pray, 'Forgive us our victimizing, as we forgive the victimizing done to us... Deliver us from evil.' The promise made by God to the first human representatives - the crushing of the serpent's head (Genesis 3:15) - has been fulfilled by the new human representative, Jesus the Messiah and Son of God.

## The New Heaven and New Earth

Jesus' Kingdom of God offers us a vision of a new world in which God's will is done on earth as it is done in heaven. Jesus claimed that the Kingdom of God was already here in his own life and ministry. Heaven was already joined to earth in his own person. In being corporately joined to Jesus, his obedience becomes our obedience, thus joining us to heaven. St. Paul says that our union with Jesus is a new creation of God. "Anyone who is joined to Christ is a new being; the old is gone, the new has come." (2 Corinthians 5:17). Christians have a future and a destiny that they know awaits them. Life will not end in emptiness. Our union with Jesus means that we too will be raised up to eternal life by God along with him. So according to St. Paul, we need not be sad in the face of death. (1 Thessalonians 4:13).

Our destiny with God is assured, because as St. Paul says, nothing can separate us from the love of God, which is eternal. Love never dies. (1 Corinthians 13:8). It is only the eternal love of God that can satisfy our hungering and thirsting for happiness and unite us to God:

> For I am certain that nothing can separate us from his love: neither death nor life, neither angels nor other heavenly rulers or powers, neither the present nor the future, neither the world above nor the world below – there is nothing in all creation that will ever be able to separate us from the love of God which is ours through Christ Jesus our Lord. (Romans 8:38-39; see Isaiah 55:1-2).

Mark's gospel is framed by two openings of heaven, each revealing something new about God – firstly at Jesus' baptism (1:10), and lastly at his death, when the temple curtain was torn from top to bottom (15:38), signifying an opening of heaven to earth. These were mere glimpses of the heavenly dimension, God's dimension, the first one implicitly revealing God's intention to make everyone his sons and daughters; the second, signifying an intimate transformative relationship between God and his people. The author of the Book of Revelation has a vision of the new creation, as outlined in the following passage.

> Then I saw a new heaven and a new earth. The first heaven and the first earth disappeared, and the sea vanished. And I saw the Holy City, the New Jerusalem coming down out of heaven from God, prepared and ready, like a bride dressed to meet her husband. I heard a loud voice speaking from the throne: 'Now God's home is with human beings! He will be with them, and they shall be his people. He will wipe away all tears from their eyes. There will be no more death, no more grief or crying or pain. The old things have disappeared.' Then the one who sits on the throne said, 'And now I will make all things new.' (Revelation 21:1-5, see Ephesians 1:10; 2 Peter 3:13; CCC 1043).

Isaiah's prophecy of the exalted Jerusalem, shining like the sun (Isaiah 2:1-5; 11:6-9; 60:1-2; 65:17-19) is a metaphor for God's new world at the end of time, and is fulfilled in Revelation 21:1-5, 22-27. The word "New" implies a radical renewal of the old creation, not its disappearance. The absence of the sea (Revelation 21:1), which symbolized primordial chaos and darkness (Genesis 1:2), means that the world is definitively rescued from chaos and disorder - "no more weeping or calling for help (Isaiah 65:19b)," suffering, and "death destroyed for ever." (Isaiah 25:7-8; Revelation 21:4). The end of suffering and death, above all, is what makes the new cosmos new. In this new creation, the "new Jerusalem coming down out of heaven from God" (Revelation 21:2) symbolizes the bridegroom Jesus coming back to earth (heaven being united to earth) to celebrate his marriage (Revelation 21:2; 19:7) with his bride (humanity), who is newly dressed with divine life – a transformation from her former nakedness. (Genesis 3:10). Those words echo God's Old Testament promises to dwell with his people Israel as their God. (See Ezekiel 37:27; Zechariah 8:8); and also his promise, that many nations will be his people, with whom he will dwell eternally. (Zechariah 2:10-11; Isaiah 19:25, 56:7; Amos 9:12). In the new creation, the people of all nations will share in the blessings of the covenant people Israel. (See Genesis 22:18).

In the foregoing passage, the voice of God comes from his throne: 'I will make all things new.' (Revelation 21:5). The renewal must come from the Creator God, who, in the beginning of creation, made the world "good." (Genesis 1:10, 12, 18,21, 31, NJB, NRSVC). God loves his good creation, so he doesn't want any of it to perish, and that includes our bodies. St. Paul says that Christians are "citizens of heaven," a heaven joined to earth, and that "Christ Jesus will change our weak mortal bodies and make them like his own glorious body." (Philippians 3:20-21). In being raised from the dead, Christ is the "first fruits" of the new creation. (1 Corinthians, 15:20, NJB). Human nature will not be changed, but renewed and perfected. Transformed human beings and the renewed earth will assume something of the heavenly dimension. Because human beings will become God-like - our bodies not being subject to decay or death - God can live in close relationship with them eternally. (Revelation 21:4). It is in this renewed world that the kingdom of God will reach its fullness and the reign of God definitively established, with Christ as King. (1 Corinthians 15:28; CCC 1060).

The renewal of "all things" (Revelation 21:5) includes the renewal of the earth itself. As a consequence of the disobedience of the first human representatives in the Garden of Eden, the earth was under a "curse," producing only metaphorical weeds and thorns, thus lacking in the fruit of righteousness. (Genesis 3:17-18). Isaiah sees the earth as if "consumed" by the "curse" of human disobedience. (Isaiah 24:4-6). Because of the obedience of Jesus, the new human representative, this curse is undone and the earth is restored to full fruitfulness, with human beings obediently discharging their mission of caring stewardship, as in the Garden of Eden– the way God always wanted it to be. (Genesis 2:15). St. Paul sees the earth being freed from its curse and sharing in the liberation of human beings from decay and death: "There was the hope that creation itself (the natural world) would one day be set free from its slavery to decay and would share the glorious freedom of the children of God." (Romans 8:21-23). God is coming down to earth to "make his home with human beings" (Revelation 21:3). For this to be possible, the earth must, in some sense, be God-like, i.e. restored and renewed to its original purpose, when God lived in harmony with the first human representatives. (Genesis 3:8).

We can only speculate as to what a renewed earth will be like. When the earth is renewed in a new creation, it might in some way, resemble the resurrected Jesus, i.e. embodying both heavenly and earthly characteristics. So is it possible, that in this renewed world, we will still enjoy the same creative pursuits, which sustained and inspired us in this life? That is possible. In the renewed heaven and earth, our experience of the wonder and magnificence of the created world, may be transformed to a level unimaginable to us now – bearing in mind that the world already reflects the glory of God. (See Psalm 8; Psalm 19:1).

It is inconceivable that this new creation could become a reality, if sin, evil, decay and death still had the power to thwart it. God would not begin, for a second time, something that could again be derailed by human grandiosity, rebellion and idolatry. No new creation could take place in a world where death and decay still held everything in their grip. This is why the resurrection of Jesus is the foundation for the eventual new creation. The new creation has already happened in Jesus, but it still awaits completion, when death will be abolished. It is in this renewed earth that the Kingdom of God will reach its fullness.

We must bear in mind, that the passages from Scripture about a transformed earth have nothing to do with science, which has its own well-grounded theories about the fate of the universe. Scripture, on the other hand, is about God's loving, spousal relationship with the whole of creation, of which human beings are a part - Jesus renewing and transforming the world with his love. The bridegroom (Jesus) is united with his bride, now "dressed" in new heavenly life. (Revelation 21:2).

## Resurrection of the Dead

"Death is a consequence of sin." (CCC 1008; see Genesis 2:17; 3:3, 19; Wisdom 1:13; Romans 5:12,14; 6:23). Even though human nature is mortal, God had destined human beings not to die. After death, Christians believe that there will be what the Church calls a "particular judgement by Christ." (CCC 1051). "We believe that the souls of all who die in in Christ's grace are the people of God beyond death. On the day of resurrection on the last day, death will be definitively conquered, when souls will be reunited with their bodies." (CCC 1052, quoting Pope Paul VI, CPG 28; see Isaiah 25:8; John 6:40, 54; 1 Corinthians 15:51-54; 1 Thessalonians 4:16-17).

The resurrection of the dead has nothing to do with the resuscitation of corpses, or bodies physically emerging from their graves. Yet, in some mysterious way, it is the bodies we have in this life that will be transformed and made incorruptible through the resurrection. (CCC 999). But what kind of bodies? St. Paul says that "when buried, the body is a physical body; when raised it will be a spiritual body." (See 1 Corinthians 15:42-45). Because human beings are loved by God and redeemed by Christ, God will not allow them to perish in the dust of the earth for ever, which was the effect of disobedience. (Genesis 3:19b). "It is the whole person who longs for eternity, and the God of love not only wants that, but effects it and is it."[148] "For I know that my Redeemer lives and that at last he will stand upon the earth; and after my skin has been thus destroyed, then in my flesh I shall see God." (Job 19:25-26, NRSVC; see Psalm 73:23f). The risen person should have some of the characteristics of Jesus after he was raised from death. He seemed to have been at home in both the heavenly and earthly dimensions. He could consume food. (Luke 24:41-42). But he could appear through locked doors. (Luke 24:36; John 20:19). He could suddenly vanish from the disciples' sight and just as suddenly reappear to them. (Luke 24:31b, 36).

In a certain sense, we have already risen with Christ, through the Holy Spirit living in us, through baptism and through our participation in the Eucharist. (Colossians 2:12; 3:1, see CCC 1002, 1003).

---

[148] Joseph Cardinal Ratzinger (later Pope Benedict XVI), *Introduction to Christianity*, (Communio Books, Ignatius Press), p. 350.

## The Son of Man will Come Again

With Jesus' first coming, God fulfilled his promises of a future Messiah who would redeem Israel (humanity). Jesus prophesied his second coming as the Son of Man, in order to bring history to a successful conclusion, to definitively put everything right. (Mark 13:24-27; 14:62). It is only God who can pronounce the final word on good and evil. History is not an unending cycle of events. The biblical understanding is that history has a goal granted to it by God.

Jesus' second coming, in which he will be unveiled in the fullness of his glory, is necessary, because of the unfinished work of his first coming. The human story continues down through history - a time of testing and "watching" (Mark 13:33; 2 Corinthians 2:11; Mark 12:38-39; Luke 21:8). This is a time of preparation for Jesus' second coming, when he will definitively establish his kingdom - his wise rule, and gather his universal family into eternal blessedness, thus fulfilling Mark 3:33-35. (See Matthew 25:32).

Jesus hasn't gone away and left us orphans. The human story does not end with Jesus' ascension into heaven. (Luke 24:50-51; Acts of the Apostles 1:9; see Isaiah 49:15-16). Jesus is still here with us through his Spirit, empowering us on our earthly journey, as we live in hope for a meaningful end to the human story, an ending that will fully satisfy human hungering for definitive rest and happiness. (Isaiah 55:1-2). Human beings can live in the knowledge that a promised land awaits them. The hope for this final rest is what gives meaning to human life. God has placed in the human heart a desire and a hope for perfect happiness, and if that were to be frustrated, life would be meaningless. Every story must have a resolution, and what we long for, above all, is a happy ending. God is the author of the human story, and he will eventually resolve everything and bring his characters (human beings) home from exile to their promised land, thus fulfilling the ancient promises to Israel, but in a sense hitherto unimaginable. (See Joshua 1:12-13; 24:13).

The account below, of the second coming of the Son of Man, from Matthew's gospel is a type of literature we have already seen in the Bible – apocalyptic, i.e. concerned with the end times. (See Mark 13:5-37). The word "apocalyptic" comes from the Greek *apokalypto*, meaning "to reveal." (See Revelation 1:1).

From 300 BC up to the time of Jesus was a long period during which Israel was ruled by foreign powers. Understandably, there was a deep longing for freedom from these oppressors. This is what gave rise to apocalyptic literature, which foreshadows Jesus, and thus looks ahead to God definitively intervening in the world, in order to put everything right. Examples of this kind of literature are found in Mark 13, the Book of Daniel, Ezekiel chaps. 38-39, Isaiah 24-27, Zechariah 9-14 and the Book of Revelation (the last book of the Bible). Instead of denouncing Israel's unfaithfulness – as the prophets previously had been doing – apocalyptic writings aimed to encourage God's people to endure their sufferings and live with hope of eventual deliverance. The theme of apocalyptic literature is that God is not indifferent to his world, nor is he powerless to intervene to achieve justice for humanity. The message is that the rule of Satan will not last forever. For Jesus, death was not the final answer from God. Neither is it for us. It is to apocalyptic that we can attribute our hope in the resurrection of Jesus as the source of our life. God will prepare a banquet for his people on Mount Zion to celebrate his ultimate victory over evil. (Isaiah 25:6-9). God does not forget his people. (Isaiah 49:14-16). God will eventually intervene to definitively overthrow evil. (Ezekiel 39:1-7, 21, 25; Daniel 12:6-13).

Apocalyptic literature is pure poetry; it should not be interpreted literally. As in the passage below, it is full of images: king, royal throne, clouds of heaven, shepherd, feeding, sheep and goats, fire. Behind the words and images is revealed the 'good news' of the eternal love, the infinite mercy and justice of the Creator God.

> When the Son of Man comes as King and all the angels with him, he will sit on his royal throne, and the people of all the nations will be gathered before him. Then he will divide them into two groups, just as a shepherd separates sheep from goats. He will put the righteous people on his right and the others on his left. Then the King will say to the people on his right. 'Come you who are blessed by my Father! Come and possess the kingdom that has been prepared for you ever since the creation of the world. I was hungry and you fed me, thirsty and you gave me a drink; I was a stranger and you received me in your homes, naked and you clothed me. I was sick and you took care of me, in prison and you visited me… I tell you, whenever you did this for the least important members of my family, you did it for me!' (Matthew 25:31-36, 40; See CCC 1038).

The coming of Jesus to judge humanity was prophesised by Jesus himself when he delivered his farewell address to his disciples. (See Mark 13:26-27). The theme of judgement is to the fore in the account depicting Christ's second coming. The scene in the above passage resembles the prophetic judgement of the pagan nations for their treatment of God's chosen people. (See Amos 1–2:1-3; Isaiah 21:1-10; 30:27-33). God's people do not escape judgement themselves, but it will be a judgement tempered with mercy. (Ezekiel 39:21-29; Joel 3). Jesus has already told the leaders of Israel that their house will be left "desolate" because of their killing of God's messengers and prophets, and because of their refusal to repent of those sins and receive forgiveness. (Matthew 23:37-39, NRSVC; see Mark 12:1-8; 14:62). We live in hope of God's merciful judgement.

The constant teaching of the prophets is that God is both merciful and just. He is merciful when people turn back to him and repent of their sins. His judgement is just, and it is mixed with mercy. (Psalm 9:8; 36:5-6; 89:14; Romans 2:12-16; 2 Timothy 4:8; James 2:13; Revelation 16:5). Judgement is a reality. God cannot ignore deliberate wrongdoing, as if it did not matter. He is angry with evil and injustice because they deface his good creation. (Romans 1:18). Evil destroys peace and security in the world. It creates the chaos of the "dark, raging ocean." (Genesis 1:2; see Psalm 46:6-11). When people take up their swords and kill, violence breeds retaliation, tit-for-tat victimizing. How can the destroyers of history think that their betrayals, murders, cheating and defrauding are never going to be judged? History has shown that a loss of belief in God, especially a God of judgement, can result in brutality on a vast scale – tyrants thinking that they can unleash reigns of terror on the earth without ultimate accountability. We all long for justice, but it is only God who can, and will, establish final justice, by vindicating and rewarding all those who suffered injustice down the ages, and by calling the perpetrators of injustice to account, so that the scales of justice may be balanced. God's justice will triumph over all the injustices committed by his creatures. (See CCC 1040). "There is an undoing of past suffering, a reparation that sets things right."[149]

There is an objection often cited today: "a loving God cannot be a judging God." And as the saying goes, we shouldn't be 'judgemental.' This seems to suggest that we should never judge other people's actions or behaviour. That cannot be right. We judge that caring for a sick person is good, for example. We judge that stealing from the person is bad. However, we should not be censorious, and we must take care that our judgements are not slanderous. The human tendency is to see a "speck of dust in our brother's eye, while paying no attention to the log in our own eyes." (Matthew 7:3). It is only God who can see fully into the motivations of the human heart. We should never seek to condemn anyone, because that has implications of self-righteousness and punishment. God sees us with understanding and compassion, and that should be our model for human interaction.

Since God is, by nature, righteous, his judgements are always just. (Genesis 18:25; Deuteronomy 1:9-18; Jeremiah 11:20). God's judgements are not condemnatory. Their goal is to reform, not condemn the human person.[150] We must distinguish between judgement and condemnation (punishment). The God in whom we believe is not a punishing God. He does not punish for wrongdoing. Although the prophet Isaiah sometimes speaks of God punishing wrongdoers, his words are to be interpreted as judgement on evil. (See Isaiah 13:11; 24:21). The God revealed in Jesus Christ suffered the blows of humanity unto death – represented in his executioners. He came back again, not seeking retribution or to punish, but to forgive us, in order to liberate us from our victimizing practices and thus unite us to himself. (See Luke 15:11-32). However, punishment in the guise of one disaster or another may result from wrong-doing. It is human beings, through their evil acts, who often bring destruction down on their own heads. In his judgement, God must name wrong-doing for what it is, and for what it is doing: defacing and destroying his good creation.

In the matter of judgement, we may take an example from the criminal courts. Having listened to all the evidence in a criminal trial, the judge names the accused person as guilty of his crimes and reminds him of the evil he has done. Sentencing the person is a different matter. That is punishment, not judgement. God desires that human society should function justly and orderly. So he has given to his human authorities the responsibility to administer justice and to impose fitting punishments on wrongdoers. (See Romans 13:1-4). It goes without saying that such punishments must always be just, and every effort should be made to rehabilitate the offending person. It looks like God goes along with State sanctioned punishment as the lesser of two evils. The alternative might be mob organized violence, and perhaps sometimes the lynching of an innocent person.

It is clear from the foregoing passage in Matthew's gospel that salvation has a communal dimension, symbolized in the gathering of the nations. (25:31). Salvation is

---

[149] Pope Benedict XVI, *Spe Salvi*, section 43.

[150] *Catholic Bible Dictionary*, (Doubleday), p. 492.

not primarily a matter of the individual seeking the salvation of one's own soul, while at the same time, ignoring the just needs of his or her neighbour. A life lived solely for oneself may lead to alienation and isolation - a divided family. (Mark 3:24-25). Unlike what Cain believed and thought, we *are* called by God to "take care of our brother." (Genesis 4:9; see Matthew 25:35).

A culture of extreme individualism represents what the Bible calls a "scattering." It is not of the will of God, who wants to bring us together as a family in which we are united by imitating Jesus' compassion for us. (Mark 6:34; 3:33-35). Thus, we have Jesus as our model, showing us that Christianity is not a selfish search for salvation, which rejects the idea of serving others. (See Mark 10:17-22). In the Old Testament God himself is depicted as a servant of humanity. (See Isaiah 42:16; 43:1-2; 44:2; 45:12; 48:17; 51:3-4; 52:10; 54:11). God wants us to imitate his gratuity by our service of one another. We are a communion in which we relate to one another – the communion of the body of Christ, into which Jesus draws all Christians, as their eternal inheritance. If we have this intimate relationship with Jesus who is alive, then we will live with him and in him. Our relationship with him draws us into his own life of service for everyone. As he gave his life in service for others, he commits us also to live for others. "Christ died for all, so that all who live might no longer live for themselves, but only for him who died and was raised to life for their sake." (2 Corinthians 5:15). Living for his brothers and sisters is living for him, because he identified with all his brothers and sisters everywhere. (Mark 1:4, 9; Matthew 25:35).

The foregoing passage from Matthew is a revelation of our eternal destiny. It looks ahead to the day when the reign of God will be established in all its fullness, all his promises fulfilled, and human beings judged on their mission of stewardship: caring for the earth and one another. (Genesis 1:28; 2:15; see CCC 1040). On that day, Jesus will return in all his power and glory, with the people of all nations gathered before him. The Son of Man will come as Messianic King, Shepherd and Judge, this time not as a vulnerable child looking for "room in the inn," but appearing in all his power and majesty, and accompanied by his angels. (Matthew 25:31; Mark 1:13b; 13:24-27; see Luke 2:13-14).

Jesus will come as King to definitively establish his reign over evil, all his enemies having been overcome, the last enemy being death. (Matthew 25:34; 1 Corinthians 15:25-26; CCC 1008; see CCC 1010). Having laid down his life for their ransom (Mark 10:45; John 10:10-11, 15b), he will come as Shepherd to gather his flock from all nations (Mark 13:24-27; Matthew 25:31; Ezekiel 34:11-12). And he will come as Judge in order to separate the sheep from the goats (Matthew 25:32-33). We have the consolation that Jesus will judge us as our brother, who cares for us. Death having been conquered, the dead will rise again in a general resurrection, thus opening the door to eternal life – a sharing in the life of God. (See Acts of the Apostles 24:15; see CCC 1020).

As a metaphor for the two classes of people assembled at the last judgement, Matthew draws on the Parable of the Sheep and Goats. (25:31b). The images of 'sheep' and 'goats' go back to the prophet Ezekiel. "Now then my flock, I, the sovereign Lord, tell you that I will judge each of you and separate the good from the bad, the sheep from the goats... I will give them (his flock) a king like my servant David to be their one shepherd, and I will take care of them." (Ezekiel 34:17, 23). Ezekiel's prophecy about God himself coming to gather his flock together and caring for them is fulfilled in Jesus, who is both king and Shepherd. (See Ezekiel 34:11-15).

The parable of the sheep and goats reveals something about ourselves, our relationship with God and with one another. There are things that only our Shepherd can see in us, and those unseen things reveal to us whether we are 'sheep' or 'goats.' How do sheep and goats differ? Sheep are timid and vulnerable creatures. They need the comfort and security of the flock. They need the shepherd to lead them on the right path. (Psalm 23:3). A sheep wandering off on its own would be lost, and easy prey to wild beasts or other dangers. (See 1 Samuel 17:34-35; Isaiah 53:6a; Mark 1:12). The sheep know the shepherd and recognize his voice. He knows and cares for each one of them. (John 10:14-15). They learn to trust him and follow him as he leads them safely to fresh pastures and restful waters, where they will have their deepest hungers and thirsts for meaningful life satisfied. (Psalm 23:2; see Isaiah 55:1-2). The human journey as a whole, however, is not always a tranquil procession through green pastures and restful streams. For both the shepherd and his flock, it is often a walk through "a ravine as dark as death." (Psalm 23:4a, NJB). Will the sheep still trust their shepherd in this time of menace and testing? They might wonder why he has to lead them through a place where the shadow of death hangs over them. But they are encouraged and comforted in the realization that his crook and staff are there for their protection. (Psalm 23:4). In losing heart, or through lack of faith in the shepherd, some sheep might become detached from the flock and wander off into the dark, ending up injured by a wild beast. (Ezekiel 34:28). Salvation does not come easily to the lone individual, who shuns help and guidance. Because the Good Shepherd loves and knows each one of his sheep, he desires that not one of them should perish. (Matthew 18:14; see 1 Timothy 2:4). With his crook and staff in his hands, he heads off into the dark in search of the lost and injured one in the nooks and crannies of the ravine and brings it back safely to the flock. (Luke 15:4-5; 10:33-35; Isaiah 40:10-11). While the sheep may feel discouraged and threatened by the death-like ravine, the shepherd can envision a glorious destiny for all of them: a prepared table and a banquet of the "richest food and finest wine" in which all will participate, at their homecoming to the house of God. (Isaiah 25:6-9; see Psalm 23:5-6).

Goats are more independent than sheep. They feel less vulnerable. While sheep are led by their shepherd, goats are led by the leading goat. The goatherd follows behind. Goats do what they want. They may trample down the good grass that the sheep prefer. (Ezekiel 34:18). Goats do not graze. They forage among the rough pastures, feeding on whatever takes their fancy. If we allow ourselves to be led by God's Spirit and faithfully follow the Shepherd, who feeds us with the best quality food and drink (Isaiah 25:6b; Psalm 23:2) - we are sheep. If we are self-willed, and feed on our own individually invented meanings, truth and goodness - we are goats. If we feel, as individuals, that we are self-sufficient, and that others should look after themselves—we are goats. If we go our own way and walk on a path marked out by ourselves alone, and away from God's guidance - we are goats. (Psalm 23:3b).

The scene at the last judgement is the time for rendering an account of our God-given mission of stewardship of the earth and of one another. (See Genesis 1:28; 2:15). The criteria for being numbered among the eternally blest are feeding the hungry, giving a drink to the thirsty, clothing the naked, releasing people from their various prisons - as the true test of faith and obedience to God. (Matthew 25:35; Mark 3:33-35; see Isaiah 58:7, 10). These metaphors: feeding the hungry, etc, recall Jesus' own mission in Galilee and on his journey to Jerusalem. His whole life was devoted to feeding all who were hungry for the blessing of a meaningful and fulfilled life, symbolised in his table fellowship and feedings in the wilderness. He clothed the naked by his transformation of all who had been excluded from fellowship with one another and with God. (See Mark 5:15). His mission on earth was good news to the 'poor.' He released people from their prisons of oppression, sickness, spiritual blindness and deafness. (Luke 4: 18-19). Jesus has the same message for all of us, 'You go, then, and do the same.' (Luke 10:37b).

All those placed on the right side of the Shepherd-King (Matthew 25:34) are his flock who have followed him faithfully and remained with him, even though their journey was often through a "ravine dark as death." (Psalm 23:4). And as he says, these works of mercy are performed for "the least important members of my family," and whoever does them, does them "for me." (Matthew 25:40). In serving his people, we are serving Jesus, because he identified with his people, even with the least important ones. (Mark 1:5, 9). "I was hungry and you fed me." (Matthew 25:35). What does the word "hungry" mean? There are two kinds of hunger and two kinds of poverty: material hunger and poverty and spiritual hunger and poverty. There is a hunger for ordinary food, but the hunger for enduring love, care and meaningful life (spiritual hunger) may be a much greater hunger in today's world. In sharing our bread with the hungry (our self-sacrificial service, talents, care), we are implementing our mission of stewardship of creation. (Genesis 2:15; Psalm 8:8-9). And we are doing it for Jesus because he identified with all hungry ones everywhere. (Matthew 25:40; Mark 1:9; see Isaiah 58:7). The least important members of his family can mean everyone who is dependent, vulnerable and in need of help in some way – literally every human being; but firstly, those closest to us, members of our families, our children, relatives, our friends, people in the wider community. What is demanded is something more than simple good works. It involves self-sacrificial service – following Jesus on his way. It begins with observance of the Ten Commandments. (Mark 10:18-19).

The service of feeding the hungry in imitation of Jesus' own feeding, releases the grace of the self-giving and forgiving Jesus to unite us to one another and to God. (Matthew 25:34; Luke 10:36-37; See Isaiah 58:7-8). God's universal family is thus definitively established (see Mark 3:33-35), comprising all who have done the will of God on earth as it is in heaven. Jesus gave his life so that all may be one. This is the union for which he prayed to his heavenly Father shortly before his death. (See John 17:11). The reward for feeding the hungry is beautifully summed up by the prophet Daniel: "Those who are wise will shine as brightly as the expanse of the heavens, and those who have instructed many in uprightness, as bright as stars for all eternity." (Daniel 12:3, NJB; see Matthew 13:43). "Instructing many" can be interpreted broadly as different ways of feeding the hungry, giving a drink to the thirsty – serving all those in need. (Matthew 25:35).

On the king's left side (Matthew 25:33) are those who remained in their self-created comfort zone, used their God-given talents for selfish purposes, refused their God-given mission of caring stewardship, and thus failed to respond to the call to service.

"The King will say to them, 'I tell you, whenever you refused to help one of these least important ones, you refused to help me.' "These, then, will be sent to eternal punishment, but the righteous will go to eternal life." (Matthew 25:45-46). The punishment of "eternal fire" mentioned in Matthew 25:41 should not be interpreted literally. Matthew's gospel mentions fire, or the "fires of hell" a number of times. (5:22; 10:28; 13:49-50; 25:46; see Mark 9:43). The word "hell" is an Anglo-Saxon translation from the Hebrew word *gehenna*, which was the name for a burning rubbish dump in the Valley of Hinnom located just outside the walls of old Jerusalem. This valley achieved its notoriety as the place where some of the kings of Judah sacrificed children by fire in order to appease the Canaanite god Moloch. (See Jeremiah 7:31; 19:26). Matthew uses Gehenna (hell) as a metaphor. Fire can symbolize a burning passion for what is right (Luke 24:32), but it can also symbolize destruction. It can thus mean self-destruction.

We struggle to grasp the idea of eternity or 'eternal life.' The Scriptures speak of God as the eternal one. (Psalm 90:2). God's love is said to be eternal. (Psalm 107:1; see 1 Chronicles 16:34, 36). Divine actions are called eternal or everlasting. So eternal life is said to be endless. But 'endless' is not a very good word in this context. Eternity does not mean earthly time stretched out for ever. Eternal life may be something like an eternal 'now.' There can be no time in eternity, no before or after, no going forward. A future implies something further to be gained. Because eternal life is a sharing in the life of God, it is life in all its fullness of perfection; there cannot be any more of it. It is life that is gifted to us through our incorporation into the body of Christ. (John 1:4; 5:21, 24; 8:51; 17:2-3). Even in the present world, believers in Jesus already have some share of eternal life, or life in the kingdom of God. (Mark 10:17). Living in the right relationship with God, i.e. by following Jesus on his way of the cross is already a taste of eternal life. (See Mark 10:21). So the idea of heaven is a way of talking about our relationship with God as we reach our destiny.

In this life, our vision of God is hidden as if in a firey cloud on a mountain. (Exodus 19:18). We see God only dimly. (1 Corinthians 13:12a). In response to our trusting and hoping, God will ultimately grant us a vision of himself, so that we will see him "face to face" and know him completely. (1 Corinthians 13:12; see 1 John 3:2). Faith and hope are then fulfilled; they are no longer necessary. There is nothing more for which to hope, nothing more to achieve. We will have life in the fullness of an "overflowing cup." (Psalm 23:5b). Of faith, hope and love, only love remains. Love is eternal. "The greatest of these is love." (1 Corinthians 13:13).

And what then of 'eternal punishment?' (Matthew 25:46a). God does not punish human beings in eternal burning fires, whether the fires are named as 'hell' or anything else. It is rather that they themselves deliberately separate themselves from God's presence (Genesis 3:8), which is the source of love, joy, and wisdom – the source of life. In a sense, they have already passed judgement on themselves. When Genesis says, "God sent Adam out of the Garden of Eden," those words are to be interpreted as judgement rather than punishment. The first human representative had already committed his act of disobedience, which was his decision to walk away from God and go his own way into hiding from God. There were consequences for Adam, one of which was death. (Genesis 2:17b). Similarly, in Matthew's account, when the King tells those on his left that they must go to "eternal punishment," this is interpreted as judgement. The punishment may be self-inflicted, resulting from decisions already made. During Jesus' first coming, people had to make a decision either to accept him or reject him. The decision they made was their own judgement on themselves. It determined whether they would be saved or not. (John 3:19; 9:39). When we look at all the horrible wars of history, and the mechanized destruction of millions of people in our modern wars, we are looking at hell. The reality of hell is something which human beings themselves create by following their own will, and from which they seemingly don't want to free themselves. In refusing to love and serve their "brother" (Genesis 4:9b), they cannot be united with God, whose image is planted in their neighbourly brother. (Genesis 1:26; see CCC 1033). Having made their choices, they may have to endure the frustration of missing out on the purpose for which they were created, which is to be eternally happy with God – "life in all its fullness." (John 10:10b; CCC 1057). The consequence of their choices may be the self-absorbed existence they have already chosen. They may self-destruct, mentally, emotionally and physically – as a kind of hell.

That being said, if it is true that human beings cannot save themselves, it is also true that God desires the salvation of everyone (1 Timothy 2:4; See Isaiah 49:14-16), and that for God, "all things are possible." (Mark 10:27; Matthew 18:14; 19:26; CCC 1058).[151] Perhaps a totally self-absorbed existence is something fairly rare, in any case. There are people who may profess to have little or no religious faith, but they love and care for their families. They sacrifice themselves for their children, in whom they place their faith and hope. They are honest in all their dealings. It doesn't make sense that God would turn his back on them in the final day of reckoning. When they appear before Jesus beyond the door of death, he will surely say to them, 'Well done, you good and faithful servants… Come in and share my happiness.' (Matthew 25:23).

The question is often asked, "Is it possible that we will see our departed loved-ones again in the next life?" It is entirely likely that God will fulfil our desires for the restoration of a union that we enjoyed in this life. Love never dies (1 Corinthians 13:7, 8a), so the love which creates a natural family in this life, may indeed, continue into the next life - for God to give this experience back to us again as an "overflowing cup." (Psalm 23:5b). This means that part of what will give us eternal happiness may be a continuation of the relationships of love we enjoyed in this life. Let us bear in mind that salvation has a communal dimension. God's love is mediated to us through our neighbour, and we, in turn, love God through loving and serving one another. This is especially so in reference to those close to us. So in the next life, God's love may be mediated, at least in part, through those whom we loved in this life. God takes delight in our good and noble desires, and if this is our hope, he surely wants to fulfil it. This is the thinking of Pope Benedict XVI: "The belief that love can reach into the afterlife, that reciprocal giving and receiving is possible, in which our affection for one another continues beyond the limits of death – this has been a fundamental conviction of Christianity throughout the ages and it remains a source of comfort today."[152] This is why we should try to keep in touch with our departed

---

[151] Re the Last Judgement, See the encyclical by Pope Benedict XVI, *Spe Salvi*, sections 41-44.

[152] *Spe Salvi*, section 48.

loved-ones. We should pray for them. (2 Maccabees 12:38-45). Prayer is like saying to them, 'We know you are there. We hope you are receiving all that God has to give you. Please forgive us if we did not fully communicate with you, or failed to forgive you in some way while you were with us.' The reaching out of our departed loved ones to us, with their own love and forgiveness may be one of the ways in which they can help us on our earthly journey. The teaching of the Church is that the faithful on earth and those in heaven form one united body (the Communion of Saints), with Christ as its head. (See CCC 947).

Our earthly journey has a final goal in a new creation, the "new heaven and the new earth," in which all evil is abolished, "every tear wiped away," human hungering and thirsting for happiness fully satisfied by a God of love and compassion, who wills that the creatures whom he created in his own image and likeness, should not perish in the dust of the earth, but are bodily raised to glory, in, and with Christ, and loved by God with an infinite and eternal love. (Revelation 21:1-7; John 6:37-40; 12:48; 1 John 3:2).

Lightning Source UK Ltd.
Milton Keynes UK
UKHW051610281221
396289UK00006B/90